D1493347

PRIVATE EYE

THE
60
YEARBOOK

For my sister, Kirstie Macqueen,
without whose support (and spare room)
none of this would have been possible.

Published by Private Eye Productions Limited 2021

10 9 8 7 6 5 4 3 2 1

First published in Great Britain by Private Eye Productions Limited 2021

6 Carlisle Street
London W1D 3BN

www.private-eye.co.uk

A CIP catalogue record for this book is available from the British Library

ISBN 978-1-901784-69-5

Designed by Bridget Tisdall
Printed and bound in Italy by L.E.G.O. S.p.A

PRIVATE EYE

THE
60
YEARBOOK

SIX DECADES OF JOKES AND JOURNALISM

EDITED BY ADAM MACQUEEN

Introduction

This is a history of the last 60 years, as seen by *Private Eye*, the UK's best-selling and indeed only satirical fortnightly magazine. Over the years the *Eye* has developed a unique mix of jokes and journalism. Both feature in this book.

THE JOKES look like this.

THE JOURNALISM looks like this.

Er...

That's it.

1960s

PRIVATE EYE ARRIVED AT THE END OF AN ERA THAT it helped hasten out. In October 1961 the war still loomed large in the life experience of every adult, Britain retained a fair chunk of her empire, Conservative prime ministers were still appointed by way of gentlemen's agreement from the ranks of Eton old boys (imagine that!), and businessmen in bowler hats with furled umbrellas could still be seen on the streets as opposed to just in cartoons. But the Britain of deference and respect for your elders had already taken a couple of hard knocks in the form of the Suez crisis and the electric guitar, and the finger-poking of figures like Bernard Levin, Malcolm Muggeridge and Peter Sellers was about to escalate into a more concerted duffing-up that became known as the "Satire Boom".

Private Eye was a key part of it, even if, in retrospect, what the public felt the magazine was saying about the Profumo scandal was more significant than anything it actually revealed. But when the boom busted, with the cancellation of TV's *That Was The Week That Was* and the replacement of the 14th Earl of Home with a Labour prime minister who was both a generation and several centuries younger, the *Eye* surveyed the fallout and just… carried on.

Three things helped it do so. Founding editor, Christopher Booker, was ejected from the top chair, moving instead to a permanent place in the joke-writing troika, alongside his

> 66 *It shows the importance to journalism of having people who are too poor to worry about money, and insufficiently senile to know that there is nothing you can do about anything. Private Eye's editors are opposed to people talking demotically among themselves and writing mandarin for the public.* 99
> Claud Cockburn, 1964

successor, Richard Ingrams, and Barry Fantoni. There were also occasional inspired interjections from new proprietor Peter Cook. And these included one stroke of genius, which became a new regular feature co-written by Ingrams and John Wells: Mrs Wilson's Diary. It plucked the prime minister out of the corridors of power and shoved him firmly into the suburbia previously inhabited by Mr Pooter: any lingering remnants of the "white heat of technology" that had swept him into power were swiftly extinguished with a good dousing of Wincarnis Tonic Wine (assuming his foreign secretary, George Brown, hadn't already finished it all and passed out on the matching bathroom mat and toilet seat cover).

It was towards the end of the decade that the other essential ingredient was finally inserted into the *Eye* mix. Veteran campaigning journalist Claud Cockburn had been recruited early on and begun to highlight police violence and spy scandals, but it was when Paul Foot (a schoolfriend of Ingrams, Booker and key cartoonist Willy Rushton) came on board that the magazine really earned its reputation for printing the stories Fleet Street, for reasons of cowardice or chumminess with those in power, declined to run. Michael Gillard, aka "Slicker", brought his unique take on the City from August 1969. And now two solid slices of journalism sandwiched the jokes in the middle of the magazine. The template for the next half a century was set.

1961

THE VERY FIRST edition of *Private Eye*, published in October 1961, took aim at the relics of the old order still prevailing over the country. Winston Churchill, only six years out of Downing Street, remained on the backbenches, and the current prime minister was the barely less venerable Harold Macmillan...

...BUT THE MAGAZINE quickly turned its guns on the new order too: here the new 44-year-old American president John F Kennedy is pictured alongside a section of the recently erected Berlin Wall.

Part 4 – FALL-OUT

You've probably been wondering, children, what Dad's always doing down in the cellar. Why Mum's white-washed all the windows. Why Grandpa keeps his umbrella up indoors. Why all your milk has to be strained through barbed-wire. Well, the answer is really quite simple.

Last week, you'll remember, we told you how to make a simple old-fashioned atom bomb out of a few old TV sets, some Sellotape and an ordinary lump of household uranium. We'd been told by Uncle Mac in Parliament that this wasn't at all dangerous.

Well, now it seems that when the Russians do it first it can be just the teeniest bit worrying. But never mind. Uncle Mac is taking every precaution. For all of you under one he has bought lots of tins of dried milk, just like in the War. I expect Daddy has told you what a super time it was in the War — so I think we might be in for lots of fun, don't you?

Just one precaution, though, we can all take. Don't eat any grass until Uncle Mac says you can.

THE AUTUMN OF 1961 saw an unprecedented programme of Soviet nuclear testing after the collapse of disarmament talks. The British government, led by Harold Macmillan, tried to reassure a nation already reeling from the cancellation of the BBC's *Children's Hour* with its cast of Uncles and Aunties.

1962

13-YEAR-OLD Prince Charles was rushed to hospital from his prep school for an emergency appendectomy on 12 February, inadvertently becoming the subject of *Private Eye's* first ever speech-bubble cover.

IT WAS ANNOUNCED that the first tests of a British nuclear device would take place on American soil – or rather, beneath it, in the tunnels of the Nevada Test Site.

Mr Macmillan revealed that American scientists were to be granted facilities for testing the effects on a population of their 15-megaton hydrogen bomb.

"We offered them Yorkshire," he concluded with a smile, "but they pointed out – and quite rightly – that the greater population density of Lancashire would make it entirely more suitable for purpose."

THE FILM VERSION of Stan Barstow's *A Kind of Loving* continued the fashion for the gritty "kitchen sink" style in fiction.

How to be a novelist

Let your pen earn you that second holiday and your Sunday Telegraph young executive 'hat'. The 'Private Eye' School of Novel Writing

Bernard Flan, né Hector St. J. Parfitt, is a typical product of the *Private Eye* school. First

of all we sent Bernard to live in the North, 'The grimy rump of England, where people really live'. Bernard spent three weeks at our Slagville school and worked for two days as an unskilled labourer in a shoe shop. He emerged with a Northern Accent, a red-brick blazer, and about eight Biros in his breast pocket.

Within Weeks Flan's First Book Is On The Stalls!!!!

A Pride of Snoggings, Bernard Flan's new novel, tells the story of William Dudd, an unskilled labourer in a shoe shop in a town somewhere in the North of England. Educated at the local Grammar school, bolshie and oversexed Dudd seduces one of the usherettes at the local Alhambra. Their ill-starred romance is played out against a background of belching factory chimneys and pubs that reek of urine.

THE LIBERALS CAUSED a major political upset by taking Orpington from the Conservatives on a 22% swing in a by-election. The rattled Tories swiftly commissioned research into the phenomenon that became known as "Orpington Man".

Statistics show that Norman Grubb of Herbert Grove, Orpington, is a typical White Collar Worker. He is married, once. He eats Golden Shred and doesn't understand Coronation Street. Lives in a semi-detached, four up, three down. Has 3.4 children, 0.6 of a small dog and 0.3 of a family saloon.

IN JERUSALEM Nazi Adolf Eichmann, the architect of the holocaust, was pursuing a vain appeal against his conviction for crimes against humanity.

THE COLD WAR continued to warm up.

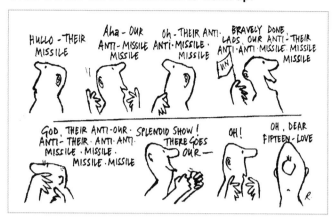

ON THE SET of *Cleopatra* in Italy, Elizabeth Taylor and Richard Burton began an affair which would ultimately see them marry – twice.

Liz and Dick hold hands

reveals LUNCHTIME O'BOOZE

Yes, the dear old Eternal City was as full of old friends as ever when I nipped over last weekend for a spot of sunshine away from Fleet Street, and the chance of scrounging some juicy little titbit about Liz Taylor's romance.

Within minutes of my arrival I had run a whole crowd of acquaintances to ground in the smoky recesses of the fashionable El Grill Harry, not a toss of a cardinal's hat away from the Vatican.

THEY WERE ALL WITH ONE ACCORD SICK AND TIRED OF THE WHOLE OVER-WRITTEN, OVER-PUBLICISED, OVER-BLOWN AFFAIR.

For three weeks Rex Froth of the Mirror, Arthur Bellifull of the People and my other friends had been crawling around on the sunsoaked beaches of glamorous SanStefano, hoping for just a glimpse of the loving couple.

AND IN THE END THEY HAD BEEN BEATEN TO IT BY SOME LOUSY ITALIAN FREELANCE PHOTOGRAPHER.

As I downed my twelfth Cinzano, my prospects of finding a story based on truth looked slim indeed...

SEVEN MEMBERS of the cabinet, including chancellor Selwyn Lloyd, lost their jobs in what became known as the Night of the Long Knives.

YOUR COUNTRY DOESN'T NEED YOU

MARILYN MONROE was found dead in her Hollywood home at the age of 36.

Showgirl mystery

The gay funloving world of London's Mayfair was shattered today by the news of the attempted suicide of gay, funloving Miss Gaye Funloving, the now well-known showgirl.

Gaye was found in the early hours of this morning by a man friend, totally nude except for black fishnet stockings, bra and panties, thinly covered by a tweed skirt and sweater, clutching a half-empty bottle of sleeping tablets.

I talked today to some of Gaye's closest friends, who told me that she had always been happy and cheerful, a 'vivacious centre of attraction' as one of them put it to me.

GLOSSARY OF TERMS

For readers unfamiliar with Mayfair-Showbiz vernacular, the following translations may be of assistance:

- For 'funloving' read 'promiscuous'
- For 'gay' read 'lonely, wretched, unhappy'
- For 'gay, funloving' read 'very promiscuous because lonely, wretched, etc'
- For 'vivacious' read 'neurotic'
- For 'man friend' read 'client'
- For 'happy' read 'drunk'
- For 'always happy and cheerful' read 'alcoholic, heroin-addict'
- For this sort of rubbish read the *Daily Sketch*.

AN INCREASING NUMBER of mothers who had been prescribed Thalidomide during pregnancy were giving birth to babies with severe deformities.

"I'm sorry, but the ethical position is quite clear. Thalidomide was a legal prescription, but what you suggest is an illegal operation"

IN OCTOBER the world came the closest it has ever been to all-out nuclear war, as the USA and Russia faced off over the siting of Soviet missiles in Cuba. President Kennedy released aerial photographs which he said revealed Russian activity on the island.

This picture could mean World War III

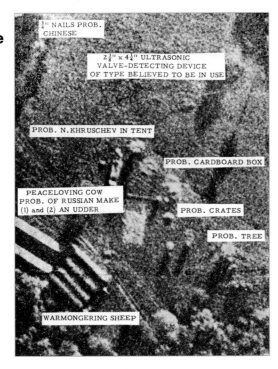

To the ordinary peaceloving reader it may look like an ordinary clump of trees in any old field. Which is, of course, what it is.

But the trained observer looks beyond the simple peaceloving blades of grass, the few freedom-hungry sheep. For when this picture is blown up 24,000 times it shows nothing less than an enormous underground missile site. On neat racks lie hundreds of nuclear missiles, each one carefully labelled with the name of an individual American city and the words "Made in Russia".

These are the secrets revealed by the ever-vigilant eye of the peaceloving U-2 pilot and the careful use of white ink in the pentagon photographic section.

THE EYE'S MAN in the House of Commons was junior MP Eric Buttock, who bore an uncanny resemblance not only to Orpington's Liberal member Eric Lubbock but also schoolboy Nigel Molesworth, from Geoffrey Willans and Ronald Searle's St Custard's books. He recorded Macmillan and opposition leader Hugh Gaitskell's reaction to the crisis.

"...sudenly there is a grate air of suspense in the Skool when old Kenerdy, he's the Hedmarster, sa 'in ten hours time orl the boys must assembl for an announcement of the gratest importanc'. evrione think it will be just another peptalk about the WALL GAME next weke but no. for kenerdy hav

ben reding about james bond single handed beting up the evil DR. who is siting on his caribean island wating to blow up cape KANaveral. so he sa to the skool 'yarroo we are going to bete up the dredded oik DR. CASTRO". Evrione think nacherally of the episode of EDEN A. who try the same thing a few yeres ago and hav to be restraned by old IKE he was hedmarster before kenerdy, and put in the san. But then they orl realise of corse Eden A. was just one of the boys but old kenerdy is Hed Man. Anihow, then evrione suk up to old kenerdy like mad esp. old MAC who sa 'the hedmarster is absolutely right wot's he done?' and old Gaters who have bene trying to be lik Kenerdy for yeres and sa 'Yaroo kenerdy is absoltly right' altho he forget he sa larst term if kenerdy ever bash up castro he wil be joly batey."

In the end, Krushchev blinked first and agreed to remove his missiles from Cuba, while the US would withdraw its own nuclear weapons from Turkey.

AFTER A CIVIL SERVICE clerk, John Vassall, was imprisoned for spying for the Russians, an official tribunal was set up to investigate the scandal.

LORD CARRINGTON, First Lord of the Admiralty, then appeared before the Tribunal to give evidence.

'I should like to emphasise from the start, that in my opinion the Vassall case has demonstrated not the weaknesses but the strength of our security system. The first time we realised that something was wrong was when someone noticed that every time our Polaris submarines – that is to say, those of our allies the Americans – put to sea, a fleet of Russian trawlers happened to be fishing for kippers (the official Russian explanation) just outside the harbour. But it must be admitted that this could have been purely coincidence. My own suspicions were really aroused when the British deterrent was one day found to have been mislaid. It was later discovered in a suitcase on the Moscow underground, and returned to our Embassy there with a note reading 'Can't think how this got here. Nikita.'

'We'd vetted Vassall before, you know. But his job was really very unimportant, you know – he was simply a sort of refuse disposal clerk, in charge of burning all classified documents after use. So it took us a long time to latch onto him. But the fact remains that we did! When we discovered that he was making long-distance calls to Moscow in office time we thought of taking him in straightaway – on the grounds that he was stealing official electricity and putting up our phone bills. But then we found that he was reversing the charges – and it was obvious that we couldn't really charge him until we were *quite sure* that he was leaking classified information. As soon as we were absolutely certain, of course, after a couple of years or so – on went the handcuffs and there we are. A happy end, I'm sure you'll all agree, to a very nasty story.'

1963

THE WINTER OF 1963 was the harshest for over 200 years.

White terror strikes havoc

Hard on the murderous toll of last month's killer smog last night Britain was again stricken, this time in the icy stranglehold of the white terror. Within minutes the entire country had been brought to a standstill by what an AA spokesman described as 'the worst winter conditions since 1962'.

Hard on the raging blizzards came the dreaded ice. Millions of motorists all over the country were forced to abandon their cars by conditions officially described by a Ministry of Transport spokesman as 'the most deadly ice since last month'.

The deadly white ice which forced millions of motorists all over the country to abandon their cars was followed later last night by the even more deadly 'black ice' – described by an RAC spokesman as 'the motorist's worst enemy'.

Hard on the 30ft drifts which covered many roads this morning came a further threat to motorists – the Great Thaw. The great drifts turned almost instantly into the dreaded slush – and a further Freeze-Up, warned an RAC spokesman, could well lead to patches of 'invisible grey ice' – notorious as the most terrifying hazard of all.

The Ministry of Transport has advised drivers to stay home in future. 'We cannot risk a repetition of this chaos,' said a spokesman.

FOLLOWING THE DEATH of Hugh Gaitskell, Harold Wilson's carefully crafted public persona helped him get elected as Labour leader.

PRESIDENT DE GAULLE refused Britain entry to the Common Market.

AN ENGLISH TRANSLATION of *One Day In The Life Of Ivan Denisovich* by Alexander Solzhenitsyn, imprisoned by Stalin but given the unexpected blessing of his successor Krushchev, was published.

The book that rocked the Kremlin

Sensational evidence has just reached this country from Russia that Mr Krushchev's regime is tottering – and that the whole Communist edifice is crumbling in ruins.

The evidence is contained in a sensational new book, published today by Snipcock and Tweed – 'Ten Minutes In The Life Of An Omsk Tram Driver'.

The book was written by Igor Szynshulevishnksa, who was once an Omsk tram driver for ten minutes himself – and its publication undoubtedly ranks the name of Szynshulevishnksa with those of Yakatinsczovich and Turgidevolomovich on grounds of sheer unpronounceability alone.

There is no doubt that six years ago this book could not even have been written – let alone published – since the events it describes are set in 1957.

IN MARCH, THE EYE made its first allusion to the Profumo scandal, soon after Christine Keeler had failed to appear to give evidence at the trial of Johnny Edgecombe. He was charged with firing a gun outside the house of well-connected osteopath Stephen Ward after Keeler refused to let him in.

Idle talk

reveals LUNCHTIME O'BOOZE

Mr Silas Jones, a West Indian immigrant of no fixed abode, was today sentenced at the Old Bailey to 24 years Preventative Detention for being in possession of an offensive water pistol.

The chief 'witness' in the case, gay funloving Miss Gaye Funloving, a 21-year-old 'model', was not actually present in Court. She had, in fact, disappeared. It is believed that normally, in cases of this type, a Warrant is issued for the arrest of the missing witness.

'Parties'

One of Miss Funloving's close 'friends', Dr Spook of Harley Street, revealed last night that he could add nothing to what had already been insinuated.

Dr Spook is believed to have 'more than half the Cabinet on his list of patients'. He also has a 'weekend' cottage on the Berkshire estate of Lord ****, and is believed to have attended many 'parties' in the neighbourhood.

Among those it is believed have also attended 'parties' of this type are Mr Vladimir Bolokhov, the well-known Soviet spy attached to the Russian Embassy, and a well-known Cabinet Minister.

'Resignation'

Mr James Montesi, a well-known Cabinet Minister, was last night reported to have proferred his 'resignation' to the Prime Minister on 'personal grounds'. It is alleged that the Prime Minister refused to accept his alleged 'resignation'. Mr Montesi today denied the allegations that he had ever allegedly offered his alleged 'resignation' to the alleged 'Prime Minister'.

Mr Silas Jones is serving his 24-year sentence in a prison of the type it is believed is a long way from Fleet Street. Miss Funloving is still 'in hiding'.

In the Dark

The public is still in the dark. And so am I, which is why I have had to compile this whole ridiculous story from other newspaper cuttings. So what?

On the day this piece was published, Labour MP George Wigg demanded that John Profumo, the secretary of state for war, make an official statement about the rumours of his involvement with Keeler – and Profumo assured the Commons that there was "no impropriety whatsoever" between them, and threatened to sue anyone who suggested otherwise.

DR RICHARD BEECHING published his report *The Reshaping of British Railways*, which recommended closing down thousands of rural lines and stations, on the grounds that they were not profitable.

Beeching to axe Balmoral
2,369,204 stations also affected

The Ministry of Transport today revealed its bombshell plans for the future of British Railways in a sensational pamphlet 'The Reshaping of Dr Beeching'.

Introducing his plan, Dr Beeching claimed that 'the only reason why a number of towns in this country still survive at all is because of the railways. This is obviously an unnatural state of affairs which I propose to remedy by closing down these towns – that is to say, railways – for ever'.

'We shall, of course,' Dr Beeching continued, 'have to work out some way of providing the public with bus services to replace the rail services. And, in many cases indeed, we shall have to work out some way of providing roads for the buses to run on. But for the moment, of course, we shall have our hands far too full with closing the railways to worry about all that yet. The public may in some cases have to wait up to two or three years for their buses.'

'We have to do that already, most mornings,' interrupted a spokesman for the public from the back of the hall.

THE LAST MASS ALDERMASTON march organised by CND set off from the capital to the Atomic Weapons Research Establishment on the Berkshire airbase.

"Eight hundred and sixty two with, three hundred and eighty four <u>without</u>, and five no milks"

AS EVIDENCE OF HIS WIFE'S infidelity during a scandalous divorce case, the Duke of Argyll presented a polaroid photo of her fellating a man whose head could not be seen in the picture. There was widespread speculation about his identity, and that of the 87 other men he accused her of committing adultery with.

What have the following got in common?

Duncan Sandys
Dominic Elwes
Douglas Fairbanks Jr.
The Duke of Argyll

ANSWER: They are all famous.

ON 5 JUNE PROFUMO finally admitted both to his affair with Christine Keeler and lying to parliament, and resigned. Keeler rapidly sold her story to the *News of the World*. *Private Eye* bought someone else's.

Macmillan confesses

Little did I know, in those happy days back in 1957 when I at last attained my life's ambition – to be Prime Minister of Britain – how tragically and terribly the whole thing was going to end. As I first walked into Number Ten, on that cold January day, everything looked bright for me. From my humble origins I had risen to be accepted in the highest ranks of society. By skilful manoeuvring at the time of the Suez crisis, I had achieved the highest honour my countrymen can bestow!

Little did I forsee how I was to betray that honour so grossly over the next seven years – until the final humiliation of my resignation!

How the country was to be consistently betrayed by my lies and evasions.

How so many of my friends were to have their names dragged in the mud of public contempt and degradation. How my government was to become notorious throughout the world for its incompetence, laxity and vile corruption.

Little did I foresee, at that time, how everyone of my policies – such as they were – would collapse in disaster through mismanagement and lack of conviction. And that eventually the little children would run through the streets, howling execration at my name and tweaking without mercy my already ludicrous moustache.

NEXT WEEK

● I flirt with Russian official 'Mr. K' and am invited to Moscow
● The night I was thrown over by de Gaulle
● The day I told Lord ***** that I preferred 'a real MAN'.

THE GREAT TRAIN ROBBERY on 8 August led to a major police manhunt.

Yard issue pictures of two more they wish to see

Arnold Feltcrumpet, aged 38 *(seen on the left)* whom the Yard wish to see. The picture on the right is how he may appear now since plastic surgery.

They are also searching for his wife Molly *(seen here on the left)*. The picture on the right is how she may look now, having been married to Arnold Feltcrumpet for 17 years.

WARD, WHO WAS CLEARLY being made a scapegoat for the whole affair, was put on trial for living off immoral earnings.

THE WARD CASE

Miss 'Q' tells of Miss 'Carriage' Mr 'X' involved *Reports MR O'B*

The hearing continued before Mr 'G', the magistrate, today.

Miss 'A', the first witness, appeared in the dock wearing dark glasses, a pink bikini and a purple wig.

She told the court how she had met DR STEPHEN WARD, the fifty year old osteopath who is charged with eighty five offences and may go to prison for sixty three years, several times in DR WARD's flat.

Dr STEPHEN WARD, who is fifty, sat passively in the dock making sketches on a pad while she gave her evidence. Dr Ward it will be remembered is a well known artist who has painted many members of the Royal Family including Princess 'F' and the Duke of 'P'.

Miss 'A' then told the court of her relationship with DR WARD, the osteopath, who is fifty.

'He introduced me to several men,' she went on, 'including Lord…'

'We don't want to hear any names' interrupted Mr 'J' Q.C., the prosecuting counsel.

Mr 'G' the magistrate then asked the Clerk of the Court, Mr 'D' the tape-recorder, to strike Miss A's evidence from the record.

Ward killed himself before the end of the trial.

ALFRED HITCHCOCK'S *The Birds* arrived in cinemas.

Films – *The Sheep*

From the first horrific moment, when cool blonde new discovery Lotte Bosom, pick-nicking on Tulse Hill with craggy Ned Fluteholder, is bitten on the shin while knitting by an elderly ewe, I sat trembling on the edge of my seat. A few more deft touches, the ghastly rape of Fluteholder's gardener by a beige ram, the stampede of sheep in the Festival Hall, the near-strangling of Miss Bosom by her own woolly vest, and the old Maestro of Suspense has us eating out of his hand. The climax, with Ned and Lotte alone in a barricaded house, listening to the sinister baa-ing outside, the rumble of sheep's feet on the roof ('It's when they stop bleating, you've got to worry,' says sturdy Ned) is almost too much to bear. I recommend this film to all who have ever kept caged sheep in their drawing rooms.

MACMILLAN FINALLY announced his resignation on 10 October. Lord Home – aka 'Baillie Vass' – emerged as his successor in a process that was not entirely clear – until *Private Eye* revealed the details.

For the first time in any consultation in history, the leading echelons of a party were asked a series of three questions, the second of which led to the third conclusion which Macmillan wanted: First 'Which candidate for the Prime Minister do you most want?' Second, 'Which candidate do you most detest?' And, third, 'To whom (pronounced Home) do you have the least objection?'

PRESIDENT KENNEDY was assassinated on 22 November. That evening, Labour politician George Brown appeared on television to pay tribute and was clearly as drunk as a skunk, with official excuses giving rise to the long-standing *Eye* euphemism "Tired and emotional".

THE FINAL EDITION of TV satire show *That Was The Week That Was* was broadcast, after BBC director-general Hugh Carleton Greene ruled that it could not be broadcast in what was to be an election year.

Election to be secret – BBC

The BBC has reluctantly decided not to mention the General Election on any of its programmes, until the whole thing is over.

This was announced by a spokesman for Sir Hugh Carleton Towers, the Director General, last night.

Said the spokesman: "It is felt that any further reference would contravene our obligation to remain impartial. We shall therefore maintain our neutrality by not mentioning it."

When asked whether the BBC would announce the date of the election when it was made known, the spokesman said "No. We feel that even this would prejudice the chances of the Conserv… I mean one or another of the three main political parties."

A high ranking official of the BBC last night refused to make any comment on the news. It is understood that he (or she) was shamelessly emotional at the time.

IN A SPECIAL EDITION he was guest-editing in August 1963, veteran journalist Claud Cockburn revealed the name of the head of MI6 for the first time. The existence of the security services would not even be officially acknowledged for a further 25 years, and the names of their heads not published until the 1990s.

NOTE TO FOREIGN AGENTS:

You think that a man called Menzies is head of what you so romantically term the British Secret Service.

> **MENZIES, Maj.-Gen. Sir Stewart Graham**, K.C.B., *cr.* 1951 (C.B. 1942); K.C.M.G., *cr.* 1943; D.S.O. 1914; M.C.; *b.* 30 Jan. 1890; *s.* of Lady Holford.
> *Educ.:* Eton. Grenadier Guards, 1909-10; Life Guards, 1910-39. Served European War, 1914-18 (despatches, D.S.O., M.C., Bt. Major). Subsequently Bt. Col. Grand Officer Legion of Honour; Grand Officer Order of Leopold, Crown of Belgium; Legion of Merit (U.S.A.); Polonia Restituta (Poland); Grand Officer Orange Nassau (Holland); Commander St. Olaf (Norway). *Address:* Bridges Court, Luckington, Chippenham, Wilts. *Clubs:* White's, St. James'.

As you will see, the fellow is 73 and does not want to be bothered with a lot of telephone calls asking which Ministers of the Crown are Scottish agents and were they instructed to go to bed with the Duchess of Argyll? The man you should ring is:

> **WHITE, Sir Dick (Goldsmith)**, K.C.M.G. 1960; K.B.E. 1955 (C.B.E. 1950); O.B.E. 1942); attached to Foreign Office; *b.* 20 Dec. 1906; *s.* of Percy Hall White and Gertrude White (*née* Farthing); *m.* 1945, Kathleen Bellamy. *Educ.:* Bishops Stortford Coll.; Christ Church, Oxford; Universities of Michigan and California, U.S.A. U.S. Legion of Merit, Croix de Guerre (France). *Address:* The White House, Nutbourne, Pulborough, Sussex. *T.:* West Chiltington 2136. *Clubs:* Travellers', Garrick.

1964

THE ARCHITECT Sir Leslie Martin was commissioned to produce a "masterplan" for London's Whitehall, which would involve knocking down almost every historical building which stood there.

The news that the Foreign Office is to be demolished has been greeted with alarm, not to say disquiet in F.O. circles (writes our Diplomatic Bag).

A spokesman for the Ministry of Works said last night: "The Foreign Office is an out-of-date body of men, quite unfitted to cope with the problems of the Twentieth Century. Many of them date from Victorian times and are suffering from damp and general neglect. Others have been kept in storage for many years. It is high time that they were demolished and replaced by an efficient contemporary structure."

PROTEST

Mr John Betjeman, the poet, has already formed a protest movement to prevent the demolition of what he called "a priceless piece of Victoriana". He is being assisted by Sir Jenkyn LeStrange (85) until recently Ambassador to Tierra del Fuego and himself a fine specimen of the neo-Gothic style. Built in 1878, he is still in very good condition and shows no sign of the ravages of time and the Death Watch Beetle which have undermined other parts of the structure.

THE QUEEN gave birth to her fourth child, Prince Edward.

FAMILY FORUM

A Royal baby for you to knit

Those of you who are lucky enough to be expecting the arrival of a little stranger in the near future should make the most of all opportunities to slavishly copy the antics of our Royal mothers-to-be (writes Muriel Prune, the *Daily Telegraph*'s Baby Correspondent).

As in all things the Royal family is setting a truly regal example and no more so than in their choice of nappies.

The Queen herself is known to favour a plain white creation specially designed by Norman Hartnell, simple but at the same time exquisite.

For her sister Princess Margaret, never afraid to be in the vanguard where fashion is

concerned, there is the Design Centre's latest triumph in exciting Swedish wood – elegant but at the same time eminently practical.

One last suggestion! – for those unlucky little wives who won't be having babies this year – Harrods are now offering special Souvenir Royal Year babies for sale – boys and girls – and once again each baby is individually stamped with the Royal coat of arms. Prices are quite reasonable, ranging from 2,000 to 5,000 guineas each.

THE UNITED NATIONS sent troops into Cyprus to try to quell fighting between the Greek and Turkish communities on the island.

A typical holidaymaker's day in the island of sun

- A morning visit to colourful bloodstained Nicosia.
- Witness the famous bombthrowing festival in the sun-drenched streets of Limassol.
- Attend the traditional Armsgiving Service at the Greek Orthodox Cathedral.
- See the Murdering of the Monks pageant – centuries-old rite beloved of the Eastern Church
- Watch the gnarled Greek fishermen knotting Turkish heads.

All this PLUS a FREE 'policeman's kit' – including knives, bombs and grenades – each one hand made in Athens.

RON DISK, the *Eye*'s "Prophet of the Pops", had news of the biggest British export in decades.

It's Oui (Yes) Oui (Yes) Oui (Yes)

The teenagers of Paris have certainly given the Beatles "un grand 'allo'" (a big hello).

Yesterday I went with them for a stroll down

the famed Champs Elysées. I say stroll, but it was more like a rugger scrum.

The French fans were everywhere. Old and young, they had all turned out to see 'les fabby whackeurs d'Angleterre' (the fabby English whackers).

One old concierge who could have walked straight out of the pages of Maigret was wild with joy. 'Qui sont les garçons avec les cheveux bizarres?' (Oh, look, there are the Beatles!) she cried in ecstasy.

THE UK'S FIRST pirate radio stations, Radio Caroline and Radio Atlanta, began broadcasting without licences from ships in international waters.

Daily Telegraph pirate ship starts transmission

The *Daily Telegraph* pirate ship, anchored of Frinton, today started transmission.

The ship, 'The Marsland Gander', which is under the control of Screaming Lady Pamela Berry, is broadcasting non-stop popular music by Souza, Sir Arthur Sullivan and Mr Percy Grainger. The music is interspersed with satirical readings from the *Daily Telegraph*'s 'Deaths' column and Mr W.A. Darlington's Theatrical Notes.

JOHN BLOOM, the flamboyant businessman who had been at the head of the "washing machine wars" of the early 1960s and whose company was in the process of spectacularly collapsing, moved into the package holiday market, with cheap breaks on the Black Sea coast of Bulgaria.

VIOLENCE BETWEEN mods and rockers raged in seaside resorts across Britain, with police complaining that they lacked the powers to deal with it.

Rozzery with Violence

By SIR ARTHUR LOONEY-BINNES, Psychiatric consultant to Scotland Yard (1953-54)

There is a great deal of misunderstanding today on the part of the public about the Police Farce. It only takes a few thousand cases of misplanted evidence and brutality for people to be up in arms demanding stiffer penalties and the return of the lash.

Having worked among policemen all my life, I think I may claim to have gained some insight into the police mind. Many policemen today come from broken homes. (I personally have seen some of the homes they have broken.)

A typical group of ton-up 'ROZZERS' (with their steel-blue uniforms and helmets) waiting for a rumble with the nattily-garbed 'PLODS'

Again some are illegitimate. The psychiatrist Dr Ephraim Ghoule even went so far as to remark to me that in his opinion 'ALL policemen are bastards'.

More recently cases of juvenile policemancy have been directly caused by the floods of police films and serials which flow from the television companies. These can have a lasting effect on the minds of young 'coppers'. Often they seek to conceal their sense of inadequacy by dressing up in strange uniforms and riding through the streets on motor-bikes with blaring radios to the terror of the law-abiding citizen.

It is pointless to think that policemen can be deterred by stiffer penalties and other repressive action. The hardened 'rozzer' will always revert to type however many years of solitary confinement he may serve.

For too long society has regarded the policeman as a brutish beast who should be kept behind bars. Medical experience has shown that provided he is treated with sympathy and understanding even the most brainless blood-crazed and doltish 'peeler' can regain some degree of self esteem and human dignity.

PRESIDENT LYNDON B. JOHNSON received approval from Congress to take "all necessary action" against the Communist regime in Vietnam. *Private Eye* demanded leadership from elsewhere.

Come off it Pope!

Says
MERRYMAN CLAPPER

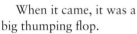

Last week the world waited impatiently for the first official statement from the new Pope – Pope Paul VI.

It came at a time of fear and crisis – Vietnam – Cyprus – The Great Prison Escape. What message of comfort would the Pope deliver to the nations in their hour of need?

When it came, it was a big thumping flop.

Under the high-sounding title 'Pacem in Terris' the Pope told the people of the world 'The Church is on the side of Peace'.

Time For Action

Is this really the sort of thing we want to hear in 1964?

I say No. For one thing, we've heard it all before. 'Pacem in Terris' is old hat. When Ho Chi so-called Minh bloodily attempts to massacre the second fleet, is it not time for a dose of the old 'bellum'?

Limited 'bellum' of course. And bellum in the best possible taste. But 'bellum' nevertheless.

And where should the Pope be, when there's a bit of bellum about?

At The Head of it of Course

In years to come, let not the Communists point their sniggering fingers and say – 'Where were you, Father, during the Great bellum?'

PRINCESS MARGARET WAS forced to evacuate the Aga Khan's yacht after it hit a rock in the Mediterranean.

What's to stop the Queen drowning?

Last week Princess Margaret narrowly escaped a watery grave at the hands of the Aga Khan.

Had it not been for our Meg's courage and leaping ability The Nation might today be swathed in black tulle.

Hazard

Today we spotlight a new peril.
WHAT IS TO STOP THE QUEEN DROWNING?

The answer: a disturbing NOTHING.

When I put the question to palace officials their report was negative in the extreme. "Her Majesty," I was told, "is a fine swimmer and completely at home in the water as she is on horseback."

That's as may be, Mr Toffee Nose Know All. But what thousands of her loyal subjects are wondering is this:

WOULD THE QUEEN BE EQUALLY AT HOME, IF LEAD WEIGHTS WERE ATTACHED TO HER BODY, AND GRAVITY ALLOWED TO EXERCISE ITS NORMAL THRUST?

"Such circumstances are of course highly unlikely," I was told.

Jeopardy

But those of us who remember being told that the Titanic would never sink will view this complacency with alarm.

If the Titanic can sink, then so can our beloved Royal Family.

DOUGLAS-HOME was swept out of power in October's general election, and Harold Wilson entered Downing Street – along with his wife.

Mrs Wilson's Diary

I was in a bit of a tizz moving into Number 10 but I'm glad to say the servants were all very kind and didn't boss me around too much.

We had a bit of a surprise when we went into the lounge. We heard a strange scrabbling noise from upstairs – and then a sudden shot. Harold ran upstairs to see what was happening and found Baillie Vass stepping out of a cupboard with a smoking rifle. "Oh, hello Mr Watson," said the Baillie, "I got locked in by mistake. I thought it was the back door." Then he rushed out of the house giggling in a funny sort of manner and Harold didn't have time to make out a bill for the damage to the lock. Mrs Vass apologised for her husband and said she hoped she hadn't left too much washing up but that Colman would look after it. It was then that I was introduced to the staff. The three footmen Colman, Prentis and Varley, Nugent my personal maid and Inspector Trimfrittering whose job is to protect Harold and be with him at all times. When after our Ovaltine (laced with a little Sanatogen) we retired for the night, I was surprised to find the Inspector lying between us. "Don't mind me," he said, "just carry on as if I wasn't here." I tried to but somehow I couldn't get to sleep with the Inspector snoring at my side. Harold tells me I will get used to him and I sincerely hope I will.

THE NEW GOVERNMENT set out an ambitious programme of legislation.

BY OCTOBER you could forget the Beatles – there was a new band in town.

Pop Scene

by MAUREEN CLEAVAGE

Introducing the Turds

I want you to meet four very young and very exciting Turds.

They're from the new Beat Centre of Rochdale and they're swinging into the charts with their first waxing 'Chain Stagger'.

Yesterday, I popped into the studio and talked to them.

The Turds are something new. Irreverent, greedy, short and acned, there is a trendy look about them that sets a 60s pace, as up to date as next year's Courreges Underwear.

The leader of the group Spiggy Topes explained: 'Actually we don't have a leader. In our eyes all Turds are equal.'

Spiggy regards the Turds' success philosophically. 'What I say is I mean about this beat business well I shouldn't think we'll be around in a hundred years' time.'

The Turds started at the bottom and are already dominating the thinking of pacey people.

I think the Turds are going to be with us for a long time. *(God help us all. Ed)*

THE NEW SECRETARY of state for economic affairs, the permanently pissed George Brown, chose a memorable phrase to describe the Swiss bankers whose currency speculation he blamed for economic chaos in Britain. The *Eye*'s proprietor took great offence.

Lord Gnome writes

I would like to begin this week by pointing out that I am in no way connected with what are known as the "Gnomes of Zurich". These persons are of foreign origin whereas of course I myself was born and bred in Middlesex. If there are any more cheap slurs of this kind, I shall not hesitate to issue writs.

A PAIR OF NOTORIOUS criminals were named for the first time in edition 68 of *Private Eye*, guest-edited by Peter Cook.

Reporters on some Fleet Street newspapers have refused to cover what everyone in the business calls 'the Kray story'. They think it is physically too dangerous.

PRIVATE EYE thinks it sensible and proper to print the names.

The two people being written about are the twin brothers, Ronald and Reginald Kray.

For ten years both have been well known figures of London life.

They are rich.

They have criminal records.

They are credited in the underworld with immense power. Criminals have 'authoritatively' told researchers that the Krays can whistle up 300 thugs for rough stuff and mayhem in half an hour. Or else it is that they can mobilize a thousand of the same in two hours.

The same sources say the Krays have at their disposal 'suicide' squads of dedicated goons, so loyal that they will risk life sentences in reckless acts of violence on behalf of their 'leaders'. The goons, criminals declared, specialize in blowing off the kneecaps of hostile elements. Or they squirt a man with petrol and toss a lighted match on him.

The Krays are known to work energetically on behalf of many charitable causes. They have unquestionably done valuable work for spastics and retarded children. They have raised and contributed funds for cancer research.

They have been in business in the East End for approximately eight years, and in the West End for approximately two. They operate the Esmeralda's Barn nightclub.

1965

DESPITE THE MOUNTING costs of the joint Anglo-French project, Harold Wilson committed to continue work on Concorde.

AMERICAN JOURNALIST John Crosby took to the pages of the *Daily Telegraph* to declare London, which was by now showing undeniable signs of swinging, "the most exciting city in the world".

London – 'In' city of the world

Script: GARY WIMPYBURGER
Photos: HELMUT FINK

Different cities at various periods in history for some unknown reason have become magnets for talent, drawing young people from all parts of the world – many not understanding fully why they have come. And after the writers, students and musicians have set the trend, the rich and the fashionable follow – the playboys, the beautiful women, the German photographers and switched-off American journalists unable to make a decent living in their own countries.

Only a foreigner and a loonie could lift up the drab and grimy skirt of Old Mother London, the London of crooked landlords, grotesque skyscrapers, tarted up pubs, traffic jams, non-existent public transport, drooling Press and sweaty pooves, and discover a swinging, switched-on, fab, geary, groovy, trendy, with-it, pace-

Some of the young pacey people who make London swing

setting, Ready Steady Goes Live, Bo Diddlyesque, Folk bluesville of a place – EARTH'S MOST EXCITING CITY.

Typical of the younger get-with-it monkey men who can be found tapping out a groovy beat at the Moody Poove is switched-on, pacey 25 year old Balliol man **Horst Weimar**, 37. Weimar owns the go ahead kinky 'Giftique' shop in Chelsea's King's Road marketing antique bus tickets, last year's British Railway's timetables, and Victorian ginger-beer bottles which Weimar picks up on the Old Kent Road for ½d apiece and sells for 39/11d. Says Weimar: 'Ten years ago I would have been in prison. Indeed I was.'

Regularly seen in Giftique is stubby shutter snapping photographer, **Stephen Hathaway-Smith**, 3'6" and bursting out of his thigh-tight goats-leather Levis. Stephen says: 'It's a load of old cobblers to say that all photographers are successful sex-maniacs. I started with an old Brownie, now I've graduated to elderly Girl Guides.'

THERE WAS OUTRAGE when Harold Wilson presented the Beatles with MBEs, with several former recipients returning their honours in protest. Meanwhile…

Pop Scene – Turds turn down peerages

At a hurriedly called Press Conference yesterday Mr Lemuel Sweat (Managing Director of 'Lemmie Sweat Orchestras Ltd') announced that the Turds (a popular singing group) had rejected an offer to become Life Peers in the recent Honours List.

Waving a letter purporting to be addressed by Harold Wilson to Spiggy Topes, the leader of the group, Mr Sweat explained: 'The Turdies are deeply committed. They feel that peers and that are inconsistent with the first half of the twentieth century. They much appreciate the offer but feel – sincerely mind – that it is out of keeping with their democratically switched-on image.'

Miming on behalf of the group, Spiggy Topes said: 'A lot of grotty groups obviously cannot resist the gilded carrot dangled by the Establishment.'

Mr Topes continued: 'We are not alone in refusing the embrace of the famous and powerful. Winston Churchill did the same. So did Earl Attlee. And the kids like that!'

HAROLD WILSON continued to burnish his "man of the people" image.

You don't have to drink it, Mike. Just wait till the photographers have gone and then I'll buy you a Scotch

THE PRIME MINISTER celebrated his first anniversary in Downing Street, skilfully papering over the cracks in his administration.

A Year of Power

HARRIS TWEED talks to HAROLD WILSON

Tweed: Prime Minister, have there been any conflicts of opinion in the Cabinet?

Wilson: Well y'know Mr Harris (or may I call you Creepydrawers?) the Tory press along with their cronies in the Socialist press have tried desperately hard to manufacture crises and so-called splits in the Cabinet. Certainly we have had our differences of opinion. No Cabinet would be complete without them. But when I read reports as I did last week about fisticuffs arising between George Brown and Jim Callaghan at a bridge-building coffee break and Frank Cousins sinking his teeth into Sir Frank Soskice's left testicle in a moment of fury, I begin to despair of the impartialty of the press.

Tweed: I don't think I read this report.

Wilson: Oh, that must have been one we managed to suppress.

WAR BROKE OUT between India and Pakistan over the disputed territory of Kashmir.

War a bad thing – The world speaks out

"PEACE OFF" SAYS INDIAN GENERAL

The world today spoke out on the blood-sodden conflict between India and Pakistan. In Washington President Johnson interrupted an important briefing session on the pattern bombing of strategic rice-growing villages in North Vietnam to speak to reporters outside his anti-nuclear bunker in Washington.

"The hearts of all peace-loving children are torn with grief and sorrow at this mindless war. Raise head to television cameras and adopt look of worried responsibility."

THE POST OFFICE TOWER, the tallest building yet built in the country, was officially opened.

It is believed that during recent winds unforeseen problems have arisen. On one occasion a GPO official whose duty is to stand on top of the tower transmitting telephone messages to Paris by semaphore, became sick and dizzy. As a result, reports appeared in some French newspapers of Princess Anne's behaviour giving rise to 'grave despondency'.

In future, the spokesman said, semaphore workers will be issued with parachutes and anti-sickness drugs.

DRAMA CRITIC Kenneth Tynan became the first person to say "Fuck" on television – or, given that he had a stammer, "Ff-f-fuck".

The BBC switchboard was jammed by viewers who had missed the 'event' and who wished to see it repeated on BBC2 at a peak viewing hour.

Brigadier Stanley Freend, KRGSPN., said: "That sort of thing is alright among men, but when these things start cropping up in the presence of women, then someone must draw the line." Brigadier Freend, who is 95, is planning to write what he described as a "stiff note" to the Queen for allowing the BBC to exist. "I did not fight in seven World Wars to see the BBC put a load of cock on the air," he said.

MRS SAXE-COBURG-GOTHA went on a royal visit to Berlin.

1966

HAROLD WILSON called a general election, hoping to improve his majority of just four. Lord Gnome threw *Private Eye*'s support firmly behind the Conservatives.

I have commissioned my own confidential sample from the well-known and impartial firm of Pollbrokers, Swizzle, Gnome & Twist Ltd of Beckenham, Kent. The result of their investigation is now before me. And encouraging reading it makes.

A cross-section sample of all classes of retired gentlefolk living in Bournemouth were asked: *Would you not agree that the Conservatives will win the next election?*
Yes (thank you for your crispy £5 note) 99%
Eh? Speak up! You must excuse me,
my hearing is a little out of focus 1%

LABOUR were victorious.

Mrs Wilson's Diary

I must confess that I was quite carried away by the emotion of Election Night in Liverpool. Harold was also carried away by Mr Kaufmann and the Inspector and laid out on his bed. He was so weary after all the thirsty work on the hustings that it was all he could do to drink seven or eight large balloon glasses of Lucozade in order to restore his lost energy and collapse on the floor of the Hotel Splendide like a felled elephant. Mr Kaufmann, a rather austere person with a bald head who has taken over as our Press Adviser, repeatedly cautioned Harold against drinking any more of the health-giving tonic drink, but Harold paid little attention, finally putting his tongue out at Mr Kaufmann and remarking "Belt up, Foureyes, or it's back to the New Statesman."

IAN BRADY and Myra Hindley's trial began at Chester Assizes amid a press circus.
Commencing April 19

*THE LORD CHANCELLOR OF ENGLAND
In Association with Lord Rothermere,
Sir Max Aitken, Mr Cecil King and Other
Distinguished Persons presents:*

The Moors Murder Trial

Special repeat performance with additional horrors

● THE MURDERS THAT SHOCKED THE CONTINENT WILL BE BROUGHT DAILY INTO YOUR HOME BY SOME OF THE WORLD'S FINEST JOURNALISTS

● BLACK MAGIC – DE SADE – AXES – VIOLENT DEATH – MORE GRISLY DETAILS WILL BE REVEALED IN THIS NEW UNEXPURGATED VERSION OF ONE OF HISTORY'S MOST REVOLTING CRIMES

● YOU WILL SQUIRM AS NEVER BEFORE WHILE DAY AFTER DAY THIS HORRIBLE SAGA IS EXPOUNDED FOR THE SECOND TIME IN ALL ITS MACABRE AND DISGUSTING DETAIL!!

Order your copies now!

JOHN LENNON announced that the Beatles were "more popular than Jesus", prompting outrage and protests across the US. The Turds were swift to respond.

Greeb raps U.S. Turds smear

Mr Len Greeb, the Manager of the Turds (a popular singing group) left his sick bed yesterday at the National Hospital for Revolting Diseases (Frith Street) to fly to New York and clear up a "misunderstanding" about remarks made by Spiggy Topes in the course of an interview with Maureen Cleavage of *The Evening Standard*.

Mr Topes, the leader of the group, was quoted as saying: "John Lennon is played out. He is finished. We are more popular than the Beatles and God rolled into one. Lennon was alright, but his disciples were thick buggers."

The widely reported remarks led to a mass burning of the Turds' records. In all over 17 copies of their new release "Eleanor Bron/ Yellow Hovercraft" were destroyed by leading American disc-jockey B.J. Wiggenstoof.

"It's blasphemy," said Mr Wiggenstoof. "J.L. is as big today as he ever was."

The controversy spread to Zambia where President Kaunda has banned all Turds recordings.

Yesterday Mr Greeb appeared on Coast-to-Coast Television to defend his group.

"Spiggy was quoted out of context," he said. "What he was trying to say was that he was deeply interested in religion and would welcome a Board of Trade inquiry."

NOW WITH A SUBSTANTIAL majority, the prime minister set about reshaping his team.

Shazamm!
The new men move in
Yes! It's Wilson's whizzkids

Britain is on the move again. Blasting away the cobwebs of apathy and Whitehall waste, dynamic young (50-year-old) Harold Wilson last week set the foundations of government shuddering with one of the most violent Cabinet reshuffles for centuries.

WOW

OUT goes fuddy-duddy Lord Longford, the shambling undynamic Irish peer who is generally admitted to have been a flop at the Colonial Office.

BOP

OUT goes toothy incompetent Sir Frank "Immigration" Soskice, Lord Privy Seal, once the doyen of Labour's entrenched Old Guard, now recognised for the senile ineffectual ditherer he is.

ZOWIE

IN comes abrasive Irish peer Lord Longford, stepping ruthlessly into Sir Frank's shoes as Lord Privy Seal. At sixty he is regarded by many as the White Hope of Harold Wilson's streamlined administration.

BOOM

IN comes rock-jawed superman Sir Frank Soskice, to dynamite the archaic fabric of the House of Lords out of the nineteenth century, if necessary, into Kingdom Come. Sir Frank is widely respected by his colleagues as a man with fire in his belly.

AMERICAN EVANGELIST preacher Billy Graham arrived in Britain on his latest "crusade".

What's wrong with British brimstone?

The NUBT (National Union of Bible Thumpers) last night protested to the Home Secretary, balding dynamic Joy Renkins, over the admission to this country of Dr Billy Graham, and his wife the Singing Nun.

The Secretary General of the Union, Dr Ronnie O'Gorman led the protest. He said: "It's a f--king liberty. I had booked Earl's Court on June 7 for my 'God Will Return

on June 8' Rally. Now I shall have to postpone it."

Asked what action he intended to take, Dr O'Gorman replied: "I am going to invite Dr Graham to come with me on the GPO Tower and then tempt him to leap off."

AS AMERICAN BOMBING in Vietnam intensified, Wilson declined pleas from his MPs to disassociate the UK from US actions.

IN THE USA, experiments with transplanting organs from chimpanzees to humans met with varying levels of success.

Medical news

From Chicago today comes news of further major breakthroughs in the Advance of Medicine. Surgeons in Gary, Indiana, grafted the leg of an elk onto a 45-year-old post office worker, Mr F.R. Faggot. "This is the first time this operation has been attempted," said Dr Krotchweiser's Public Relations Officer. "Mr Faggot is on the danger list admittedly and will in all probability die, but the elk, apart from a mild limp, is in fine fettle."

In Rolla, Missouri, a gorilla's head has been successfully transplanted onto the body of a 73-year-old school teacher Miss Lisa Gamely who lost her own during a Biology Class. When asked how her mind was working after the operation, Miss Gameley's voice was clearly heard saying that the H-Bomb should be dropped on Hanoi and Peking. Friends were surprised and shocked as Miss Gamely had for many years been a Chinese Communist Agent, but as these were her and the gorilla's last words, conjecture ceased.

SOUTH AFRICAN prime minister Hendrik Verwoerd, the architect of many of the party's apartheid policies, was assassinated.

THE EYE STUBBORNLY refused to get excited about the football World Cup, which England won.

TV

5.0-6.30	WORLD CUP PREVIEW – Who? What? Why?
6.30 -7.00	UNITED – The Story of a Football Team
7.00-9.00	WORLD CUP – England v. Argentina *(repeat)*
9.00-10.00	WORLD CUP – Highlights.
10.00-10.30	Show Jumping from the White City
10.30-11.00	Suivez la Piste. *(Follow that Wyndham-Ghoulie)*
11.00-11.02	Is Britain Falling into the Sea? Economic discussion.
11.02-12.30	WORLD CUP. Will it ever end?
12.30	Close down.

PRIVATE EYE WAS the first publication to point out that Harold Wilson's image was an illusion in June.

Journalists are an unobservant lot, indeed yes, but you'd think that somebody, by now, would have made the elementary observation about the Prime Minister's face furniture (viz. it's not what it seems). But no, because we all know that Harold Wilson smokes a pipe and got those sexy pouches under his eyes by poring over letters from Ian Smith during the midnight hours, nobody has noticed the obvious: Harold Wilson rarely smokes a pipe, and wears glasses.

When the prime ministerial car sweeps up to the door of No.10, the steps of a VC10, or wherever, Harold Wilson has an automatic gesture. Just before the photographers close in, he whips off his glasses, consigns them to his left hip pocket, and extracts therefrom an unlit pipe, which he thrusts dynamically between his teeth.

IN SEPTEMBER, THE EYE revealed details of what went on inside the government's germ warfare laboratory, Porton Down.

Pneumonic plague is highly infectious; as has been proved with experiments with the creatures from whom the disease originates, black rats. A relatively small quantity of germs kills a very large number of people. Death is very quick – there is very little time for inoculation – and also very painful The kind of thing, in fact, which the Reds thoroughly deserve.

One vast room at Porton Down contains a large number of hermetically sealed cabinets, which look like 2-gallon glass jars. Inside a mass of orange fluid, constantly churned, containing a perpetual stream of active plague bacilli. Each cubic millimetre of this fluid contains twenty million lethal bacilli; so a 2-gallon jar contains rather a lot of potential death.

An ordinary two-seater reconnaissance plane, equipped to spray crops, could 'make a mistake' with its navigation and quietly spray about 50 gallons of Porton's orange fluid in a key area; thus ensuring the end of an army, a city or even, if you wanted to get it over with, every single person in the world.

The magazine's editor Richard Ingrams was phoned by the Home Office shortly after the article appeared and informed "that the Home Secretary 'took a very dim view' of the article, that 'one or two points struck home' and asking, in the interests of security, if we would kindly refrain from publishing anything similar".

1967

HAROLD PINTER'S *The Homecoming*, which had transferred to Broadway, swept the board at the Tony Awards.

Man in the News

HAROLD PINTER talks to BASIL MEAB

I met Mr Pinter in a basement tea-room in Letchworth. This is a recording of our conversation.

Meab: Good afternoon, Mr Pinter.

Pinter: *(after long pause)* Ah!

Meab: It's Meab of the *Eye*.

Pinter: Oh, I thought you'd been drinking.

Meab: Mr Pinter, having just seen your *Accident* and your *Basement*, I was wondering just how it is you manage to convey the underlying menace of existence. The stoat under the middle-class dining table, so to speak.

Pinter: Oh yes.

Meab: It seems almost as if you say more with your silences than with your words.

Pinter: *(breathes meaningfully for 8 minutes)*

Meab: Quite Mr Pinter. At times you have the uncanny accuracy of a tape-recorder in catching the nuances of human relationships in the Britain of the 60s.

Pinter: *(hums slightly and changes reels).*
(Enter Florence Scriggle, Proprietress of Ye Olde Tea Basement)

Scriggle: Tea and cakes for two is it?

Meab: No cake for me thank you.

Pinter: *(His face working with subdued fear)* Do you use tea bags?

Scriggle: *(whose fluting laugh ill-disguises her subdued threat)* No.

NOW PROMOTED to foreign secretary, George Brown continued to behave erratically.

THE TORREY CANYON tanker ran aground and broke up off the shore of Cornwall, spilling 100,000 tons of oil.

PROMOTED FROM postmaster-general to the recently created position of minister of technology, Tony Benn was causing quite a stir.

Benn's Hoverbritain

In his office on the 413th floor of the gleaming new Technology Tower, we talked this week to the man who is putting the 'New' back in the 'New Britain', Mr Anthony Wedgwood Hoverbene (or 01-346-2167, as he prefers to be called.)

Before the interview began, Mr Hoverbene rather surprisingly asked for a minute's silence for prayer and meditation. He crossed the room and knelt on a small inflatable rubber model of a Hovercraft, before an illuminated mock-up of the Concorde airliner.

"Technology," he confided, when he had finished, "is to me a spiritual affair. It liberates the soul from the enslavement of the ordinary human world. Take the telephone." "Thank you very much," I murmured, somewhat bewildered by this strange request, and crammed the instrument into my already bulging briefcase.

"You see," he went on, "I've been attacked by normally quite sensible people for my scheme to abolish all street names and addresses and replace them with a simple code of 54-digit numbers. But what they don't realise is that this simple idea would save the Post Office £57,000 million-a-year – because no one would send letters any more."

THE SIX-DAY WAR broke out between Israel and its Arab neighbours, causing alarm in the Wilson household.

We had just finished tea and I was clearing the things away with Harold watching the news on the TV when he came rushing through into the kitchen biting on his pipe and waving his hands about in an agitated fashion. "Whatever is it?" I could not but remark. "I trust your poll has not dropped off again." "Great heavens woman," he replied, "a crisis of amazing dimensions looms over the Middle East. The whole world hangs poised on the edge of a precipice. I have just seen it announced on the television. Kaufmann! Get Mr Brown on the line at once and Gladys, be so good as to look out my Reader's Digest 'Atlas of the World in Full Colour'. I fancy it is in the den along with the 'History of the World in Pictures'." I did as I was bid and returned to find Harold speaking agitatedly to Mr Brown over the scrambler. "No George," he was crying, "I tell you a crisis looms. Look I have seen the BBC News. Kindly get on to the Foreign Office and find out which side we are on."

THE WAR ENDED with Israel having massively enlarged its territory.

COME TO ISRAEL
AND SEE THE PYRAMIDS

Issued by the Israeli Tourist Office

FOOT AND MOUTH disease was spreading across the country.

As Britain's cows fall coughing to the ground the man who could have stopped it all is on the plane to New York to seek pastures new.

For years Col. Wemberley Threbb has been clamouring for Government support of his unique hovercow system.

Like all great ideas it seems incredibly simple. By harnessing the sun's rays with conical mirrors attached to the backs of Britain's cattle, they can be borne an inch aloft by powerful jets strapped to their hooves.

What was the reaction of the British Government to the Colonel's modest request for £80million?

A blanket No and a brusque brush off.

If Britain's cows had been hovering over the ground, the Foot and Mouth virus spread by infected copies of the *Daily Express* could never have gained a stranglehold on our native udders.

TRANSPORT MINISTER Barbara Castle launched the breathalyser, allowing police to check on drivers' alcohol levels.

That B Test

Sir,

What in heaven's name is going on? One thing is certain, I have now gone completely off my head.

Things have come to a pretty piss (whoops, sorry) when I am no longer allowed to sally forth of an evening with a skinful of sack, not to say a sackful of skin, and drive my souped-up Aston Ferrari round the highways and byways of our native heath knocking people down without being waylaid by some dunderhead flatfoot and told to breathe into a beastly bag and I refer in no way to my lady wife who shall remain blameless as far as these activities are concerned.

I certainly did not fight in the battle of Agincourt (*you amaze me – Ed.*) to see the liberty of the British citizen undermined and blown out of court by the forces of tyranny in this brutal and degrading manner.

Rise up Britannia!

Throw off the shackles of the dictator Barbara Cartland.

Yrs. etc.

HERBERT GUSSETT,

Johnson Home for Distressed Gentlefolk,

Nabarro, Gloucs.

BRITAIN ONCE AGAIN applied for membership of the European Economic Community.

AS THE FINANCIAL crisis worsened, chancellor Jim Callaghan announced that sterling was to be devalued, a complete reversal of government policy. Few were convinced by Harold Wilson's claim that "it does not mean, of course, that the pound here in Britain in your pocket or purse or in your bank has been devalued".

POUND CRIMES TRIBUNAL

Callaghan pleads not gilt-edged

Mr James Callaghan accused of crimes against the pound pleaded not guilty yesterday when his trial opened at Vestmeinster.

"I never opposed devaluation," he sobbed. "I was only taking orders from above. We had no choice in those days. It was our job to defend the master currency."

Mr Callaghan blamed the sequence of events on his Operation Overlord Adolph Wilson who he described as "a group of sinister men embarked on an insane mission of power".

"You would have done the same," he told prosecuting counsel in emotional tones. "Anyway none of us knew what was really going on. We simply took orders and carried them out."

When the trial resumed this afternoon the accused was asked if he cared about the countless millions of pounds which had been lost.

"Nothing you can do will bring them back," he said.

He was carried from the court weeping.

PRESIDENT DE GAULLE vetoed the British application to join the EEC.

Yes, it's oui say British

Foreign Office spokesmen are undeterred by de Gaulle's latest rebuff to British hopes of joining the Common Market (writes Our Man in the Pissoir LAURENCE OLIVIER TODD).

They go so far as to regard it as a positive welcome to Britain by the French.

"A lot of the difficulty springs from the translation problem," murmured a Whitehall man. "When the General says 'Non', it could mean a lot of things including the various forms of Yes which strike deep into the heart of every living Briton.

"Then again a good deal of misunderstanding has arisen about the General's reported statement that 'Britain is a pathetic bankrupt nothing with no clothes sitting shivering in an ocean of despondency and misery'. Even if the General said this, and we only have the word of 2,000 reporters that he did, the words referred to contain, if anything, boundless praise for our achievements and economic stability."

SOMEWHERE, A VERY LONG way from the *Private Eye* office, the Summer of Love was happening.

THE SEXUAL OFFENCES ACT decriminalised homosexual acts in private between men over the age of 21.

1968

AS THE ECONOMY continued in the doldrums and the new chancellor slashed public spending, a patriotic "I'm Backing Britain" campaign was launched.

It was revealed today that long before the Surbiton typists initiated the 'I'm Backing Britain' campaign, the staff at Gnome House had been working overtime for no extra pay.

Typists, waiters, chefs, chauffeurs, cigar cutters and game keepers employed at Gnome House have been clocking in at 2.00am in 'a purely voluntary effort' to help Britain in her hour of need.

Lord Gnome, supporting the 'I'm Backing Britain' movement, has also started a fund to send Simon Dee to the uninhabited island of Depression in the remote Pacific.

IN MARCH, PROTESTERS against the Vietnam War attempted to storm the American embassy in London, with stones and smoke bombs thrown.

War effort to be stepped up

A million more students are to be drafted and sent out to Grosvenor Square a spokesman for the Guevara is Alive and Living in Hanoi movement announced today.

The announcement follows increased pressure from the hawks in the movement to end the war and bring the American Embassy and the police to their knees.

Mr Tariq 'Tin Pan' Ali, President of the Light Up an Embassy group, is determined to fight the war to a finish despite the heavy loss of life and the mounting criticism within his party.

Heavy casualties were inflicted in the recent offensive when small bands of disciplined policemen beat back the Light Up an Embassy forces who retreated in confusion, not to say Black Marias.

Our Military Correspondent Writes
The despatch of a million more men to Grosvenor Square is unlikely to bring the end of the war nearer.

Time and again events have shown that mere numbers are ineffective when it comes to overpowering a band of highly disciplined thugs under the command of Insp. 'Knacker of the Yard' Knacker.

Charlie Fuzz, as he is known to the Ali forces, is a determined enemy who with only a wooden truncheon can wreak havoc in a couple of minutes. While the L.U.E. depend on a complicated and clumsy chain of supplies, Charlie can keep going for days on a pork pie and a packet of crisps.

CONSERVATIVE MP Enoch Powell made his notorious "Rivers of Blood" speech, attacking immigration and legislation that would outlaw racial discrimination.

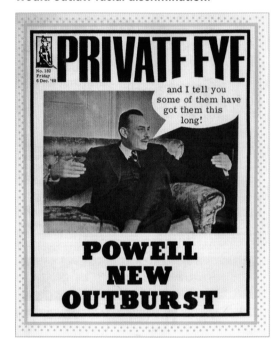

POWELL WAS PROMPTLY sacked from the shadow cabinet by Ted Heath.

What the Paupers Say

Dear Sir, I am no racialist but before readers condemn Mr Powell, let me relate a story which a friend of my aunt's was told by her brother-in-law who claimed to have heard it firsthand from Mr Powell himself.

Apparently an old lady of 103 was set upon one night as she was practising her violin by a gang of coloured men dressed in tinsel robes and told there and then to sell them her house for only 5/7d.

When she objected she was stripped naked tied up in a copy of the *Daily Express* and pushed through her own letter box where she was left while crowds of little piccaninies danced round shouting and laughing.

She has since died.

Yours,

Arthur Basildon, The Vicarage, Watford.

Dear Sir, I am no racialist, but this tiny country of ours, already bursting at the seams, can simply not afford to absorb ANYONE else, coloured or otherwise.

Yours,

Enid Benson-Thatch, Carry on up the track past Ben Nevis for ten miles and it's across the grouse moor, a little to the left with the yellow gate. Two pints next Tuesday please, Scotland.

AFTER MANY, MANY threats to resign from the government, George Brown finally did, much to the regret of part-time poet Mrs Wilson.

> *We see your little empty chair*
> *Deserted by the grate*
> *Your breath still lingers on the air*
> *Your crumbs upon the plate:*
> *We may have had our little tiffs*
> *At loggerheads have been*
> *You may have stolen all our Whiffs*
> *And drunk the Windolene*
> *But now that you have gone, alas,*
> *We miss you very much*
> *Let's hope, whatever comes to pass*
> *That you will keep in touch.*

Harold does not seem to share my nostalgia for the boisterous evenings with the Browns, and although I like the Jenkinses very much I fear Roy lacks the spirit of uninhibited fun and sunny laughter that blew into the house when George came to call. My oh my, how we laughed. At the time it was not always easy to forgive the breakages, and sometimes, when I was mopping out the bathroom, I vowed that I would never allow him over the threshold again. And yet, and yet. I do not believe that I have ever seen anyone with such an innocent and childlike mien as when he fell asleep, as he often did, during a fact-finding nightcap, on the lounge floor.

STUDENT PROTESTS erupted in Paris and came close to toppling de Gaulle's government...

...WHILE SEVERAL BRITISH university campuses saw "sit-ins", with students declaring a "state of anarchy".

The Clapham Commune

SID TRAIN (*Reader in New Left Sociology at the Public Library, Watford*)

Just over a week ago, students at the Clapham Day Nursery decided they had had enough. They occupied the premises and politely informed Miss Enid Croat, Chief Superintendent of Infant Studies and meals monitor, that she should bugger off before she got thunked on the bonce with a yoyo.

What followed has now passed into history. The infants took over the running of the school, only maintaining contact with the outside world via a Kiddiephone Walkie Talkie kit.

Lessons in the conventional sense have been abolished; the children serve their own meals, collect their own dinner money and wipe their own bottoms. It is a revolution in educational technique.

Nothing can ever be the same again.

THE COVER FOR John Lennon and Yoko Ono's album *Two Virgins* was, er, unveiled shortly after the couple's arrest on drugs charges.

RUSSIA SENT TANKS and troops into Czechoslovakia to crush Alexander Dubcek's efforts to liberalise the regime in the Soviet satellite state.

Letters to the Editor

Gosh Sir, We think what is happening in Czechoslovakia is jolly exciting and if the beastly Russians start poking their nose in like they did in Hungary, we all think it would be jolly unfair and chaps might get hurt.

Love from,

Bertrand Russell	Paul Johnson
Kingsley Amis	Henry Moore
Max Beloff	N.F. Mott
Lennox Berkeley	Soper + Mervyn Southwark
Benjamin Britten	Bridgid Brophy
David Carver	Stephen Spender
Hugh Casson	Philip Toynbee
Robert Conquest	David Watt
Stuart Hood	Arnold Wesker
Angus Wilson	Elizabeth Jane Howard
Julian S. Huxley	Peregrine Worsthorne

Esteemed Sir, The Supreme Praesidium of the Central Committee of the Communist Party of the Soviet Union has learned with dismay of the views of your most honoured British intellectuals with regard to the Czechoslovakian problems. In view of this quite unexpected show of force we are decided to withdraw all troops and to desist entirely from any further attempts to suppress the heroic fight of the revisionists.

Your humble and obedient serfs

A. Kosygin, L. Brezhnev, N. Krushchev (retd.)

The Kremlin, Moscow.

(STOP PRESS: Russian tanks invade Prague. Millions believed dead.)

MIXED-RACE CRICKETER Basil D'Oliveira was excluded from the England team for a tour of apartheid South Africa amid much dissembling about the reason why.

That *Times* editorial in full:
A surprising decision

The decision of the Committee of Reindeer Games Selectors to ban RUDOLPH the so-called Red Nosed Reindeer from joining in their games has given rise to widespread disquiet in many quarters. Here is a reindeer who has distinguished himself throughout the season as a player of exceptional quality. Why, therefore, has he been excluded from the games?

The explanation which is being advanced by some critics is that the decision represents a concession to prejudice against MR RUDOLPH's personal appearance and in particular his unnaturally rubicund proboscis.

Such charges must always be treated with caution. The Reindeer Selection Committee has stated categorically that "the games team has been picked solely on a consideration of form". The Committee must immediately be exonerated from any suggestion of prejudice. In the circumstances it is most unlikely that MR S. CLAUS will fail to uphold their decision when he comes to selecting a team for driving his sleigh this winter.

FIVE YEARS AFTER masterminding the Great Train Robbery, Bruce Reynolds was arrested in Torquay where he had been living under the name of Keith Hiller.

Hitler arrested in Torquay

A twenty-five year long search, covering all five continents of the world, came to an end early this morning with the arrest in a luxurious Riviera-style villa near Torquay, Devon, of Adolf Hitler.

The arrest comes as a personal triumph for Inspector 'Knacker of the Yard' Knacker, who has made the search for Hitler his own lifelong crusade. Said Knacker yesterday, "Let's just say – I'm very happy at the way it's worked out".

Neighbours of the Hitlers in exclusive Brazilia Drive were shocked to learn that the quietly-spoken, retiring man who they knew simply as 'Der Fuehrer', was a wanted criminal.

Said next-door-neighbour, Mrs Cynthia Glarb, a retired widow, "Oh yes, I knew Mr Hitler well. I would never have dreamed that he could have been mixed up in a thing like the Second World War. We knew him as just a kindly old gentleman with a love of animals, who had obviously been in the services. You could tell that from all the medals he wore and his habit of saluting everyone with his arm in the air."

PAUL FOOT POINTED OUT **in February that the government had broken an arms embargo by allowing the sale of Beagle light aircraft to South Africa.**

Mr Peter Masefield, Chairman of the British Airports Authority and of the Beagle Aircraft Company, told the *Financial Times* 'The aircraft is civil and unarmed'. It would be used 'chiefly for air sea rescue work and for the fishery patrols'. The biggest sale recorded yet for Mr Masefield's Beagles was to the Royal Air Force, who bought 20 Beagle 206s 'for military production conversion'. The military uses of the aeroplane are now so well established that the Beagle 206 was listed in the 1967 edition of Flight International's Military Aircraft survey.

A leading air correspondent told *Private Eye*: "If you wanted to keep an eye on a gathering in the bush, there is no better plane than the Beagle to do it from." Even the British Conservative Party is on record against selling South Africa arms for such purposes.

THE EYE REVEALED **more about the chemical weapons being produced by government scientists in July.**

"Under the auspices of Porton Down, two main types of gas are manufactured at Nancekuke, near Portreath in Cornwall. The first is the 'harrassing agent' CS, a substance which is extensively used, often lethally, in Vietnam, and was indispensable to the Paris police recently. The CS is exported, at a benefit of about £250,000 a year to the British balance of payments. A considerable quantity is held over for 'selected forces' of English and Scottish police, which stockpile large supplies.

British CS was almost certainly not used in Paris, since each British CS grenade carries about 40 grams of the stuff, while the French police grenades last May carried only 1 gram each. Should CS be used by the British police, in other words, each grenade will be forty times more powerful than those used with such effect in France.

The Nancekuke factory also produces 'V' agents – a gas which is instantly lethal if applied in the smallest quantities. 'V' agents packed into artillery shells or warheads could devastate an entire nation with minimal effort."

THE COLLAPSE OF RONAN POINT, **and its implications for the 10,000 or so people living in around 30 other tower blocks built to the same design, came under Foot's scrutiny in August.**

The preliminary report of the consulting engineers Bernard L Clark and Partners concluded the explosion was not a particularly violent explosion. While the contractors estimated the pressure of the explosion at a fantastic 600 pounds per square inch, the Clark Report puts it at nearer 3 pounds per square inch. Clearly if a small explosion of 3lbs PSI can knock down a section of 22 stories in a building like Ronan Point, something is very wrong indeed.

There was therefore some anxiety among onlookers as the Building Research Station experts started piling up the weights on a two storey block designed exactly to resemble Ronan Point. To their astonishment, the crucial joint fractured at a mere 1.6lbs PSI.

The block of flats at Ronan Point is built under a system originally devised by the Danish building firm Larsen and Nielsen. The system was devised for relatively low-storey buildings, seldom more than five or six storeys high and usually less, but it soon caught the attention of British firms, who bought up licences and started to interest local authorities in "sky-rise" Continental-style blocks which could be built relatively cheaply and quickly. For these new building systems there was no established code of safety, nor even a code of regulations for the construction process.

The outer walls of most Larsen Nielsen-style blocks in this country, which bear most of the weight of the 22 storeys, are six inches thick, compared with the 18 inches recommended. The four-ton floor slabs are fitted into slots in the walls. One and a quarter inches of the slab rests on the wall on each side, and the gap is filled with concrete on the site, thus making a 'joint'. There is no other tie between the wall and the floor, so that if the wall is pushed out by a quarter of an inch or more, the new concrete almost certainly splits and the floor falls in. The fall will almost certainly release the floors above and below from the grip of the wall panels, leading to what is known in the trade as "progressive collapse". Wind could disturb the building. Subsidence of merely an inch at the base of the building would bring it tumbling down. Or fire. And one of the findings of the Clark Report was that the building did not meet the standard fire regulations.

1969

AS RUPERT MURDOCH took over the *News of the World*, Lord Gnome welcomed him to the ranks of British proprietors.

Gnome

A glance at any one of Mr Murder's highly respected Australian journals should be enough to dispel lingering doubts about his claim to be regarded as one of the greatest living beneficiaries of the human race.

I need only mention the weekly paper of opinion and comment "Bust" which circulates widely in Sydney.

Peeping furtively through a specimen copy of this admirable publication the eye alights upon such inviting headlines as 'Do Mini-skirts Excite Rapists?' or 'Wife Served Meals Nude'. The reader is left with the strongest impression of controversial issues discussed in a sober and responsible spirit.

BERNADETTE DEVLIN WON a by-election in Mid-Ulster, becoming Westminster's youngest MP at the age of just 21.

The laughing Colleen swings in

By LUNCHTIME O'BOOZE

Not since the young William Pitt stormed the citadels of power at the age of 8 in 1791* has there been anything like it in the history of Parliament.

At the age of 16 a young bright-eyed mini-skirted lass from the bogs of Ireland has swung into Westminster like a blast of hot air.

Her name is *(Cont. p94)*

*Check with Daily Telegraph Information Service. Ta.

What are you going to be when you grow up ?

BARBARA CASTLE, now minister for employment, set out controversial proposals to curb trade union powers in a white paper "In Place of Strife". Not everyone was convinced by them.

A special White Paper entitled 'In Place of Trade Unions' published last year set out the guidelines for a realistic approach to industrial problems.

The proposals contained in this White Paper were tough; they had teeth; and they were pushed through in the face of remorseless opposition from A.N.U.S. (the Amalgamated National Union of Satirists); but they were vitally necessary if the wellbeing of… the nation was to be preserved.

The tough unpopular measures were as follows:

1. An immediate reduction in working hours.
2. A statutory 50% increase in all wages and salaries.
3. A compulsory two-month holiday period for all employees (replacing the previous two-day arrangement).

It will be seen that this document does not by any means go all the way in dealing with costly industrial disputes.

But at least it represents a courageous attempt to make a start in the vital task of overhauling our outdated attitudes.

KENNETH CLARK'S *Civilisation*, a history of Western art, began on BBC2.

Part 79: The pundit as hero

By SIR MICHAEL ANGELO

(24 hours signature tune. Camera tracks back to reveal Sir Michael standing at the end of an interminable corridor).

ANGELO: I am standing on the spot where television came to one of its major cross-roads, Corridor B in the great BBC Television Centre. Last week, you may remember, we saw how television had entered a new Dark Age, which could hardly be described as civilised. The naïve and simple faith of the men who had produced such masterpieces as *Z-Cars* and *The Black and White Minstrel Show* had lost its way. The limitations of their simple techniques were no longer enough to sustain the interest of the civilised world. Men were unconsciously seeking new ways in which the old truths could be expressed.

(Camera cuts to contemporary print of white-coated technologists grappling with elaborate machinery.)

Shape, motion and light – all these techniques had been mastered. It seemed that there was nothing new. But then, as we have so often seen before, came one of those rare moments which alters the whole course of civilisation. Like the frescoes of Giotto or the discovery of perspective by Spaggetthi di Bologna, the invention of colour television completely changed our way of looking at the world.

(Picture of Val Doonican is shown first in black and white and then in colour.)

What a glorious world was opened up to the artists of the age! No longer were they confined to the subjects and images dictated by tradition. Now they could explore the entire kingdom of nature – a nature where grass was green, the sky was blue and Fanny Cradock's fish fingers could be seen at last in their true shade of bilious orange.

NEIL ARMSTRONG and Buzz Aldrin became the first men to set foot on the moon. Except for an intrepid *Eye* correspondent who had got there first.

Gnome

Another amazing scoop has been achieved by myself after lengthy negotiations in America – the story of man's first steps on the moon BEFORE THEY ACTUALLY TAKE PLACE.

The full story headed 'I SET FOOT ON THE MOON' by world famous Lunchtime O'Booze MBE will be published in the next edition of my organ.

It will tell for the first time ever the amazing story of man's tentative exploration of the moon's surface.

Needless to say there have been plenty who are prepared to scoff at this personal triumph; there have even been those who go so far as to suggest that there is an element of deception in Mr O'Booze's brilliant despatches from the moon's surface. Such people do little more than betray their abysmal ignorance of matters scientific.

The moon is, as any schoolboy knows, two million light years away. It follows that events taking place on the moon do not accord with our own earthly time scheme.

It is perfectly possible, therefore, for things that lie in our future to have already occurred on the moon. Mr O'Booze's awe-inspiring journey is in lunar terms old hat; but to some dim eyes here on earth, it appears, by a process of 'time-space illusion' to lie in the future.

It is a sign of the intellectual dearth inherent in my many critics that it should prove necessary for me to acquaint them with such elementary scientific facts.

E. Strobes
pp Lord Gnome,
Lunar Orbit Station 71b,
7 June 2001

TWO WEEKS LATER...

Private Eye first with moon pictures
"Triumph" – Gnome

The amazing *Private Eye* picture, showing on the left 'The Sea of Absurdity'. The picture has been described by Russian scientists as 'Bogus to say the very least'.

World Acclaims *Private Eye* Scoop

The *Private Eye* achievement was acclaimed throughout the world's Press within seconds of the publication of the amazing photographs.

WASHINGTON: 'The Smallholder's Echo' wrote: "*Private Eye* is a humorous magazine appearing fortnightly."

PARIS: 'Le Canard Enchaine', famed satirical organ, wrote "Not since the days of Louis Quatorze..."

STOCKHOLM: 'Het Dageblat' commented: "Het os der grosse bøllsøp søns grondma køt her tøts in der møngel."

THE KRAY TWINS were found guilty of the murders of George Cornell and Jack "The Hat" McVitie and jailed for life, amid questions about how they had evaded prosecution for so long.

NOT TO BE OUTDONE, O'Booze's new colleague made her debut discussing the only subject of the moment (herself).

A NEW VOICE IN THE EYE

Down to earth with Glenda Slagg

So President Nixon can call up the astronauts on the moon's surface three million miles away and be put through with scarcely a second's delay.

But when I try to phone my editor and tell him that I can't think of anything to write about so is it alright if I churn out 2000 words on Come Off It GPO What's Wrong With Britain's Telephones, I get an engaged tone.

When I do get through I am told he's in the boozer and not on any account to be disturbed.

WAKE UP EDITOR! Wake up John Stonehouse! Men may be able to get to the moon but for the ordinary housewife in the street... *(cont. p.94)*

TROOPS WERE SENT into Northern Ireland for the first time on what was meant to be a "limited operation" to help restore law and order after weeks of sectarian violence, aggravated by the partisan nature of the Protestant police reserves, the 'B Specials'.

Ulster: We name the guilty men

Behind the so-called talks of the so-called Civil Rights movement lurks a vast international conspiracy planning to overthrow all that we know as so-called civilisation today.

Who are these men who are plotting Armagh-geddon?

As a result of an exhaustive 24-hour drinking probe with highly-informed sources, believed to be not a million miles from Det. Sgt. Leasco O'Pergamon of the 'M' Specials, I am now in a position to name the guilty men.

They are:

1. **Miss Bernadette Devlin**, 21, the conspirators' 'cover girl'.
2. **Eamonn O'Lenin**, 16, a former Botany student at the Londonderry College of Technology. O'Lenin is the founder and only member of the Ulster Committee for Universal Democratic Friendship.
3. **Sunday O'Telegraph**, 17, unemployed building worker, part-time hooligan, and member of the 'Violence for Peace in Ulster' movement.
4. **Gerry Mander**, 16, editor of 'Baton', organ of the militant 3-strong Trotskyite Alliance for Chinese-Ulster friendship.
5. **Paul Trot**, 33, journalist son of U Trot, General Secretary of the United Nations Darts Club and a regular contributor to the militant, Albanian-financed Mao-ist fortnightly, *Private Eye*.

IN THE COMMONS, Enoch Powell outlined his vision of Britain's future yet again.

Powell's new bombshell – '100% coloured births are coloured'

According to the latest statistics 100% of the children born of coloured immigrants are themselves coloured.

This was the shock statistic introduced by Mr Enoch Powell into a House of Commons speech today.

BONFIRES

"It is a staggering fact," said Mr Powell, "which we ignore at our peril. In 25 years time coloured babies born today will be 25 years old." Mr Powell went on to state that in areas where there had been wide-scale coloured immigration the numbers of coloured births were higher than in other areas.

HOLOCAUST

Another amazing statistic produced by Mr Powell shows that young immigrant women between the ages of 17 and 30 have more children than white women aged 70-95.

"If this continues," says Mr Powell, "there will be civil war within our lifetime.

"Unless the death penalty is reintroduced for all those guilty of immigration, such a funeral pyre will be lit as will be beyond the comprehension of generations to come."

Further statistics revealed that less than 1% of Mr Powell's brain was grey matter. The matter is to be looked into.

AN UNPRECEDENTEDLY intimate documentary, *The Royal Family*, was broadcast ahead of Prince Charles's investiture as Prince of Wales.

JOHN LENNON returned his MBE to the Queen, "as a protest against Britain's involvement in the Nigeria-Biafra thing, against our support of America in Vietnam and against Cold Turkey slipping down the charts".

Spiggy sends back medal

Spiggy Topes leader of the Turds a popular singing group has sent back his Toytown coronation medal to Buckingham Palace.

With it he has sent a letter in which he registers a "strong protest" against "the way in which things are going man".

Says the letter:

Dear Thing, You probably don't remember me, but I once waved to you when you opened the new extension to the public library at Neasden in 1947.

I am sending back my medal as a symbol of the world's hang-up. Nothing personal mind, but I cannot do gigs wearing my medal knowing that hundreds of Turkeys will be slaughtered this Christmas in the name of peace.

Are you reading me, Your Majesty?

A Palace spokesman said last night: "We have received Mr Topes's letter and paid the postage due. Her Majesty was deeply touched by his good wishes."

ANYTHING CONTINUED to seem possible.

"I've got this fantastic idea for an idea, man"

AFTER THE CARIBBEAN ISLAND of Anguilla declared independence from neighbouring British colony St Kitts, Harold Wilson and his foreign secretary Michael Stewart dispatched paratroopers to retake the island. Mrs Wilson watched proudly.

"Where did you say it was?" Harold continued, taking down the Reader's Digest Atlas of the Universe with revised Moonmaps from the tooled oak-style Maples Bookerama by the television. "Anguilla, Anguilla, were are we? Ah yes, here it is, just south of Madrid." "No, no," interposed little Mr Stewart, fingering his tie, "it is an island in the Caribbean, or so I am informed by my experts on the Desk. It would seem that self-styled President Webster declared

U.D.I. some time in 1967. Might I suggest that we lodge a mild protest at the UN?"

"Wait a moment," Harold replied, poring once more over the map. "here we are: Anguilla Pop. 6,000. What's that you say? Protest? My dear Stewart, as you are no doubt aware, this week sees the hundredth anniversary of the birth of Neville Chamberlain. Those of us who have lived through these troubled times will know full well the penalties that befall those who are prepared to compromise with the dictators. Are we to stand idly by while evil men wave the mailed fist of derision at the forces of democracy and peace? While the lion's tail is twisted beyond endurance by power-mad tyrants intent on world domination? This President Whitlock, who does he think he is?" "Webster, Prime Minister, Webster," soothed the silver-haired satrap. "Whitlock, Webster, Nasser or Hitler, style themselves how they will, we know their type. If we give way now we shall pay for it later with millions dead and our cities devastated to rubble. I am surprised, Stewart, that you have so little regard for the lessons of history."

"Kaufmann," Harold shouted, thrusting his hand inside his waistcoat in a belligerent manner, "ring up Dickie Mountbatten and ask if he'd be interested in becoming Allied Supremo of an amphibious task-force designed to bring this sabre-rattling Mussolini grovelling to his knees." Unfortunately, Lord Mountbatten was already booked for Late Night Line Up and was unable to accept. However, Mr Healey came round at once and was delighted at the suggestion, as it would give them a chance to try out the new Peewit inflatable Hovertank, and as the army, all fifty-seven of them, were getting a bit bored sitting about in their luxury Butlin-style Cookhouse on Salisbury Plain.

SENATOR EDWARD KENNEDY admitted that he had driven into a tidal lagoon on Chappaquiddick Island and then left the scene despite his passenger Mary Jo Kopechne being trapped in the submerged car. He didn't report the accident until after her corpse had been found.

You Kennedys can get away with murder

IN DECEMBER it was announced that after months of cover-up, US Lieutenant William Calley would stand trial for the murder of 109 men, women and children at My Lai in Vietnam.

That massacre – you write

Dear Sir,

Surely after this lapse of time it is to be doubted whether the true facts of the so-called Bethlehem Massacre will ever be known. I have had some experience of this kind of thing myself, and know how such matters can get blown up out of all proportion. Despite the alleged existence of alleged eyewitness accounts of the alleged incident, the full story will never be known, and I suggest it is time we washed our hands of the whole affair.

I remain, sir, yours faithfully,

P PILATE (Governor, retd) The Villa, Aston, Britannia

AUTHORITIES IN AMERICA did their best to distance themselves from the atrocity.

The Sharon Tate murders and the killing of Black Panthers by Los Angeles police were "isolated incidents" and not typical of the conduct of Americans in America, a White House spokesman said today.

The statement was plainly designed to quell the world-wide sense of outrage following news of these latest atrocities by American citizens.

The spokesman commented: "Inevitably America has a brutalising effect on people, and some unstable elements run amok. But we are convinced that the Government policies are right and we intend to continue on the same lines." World reaction to the atrocities however has been uniformly unfavourable. A leader in the Hanoi Daily Telegraph comments: "Here is ploof at last if ploof were needed that it is time for the Amelicans to get out of Amelica."

THIS YEAR a new *Eye* tradition which would last for decades began: being forced to print apologies to businessman, bully and crook Robert Maxwell. The first, over suggestions he, er, tried to intimidate journalists who wrote about him, appeared in August as he was being booted out of his company Pergamon due to dirty dealings over a takeover. His legal threats were very effective, as this photobubble from the very next issue demonstrates.

If there's another word about bouncing Czechs I'll sue.

UP-AND-COMING historian David Irving was profiled in January.

In his university days in the late '50s, Irving had great pretentions as a journalist and became editor of Imperial College's glossy magazine *Phoenix*. The paper started a regular feature about old boys, and readers were surprised to notice that the first old boy selected was a Nazi. They were even more surprised when yet another Nazi old boy got treated to a further write-up. In a journal called *Carnival Times* Irving included in the magazine a special supplement containing political cartoons and comments along the line of the editor's extreme Right-wing views, articles defending apartheid and dictatorship in Europe. Irving said at the time, "I belong to no political party. But you can call me a mild Fascist if you like."

AND ANOTHER NEW and promising subject emerged in December in the form of the newly-elected MP for Louth.

Jeffrey Archer worked as a fund-raiser for the United Nations Association from July 1967 to February this year. For the period July 1, 1967 to July 31, 1968 Archer had claimed more than £1,700 in personal expenses, a sum which was regarded as "generous" for an organisation which relies on voluntary funds. An inquiry was launched into the expense claims, not all of which were found to be satisfactory...

Some of Archer's expense claims were for the entertainment of Sir Gerald Duke, a retired Major General, and Sir William Oliver, former High Commissioner in Australia. The two knights are now Archer's partners in in a firm called Arrow Enterprises which was formed on April 29, 1968, in the names of Jeffrey Archer and Humphrey Berkeley, chairman of the UNA. Berkeley denies any knowledge of his partnership in Arrow. A document was placed at Companies House to the effect that Berkeley had resigned his directorship. The signature bearing Berkeley's name on this form is clearly not written by Mr Berkeley.

1970s

THIS WAS THE DECADE WHEN THE *EYE* BECAME dangerous. In 1972 it took its first major scalp when Reginald Maudling was forced to resign as home secretary after managing to get himself embroiled in not one but two major scandals the magazine had unravelled over the years. In 1978 it claimed another when it revealed police were poised to arrest the former Liberal party leader Jeremy Thorpe on suspicion of conspiracy to murder his ex-boyfriend. And in between it made itself such an irritant to the inhabitants of Downing Street that some of them were party to a plot to destroy it completely.

Ted Heath was content just to moan. "*Private Eye* could never forgive me for the fact I didn't go to a public school," he groused, leaving editor Richard Ingrams to explain that his "Grocer Heath" nickname actually came from "all those early Common Market negotiations when the whole thing seemed to revolve around what we would pay for cat food and that kind of thing".

> " *Private Eye is like Sellotape. Maddening like Sellotape, messy like Sellotape, imperfect like Sellotape, and horrid like Sellotape, it is nevertheless indispensable like Sellotape; and above all, it resembles Sellotape in that we cannot imagine how we got on before it existed.* "
>
> Bernard Levin, 1974

But Harold Wilson and his equally paranoid political secretary Marcia Williams (created Lady Falkender on the pair's return to Number 10 in 1974) became deranged with the conviction their conversations were being leaked to the *Eye* as part of a "smear campaign". Falkender even attempted to have Robin Butler, who would go on to head the entire civil service as cabinet secretary, booted out of Downing Street because she suspected him of "lunching with *Private Eye*", and Wilson blocked one nominee from the notorious "Lavender List", which featured honours for at least two actual criminals, because he was suspected of being "too close to *Private Eye*".

When the magazine proved impervious to the threats of their lawyer and fixer Lord Goodman, a different plan was concocted. In 1976 the millionaire gambler and businessman, James Goldsmith, hit the *Eye* and its distributors with more than 100 libel writs which were explicitly aimed at putting it out of business. He even sued Ingrams and hack Patrick Marnham for criminal libel under a long-dormant law dating from the sixteenth century, which could have put them both in prison. Though nominally about Marnham's article on his role in the disappearance of murder suspect Lord Lucan, it was widely believed that Goldsmith was acting on behalf of his friends in Number 10: prime ministerial advisers were openly discussing Goldsmith being "prepared to put up £250,000 to destroy *Private Eye*", and his action ensured his own spot on the Lavender List when it appeared mid-litigation. Goldsmith settled all his cases in 1977, but not before they had sent him as demented as his Downing Street pals: he took to referring to the *Eye* as "a pus seeping through the system". If so, it was a remarkably popular pus: the magazine ended the decade with its highest readership yet.

1970

GENERAL ODUMEGWO OJUKWU, leader of the breakaway Biafran republic, fled the country ahead of its surrender to Nigeria. The Red Cross estimated that up to 10,000 Biafrans were dying of starvation every day.

> And with me gone, comrades, there'll be one less mouth to feed

BYE BYE BIAFRA

YOUTH UNREST CONTINUED, and began to spread to other sectors of society as prices rose and the government resisted claims for higher pay.

Demos and Molotov cocktail parties 1970

March 13: The Vice-Chancellor of Warwick University at home to the International Youth for Anarchy League and other organisations. Bring a bottle.

March 30: The Senior Proctor of Oxford University and Warden Sparrow at home, Clarendon Building 6.00pm – 9.00am, all-night sit-in.

April 28: The Rt. Hon. Harold Wilson and Mrs Wilson at 10 Downing Street, a small party for teachers and nurses.

June 5: Viet Cong Solidarity Committee, Grand Ball-in, Grosvenor Square. Demonstrations by Metropolitan Police dog-handlers and show jumpers. Fancy dress will be worn. 2pm – whenever the fuzz break it up.

July 12: Mr Justice Lawandorder, at the Central Criminal Court, a small party in aid of the Welsh Traffic Signs for Wales Committee. 3-6 (months, to run concurrently).

PAUL McCARTNEY issued a court writ to dissolve "the business carried on as the Beatles and Co".

Spiggy to quit Turds shock sensation

The world was stunned yesterday by the news that Spiggy Topes is no longer leader of the Turds, a popular singing group.

The sensational news came in a statement issued at 12.43 local time from the offices of Nipple, the Turd's multi-million pound business corporation, in fashionable Jimmy Savile Row.

Speaking frankly to me yesterday in a candid, exclusive interview given at his £250,000 exclusive, Tudor-style Neasden-on-Thames mansion, Topes said, "Basically, there is no split between us. It's just that I can't stand the sight of them any more."

In The City with 'Jobber'

Turds fell heavily this morning following the shock news of the Topes statement, but strengthened later and finished firm.

TO EVERYONE'S SURPRISE, Ted Heath won a comfortable majority in the General Election in June. He gave a young female politician her big break with a cabinet job.

The new names you'll be hearing about

Minister of Education
MRS MARGARET THATCHER

Behind a deceptively naïve and priggish exterior, friends say she is inclined to be a little naïve and priggish. Widely tipped to be the first woman on the moon, she knows little about schools or universities, which insiders say "will enable her to start without preconceptions". A grammar-school girl herself, she has a brilliant mind and knows the faults of the state system from the inside. (Her own children go to private schools.) Very much the new progressive type of Tory woman – she is keen on the Eleven Plus and driving her car.

CRACKS WERE BEGINNING to appear in the marriage of Princess Margaret and Lord Snowdon.

> What's all this about us rowing in public ?

> Shut up you fat bitch and keep smiling

FOLLOWING CLASHES in Notting Hill, the Community Relations Commission accused London's police of racial prejudice.

Notting Hill says Carry on Knacker!

Despite widespread criticism from Race Relations officials, Insp. "Knacker of the Yard" Knacker will remain as head of the notorious "Darkie Basher" division of Notting Hill Police.

Said Knacker: "I have nothing against these nig-nogs, but they are a bloody nuisance if you ask my opinion."

It is believed that the controversial Inspector may have been over-enthusiastic in carrying out his duty. "And that is not all he has carried out," a West Indian resident told me. "He carried out all my furniture last week for forensic analysis. That was the last I saw of it."

Another resident who asked to remain anonymous is 43-year-old part-time hospital patient, Mr Underground Conductor. He told me that he had been sitting watching the television one night with a few friends when the controversial Inspector swooped, along with 70 members of the controversial "Darkie Bashers".

Shapely 26-year-old Mrs Nigella Conductor was subjected to a lightning "frisk" whilst her male relatives were given an impromptu demonstration of modern police techniques.

Denying these and many other allegations of police brutality, Insp. Knacker said, "There is obviously some misunderstanding here. Many of these wogs, no disrespect intended, do not speak English proper like and therefore you could be easily misled by what they say into thinking that irregularities may have occurred in the line of duty.

"One other thing I should point out is that some of these spades are difficult to see in the dark and it is only too easy for a constable to bump into them by accident."

KEN LOACH'S "KES" proved itself a cut above most other films on offer.

Cinema Goround

NEASDEN GAUMONT

NES (AAIAA) Moving documentary-style essay about a young Neasden boy who tames a budgerigar in his back garden. The drab landscape of Neasden is beautifully photographed by Garry Baldie. Director Len Koach puts himself in world class, but Neasden dialect sometimes hard to follow. Plus full supporting programme of advertisements.

NEASDEN ESSOLDO

YOU CAN HAVE HER ANY TIME YOU WANT (XXX) 2.15, 3.45, 4.40, 5.15, 6.15, 7.40, 8.45, 9.50, 10.16, 11.27 (special late perf. Sats)

A CYCLONE and the subsequent floods killed hundreds of thousands of people in East Pakistan.

FLOOD DISASTER
The planes fly in

From all over the world they were flying in today, to the 1,000 miles of misery and mud that is flood-torn East Pakistan.

Planes, ships, helicopters – no effort or expense was being spared in the all-out bid to bring the vital lifelines of the world's press and television to the site of the worst disaster in history.

By early today the first wave of helicopters was circling the worst-hit areas of devastation, taking the vital pictures for which the world has been eagerly waiting.

Some courageous reporters were even requisitioning inflatable dinghies in their anxiety to reach the stricken villagers for on-the-spot interviews before it is too late.

AS IT WAS REVEALED that 8.8 million working days had been lost to strikes during 1970, industrial action by power workers led to widespread black-outs – and printers stopping the *Evening Standard*'s presses because they objected to a cartoon by Jak about their fellow trade unionists.

CORRUPTION AND BRIBERY on an epic scale began to be revealed by the *Eye* in April, with the first stirrings of a scandal which would lead within three years to the jailing of businessman John Poulson, the resignation of home secretary Reginald Maudling and the creation of the MPs' register of financial interests.

Mr John Poulson, a millionaire from Pontefract, until recently controlled one of the biggest and most powerful architectural practices in the world. Mr Poulson is a Licentiate of the Royal Institute of British Architects, and so has never had to pass an exam to qualify as an

architect. Nor is he qualified as a consulting engineer, though the firm JGL Poulson Associates, Consulting Engineers, has been operating since 1965. He is however a brilliant entrepreneur.

His firm was consultant to the enterprising Bradford-based Arndale Property Trust, which specialised in developing city centres and spread from its base at Bradford to the North East, to Scotland and even further south (Camberley, Tunbridge Wells, Luton). Apart from city centre development, Poulson's specialised in hospitals and swimming pools.

Mr Poulson set himself diligently to work, to establish contacts with local authorities who could be kept in touch with his firm's potential. For his contact with Labour authorities, Mr Poulson depended increasingly on the help and advice of his friend and colleague Mr T Dan Smith, the leader of the Labour majority group on Newcastle-on-Tyne Corporation and Chairman of the Northern Economic Planning Council. Dan Smith himself set up a number of public relations companies, which helped him in his work as link-man between developers and Labour local authorities.

Smith's companies sought to interest local authorities in a new craze, system building, while Poulson's helped to design some of the new system-built complexes, notably four blocks containing 521 houses at Felling, Co. Durham, built under the Larsen Nielsen system, which proved itself at Ronan Point. More important, both men saw the need for an indigenous British system, and in July 1964 a company was formed called Open System Building Ltd, whose founding directors were Mr and Mrs T Dan Smith.

In April 1966 OSB Ltd, which had moved its registered offices to Poulson's London office, was joined by a new distinguished chairman, Sir Bernard Kenyon, who at time of joining was clerk to the West Riding Council. Five months later, a new director joined the board – Mr Martin Maulding, who had left Oxford two years previously with a pass degree in politics, philosophy and economics and his experience in architectural consultancy was slim. His full value to the board was probably not realised until the following July when his father, the Rt. Hon Reginald Maulding, MP, deputy leader of the Opposition, joined the board. To complete the family picture, Caroline Maudling, Martin's sister and Reginald's daughter, and Mrs Beryl Maudling, Reginald's wife, bought substantial shareholdings in the company…

IN NOVEMBER the *Eye* began looking into another business in which the home secretary had become embroiled.

The recent much-publicised financial difficulties of Jerome Hoffman's International Investors Group have been under close scrutiny by the authorities. Hoffman's debts in this country are reckoned at up to £200,000.

Last August, as Hoffman's company came under the glare of publicity, Reginald Maudling resigned from the Presidency. He has since tried to give the impression that with his resignation he severed all connections with the Fund. On the contrary, however, Maudling has remained on good terms. He retained 50,000 shares in the company given him by Hoffman, and continued to take an active interest in IIG management. After the Tories won the election last June, the September IIG House journal carried a whole-page feature entitled CONGRATULATIONS REGGIE!

Somehow, Mr Maudling did not appear over-grateful for this eulogising. As the clouds over IIG began to darken, so Maudling's friendship with Jerome Hoffman began to cool. He tried to sell his shares in IIG, only to find that he had been given them on condition that he could only sell them back to the company. Hoffman refused to buy them back and Maudling was stuck with the connection. All he can do now is hope that Hoffman gets out of the country as fast as he can…

Hoffman, after going on the run, was subsequently jailed for fraud in America.

1971

BRITAIN CONVERTED to decimal currency, with the *Eye* going from 2 shillings to 10p a copy.

Those new coins – You write

From Sir H. Gussett

Sir, I am sure many readers will have been baffled, as I was, by the proposed new coinage. May I offer them a simple method of do-it-yourself conversion. Simply take any sum, say £12 18s 11d, and to convert it to its decimal equivalent, perform the following simple calculation. Add all the digits together. Then reverse the sum, making £11 18s 12 (or £11 19s 0) and multiply this by the former figure. The result will be exactly 152 times the required decimal figure. A straightforward exercise in long division will then yield the desired answer.

You may wonder how to remember the different stages of this calculation. I have therefore devised the following simple mnemonic, based on the words D-Day. D-Double the sum involved. D-Divide by 152. A-the answer you require. Y-You're home and dry!

I remain, Sir, in a state of confusion
HERBERT GUSSETT.

ASCOT RACECOURSE issued new dress rules. The *Eye*'s top columnist had her say.

Here she comes – It's Glenda Slagg

■ Blimey O'Reilly!!! Whatever next? So his Grace the so-called Duke of Norfolk has given the thumbs down sign to hot pants in the Royal Enclosure, Ascot.

Not for the first time has this old leftover from the Middle Ages tried to hold up the March of Progress, in this case the biggest thing in fashion for donkey's years!

Come off it, Dukie!! We're not ALL a hundred years old!! The world has come a long way since the lobster blushed because it saw Queen Victoria's bottom!!! (Auntie Glenda's little joke).

■ Don't women look silly in Hot Pants!!! For my money these ridiculous garments are the biggest hoax ever to be perpetrated on the daft British female!!

If I had my way these shorn off shorts would be banned by law from *all* public places.

THE THREE EDITORS of underground magazine *Oz* were jailed on obscenity charges by a judge who had shown every sign of being absurdly prejudiced against them throughout the trial.

THIS JUSTICE SHOULD BE SEEN TO BE DONE

Judge
Michael Argyle
A recent portrait
To avoid prosecution under the Obscene Publications Act, the obscene parts have been blacked out

LOCAL MP MARK WOODNUT devoted himself to preventing a recurrence of the Isle of Wight pop festival, at which Bob Dylan and Jimi Hendrix had appeared in previous summers.

IOW 'Black Death' peril threat, MP warns

The Black Death could kill millions if the Isle of Wight pop festival is allowed to continue, Mr Mark WoodnutifIwasyou, Conservative Member for the Island warned yesterday.

"I have been assured on the highest authority," he told reporters, "that if Messrs Burnt Fingers Ltd are given permission to go ahead with their so-called Festival we could see a recurrence of scenes unknown since the time of the Dark Ages.

"Last year," he recalled, "millions of teenagers jumped naked into the sea in scenes unparalleled since Nero's Rome.

"This year, I cannot say what horrors may lie in store for the residents of this so-called island paradise. Drug-crazed, Charles Manson-style murderers running amok in every boarding-house back garden. Killer rats, immune to all known chemical poisons, attacking innocent colonels in bath chairs. Giant dinosaurs of a type not known for millions of years roaming through the undergrowth and trampling on the Floral Clock at Ventnor."

THE EMPEROR OF JAPAN made a state visit to London, despite furious protests from former prisoners of war who had suffered at the hands of the soldiers under his command during the Second World War.

The lovable old gent they called the Führer

To anyone under 40, the name Adolf Hitler probably means precious little. But there are still some old fogeys around who may conceivably resent the state visit this week of a man who in his day was widely held to have been responsible for World War Two.

Today, as he shuffles to and fro in his carpet slippers, amid his collections of prizewinning chrysanthemums and priceless old masters, picked up for a song (believed to be the Horst-Wessel-Lied) during the war years, few neighbours recognise the man they once worshipped as a divine being.

TED HEATH and his chief negotiator Geoffrey Rippon agreed terms to take Britain into the EEC.

Yes, it's Oui

"We're going in!" That was the message today from a tired but smiling Mr Geoffrey Rippon, as he beckoned reporters to follow him into the Beefeater Bar of Ye Olde Redde Barrelle, the new British-style pub which has been flown over specially from Neasden High Street as part of European Conservation Year.

"Make no mistake about it," he told me, "this is the breakthrough we've all been waiting for. It's pretty well all sewn-up."

Certainly the faces of officials I spoke to today carried their own message of optimism and even ecstasy at the way the talks have been progressing.

"If things go on like this," said one, "we should be home and dry by Christmas. The vital question of Mauritian molasses, for so long the big stumbling block, has finally been cleared up. And there only remain now a few minor details to be cleared up – New Zealand butter, devaluation of the pound, abolition of the Monarchy, 200% rise in food prices, disappearance of the House of Commons, suicide of Enoch Powell, that sort of thing."

A COMMITTEE SET UP by former cabinet minister Lord Longford to investigate pornography got down to work.

Gnome committee on Longford meets

Lord Gnome's Committee to investigate the possible harmful effects of Lord Longford met today at Gnome House.

The "Study Group", as it will be called, includes such well-known figures as the Bishop of Neasden, Basil Brush the TV Personality, Mr Perishing Worthless the Journalist and the Nawab of Twat, 43.

In his opening address, Lord Gnome said that as far as he was concerned his mind was closed to the subject of Lord Longford. In recent weeks it was impossible to open a newspaper without seeing Lord Longford, in one form or another, on almost every page.

There was no doubt that this caused widespread offence and could be harmful to the young. In his view, Lord Longford should be confined to the House of Lords, where he would be available on request only to bona fide researchers and anthropologists.

THE GOVERNMENT introduced a policy of internment without trial for suspected IRA supporters, and were surprised to find that both resentment and violence increased in Northern Ireland.

'IRA hit for six'

"Not a single member of the IRA is left alive north of the Equator," claimed a tired but triumphant General Syngman Ree-Smogg, General Officer Commanding the British Army of the Boyne, yesterday.

His proud boast followed the sensational dawn swoop in which over 3,000 of the most dangerous men in Ulster were arrested and interned for an indefinite period.

"We've got the lot," said the General. "You can take it from me that there'll be no more trouble in Northern Ireland for quite a while." As he spoke, a high-velocity nuclear device exploded, sending a shower of tin-tacks into the General's recumbent form, where it lay beneath his desk.

Meanwhile, a hundred years away across the city, 3,000 journalists and TV men packed into the tiny suburban front-room of 2031 Ballyneasden Estate, the top-secret hideaway home of the most wanted man in Ulster, Lunchtime O'Buzo of the Irish Republican Army.

"We mean no harm to anyone," said the self-styled Generalissimo, in his gentle Irish brogue, toying lightly with a .45 pearl-handled revolver. "But so long as there's a British soldier alive on Irish soil, we shall kill him."

As he spoke, the Sacred Heart cuckoo clock on his mantelpiece sang six *Ave Marias*.

"Holy Mary," he lashed out, crossing himself devoutly, "you'll please excuse me, gentlemen, or I shall be late for mass now."

1972

ON WHAT BECAME known as Bloody Sunday, British troops opened fire on unarmed protesters in Londonderry, killing 13 people, and then immediately set about covering the whole thing up.

MAJ. GEN SIR SANDY 'BLOODY' SANDYS, Officer Commanding 14th Battalion the Parachute Regiment (The Paranoids) explains:

I'd like to take this opportunity, errrr, to clear up what happened the other day.

These are the facts.

At approximately 1400 our men came under severe bomb and mortar attacks from the trenches. Through my binoculars I could quite clearly see the tanks and armoured vehicles advancing across no man's land.

I gave instructions, in accordance with the Green Card issued to all paratroopers with abnormally low IQs, to fire a warning shot into the bodies of the hooligans, many of whom were by now retreating in a pretty cowardly fashion, showing the lack of pluck which is typical of the hooligan.

Errrr. Now then. *(Scratches moustache)*. To my certain knowledge, only one shot was fired. Any questions?

Q: General, if only one shot was fired how is it that thirteen people were killed?

Good question. I think this shows that the modern Para is a first class shot and a first class soldier. *(Beams)*. Thirteen with one bullet. Not bad shooting, what what?

ROBERT MARK was appointed as Metropolitan Police Commissioner with a brief to root out corruption. The head of the Flying Squad, Ken Drury, was suspended from duty after reports he and his wife had been on holiday to Cyprus as guests of a Soho pornographer.

Knacker suspended

by Our Crime Team
Ron and Reg

"I am deeply shocked," said quietly spoken Chief Insp. "Knacker of the Yard" Knacker following the news that he had been temporarily relieved of his duties pending an impartial police inquiry to be headed by his son, Supt. "Nipper" Knacker.

Speaking from the Knickerama Nudiebar in Lower Norwood, the Inspector said, "I have never been suspended before. It is another nail in the coffin of democracy to my way of thinking."

Knacker's controversial method of tracking down criminals by living with them for several months in tropical resorts, has come in for veiled criticism in some quarters.

But Knacker says, "Some people just don't seem to realise the truth of the old saying 'It takes a thief to catch a thief'.

"As to the allegations of bribery all I ask is this: 'Do the public want to see notorious criminals going round with bulging wallets?

"Would they not prefer to see the money in the safe hands of the police?"

AS A STRIKE BY MINERS dragged on into its second month, the government declared a state of emergency. The use of electricity to heat shops, offices and restaurants was banned, and householders were told they must only heat one room in their homes and "lights should only be used where essential".

TV rushed to hard-hit areas

Emergency supplies of *Dr Finlay's Casebook*, *On the Buses* and the *Blacked-out Minstrel Show* were rushed to several parts of the country yesterday, following the news that millions of people had spent several hours without television.

Said a typical householder, Mr Humphrey Daft of Leeds, "We have never known nothing like this. It was terrible."

But not all viewers were as lucky as Mr Daft. The films arrived too late for Mr Enoch Finger, a retired mattress-spring bender of Robertsbridge, Staffs.

He died before supplies of the *Golden Shot*, which he needed daily in order to keep alive, could reach his home in Grimsby, Devon.

Said a neighbour, "Mr Finger lived alone with only his wife and seven children to keep him company. These miners should be made to see just what they are doing to people like Enoch. And how would they like to spend hours of every day in the dark with just a flicker of light to show them the way?"

NEW YARD CHIEF

Morning Constable!

I am not obliged to say anything till I have spoken to my solicitor.

MASS PURGE

WITH DOCKWORKERS the latest to go out on a long-running strike, the prime minister attempted to negotiate a way forward with Trades Union Congress boss, Vic Feather.

AS VIOLENCE CONTINUED to escalate, the government pushed out Northern Ireland's prime minister, Brian Faulkner, and imposed direct rule from London.

A Message from the Managing Director

Hullo. I'd just like to take this brief opportunity to bring you up to date with regard to the situation as far as our Irish branch is concerned.

For quite some considerable time, we have been experiencing difficulties of a serious nature in this branch.

What I have done now, quite simply, having given the matter a great deal of to-ing and fro-ing in my mind, is to ask Mr Faulkner, formerly our Managing Director (Northern Ireland), to resign and this he has now done though I regret to say not in such a manner as I would have expected from a man who has occupied such a senior post in the Heathco complex.

In his place I have asked Mr Whitelaw to take charge. All of you will be familiar with Bill Whitelaw. Quite frankly you couldn't hope to meet a nicer chap. If there's anyone I know who can smooth out this situation it is Bill Whitelaw. I am sure everyone wishes him all the best.

But let one thing be clear. This is my final attempt to sort this one out. If the troublemakers – and some of them are little better than a pack of animals to my mind, the way they carry on – continue to spoke the works, then I shall shut the whole bloody shop up once and for all and leave it to the people on the spot to pick up the pieces as best they can and it won't be any use coming crying to me.

■ By the way, as you may have seen from the OUT OF ORDER notice, we are still experiencing teething troubles with the Automatic Plastic Beaker Disposal Unit in the canteen.

Obviously it was not working during the blackouts. But it did not stop some of you ramming beakers into it until it is now completely useless and will have to be overhauled which will cost I might add several hundreds of pounds.

E. Heath, Managing Director

CABINET MINISTER Geoffrey Rippon was dispatched to Uganda in a fruitless attempt to dissuade dictator Idi Amin from expelling the country's Asian inhabitants, many of whom had British passports.

End to round-the-world shuttlecock victim drama horror

Mr Geoffrey "Geoff the Rippon" Rippon, the unwanted cabinet minister, can stay in Britain for a limited period. This was the Home Office reaction to the tragic story of the fly-away trouble-shooter who for the last two weeks has flown from airport to airport looking for someone to talk to him.

It is now nearly two weeks since Rippon boarded a plane at Heathrow and flew to Uganda. But Ugandan officials turned him back and he was re-routed to neighbouring Kenya, where he hoped to speak to President Kenyatta.

But once again it was heartbreak for Rippon as burly Jomo refused him entry. He has now been given sanctuary in London for "compassionate reasons".

In Wolverhampton, Mr Enoch Powell lashed out at what he called "this terrifying flood of Rippon which could engulf the whole country in a raging holocaust unequalled since the time of Caligula". Militant dockers later came off strike to march in support of Mr Powell.

DESPITE FEARS of how the public would react, 27,000 of the refugees were welcomed to Britain.

FORMER PRIVATE EYE columnist John Betjeman was appointed poet laureate. A fellow poet, recently recruited to the magazine, paid tribute.

To Sir J.B.

A Tribute On His Appointment To The Laureateship

Hats off to you, Sir John!
So they have made you
Laureate at last. Well,
Of course I'm mildly
Disappointed I won't deny it.

It's a job that I wouldn't
Minded have doing. But no
Hard feelings.
You are the older man let's
Face it. I am a mere stripling.

I have no doubt that some day
Providing of course that I keep
On working at my poems
And don't give up like so many
That I shall pick up the phone
And hear Her Majesty's fluting tones
Saying 'Hallo there, E.J.
Thribb! The job is yours
At last'.

But that's all in the future.
I mustn't let my imagination
Run away with me, must I?

E.J. Thribb (17)

ARAB TERRORISTS broke into the Israeli team's accommodation block at the Munich Olympics, killing two athletes and taking nine hostage. They demanded safe passage out of Germany to an Arab country and got as far as a military airport before police opened fire. All the hostages were killed in the resulting shoot-out.

Munich Tragedy – 'How I would have stopped it'

Inspector "Knacker of the Yard" Knacker hit out today against the Bavarian police who were involved in the recent massacre at the Olympic Games in Munich.

"The British Bobby takes a lot of knocks, but never before have I seen eleven Israeli athletes gunned down in my manor," the Inspector said.

"From the start it was obvious these Arabs meant business. This is how I would have tackled what they are calling 'the Munich mix-up'. I would surround the building with policemen dressed in tracksuits. Under cover of darkness after parleying with the suspects I would have

agreed to escort them by bus to three helicopters and thence proceed in a northerly direction to a nearby airport. Then my carefully-trained team of snipers would open fire."

When it was pointed out to the inspector that his plan was identical to that followed by the Munich police, he became incensed and pressed a red button. Immediately a number of policemen disguised as Olympic athletes seized the assembled pressmen at gunpoint and escorted them to a waiting hovercraft while the world held its breath.

TED HEATH TRAVELLED to France to finalise arrangements for Britain joining the EEC, as the leaders of its nine members pledged themselves to closer union, including a common foreign policy and shared currency.

Hullo.
As you probably know I've been away at a conference in Paris sorting out the final details of the merger between our company, Heathco, and the large continental combine, E.E.C. Ltd.

To hear some people talk you'd think Heathco is going to be the junior partner in the new set up and that we're going to have company policy decided for us by these other chappies.

Such views are utterly and totally incompatible with the facts with regard to this one. I would like to state categorically once and for all: THIS NEW ARRANGEMENT DOES NOT, I REPEAT NOT, MEAN THAT WE ARE GOING TO BE TOLD WHAT TO DO BY A LOT OF FOREIGNERS.

And here's another thing. I haven't fixed up this merger for my own benefit. The whole idea is that everyone gets a fair crack of the cake.

So let's pack in the moaning and get on with the job for heaven's sake.

◾ Now, a word or two about the new Automatic Plastic Beaker Disposal Unit which we are installing in the canteen. It is the very latest model made by the Phuwatascorcha Co Ltd, something of a big noise in the APBDU world.

Unfortunately the instructions are printed in Japanese, which I must say hasn't helped matters.

It now appears that we are missing the interlocking compressor rods which are vital to the proper functioning of the machine, and which are stuck down at Tilbury. I need hardly point out, do I, that so long as the incomplete unit remains in the canteen, staff should keep well clear at all costs.

E. Heath, Managing Director

A HANDFUL OF MILITANT shop stewards attempted to get themselves jailed for illegal picketing in the hope that it would prompt a general strike, but the government's Official Solicitor intervened to prevent them becoming martyrs.

Kray Brothers Released

Intervention by Official Solicitor

Amidst emotional scenes unsurpassed since D-Day, Ronald and Reginald Kray, the popular East End knee-breakers, were released from prison today. There was community singing as the Krays were shouldered by their workmates and carried to a waiting flower-decked tank.

The release of the Krays followed a surprise intervention by the Official Solicitor, Mr E. Tharg. Mr Tharg told the court that the Krays' release had no connection with recent threats to "do up" Mr Heath and other members of the government.

Mr Tharg added that the release of the notorious 'Mile End Two' could well help to bring peace to London's strife-torn dockland.

AFTER TALKS WITH THE CBI and TUC failed, the government announced a compulsory 90-day freeze on prices, rent and wages in a last-ditch attempt to curb inflation.

70-80-90 Days: Brrrr! What a freeze up!

WHAT IT WILL MEAN

Prices: From today everything will cost more as a result of shop keepers putting up their prices in order to avoid the freeze. But not from tomorrow.

Wages: No one will ever get any more money ever again. If you are earning sixteen pounds now you will be earning sixteen pounds for the rest of your working life.

ONLY by then your sixteen pounds will be worth £2.50 as a result of price rises brought about by the freeze.

THEREFORE you will be saving yourself over £13 a week.

What happens after the freeze?

The freeze will be lifted after 90 days in order to enable prices to go up as a result of the introduction of VAT when we join the E.E.C. *(See 'Vat It Vill Mean', p.94)*

EVERYTHING seemed to be falling apart.

WHILE-U-WAIT REPAIR SERVICE

"You wait about six weeks"

Considering the number of reporters who crowded into the County Court at Wakefield, Yorks, on June 13th to hear the bankruptcy petition of Mr JGL Poulson, the coverage of proceedings was disappointing. Mr Poulson suggested in court that the parlous state of his architectural practise, which four years ago was the biggest in Europe, had to some extent been brought about by unfavourable publicity in *Private Eye*. The Official Receiver at Leeds and counsel for the Bankruptcy Trustee, representing Poulson's many creditors, revealed that the continued deterioration of Poulson's finances toward the end of the 1960s did not deter him from making generous payments to a number of prominent individuals in politics and the civil service.

In June 1969, for instance, Mr Poulson paid £20,000 to Mr T Dan Smith, who was then chairman of the Northern Economic Planning Council, for "expert advice". Mr T Dan Smith was acquitted last year at the Old Bailey of offering money to the leader of Wandsworth Council in exchange for a public relations contract. The leader of the council concerned, Mr Sidney Sporle, is in prison for corruption offences which include receiving money in exchange for giving a PR contract to T Dan Smith's PR firm.

Another payment in 1969 went to Mr J H Cordle, Conservative MP for Bournemouth East. He told *Private Eye*: "The money was not paid to me. It was for expenses incurred on his behalf when I introduced him to President Tubman of Liberia…"

At the hearing, Mr Poulson was asked about a payment of £8,053 to a Mr W G Pottinger, described as a "high-ranking civil servant". Asked by *Private Eye* about the payment, Mr Pottinger said: "It was a gift. Mr Poulson is a close family friend of mine…"

Finally, there is the complex question of the involvement in Mr Poulson's affairs of Mr Reginald Maudling, now Home Secretary…

Just over two weeks later, Maudling resigned from the cabinet after police launched a criminal investigation into Poulson. Cordle was eventually forced to resign from parliament over the scandal. Pottinger and T Dan Smith, as well as Poulson himself, all ended up in prison.

1973

IN WE WENT!
Fanfare for Europe
A nation-wide festival to mark the entry of the United Kingdom into the European Community

● Exhibition of contemporary Danish book and magazine production at the "Books and Mags" shop, Mintoff Yard, NEASDEN. "Brøwsers Welkømmen".

● Radio Luxembourg – Special non-stop broadcast of contemporary popular music and advertisments, relayed from this historic Duchy in the heart of the Common Market.

● Danish Blue Cheese – Special display at all Sainsbury's cheese counters, NATIONWIDE.

● Italian ice-cream – special "Common Market Introductory Offer" mobile exhibition. Vans will travel through all parts of BOLTON, ROCHDALE and HALIFAX. "Stop 'em and buy one!"

● French cricket – special display by the boys of St Pederast's Preparatory School, BAGSHOT.

● "Common Market Cavalcade", M4 MOTORWAY. Hundreds of cars driven by ordinary men and women will pass special "Vu-points", including many cars of famous foreign makes such as Fiat, Volkswagen, Peugeot etc.

THE NATION'S GAS WORKERS were the latest to go on strike over pay, closely followed by teachers, train drivers, workers on Ford's assembly lines, civil servants and hospital staff.

Hullo.

I expect many of you, like me, are undergoing considerable inconvenience to put it mildly as a result of quite frankly the most bone-headed state of affairs that it's been my unfortunate privilege ever to have been involved with.

Quite honestly I've had it right up to here with these chappies who think they can jump the queue and throw spanners in the works as and when they so feel the urge.

Well I've got a message for them: THIS TIME THERE'LL BE NO GIVING IN. If these stupid sods think they can be made an exception of, then quite frankly they've got another think coming to them.

And while we're on this subject I am perfectly well aware that the Gas Dept. are not the only

bunch of layabouts who think they're getting something extra special with regard to this one.

Blimey O'Reilly! You don't have to tell me that as soon as we've got this little lot sorted out there'll be some other bunch of Charlies banging on my office door wanting more than their fair share of the Heathco cake.

You're all the same, you people. You expect somebody to come along and do it for you.

■ Some of you may be wondering why there are now five APBDUs currently stacked in the works canteen. The answer is quite simply that no sooner had we cancelled our order from the Phuwatascorcha Co (Japan) Ltd and ordered a pricey British replacement from Vendomatic, a bloody great juggernaut arrived loaded with three fully assembled de luxe Phuwatascorcha models. It is enough to give a fellow the screaming ab-dabs.

Edward Heath, Managing Director

A CEASEFIRE was declared in Vietnam.

At last! It's peace

Peace with honour. Yes, that was the message from a tired but triumphant President Nixon last night.

When the news reached Vietnam, shots rang out all over the country and churches fell to the ground as hordes of soldiers thronged the battlefields and joined in a thanksgiving massive bombardment. Complete strangers blew each other's brains out. Old-age pensioners joined hands with teenagers as they fled from burning villages (cont. Parallel 94)

STANLEY KUBRICK withdrew his film *A Clockwork Orange* from the UK following reports of copycat violence.

"That's my son. He was terribly influenced by the Clockwork Orange film"

FOUR WHITE HOUSE AIDES resigned over their roles in the Watergate break-in, as the scandal crept ever closer to the President himself.

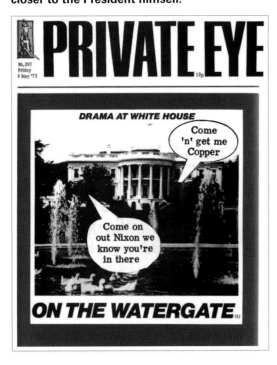

HEATH LAUNCHED phase 3 of his pay policy.

I WANT YOU ALL EACH AND EVERY ONE OF YOU TO THOROUGHLY READ THROUGH THIS VERY CAREFULLY SO AS TO SEE HOW IT WILL AFFECT YOU.

Heathco will permit pay rises up to and not exceeding 7% of a total gross take home pay. This is an across the board measure which applies as much to the senior executive as to the chappie on the shop floor.

Let's get this straight. This is your last chance to sort this one out. I've done my bit. God Almighty! I've spent literally hours in the evenings going through the books and going through the fine print with a tooth-comb to make sure that everything is ironed out.

If you people want Heathco to carry on now it's up to you. You've brought this Phase 3 on yourselves and all the other bloody phases. Until you can learn to behave yourselves and stop bellyaching on, every hour of the day and night, then you'll just have to be told what to do.

▓ *I would like to put you in the picture with regard to the canteen being closed last week.*
It transpires that owing to changeover to metrication, the new Vendomatic APBDU is made with a larger input-filter and all our beakers are BSM (British Standard Measure). In other words the beakers are TOO BLOODY

SMALL. But of course no one told us at this end.

Nor I may say did people have enough sense once they realised the beakers were the wrong size to refrain from inserting them into the beaker-receiving chute, with the result that by about half past four on Friday afternoon the canteen floor was about a foot deep in a mixture of tomato soup, hot chocolate and tea.

Words fail me.

E. Heath, Managing Director

THE ARAB STATES put up oil prices by 70 percent in protest at US support for Israel in the Yom Kippur war. At the same time the National Union of Miners imposed an overtime ban in protest at a pay increase offer of a mere 16.5 percent. A State of Emergency was declared by the government.

FUEL AND POWER EMERGENCY

How to save fuel in the home

Extinguish all fires, especially those that use gas, coal, oil and electricity.

Turn out the light. If everyone in the country uses no light at all, supplies of electricity could last indefinitely.

Put on as many clothes as you can. At present there are no restrictions on how many clothes you can wear.

Set fire to your house by rubbing two pieces of wood together. One blazing house will provide much-needed warmth for hundreds of people, in addition to creating vacant sites suitable for office development.

Climb into bed. But do NOT use hot water bottles, as an acute water shortage is imminent.

Try and die as soon as possible. This can be done by starvation. Your early death will help Mr Heath to win the next election.

BOMBS WERE SET OFF in shopping centres and stations in London, Solihull and Birmingham. The *Eye*'s new columnist was having none of the official explanations.

The Controversial Voice

Every week Dave Spart, General Secretary of the National Amalgamated Union of Sixth Form Operatives and Allied Trades and editor of "Strike", talks frankly and outspokenly about the facts behind the news.

It is predictably assumed by the capitalist media that the IRA are behind the recent wave of so called bomb outrages i.e. the explosions of letter bombs and so forth etc. but this is to totally ignore one vitally important factor i.e. that acts of violence though to my mind counterproductive are an inevitable consequence of the current economic crisis inherent in late capitalist society notably er price increases 14% mortgage rate rampant flouting of price controls by the Tory (*cont. p94*)

AS THE SITUATION with both the miners and OPEC got even worse, the government was forced to implement a three-day week.

The Emergency – an official announcement

THE 3-DAY WEEK – WHAT IT MEANS

From today, everyone in Britain will only be working for three days a week (with the exception of certain exempt classes of person listed below).

EXEMPT PERSONS

Unemployed
Old-Age Pensioners
E. Heath Esq
Vicars
All workers who are on strike.

REMEMBER – THE SURVIVAL OF YOUR COUNTRY DEPENDS ON EVERYONE PULLING TOGETHER AND NOT WORKING FOR LONGER THAN THREE DAYS.

HOW CAN I HELP?

Thousands of men and women are urgently wanted by the Government to act as "Work Wardens". Their job will be to keep a 24-hour watch and institute summary on the spot fines of up to £200million on any idle layabout who is found working.

This Announcement Is Issued By The Department For Non-Trade and Industry.

URI GELLER SHOT to fame by spoiling some cutlery on a chat show.

Tiny genius rocks universe shock

by Our Science Correspondent **Patrick Bore**

Make no mistake about it. Since last week's sensational Dimbleby Bore-In appearance by 22 year-old Israeli-born Uri Nargs, the universe as we know it will never be the same again.

Not since Sir Isaac Newton shot the apple off his son's head at the age of two and a half has the world of science been so rocked to its foundations.

From the moment Uri succeeded in bending a common or garden teaspoon in front of 15 million TV viewers, hardbitten scientists have had to throw out almost every existing theory about the way the world works – not to mention their cutlery.

Uri Nargs

For thousands of years, scientists have argued that spoons are straight.

Now they have been proved wrong.

A ROYAL WEDDING provided some brief respite from the gloom.

Exhausted, Anne flung herself down on the satin quilt of the old Mountbatten four-poster in the Royal Suite of HMS Britannia. Now at last it was all over. She was Mrs Phillips.

The north wind was getting up now and Britannia began to roll on the mounting waves. She could hear the feet of sailors overhead as they rummered down the jauntlings and pulled tight the gillards. Soon Mark would be with her, his strong manly form would hold and protect her, while outside the black night roared and the mighty billows thundered with a passion to match their own…

Yes! Now she heard his familiar footstep on the wooden ballons! Her heart began to beat faster and faster. The boat was rocking like a cradle. The door burst open and Mark rushed towards her, his jaw set strong and firm.

"Darling!" she cried. "Darling!"

With a strange yet thrilling unearthly cry he ripped his collar open. And then, with fierce staring eyes, he staggered past her into the bathroom, and Anne heard the unmistakable sound of her husband in the grips of uncontrollable sea-sickness.

Was it the end – or was it only the beginning?

NOVEMBER BROUGHT inflammatory news about the regeneration of London's docklands.

On the evening of Sunday 4 November, fire broke out in a warehouse in east London. The building in question, 'B' warehouse on St Katharine Docks next to Tower Bridge, was protected from demolition as one of our finest examples of dockland architecture. It stands at the centre of an enormous redevelopment scheme, Taylor Woodrow's World Trade Centre. During the past year, Taylor Woodrow have been seeking permission to gut the interior of 'B' warehouse and add another 107,000 square feet of offices to their plan. This would increase the value of the site by £30m, but shortly before the fire the Greater London Council Historic Buildings Board refused to allow them to gut the building.

Thankfully, Taylor Woodrow consider that the conversion of the warehouse is still possible, and Peter Drew, the managing director of the project has authorised the extensive demolition of the interior.

Until 1969 the 25 acres of St Katharine Docks was owned by the Port of London Authority. The PLA sold the land to the GLC for the knockdown price of £1.5m, in the belief that it was to be used for public housing. Taylor Woodrow were granted a 125-year lease. Their scheme was to include 378 private homes, 300 council homes (to be paid for by the GLC) and a 776-bedroom hotel. 'B' warehouse was to be preserved intact and converted into a 262,000 square foot "export centre". This scheme was approved by Environment Secretary Peter Walker within 48 hours of being submitted, instead of the usual six months, despite the fact that the original outline planning permission from the local council had instructed that the site should contain no more than 3,000 square feet of offices.

Then in 1972 Taylor Woodrow acquired two adjoining acres, including 'C' warehouse, from the PLA at a knockdown price. For some reason the PLA were under the impression that 'C' warehouse, which was also a protected building, would be preserved, but Taylor Woodrow were informally discussing with Shell-Mex a possible tenancy in the huge office block which they intended to build in its place.

The fire is one of an unexplained series which have caused the destruction of a number of warehouses in the last year: a number of fires between Wapping Dock Stairs and New Crane Stairs destroyed warehouses whose sites have now been cleared for redevelopment. In March a fire in Dock Street destroyed a factory adjoining a new development. Another fire next door broke out last month, four weeks after the building had been listed for preservation following an attempt by the owners, Leopold Joseph Properties Ltd, to demolish it. In August there were four more fires. On October 9 fire broke out in another warehouse in Wapping High Street, also "listed" by the DoE. The remainder is to be demolished, meaning that virtually the whole stretch of riverside from Tower Bridge to Wapping Police Station is now idle, derelict and ripe for development.

IN DECEMBER, IN A REPORT on the connections between bullying landlords in Brighton and fascist groups, the *Eye* drew readers' attention to one particularly unsavoury character.

Peaceful, law-abiding citizens who live in Brighton have been greatly alarmed at the recent increase in illegal evictions of tenants by landlords and landlords agents. One keen local property developer with a propensity for violence – and an obvious dislike for Jews – is 27-year-old millionaire Nicholas van Hoogstraten. He served a four-year prison sentence for throwing a hand grenade into the residence of the son of a local Sussex Rabbi, only completed 12 months ago. As recently as last week, Hoogstraten was described by a judge as "a sinister figure who is thoroughly dishonest".

Hoogstraten has nasty methods of evicting tenants. In July the Williams family returned to find their beds, furniture, mattresses, clothing, wardrobe and tables thrown out into the street and back garden. Every window and window-frame, except the ground-floor front, was removed and even the lock on the front door had been changed. When Mrs Williams returned she was told through the door to "fuck off unless you want to be cut to ribbons".

Hoogstraten told a reporter, "It's the best bit of fun we've had for some time. It was a real blitz operation. You can go so far legally and then it's no good messing about any more. I couldn't care a toss what anyone tries to do. I'm an expert on this kind of operation. I showed them how it should be done."

Hoogstraten's career of bullying and rampant illegality went on for a further 30 years before he was convicted of the manslaughter of a former business associate who was trying to sue him: he was later cleared on appeal, but a civil court found him responsible for the death. He refused to pay the costs and compensation he was ordered to and later emigrated to Zimbabwe, where he became a close associate of Robert Mugabe.

1974

AS THE STRIKES and the three-day week dragged on into the new year the *Eye* offered a useful new novelty item.

The Gnome Magigraph

Just cut out and paste to a piece of stout cardboard.

Looked at normally the Magigraph gives an instant, 100 percent accurate, at-a-glance picture of:

- value of pound sterling
- Britain's coal stocks
- Financial Times share index
- Mr Heath's popularity
- Britain's growth rate
- route taken by Hillary and Tensing on descent of Mt Everest 1953

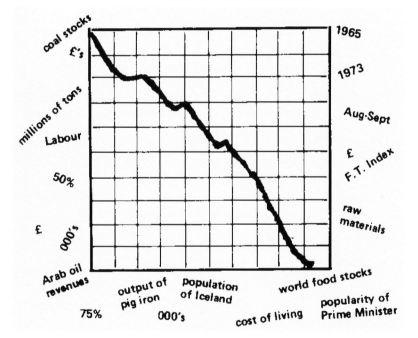

Now simply rotate your Magigraph 90 degrees anti-clockwise or look at it in an ordinary household mirror, and get an equally accurate month-by-month record of:

- Britain's import bill
- unemployment
- rate of increase in wage demands
- mortgate rates
- interest on overdrafts
- national debt
- price of Concorde
- school fees at Eton
- route taken by Hillary and Tensing on ascent of Mt Everest 1953

UNABLE TO BREAK the miners' strike, Ted Heath finally gave in and called a general election, asking "who governs?".

THEY DECLINED to do so, returning a hung parliament. Several days of negotiations followed between the Conservatives and Jeremy Thorpe's Liberals, during which Heath refused to vacate Downing Street. He finally departed in the same week that Japanese soldier Hiroo Onoda emerged from three decades hiding in the mountains of the Philippines, finally persuaded that World War II was over.

The final surrender
Election now over – official

29 years after their Party's crushing defeat in the 1974 election, the last survivors of the once-vaunted Conservative Government finally surrendered last night. At their head, defiant to the last, was their leader – Lieutenant-Colonel "Glo-sah" Hiroheathco.

For the last 29 years, Glo-sah and his tiny band had apparently been completely unaware that their side had lost the election. Every effort was made to let them know that it was "all over". Newspapers spelling out news of the defeat were regularly delivered to their hideaway at Number ten, Downing Street.

But still Glo-sah held out.

WILSON ACTED SWIFTLY to end the strikes and restore a full working week.

Mrs Wilson's Diary

I was just shaking out the Brumas-style simulated fluff lounge mat at the front door the other morning when a small dapper individual approached with a neat grey suit, well-polished shoes and carefully parted Brylcreemed hair. He carried a clipboard and and was licking the top of a freshly sharpened pencil. "Ah, Madam," he vouchsafed with an ingratiating smile, "I've come about the Electricity."

"Oh, please come in," I remarked. "I will get you a copy of the *Methodist Women's Weekly* to put on the chair so you can see to read the meter."

"No, Madam," replied the official, "you misunderstand me. I am head of the TUC. Murray's the name, Len Murray. I think you and I will be seeing quite a lot of each other in the days to come."

Harold unfortunately was tied up with his Kung Fu exercises, so I asked our new press secretary Mr Haines to bring in a few fancies and a fresh pot of Sainsbury's Rapid Brew. We were reminiscing about the good old days with Mr Feather and the time he nearly came to blows with Barbara Castle in the front room at Number Ten, when Harold bounded in, wearing his brand new art-silk Yamaha Karate Gown. "Ah, Murray," he exclaimed, "not a moment too soon. You have seen the budget, I trust. Everything you ever dreamed of, handed to you on a plate."

THE BRITISH BOARD of Film Classification gave the *Exorcist* an X certificate, uncut, despite warning that "It is a powerful horror movie. Some people may dislike it."

A GUNMAN ATTEMPTED to kidnap Princess Anne and hold her for ransom, shooting two policemen, her chauffeur and a passer-by in the process. The *Eye*'s diarist was impressed.

Auberon Waugh's Diary

We hear a lot about the heroism of the victims of violence on these occasions, but very little, for some reason, about the heroism of the criminals. If Ian Ball had succeeded in outwitting all the armed policemen and brave chauffeurs protecting Princess Anne, if he had managed to evade all the public-spirited passers by and heroic journalists or her invisible bodyguard, he would still have had to spend anything up to a month closeted alone with the young lady and her speechless, smiling husband until the £3m ransom money arrived.

It was this sort of courage, this willingness to take risks and face unmentionable horrors in the cause of profit which once made the foundation stone of our country's commercial empire. It may be true, as our detractors say, that Great Britain has only got one Ball, but at least we should be proud of the one we've got.

RETIRED SOLDIER and extreme right-winger General Sir Walter Walker put himself, and his organisation Civil Assistance, forward as the saviour of the nation from communism.

For your eyes only – Top Secret

Copy to: Chapman Pincher, Sir Arthur Bryant, Enoch Powell, Chief of Staff UN, Lt Col (rtd.) "Buffy" Frobisher, His Royal Highness the Emperor Roscoe.

Like many ordinary English lunatics I cannot help feeling actively aware of the very grave threat that confronts this island at this moment in time from the activities of subversives and traitors who have wormed their way into the very fabric of this country.

Wherever we look today we see the lack of the smack of firm leadership in high places. No one doubts that a crisis of quite unprecedented proportions now looms over us all, threatening to engulf every man, woman and child in a holocaust of unfathomable horror. At a meeting convened in the Rhodes Boyson Bar of the Olde Bernie Inne, Watford, it was decided by those present (H. Gussett and B. Frobisher, codenames 'Falcon' and 'Rhino') to launch a nation-wide Security Task-Force with full operational powers.

The organisation is to be known as "Operation Gussett". The principle will be to train men and women in the basic tasks of manning Nuclear Power Stations, Advanced Passenger Trains, Inter-Continental Ballistic Missile Bases and other vital services.

Yours faithfully,
Sir Herbert Gussett,
Somewhere in the Goat and Compass, Bletchley.

CHIA CHIA AND CHING CHING, two giant pandas presented to the nation by Mao Zedong, showed every sign of enjoying their new home at London Zoo – but not each other.

A SPATE OF IRA attacks culminated in the bombing of Westminster Hall, the oldest part of the Houses of Parliament.

Hogg explodes – many hurt

The Palace of Westminster was wrecked today when the former Lord Chancellor, Lord Hailsham, exploded without warning. Eyewitnesses said it was the worst explosion they had ever seen.

One member of the public, who was treated for burns and shock, later described what happened: "We were just sitting quietly in the public gallery when I noticed a strange rumbling coming from Lord Hogg. He was talking about those IRA men in Ireland – and then suddenly there was the most gigantic explosion. The last words I caught were Lord Hogg saying that people who commit treason can still be hanged – and then everything went black.

The famous Lord Hogg was perhaps the finest of his kind in Europe. A massive structure supported by gigantic trunnions, the Hogg was a unique survival from the distant past.

DESPITE AUBERON WAUGH'S discouragement, voters returned Wilson as prime minister with a majority of just three in the second general election of the year.

Thursday

I would advise everybody against voting in this ridiculous election between teams of twittish nobodies for posts which carry no importance or authority on the British scene. Apart from anything else, there must be some danger of catching infectious diseases in the polling booths, or whatever they're called. One never knows who has been there before one.

Friday

In the new spirit of austerity I take an Underground train from Islington to Tottenham Court Road. One would have thought that at least the lower classes would look happy to have won again, but they look absolutely wretched. Perhaps they always do, but in that case the whole thing seems a waste of time.

SIMILAR SENTIMENTS – accompanied by the suggestion that birth control should be pushed on the lower orders because "our human stock is threatened" – scuppered Sir Keith Joseph's chances of succeeding Heath as Conservative leader...

Sir Keith – 'I was robbed'

An angry Sir Keith Joseph last night issued a furious statement accusing the press of "gross distortion".

"It is quite intolerable," he lashed out, "that my statement of yesterday, seeking to correct the blatant misrepresentation of my speech last Saturday, in which I sought to clarify my remarks of the previous Thursday, should have been so wilfully taken out of context."

...BUT MANY PEOPLE shared his pessimistic views of modern life.

"We can do without your down-to-earth realism, Henshaw"

LORD LUCAN went on the run, wanted for the murder of his children's nanny and attempting to kill his own wife. The facts of the case were recounted in a new *Eye* feature.

Great Bores of Today

"Apparently the papers have got it all wrong according to this pal of mine at the office who shares a flat with someone that knew a friend of the Nanny and he says that what actually happened is that he came round that night to pick up the dog which wasn't mentioned by any of the papers because if you look at the letter that his mother sent to the wife it's perfectly obvious that the Nanny was involved with the business with the children but anyway it was her day off so he couldn't have known and another thing which no one seems to have noticed is that if he was going to leave the country he would have needed his passport that wasn't mentioned in any of the papers oh was it? Oh I didn't see that oh well anyway according to this man…"

TOWER BLOCKS WERE springing up all over.

New look for Square shock

Plans went on show today for a new-look Trafalgar Square. The £30 millon redevelopement will demolish the outmoded Victorian structure known as 'Nelson's Column' and replace it with an office block of similar proportions.

The block is to be constructed entirely of glass to allow a clearer view of Concorde as it flies over the Shell Building. It will be surmounted by a larger-than-life fibreglass replica of Richard Seifert, the legendary architect who "turned a blind eye" on most of his buildings.

NO SOONER HAD Harold Wilson returned to power in March than the *Eye* picked up on difficulties among his staff.

A writ has been issued against the Civil Service by the widow of Arthur Norman "Michael" Halls, formerly Wilson's Principal Private Secretary. Mrs Halls is claiming that her husband died in 1970 as a direct result of overwork and strain incurred while working for Wilson. Mr Halls was 54 when he died of a heart attack.

Mrs Halls now claims that her husband had to perform duties which had nothing to do with his civil service work. Part of his brief was, apparently, to act as liaison between Wilson and his highly-strung secretary, Marcia Williams.

Mrs Halls says that one evening her husband came home and said Harold and Marcia had had a raging row. Wilson rang later that night to say "she's finally gone, screaming her head off". Another time, Mrs Williams rang Mrs Halls up: "She said that if Michael did not get her telephone mended immediately she would bring down the government."

ALMOST IMMEDIATELY the all-powerful Williams and her brother, a property speculator, dragged the prime minister into a scandal over lucrative land purchases in Wigan. The *Eye* provided some background details which no other paper would report.

No matter how indiscreetly Williams and her brother Tony Field behave, Wilson can never quite make up his mind to sack her. Her influence over the prime minister is extraordinary. It first became apparent in 1967, when her two chief competitors for Wilson's ear departed Downing Street. Shortly before Michael Halls' death he is reported to have said to Wilson, "I can't stand that woman any more. Four years is enough." Wilson replied, "Four years? I've had fourteen years." Wilson's chief adviser George Wigg also fell out with his old friend and left for the House of Lords.

With Wigg gone, Wilson let Williams's views overrule those of Burke Trend, the cabinet secretary. He consulted her constantly about government appointments. Secure in her position, Williams pursued two new interests: she invested £7,000 in her brother's land and slag firm, and she started an affair with Walter Terry, then political correspondent of the Daily Mail (now political editor of the Daily Express). She became pregnant and secretly had a child, born in

August 1968. In the later stages of her pregnancy, since she could not come to her office in Downing Street, boxes of official papers were sent over to her flat and were sometimes taken in at the door by the political correspondent of the *Daily Mail*.

Her influence is shown by Wilson's reaction to the land reclamation story: instead of a "personal statement" in the House he made a "ministerial statement" on a matter which had nothing to do with his ministry since all the events took place when he was in opposition. He took Williams' advice against that of his cabinet colleagues and defended Tony Field's behaviour – and thereby associating himself with it.

The fact is that when Field was working for Wilson as unpaid office manager between 1970 and 1973, he was using the leader of the opposition's office to set up land deals which were netting himself and his sisters, Marcia Williams and Peggy Field (secretary to Mrs Wilson), a profit on purchase price of between 200% and 350%.

Wilson's reaction to the scandal was not to fire Williams, but to raise her to the peerage as Lady Falkender.

IN NOVEMBER, THE EYE reported developments in the business career of Labour MP John Stonehouse.

Out of ministerial office in 1971, Stonehouse was taken on as a Development Director for War on Want, where he was greatly involved with the problems of Bangladesh. After leaving the following August Stonehouse set up the British Bangladesh Trust to provide banking services for the 70,000-strong Bengali community in Britain. When it went public BBT featured a convivial photograph of the Bank of England discount department man in a double-page Bengali advertisement without approval from the Bank, and falsely assured potential investors that the Bank of England would give permission for the Trust to change its name to British Bangladesh Bank. How many investors knew that the Chairman of BBT, John Stonehouse, was also the company's landlord via his private company, Export Promotion & Consultancy Services?

In March 1974 the Trust was incorporated into the London Capital Group. One director was Keith White, who had worked for 25 years at the Westminister Bank but resigned in July this year. White is now suing Stonehouse for the specific performance of an oral agreement made in April 1974 for the sale of 1,012 £10 shares in the company or for damages in breach of said agreement. No date has yet been fixed for the hearing of the case.

STONEHOUSE PROMPTLY hit the *Eye* with a libel writ and notice that he was seeking an injunction to stop them reporting further on his business affairs, then announced that he was going swimming off a beach in Miami – and disappeared. The magazine was sceptical.

According to Miami police detective Lt Mike Miller, "There are factors in this case we do not understand. We are checking every possibility. At the moment Mr Stonehouse is a missing person. It is unprecedented for a drowned man's body not to turn up in Miami within a day or two."

The FBI have asked Scotland Yard for a confidential report on the politician's business and financial status.

Shortly before his "disappearance", Stonehouse took out several substantial life insurance policies. According to *Eye* informants, one of these was with a large City firm for £20,000. The firm contacted a doctor and asked him to examine the Labour MP. In his view Stonehouse was mentally unstable and showed distinct schizophrenic tendencies.

Stonehouse turned up, very much alive, in Australia a month later. He claimed to have suffered a "mental breakdown" in 1973 which resulted in him living long periods of his life under an identity he had stolen from a dead constituent. He was subsequently convicted of 18 charges of fraud and theft, several of them relating to his financial dealings with Bangladesh.

1975

MARGARET THATCHER thrashed four male opponents in the election to become the new Conservative leader, and nothing would ever be the same again.

THE DAILY TELEGRAPH
Friday ~~August 3rd 1965~~ February 11th 1975

The right choice

The election of ~~Mr Heath~~ Mrs Thatcher brings a welcome end to a period of uncertainty for the Conservative Party. In electing ~~Mr Heath~~ Mrs Thatcher there can be no doubt that Tory MPs have made the right choice. ~~He~~ She will bring to the task a welcome toughness and a steely determination. ~~Mr Heath~~ Mrs Thatcher is by no means a Tory of the old school.

~~He~~ She has risen to ~~his~~ her high position from humble origins – ~~his~~ her father was a ~~boatbuilder~~ grocer – via a successful career at Oxford. ~~He~~ She has therefore a well-founded respect for the old-fashioned virtues of self-help and a proper pride in achievement, which are much needed at this present time. Above all, in ~~Mr Heath~~ Mrs Thatcher the Tories have a leader who is likely to prove to be more than a match for Mr Wilson. There can be no doubt now that the latter will have to look to his laurels.

INDUSTRY SECRETARY Tony Benn was pushing for the nationalisation of failing car company British Leyland, along with almost everything else.

CAMBODIAN LEADER Lon Nol fled the capital, leaving it open to Pol Pot's Khmer Rouge.

Lon Don: The end in sight

An eerie silence now hangs over the capital of what was once a proud nation.

On the surface things look normal. The streets are filled with uncollected rubbish. The news-stands are plentifully stacked with Soft Porn. A familiar headline "Phew! What a Scorcher!" announces the onset of the Warm Season, as if this was like any other time.

But beneath the routine of day to day life in Lon Don things are very far from normal. Nobody seems to know what is happening. In the bars and cafes the wildest rumours circulate freely – the Army is going to take over; the currency is about to collapse. The mounting fear of the bourgeoisie in Lon Don is of the growing power of To Nee Ben, the fanatical left wing leader, who has already occupied many of the key strategic areas including the vital shipyards and now the car industry. Most Lon Doners no longer expect that the capital will survive more than a few more weeks.

Meanwhile there is no doubt of one fact. Many people are already preparing to leave the capital. Those who could do so have already left, taking with them as many of their possessions as they could pile into the back of their Kor Tee Nas (the most popular make of local car).

Observers here point to the growing isolation of President Wis Lon. Last night his priceless collection of 20th Century Woolworth Flying Wall Ducks was dispatched to his Scilly Island hideaway. But he himself, official sources say, is determined to remain in office until the last minute.

IN A NATIONWIDE referendum, Britain gave an overwhelming "Yes" to staying in the European Community – although some grumbled about the leading nature of the question asked.

DON'T YOU THINK THAT THE UNITED KINGDOM SHOULD STAY IN THE EUROPEAN COMMUNITY?

YES ☐

HAROLD WILSON PROVED unwilling to impose statutory wage controls and cuts to public spending, which the Treasury insisted were vital to get rampant inflation and a haemorrhage in the value of the pound under control – even when he was hoicked mid-speech from the Royal Agricultural Show to deal with the crisis.

Mrs Wilson's Diary

A messenger came running in, and attempted to force his way through the plump yeomen listening politely to Harold's speech. He finally reached the podium and handed up a telegram to Harold who opened it, and with a strangled cry plunged out of view behind the bank of potted Granny Goodman Dwarf Apple trees. A moment later Mr Haines was by my side, and ushered me through the glazed audience as the band played on.

Harold's mood, as Mr Haines and Lady Forkbender climbed into the front of the Mini, was more disturbed than I have seen it for many years. His face was pale, and beads of sweat stood out upon his brow. "Step on it, Haines," he cried in desperate tones, "the Pound is at its lowest ever and still plummeting! I must get back to restore confidence!" He sat, staring wild-eyed, and chewed his fingernails, until Lady Forkbender brought a phial of capsules out of her handbag and passed one to him, saying that she always used them when things got on top of her.

Whatever the palliative, it appeared to have a marked effect on Harold, and when we reached the outskirts of Swindon, he insisted on Mr Haines making a long detour to a public house where we were all able to sit outside between the toilets and the garage while Harold quaffed a Jumbo of Malt Drain's Four Star Executive Special, ignoring Lady Forkbenders warning that he should not drink on top of his pills. After a brief altercation, during which Lady Forkbender became highly distressed and began to tremble, Harold sent Haines back into the Lounge to buy another round of drinks. He returned with a tin tray and intimated that we must soon be getting along as Mr Healey was waiting for him at Number Eleven with the foreign bankers.

Harold gazed at him for some time with a beaming smile, and then took a long swig of the Executive Drink which left a moustache-like crust of white foam on his upper lip. "Haines," he remarked. "Here is Ten p. Ring Denis, there's a good chap, and tell him that I do not believe in interfering with the day-to-day problems of my Ministers. He must do as he sees fit."

As the factotum hurried away, he turned to me and observed, "You know, Gladys, when you have been through two or three Sterling crises, it doesn't have the same excitement any more somehow…" His voice trailed away, and soon a rhythmic snoring sound informed me that he had gone to sleep.

SHOES APPEARED to be the only thing on the rise.

"They moved me and the kids from the old shoe into this new high-rise one"

DAVID FROST ANNOUNCED that he had signed an exclusive deal for a series of interviews with ousted president Richard Nixon, but refused to say how much he had paid for the privilege.

EXCLUSIVELY RECORDED FOR GNOMEOVISION

David Frost talks to Richard Milhous Nixon

FROST *(for it is he)*: Hullo and welcome. It's a very great joy to be able to welcome back someone who has been absent from our screens for far too long – myself. In addition tonight, it is my very great pleasure to welcome one of the best-loved human beings it has ever been my privilege to meet – the one and only PRESIDENT NIXON! *(wild dubbed applause)* Mr President, you're looking absolutely terrific and bronzed and relaxed. It's a very great joy, if I may say so, to see you looking so well. And I'm sure that the millions and millions of viewers who I hope will be watching us all over the world will agree that it really is fabulous the way you seem to have recovered so completely from all those agonising problems you had to deal with a year or two ago.

NIXON: Well, David –

FROST: Mr President, although the very last thing I want to do is to go back yet again over those moments of agony a year or two ago… please don't answer this if you don't want to… but, looking back over that whole unfortunate turn of events, what memory do you cherish most from those days?

NIXON: Well, David, I so well remember the day when we all celebrated Christmas together at the White House. Just you and me, and Pat and the kids, and your wonderful Mom, and the tree there bedecked with gifts in the corner, chestnuts roasting on an open fire.

FROST *(sobbing uncontrollably)*: Super, wonderful, here's your cheque. God bless you, Mr President.

THE QUEEN OFFICIALLY set the first North Sea oil pipeline flowing.

SADLY, PREDICTIONS that this would cure all Britain's economic ills proved premature.

'Britain round the bend' – Healey's cheerful forecast

Yes, Britain is round the U-turn – and from here on in, it's prosperity all the way! That was the shock forecast yesterday from Chancellor Denis Healey, speaking in white-tie-and-tails to a dinner of City businessmen.

"Make no mistake about it," said Mr Healey, "we have bottomed out. The worst is now behind us, and we shall soon begin to see the upturn in world trade which in association with North Sea Oil will spell the road to the light at the end of the tunnel of love."

Mr Healey was then carried from the hall by a cheering group of businessmen in white coats.

Our Economics Editor comments:
Although all Britain's troubles are now over, it may be some time before we notice real signs of recovery. I understand that unemployment is likely to reach five million by the end of the year, and that inflation may hit 40%.

Investment too will continue to slump, and the pound is expected to hit a new low. Treasury forecasts indicate further widening of the trade gap, and it now seems almost certain that by the middle of next year the Government will find it impossible to make further borrowings to cover the record public spending deficit.

Other than that, it's good news all the way!

SO MANY DIFFERENT revolutionary groups were holding so many hostages for so many different reasons it was hard to keep track.

Great Bores of Today

"...Meanwhile in Buenos Aires there is no news of the kidnapped Czech anthropologist Dr Tibor Weeterbicz who is being held by members of the P.B.N. Peron separatist movement demanding the release of five political prisoners. In Milan the deadline set for the execution of the three bank hostages held by armed gunmen expires at noon today. After appealing to the gunmen for clemency Senor Ruffino Fanfarni the Minister for Internal Affairs said he was hopeful of a satisfactory conclusion to the situation. There is still no further news concerning the whereabouts of Dr Gunter Cabwallander the Belgian industrialist missing from his home since last Friday. Police believe that breakaway members of the S.H.F. splinter group are responsible. News is just coming in that the Swedish consular official Mr Gottlob Nogstrum held hostage by members of the Borneo Liberation Front for the last three years is to be released after conciliation moves by UN officials. Meanwhile there is still no news of the fifty two..."

THE YEAR ended with yet another escalation in the IRA's bombing campaign.

MRS THATCHER reappointed Reginald Maudling to the front bench as shadow foreign secretary, to the *Eye*'s disgust.

The Lazarus-style rise has been met with something less than ecstatic rejoicing, not dispersed by Mr Maudling's defence that "all of us can be taken in from time to time". The fact he was "taken in" twice in a brief four-year span by two such men as Poulson and Hoffman may explain some of Fleet Street's reserve. But that is as nothing to the feelings in Scotland Yard. The specially set-up Poulson Squad have for many months been probing various aspects of Maudling's involvement with the greatest corruptors of public officials Britain has ever known. Since well before Christmas a decision has been awaited from the Director of Public Prosecutions on the detailed reports submitted by Yard detectives. It would now seem that a decision has been taken. But no one bothered to tell the police. In consequence, police irritation has been expressed somewhat forcibly to the DPP.

Maudling was sacked by Thatcher two years later; a year after that a parliamentary inquiry found him guilty of "conduct inconsistent with the standards which the House is entitled to expect from its members" over his dealings with Poulson.

IN DECEMBER, Auberon Waugh made a rare excursion into pure fact in his diary.

West Somerset is buzzing with rumours of a most unsavoury description following reports in the *West Somerset Free Press* about an incident which occurred recently on Exmoor. Mr Norman Scott of North Devon, who claims to have been a great friend of Jeremy Thorpe, the Liberal statesman, was found by an AA patrolman weeping beside the body of Rinka, his Great Dane bitch, who had been shot in the head.

Information about this puzzling incident has since been restricted, on Home Office orders, but a man arrested at London Airport on a firearms charge will be appearing before Minehead Magistrates on December 19th, when we may learn more.

My only hope is that sorrow over his friend's dog will not cause Mr Thorpe's premature retirement from public life.

In a series of reports over the following two years, the *Eye* would do much of the untangling of the web that connected the Liberal leader to the assassination attempt.

IN THE SAME ISSUE, the *Eye* carried a report on Lord Lucan's disappearance which would prove far more significant for the magazine than it at first seemed.

Detective Chief Superintendent Roy Ranson of Scotland Yard remains baffled, and his efforts to trace the murderer of Sandra Rivett, the Lucan nanny, have not been assisted by Lord Lucan's beautiful friends. From the beginning the police have met obstruction and silence from the circle of gamblers and boneheads with whom Lucan associated. On the morning after the murder John Aspinall held a lunch so they could decide "what to do if Lucan turned up". He received several offers of money to help the fugitive Earl. At the lunch were Lucan's stockbroker, Stephen Raphael, Billy Shand-Kydd, who is married to Lady Lucan's sister, and Jimmy Goldsmith, the Old Etonian millionaire who is now in charge of Slater Walker...

The article resulted in Goldsmith serving over 100 writs on the *Eye*, its printers, distributors and stockists, attempting to have editor Richard Ingrams and hack Patrick Marnham imprisoned for criminal libel, bringing a number of injunction actions and tying the magazine up in eye-wateringly expensive legal actions for the next 18 months.

1976

THERE WERE signs of further cracks in the Downing Street machine.

Mrs Wilson's Diary

I had hoped for a peaceful new year at Chequers, but as I brought a tray of Goolagong Old Smokey HB Tips from the pantry I was surprised to find the Canasta cards scattered over the floor, and Harold standing defensively with his back against the Aga. "Say that once again and I will forking brain you," Lady Forkender was remarking, brandishing an empty saucepan in one trembling hand. "Go on, say it!"

Harold seemed unruffled. "I merely pointed out," he avowed, "that by awarding the Order of the British Empire to a glove puppet called Sooty there might be some danger of my becoming a laughing stock."

At this, Lady Forkbender struck him a playful but resounding blow with the saucepan, burst into tears, and stormed out, while Harold snatched up his Jeroboam of Spanish Fly Wincarnidillo and followed her upstairs, muttering to himself in a hostile vein.

THE LEADER of the opposition did wonders for her image with a speech denouncing Soviet Russia, and was in turn denounced by Moscow as the "Iron Lady".

London housewife attacks U.S.S.R: 'Millions feared dead'

At 6.42pm yesterday evening, a London housewife, Mrs Margaret Thatcher, launched an all-out attack on the world's largest military power, the Soviet Union. Wearing only a cashmere twin-set and stout brogues, Mrs Thatcher set out across the snowy wastes that separate the so-called Free World from the grim monolith that is Soviet Russia today. A handful of friends and supporters watched apprehensively as "Battling Maggie's" diminutive silhouette drew nearer to the massive watchtowers, minefields and barbed-wire fences that mark the Iron Curtain. A thin cheer went up as she began threatening the 200 divisions drawn up on the other side of the wire with her handbag.

Minutes later, the Kremlin issued a statement deploring "this totally unprovoked and dastardly act of aggression, which has brought the whole world to the brink of nuclear holocaust".

NORMAN SCOTT went public with his claims about Jeremy Thorpe, and the money he had been paid via intermediaries over the years to keep quiet.

Gnome

I have, needless to say, been appalled and distressed by the gutter press stories concerning my alleged relationship with a Mr 'Sweety' Roughtrouser. In particular, suggestions that sums of money were paid, at my instigation, to Mr Roughtrouser by Mr Emmanuel Strobes have caused me unprecedented mental anguish.

Mr Strobes has now made it clear why he was paying Mr Roughtrouser a sum of £10 a week. In a statement sent to me, Mr Strobes says, "I once saw Mr Roughtrouser from a bus window, and felt very sorry for him. That was why I paid him the money."

As to Mr Roughtrouser's allegations concerning his relationship with myself I can only repeat that there is not a single word of truth in anything that he has said.

My legal advisers, Messrs Sue Grabbit & Runne have already issued 973 writs against a wide assortment of editors, printers, publishers, newsagents, tobacconists, train drivers, string manufacturers and all others who are responsible in any way whatsoever for the dissemination of these vile untruths.

EXTERMINATE – DESTROY

THE NATIONAL THEATRE finally opened on London's South Bank.

Gala opening for National Car Park

The multi-level, all-concrete car park, designed by architect Denys Neasden, is the largest and most expensive of its kind ever built. As well as space for 3,500 cars, the building contains 50,000 feet of air-conditioned offices, luxury flats, a shopping centre, a multi-racial uni-sex 'toilet complex', 14 bars, six restaurants and a casino.

There is also a small theatre in the basement.

ON 16 MARCH Harold Wilson took everyone by surprise by abruptly resigning as prime minister. He was replaced by Jim Callaghan.

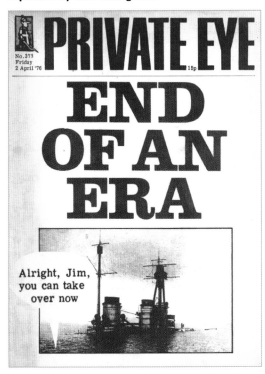

PRINCESS MARGARET and **Lord Snowdon** announced their separation in the same week.

Who will succeed?

So Lord Snowdon bows out – after 15 turbulent years holding down what has been described as "the most gruelling job in Britain" – being married to Princess Margaret. Who is likely to succeed him? A clear favourite must be the "caretaker" candidate, **Roddy Llewellyn** – youth is on his side, and his strong family connections with horses must endear him to his prospective sister-in-law.

But making a strong late bid is former prime minister **Ted Heath**. In his favour – the fact that he is unemployed and has never been married before. Against him, however, is his difficulty in speaking the "Queen's English", which he pronounces with a strong foreign accent, like the late Duke of Gloucester.

LADY FALKENDER denied having any part in Wilson's "Lavender List" of resignation honours for various crooks and shysters including James Goldsmith.

From Her Grace the Dowager Duchess of Forkbender O.M.

Sir – I am writing this letter to you personally to let you know just how totally shocked and disgusted I was to read in your paper the comments that you make about my late employer's peerages. Quite honestly it reminded me of *Private Eye*, the way you are just going on and on about Sir Harold's list, thereby showing that you have no ordinary human feelings or decency.

And another thing, while I am about it. As for your insinuations that I was totally responsible for picking the names of people like Sir Sigmund Sternberg and Sir George Weidenfeld for these honours, it is totally ridiculous. I hardly know Sir George, except for having met him a few times when he was publishing my book. And as for making David Frost a knight, well it is true that he and I are quite friendly, but as you would have seen if you'd even bothered to read your own newspaper properly, he wasn't even on the Honours List in the end, because we were told to cross his name out.

Anyway, it is completely ridiculous to suggest that I was ever in the sort of position where I could have been so powerful as to recommend people's names to the Prime Minister for honours anyway. I was only working in the background, in a humble capacity, slogging my guts out twenty hours a day while he and his cronies like Kagan and all those other people he's given peerages to who didn't deserve them were swanning around, living it up and getting all the publicity.

Oh no, poor little juggins here didn't get any credit for all the responsibility I was carrying running the country – although I suppose to be fair he did give me a peerage in the end, but only after I'd threatened to spill the beans on one or two things which I won't go into here. And I still could if it came to that, so certain parties better keep their noses clean, if you get my meaning?

Yours sincerely,
Marcia Forkbender (LADY)

SKINHEADS ROAMED the streets of Britain.

"These are fine, I'll take these"

BRITAIN BASKED in an unprecedented summer heatwave…

Great Bores of Today

"… apparently it was 95 yesterday in central London but it's definitely hotter than that today I would say is the hottest since Sunday and Sunday was bloody hot believe you me well I'll tell you how hot it was Sunday they were putting sand on the roads to stop cars getting stuck in the melting tar and that was the Sunday morning heaven knows what it was like by the afternoon our bedroom even with all the windows open was like an oven I didn't sleep a wink from the moment I pulled the blankets over my head but today I think it beats the lot definitely hotter than Sunday shall I tell you how hot I think it is today…?"

…CAUSING WATER SHORTAGES and hardship for families across the land.

Auberon Waugh's Diary

In the afternoon the chairman of Wessex Water tells us that all households must take a bath together to save water, so although I and most of my family have already had baths in the morning we solemnly climb into the tub together: myself, my dear wife, our seven children and the faithful old cook, who has been reading the *Observer* again and is in a highly excited state.

It is a most disagreeable experience. Afterwards, we are told we must use the bathwater in the garden, but when we empty it over a rhododendron bush the flowers drop off, then the leaves turn brown and the whole tree recedes slowly into the earth.

DENIS HOWELL was appointed as Minister for Drought, and strict new regulations introduced to deal with the water crisis.

The Drought: Emergency Measures

1. **Drinking.** This will cease forthwith. Persons believing themselves to be suffering from dehydration should apply in writing to the Special Advisory Centres which are to be set up in the coming weeks.

2. **Washing.** A booklet entitled *Hints To Those Wishing To Effect Rudimentary Ablutionary Procedures In A Zero Humidity Situation* is to be published early next year by Her Majesty's Stationery Office. In the interim, basic skin-cleansing can easily be effected without the use of water. Soap will be found to liquefy at temperatures in excess of 400° Fahrenheit (23° Centigrade). The soap should then be rubbed over the body in the normal way and rinsed off by running at speed through the nearest forest fire.

3. **Pets.** Domestic Animals will be found to be a valuable source of liquid. By careful squeezing, an adult gerbil can be made to produce several spoonfuls of drinkable liquid.

4. **Perspiration Centres.** Voluntary perspiration centres, where donors can give perspiration for use in emergency thirst cases will be set up in due course in all major urban areas. The centres will remain open from 7.00 to 8.30am on the first Saturday in the month, or by application in writing to the relevant authorities (see H.M.S.O. booklet *The Relevant Authorities 1977 [Amended]*).

THE DEPARTMENT OF TRADE was kept busy investigating the international business buccaneering of such figures as Tiny Rowland, Jim Slater and Edward du Cann.

Who are the Gnomrho men?

A Private Eye key guide to the men behind what they're calling 'The City Scandal of the Century'

MR 'TINY' GNOME

No pictures are available of the elusive multi-millionaire who built up the giant Gnomrho conglomerate.

MR E. STROBES (Gnomrho's 'Mr Fixit')

No pictures are available of this former war-time Commando ace who is reputed to "know everybody in the world" from Mr Aristophanes O'Booze, the Irish-Greek tanker king, to Mr Adnan Kashandkarri, the Lebanese-born friend of Mr Harold Lever MP.

SIR HECTOR CONGLOMERATE

It was his VAT return of 1971 that sparked off the great "Karrirsteinfontein Treacle Mine Row" which ended in the resignation of "Monty" Swinefever from the board of

Amalgamated Chemicals, thus precipitating the collapse of United Holdings (Cayman Islands) Ltd, the company which paid a £193 million "golden handshake" to Sir Wallingford Gibberish, the former Conservative Parliamentary Under-Secretary, who was brought in by the Hon. Angus Steak-House, brother-in-law of the Duke of Gloucester, following the notorious "Gussett Telegram Affair" of 1969, which later prompted Mr Edward Heath to describe Mr Jim Slater's private share scheme for impoverished Conservative Prime Ministers as "the highly acceptable face of capitalism, but if there is any mention with regard to this in the media I will come down on the lot of you like a ton of hot bricks", which in turn led to the amazing "Ton of Hot Bricks Affair" in which *(cont. p94)*

CHANCELLOR DENIS HEALEY was forced to apply for the maximum available loan from the International Monetary Fund (IMF) in order to bail out the British economy.

A WELL-REFRESHED Bill Grundy interviewed the Sex Pistols on his ITV teatime show, ending his own career but kicking off their own in style.

Gnome

My attention has been drawn to a distressing incident which marred the prestigious *Roond 'n' About* programme, broadcast on Gnomevision TV last Thursday. During the transmission a pop group known as "The Horrible Yobs" mouthed a number of obscenities, thereby causing intense distress to countless viewers up and down the land.

It has been pointed out that The Horrible Yobs are at present under contract to the GNOMEMI (Gnome Electrical and Money Industries) company to make a series of long-playing records.

GNOMEMI associate ourselves wholeheartedly with the public apology made by the Gnomevision company for the distressing conduct broadcast.

Nevertheless, we genuinely feel that on this occasion The Horrible Yobs were incited to opprobrious behaviour by the interviewer, Mr William Pissartist.

GNOMEMI's confidence in The Horrible Yobs as a group reflecting current moods which acts as a healthy and necessary focus for pent-up aggression remains un-impaired.

In the light of the above, we shall continue to cash in on these revolting people.

THEY WERE FAR from the only new phenomenon causing anxiety to the elderly.

Beat the muggers!!

Centurion-style TANK

You need never feel afraid of going home in the dark again with a genuine Army Surplus Centurion-style TANK.

Be safe in the streets, like Grandma used to be! It's the ultimate answer to Soccer Hooliganism, Rising Crime, VAT Officials, Jehovah's Witnesses etc. Just climb into your easy-to-operate 150-ton, all-British-made "tank" and it's "All Systems Go"!!

*Only £2,500,000 each (plus p&p)

BUT ONE MORAL CAMPAIGNER was doing her best to turn the tide, announcing that she would be bringing a private prosecution for blasphemous libel against *Gay News*.

Say goodbye to dirty blasphemy!

"I couldn't believe my eyes," writes Kidderminster housewife Mrs M.W. "It was the filthiest thing I've ever set eyes on. And don't get me wrong. I have to handle dirty articles every day of my life."

But then Mrs M.W. discovered nature's own remedy – age-old "Blasphemous Libel", based on a secret recipe devised by monks in the Middle Ages.

"It was like a miracle," says Mrs M.W. "Within months all the dirt had vanished – nasty poove stains and all."

1977

THE SILVER JUBILEE year kicked off with the publication of *Majesty*, a revelatory new biography of the Queen by Robert Lacey.

EXCLUSIVE TO PRIVATE EYE

Travesty, the book the whole world has been waiting for

Ever since she was a little girl the Queen has liked dressing up. On one day in May 1933, an old friend of the family called at Clarence House to find her standing at the window wearing the uniform of a Field Marshal in the Bulgarian Navy.

After 25 years on the throne, the Queen knows much more about politics than any Prime Minister. She once startled Harold Wilson by asking why Arthur Bottomley wore red, white and blue braces. For once, Wilson was stumped for a reply. "To keep his trousers up," she quipped with her legendary wit, and threw a Corgi at him.

The Queen sleeps in a four-poster bed which she takes round with her wherever she goes. The Duke of Edinburgh sleeps downstairs in a hammock. The Royal Corgis sleep in the kitchen along with Lord Weidenfeld and other members of the Royal Household.

FOREIGN SECRETARY Tony Crosland suffered a stroke and died.

The Alternative Voice

with DAVE SPART
Nothing has been more nauseatingly hypocritical to my mind than the literally yards of rubbish printed by the media saying that Tony Crosland literally worked himself to death which is a blatant insult to millions of members of the working class i.e. miners, car workers, students etc. who know what real work is i.e. getting up early in the morning and slaving for the bosses, instead of sitting around in large cars, smoking cigars and drinking wine, with working people having to wait on you hand and foot, which is all that Crossman ever did let's face it, with all due respect *(cont p.94)*

HE WAS REPLACED by a promising youngster.

Glenda Slagg

Mmmm! Doctor David Owen!! (In case you've been to the moon just lately, he's the new fab Foreign Secretary who in a few minutes has set

the whole of Africa a-hummin' like it's never hummed before!)

Those Rhodesians jus' didn't know what had hit them when Dishy Doctor David flew in for last-ditch talks.

Wowee!! They hadn't seen nothin' like this since Cecil Rhodes!

"Kissinger Schmissinger!" said one chocolate-coloured gal who had just got a load of the Flying Doctor with the Mostest. I agree!!

DOWNING STREET HOSTED an international summit on the world economy, from which new US President Jimmy Carter emerged, saying, "Now we must act as well as talk."

FACING A NO-CONFIDENCE motion from Mrs Thatcher, Jim Callaghan managed to stave off the prospect of a general election by agreeing the "Lib-Lab Pact" with David Steel's party.

Yes, Jim swings it!

In the most sensational development to rock British politics since the invention of the Gladstone Bag, Mr David Steel last night "signed terms" with Mr Callaghan which spell an end to 5,000 years of Parliamentary democracy.

Scenes of pandemonium broke out at the

House of Commons, when the terms of the Liberal "Big Deal" were at last revealed. The shock terms are:

1. That Mr Callaghan's secretary will agree to ring up Mr Steel once a month to tell him how things are getting on.
2. Mr John Pargs, economics supremo of the tiny 3-member Liberal Party, will be given free access to all Treasury car parks.
3. This offer does not constitute a contract.
4. Jim Rules – OK?

An emotional Ms Thatcherette, self-styled supremo of the so-called Tory Party, described the deal as "a dirty rotten trick". Mr Steel was "very naughty", she went on, adding that it was "not cricket".

25 YEARS ON from the Queen's coronation, the nation rejoiced.

Great Bores of Today

"…I won't hear a word against Her myself I say jolly good luck to Her I wouldn't do Her job for all the tea in China just imagine it I mean She couldn't do what we're doing now no it's easy for people to knock Her She can't answer back but I wouldn't do Her job for anything I feel sorry for Her I mean just think of it having to smile and wave all the time and open those hospitals not to mention having to listen to lots of boring people going on and on and having to pretend to look interested at some terrible fellow boring on about something you couldn't care less about no I say good luck to Her she deserves every penny she gets…"

THE CELEBRATIONS coincided with the height of a notorious industrial dispute…

Queen to visit Grunwick

Her Majesty the Queen will today become the latest visitor to the famous Grunwick Film-processing Studios, as part of her Jubilee Tour of North-West London.

The Queen, accompanied by the Duke of Edinburgh, will see for herself the now-familiar scenes of "pickets" and "police" engaged in their traditional "clashes" outside the factory gates, watched by newsmen and tourists from all over the world.

Her Majesty will wear special "protective clothing" as she watches the highspot of the show, the arrival of the "works bus".

At this point, hundreds of screaming pickets surge forward in order to exercise their democratic right of "interviewing" the "blacklegs" with the aid of milk-bottles and lengths of lead piping.

Her Majesty will then witness the ancient ritual of "smashing the pigs", in which young policemen exercise their democratic right to fall on the ground with blood pouring from their heads.

…BUT ALSO, more pleasingly, with a British win at Wimbledon.
Lines on the Wimbledon Victory of Virginia Wade in the Women's Singles

Quiet please!

So. Congratulations
Then Virginia
Wade.

Or Ginny as
You are better
Known in
The popular
Press.

For years you
Have struggled
To achieve
This goal.

Now in Jubilee
Year in the
Presence of Her
Majesty the
Queen you
Have at last
Succeeded.

4-6
6-3
6-1

These simple
Figures do not
Tell the whole
Story.

But there is
Not enough room
In a poem for
Anything more
Specific.

E. Jervase Thribb (17)

THE EX-PRIME MINISTER kept expounding wilder and wilder conspiracy theories to anyone who would listen to him.

AN EPIDEMIC OF FOOTBALL hooliganism was sweeping through Britain's stadiums.

Neasden chairman lashes fans

Neasden Chairman, local Launderama magnate Brig. Buffy Cohen, today hit out at club fans (Sid & Doris Bonkers) whom he described as "a pack of wild beasts on the rampage".

He told reporters, "I will not allow these monsters onto the terraces of the Bridge. They have made Neasden a byword for bestiality and violence."

The Brigadier's outburst followed last Saturday's shock scenes in which the Bonkers launched a bazooka attack on "Balon's Hot Dog Stand" following referee Sid Himmler's controversial decisions to have "Baldy" Pevsner arrested for gross indecency only five minutes after kick-off.

Following a full-scale board meeting, Neasden's manager, tight-lipped soccer supremo Ron Knee, 59, revealed that plans were under way to dig a "Colditz-style" tunnel from Neasden Station leading direct to the local Magistrate's Court.

LATE SCORE

Dollis Hill 1, Neasden 0. Match abandoned.

ELVIS PRESLEY died at the age of 42 and the weight of 25 stone.

The Wayside Pulpit *with the REV. J.C. FLANNEL*

I expect all of us have heard by now of the tragic passing of the Big E, as I believe he was known among his many devoted fans. But, you know, at this time, I think all of us can learn something from the life on earth of this "prophet of the pops". Was it not he who sang of the Heartbreak Hotel, situated, you will recall, "at the end of Lonely Street". Are we not all of us residents, in some sense, of that street? And again, he tells us, in another of his songs, "Return to Sender". What better reminder for all of us, that we too must one day return to He who sent us? And now, Hymn 94, in the Nashville Hymns for Rocking Christians, *We Are All Shook Up, In A Very Real Sense*.

PRINCESS ANNE gave birth to the Queen's first grandchild.

Auberon Waugh's Diary

Rumours which continue to reach me that there is something terribly wrong with Master Peter Phillips can only be strengthened by the Queen's decision to have him improperly christened in a drawing room at Buckingham Palace, instead of publicly in Church.

First reports that the lad was born with five legs can surely be discounted. It is quite normal for the male organ to appear disproportionately large in new-born infants. The truth may be much more simple: that Princess Anne has given birth to a centaur. IF so, it is hard to decide whether one should congratulate her on her good fortune or commiserate with her. The best thing is surely to enter him for Eton and for Fred Winter's stable at Lambourn and decide which is more suitable at the time.

THE EYE MARKED the death of Sir Eric Miller *(see journalism, right)*.

RIOT SHIELDS were deployed by police for the first time on the mainland during clashes in South London between National Front marchers and those opposing them.

"That's the trouble with Sundays around here – nothing ever happens!"

IN FEBRUARY the *Eye* uncovered some intriguing details about businessman Eric Miller, and his connections to several of their favourite targets.

The ill-fated firm of Labour Party Properties, set up in 1969 to buy and manage property "for the purpose of assisting directly or indirectly the work of the Labour party" now seems almost certain to be forced into liquidation, causing considerable embarrassment to the Party, the government and last but not least James Callaghan. Its last annual accounts declare a loss of £30,735, and its auditors point out that "in the present uncertain conditions of the property market, we are unable to satisfy ourselves that the Balance Sheet does not overstate their worth".

Directors include founder-member of the "Marfia" and millionaire Sir Eric Miller, chairman of Peachey Properties, knighted in Wilson's resignation honours.

Despite his recent Labour links, Miller has also hedged his bets by maintaining contacts with the Tories. Former Shadow Foreign Secretary Reginald Maudling's Hertfordshire home was sold some years ago to Peachey Property Corporation in a deal which has some singular characteristics. Purchased by Maudling for a reputed £9,000 in 1950, Bedwell Lodge was sold to Peachey for only £3,000 soon after the Labour party's 1964 election victory. Peachey then leased it back to the Maudlings, allegedly at the most advantageous rental of precisely £2 a week, and

assumed responsibility for all repairs. Peachey also paid John Poulson to build a swimming pool at the property at a cost of £8,000.

Miller resigned from Peachey at the end of March after the board queried his misuse of company money. The *Eye* was in prophetic mood.

Sir Eric Miller is the second of Sir Harold Wilson's personal friends to come under something of a cloud. The other was Lord Brayley, formerly Wilson's Army Minister, who was facing fraud charges when he died in March. No one has suggested that Sir Eric will undergo a similar fate.

He did though. As well as lengthy ongoing investigations in the *Eye*, Miller was the subject of fraud inquiries by both the police and the Department of Trade when he shot himself that September.

THE GROVEL COLUMN reported on royal romances in November.

Hacks working for Rupert Murdoch have been pestering me for the identities of the married ladies who have caught the eye and fancy of the Heir to the Throne, Prince Charles, but I have demurred. *Eye* readers, however, may wish to know their names. His fancies include Camilla Parker-Bowles, a member of the Cubitt building family and wife of Household Cavalry officer Andrew, a former escort of Princess Anne.

1978

PRINCESS MARGARET'S affair with toyboy Roddy Llewellyn boosted both the public mood and the country's tourist trade enormously.

EVERYONE WAS STILL talking about a film released at the end of the previous year.

Wayside Pulpit

The REV. J.C. FLANNEL writes:

You often hear it said that fewer and fewer people these days are going to see Star Wars. In this day and age, there are so many things to distract us; demos, discos and bingo-parlours, that the really important things in life often tend to be put to one side. We say, "We'll go to Star Wars next week". But somehow, when next week comes, our good resolution is quite forgotten.

But, you know, just because people aren't going to see it, it doesn't mean that Star Wars has lost its relevance for modern man. The great battle between Good and Evil goes on in all our lives, just as it always did.

And now we say the responses on page 14 of your Series 94 Service Book:
THE PRESIDENT: The Force Be With You
THE CONGREGATION *(Mrs Ethel Betjeman, 105)*: And Also With You.

IN ITALY, far-left terror group the Red Brigade took the former prime minister hostage, demanding the release of imprisoned members of their group.

Auberon Waugh's Diary

It has not been a good year for former Prime Ministers, with Mr Bhutto of Pakistan sentenced to hang and Alberto Moro imprisoned somewhere by frenzied Lefties who are no doubt haranguing the poor man about Chile, international combines and other recondite topics of that sort. The great question in all our minds is whether it could happen here. Grocer Heath might seem to offer a tempting target. Perhaps would-be kidnappers are intimidated by the thought of being shut up with him, while would-be assassins pause to reflect on the mess he would undoubtedly make if blown up.

Predictably, Pope Paul has offered himself as a replacement for Mr Moro.

One day the penny will drop that kidnappers don't want him for the good reason that he would not be worth more than a tin of sardines and a plastic medallion of Pope John in exchange.

I suppose it is time I did my duty and announced to the world that I am prepared to exchange myself for the Pope. But I have a terrible feeling he may accept.

OUTPUT AND QUALITY both continued to plummet at British Steel despite the best efforts of chairman Sir Charles Villiers.

State boss hits back at critics of £20 billion-a-day loss

Sir Humphrey Noggis, £60,000-a-year Chairman of the British Air and Water Corporation, today lashed out at critics of Britain's loss-making nationalised industries.

Asked on the BBC phone-in show *Line Engaged* if it was true that the BAWC was likely to lose £24,000 million during this financial year, Sir Herbert replied, "Oh no, no, no, no, no. We don't look at it like that at all." Pressed by the interviewer Ron String to defend the BAWC's "gross overmanning, appalling strike record, disastrous productivity, and failure either to make or sell anything at all since 1968," Sir Hubert said: "No, no, no, no. That's not the point. We're doing a lot better than some of our competitors overseas. If you look at Uganda, for instance, or Outer Mongolia, you'll find that production of micro-dot nuclear processing plants is almost zero. So don't let's get things out of proportion."

Asked if it was right that he should be given a 400% increase in his already ludicrous salary for running an industry that contributed nothing to Britain at all, Sir Humbert replied: "It would be wrong to see these figures out of perspective. Compared with many oil sheikhs, I am virtually on the bread-line."

LEONID BREZHNEV continued to serve as Soviet leader, despite being at least two-thirds dead and 80% proof.

THE LEADER of the opposition was working hard to boost her image with the public.

'I love a good cry' – Iron Lady's shock claim

In an article published in today's issue of *Womanperson*, the Conservative leader Mrs Thatcher admits frankly that she likes nothing more in life than ironing her husband's pyjamas. "Now that I am Tory leader, however, I don't have much time to do that sort of thing."

Mrs Thatcher also admits that she likes nothing more (apart from ironing her husband's pyjamas) than having a good cry at the local Odeon on Saturday nights. "It is such a shame they had to close it down and turn it into a bingo hall," she says.

She also admits that she likes nothing more than going down to her local bingo hall, to iron pyjamas and have a good cry. "But of course it's very difficult to fit that kind of thing in nowadays," she says, "what with my engagements up and down the country and all these interviews with women's magazines."

WITH SUPPORT FOR THE National Front at its highest-ever level, racists remained convinced that being in Britain was a privilege.

Major Daily Mail Poll Reveals 97% of Immigrants Say 'Yes' to Repatriation

A shock poll carried out for the *Daily Mail* reveals that well over nine in ten of Britain's coloured people want "to leave this country as soon as possible". The question put to more than 15 coloured immigrants in areas such as Brixton, Walsall and Bradford last week was: "If the Government under Mrs Thatcher were to give you a million pounds, and a first-class air ticket to the sun-drenched tax haven of your choice, where you could spend the rest of your life lying around by swimming pools, drinking Bacardi and Cokes and having your every need catered to by bevies of gorgeous lovelies, wouldn't you want to get out of this dreadful, snow-bound hell-hole of a country as fast as possible?"

An unbelievable 97% of those questioned gave their answer as "YES".

The message from Britain's coloured people is clear. They want to go. The sooner they can get out the better. Britain is on the skids. (*Can this be right? Ed.*)

THE RECENTLY ELECTED Pope John Paul I, who took his name in tribute to his two immediate predecessors, also swiftly followed their example by dying.

Lines on the Death of Pope John Paul I

So. Farewell then
Pope John Paul I
After only thirty-
Four days.

John Paul.
A name chosen
From
Your predecessors.

Keith suggests that
The next Pope
Should be
Called

John Paul George
And Ringo.

But I consider
That remark
Is in poor taste

Under the circumstances.

E.J. Thribb (17½)

CALLAGHAN DECIDED not to opt for an autumn election, erroneously believing things were going to get better for his government by the spring.

That's what I'm afraid of Brothers

BUT INDUSTRIAL relations were worsening...

TUC calls for 'No-day week'

by Our Industrial Correspondent **Maurice Marina**

By 64,782,219 votes to one, the TUC yesterday approved what Mr Clive Jenkins described as "a plan for a better Britain".

The package envisages:
- A new 'no-day week'
- Eight months, paid holiday a year for every trade union member
- A new, across-the-board, index-linked minimum wage of £500 a week
- A new index-linked pension structure to permit retirement on full pay at 23.

Mr Alan Vole, General Secretary of QUANGO (Quite Unemployed Association of No-Good Operatives) brought delegates cheering to their feet with his claim that, "Brothers, we are an idealistic movement, fighting for the rights of the under-privileged, or we are nothing."

...CASTING a shadow over preparations for Christmas.

MARCH BROUGHT more news of the Norman Scott investigation.

Over the last month or so the Director of Public Prosecutions, Thomas Hetherington, has been (metaphorically of course) wetting his pants over what is becoming known as "The Shot Dog Mystery" or "The Hound of the Liberals". Andrew Newton was convicted of violence against the dog, against Scott, and was sentenced to two years imprisonment. And there, the DPP might well have felt, the matter ended. But not so. For now new papers are arriving in his office almost every week arising from Newton's statement, after coming out of prison, that he had intended to kill Scott, and that he had been paid £5,000 to do so by people closely associated with the Liberal Party.

The policeman in charge of inquiries into the case, one Supt. Michael Challes, is very anxious to avoid the criticism that he is part of a "cover-up". Mr Challes' papers to Mr Hetherington have been remarkably frank. Mr Challes wants in one of his more memorable phrases to go "all the way". Not to put too fine a point on it, he wants arrests for conspiracy to murder.

By July it seemed he was about to get his way.

Mr Thorpe has been interviewed by police but did not endear himself to them. He is known to police investigators as "the ditto man". He answered every question with the one word, "ditto", in reference to his earlier statement that he had been told by his advisers to say nothing at all.

Mr Peter Bessell, former Liberal MP and former friend of Thorpe, was, on the other hand, very cooperative. He told police that at a meeting at the House of Commons in 1968, Thorpe had said of Scott "We'll have to get rid of him." When Bessell protested, Thorpe replied: "It's no worse than shooting a mad dog." A grimly accurate prophecy, as it turned out. Bessell was sure, and is sure, that Thorpe was serious in this suggestion. He remembers several conversations with his leader about various ways in which Scott could be "done away with".

Thorpe, according to Bessell, was sure that the best man to do the job was David Holmes, a close friend. Bessell remembers a meeting in early 1969 during which Thorpe suggested Holmes pose as a reporter hunting for dirt about Thorpe, get Scott drunk, kill him and drop him down a tin mine. In 1970 there was another wild plan, passed on by Holmes to Bessell in

America, to "lure Scott over here and finish him off in the Everglades".

As the elections of 1974 approached, Thorpe became more and more determined on his plan. Holmes contacted a business associate, John Le Mesurier, and asked him to hunt around for a hit man. Le Mesurier contacted George Deakin, who through other contacts found Andrew Newton, who agreed to bump off Scott for £10,000.

Perhaps the most devastating evidence uncovered concerns the raising of money to pay for all this. It seems that Jeremy Thorpe approached his old friend Jack Hayward, a millionaire much of whose business dealings are conducted in the Bahamas, and asked if he could spare £10,000 for "election expenses". The money was paid in November 1975, exactly a month after the murder attempt on Scott by Newton. When he asked why he wasn't expected to pay his donation, as he usually did, straight into Liberal Party funds, Hayward was told that these were "special expenses".

Thorpe immediately threatened to sue the *Eye* for criminal libel and reported the magazine to the Attorney General for contempt of court – but was arrested for conspiracy to murder a fortnight later. In November magistrates committed him, Holmes, Le Mesurier and Deakin for trial at the Old Bailey the following year – but at that stage the *Eye* identified a potential problem.

The decision by Mr George Deakin, the amusement machine businessman, to lift reporting restrictions in the Thorpe trial is easily explained. He was the only person around who wasn't likely to get lots of money. Hacks have been wheeling and dealing for the bodies of witnesses, defendants and anyone else with a story to tell.

The *Sunday Telegraph* surprised the field with a shock signing of key prosecution witness Peter Bessell for £50,000. Negotiations of a similar kind are believed to have been opened with defendants David Holmes and John le Mesurier. Witness Andrew Newton has already had large sums of money, the latest £2,000 from the Canadian Broadcasting Corporation.

Thorpe's defence went on to portray Bessell and other witnesses as hopelessly compromised by their financial deals with the media, a major factor in all four defendants being found not guilty the following year.

IN APRIL, SLICKER BEGAN to raise doubts about financial phenomenon BCCI.

There has been more than a little eyebrow raising in banking circles over the curious mixture of explosive growth, controversial associates, unusual clients and general mystery which makes up the Bank of Credit and Commerce International, possibly the world's fastest-growing bank.

For some time there has been considerable City interest as to who exactly owns the bank, given that its ownership disappears into a maze of nominee names and companies in the Cayman Islands and Luxembourg, both locales with a frosty welcome for the seeker after truth.

BCCI was formed by Pakistani banker Agha Hasan Abedi, its president. Until recently the only known investor was the Bank of America, the world's largest bank, which owns 24% of Bank of Credit and Commerce International Holdings (Lux) which in turn owns BCCI. The remaining shares are said to be spread among Abedi and a gaggle of rich investors from Saudi Arabia and the United Arab Emirates, including the ruler of Abu Dhabi, Sheikh Zaid.

However, the identities of these important people are not known either to the Bank of England or the Department of Trade who are responsible for the banking sector in Britain.

BCCI is rumoured to be the custodian of up to $200 million in deposits for Sheikh Zaid and his family. According to one Arab banking source, BCCI obtained this money by the simple device of outbidding every other bank for the deposit interest it was prepared to offer when Sheikh Zaid decided some years ago that to the highest bidder would go his oil wealth. Now this may be envy talking. But if true, it suggests that Sheikh Zaid at least will not be a happy man if things do not continue to go up and up for BCCI.

BCCI finally collapsed in 1991, when the Bank of England forced it to close its UK operations, with investors – including a number of British local councils – losing hundreds of millions. It subsequently emerged that the bank had debts of £5.6bn, and had stolen £1bn from Sheikh Zaid's personal account. It had been able to get away with crimes including fraud, money laundering on a massive scale and involvement in the international drug trade for years, due to the carefully designed set-up Slicker had identified, which allowed it to evade the regulatory powers of central banks and operate in jurisdictions with high levels of financial secrecy.

1979

WIDESPREAD STRIKES plunged the country into what became known as the Winter of Discontent, despite the prime minister denying any "mounting chaos".

PRIVATE EYE

No. 446
Friday
19 Jan. '79
25p

JIM SINGS

Do you know the country's in a terrible mess?

You hum it and I'll soon pick it up

A very old joke I'm thinking

HE RESISTED DECLARING an official State of Emergency, fearful of how the unions would react.

Government to declare 'State of Bliss'

In a shock move to meet Britain's growing crisis, the Government last night declared a "state of bliss" to come into effect from midnight.

WHAT IT WILL MEAN:
- No more juggernauts, cars or buses to make Britain's roads "a living nightmare"
- *Sunday Times* to remain unpublished
- Motorways to be "ploughed up" and used for intensive hallucinogenic mushroom farming
- All noisy, polluting aircraft to be grounded indefinitely
- Everyone to remain at home "until further notice", making their own entertainment and growing their own vegetables of the type no longer available in shops.

MEANWHILE, the increasing piles of rubbish bags stacked up in the streets were hindering many people from going about their daily work.

"Like a good time, dearie?"

IN IRAN, the Shah was deposed by supporters of Ayatollah Khomeini.

Around the World with Glenda Slagg

■ Come off it, Ayatollah Khomeini!!! Who'dja think ya tryin' ta kid?? Sitting there in Paris combing your beard and a-prayin' to Allah all day long!!!

■ Pull the other one, Ayatollah baby!! Give me the sexy Shah any day!! At least he's got a bit of class. With his grey hair and millions of pounds he's the kind of guy I could go for!!! Geddit???

■ Hi there, Your Magnificence!?!!! If you're looking for a little Shangri-La give us a call. You can ski down my slopes any day!!!?

SEX PISTOL Sid Vicious died of a heroin overdose.

Obituary – Mr S. Vicious

The death is reported from New York of Mr Sidney Vicious, the distinguished "punk" musician. He was 15.
Our Musical Critic Mr William Mann writes:
It seems hardly three weeks ago that Mr Vicious first laid claim on our attention by murdering his companion in a New York hotel room while under the influence of hard drugs. But it is perhaps for his music that he will be best forgotten.

THE CONSERVATIVES won the general election, and Margaret Thatcher became Prime Minister.

HER HUSBAND DID not appear delighted by the development.

10 Downing Street
Whitehall

Dear Bill,

As you may have seen in the Telegraph, all hell has broken loose around here since we were last able to have a chat over lunch that day at the Army & Navy. M. has become Prime Minister, and it's caused no end of a flap. Telephone never stops ringing. All my daffs got trampled by a lot of bloody pressmen on election day. I actually spotted some photographer-johnny nipping up the fire-escape trying to catch Carol starkers in the bath, dirty bugger.

To cap it all, we've now had to ship the whole shooting-match over to Number Ten, and I don't know yet whether I'm coming or going. The bloody fools from Pickfords seem to have lost that set of Ping Irons Burmah gave me when I handed in my cards. What with decorators, policemen and politicos running about all over the place, Number Ten is the worst shambles I've seen since the Dieppe show in '42. What's more there doesn't seem to be a decent local, and they've even got some Ministry of Works chappie called Boris to take care of the garden, so any hope I had of taking off a peaceful hour or two in the greenhouse is out of the window.

Anyway, so sorry I couldn't make it on Tuesday. M. insisted I turn up for some kind of State Opening of Parliament or other. I had assumed that now the election was over I would be excused this kind of thing, but oh no. I had just carried my spare clubs out to the jalopy, when heigh ho! Up goes a window, and M. is giving me my marching orders. It's off to Moss Bros for the full kit, and then on to the Commons. What a place, Bill! If you ask me, it's just an antiquated rabbit warren – miles and miles of corridors, with chaps in evening dress wandering round like a lot of super-annuated penguins, and not a decent watering hole to be found.

Do tell Monty and the Major that I am definitely on for the 24th. I've checked with M.'s secretary, and there's absolutely nothing in the book. So see you for a few pre-match snifters at the 19th!

Yours Aye, Denis

SIR JOSEPH CANTLEY, the judge at Jeremy Thorpe's trial for conspiracy to murder Norman Scott, delivered an astonishingly biased summary to the jury.

That Summing Up

Ladies and gentlemen of the jury. It is my duty to advise you how you should vote when you retire from this court. In the last few weeks we have heard some pretty extraordinary allegations being made about one of the most distinguished politicians ever to rise to high office in this country – or not, as you may think.

We have heard, for example, from Mr Bessell – a man who by his own admission is a liar, a humbug, a hypocrite, a vagabond, and a loathsome reptile. You may choose to believe the transparent tissue of lies which streamed from his lips in the witness box, if you wish. That is entirely a matter between you and your conscience.

Then we have heard from Mr Scott – a scrounger, a parasite, a pervert. It would be hard to imagine, ladies and gentlemen, a more pitiful, discredited and embittered man, or a more unreliable witness upon whose testimony to convict a man whom you may think should have become Prime Minister of this country.

Over the evidence of Mr Newton, the so-called "hit man", I would prefer to draw a discreet veil. He is, as we know, a man with a criminal record, a piece of refuse unable to carry out even the simplest murder plot without cocking it up.

One further point. You will have noticed that three of the defendants have chosen, very wisely, to exercise their inalienable right not to go into the witness box to answer a lot of embarrassing questions. I will merely say that you are not to infer from this anything other than that they consider the evidence so flimsy that it was scarcely worth rising from their seats to waste breath on denying these extraordinary charges.

You are now to retire to consider your verdict of "Not Guilty".

THE EYE'S MAN IN COURT watched what happened next.

Auberon Waugh's Diary

Thursday

The jury is still out. Thorpe apparently spent the night in hospital in Brixton Prison with an upset stomach. Just occasionally, I too have suffered from an upset stomach and it can be quite disagreeable, although it has never occurred to me to go to hospital for it.

The other three defendants, being of a lower class, spent the night locked in a single cell. Although not by nature a left-winger, I feel something in this case stirs the latent Robespierre in me.

Friday

The verdict. Thorpe declared not guilty, as we all knew he would be. How could it have occurred to any of us for a moment that he was anything but innocent?

Speaking for myself, I think it may have been something to do with the double-breasted waistcoats he wears. At my school, prefects were allowed to wear these absurd garments as a badge of office. So many of them were hypocrites, sodomites and criminal psychopaths that I understandably jumped to the wrong conclusion that Jeremy Thorpe might just possibly be one too.

Now we know otherwise, perhaps he will consider wearing more conventional clothes in future.

THE IRA MURDERED the Queen's cousin, Lord Mountbatten, two members of his family and a teenage crew member by blowing up the boat they were in. Foreign secretary Peter Carrington and Mrs Thatcher were quick to condemn the atrocity – as was her husband.

10 Downing Street
Whitehall

Dear Bill,

Well, we live in stirring times, no doubt of that. This Mountbatten business has been pretty sickening all round: apart from anything else I'll have to scratch the outing to Hunterscombe. Peter Carrington told me that from now on if I go anywhere out of doors I have to have some bloody Special Branch man in a dirty mac traipsing about in my wake, shaking the clubs out every time I want to play a shot, and peering through the window, no doubt, at the Nineteenth, to avert foul play. Things have come to a pretty pass, Bill, when a chap can't even take the clubs for a walk because some thick-headed Irish hooligans want to play silly buggers.

The funny thing is, the Boss seems to be having a bit of a ball over the whole thing. No sooner had the balloon gone up than our enterprising Italian friends from Saatchi's were

round with the kit: full camouflage flak jacket and khaki bloomers for a whistle-stop tour of the black spots. The name of the game, obviously, was showing the flag. Usual guff about hot pursuit, M. determined to get on top of the gunmen, Carrington banging on about not giving in to the men of violence, and if we pull out there'll be a bloodbath.

Well, what the hell does he think is going on at the moment? That's what I'd like to know. But it's no use talking to these politicos, Bill, that's what I've discovered. The whole thing's as plain as a pikestaff to you or me, but they can't see it.

My best to Daphne.

Yours, Denis

THE SQUATTING MOVEMENT reached its height, with an estimated 50,000 people living rent-free in properties that did not belong to them.

THE MAN WHO HAD become known as "The Yorkshire Ripper" killed his 12th victim.

Ripper – Knacker claims 'We're almost there!'

"Make no mistake," said a tired but triumphant Inspector Knacker of the West Yorkshire police, "the so-called Ripper is as good as in the bag."

The Inspector's confident prediction came only hours after the Yorkshire Ripper had claimed his 495th victim.

"We are almost there," said the Inspector. "We know everything about this man, except who he is. My lads have performed a super-human task in narrowing down the field. We have a short-list of just two million possible suspects, and we are constantly adding to that list."

AT A COMMONWEALTH conference in Zambia, Mrs Thatcher brokered a deal to introduce black majority rule in Rhodesia – or as it would henceforth be called, Zimbabwe.

That Rhodesia peace plan in full

1. That a conference shall be held somewhere in the near future with regard to this one.
2. That a new election shall be held in which either Mr Nkomo or Mr Mugabe shall be declared the winner.
3. That Smithy shall be deposed of double-quick.
4. That all armed forces in Rhodesia-Zimbabwe shall be disbanded immediately.
5. That the troops of His Excellency General Mugabe shall be given a totally free hand to bring peace in our time to Rhodesia by whatever means they see fit.
6. That his Imperial Holiness Field Marshal Mugabe shall be awarded the VC to bring him into line with other Commonwealth leaders.
7. That Zimbabwe-Rhodesia shall hereinafter be known as Mugabwe.

IN IRAN, THE SHAH was deposed and an Islamic Republic declared under Ayatollah Khomeini. The US embassy in Tehran was stormed and its staff taken hostage.

Why don't we go back to your place and start World War Three?

IN MAY, THE EYE followed up the revelations of a local paper.

There is not an important newspaper or TV station in the land which has not received a copy of the May issue of the *Rochdale Alternative Paper,* with an article which describes some unusual behaviour on the part of Cyril Smith, Rochdale's newly-returned Liberal MP. The allegations are substantiated by a number of sworn statements and carefully recorded interviews, but they have so far not been published anywhere else. Nor has any writ for libel yet been issued by C. Smith.

The article refers to the Cambridge Boys Hostel, opened by the Rochdale Hostel for Boys Association, of which Cyril Smith was secretary. It publishes extracts from three men, all living in Rochdale and then homeless apprentices who were staying at the hostel. The first man says that he had missed a day off work, which was against the hostel rules. He was reported, and interviewed by Cyril Smith.

"He gave me the choice between accepting his punishment or leaving the hostel. I said I would accept his punishment. He told me to take my trousers and pants down and he hit me four or five times with his bare hands on my bare buttocks."

The second man says "Cyril Smith found that I had taken some money. He told me to take off my trousers and pants and bend over his knee. He hit me many times with his bare hand, and I pleaded with him to

stop because he was hurting me. This took place at the hostel. Afterwards, he came into my bedroom and wiped my bare buttocks with a sponge."

Another man says "I was given a kind of medical examination by Cyril Smith. He told me to take my trousers and pants down. He held my testicles and told me to cough." The *RAP* editors say they have four other sworn statements from men who allege similar spankings or inspections.

In 1970 a young man was interviewed at Risley Remand Centre, and told police about punishment he had received from Smith. A full-length police inquiry followed. Smith was interviewed and vigorously denied all the allegations put to him. The police inquiry was completed, and a file prepared. What happened then is not clear. The Director of Public Prosecutions says "The DPP cannot trace such a case being referred to us, but cannot confirm or deny receiving it." The police declined to comment.

Whether or not the file went to the DPP, it was kept for some years at the police headquarters at Preston. In March 1974, during discussions about the possible formation of a Con/Lib coalition after the general election of that month, the Special Branch copied the file and took it to London.

With the honourable exception of the *New Statesman*, not a single other media organisation followed up this story until Smith's death in 2010, after which the full extent of his sexual abuse was revealed.

JUNE BROUGHT disturbing news from Jeddah.

Ronald Smith, a former Leeds policeman, has been here for several weeks: his daughter Helen was found half-naked and dead on May 20. The official version, strongly supported by the Foreign Office, is that Helen fell to her death while making love to a young Dutchman on a balcony. Ronald Smith is convinced that Helen was murdered, and her body placed on the ground as though she had fallen.

On arrival he went to the privately owned Bakhsh hospital where his daughter worked, and studied the top-floor apartment next door but one to that from whose balcony the couple were supposed to have fallen. The balcony wall was high enough to ensure that no one, however drunk, could possibly have fallen from it.

Smith's doubts were reinforced by a short 10-minute interview he was allowed with Richard Arnot, the British consultant, who works at the Bakhsh hospital, and at whose flat Helen attended a party on the night of her death. Dr Arnot and his wife Penelope are both held in custody by the Saudi Arabian police on charges related to alcohol which, it is alleged, was being illegally consumed on the night Helen died. Arnot said that the bodies of Helen and the Dutchman had been spotted by "two men at the party" who "went onto the balcony to watch the sun rise". Smith knew this to be unlikely: he had seen that the only balcony from which the bodies would have been visible faced due west.

Smith then went to the public mortuary. From his experience in the police, he knew what to expect of a body which had fallen from a fourth storey. "Her face, head and neck," he says, "were perfect, except for a small hole in the centre of her forehead, above the right eye, which had forced the eye back into the brain." The dead girl's left hand was held up across her face, as if to protect it. The hand was extensively bruised. So were her thighs. Her right hip was fractured.

He demanded an autopsy, which confirmed that there were no multiple fractures of the type which might have been expected from a steep fall. Death had been caused by bleeding due to internal injuries.

Eight nurses, doctors and consultants at the hospital have provided Smith with tape-recorded statements about Helen's death. All thought she had been murdered.

One of Penelope Arnot's closest friends here in Jeddah is Gordon Kirby, vice-consul at the British Embassy. Kirby had arrived at the hospital at six on the morning of the deaths. He took a statement from Penelope Arnot. Smith went to the British consul and

demanded to see the statement. He refused. In a rage, Smith insisted on seeing the British Ambassador. He got as far as the charge d'affaires, Michael Weston, who told him that he had strict instructions from the Foreign Office not to let Smith – or anyone else for that matter – see the statement.

Mr Weston explained that Anglo-Saudi relations were of the utmost importance, and that it would be very silly of anyone to do anything to damage them. Smith's certainty that his daughter was murdered is strengthened by what he sees as the determination of British officials in Saudi Arabia to protect her murderers.

Ron Smith's campaigning resulted in a change to the law obliging coroners to investigate deaths abroad (*see 1982*).

THERE WAS SOME intriguing publishing news in September.

Last week the deputy managing director of the publishers Hutchinson's received a phone call from the distinguished libel lawyer Michael Rubinstein. He was ringing, he said, in connection with a book, *The Climate of Treason* by Andrew Boyle, to be published next month. He said he had reason to believe that it may contain defamatory references to a client – who, after huffing and puffing, he admitted was Sir Anthony Blunt, the Queen's advisor on paintings and drawings and Surveyor of the Queen's Pictures, 1952-72.

Rubinstein has been told that he cannot read the book in advance of publication. The reason for Sir Anthony's concern is not immediately clear. The book, which does indeed contain many references to Sir Anthony, traces in greater detail than hitherto the background to the Burgess-Philby-Maclean story. In doing so it introduces the so-called "Fourth Man", another senior official in the British Intelligence Service who was a long-serving Russian agent. This fourth man is referred to throughout by Boyle as "Maurice", the code name by which he was known to the Russians.

What has this to do with Sir Anthony Blunt, who, during the war according two *Who's Who* was at the War Office?

In November, eight days after the *Eye* had made things more explicit ("The Blunt truth is that "Maurice = Sir Anthony Blunt"), Mrs Thatcher confirmed in the Commons that he had indeed been a spy for the Russians, and that the security services had known and covered the truth up for 15 years. His knighthood was annulled by Buckingham Palace minutes later.

1980s

THE EIGHTIES IN BRITAIN WERE DOMINATED BY the figure of one woman. And in *Private Eye*, by her husband.

Dear Bill, the letters of prime ministerial consort Denis Thatcher to a golfing chum, were another product of the dream team of Richard Ingrams and John Wells. They established a comic persona that the real Denis was more than happy to play up to in order to dispel any suspicion that he was pulling the strings of the nation's first woman leader, and allowed the *Eye* team to create what was in effect a long-running sitcom which quietly chronicled the epic political events of the decade, even as readers thought they were just enjoying several snifters of electric soup.

It was also the era when Britain's manufacturing and industrial base was pushed aside in favour of high stakes financial buccaneering – something that was also evident in the arena where the *Eye* spent much of the decade, the libel courts. "The 1980s were extraordinary: some years we had up to a dozen actions or so. We used to get hammered," remembered then managing editor Dave Cash.

Several subsequent changes to the law mean that suing for libel has become both more risky and less potentially lucrative, but the degree to which the playing field was tilted against the defendants was demonstrated by the case brought by Sonia Sutcliffe, wife of serial killer the Yorkshire Ripper, over the claim she had been negotiating with newspapers to sell her exclusive story (she had). She was allowed to bring a libel claim a full six years after the story appeared and supposedly did such damage to her reputation, and when the jury found in her favour they – and not the judge – were allowed to award her an eye-watering £600,000 in damages, close to 100 times what surviving victims of her husband's vicious hammer and knife attacks had been awarded in criminal compensation. The *Eye*'s young editor, Ian Hislop, appointed five years after the story was published and one year before the writ was produced, promptly and memorably announced that "if that is justice, I'm a banana".

In the Sutcliffe case, the damages were subsequently reduced to a more manageable £60,000. But at least she only sued once: one man, the bully, thief, swindler, serial apologist for murderous dictators and part-time newspaper publisher Robert Maxwell, kept dragging the *Eye* back through the law courts. He sued over a story suggesting he was wangling for a peerage. He sued over a story about his helicopter company. He sued over stories about his newspaper company. He sued over a cartoon. He sued over a lookalike on the letters page. And finally he sued over the "very serious injury to his feelings and reputation" caused by a report that he was fiddling the *Mirror* pension fund, weeks before it was publicly revealed that he had looted it of £440 million. Fortunately for all concerned, by that point he had fallen off the back of his yacht and died, which was probably the only thing that could stop him from winning that case too.

> " *Journalists may read it because it strays over borders, takes off lids and peers into things. The public reads it because it is the only regular funny periodical readily available in Britain. When it stops being funny, they will stop reading it.* "
>
> Stephen Fry, 1986

1980

STEEL WORKERS WERE the latest to go on strike over job cuts.

"Right lads – remove those secondary pickets"

BUT THE WORLD was looking to the future.

It's the decade of the chip

It's no larger than a pin-head. But make no mistake. In the decade that lies ahead, the silicon chip will change all our lives more than anything since the invention of the wheel. In a million different ways this tiny micro-miracle, no bigger than a three-penny bit, will transform the lives of every man, woman and child on the earth today.

From Shanghai to Shepton Mallet, they're calling it the biggest thing since the invention of fire by stone-age man. Make no mistake. Thanks to the silicon chip revolution, nothing will ever be the same again.

What will it mean to you and me – this astonishing atom-age breakthrough, no bigger than a nuclear power station? This is what the experts predict:
● Millions of jobs will be created overnight to cope with the expanding needs of micro-chip technology
● Millions will be thrown out of work overnight by the deadly chip, which poses the greatest threat to civilisation since the hydrogen bomb.

MRS THATCHER – and her husband – were greatly exercised by the Russian invasion of Afghanistan, and proposals for a boycott of that summer's Olympics in Moscow in response.

Dear Bill,

M. is frightfully steamed up about the Russian Bear. Quite right too, in my book. As one who knows his Burma and has seen Johnny Gurkha on the job, I see the whole thing as crystal clear. Peter Carrington dropped in the other night with his missus for a bite, and while she and M. went off to powder their noses I took the opportunity of putting in my two pennyworth. As I told him, with the help of the very serviceable *Reader's Digest World Atlas and Restaurant Guide*, your Tunbridge Wells friend kindly slipped into my arms after that shindig at the Pantiles, Warm Water Ports is the name of the game. Ever since the days of Ivan the Terrible, I explained over a tincture or twain, what the Rusky has always craved is somewhere to keep his fleet where it isn't too cold. What more natural then than for the Red Menace to come rolling through the Khyber, next stop Colombo, and there's your W.W.P.?

Carrington seemed very receptive to my little geography lesson, drumming his fingers on the tabletop and looking at the ceiling, always a sign in my experience that the little grey cells are working flat out. I was emboldened to suggest something short and sharp: no earthly use withdrawing our show-jumping team from the Olympic Caper, only leave the way open for the Japs to nab all the silver pots and trophies. Far better a quick blitz with half a dozen I.C.B.M.s, only language these chaps understand. Witness A. Hitler, failure to deal with menace of.

I could see Carrington absorbing all this, eyes tightly closed in concentration. Hope it at least provided a salutary antidote to what he gets fed by the assorted Moles, Pinkoes and Wooftahs at the F.O.

However, when we joined the Boss and Lady C. for the After Eights, the conversation turned to the rights and wrongs of index-linked perks for non-residential ex-industrialists. I now learn that as far as the Red Menace is concerned, there are plans afoot to cancel the forthcoming visit of the Leningrad Formation Ice-Skating Team. That'll stop the Mongol Hordes in their tracks, eh Bill? Poor old Colombo is all I have to add.

Yours, holding the fort,
Denis

FIVE MONTHS INTO a hostage crisis that saw 52 American diplomats being held in Iran, President Jimmy Carter was prepared to consider almost any means of freeing them – but without success.

SAUDI ARABIA THREATENED to cut off diplomatic relations with Britain over an ITV drama-documentary, *Death of a Princess*, which depicted a member of their royal family being executed alongside her lover for adultery.

The Saudi Telegraph
Storm grows over 'Princess' film

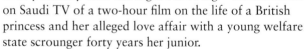

The English-speaking world was up in arms yesterday after last night's showing on Saudi TV of a two-hour film on the life of a British princess and her alleged love affair with a young welfare state scrounger forty years her junior.

I understand that the British Royal household has taken "grave offence" at the film. A British Palace official yesterday claimed that it was a "disgraceful attack" on the traditional beliefs of millions of Anglicans throughout the world. He pointed out that Princess Margaret is the sister of the head of the Church of England, and therefore a person held in deep reverence by all devout Englishmen.

Last night Lunchtime O'Nobooze, the producer of the award-winning film, was unrepentant. "While making *Princess*," he said, "we spoke to more than ten million people, tape-recorded thousands of interviews and shot over 500 miles of film. I agree that the end-product is a load of rubbish, but no one can deny that investigative journalism of this type has a vital role to play in bringing about World War Three."

OVER ON THE OTHER SIDE, an American import had become a huge hit.

GLENDA

★ J.R.!!!!?!!
Aren'tchasicktadeath of him?
With his ten-gallon hat and his false teeth he's gotta be the jerk of the year, geddit???
Give us a break, mister!!
Get back to *Dallas* and put a sock in it!!?! OK?!??

★ J.R.!?!?
Don'tcha love him?
With his come-and-get-me smile and his long silk dressing gown he's my idea of a real Texan – if that's not Texan the imagination, geddit??
Hi there, cowboy!?!
Here's a gal that's just dyin' for some of that old time southern comfort!!?!
Mmmmmmmm!?!!!

★ Who shot J.R.???
Who cares?!?! Not me, mister!?!!

THE SAS STORMED the Iranian Embassy in London, bringing to an end a six-day standoff and releasing 19 hostages – but, controversially, killing all but one of the hostage-takers.

10 Downing Street
Whitehall

Dear Bill,
I don't think I've had the chance to put pen to paper since the dust-up at Prince's Gate. Best thing since the Coronation. By the by, did you feel a mite let-down by the Home Sec after the curtain finally descended? As I said to M., why couldn't old Whitelaw come straight out with the joyful tidings about the wog cull, i.e. that the little fellows had been lined up in the corner and rat-a-tat-tat, and that the only reason the last one got out in one piece was that they thought he was one of ours? Instead of which we get this pussy-footing stuff about sub judice and the Ministry of Defence. If I'd had any say in it they'd have lugged all two and a half brace of them out, and had our masked friends from the SAS round for a photo-call with their boots planted on the day's bag, what, Bill? I'm beginning to think Whitelaw deep down may be a bit of a wet. A decent enough old stick and a demon with the mashie, no doubt, but inclined to fluff his putts.

WITH UNEMPLOYMENT at a record **1.6 million,** Mrs Thatcher and her industry secretary, Keith Joseph, announced the creation of seven "Enterprise Zones" with special economic measures to encourage job creation.

MICHAEL FOOT WAS ELECTED as Labour leader – just as a successor to Tom Baker in the Tardis was announced.

Foot is new Dr Who

The 67-year-old Michael Foot is to be the new Dr Who, it was revealed today. The part of the eccentric doctor who spends his life in another world was left vacant when James Callaghan decided last month that he had "had enough".

Said Foot, 67, "I am over the moon. It is a part I have always coveted and it is a great honour to be chosen."

In his first series, Foot, 81, will do battle with the ruler of the dreaded Tory Party, the extraordinary so-called Leaderene, a statuesque blonde with staring blue eyes and a high-pitched mechanical voice.

Meanwhile a question-mark hangs over the dog-like robot K-Benn, which has proved an especially unpopular feature of recent stories. "We shall just have to see," said Mr Foot, putting on his long scarf and disappearing into the Tardis.

AUBERON WAUGH was unimpressed.

Foot is a perfectly decent fellow if you can get him alone. It's only when he's showing off to the lower classes that he becomes insupportable. But what terrifies me is the sort of adulation he receives from soppy people of every age group, as if he came from the Osmond singing family instead of from the family of a jumped-up Cornish solicitor and Lord Mayor of Plymouth.

I see the makings of a Footsville Massacre, with groupies clambering over each other to drink cyanide as the world comes crashing down over his silly, quivering Cornish ears.

IT WAS REVEALED that Prince Charles had a new girlfriend – one Diana Spencer.

Nigel Dempster's Daily Mail Diary

The new girl in Prince Charles's life

Make no mistake about it. This time it's for real. What is she like – the new girl in the life of the heir to the throne? She is 19-year-old lissome, nubile Lucinda Nubile-Lissome, daughter of Lord Dartmoor. Although Lucinda and Charles have not yet met, close friends are convinced that she is the girl whom Charles will marry. Yesterday Lucinda took her first tentative steps along the tricky road that could lead to the throne of England. She posed for photographers outside the Chelsea boutique where she has worked since yesterday morning. Asked about her whirlwind romance with the man she has yet to meet, she replied diplomatically: "I don't know what you're talking about." Perhaps the strongest point in favour of Lucinda becoming the next Queen of England is that she is the only 19-year-old virgin left in the country [*shurely shome mishtake here? W. Deedsh*]. Prince Charles is 31.

JOHN LENNON was assassinated in New York.

The Genius that was Spiggy

What can one say about a man who towered amongst giants, who seemed to epitomise all the cultural aspirations of the post-war generation of the world's youth more than anyone else?

Vietnam, Watergate, Biafra – Spiggy's music spoke for a whole age, encapsulating the whole ethos of protest which sprung up in the post-war era as a deeply felt reaction to the age of the nuclear threat.

Of the four Turds, Spiggy was the mystic, the philosopher. When he wrote such lyrics as:
Big fat man in a submarine
Don't you think you're in a dream
he was expressing the sense of meaning which many were searching for in the use of hallucinogenic drugs. He was also the group's political spokesman, articulating a deeply felt commitment to peace and love as an alternative to war and hatred, as we can see in such songs as Petrol Bomb Man:

Millions of people milling around
Trying to find what can't be found
Love is what it's all about
Hate isn't.

Not since Beethoven and Schubert
(cont. p94)

IN MAY, THE EYE NOTED a few facts about Irish Taoiseach Charles Haughey which the press in his own country seemed anxious to ignore.

If Charlie has achieved little else since he came to office, he has succeeded in gagging the press. One of his regular indiscretions takes place almost literally under the noses of Dublin hacks, and not a cheep of it has appeared in the prints. This is his drawn-out, blowing hot-and-cold affair with *Irish Independent* scribbler Terry Keane whose husband Ronan, a judge, is said in Dublin to hand out Draconian sentences at those times when his wife's frolics reach their peak.

Haughey's affair – memorably described in another *Eye* piece as "horizontal jogging" – was not revealed in Ireland until Keane herself went public in 1999.

THE EYE EXCLUSIVELY revealed disturbing details of a top diplomat's arrest in October.

Sir Peter Hayman, KCMG, CVO, MBE ended a distinguished career as a British High Commissioner in Canada from 1970-74. Previously he held a series of highly delicate posts, including Assistant Principal to the Ministry of Home Security, Personal Assistant to the Chief Staff Officer to the Minister of Defence, member of the UK delegation to Nato, Director-General of British Information Services New York and perhaps, most crucially, Minister and Deputy Commandant in the British Military Government of West Berlin, 1964-66.

Such a combination of defence and foreign office postings almost invariably indicates an intelligence background. Sir Peter would certainly have had access to top secret papers. A risk to security lay in the fact that Hayman was a sexual deviant who kept explicit and detailed diaries cataloguing years of his sexual activities which involved every conceivable perversion. The diaries, along with articles of female clothing and pornographic photos, were found in a sparsely furnished flat in Notting Hill by Porn Squad officers who raided the flat in the summer of 1978.

The police raid followed the discovery of a bulky package of obscene material addressed to a "Mr Henderson" on a bus. Police also discovered that Henderson, who was in fact Hayman, was a member of the Paedophile Information Exchange and frequently entertained prostitutes at the flat. Hayman appears to have used PIE in order to locate other deviants for correspondence purposes.

Hayman's role emerged after two men were conditionally discharged for three years after pleading guilty to sending obscene material through the post. The decision not to prosecute Hayman, who was certainly as guilty as the other two, came from high up, much to the disgust of DPP Tony Hetherington's aides and also the policemen involved in the case. They were told that this was "no reflection on the evidence."

The diaries – some 46 quarto size books of 80 pages each – clearly refer to Hayman's period of office in Canada. But MI5 and MI6 are deeply worried about how much further back Hayman's activities extended – and how public did he make them?

In fact, former cabinet secretary Lord Armstrong testified to the Independent Inquiry into Child Sexual Abuse in 2020 that "neither the Foreign and Commonwealth Office, the Cabinet Office nor the security service knew anything about the matters in the article until it was published" in *Private Eye*. Papers show that Mrs Thatcher strongly advocated keeping the matter secret, but it was to no avail: five months later Hayman was publicly named under parliamentary privilege by Conservative MP Geoffrey Dickens. The correspondence he had exchanged included vivid fantasies about "the systemic killing and torture of young people and children".

NOVEMBER BROUGHT the latest news on someone the *Eye* had been following since student days.

Historian David Irving is about to re-issue his famous book, *Destruction of Convoy PQ17*. The news comes at a time when the infamous historian – whose books are treated respectfully by many distinguished reviewers – has at last emerged in his true colours as a fascist.

Irving has written a whole series of books, all to do with topics related to World War II, and all adopting a "revisionist" approach to history. His normal technique is to insert at least one sensational lie into a normally well-researched and factual book. The effect is to obtain for its author a great deal more publicity than he would usually get by provoking a spurious controversy. The most obvious example is his contention that Adolf Hitler knew nothing about the Final Solution.

It was not until 2000, when Irving sued Deborah Lipstadt for calling him a holocaust denier and lost spectacularly, that the full extent to which he had distorted historical evidence and relied on forgeries to push his claims of Hitler's innocence in the genocide was established.

1981

PETER SUTCLIFFE was arrested and charged with the series of 13 murders attributed to the "Yorkshire Ripper" over the previous five years. It emerged that he had been interviewed by police on nine different occasions, but they had failed to make vital connections.

Parky meets T'Ripper

PARKY: Good evening. My guest tonight is a villain, a monster, a man so evil that words fail me. Ladies and gentlemen – the Yorkshire Ripper!

(A hail of catcalls, boos, whistles and screams as the Ripper enters, together with a very little clapping)

PARKY: You are responsible for the most horrific and cold-blooded series of murders this century, are you not?

RIPPER: 'appen.

PARKY: I expect there must have been some really funny moments during your hideous life of crime.

RIPPER: Oh aye, Michael, I've had some laughs. I remember one time in Leeds or Bradford – these places all look much the same at night – when I was out skulking around and this policeman came up to me. Well, I thought I'd really bought it! But all he said to me was, 'Haven't got the time, have you?' I often laugh about that one!

PARKY: And you're not afraid of being arrested here tonight?

RIPPER: Not at all.

ANNOUNCER: *That programme, which was a filmed recording, was a repeat. Would anyone who saw this programme and can identify anyone on it please contact Yorkshire police immediately?*

THE ENGAGEMENT of Prince Charles and Lady Diana Spencer was announced – and Sylvie Krin was there to chronicle the heir to the throne's last-minute doubts.

Born to be Queen

VENETIA BARKWORTH-SMYTHE stood alone in the morning room of Piggott's Lodge, the lavish Berkshire home she shared with her racehorse-trainer husband Derek. Her soft limpid eyes strayed to the French windows. The Orumulu clock behind her struck 11. The Prince was cutting it a bit fine, she thought. Derek's plane was due into Heathrow in an hour's time. He would be in Hungerford by 2.

Then the door behind her opened and His Royal Highness Prince Charles, looking spruce and well-groomed in his check sports jacket, strode purposefully into the bright sunny room.

"Morning, Venetia," he beamed. "Beautiful day, isn't it? I've just… I mean, I've often wished I could paint."

Venetia smiled reassuringly. "You do so many other things so well, Charles."

There was an awkward silence. She knew with her woman's intuition that he had something on his mind.

"Ahem!" coughed the Prince. "There's something I think I ought to tell you…"

She leaned forward. "Let me make it easy for you, Your Royal Highness," she soothed. "You're trying to tell me that you are planning to marry – and that it will mean an end to our happy times here together."

The Prince fidgeted nervously and began to fiddle with the knot on his tie.

"Let me say if I may, Your Majesty," she intervened, "that I entirely understand. And I will always treasure the memory of our wonderful times together."

She rose, and planted a chaste kiss on his forehead.

✳   ✳   ✳

This would be the last time he would make the journey from Hungerford, reflected Charles as he thundered down the fast lane of the M4.

Was there a tinge of sadness? Perhaps. After all, Venetia had been good to him. A woman of the world, she had taught him the ways to please a woman. For this alone, he would owe her an eternal debt of gratitude.

But as from today he would knuckle down

to his Royal duties. Diana would be at his side, her innocent young eyes gazing at him in rapt adoration.

This was to be it from now on. That was what his parents wished. Even now elaborate plans were being drawn up for what newsmen were calling the Wedding of the Century.

A married man. Duties to the throne. Pomp and circumstance.

A Beefeater hurried forward to take his bags as he pulled into the courtyard at Windsor. Was it his imagination, or had dark clouds begun to gather over the castle's battlements?

The Prince strode swiftly towards the library where he knew he could be alone. "Bring me a drink, Wheatcroft," he cried to an aged retainer. "A large brandy. And be quick about it!"

He had promised to phone Diana. He crossed the library floor to the ornate enamelled telephone, a present from King Otto of Bavaria to Queen Victoria.

Where would she be? He could try the flat, but that might mean talking to one of those half-witted giggling girls she shared with.

The address book fell open under B. As if in a trance he found himself dialling the familiar Hungerford number.

"Hello? Hello? Derek Barkworth-Smythe speaking – who is this?"

Hastily the Prince placed a royal finger on the receiver rest and cut off the call. A sharp *brrrr!* sounded through the library, as if echoing the chill that had suddenly gripped his heart.

To be continued…

FOLLOWING ASSASSINATION attempts on President Reagan and Pope John Paul II, several blank shots were fired at the Queen during Trooping The Colour.

"Why aren't you out shooting famous people?"

RIOTS BROKE OUT in Brixton, with the Met strongly denying claims that they were the result of police harassment of young black people.

Why, Oh Why? Day 17 of 'The shame that was Brixton'

At an impromptu press conference in South London, a tin-helmeted Inspector "Knacker of the Yard" Knacker yesterday refuted charges of 'over-reaction' in response to the recent non-race riots in Brixton.

"We have a duty to all members of the community, black or white, but mainly white," said the Inspector. "It must be remembered that this area has the highest crime rate in the world. That is why Operation Wogsmasher was brought into operation last week before the first sign of trouble.

"Since we arrested 90% of the black population, the crime rate has shown a dramatic decrease, which shows to my mind that these methods are 100% effective. In fact there is hard evidence, unconfirmed as yet, that the trouble last week was the work of outside elements of an entry-ist nature. Molotov Cocktails are not something you can run up overnight out of a few old milk bottles full of petrol with a rag stuffed in the top. They are a highly sophisticated piece of modern weaponry which may have been manufactured in the Eastern bloc, and exported to this country via Libya."

KEN LIVINGSTONE BECAME leader of the Greater London Council.

Man in the News

KEN LENINSPART

What is he like – the man they are calling the new "Mr London"? Ken Leninspart, the newly elected leader of the GLC, is 23 and lives in Neasden, in a one-room bedsitter over a launderama. Outside 4876 Tesco Road, a rusting bicycle is chained to a dustbin. Leninspart does not own a car, and does not see why anyone else should. His bedsitter is furnished with the austerity of an H-block cell. The only furnishings are a signed photograph of Tony Benn and a small tank of newts. Since his wife left him five years ago, Leninspart has lived alone, except for his newts, in what with a rare flash of humour he calls "a single person family situation". He is currently a member of seven London councils in addition to the GLC and lives off the £52,000 a year he receives in expenses and allowances.

What is London going to be like now that Leninspart and his allies have attained supreme power? "Er, basically," he says, "we are going to totally abolish bus fares etc. This will mean totally free transport for working people, i.e. blacks etc. Next we are going to ensure they get the services they deserve, i.e. more play-group facilities, proper amenities for one-parent families, gay rights advisory centres etc."

Ken Leninspart is 19.

MORE RIOTS BROKE out in Toxteth in Liverpool, and then in several other cities across England, to the distress of home secretary Willie Whitelaw.

MRS THATCHER RESHUFFLED her cabinet, with a decisive swing to the Right.

10 Downing Street
Whitehall

Dear Bill,

As you will have seen from the press, I made quite a little killing at the betting shop on the Massacre of the Wets. Old Cemetery Face Gilmour was given short shrift, likewise Fatty S. and poor old Carlisle, and the Boss is cock-a-hoop about her victory over Old Farmer Prior, who is even now buckling on his bullet-proof underwear en route for Belfast.

M. has now wheeled out some snotty little ex-airline pilot called Tebbit to wield the big stick. He started off well enough, telling all and sundry to bloody well pull their socks up, get on their bikes and work harder. Needless to say, some wag pointed out that if they hadn't got any work in the first place, how the hell could they do it any harder? Personally I thought that was a bit cheap, and anyway, when a new chap comes in, albeit up through the ranks, you should give him a moment or two to collect himself before pulling his trousers down.

THE HAPPY DAY arrived – but the bride's famous step-grandmother was not invited.

Lines Written on the Nuptials of HRH the Prince of Wales and Lady Lavinia Tharg *(please check old bean, I may have got the name wrong – J.B.)*

By Sir John Betjeperson

From Uxbridge and from Potters Bar
From Morden and from Kew
See them come from near and far
To get a royal view.

Nothing beats the crowded pavement
Here on leafy Ludgate Hill
Now we know what 'royal wave' meant
Golly, what a real thrill!

Ring out the bells in jubilation,
Now they're well and truly hitched.
Not since Brenda's coronation
Have we all been so bewitched.

But as we all carouse and wassail
To celebrate this glorious day,
In tower block and ducal castle,
Drinking half the night away,

Spare a thought for one old lady
Sitting all alone and glum.
Couldn't get a cheap away-day
So she said she couldn't come.

Barbara Cartland, don't you love her,
With her feather-boa'd hat.
Lady Dartmouth's dear old mother,
All of eighty – fancy that!
(It's not awfully good, is it? Put it in if you like. Cheerio! J.B.)

TONY BENN'S bid to unseat Denis Healey as Labour's deputy leader failed, and did little for party unity at their conference in Brighton.

ITV BROADCAST A LAVISH adaptation of *Brideshead Revisited.*

Bargshead revamped

(Appalling baroque-style music of the type usually heard in commercials for hair lacquer. Large agreeable country house hoves into view)

NARRATOR: That autumn I came back to Bargshead for the last time. Sebastian had sent me one of his telegrams. "DARLING CHARLES, COME AT ONCE, SOMETHING TOO GHASTLY HAS HAPPENED. MUMMY'S JOINED THE MOONIES." I left Bayswater at once.

(Shot of a vintage steam train puffing through countryside)

VOICE OF JIMMY SAVILE: Businessmen and businessladies, you don't need me to tell you what a strain it is travelling to Manchester in a vintage car. Why not take my advice – travel by L.M.S.

(Vintage car drives up three-mile drive to large house [see above])

NARRATOR: Bargshead had never looked more beguilingly ravishing than on that fateful October evening. I had a strong sense of foreboding as I walked into the library.

(Finds corpse lying in front of library fire. Sebastian sprawled senseless on sofa, surrounded by empty brandy bottles.)

COMMERCIAL BREAK

(More Vivaldi-type music over shot of gondola drifting down Grand Canal, Venice. Sebastian and Charles lie entwined in each other's arms)

VOICEOVER OF SIR JOHN GIELGUD *(singing in quavering falsetto)*: Just one Cornetto, give him to me, Delicious soldier of Italy…

VOICEOVER OF LORD OLIVIER: Take an autumn break in Venice like Lord Sebastian and his good-looking young friend – not forgetting Aloysius the Teddy Bear. Just £395 all-in from Thomson's Holidays.

PART TWO

(Pamela St John Stephenson walks naked down very long marble staircase)

ALEC CLIFTON-TAYLOR *(for it is he)*: Just look at this wonderful staircase, truly one of the glories of late 18th-century domestic architecture in this part of England.

(Handel-type music swells to climax. Lord Sebastian enters with Charles)

CHARLES: Who is that dreary little member of the middle classes going on about the stairs?

SEBASTIAN: Oh, I don't know. Someone of Mummy's. She's always allowing these television people to infest the house nowadays.

(Outside another vintage car screeches to halt. Sir Alec

Guinness gets out, in muffler, and is shown into Blue Drawing Room)

LADY MARCHMAIN: Ah, Mr Smiley – so good of you to come down from London to try to rescue our little serial. *(Guinness gives enigmatic smile)*

LADY MARCHMAIN: It's just that there's a frightfully dreary little man called Samgrass whom we were rather hoping might turn out to have been a KGB recruiter. It would give a tremendous twist to our story if he was trying to get poor Sebastian to work for the Russians. He's got everything going for him – he's gay, he's got a drink problem, and he's got this friend at Oxford called Anthony Blanche who seems fearfully fishy.

(Yet another vintage car crunches to a halt on drive. Out jumps Ian Carmichael in exquisitely cut Lord Clark-style suit. He is shown into Red Drawing Room where a gentleman from Combe Florey is counting cheques. Continued after commercial break number 94)

SHIRLEY WILLIAMS overturned a 19,000-strong Conservative majority in Crosby, in the first victory for the newly-formed SDP.

Great Bores of Today

"… I don't know but I'll probably vote for the SDP next time I mean the other two parties have completely failed and I really think that these people do offer something different I have enormous respect and admiration for Shirley Williams who I think has shown tremendous courage and they're very good you know on housing and welfare and so forth it really is very exciting what they're doing making a real change in the whole political thing breaking up you know this old way they have of doing things and offering a genuine alternative you know that hasn't been tried before because everything the other parties have tried has just failed that's why I think we should all vote SDP…"

LABOUR LEADER MICHAEL FOOT was criticised for his scruffy appearance at the Service of Remembrance at the Cenotaph.

Picture the scene, Bill. Sun streaming down Whitehall, a few last brown leaves scratching along the pavement, the note of the bugle dies away, the great bell tolls and a solemn silence falls over the heart of the Empire. Then, blow me – Worzel, who has already attracted a good many black looks from the Royal Box for turning up in a silly tie and some kind of German donkey jacket out of a Millet's sale, begins to fidget, pick his nose and scratch his arse as if waiting for the Number 11 bus. When it comes to the wreath-laying he shambles up in his brothel-creepers and plonks it down like a poor old codger putting the empties out and totters back to resume his monkeyhouse act at the Proprietor's shoulder.

I expected Margaret, when we got indoors, would be fit to be tied, but not a bit of it. Old girl cock-a-hoop, large stickies all round. Points out the whole thing has been on the telly, Worzel must have been losing votes like air out of a burst tyre. I couldn't help feeling a bit sorry for Foot all the same. Reminded me of that time Ginger Withers turned up at the Burmah Christmas Lunch wearing a dinner jacket when it said Informal on the card and we all threw bread rolls at him just to drive the point home. Personally, I blame the wife.

UP-AND-COMING PUPPETEERS Fluck and Law commemorated Foot's appearance on the *Eye*'s Christmas edition – and also provided their take on Rupert Murdoch (*see opposite page*).

TOP-SECRET INFORMATION came out in January about Rupert Murdoch's bid to buy the *Times* and *Sunday Times*, which sellers Thomson Newspapers claimed were both running at huge losses.

Trade Minister John Biffen knows the facts about the *Sunday Times*. So does Rupert Murdoch. The facts – that it is a money machine of highly lucrative proportions – are contained in the confidential documents drawn up by Thomson and its advisors, bankers S.G. Warburg, last November. The quasi-prospectus was supplied under conditions of great secrecy to potential bidders only. *Private Eye* has obtained access to the documents, which show what everyone outside the cosy trio of Thomson, Murdoch and the Government suspects – that the *Sunday Times* is not only viable but stands to become a major profit-earner for the debt-laden Murdoch empire.

More importantly, they demonstrate that the *Sunday Times* can be shown to have been a money-maker in 1980 – therefore making a reference to the Monopolies Commission almost mandatory under the Fair Trading Act.

The Information Memorandum shows revenue for the two newspapers, supplements and other interests is forecast as rising from £89,240,000 last year to £100,630,000 this year and £158,480,000 by 1983. The effect of this rise, combined with the introduction of new technology and certain redundancies, would be expected to reduce the expected £12 million trading loss for 1980 by two-thirds in the current year and replace that by a turnaround to an £8 million profit in 1982 and £14.3 million in 1983.

These figures are taken after deduction for the group fixed costs – the factor Mr Biffen relied on so heavily when telling critics of the deal why the *Sunday Times* was not viable even if it did make money. However, the Thomson/Warburg figures estimate that these costs – interest, rates, overheads – would be more than absorbed by profits from 1982 onwards.

Another curious aspect of the way Thomson drew up its figures is that the group fixed costs are allocated almost equally between the two papers. Yet the *Times* has been the persistent money-loser. It also employs more people and costs more in rent. Thomson also increased the burden on the *Sunday Times* by putting up the rent on its Gray's Inn Road offices from £375,000 to £796,000.

Removing a large part of these fixed costs – which would be the result of a Thomson sale to Murdoch –

would greatly increase the profitability of the *Sunday Times* and even the *Times*. Murdoch knows this. And he also knows that these forecasts allowed for none of the draconian economies he is now proposing. He is looking for redundancies of 25-35% overall, 10% from the journalists, a two-year wage freeze and the supplements' printing to be moved out of London.

These are the figures John Biffen ignores on the lame excuse that he is not able to look at future prospects, only the current experience when saying the *Sunday Times* is "not economic as a going concern" under the terms of the Fair Trading Act.

In the event, Mrs Thatcher's government waved through the sale without referring it to the Monopolies Commission, receiving slavish support from all Murdoch's papers for years afterwards in return. Murdoch implemented massive redundancies, and switched production of his papers to a new, more technologically-advanced plant in Wapping, dispensing with the print unions as he went.

IN AUGUST, THE EYE revealed some worrying – and one, in retrospect, less worrying – facts about Conservative MP Harvey Proctor.

The deeply unpleasant MP for Basildon, Harvey Proctor, is so far right he is halfway across the North Sea. A former Assistant Director of the Monday Club,

Proctor was once thrown off the Tory list of approved party candidates because of his anti-black, anti-Grocer views. He recently attacked the Home Secretary in a speech at Caxton Hall on 18 July. His call for Whitelaw's resignation came in a vitriolic racialist attack on the black communities in this country, perverting the truth and laying the nation's ills on these immigrants. His 'final solution' was a recipe of deportation, compulsory repatriation and the repeal of all race relations legislation.

Proctor made his speech before a selection of the most looney and dangerous rightwingers ever to gather under one roof since the late Sir Oswald Mosley and his fascist scum were at their peak.

Joe Pearce, the editor of the National Front magazine *Bulldog* and himself up on several charges connected with racist literature, was in attendance. So was wizened old crone the Dowager Lady Birdwood, remembered for her links with the National Front and the more insidious Column 88, a fascist paramilitary group, some of whose members are currently in prison for the illegal possession of arms and explosives. Even the breakaway N.F. was represented in the person of Paul Kavanagh of the Constitutional Movement. Don Martin represented the British League of Rights. But the most interesting spectators were Steve Brady and Jimmy Styles, recently shown by *World in Action* to be operating as gunrunners in the UK, and part of a group giving shelter to right-wing international terrorists. Finally there was Tony Malski, the half-wit who planned to place bombs amongst the black community in Notting Hill at the coming Carnival.

The vote of thanks was given by Andrew Fountaine, the only man in Tory party history whose adoption as a parliamentary candidate was overruled by Central Office because of his antisemitic and Nazi leanings.

Like many fascists, Proctor is a raging homosexualist. His former longstanding boyfriend Terry Woods has recently been ringing several newspapers about the treatment Proctor has dealt to him. He says he has been kept by Proctor for over seven years, since the age of 19 when he was a minor.

Proctor was convicted of gross indecency with men under the age of consent – then 21 – in 1987, after resigning as an MP following a tabloid exposé. He and Terry Woods are still partners 40 years later.

1982

MARK THATCHER, son of the prime minister, disappeared for several days in the Sahara desert during a car rally.

10 Downing Street
Whitehall

Dear Bill,

Thank you for your condolences on the safe return of the son and h. Honestly, what a prize twerp! I washed my hands of the little blighter years ago, and when the Boss told me he was intending to drive across Africa with some fancy French bint he'd picked up in the pits, my response was that he could go to hell in a handcart for all I cared. Next thing I know, M. is hammering on my door at some unearthly hour to say she has just heard that the little bugger has been missing for four days and what was I going to do about it? Answer, turn over and go back to sleep. Cue for maternal hysteria, call myself a man etc. Waterworks turned on, hanky out, wailing and gnashing of teeth, all culminating in yours truly agreeing to jump on the first Laker to Timbuctoo in search of Prodigal Son.

Touch down desert airstrip, a real dump if ever I saw one. Reptiles have beat us to it andare drinking the place dry. Would you believe it, ten quid for a single? Obviously, mine host Ali Baba had seen us coming.

Thanks to Boss hoisting storm cones, the entire Algerian airforce in the shape of three helicopters and an old Hercules was grinding through the sky overhead. One of the pilot johnnies said would I like to go aloft in his kite for a shufty, and before I knew it we were bucketing about in inky blackness and it crossed my mind that given a fair wind the Boss might soon have to send out another search party to bring in yours truly. When we eventually returned empty-handed to the bar, bugger me if young Mark isn't sitting there with a carefully nurtured growth of beard drawling away to the reptiles and clearly seeing himself as hero of the hour. First opportunity I got I gave him a pretty largish piece of my mind. Absolutely no response. Sulky look, not his fault if parental brigade overreacts, he and Mamselle Fifi perfectly happy sitting in the desert waiting for the local AA man to turn up.

I ask you, Bill!

FREDDIE LAKER'S eponymous low-cost airline collapsed, despite members of the public offering their pensions and pocket money to try to keep it afloat.

Gnome

I have been deeply touched by the many messages and offers of help from members of the public following the tragic closure of Gnomair Ltd.

In the last 24 hours literally thousands of letters, telegrams and donations have flooded into my offices at Gatwick airport, many of them from ordinary travelling members of the public. An Old Age Pensioner from Hartley Witney wrote, "£1 is all I can spare but please accept it as a token of my heartfelt admiration for the greatest buccaneering Englishman since Sir Francis Drake." Cheques should be sent to me at the address below. God bless you all!

Lord Gnome
Account 51746(D)
Banque de Vadus
1009 Rue des Entrepreneurs
Zurich, Switzerland

ARGENTINA unexpectedly invaded the Falklands – and Britain, with most of its armed forces on the opposite side of the globe, was not in a position to do much about it.

FEELINGS ran high.

Glenda Slagg – *Fleet Street's Hot Potato*

Hats off to the Falkland Islanders!!! (Don't tell me you
haven't heard of them, mister??!)

When it comes to guts, those guys and gals have got it!!!

We're right behind you, Maggie, me dear!?!

Geddit???

* * *

Falkland Shmaulkland, who cares!?!?!

Ok, so the Argies have taken them over in the middle of the
night!?!! So what???

Don't cry for me, Argentina?? You must be joking!?!

A TASK FORCE was swiftly dispatched.

Aircraft Carrier HMS Invincible *(shortly to be renamed the
Dame Edna)* Built 1956-1981, sold to Australia 1982

HMS Hermesetas *(dissolves instantly in hot water – geddit?)*

SS Canberra *(passenger liner converted to ITN studio and
other uses)*

SS The Sir Peter Parker *(converted Sealink ferry)*

The Woolwich Experience *(converted Thames ferry)*

Cutty Sark *(by permission of the GLC and the National
Maritime Museum)*

Assorted Requisitioned Pedaloes, Punts, Kayaks,
Used Grapefruit Skins *(by kind permission of
Marnham's Aquapark, Morecambe; Betjeman's Boat
Hire, Walton-on-the-Naze; the Wessex Water Authority)*

Submarines: HMS Dungeness B *(nuclear-powered, slightly
leaking)*

HMS Despicable *(shome mishtake shurely? Ed)*

HMS Ludicrous *(shee above)*

The Loch Ness Monster

US SECRETARY OF STATE
Alexander Haig travelled to
London to attempt to broker a
diplomatic solution.

BRITISH MARINES SWIFTLY recaptured the island
of South Georgia, and Mrs Thatcher ordered the nation
to "rejoice!".

Special Gnome Offer

Now you can have a lasting
memento of perhaps the
greatest naval victory of
all time – the historic
Battle of Grytviken
(1982) in which 17 naval
warships single-handedly
defeated the massed
penguins and scrap dealers
of South Georgia, with this
series of hand-painted
commemorative dinner plates.

Plate Number Three

1. *Members of the Special Boat Squadron go ashore at
Weidenfeld Bay to reconnoitre the territory*

2. *The very rare Antarctic Parrot (Paraquat Antarctica
Antarctica), found only in the sheltered marches of
South Georgia*

3. *The guns of HMS Despicable open fire on the
Antarctic Parrot*

4. *Argentinian scrap merchants hand over their arms to
Rear Admiral Sir Sandy Nutcase RN.*

5. *Mrs Thatcher announces the great British victory to
cheering crowds of ITN cameramen*

6. *As old-age pensioners join hands with teenagers and
dance in the streets, a statue of Sir Sandy Nutcase is
unveiled in Trafalgar Square*

These highly desirable plates are only available in a limited
edition of 500,000. Buy now!

RETAKING THE FALKLANDS themselves proved rather more difficult. The *Sun* was in full-throated support, reporting the sinking of the Argentine cruiser *General Belgrano* beneath the headline "Gotcha"...

What the SUN says:

MICHAEL FOOT – Is hanging too good for him? p.12
THE TV TRAITORS – p.4
KILL AN ARGIE – And win a Metro! Details p.11
PLUS: IS THE POPE GAY? 10 tell-tale signs
SEX SECRETS OF THE BARBICAN
FLEXIBLE ROSTERING – ASLEF wives to ration love

There's more and more fun – in the SUN

...BUT THE GOVERNMENT felt the BBC's coverage left much to be desired.

Portlands under siege

Mrs Thatcher yesterday ordered a massive air-and-ground attack on the BBC. As thousands of marines stormed through the corridors of Portland Place blasting at anything that moved, an armada of vertical take-off Conservative MPs bombarded outlying BBC outposts all over West London.

Urging his forces to "resist the enemy to the last drop of their blood", the BBC leader Director-General Galasdieri Milnas ran up the white flag and surrendered to the men of the Special On-The-Air Service, the SOS.

THE ARGENTINES surrendered on 14 June.

The final victory

A pooled despatch from SIR MAXWELL HASTINGS V.C.

Today I watched with my own eyes as British forces reoccupied the last remaining South Atlantic territory still in Argentine hands. It was dawn as detachments from the 14th Paras, 12th Gurkhas, 4th Special Patrol Group and 2nd ITN Camera Battalion massed for a dawn swoop on the tiny but impregnable 12' by 12' island fortress of South Marmite Island.

An as yet unnamed number of casualties were sustained as the troops scrambled desperately for room to stand upright on this piece of rock little bigger than a billiard table.

And yet later that evening, when room had at last been found on the few square inches of rock to raise a flagpole proudly carrying the Union Jack and a signed photograph of the Princess of Wales, there was a feeling that it had somehow all been worth it.

As battle-hardened Staff Sergeant Garry Cabwallander put it to me, with tears in his eyes: "Excuse me, you're treading on my foot." Rear Admiral Sandy Nutcase is 62.

OVER 900 PEOPLE had been killed.

PRINCESS DIANA GAVE BIRTH to a son, **William, despite ignoring Auberon Waugh's advice to banish Prince Charles from her bedside**.

The reason that husbands have always been kept away on these occasions lies deep in our surviving links with the animal creation. The humblest female mammal always seeks privacy to give birth, and male rats are so outraged if they find themselves present that they eat their young.

No doubt the Prince of Wales would be able to restrain himself from eating the next Heir to the Throne. So abject have English males become, he will probably just blush to the roots of his hair. But I believe that Captain Phillips, who was bossed into watching his wife produce Baby Susan – ate a polyester teddy bear and two plastic ducks, no doubt in some confusion about what he was expected to do.

Mr Harold Brooks-Baker, managing director of Debrett's, claims that so few babies are now being born as a result of these uncouth practices that the Western European nations will soon disappear.

A BRAND NEW cheese was launched.

A Doctor Writes

As a doctor, I am often asked, "Doctor, is there any known cure for Lymeswold?"

Well, the short answer is no. Lymeswold is a new and relatively virulent form of cheese which once caught can never be totally eradicated.

What happens is that Lymeswold, or *dolcis lattus supermarketensis*, is picked up all over the place, most commonly in the supermarket. The carrier brings it home where it is often given to the whole family.

If you think you have Lymeswold then you should consult your doctor.

Next week: Fishbones – what risk to they pose to the Queen Mother?

AN INTRUDER BROKE INTO the Queen's bedroom at Buckingham Palace.

CHANNEL 4 WAS LAUNCHED, with a schedule designed to "appeal to tastes and interests not generally catered for by ITV".

4.45 *Jolly Boateng Weather.* New quiz programme on race relations, chaired by Paul Boateng of the GLC.

5.15 *News for the Mentally Handicapped* (pictures only)

5.20 *Case Book.* Social workers talk frankly.

6.30 *News In-Depth.* TV's first ever programme that looks at the news in-depth.

7.30 *Pink Knickers and Purple Tights.* A light-hearted all-women revue on themes suggested by the week's news, starring Libby Grobes, Jan Herpes and Polly-Esther Tweedie.

8.00 *TV Scrabble.* Alan Coren invites scrabble players from all over Britain to compete for the coveted Channel 4 Scrabble Goblet 1982.

8.30 *International Drama on Four '82: Cavern.* A film by Mike Leigh. Kevin and Les, two unemployed, mentally handicapped glue-sniffers from Neasden decide to take up potholing – with unexpected consequences.

9.20 *News for the Blind* (sound only).

TWO HORRIFIC BOMB ATTACKS by the IRA in the same day killed 11 soldiers and seven cavalry horses in Hyde Park and Regent's Park.

THAT IRA OUTRAGE

Words Fail Us!!!

THE SUN SAYS: We cannot find words to express our feelings about the latest IRA bombing, so here is a picture of a naked lady.

SOVIET LEADER Leonid Brezhnev died, and was succeeded by Yuri Andropov, who was only nearly dead.

Brezhnev – The world mourns

by Our Moscow staff **Lunchtime O'Snowonhisbooze** and **Phil Kimby**

Millions of ordinary Muscovites wept openly in the streets today when news broke of the death last month of their beloved leader at the age of 187.

Millions more queued openly in the hope of being able to buy a tin of old salt fish from the world-famous luxury department store Marx and Sparts (open alternate Wednesdays for sale of odd shoes only).

More than anyone else, Brezhnev was the man who dragged the Soviet Union out of the drab, uniform, fear-ridden fifties and into the drab, uniform, fear-ridden eighties.

To millions of Russians, President Brezhnev was a liberalising force. Under his rule it became permitted to watch colour television and to wear Western-style braces, although supplies of both are not yet available in Russia.

TWO BLOCKBUSTERS dominated cinemas.

This strange looking little creaure with his loin cloth and glasses came to earth to change the face of history. He preaches love and non-violence. The authorities persecuted him. His only weapon was a pointing finger.

He was lost. He was afraid. He was thousands of miles from home and millions of pounds overdrawn. He was Sir Richard Attenbore. *(Shome mishtake here surely? Ed.)*

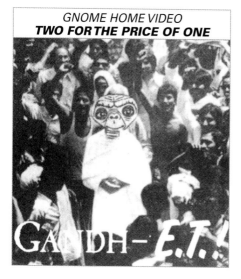

JUNE BROUGHT NEWS of the all-powerful leader of the miners' union.

King Arthur Scargill is moving into a 25th storey £125 a week sumptuous flat in Shakespeare Tower, Barbican EC2 and has warned his petrified staff never to reveal his new address.

Rent and rates for Scargill's new abode come to £5,500 p.a. Amenities include a 24-hour Porter Service.

Administrators of the Barbican site have tactfully put Scargill in a separate block to that accommodating Unemployment Secretary Norman Tebbit, who resides in Lauderdale Tower. From his citadel window Scargill will have a perfect view of the filthy capitalist City, including the Royal Exchange, the Bank of England, Mansion House and other bastions of monetarism.

Thirty years later, Scargill's bitter battle with the NUM over whether they should still be paying all expenses on his Barbican flat went all the way to the High Court, where he lost.

AS RON SMITH SUCCEEDED in getting an inquest into the death of his daughter Helen, further disturbing details emerged of the night she died.

The Dutch captain, Johannes Otten, who met his death with Helen Smith, was insured by his employers with Rocloffs, a reputable Rotterdam firm. When Otten's parents claimed on the policy, Rocloffs undertook an investigation into the circumstances of his death. Interviewed by investigators, the German divers present at the Arnots' party admitted that there had been a fight involving Otten – an admission that clearly contradicted earlier statements which they gave to the BBC and ITN.

Meanwhile further evidence about the real nature of the Arnots' party has come from Mr Alexander O'Brien, a former Lockheed engineer in Jeddah. He told of a visit he received that night from his fellow Lockheed employee, Dr Alan Kirwin, who arrived at his house looking fraught and asking for booze. The party at Richard Arnot's flat, he said, was getting out of hand. Arabs had started to arrive in some numbers, bringing hash and other drugs. He'd left early because he didn't want to get involved. But Kirwin now claims he has never heard of O'Brien – which is odd, because he can give a very good description of the doctor, and Mrs O'Brien too remembers him coming to the house that night.

From Dr Arnot downwards, everyone has always insisted that this was a quiet little get-together in which a few divers came together to wish farewell to their colleague Tim Hayter, who was due to leave Jeddah the next day. In the course of this, it is suggested, Helen and Johannes Otten slipped out on the balcony for a cuddle, and toppled over silently to their deaths.

But O'Brien's story coincides remarkably with the so-called "Iliff Report", an internal Foreign Office investigation revealed in the *Sun* in September 1980. That claimed there had been during the course of the night more than 80 people at the party, and that drugs had been circulated as widely as booze. Gordon Kirby, vice-consul in Jeddah at the time of the deaths and a close friend of Penny Arnot, told a British journalist that he had been "cleared" by the report, and that it had revealed Helen had probably been murdered by a young Saudi with important connections in high places. There are other examples of high-ranking young Saudis being protected by diplomatic niceties and downright cover-ups when they have killed expatriate guests.

The name "Iliff" was given to the British journalist as the man who held the inquiry, but no Iliff has yet been discovered either in the Foreign Office or the police.

O'Brien also remembers being told that the flat of a paediatrician, Dr Sarchal, who hails from Iraq and who spent much of his time on leave was often used as a sort of sex annexe for the Arnot parties. He had been engaged in a short tempestuous affair with Helen which broke up when he revealed he was married. But Helen almost certainly had a key to his flat. If the party did "spread" downstairs, and a fight took place in which Helen and Otten were murdered, a mystery is cleared up: according to the pathologists who have now seen Helen's body her injuries indicated a fall from much less than 70 feet if she fell at all. One has guessed at 12 feet as the maximum distance for the fall. Sarchal's first-floor balcony is exactly 12 feet from the ground.

In December the inquest into Helen Smith's death, held in Leeds, returned an open verdict. Ron Smith refused to allow her body to be cremated until the full circumstances of her death had been established: he relented in 2009 and died two years later, still convinced that his daughter had been murdered.

1983

THE DISASTROUS launch of breakast service TV-am coincided with the Franks report clearing the government of any blame over the Falklands invasion.

Breakfast TV – Maggie not to blame

The present government was in no way to blame for the disaster of breakfast television, Lord Franks concludes in his report published today.

What was described as "a terrible national humiliation" took place as the result of "a series of improbable events which could not have been foreseen by anyone of common sense or even Mrs Thatcher," Lord Whitewash continued.

His report admits that "long before the actual arrival of Breakfast Television on 17 January 1983, there were countless indications that something of the kind might be imminent". The *Radio Times* even carried a special 12-page supplement in full colour the previous week headed "Everything You Want To Know About Breakfast TV", including dates, times, maps and profiles of the stars.

But despite these indications, Lord Frankenstein, 89, finds that the government was "totally justified" in dismissing the possibility of breakfast television as "a remote fantasy".

POLICE HUNTING ESCAPED prisoner David Martin shot and severely injured unrelated film editor Stephen Waldorf instead.

'Some mistake' admits Knacker

Wanted killer   Victim

A repentant Inspector "Knacker of the Yard" Knacker yesterday told reporters that there had been "an error of police procedure" which led to the shooting of an innocent man.

Said Knacker: "We deeply regret any death that this member of the public may suffer as an indirect result of my lads firing point blank into him."

Asked why seven armed men had simultaneously opened fire on a passing bus full of people the Inspector said, "It was a miscalculation on the part of my lads, who were following normal police procedures."

Asked precisely what these procedures were, the Inspector clarified: "The British Bobby, as is traditional, does not carry fire arms and is instructed not to use them unless he is fully convinced no one is looking."

THE BERMONDSEY by-election took place, with the Liberals disclaiming responsibility for eye-wateringly homophobic leaflets about the Labour candidate which helped their own not entirely heterosexual Simon Hughes to victory.

Gnome

Whatever one thinks of the Labour candidate in the Bermondsey by-election, Mr Peter Tatchell, it is surely utterly disgraceful and deplorable that he should be made the victim of a personal smear campaign.

Leaflets headed "Which Queen would you vote for?" and giving credence to the charge that Mr Tatchell is a "Gay Rights" campaigner have been spread around the constituency by an unidentified opponent. I do not know whether or not Mr Tatchell is a "Gay". What I do know is that the question of whether or not he is a sexual pervert is utterly irrelevant to his political views. His disgusting proclivities, if indeed they are such, have nothing to do with the campaign.

I would like to deny categorically that I myself am responsible for printing this disgraceful smearsheet with its totally unsupported allegation that Mr Tatchell is a revolting poof.

E. Strobes, pp Lord Gnome

DERBY-WINNING racehorse Shergar was stolen, and a £2 million ransom demanded for his return.

THE NUCLEAR ARMS RACE accelerated as President Reagan proposed a "Star Wars" missile shield to protect America from Russian attack.

"Oh no! Not on bloody washday!"

MEANWHILE, under Ken Livingstone, the GLC continued to spend public money in ways that weren't to everyone's taste.

Those controversial GLC grants in full

£15,000 to Turgis Green Lesbian Citizens Band Radio Workshop; £25,000 to the Jill Tweedie Hostel for Disabled Gay Single-Parent Mothers, Tufnell Park; £45,000 to the Dollis Hill Women's Support Group for International Abortion Year; £350 to the Daily Telegraph 'Save the Doyly Carte Opera' Campaign *(shome mishtake,* *shurely? W.D.);* Lewisham Under-Fives Sexual Awareness Play Group £25,000; King's Cross Prostitutes Collective Say No to Pershing Action Committee £30,000; The Irish National Animal Liberation Army Bombs For Peace Centre £25,000.

RUPERT MURDOCH SPENT over a million dollars on the *Hitler Diaries* with the intention of serialising them in the *Sunday Times* – only for them to turn out to be forged (he published them anyway).

Exclusive to *Private Eye*

26 August 1938. O mein Gott. Vot am I to do about this unspeakable little man Gerbils? Vot a vulgar man he is to be sure, mit his club-foot und his lies. If he goes on like this, our beloved fatherland may soon be dragged into war.

12 July 1940. O mein Gott – vot in Himmel am I going to do with this schweinhund Goring, mit his crazy ideas about droppink bombs on London? Ze English are a nice bunch of guys, mit zere cricket, ze old school tie und ze Duke of Windsor.

15 June 1944. O mein Gott! Vot a mess zis dumbkopf Himmler is landing us into, viz his mad schemes for invading Russia. If things go on like zis, I tell you, it will all end in tears.

21 July 1944. Donner und Blitzen! Mein little bomb plot to blow up all my colleagues is alles aufgekocht. Instead of Gerbils, Goring and co. all being blown into ze smizzereens, instead it is none ozzer zan your old chum who is getting it in ze neck, not to mention ze arm. Now how am I going to finish zese very important diaries for ze *Sunday Times*?

A GENERAL ELECTION campaign kicked off.

MRS THATCHER WENT INTO IT with an obvious advantage…

'Falklands not an issue' – Maggie's shock claim

Mrs Thatcher today made it plain that she had "absolutely no intention whatever" of making last year's Falklands crisis the central issue in the election campaign. "I want to make it abundantly clear," she told an audience of cheering servicemen and their wives at Aldershot, "that the tremendous victory won by our boys in the South Atlantic exactly a year ago should not be used to make cheap political capital in this election."

As massed bands began to play "Land of Hope and Glory", Mrs Thatcher removed an onion from her handbag and went on: "It would be little short of a tragedy if the splendid achievements of the task force and the government which had the courage and vision to send it on its sacred mission were to be made mere pawns in a political argument."

…AND THE WHOLEHEARTED support of certain sectors of the press.

Daily ✠ Mail

Shock finding by doctors: A.I.D.S. threat to Labour voters

ON OTHER PAGES: ● Maggie saves child's life
● Foot lashes O.A.P. with stick

SHE WAS RE-ELECTED by a landslide with a 144-seat majority, much to her husband's delight.

10 Downing Street
Whitehall

Dear Bill,

Well, that's it! What a ballcrushing disaster! In all my wildest nightmares I never visualised it being quite as bad as this. Another five years of guaranteed hard labour as a tailor's dummy being wheeled on to grin to order every time the Boss plays host. I did think of approaching Top Management with a strike ultimatum, proposing a minimum three months in six off the leash, all expenses paid and a company flat in sunny parts, but the Boss is still in overdrive after Friday morning's results and shows no sign of shifting into a lower gear.

Still, as Boris pointed out over a crate of his widowed mother's plum vodka, at least we now have the chance to crack down on the trouble-makers, pack up the railways and other drains on the motorist's pocket, remove tax from heavy spirits, hand over the NHS to Bupa, introduce imprisonment without trial for all shop stewards, bring back

the black cap and other long overdue middle-of-the-road reforms. I noted down a few of these ideas on a paper doily and stuffed them under the door of little Bertie Mount, Margaret's one-man think tank. And as you will see from the reshuffled cabinet, some of my notions are beginning to trickle through.

AMONGST THE "WETS" purged from her cabinet was foreign secretary Francis Pym.

MRS THATCHER ANNOUNCED her intention to abolish the Greater London Council at the same time it emerged that long-serving character Len Fairclough was being written out of *Coronation Street*.

Red Ken 'to be killed off'

The popular TV personality Kenneth "Red Ken" Livingstone, who plays the part of the zany Chairman in the long-running farce GLC, is to be written out of the series, it was revealed today. The Prime Minister, Mrs Thatcher, has apparently decided that the public have "had enough" of Red Ken and his mad antics.

Scriptwriters at Tory Central Office are now racking their brains for ways to kill off the popular hero in the long-running soap opera. One possibility is that he will be blown up by mistake by his friends in the IRA, or eaten alive by his collection of newts.

However, the most likely scenario is that the government will simply ditch the whole of the GLC.

MRS THATCHER DECLINED to use the NHS for an operation on her retina, which she announced had been more than successful.

PRESIDENT REAGAN LAUNCHED an invasion of Grenada without telling Mrs Thatcher, much to her fury.

An exclusive Private Eye reconstruction of how the crisis unfolded

Friday October 17th
President Reagan rings up and tells Mrs Thatcher that he has got an amazing idea about invading a little island, the name of which escapes him, and that there must be a lot of votes in it. Mrs Thatcher patiently explains that she has already had her election and doesn't need any more invasions today, thank you.

Monday October 20th
Mrs Thatcher reads in *Daily Telegraph* that US marines are storming ashore on Grenadian beaches. She at once telephones Washington.

Mrs Thatcher: Why wasn't I told?
Reagan: Who is this speaking, please?
Mrs Thatcher: Come along, Mr President, don't shilly-shally. I'm flabbergasted.
Reagan: That's funny, you sound just like Mrs Thatcher. *(Hangs up.)*

JANUARY BROUGHT the first of many *Eye* reports on a dangerous drug.

Dista products, the company which had such a conspicuous success in publicising the wonders of the lethal arthritis drug Opren which was banned last August, is equally capable when it comes to the suppression of crucial information on its products.

When Opren was just a twinkle in the eye of the company's researchers, Dista produced a drug named Distalgesic which was also used in the treatment of arthritis. Within a few years, the company achieved a massive sale of some 20 million tablets in Britain alone, which meant incredible profits for Dista and, ultimately, its parent company Eli Lilly in America.

It was in 1979 that the medical world first began to wake up to the fact that this "easy to swallow little shape" was causing a huge number of accidental deaths. Specialist medical journals started taking a critical look at the drug. The Birmingham coroner, Doctor R. Whittington, wrote a piece in the *British Medical Journal* pointing out that as few as 10 tablets (four over the recommended dosage) could cause death, whereas double or even treble the amount of aspirin would not have the same effect.

A number of doctors wrote to the *BMJ* saying that "the drug was the commonest cause of death in those cases referred to forensic medical departments". They urged the company "to restrict the promotion of this dangerous product".

Dista reacted to all this unfavourable publicity in a most curious way. Instead of publicising the danger of the drug and actively alerting doctors to the precise number of tablets which constituted an overdose, they simply set up the Distalgesic Steering Committee, whose sold aim was to limit and suppress damaging publicity. They drafted a number of pompous and uninformative letters to send to editors. And they created the Dista Achievement Award which was open to all sufferers of arthritis. Lasting over several months in 1979/80, the award got a great deal of advantageous publicity in the local press and did what it was meant to do – deflect attention from the Distalgesic deaths.

The drug is still killing people on a regular basis and there is no restriction on its prescription. Its main ingredient, Dextropropoxyphene, is an opium-like compound which causes the nervous system and lungs to relax. Taken with drink, the drug becomes especially difficult to treat and even intravenous antidotes have been known not to work.

Warnings about the drug's effect were strengthened following a review by the Committee on the Safety of Medicines in 1985, but it was not finally banned as a result of "the high fatality rate involving both intentional and accidental overdose" until 2005.

THE BUSINESS CAREER of the prime minister's son came under scrutiny in March.

Mark Thatcher has formed an intriguing association with an Argentinian commodity broker engaged in fixing arms deals in Central and South America. Towards the end of July last year, just weeks after the end of the Falklands conflict, two arms dealers in Dallas received a Telex from the broker, Leonidis Horacio Walger, advising them "I am a close friend of Mark Thatcher who, for obvious reasons, is also highly well-connected in other parts of the world." Walger was offering himself to the Texans as a go-between to secure arms deals.

Ex-Special Forces Major Richard Meadows, who has an outstanding military record, met Walger in London last August to discuss a deal. Walger told Meadows that he kept Thatcher around because of his contacts. He didn't consider the PM's son too bright and indicated that he had to push "business" Mark's way to keep him going.

Walger is an Argentinian, resident in Britain, and runs a commodity company called Cominter (U.K.) Limited from the City. On documents filed at Companies House several other Argentinians appear.

Reports about Mark Thatcher's dodgy dealings and shameless trading on his mother's name became so commonplace by the time of the 1987 election that her press secretary Bernard Ingham recommended the best way he could help the campaign was to leave the country. In 2005 he was convicted and given a four-year suspended jail sentence in South Africa for his part in funding an attempted coup in Equatorial Guinea.

IN MAY, THE EYE REVEALED details about the Federation of Conservative Students.

This sticker is an example of the handiwork of certain members of the Federation of Conservative Students: Marc-Henri Glendenning (current FCS vice-chairman), David Hoile (a white Rhodesian

currently at Warwick University) and Brian Monteith (this year's chairman). Monteith is very keen on this form of propaganda, having put out a poster in a student election that claimed one of his political opponents was a paedophile. These psychopathic scurrilities bear no printers mark which makes them illegal. This is a characteristic they have in common with Monteith's most interesting work to date, the "Which Queen do you support?" pamphlets distributed in Bermondsey during February's by-election.

Monteith was not in London at the time but was attending the Yorkshire Area Dinner. However he announced at the dinner that at that very minute the leaflet was being distributed in Bermondsey by Conservative students. He added "I use that term loosely."

The FCS was disbanded by party chairman Norman Tebbit in 1986 after he concluded that it was too extreme.

THERE WAS NEWS of a top jockey in July.

Lester Piggott, one of the world's richest sportsmen, has had a little problem with the tax man. Investigations have been carried out into the question of his substantial overseas earnings.

Following close attention to his affairs by one of the Revenue's Special Offices, a settlement is expected to be agreed which will result in the miserly millionaire having to part with a sum approaching £200,000.

The earnings concerned were apparently channelled through a Cayman Islands company. However, the Revenue took the view that they were still liable for taxation here.

The Revenue's willingness to make a settlement and not to insist on much greater penalties is unusual, for this is the second occasion on which the punter's favourite has come to their attention. The first was in the mid-1970s when there was a little misunderstanding regarding the overlooking of certain overseas earnings. That time the settlement was nearer £100,000.

In 1987 Piggott was jailed for three years for failing to declare income of £3.25 million to the Revenue, instead channelling earnings under false names through bank accounts in the Cayman Islands, Switzerland, the Bahamas and Singapore.

ALSO IN JULY, the *Eye* carried details of the death of Roberto Calvi, a banker whose clients included the Vatican and the Italian mafia, who was found hanging from the underside of Blackfriars Bridge in London.

The open verdict returned in the inquest on Roberto Calvi, former President of the bankrupt Ambrosiano bank, must have come as a shock to the police. "We treated it as suicide from the word go," explained Detective Inspector John White, and went on to make it clear that City of London policemen such as he do not readily change their minds.

Mr White's assessment of the death paid remarkable tribute to the athletic powers of the 62-year-old banker who, according to his son, had not taken any exercise or played any sport for some 20 years.

He also suffered from vertigo, but had still been able, after walking unobserved for four miles down the Thames, a river he hardly knew, to go down twenty feet from the pavement under Blackfriar's Bridge to the water's edge, to jump onto a plank at the bottom of some scaffolding, to mount the scaffolding to a place where he could attach a noose to his neck and then hurl himself towards the water and his death.

This would have been an astonishing achievement at the best of times, but Mr Calvi managed to do it with a hefty brick in both of his pockets and, most amazingly of all, with another brick shoved down his flies.

Moreover, Mr Calvi managed his acrobatics without getting his fingers dirty. His beautifully manicured hands were perfectly clean, and there was no sign of the bricks or the rusty scaffolding poles in his fingernails, or on his clothing.

In 2007, an Italian court finally found that Calvi had been murdered – but failed to convict anyone of the crime.

IN OCTOBER, the Grovel column offered intriguing news of one of Mrs Thatcher's favourite colleagues.

Why was Cecil Parkinson asked to step down as Tory Party Chairman? I can assure readers that it had nothing whatever to do with his marital difficulties which have recently caused raised eyebrows in Tory circles.

Now comes the news that Parkinson's fun-loving secretary Ms Sarah Keays is expecting a baby in three months' time.

Having failed to persuade Keays to abort his baby, Parkinson admitted their long-running affair (although not his frequent promises to divorce his wife and marry

her) and resigned from his new job as trade and industry secretary. The following issue exposed some of his subsequent false claims about his behaviour.

An exclusive article in the *Sunday Times* displayed an intimate knowledge of Cecil Parkinson's affair with Sarah Keays, accused her of deliberately trying to ruin his career and praised his superhuman fortitude during the election, with "that woman" ringing him up twice a day begging him to divorce his wife. Great excitement spread in the office when word spread that Parkinson himself had telephoned the *ST*'s brand new editor, Andrew Neil. *News of the World* editor Derek Jameson was offered the opportunity to share the "exclusive", and believed he was going to get Parkinson's very own words.

When the story appeared, however, there was consternation. For the unsigned article – political correspondent Michael Jones refused to allow his name to appear – was full of quotes from "Parkinson's friends", none mentioned by name. There was a stormy meeting on the back bench and a deputation went upstairs to see Neil, who denied that he had spoken to Parkinson. The next morning he told TV-am he had in fact had a "private conversation" with him, but it had nothing to do with the "exclusive story".

It is clear that there are no such people as "Parkinson's friends". No other newspaper has been able to contact them, despite teams of hacks working on the story.

Parkinson himself claims that he has never talked to the press about the relationship, whereas Sarah Keays "betrayed" her side of the bargain. But he has clearly also forgotten about his 40-minute conversation with Peter Simmonds, political editor of the *Mail on Sunday* who wrote a long and sympathetic article about him last week.

1984

SCIENTISTS WARNED that a "greenhouse effect" was trapping record levels of carbon dioxide in the atmosphere, leading to global warming.

SOVIET LEADER Yuri Andropov dropped off the perch and, as was becoming traditional, was succeeded by the only marginally healthier Konstantin Chernenko.

Speculation grew last night over the health of Soviet leader Konstantly Aboutopopov, 117, following the shock announcement from Tass that he has "a slight cold".

Secretary Aboutopopov has not been seen in public now for over four days, since the funeral of his predecessor Yuri Thelastonetodropov, 124.

Already hundreds of world leaders are preparing to stay on in Moscow in the hope of being able to save thousands of pounds in airfares by attending two state funerals on the same ticket.

TORVILL AND DEAN'S victory in the winter Olympics made Ravel's Bolero as suddenly popular as the works of George Orwell had become in his eponymous year.

New from Snipcock & Tweed
Orwell & Dean
by ERIC BLAIR-PEACH

Latest reprint in the Snipcock & Tweed 'Modern Classics' Cashin Series.

Includes: *Coming Up For Ice*; *The Road to Wigan Skating Rink*; *Down And Out In Sarajevo and Los Angeles*

THREE HUNDRED police were dispatched to help evict the peace camp that had grown up around the RAF base at Greenham Common, where US Cruise missiles had been installed.

This Romantic England No.94
The Greenham Women

The English countryside knows no more colourful sight than the groups of anorak-bedecked peace-women who traditionally cluster around Greenham Common in Berkshire.

Once a week, a strange ritual is enacted, its origins lost in the mists of time. The burghers of Newbury send "officials" to "expel" the women from their traditional roosting ground. Amid much squawking, the burly bailiffs "move in" to dismantle the primitive shelters in which the women and their offspring have made their nests.

All this is traditionally watched by a large crowd of local residents, who emerge from their large residences behind the rhododendrons and say things like "About bloody time" and "It's the least the council can do considering the rates we pay."

A few minutes later, as the Council officials' Cortinas disappear down the leafy lane, the women re-emerge and begin the age-old process of reassembling their quaint shelters.

THE NATIONWIDE miners' strike began, in protest against pit closures rather than for the reasons posited by Auberon Waugh.

All my coalminer friends are up in arms against the government's new idea to send women down the mines. They are terrified that their wives will discover what a cissy job they have. Many miners nowadays spend their entire shift in the palatial underground hairdressing salons, having their faces massaged and toenails polished as they moan quietly to each other about the oppression of the working class. Then, after they have been delicately sprinkled with coal dust from an outsize powder puff, they come to the surface bleary-eyed and ready for the first round of Black Velvet at t'Club.

My old father spent thirty years down the mine at Dunks Colliery, Lancashire, and never came up. Some say he grew so fat with all the snap and tiffin they brought him he couldn't fit in the cage, but we never really discovered. In the end they closed the colliery and left him down there. It was very sad for the family.

NATIONAL UNION OF MINERS boss Arthur Scargill dispatched flying pickets to attempt to force workers in the Nottingham coalfields to join in the strike, despite the lack of a national ballot on the action.

VIOLENCE BROKE OUT between pickets and police, but Mrs Thatcher stuck resolutely to her line.

That Thatcherama in full

Sir Robin Day *(for it is he)*: Prime Minister, this miners' strike seems to be in the news quite a bit. What do you think about that?

The Maggatollah *(for it is she)*: You know, Robin, I think our police have been absolutely wonderful. Everyone agrees with me on that. The police have done a quite superb job. I'm sure that we all want to congratulate them on their marvellous achievement.

Day *(peers at clipboard)*: Can I move on now to the economy. Some people have said that it's not going too well, unemployment still a trifle on the high side, that sort of thing. What do you feel about that, Mrs Thatcher?

Maggie: I think the police have done an absolutely wonderful job, and I am sure everyone will want to thank them.

Day: But on the question of the economy, Prime Minister – could I come back to that?

Chief Maggi *(adopting serious tone and speaking very slowly)*: I think that it's so easy to criticise the police when all they are trying to do is defend the absolutely

basic human right of everyone to go to work, and I would just like to take this opportunity to say what a tremendous job the police are doing.

Day adjusts bow tie and promptly falls asleep. End of interview.

THANKS TO A NEWSPAPER campaign, South African runner Zola Budd was fast-tracked with a British passport, allowing her to run for Britain in the summer Olympics.

The *Mail* salutes Zola

Make no mistake! Today I saw with my own eyes one of the most extraordinary record-breaking feats in the history of British Passports.

No wonder they are calling Zola Budd the human streak of lightning. In a time of precisely 10 days 7 hours 49 minutes and 27.63 seconds, this tiny bare-footed tornado became the world's fastest ever passport-getter.

MPs gasped as in a spurt of phenomenal energy South African-born Zola burst through the red tape.

Doesn't it make you proud to be South African? *(Shome mishtake shurely?)*

THE INDIAN prime minister ordered troops to storm the Golden Temple at Amritsar, which had been taken over by Sikh militants, soon after Steven Spielberg's latest blockbuster hit cinemas.

SHE'S BACK
Indira Gandhi and The Temple Of Doom

Pogroms daily

THE BBC BROADCAST a harrowing drama depicting the run-up to and aftermath of a nuclear strike on Sheffield.

Auberon Waugh's Diary

I switch on the television halfway through a ghastly programme about life in the north of England. All the homes are in a state of disrepair and many have collapsed altogether. Among the despairing, apathetic population, many have hideous mutilations of the skin, none can talk properly, and all spend their time queuing in the cold outside medical centres and whining about the treatment they receive which is, I must admit, pretty bad. Few people ever visit the region, as I do, and many viewers will be horrified to learn how bad things are from this film, which is for some reason called Threads.

AN IRA BOMB TORE through the Grand Hotel, Brighton, which was hosting delegates to the Conservative Party Conference, including the Thatchers. Five people, including one MP, were killed and 31 injured, in some cases resulting in permanent disability.

10 Downing Street
Whitehall

Dear Bill,

Very decent of you to ring. Your concern much appreciated. I'm afraid I can tell you very little about the 'incident' itself as I had retired to bed following a pretty heavy fringe meeting of the Conservative Friends of Grape and Grain, at which I had perhaps done a little too much research. Hardly had my head touched the pillow than I was plunged into a dreamless state of oblivion from which I was only woken by the Night Porter telling me that the Grand had collapsed during the night, and would I please make my way quietly down the fire escape.

The Boss, needless to say, took the whole thing very much in her stride, and after a few comforting words to the Boys in Blue, resumed the preparation of her speech to Conference. I myself tottered down to the TV Lounge, where a jolly Red Cross lady was ladling out medicinal snorts to those suffering from shock.

The wets had been popping out of the woodwork berating the Proprietor for her lack of compassion etc, but all that now forgotten in the Warrior Queen Reborn scenario: show must go on, men of violence whether in the bogs or down the mines to be resisted to the last breath, law and order to be upheld, Old Bill given pat on back, but delegates never to forget that M. deeply concerned about the plight of unemployed etc. All of which may or may not be true, though in my experience compassion has never come all that high on the Boss's list of Top Ten Virtues. As for Lawson next door, he is about as compassionate as a traffic warden with a hangover, if you ask me.

Yours in one piece,
Denis

INDIRA GANDHI WAS ASSASSINATED by her own bodyguards, and riots followed in which over a thousand people were murdered.

To the Editor of the Daily Telegraph

Sir – like so many of your readers, I was delighted to see that the BBC have decided in their wisdom to repeat that wonderful series *The Jewel In The Crown*. But am I alone in regretting that the producers have seen fit to rewrite so much of the original series?

For instance, in the episode where the train carrying the ashes of Col. Merrick is stopped in the middle of the Punjab and boarded by hundreds of bloodthirsty Hindus who pull

some unfortunate Sikh from under a seat, cover him with petrol and set fire to him, where was the delectable Sarah Layton? And why, oh why, was it necessary to change the name of the hero, Mr Harry Kumar, to Rajiv Gandhi? Surely Sir David Attenborough should know better.

As one who has been out East, I can say what a tragedy it is that these BBC-wallahs could not let sleeping dogs lie, and give us the medicine as before.

Yours in protest,
SIR HERBERT GUSSETT,
Pankottage, Amritsar Close, Wilts.

DESPITE SEEMING increasingly semi-detached from reality, Ronald Reagan was re-elected for a second term.

HORRIFYING TV NEWS reports on the famine in Ethiopia prompted charitable giving on an unprecedented scale. The *Daily Mirror*'s new proprietor Robert Maxwell leapt on the bandwagon by travelling to the country in person, then complaining that he hadn't been shown enough deference by officials there.

Famine horror latest – Maxwell flies in

A beaming, ebullient Cardinal Robert Maxwell, leader of Britain's four million *Mirror* readers, today flew into the capital of famine-torn Ethiopia to distribute millions of free bingo cards to the starving people of this unhappy land.

Plainly shaken by his plane ride, the Captain told his startled Ethiopian hosts, "This is your lucky day – do you realise that I could soon be making one of you a Bingo Millionaire?"

After presenting his hosts with a signed copy of *The Complete Speeches of President Chernenko*, Captain Maxwell left for a 15-course fact-finding dinner at the Addis Ababa People's Revolutionary Hilton Hotel.

THE MINERS' STRIKE wore on.

IN JANUARY, SLICKER suggested a more sceptical approach to a City bigwig might be in order.

Any publicity is good publicity so long as you spell the name right, declared Hollywood mogul Sam Goldwyn, and no one has taken the motto more to heart than that devout self-publicist Robert Maxwell. For the "Bouncing Czech", all publicity, especially in the City columns, is good as long as you don't spell the name Jan Ludvik Hoch. And nowhere in the City can he count on greater and more faithful support than in the columns of the *Sunday Telegraph*, where barely a month goes by without some fulsome reference, be it a recommendation for the shares in British Printing & Communications, disclosure of his latest deal that never was, or revelation of the next all-important business "event". But then, the Bouncing Czech is one of the *Sunday Telegraph*'s magic circle of City wizards whose every deal, real or imagined, is assiduously forecast or commented on.

What is not recalled is the view taken of the same Robert Maxwell by the DTI inspectors when they examined his running of Pergamon Press, then a public company.

In 1971, in their interim report, Owen Stable QC and chartered accountant Sir Ronald Leach made their now-famous assessment that Maxwell was "not in our opinion a person who can be relied on to exercise proper stewardship of a public quoted company". Despite that, 10 years later Maxwell took over at BPCC and has indeed turned the company and the shares round.

But certain less well remembered comments by Stable and Leach make strange company with the constant puffery that goes on in the *Sunday Telegraph* and other City pages of a man they described as having "an apparent fixation as to his own abilities". The 1971 report concluded: "Mr Maxwell at all times regarded the price at which Pergamon shares were quoted on the Stock Exchange as of paramount importance." The inspectors returned to this theme in their concluding report in 1973: "We were convinced that it was Mr Maxwell's overall purpose to establish an artificially high value for Pergamon's shares in the stock market, and we are convinced that the exaggerated claims, the over-statement of profits, and some of the transactions between Pergamon and the family private companies were all means to that end." The inspectors also made reference to how Maxwell was "extraordinarily astute in financial transactions not only in their conception but also in their treatment in the accounts", to his "ingenuity in providing ever-ready justifications or explanation" and to his attempts to "shift responsibility onto others".

In 1991, after Maxwell's sudden death, it was revealed that he had been looting his newspapers' pension funds in order to prop up the company's share price, and that his entire business empire was built on theft and fraud.

IN THE SAME MONTH, the *Eye* turned the spotlight onto a political lobbying firm.

Parliamentary lobbying is not a well-developed skill in the United Kingdom. In the USA, lobbyists are accepted, gratuities freely given to politicians and favours delivered. So when a fully-fledged American look-alike appears on the scene, people in politics take some interest.

Ian Greer and Associates is a public relations company based in Buckingham Gate. Greer's many clients include City folk, lead-in-petrol promoters, fishing interests, a brewery and a drug company. And not a few MPs are grateful for its financial support.

Walter Johnson, the former MP for Derby South, was associated with Greer in a campaign to maintain the lead level in petrol. Greer's client, Associated Octel, was clearly worried about the loss of income should lead levels be reduced by statute. Mr Johnson told the *Eye*: "I knew I was packing up after the next election and it was a chance to earn some extra cash – nothing wrong with that." Originally it was Johnson's intention to collect his £1,000 by having Greer pay for a holiday. Now he prefers it in quarterly instalments for tax reasons. Another MP, Ian Sproat, has reason to be thankful to Greer, who gave him money for his election campaign. He lost. Greer is also very close to the right-wing MPs Neil Hamilton and Michael Grylls.

When approached by the *Eye*, Ian Greer was at pains to point out that he valued advice from many MPs, and those that were regularly contacted were, he felt, entitled to some remuneration. He wished to make it clear that any funds for MPs' election expenses came through his many friends in the City and not necessarily through his clients.

Greer's payments to Michael Grylls and, particularly, Neil Hamilton, made in the form of picking up bills for furniture, artworks and holidays for him and his wife Christine, became a very big story indeed when Mohamed Fayed blew the gaff on the "cash for questions" affair a full decade later in 1994.

THE EYE POURED cold water on rumours about the home secretary in June.

The "Cabinet Minister Scandal" that surfaced briefly in the press last week after a lobby briefing by Mr Bernard Ingham, Mrs Thatcher's press secretary, relates to Home Secretary Leon Brittan.

The story is an old one which has been around in Fleet Street for some time and has already been widely discounted as false. As long ago as November 1983 the *News of the World* investigated the story and decided there was nothing in it. In January the *Mail on Sunday* also looked into the rumours and reached the same conclusion.

The reason for the sudden resurgence of interest last week is thought to be not unconnected with MI5 and the Libyan Embassy siege in April. The CIA in London has long taken an interest in Libya, having a special desk here. Information from Libya, together with radio and other intercepts, was correlated in Langley, Virginia and forwarded on to London.

As has so often happened, MI5 failed to evaluate the situation. The Special Branch were not warned and the demonstration went ahead with the tragic shooting of WPC Yvonne Fletcher. Brittan took most of the flak in the resulting furore and he decided to make enquiries with a view to a big shake-up in MI5.

The MI5 spooks and loonies who object to having a Jewish Home Secretary retaliated by resurrecting the Brittan smear and spreading it around Fleet Street.

As a result, Ingham "briefed" the lobby hacks, threatening writs if anything was published. In the meantime newspaper editors were phoned by the Home Office Press Officer and Downing Street and warned not to publish anything.

All this only created an atmosphere of hysteria which has not helped in any way to kill the smear.

The fake story was resurrected 30 years later in the mish-mash of made-up accusations by "Nick", aka Carl Beech, who falsely claimed to have been the victim of a paedophile ring in Westminster. Brittan died during the investigation, never finding out that the police had concluded he had no case to answer.

1985

PARLIAMENT – albeit only the House of Lords – was televised for the very first time.

INVENTOR Sir Clive Sinclair launched his Sinclair C5, a single-seat electric-powered tricycle intended to replace the car. Imitator Lord Gnome followed suit.

This is the remarkable Gnome XL 417 Shoemobile

The biggest revolution in getting from A to B since Clive Sinclair invented the wheel.

It needs no petrol. Just one small 1.5 volt alkaline battery in the back of the shoe is all you need to get you on the road.

You need no insurance. No driving licence. No seat belts, no crash helmet, no gear changes, no mirrors. You just put it on, press a button, and hey-presto, your electric-powered Shoe-mobile will do the rest.

The XL 417 has a cruising range of up to 10 yards on just one battery. If you need to travel further than this, just take a supply of further batteries and you can travel virtually around the world (providing your pockets are big enough for all the batteries). The Gnome Shoemobile has been aerodynamically styled to provide protection in most weather conditions, although use in snow, ice, rain or wind is not advised.

DESPITE A JUDGE'S direction, an Old Bailey jury found civil servant Clive Ponting not guilty of breaking the Official Secrets Act by leaking information about the sinking of the Belgrano during the Falklands War.

"And is that the verdict of you all?"

IT WAS TIME for yet another Russian leader.

Speculation mounted today over the health of Soviet leader Konstantin Chernenko, 107, when Russian news agency Tass issued a series of bulletins pronouncing him to be "in perfect health following his recent death".

Further statements throughout the day, accompanied by solemn music, claimed the Soviet leader had recently been ski-ing in the Caucasus, hang-gliding in the Urals and break-dancing in Red Square.

STOP PRESS: Mr Mikhail Gorblimov has emerged as the new leader of the Soviet Union. Kremlin experts have hailed him as an entirely new figure in the history of Soviet politics, in that he is considerably younger and less dead than any of his predecessors.

PRINCESS MICHAEL of Kent's father was revealed to have been an SS officer.

Yes, it's Glitzy Glenda Slagg – Fleet Street's Princess Di

Hats off to Princess Michael?!!??! So what if her old man was a Nazi!?!!?? None of us is to blame for what our Mums and Dads got up to before we were even born!!!?!! (Geddit?)

Thank Gawd this Right Royal Lady has got a heart big enough to cope with all the muck that Fleet Street can fling at 'er!!?!!

No wonder when she went on TV the whole country was won over to her side!?!??! God Bless You, Ma'am!!!

Did you see Princess Michael a-whingin' and

a-cringin' on the telly??! Tell us another one, Fraulein von Heineken – or whatever your real name is!?!! Of course you knew all along that Daddy was a Storm-Trooper in his spare time!?!!! Everybody did!!!?! Take a tip from Auntie Glenda, Mein Liebling!!?!! Clear off back to Bolivia where you belong!?!!

THE MINERS' STRIKE came to a sorry end, despite the best efforts of NUM leader Arthur Scargill.

41 PEOPLE WERE KILLED when a wall collapsed in the Heysel Stadium in Brussels as British football hooligans attempted to reach opposing fans.

'I Blame the hooligans' says no one

In a shock statement not made by anyone last night, the blame for the Brussels disaster was laid firmly on the heads of the soccer hooligans who caused it.

There was an immediate outcry at the suggestion the hooligans bore some responsibility for the tragedy. Laurie Driver, Professor of Crowd Sociology at Neasden Polytechnic, said, "It is all too easy to put the blame for acts of soccer violence on the people who committed them."

ON OTHER PAGES:

I blame the parents – p7

I blame the brewers – p8

I blame the ambulancemen – p9

I blame the media – p10

I blame Thatcher – p11

POLICE VIOLENTLY PREVENTED a "Peace Convoy" of New Age travellers from reaching Stonehenge to stage a free festival.

YE ANGLO SAXON CHRONICLE

Fhock fcenes as pagan hordes lay wafte Weffex

Not since ye Viking hordes came over from Denmark for ye European Cup has England seen such a horrific gang of lawless marauders. With their long hair, unkempt beards and droopy moustaches, they have struck fear into ye heart of every honest yeoman and churl in the fair countryside of Wiltshire.

Yesterday ye Saxon forces, under their renowned chief "Inspector" Knucka, met ye pagan army face to face in a mighty battle at Stonehenge. Ye pagans were put to flight and their wagons had their windows smashed by zealous guardians of ye law. But following widespread criticism of Knucka's "over-reaction" in ye media, ye chief hath ordered his lads to "keep a low profile".

ON UTHER PAGES: *A wagon-driver writes – "String ye buggers up, it is ye only language these hippies understand."*

THE POPPLEWELL INQUIRY into safety and crowd control at football grounds, set up following the fire that killed 56 spectators at Bradford City's ground in May and the killing of a teenage boy during violence at a Birmingham City match the same day, delivered its verdict.

These are the shock recommendations put forward by Britain's most controversial judge, Mr Justice Popplecarrot

1. All bona-fide football supporters to be tattooed with identity numbers, and ball and chain to be worn on match days.

2. Misleading signposts to be erected on approaches to grounds to divert supporters away from stadium.

3. All players to be issued with false beards to confuse supporters, thus preventing them from indulging in partisan behaviour.

4. Closed circuit TV monitors to be installed in all police cars to enable officers to watch the match in comfort.

5. In order to reduce fire hazards, all matches to be played wherever possible under water.

6. In future, cricket to be played instead of football at all grounds. "It is a much more civilised game," explained the judge. "I played it at Oxford and we never had any trouble with these hooligan chappies."

Mr Justice Popplecarrot is 81.

LIVE AID, a pair of transatlantic rock mega-concerts, was staged to raise funds to fight famine in Ethiopia.

Turds re-united
Moving scenes at Live Aid marathon

It was down memory lane for thousands of pop fans when the legendary Turds, a popular singing group from the early Sixties, were reunited for a few poignant moments at Wembley yesterday.

Looking very much the same, only considerably older, the Turds bounded onto the stage amidst hysterical screams of "Who are these old bores?"

Lead singer Sir Spigismond Topes commented, "The Turds broke up long ago. But we firmly believe we have a moral duty to come together to help end the war in Vietnam."

Sir Spigismond is 64.

FOUR AIR CRASHES in a single month left 720 people dead, the highest number of air fatalities in history.

Plane arrives – drama at
Heathrow airport

There were shock scenes last night when BA Flight 730 from Manchester-London landed safely on runway 2.

Said an official, "We have no idea how this happened. A group called British Airways is claiming responsibility."

This was the timetable of events in what is being called the Heathrow Drama:

0930 – Flight 730 takes off from Manchester

1030 – Flight 730 lands safely at Heathrow

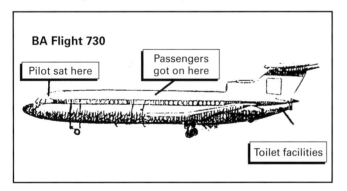

BA Flight 730

Pilot sat here

Passengers got on here

Toilet facilities

THE TITANIC WAS LOCATED, and photographed, on the sea bed.

The 73-year-old remains of President Reagan should be left undisturbed, according to a team of salvage experts who have discovered him lying peacefully at the bottom of his bed.

The wreck of the Reagan, who when launched was described as "unthinkable", was recently located in almost perfect condition. But despite campaigns to raise him, relatives and supporters are adamant that he should be left undisturbed "to sleep in peace".

Presidential spokesman Larry Speakes said last night, "This makes absolutely no difference to the up-coming meeting with Mr Gorbachev which will go ahead as planned."

THE BBC GOVERNORS caved into pressure from home secretary Leon Brittan and banned a documentary about Northern Ireland the government claimed would give the IRA "the oxygen of publicity". BBC journalists went on strike in response.

Those BBC letters in full

Dear Man in Suit,

It has been drawn to my attention that the BBC has recently made a so-called documentary programme in the series *Great Lunatics of the World*, featuring an interview with Mr Seamus O'Letter Bomb, so-called Commander In Chief of the Provisional IRA. While in no sense would I wish to pre-judge the contents of this programme in any way, I have no doubt that were it to be publicly shown, it would have the most catastrophic and damaging repercussions in all sorts of ways which I scarcely need enlarge here.

While I recognise and respect to the full the total editorial independence of the BBC and its freedom to broadcast any such thing as it may deem proper, nevertheless I hereby give fair warning to all you Trots and Pinkoes down there at BH that you'd better pull the plug on this one pretty smartish, or you can kiss goodbye to that £85 licence fee you want next year.

Yours sincerely,
S. BRITOIL,
Home Secretary.

Dear Sir Slimeswell,

I am in receipt of yours of the 29th ult. with regard to the controversial so-called programme relating to Mr O'Timing Device.

The Board of Governors have given very long and careful lunches to your views, and whilst we would like to make it crystal clear that the BBC retains complete independence in all matters relating to broadcasting policy, nevertheless in this particular case we have decided that, taking one thing with another, the time is not ripe to show the programme in this particular form, far better to put out yet another episode of *Wogan*, yes sir, no sir, whatever Mrs T. wants sir.

Yours sincerely,
M.I. Suit,
Chairman, BBC.

A MUSIC FORMAT launched three years earlier was going mainstream (with a little bit of help from Dire Straits).

HEATH

Great Bores of Today

"... it seems expensive now but the price is coming down all the time and the discs themselves are fantastic the quality of the recording is so superior to the old LPs and tapes and you can get anything pretty well classical pop jazz they're even reissuing some of the old favourites and the real bonus is they don't scratch there's no surface noise whatsoever you can do anything with them leave them lying around it's all done by lasers you don't even need needles you can even get a Compact Walkman this mate of mine has got one and he says once you've heard it you never want anything else you should hear the new Madonna album on it..."

MRS THATCHER reshuffled her cabinet.

BBC Political Correspondent John Cole reports

Hondootedly Mossis Thatcher alf garnett molto adagio rastafarian No Meejor chenges in Cobinet. As predicted Moster Tobbit rambo adrian mole general buhari repleeces John Solwen Gommer as Party Cheermon. Nigella horatia Moster Sossil Porkinson hon detoit kalamazoo jasminium nudiflorum hoops of comebock dushed. Legover multifarias violet bonham carter nelson mandela bockbench desappointmunt. Tinker tailor soldier spy Moster Potrick Jonkin typhoon ella duran duran lucca della robbia skeepgoat for Mossis Thotcher's matropulitan council obolition innuendo de facto rumbaba sena qua non see you later alligator Lord Yong weetabix *(cont. p94)*

THE NEW POET LAUREATE, Ted Hughes, was proving an awkward fit for the job.

Lines on the Eighty-Fifth Birthday of the Queen Mother

by Sir Tedwyn Hughes, Poet Laureate

> Under Gowrie Crag
> Stands the Rock
> Upfaced
> Granite eyed
>
> Rocky
>
> Lichen creeps
> On Rocky's face
> Scum of moss
> His only beard
>
> Skeleton of weasel
> Plucked dry by
>
> Owly
> Old Owly
> *(We had this last time. Ed.)*

NEW HOME SECRETARY Douglas Hurd had to deal with riots in Birmingham and London sparked by heavy-handed policing.

IN MARCH, THE EYE took a trip to Liverpool, aka Murky-side.

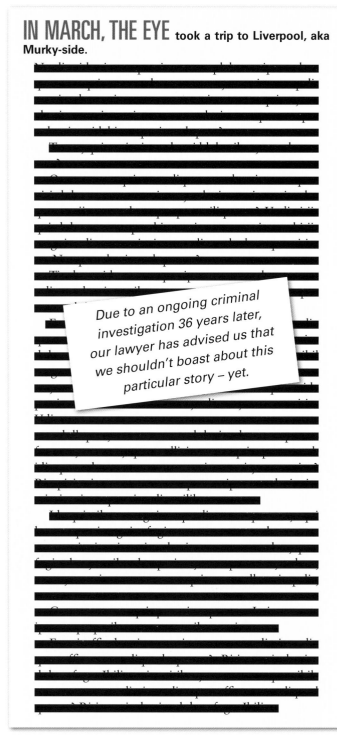

Due to an ongoing criminal investigation 36 years later, our lawyer has advised us that we shouldn't boast about this particular story – yet.

THERE WAS NEWS from a far-left group in October.

That bizarre sect, the Workers' Revolutionary Party (known to *Eye* readers as The West End Revolutionary Party – TWERP) has recently expelled its 72-year-old founding father and cult figure, Gerry Healy. But press reports of the strange goings-on have been wide of the mark. The TWERP daily organ, *Newsline*, came closest to the truth when it stated: "He abused his power for personal gratification."

Healy has long been one of the more colourful figures of the political fringe. He recruited West End stars Vanessa and Corin Redgrave to his party, and his main drive was to get more actors and actresses into the sect. The dockers were forgotten, the miners ignored. The actor's union Equity became his favoured hunting ground.

Now TWERP sources reveal that what has taken place is a Ugandan coup. Healy's penchant for Ugandan discussions with young women has been no secret within TWERP. Recently, however, he went too far in attempting to force himself on a young woman member. The victim was outraged and began to talk openly of "sexual harrassment" and rape. Within a few days, other women began to recount their vile experiences with Healy. The climax came when no less than 28 TWERP ladies wrote a letter to the Central Committee demanding protection against Healy.

The dirty old man's most avid defenders were the Redgraves. Vanessa argued, "What has all this got to do with politics?" But when the affair prevented *Newsline*'s appearance for 10 days the members realised that something was up, and Healy was unceremoniously expelled.

The TWERP, whose membership is under 1000, could now split into pro- and anti-Healy factions. Question: who will keep the cash and the expensive printworks? This question can only be resolved in Tripoli, which provided both. Healy's chances are slim. Colonel Gadaffi is known to dislike rapists and offenders have been dealt with severely.

Healy supporters – including Ken Livingstone maintained right up until his death that the accusations had been part of an MI5 plot to break up the WRP.

1986

A CABINET DISPUTE over the future of Westland Helicopters resulted in the dramatic resignations of both Michael Heseltine and Leon Brittan.

10 Downing Street
Whitehall

Dear Bill,

Don't ask me what's going on. Apparently there's this little whirly-bird company down in Yeovil that nobody's ever heard of who got into a spot of bother on the liquidity front. Along comes Sikorsky offering a helping handful of dollars saying they'll buy up the whole bang shoot and keep the yokels in employment making Yankee choppers. Westland board thinks it's Christmas, Rolls Royces out of hock, skiing holidays uncancelled.

At this juncture, however friend Tarzan springs to life, seizes a length of knotted liana and swings into Whitehall, smelling fresh meat in the shape of Mr Britoil, whose rubber stamp is even then poised over Uncle Sam's rescue package. Grunt, growl, snarl, and he swoops away from tree to tree alerting the Euro-monkeys to see off the marauding Yanks.

It wasn't long before Brittan appeared at our front door, dusting himself down, Adam's apple going up and down like a yoyo. "It really is intolerable, Prime Minister, all this was agreed in Cabinet etc. etc., do we accept principle of collective responsibility or do we not?" Next thing at Cabinet the Boss was giving Tarzan the full force bone-rotting gamma rays, and our flaxen-haired friend stormed out in a carefully planned impromptu resignation. Since when he has been on all four channels simultaneously twenty-four hours a day, a foolish thing to do as people soon get sick of seeing the same face night after night: look what happened to that Irish Johnny with the dimples who used to be the bee's knees at the Corporation and now no one's got a good word for him.

All the same, for a few days things did look pretty sticky from this end. The old girl threw herself across the body of Brittan only for it to turn out that the whingeing arsecreeper had leaked some damning letter about Tarzan to the reptiles. Now people can't accept that she knew about it when the talk in and around her office was of little else for several days. With any

normal person I agree this would be incomprehensible, but what no one can haul in is that she never listened much in the past to what other people were saying, and nowadays not at all. So it's perfectly possible that her presswallah Ingham shouted it in her ear on numerous occasions without it making any impact on her cerebellum. Even on our honeymoon, I recall, she asked me to put things in writing and shove them under the door, and to this day I've still no proof she ever read them.

Yours aye, Denis

THE GLC was finally abolished.

IAN BOTHAM was suspended from international cricket after admitting smoking cannabis.

The cricket world was rocked to its foundations yesterday by allegations that England all-rounder Ian Botham had been involved in an all-day cricket match in which wickets had been "taken" and runs '"scored". It was alleged that some of his bowling bouts lasted for days on end, leaving him so exhausted that he was incapable of performing properly in the official sex orgies and drug-taking sessions.

IN AN OVERNIGHT FLIT designed to defy the print unions, Rupert Murdoch transferred production of all his newspapers to a new automated plant in Wapping.

Gnome

I am delighted to be able to repo report that my organ has been successfully transferred l‡ck st‡ck and ba½½rrelt, o a disused sewage far farm on the outskiVRts of NeNsde farm on the outskiVRts of NeNesden.

Here the future of the BRitish Presswill be re-shaped =ransforming into aD dnynamic new froçè fœ¬[§Δ§∞Ø f£orged in the w h i t e h o t heat of the modern technological evolution.

The move grings go a grend the long unhappy era in6whih 8my3 manage½s have struggled invain awith the outdated and obstructive methods of the prinT UNions.

e. Strobes
PpP Lord Ghome
The Old Sewwage Farm,
Neasden.

FOUR DAYS AFTER it happened, the Russian authorities admitted that the Chernobyl nuclear reactor had exploded and was still on fire.

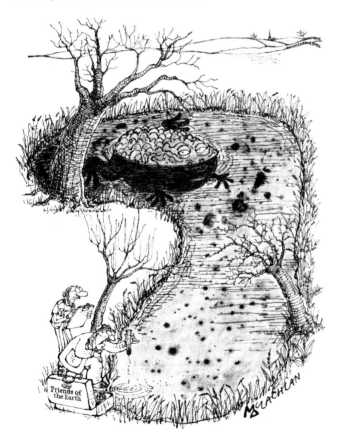

"The Government says that the radiation is quite harmless"

SOUTH AFRICAN PRESIDENT P. W. Botha introduced an indefinite state of emergency and ordered the arrest of thousands of black activists, church workers and trade unionists. Mrs Thatcher's government steadfastly resisted international calls to impose sanctions on the country.

PRESIDENT REAGAN launched an air strike on Tripoli in response to a series of terror attacks.

That Libyan raid: Glossary of Terms

WHAT THEY SAID	WHAT THEY MEANT
The mission was 100% successful	*We really screwed it up*
Surgical precision	*All our bombs hit Libya*
We hit only selected military targets	*Tough luck on those embassies, schools, hospitals, etc*
We had no intention of killing Gadaffi	*We missed*
We have made a major contribution to effectively reducing terrorist capability in the world	*Cancel your holiday plans*

MEANWHILE, 32 COUNTRIES refused to compete in the Commonwealth Games in Edinburgh in protest at the UK's refusal to join a sports boycott of South Africa.

"Bloody blacks – not coming over here!"

PRINCE ANDREW married Sarah Ferguson.

Gnome Special Royal Wedding Microwave Offer

Yes, it's your chance to celebrate the Happy Day with this fabulous and imaginative Gift Offer. Direct from Gnome Leisurewear Enterprises we bring you the Andy 'n' Fergie Microwave Experience.

The Gnome Souvenir Microwave is guaranteed to cook you a Right Royal TV Supper in literally seconds! Not only that, but in years to come, your children will come to look on it as a glorious reminder of the unforgettable Royal Wedding of 1986.

Choose from these exciting colours: Dark Brown.

Send £3,999 cash only to Gnome Microwave Offer, PO Box 347, Cleethorpes, Lincs.

NEW NEWSPAPERS – the *London Daily News, Today,* the *Independent* – were bursting out all over the place.

Gnome

I am pleased to be able to announce that I intend to launch at least ten new London evening newspapers during the next twelve months.

As readers will know, I already control the mass-market *Evening Gnome* which sells in excess of 400 million copies daily. The *Evening Gnome*, however, caters for a distinctive AB readership with a special appeal to commuters, office

workers and the deceased. The *London Strobes*, which is due to appear on the streets later this year, is designed to relate to a younger category of readers with an interest in such contemporary pehnomena as pop music, glue-sniffing and sexually transmitted diseases.

The *London Wino*, which is due to be launched in 1989, will be aimed primarily at the growing alcoholic market and will have special direct delivery services to selected bomb sites. Details of several other papers will be announced shortly.

E. Strobes

pp. Lord Gnome

A FURORE BROKE OUT over a children's book called *Jenny lives with Eric and Martin,* a copy of which was found in the possession of the Inner London Education Authority.

Remove this book now! 'Blatant Propaganda' claim

A new book *Harry Lives With Charles and Diana* has been widely distributed amongst children and "susceptible young people", Labour campaigners revealed today. The book, written by Sir Arslickair Brunette and published by Monarchist Press, shows a small boy called Harry apparently living with two members of the Royal Family.

Deidre Spart, chief co-ordinator of Harringay Lesbians Against the Police Advisory Action Committee, said, "This book is blatant propaganda for the Royal lifestyle, portraying a child growing up in a totally unnatural environment which cannot be healthy for him."

But an unrepentant Sir Arslickair said, "My book is a genuine attempt to portray Royals in a sympathetic and positive way. There is still a great deal of prejudice against the Royal community, and young people should be introduced at an early stage to the idea of Royalty as something perfectly natural."

CITY TRADING was deregulated and computerised in what was dubbed the "Big Bang".

Yes! It's the Big Bore

The financial world was rocked to its foundations today by the introduction of the so-called Big Bore, a series of the most far-ranging and boring measures ever introduced.

What it means in layman's terms is:

- HUNDREDS of young men in suits being even more boring than before

- FILM on the News every night of boring men in shirt sleeves ringing up other boring men in Japan

- THOUSANDS of boring articles in newspapers saying "What it means in layman's terms is this…"

MEANWHILE, THE GOVERNMENT'S sale of shares in British gas, and its ubiquitous advertising campaign, was proving more popular than the new presenter of Radio 2's Breakfast Show, Derek "Sid Yobboe" Jameson.

> *If you see Sid tell him his Radio 2 show is a load of rubbish*

DEPUTY PRIME MINISTER Willie Whitelaw was put in charge of a cabinet committee to consider what the government should do about the AIDS emergency.

A Non-Doctor Writes

As a Cabinet Minister I am often asked to do things about which I know absolutely nothing. Take this AIDS business. My advice to the public is to avoid AIDS at all costs. I understand that some of you chaps out there do some pretty rum things to each other which I'm not going to go into here, but I think you all know what I'm talking about, eh? *(Takes out condom.)* However if you insist on... er... you know... we're all men of the world... er... you'd better put on one of these little fellows. The way to get hold of these is to go and have a haircut and wait for the barber to say "Is that all, sir? Would you like anything for the weekend?" So that should take care of things.

"OK, that's sorted out the homosexuals, now let's have a go at Estate Agents"

JEFFREY ARCHER RESIGNED as deputy chairman of the Conservatives, after the *News of the World* exposed him paying money to prostitute Monica Coghlan.

Top Tory not to resign shock

A leading Tory newspaper proprietor, Mr Rupert Murdoch, said last night at his luxury penthouse suite that he would not resign following allegations that he had "paid off" a Miss Monica Legover via a shady intermediary, Mr Aziz Wikidway.

In a plot that reads like the fiction he himself publishes in his series of popular newspapers, a taped phone conversation reveals Mr Murdoch agreeing to meet Mr Azizway at the "Dog and Chequebook" public house in Fleet Street, a favourite venue of winos and criminals. The conversation went like this:

LEGOVER: Bring the money in used fifty pound notes.
MURDOCH: How will I recognise him?
LEGOVER: He is a shifty looking Arab with a moustache. How will he know you?
MURDOCH: I'm a shifty looking Australian in a dirty mac.

Last night Mr Murdoch said: "I have done nothing wrong. I will continue to serve Mrs Thatcher to the best of my abilities."

THE CONSERVATIVES' deputy chairman was still an embarrassment in April.

The problem of Jeffrey Archer continues to baffle the Prime Minister's advisers. His recent visit to the West Country to drum up fading Tory hopes has proved what he can still get up to. In Cornwall at the end of his tour he gathered a gang of journalists and faithful young Tories around him and told them of a terrorist attempt to assassinate him. An explosive device had been found on the moorland road where his car was due to travel. The police had stopped his car and switched him to an unmarked one so that the terrorists would be fooled. They whisked him to a Totnes hotel where all the rooms were searched by sniffer dogs for explosives. The same happened later in Plymouth. At his meeting in Totnes, the novelist went on, there were 40 plain-clothes policemen in the meeting, all with eyes and ears open for an expected attack. The Totnes Terror, he went on, was safely contained.

One freelance journalist in the company decided the story needed checking. This revealed that there had been no device anywhere in Mr Archer's route, no rumour of any such device, nor the slightest suggestion of one. The cars had been switched because Mr Archer was late. There were no sniffer dogs used in any of the hotels used by Mr Archer anywhere on his tour. And the number of policemen deployed at his Totnes meeting was not 40… but four.

Orders have now gone out from Downing Street to "shut that bloody little man up".

Archer resigned as Tory vice-chairman in October after being exposed as paying money to prostitute Monica Coghlan, but continued – to his eventual detriment – to make up false accounts of the circumstances leading up to the incident.

MAY BROUGHT NEWS from Westminster council.

The consequences of being the Thatcher government's most obedient tool are becoming evident at Westminster City Council where the gallant high Tory priestess, Lady Shirley Porter, is at the helm. An unprecedented exodus of council officers at all levels has left yawning gaps resulting in a number of botch-ups – particularly in the housing department. In the department's grants section a series of internal audits and inquiries have revealed disturbing irregularities. The most striking example is the £560,000 improvement grant awarded to private developers Firstcross Ltd for Ashworth Mansions in Maida Vale where the subsequent audit report led to the resignation of grants surveyor John Higgs, and a further internal inquiry into all grant schemes supervised by him. Its results are eagerly awaited by opposition councillors.

While the housing department dispenses lashings of loot in grants, it is at grassroots level where the squeeze is really biting. Last year the capital housing programme was reduced by £3.3 million (13.3 per cent). Not only are essential repairs not being carried out in the remaining council stock but gross understaffing at area offices means the day-to-day running of council estates is virtually non-existent. One woman pensioner has been waiting since 9 January for a two-bar electric fire to be delivered. Her council flat has been unheated throughout the freezing weather.

Porter was later shown to have run a gerrymandering policy of deliberately neglecting and selling off council properties while prioritising services in areas where likely Conservative voters lived, including placing homeless families in tower blocks known to be riddled with dangerous asbestos in a Labour ward. She and five colleagues were ordered to personally pay the £31 million cost of the illegal policy plus interest (*see p155*).

THE REAL STORY behind the suspension of Greater Manchester's deputy chief constable was revealed in June.

Joke of the month is the widely publicised notion that the disciplinary charges against John Stalker have nothing to do with his inquiry into the "shoot to kill" policy of the Royal Ulster Constabulary. The joke has led to much laughter in senior ranks of the RUC, who were becoming increasingly worried by Stalker's refusal to "play the Orange game" the way he was expected to.

Stalker was appointed in 1984 after persistent complaints from the Social Democratic and Labour Party about the involvement of the RUC in assassinations at road blocks. The SDLP allegations came after the trials in 1982 of RUC men for the murder of suspected terrorists: it was plain that the police had decided the "rule of law" was far more expensive and inefficient than simply stopping suspects at roadblocks and spraying their vehicles with machine gun fire. One of the key issues of the Anglo-Irish agreement which Mrs Thatcher signed with the Irish government last year was that the squads should be brought to book.

Stalker was appointed chief of the inquiry into the "shoot to kill" scandal and he selected some of the toughest officers in his force and others to help him. It did not take him long to discover that the policy was not the work of a few mad extremists who had slipped into the RUC, but was approved at a much higher level. An interim report last August to the DPP recommended that several top RUC officers should be prosecuted. This prospect appalled the authorities, the RUC, the DUP and the official unionists. In the government, ministers and civil servants were outraged that, in spite of all the hints to the contrary, Mr Stalker still insisted on telling the barefaced truth. He was insisting on pressing charges against the RUC. So Stalker had to be stopped.

And so the government reached for old friends, the intelligence wing of the security service. MI5 in particular were worried that Mr Stalker might have stumbled on their own involvement in the "hit squads" and the lessons they gave to the RUC about how to knock out a suspect driver and his passengers at close range. MI5 were brought in to "rubbish" Stalker and get rid of him before his report was published.

They have uncovered his friendship with a Conservative businessman and the fact that he has been known to drink in a bar frequented by convicted criminals. This has caused much mirth in Manchester masonic halls, where the new game is to try to think of a top policeman in the city who hasn't drunk in the same bar as convicted criminals. This is plain, simple "black propaganda". And it has worked wonders.

After being cleared of any disciplinary offences, Stalker was reinstated to his job in Manchester – but not the shoot-to-kill inquiry. Its final report has never been published.

IN NOVEMBER, THE EYE had the background story to the book the government was trying to ban.

Eye readers will recall a long string of articles during the middle and late 1970s which exposed a deep split in the security services, especially MI5. In the clandestine hothouse that is the world of secret agents, a new breed of spy had been hatched: deeply political, very reactionary and fundamentally suspicious of any elected government, especially a Labour one.

Such people saw Russian agents everywhere, especially in their own ranks and most especially at the very top of their own ranks. This new breed of NCOs were suspicious of their "officers" whom they believed had all come from universities where they had probably slept with the likes of Anthony Blunt and Guy Burgess.

By the mid-1970s this group had grown to substantial proportions, and was able to carry out "field actions" on its own initiative, without consulting the hierarchy. Its members had become hysterical at the growth of the Left (and the trade unions) during the Heath administration. They determined, if necessary, to challenge the government rather than allow such strength to grow.

Their activities caused much concern in Harold Wilson's Downing Street from 1974. Wilson became convinced that MI5 was gunning for his government and himself, even tapping the phones in Number 10. Meanwhile the Young Turks in the security service, who liked to call themselves "The Guardians", were also busying themselves in the Conservative Party. They were determined to get rid of Heath, whom they saw as a traitor, and they joined enthusiastically in the campaign for Mrs Thatcher.

But their most anxious propaganda was directed to their own organisations, and especially to the unlikely theory that their former boss, Sir Roger Hollis, was a Russian spy. This theory was floated with greater and greater enthusiasm in all the areas where the Guardians had some influence. It was taken up by Chapman Pincher and "Nigel West" (Rupert Allason) in their own third-rate accounts of the security services. No one was greatly impressed, and indeed the Hollis theory has been well and truly laid to rest in Phillip Knightley's recent book on the spy world.

The leader of the Guardians was Peter Wright, the sour old spy who is now planning to publish his memoirs in Australia. Most of the hoo-ha about this book suggests that Thatcher and Co are worried about what it may or may not say about Sir Roger Hollis. Not so. In a statement in 1981 she disposed of all this in the House of Commons. What worries her is what the book might say about MI5 splits in general, and about Mrs Thatcher in particular. Her apostasy has infuriated the Guardians and Peter Wright. He sees her as another traitor in the Heath mould, and has included in the book the details of his faction's support for her when she came to office. Thus the prime minister might be confronted in election year with support from a most unwelcome and embarrassing quarter.

The government undertook several legal actions to ban the sale or reporting of Wright's book *Spycatcher* in England and Wales, but since it was still available everywhere else including Scotland, this proved rather ineffective, and the ensuing publicity ensured that when the ban was finally dropped in 1988 it was a bestseller.

1987

THE CHIEF CONSTABLE of Manchester, James Anderton, who had previously declared that AIDS patients were "swirling in a human cesspit of their own making" announced that God was using him to do His work for Him.

'God is behind me' says top cop

An angry Inspector "Knacker of the Yard" Knacker today hit out at critics of his controversial policing style. "There is no crisis of confidence," he told reporters. "The Archangel Gabriel has appeared unto me in a dream while I was driving along the M62 and said unto me, 'Knacker, my son, you stay on and get rid of that creep Stalker'."

In recent months, the Inspector has come increasingly under fire for his controversial decision to deploy three million officers to track down the elusive AIDS virus, which he believed to have landed from outer space somewhere on Saddleworth Moor.

"I frequently hear voices," the Inspector told newsmen, speaking through his controversial beard. "Usually they are telling me that I am barking mad and off my trolley, but I ignore them."

PRIVATE EYE

GOD TALKS TO KNACKER

You're fired

SOME WILD CLAIMS were bandied around as election day approached…

What Labour *really* plans

When Ken Livingstone wins the General Election for Labour he will implement the following secret manifesto:
● ABOLISH the House of Lords
● INTRODUCE a compulsory quota of homosexuals into the Cabinet
● KILL the Queen and "re-educate" Princess Diana to become a coal-miner
● INVITE Mr Gorbachev to invade Britain and make himself head of a Soviet Republic
● ER…
● THAT'S it.

(The above facts have all appeared at one time or another in the imagination of Brigadier B.J.F. Buckingham-Gussett, Chairman, Loons of Industry)

This Advertisement Is Issued By Aims Of Industry, A Non-Aligned Group Who Support The Tory Party.

…AND MRS THATCHER was returned by yet another landslide.

10 Downing Street
Whitehall

Dear Bill,

As you may have gathered from the TV news, all my worst fears have been realised. Boss slavering to go on and on and on, and no earthly chance of putting the feet up in Dulwich. All I have before me now is a life sentence, rather like that Klaus Barbie cove across the water.

For one glorious moment it looked as if Superginge Kinnock was about to open my prison house door and sweep the Boss into oblivion. The old girl got very jittery and started to take it out on the wretched Saatchi twins, accusing them of making her wear the wrong shoulder-pads and speak in a soft unnatural voice. Insisted they produce some ghastly little coke-sniffer in red-framed spectacles by the name of Bell to come in and take charge of the Final Push. Meanwhile Smarmy Cecil is back, and shimmering about, whispering in the boss's ear like some ghastly floor-walker from Moss Bros.

Yours in Spandau,
Denis

EIGHT YEARS INTO her rule, Mrs Thatcher suddenly discovered an interest in urban deprivation.

MICHAEL RYAN'S RAMPAGE in Hungerford in which he shot 14 people dead was followed by the customary moral panic about "video nasties".

Gnome

The decision by British Gnomeon Films Ltd to release the film *Crazy Gunman* this week has been criticised by a number of no doubt well-intentioned busybodies in the wake of the Hungerford killings.

Let me stress again that no one has ever established a link between violence on the screen and violence in real life. As the distinguished film producer and Chairman of the Murdered Policemen Memorial Trust, Mr Michael Winner, has pointed out, Shakespeare himself included scenes of explicit sex and violence in his plays. Mr Winner's films such as *Gunpoint Rape* and *Gunpoint Rape II* are in the same tradition.

Hungerford or no, this is still a free country, and we must cherish our time-honoured freedom to amass huge fortunes by pandering to the basest urges of our fellow citizens.

E. Strobes
pp Lord Gnome

JEFFREY ARCHER WON his libel case after an extraordinary summing-up from the judge, who plainly had the hots for his wife.

MR JUSTICE COCKLECAULFIELD

Ladies and gentlemen of the jury – for the past three weeks it has been our dismal and unpleasant duty to listen to the lies and evasions of a group of persons whom you may well think might best be described as a wog, a tart and a bunch of smut-pedlars. On the other side of this unfortunate case we see a man who has occupied one of the highest offices in the land, enjoyed the confidence of no less a person than our beloved Prime Minister, run 100 yards for his country in under ten seconds, a man whose literary gifts have long since placed him in the forefront of British letters. Is it likely, we have to ask ourselves, that a man with such a distinguished record in two world wars, would wish to seek in the still hours of the morning the dubious solace of cold, joyless, rubber-insulated, double-glazed intercourse in a room no larger than a man's hat, with rats and bats crawling through the wainscotting, gibbering their horrid message of despair unto the nations of Judah?

If you think this is possible, then think back, if you will, to the vision which came upon us in this courtroom only three days ago. Was she not called Mary, like unto the Mother of our Lord? Did we not sense the odour of sanctity, an unearthly fragrance in the Courtroom that day, like unto the spring flowers in the vale of Hebron? Would any man who had the good fortune to have wedded and bedded this fairest of the fair, this gorgeous, pouting, phew what a scorcher… where was I?

Oh yes, I must now turn to the disagreeable matter of Mr Kurtha, the chief liar for the defence. Mr Kurtha, you will remember, admits to being colour blind. I have no hesitation in telling you that I am not. I see that Mr Kurtha is neither grey, nor green, nor even blue. He is brown – which I think is all we need to know about the reliability of his evidence.

I need hardly remind you that the editor of the Daily Smut has, very wisely in my view, decided to remain as silent as the grave. That is his legal right, and you must read nothing into his silence beyond the fact that he is obviously a shifty little fellow who's got something to hide.

So remembering these people – and also the delightful members of the upper-middle classes that have come before us in the witness box – you must consider the sum of money to be awarded to Mr Archer when you find him innocent. It is not within my powers to advise you on this, but about half a million should do it I would say, would you?

BEARDIE BUSINESSMAN and self-promotion specialist Richard Branson failed in his latest record-breaking attempt to cross the Atlantic by balloon.

"It's always dangerous putting a prick in a balloon"

PRESIDENT REAGAN CLAIMED not to remember being told details of a plot by his officials to secretly sell arms to Iran and use the proceeds to fund Contra rebels in Nicaragua.

Worried about Memory Loss?

Improve your powers to forget

More and more people are finding that they have things they want to forget – like the fact that they once sold arms to Iran and smuggled the money to a lot of Nicaraguan bandits who are up to no good in the jungle.

Now, at last – thanks to a new technique developed in America – you too can learn to forget instantly all those inconvenient little details that keep you awake at night and get you impeached.

"I owe everything to this wonderful technique", says R.R. of Washington DC. "What's it called again?"

TWO OVER-ENTHUSIASTIC paediatricians diagnosed 121 children in Cleveland as sexual abuse victims, causing them all to be removed from their families by social services and, when local children's homes ran out of space, housed in a hospital ward.

Mystery of missing children

Thousands of anxious parents this afternoon besieged the Hamelin Town Hall demanding the return of their children, who were last seen disappearing over the horizon with Dr Piper, a social worker specialising in child abuse.

One parent said, "It is true that we requested Mayor Heineken to rid the town of the plague of child abuse, but he had no right to appoint a so-called Pied Piper to abduct thousands of our children."

Last night, a plainly upset Mayor Heineken blamed the well-known old crone of Cheildlein, Frau Enid Rantzen, for hypnotising the townspeople into believing they were all molesting their children.

"BLACK MONDAY" saw a massive global stock market crash, just three days after a hurricane devastated Southern England.

LORD GNOME APPEAL
Plant a Yuppie Week

As Britain recovers from the worst-ever storm since records were kept, we see a land in which thousands of Yuppies have been uprooted, blown over and are now lying tragically on their backs, waiting to be cleared away.

We have all seen pictures of the appalling scenes in Threadneedle Street where some of Britain's finest men in suits, some as old as 23, were blown out of their minds and crashed down onto Porsches and empty champagne bottles.

In some cases it will take hundreds of years before we can look forward to seeing a new generation of overpaid prats towering above their VDUs, their arms waving gently in the air conditioning, their braces glistening scarlet and gold in the afternoon sunshine.

Now Lord Gnome is appealing to you to play your part in this great act of national regeneration.

- Just £100,000 is enough to fill the filofaxes which will enable ten Yuppies to grow their investment portfolios.
- £1 million is enough to set one Yuppie back on his feet in the style to which he has become accustomed
- £100 million will be stolen by Ernest Saunders and spent on Guinness shares

Send Cash now to the Lord Gnome 'Plant a Yuppie' Appeal, c/o E.Strobes, pp Lord Gnome, the Window Ledge, 14th Floor, Gnome House

"I told you never to ring me at the office!"

THE GOVERNMENT CONTINUED to humiliate itself through various international courts over Peter Wright's *Spycatcher*.

EXCLUSIVE EYE OFFER
Buy the book that no one else dares to print

Eye Catcher
by Peter Wrightwingloony

The inside story of how Britain's intelligence community set out to "destablise" a Prime Minister – by making her appear a complete idiot all over the world.
WARNING: you must take this book to Scotland before you are allowed to read it.

THE SDP-LIBERAL Alliance fell apart spectacularly.

Steel and Owen kiss and make up

Former Alliance partners David Steel and David Owen met yesterday for what a spokesman described as "a really

friendly and even affectionate lunch between two old friends". Both men were apparently confident they had "made their point" during the full and frank exchange of soup and bread rolls.

As the two men left, they smiled to reporters. A relaxed and beaming Dr Owen said, "I hope that's the last time I ever have to sit in the same room as that slimy little creep Steel." Mr Steel, plainly delighted by the outcome of the meeting, told newsmen, "Thank God we've got rid of that arrogant, big-headed, self-seeking twit, so that I can be the leader."

A HORRIFIC FIRE BROKE OUT in King's Cross Underground station in London in which 31 died. Management did everything they could to deflect the blame.

Smoker to blame for King's Cross blaze

Newly discovered evidence points to a smoker being to blame for Britain's worst peace-time disaster since the sinking of the *Lusitania*. An LRT spokesman said last night, "All our thinking so far is pointing to a cigarette as the cause of this terrible tragedy. Wild talk about out-of-date machinery, understaffing and inadequate safety precautions is just a smokescreen.

"We are almost 100% certain that the disaster was caused solely by an anonymous smoker who blatantly defied our regulations by discarding his cigarette onto a pile of petrol-soaked rags next to a ton of garbage on a wooden escalator... whoops – that last bit was off the record."

When asked for evidence, the spokesman stated that he could not discuss it as the whole matter was sub judice owing to the official inquiry, and would remain so until everyone had forgotten about it.

THERE WERE RUMOURS of problems in a royal marriage.

"They're so life-like – the way they don't talk to each other"

DECEMBER SAW PRESIDENT REAGAN and Soviet leader Gorbachev sign a historic treaty to reduce the number of nuclear missiles they both held.

Peace on Earth – It's official!

Astonishing scenes have been unfolding in Washington since the first sighting on Tuesday night of a "bright light" in the East, rapidly approaching Andrews Air Force Base. Millions of hacks who were peacefully tending their drinks by night rushed out to see this wonder that had come to pass.

And behold, there stepped forth from the Ilyushin 62 a shining figure, the Angel Gorbachev, and he saith unto them, "Fear not, for I bring you Glasnost of great joy, which shall be unto all nations."

And suddenly there was with the Archangel Mikhail a heavenly host of interpreters, arms experts and "cultural attachés" carrying sawn-off Kalashnikovs under their raincoats, singing "Peace on earth, goodwill to all men, glory to Gorb in the highest."

THE EYE KICKED OFF its coverage in May of a scandal that stretched on for decades.

Health Minister Norman Fowler has been insistent about the caring Conservatives' excellent record in combating AIDS. Regular announcements have been made about just how many millions are being spent on fighting the spread of the disease, treating more than 750 identified cases and improving public awareness. However Fowler, like his predecessors, conveniently ignores how the Thatcher government's refusal to spend money was a prime factor in more than a thousand British haemophiliacs being given the AIDS virus – courtesy of the NHS and contaminated American blood products Britain was not supposed to need. Indeed, Fowler recently argued against compensation to those haemophiliacs at risk through NHS treatment.

The human cost so far is that 23 haemophiliacs are dead and 100-200 could die. Yet most of those deaths could have been prevented. They died not through ignorance but ideology. Ironically, far from saving money – as was intended – the taxpayer has had to spend millions a year on imported blood products while waiting for the completion of a new blood products laboratory which will cost three times what was estimated in 1979.

Haemophiliacs require regular supplies of the blood clotting agent Factor 8 to prevent crippling bleeding incidents. In the early Seventies a form of concentrated Factor 8 became available, offering the opportunity of home treatment for the first time. However, while the National Blood Transfusion Service could ensure enough donors to provide the plasma from which Factor 8 is extracted, facilities for collecting the plasma and producing the concentrate were wholly inadequate. So in 1973 the NHS began importing Factor 8 from commercial blood products companies, mostly in the United States. It was very quickly realised, when the first outbreak occurred among British haemophiliacs a year later, that the US products unfortunately carried a high risk of hepatitis. This was inevitable as the plasma donors were mostly drug addicts, derelicts and the poor, drawn from the Skid Rows of American inner cities by the offer of a few dollars.

In 1975, the then Labour Health Minister Dr David Owen announced a £500,000 programme to achieve self-sufficiency and a safer Factor 8. But demand pushed well ahead of the target set – as had been predicted by those treating haemophiliacs, but ignored by the department of health and the NBTS. It became clear that the three existing English blood product laboratories were unable to cope with the burgeoning demand. By the time the first US AIDS case was diagnosed in 1978, Britain was still importing more than half its needs at a cost of over £1 million a year.

Conservative Health Minister Dr Gerard Vaughan's answer was privatisation. A British drug company should take over the production of blood products. This was swiftly abandoned amid howls of protest. The fast backpedalling Vaughan came up with an alternative which both suggested the government was tackling the problem while spending little: in 1980 he announced a £1.25 million improvement programme for the inadequate laboratory at Elstree which would double production of Factor 8. The target date for self-sufficiency was moved back to 1983.

To actually rebuild Elstree was now going to cost nearer £20 million, and there was no support from the Cabinet for such large-scale spending. It was not until 1982 that they agreed to a new facility – with self-sufficiency now promised for 1984. Meanwhile the first AIDS case had been reported in Britain three years earlier, and US doctors had long been warning of a new and deadly disease. The target was adjusted again a year later, to 1985 – but by then hundreds of haemophiliacs were already infected.

By 1985 imports were – as now – still accounting for 60% of Factor 8 supplies at a cost of £5 million a year. Now it was the turn of a new Health Minister, Kenneth Clarke, to make a prediction – he said 1987 would see Elstree in full production and self-sufficiency finally attained. Meanwhile, we continue to import Factor 8 from American companies who have had to recall batches because plasma donors have died of AIDS.

Elstree finally opened last month – at a total cost of £55 million. It will reach full production in summer 1988, the new date for that mythical target of self-sufficiency. Whether this forecast is any more correct than all the others remains to be seen. But for many haemophiliacs, it is already much too late.

A full public inquiry into the contaminated blood scandal finally opened in 2019, by which point it was estimated that 30,000 patients had been infected with HIV or hepatitis, and around 3,000 had died.

OCTOBER BROUGHT news from the inquests into the 193 people who died when the *Herald of Free Enterprise* ferry sank seven months earlier.

A majority of the bereaved families want to see the company which ran the ferry, Townsend Thoresen, and the Department of Transport brought to book. They are not impressed with the arguments of P&O chairman Sir Jeffrey Sterling that the doors of the ferry were meant to be closed and the fact they were open was all the fault of two or three members of the crew. The families' lawyers drew attention again and again to evidence from the Sheen Inquiry into the disaster that the company consistently ignored recommendations to make quite sure, by way of warning lights on the bridge etc, that the doors were shut on every voyage. The company designed the new class of ferry, with new doors which unlike the old doors, when open could not be seen from the bridge. More than one master made application to the company for a very cheap device which would warn the bridge if the doors were open. The company, to save time and a tiny amount of money, refused.

When Dover coroner Richard Sturt found that the company was "too remote" from the disaster to merit prosecution for manslaughter, the families' lawyers went at once to a judge in chambers to seek to get the ruling overthrown. The judge found for the coroner.

The jury were then faced with the coroner's direction that a verdict of "unlawful killing" would apply only to the crew members. They chose to bring the verdict in anyway, in the hope that the resulting confusion would result in the company being prosecuted. In this hope, they were at once party vindicated by a finding in the High Court by three judges that a company could, in certain circumstances, be found guilty of manslaughter.

This judgment led the National Union of Seamen and individual lawyers for the families to talk at once of private prosecutions of the company and its former directors. This in turn has led the company, advised by their former allies in the Department of Transport, to seek to challenge the "unlawful killing" verdict in the Divisional Court.

The terror for the company and the Department of a private prosecution is based on the fear that the families' lawyers will get their hands on all the evidence. At the Sheen Inquiry, and to a lesser extent at the inquest, the information about the disaster and the company's safety record was firmly controlled by the Department of Transport.

As the *Eye* has pointed out several times over the past few months, the company and their directors have for many years been hand in blouse with the Department. The giant cover-up which has taken place has been masterminded by the Department, with the full knowledge of Ministers. Questions were not properly put, let alone answered, at the Sheen Inquiry, because the counsel to the inquiry, the man in charge of what questions were asked, was briefed and paid by the Department of Transport.

P&O (as Townsend Thoresen had been rebranded) finally stood trial for manslaughter in 1990 along with three specific members of staff and four members of the *Herald*'s crew. The case collapsed and the judge directed the jury to find the company not guilty – but this led to changes in the law to allow prosecutions for corporate manslaughter.

SLICKER ISSUED an early warning in November.

There appears to be considerable interest all at once in the state of financial health at investment brokers Barlow Clowes & Partners, best known for its "tax efficient" dealings in Government stocks. Its particular wrinkle – a modern-day form of "dividend stripping" involving selling Gilts cum-dividend and thereby taking the payment as capital not income – was ironed out by a recent Finance Act change. However, it now seems that a number of official sources are eager to know more. No doubt any query, should one be made, can and will be dealt with to everyone's complete satisfaction.

Barlow Clowes collapsed in May the following year, leaving investors £170m out of pocket. In 1992, its fraudster founder Peter Clowes received a ten-year prison sentence for theft.

1988

THE MOBILE PHONE menace began.

Great Bores of Today

"…hello… hello… can you hear me? Is that you, Jenny? It's Ralph here… just to say I'm on the train and they've announced that it's running on time and it's due into Liverpool Street at 9.34 could you look on my desk and you'll find David Peebles' number he's due to meet me at the station outside the Sock Shop and let him know that we're running on time and I'll be there at 9.34 as agreed but if there is any hold-up later on I'll get back to you no messages? No I suppose it's a bit early if you want me you've got my number here haven't you? I'll be on the train at this number as I say…"

THE SAS SHOT dead three IRA men in Gibraltar, and the government immediately briefed that they had been planting a bomb – before changing their story.

I see rock shoot out

by LUNCHTIME O'BOOZE
(as told by the Ministry of Defence)

Today, in the quiet, sleepy sunlit streets of Old Gibraltar, I saw with my own eyes the MoD handout which spelt out the details of the amazing prevention of the world's greatest-ever atrocity by key members of Britain's crack STK (Shoot To Kill) Squad – motto: Who Dares Question Us?

Make no mistake, had this IRA "super-bomb" been detonated, it could have killed every man, woman and child for 50 miles around, not to mention the famous Barbary Apes which, according to ancient tradition, would have meant the end of the British Empire and indeed civilisation as we know it. The arrests, the successful defusing of the bomb and the fact that the entire terrorist gang are now in police custody and providing vital information on the inner workings of the IRA high command, means the brilliantly planned operation has been a complete success.

LATE NEWS: MoD sources have clarified that due to certain "gestures" made by the terrorists consistent with the unleashing of millions of killer bees which could have reduced Gibraltar to little more than a barren rock sticking up out of the sea, the only course of action open to the SAS had been to shoot three of the terrorists, let the fourth escape and forget that the bomb was actually 60 miles away in Marbella at the time.

NINE YEARS INTO her reign Mrs Thatcher was in no mood to listen to anyone.

Maggie plans reshuffle

The Prime Minister is believed to be planning a "major Cabinet reshuffle" to revitalise her government's lacklustre performance.

OUT will go Sir Geoffrey Howe, in the doghouse following his recent controversial "101 percent loyalty" to Mrs Thatcher. In his place as Foreign Secretary, Mrs Thatcher intends to install newcomer Mrs Margaret Thatcher.

OUT will go rebellious Chancellor Nigel Lawson, who angered the Prime Minister with his notorious "God bless you, ma'am" speech. In his place, the Prime Minister will become her own Chancellor. Mrs Thatcher is also expected to sack Nicholas Ridley, John Moore, Kenneth Baker and all other ministers, on the grounds that she is "far better equipped to carry out their jobs than they are".

MICHAEL JACKSON arrived to tour the UK, looking less like himself than ever.

"Frankly, Michael, I think it's possible to take cosmetic surgery too far"

RUPERT MURDOCH ANNOUNCED that he would launch Sky TV on the Astra satellite service, alongside various enticingly unregulated broadcasts from the Germany, Scandanavia and the Netherlands.

How it works

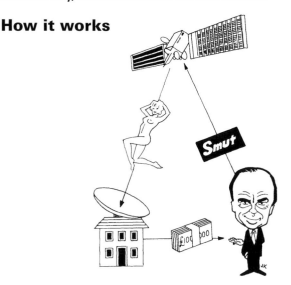

IN A SPEECH IN BRUGES, Mrs Thatcher came out decisively against the prospect of a federal Europe that had been suggested by European Commission President Jacques Delors.

10 Downing Street
Whitehall

Dear Bill,

Boss is at present on the warpath against the U.S. of E. Little Mr Tinker Bell is of the opinion that there are a good many votes to be had out of hammering the Frog, apart from which one whiskery little onion seller, Monsieur Zut Alors, has got up her nose in a big way by calling for an end to all customs barriers and full integration under Brussels by 1992. Understandably, M. feels this would do her out of a job.

I was with the Boss when Sir Alastair B. announced it on *News at Ten*, and I have seldom seen her so enraged. "How dare this snivelling Bolshevik interfere in our affairs?" she carolled, absent-mindedly emptying a largish brownie which I had poured out for myself. "We did not fight in two world wars to be dictated to!" A strange light came into her eyes, and with a sinking feeling I recognised that another Crusade was about to be launched.

The following morning Greaser Hurd hit the doormat at sparrowfart and was informed in no uncertain terms that he was outraged about the proposed abolition of frontiers. How did these Europeans think, Margaret demanded, that we could arrest IRA terrorists if there were no international barriers? It was on my lips to point out that such

international barriers didn't seem to have made a blind bit of difference when it came to rubbing out the Bogtrotter, but I could see Hurd putting on his concerned look and nodding his head like a dog in the back of a car. Lord knows where this one's going to end.

Yours in the tin helmet,
Denis

NEIL KINNOCK attempted to pivot the Labour party in a more electable direction.

The Labour Party – An Apology

In a number of statements over the years Mr Neil Kinnock may have inadvertently given the impression that he was in some way in favour of nuclear disarmament.

At the time the statements were made Mr Kinnock considered that there was no way forward and that the chances of his winning the elections were very slight. However, in the light of recent international developments and opinion polls, he would therefore like to make it abundantly clear that everything he has said in the past is to be completely dismissed, and he apologises for any inconvenience caused to voters.

N. Kinnock (on behalf of himself), Walworth Road.
LABOUR – LET'S NUKE 'EM NOW!

FLAMBOYANT JUNIOR health minister Edwina Currie was forced to resign after collapsing the chicken farming industry by incorrectly telling the public most eggs were affected by salmonella.

THE HOME SECRETARY banned broadcasters from airing the voices of Sinn Fein leaders such as Gerry Adams, as well as leaders of ten other republican and loyalist organisations believed to support terrorism.

News at Ten

BONG...

Sir Alastair Brunette: Douglas Hurd cracks down on an organisation we cannot name.

BONG...

Millions of Republicans dance in Belfast Streets.

BONG...

And we have an exclusive interview with a bearded man whose initials are G.A. which we are not allowed to show you.

(Shot of man in glasses being pushed onto doorstep at Number 10)

Hurd: What I have been told to say is that we are absolutely fed up with you-know-who getting all this publicity on the television, and the Prime Minister is absolutely determined that these chaps must never be mentioned again.

(Film of man with beard making speech)

Brunette: We are not allowed to show you what this man with a beard is saying, but he is saying that he is delighted with the huge propaganda victory handed to him on a plate by the government and is available to do interviews with American media teams for the rest of the year.

(Sound of bomb exploding off camera)

Sir Sandy Gall: And we're just getting news of a huge explosion in Central London. Some people we are not allowed to mention have claimed responsibility. We will keep you informed of any further developments, though not of course saying what they are.

A BUBBLE was swelling in the housing market.

IN MARCH, THE EYE had news of the criminal trials resulting from the Guinness share-trading fraud.

The news that Christopher Buckley, a prominent and independent Manchester lawyer, is to represent Ernest Saunders, former chairman of Guinness, charged with various crimes including theft, has sent a shiver down the backs of all sorts of blue-bloods in the City. Mr Saunders, shocked at his legal bill, is now said to be "cutting up rough".

The fear in the City has always been that instead of pleading innocent or apologising and hoping for what is known as a Collier sentence (re Geoffrey Collier, the master swindler from Morgan Grenfell who got off with a measly fine) Saunders might suddenly "do a Maundy". This expression refers to the late Maundy Gregory who sold honours mainly to rich Liberals. When he was found out and charged he threatened to spill the beans on his famous clients. The result was aristocratic panic, a word in the magistrate's ear, a guilty plea, a three months' sentence, six weeks in prison and a hefty pension for life paid through a secret account in Switzerland, provided Gregory kept out of the country and his mouth shut.

If Ernest Saunders "does a Maundy" there are fears that he may be naming names which will not only affect some very famous stockbrokers in the City, but might reach higher still, indeed into Downing Street itself.

Saunders received a five-year sentence for theft and false accounting in 1990, but this was halved on appeal after he was diagnosed with "pre-senile Alzheimers" – a condition from which he amazingly made a full recovery after being released from prison, and returned to a business career.

THE SAME MONTH brought details of the extraordinary lengths Robert Maxwell was going to, to prevent an accurate biography of him being published.

For several months Maxwell has been anxious about the contents of *Maxwell, the Outsider* by BBC journalist Tom Bower. Just after midnight on Tuesday 22 February, publisher Aurum Press was put on notice by Maxwell's solicitor Lord Mishcon that his client would be seeking an injunction on the Friday to prevent the *Sunday Times* from publishing the serialisation. The application was formally withdrawn within a couple of hours. Booktrade weekly *Publishing News* printed a spineless apology which was reported in Maxwell's *Daily Mirror*, claiming that in an interview Bower had accused Maxwell of "intimidation" – which he had not. This was the subject of a second libel writ issued by Bower against Maxwell (the first was over a letter Maxwell sent to Andrew Lloyd Webber, owner of Aurum, which he followed up with three disparaging items about Lloyd Webber in the *Sunday Mirror*). A third writ from Bower followed for calling him a "perjurer" on *Start the Week*.

On 1 March Bower and Aurum turned up at the High Court ready to answer Maxwell's charges of libel and breach of confidence. Maxwell's QC requested an adjournment until the following Monday because Bower's affadavit had given rise to 38 points that Maxwell intended to challenge: the following week he announced that he had decided to drop his application for an injunction, and there was therefore no need to discuss the 38 points.

In the meantime Maxwell had actively begun to intimidate booksellers across the country. He phoned the managing director of W.H. Smith, Simon Hornby, to tell him he would not renew Smith's contract to distribute the *Mirror Group* titles to newsagents if it sold *The Outsider*. Tim Waterstone has complained that Maxwell has been ringing him hourly and asking him why he wants to ruin a longstanding relationship, intimating that if he were to bring litigation against Waterstones it could jeopardise the company's public flotation scheduled for next year. As a result Waterstone is not only selling the offending book, but is refusing to deal with reps from Maxwell's Macdonald Futura for the time being.

THE EYE BEGAN POINTING OUT home truths about the Gibraltar shootings in May.

A simple point appears to have been overlooked in the volumes of controversy about the shootings in Gibraltar. The operation against the three IRA terrorists shot there could not have been an arrest operation, because the security services (including the SAS) have no powers of arrest.

In Gibraltar, the only people with a special power of arrest are the police. And the police didn't play a role in the shooting of the IRA three.

One might think that the current argument about whether there is an official "shoot-to-kill" policy would have taken place eight years go, after the Iranian embassy siege. But it didn't. This was mainly because, in all the jubilation at the successful rescue, no newspaper was unpatriotic enough to make anything of the fact that at least two terrorists had been killed by the SAS after they had thrown away their weapons and surrendered.

The point was briefly raised in the *Sunday Times*'s instant book on the siege, and just as briefly dismissed: "The soldiers were instilled with the conviction that even gunmen appearing to surrender could still detonate an explosion."

Eight years later, exactly the same argument is being trotted out again.

IN JUNE, SLICKER had some observations about the winding-up of Barlow Clowes.

For years now, stretching back to the 70s, the ever-sleeping, rubber-toothed watchdogs of the Department of Trade and Industry have shown no enthusiasm for using the increasing regulatory and investigatory powers given to them in successive Companies Acts. Those in charge of the DTI's supervisory functions have always preferred to rely on that good old Civil Service motto: better no action than a wrong action.

The luckless clients of Barlow Clowes, who have lost at least £138 million, are not the only ones who have paid the price of that spineless policy. When confronted by such devious or veteran con-artists as Alex Herbage of Caprimex (now in jail in Florida after defrauding more than £20 million); Neal Bruckman of Trafalgar Capital (in jail in Massachusetts but not for costing investors over here £2 million); Chandler Singh of Ravendale (still alive and well and living in Britain despite costing investors more than £1 million); and Robert Doorn of Signal Life (long gone with £7 million), the DTI response was always to do nothing until it was too late. It was not prepared to take away licences, fearing a successful legal challenge. Always, despite complaints from investors, information from other law enforcement or regulatory agencies or warnings in press publicity, any of which might have prompted intervention, the Department of Temerity and Inaction has preferred to sit on its hands while the fraudsmen made off with the public's money.

Hiding behind a variety of legalistic excuses such as "insufficient evidence" (they always want to find the conman not just with his hands in the till, but to ensure he is taking the money out not putting it back) or lack of jurisdiction, the DTI has singularly failed to prevent one major fraud in the past decade.

In December 1989 the government confirmed that "the regulatory machinery was inadequate" and announced it would be making "substantial ex gratia payments to all investors who have suffered loss" after the DTI was proved to have ignored a number of warnings that Barlow Clowes was dodgy.

IN AUGUST, HOWEVER, Slicker was able to provide details of one thorough inquiry that the DTI had completed.

All at once, from those who rushed to support the Harrods Pharaoh Mohamed Fayed – mostly in return for large fees and generous hospitality – can be heard if not the sound of silence then the sounds of doors being locked and faint footsteps disappearing down the corridors of power. The cause of all this activity? The forecast imminent report from the DTI on how the Pharaoh and his brothers came to own House of Fraser and thereby Harrods in 1985 and the truth behind the claim that they merely withdrew £615 million in cash from the "several billions" (Kleinwort Benson copyright) in their Swiss piggy-bank, the product of one of Egypt's oldest family fortunes.

Just how and where the £615 million came from – one favourite theory is a back-to-back loan perhaps facilitated by a power of attorney from the Sultan of Brunei and then refinanced using Harrods as security – is still not clear. What is clear is that there was never any fabled Fayed family fortune built up by fathers or grandfathers. Those who knew the Fayeds and their civil servant father have buried that myth.

The scathing report confirming this was not released for a further 18 months, and Fayed spent a further four years going all the way to the European Court of Human Rights attempting to get it overturned – yet more evidence of the DTI inspectors' conclusion that he was determined to "create a new fact: that lies were the truth and that the truth was a lie".

SOME INCONVENIENT TRUTHS that ought to have come out at the Gibraltar shootings inquest were pointed out by the *Eye* in October.

For days after the shooting, and indeed for most of the spring and summer, the MoD in Britain and the police and security services in Spain were all assiduously spreading the story that Farrell, McCann and Savage were tracked by the Spanish police from the moment they landed at Malaga airport right up to the point where they drove up to the frontier at Gibraltar. Countless newspaper and television reports, all springing from "official briefings", said so. Senor Augustin Valladolid, a spokesman for the Spanish intelligence service, gave a 90-minute briefing to Thames Television before their programme *Death on the Rock* was made, telling them the police followed the terrorists' car right up to the frontier. In Britain journalists known to be friendly, to the army were given special briefings at the MoD's public relations department, repeating the fact that the Spanish police never lost the three suspects from the moment they landed in Malaga.

As the SAS gunmen were prepared for the inquest, however, a dreadful thought occurred to their superiors: if the car had been tracked to the border, why were the three suspects not arrested there? Why were they allowed to drive their car, which might have contained a bomb, right into the heart of Gibraltar? What possible reason could there have been, unless the whole operation was indeed a trap?

And if it was a trap, might not an inquest jury decide that the plan was to allow the three onto the Rock in a car which everyone knew contained no explosives at all, and shoot them down?

The entire story was suddenly and inexplicably changed. By the time the soldiers came to the inquest, the "tracking to the border" had never happened! The MI5 officer in charge of the operation solemnly told the coroner that the Spanish police had "lost" the terrorists somewhere outside Malaga, and the car wasn't identified until it was seen in the square on the Rock. This was dutifully confirmed by a senior officer from the Gibraltar police.

What had the Spanish police to say about this sudden and unheralded attack on their competence? For a time it was put about that the Spanish police and intelligence services, nobly brushing aside their historic hostility to British jurisdiction on the Rock of Gibraltar, would appear before the coroner to clear the whole matter up.

In the middle of the inquest, on 22-24 September, Prime Minister Thatcher went on an official visit to Spain. She spent a long evening in private discussions with Spanish Premier Gonzalez, which was described as "very successful".

From that time on, it was suddenly clear that the Spanish police would not appear. No evidence was given from Spain to confirm the astonishing new news that the police had "lost" the terrorists. All that was left was for the government press to tell exactly the opposite story to the one they told their readers at the time, which they dutifully did.

1989

A DEADLY THREE-TRAIN pile-up in Clapham Junction, the downing of a Pan Am jumbo jet over Lockerbie and another plane crash on the M1 kept a suddenly hyper-sympathetic Mrs Thatcher busy.

A FORMER LIVING GOD became a formerly living man.

Haiku Corner

In Memoriam Emperor Hirohito

Ah so.
Farewell then
Emperor Hirohito.

E.J. Thribb (17½ syllables)

THE AYATOLLAH KHOMEINI issued a fatwa calling for the killing of Salman Rushdie and anyone involved in the publication of his book *The Satanic Verses*, which he described as "against Islam", and a $1 million bounty was put on the author's head.

Million$ to be won!

In the Greatest Giveaway Game of All Time
Some of the greatest cash prizes ever have been offered by various bearded Iranian loonies in the world's first religious bingo game.
TOP PRIZE
● $3,400,000 offered by Ayatollah Khomenei of Tehran to the first Muslim who manages to "cast utterly into hell and outer darkness the vile infidel dog Salmonella Rushton"
2ND PRIZE (open to non-Muslims)
● $1,000,000 offered by Ayalottah Khomoney for anyone in the world who manages to "remove from the face of the earth the blaspheming bastard Solomon Grundie". Plus a holiday for two in the mosque of your choice.
BECOME A MULLAHIONAIRE!!

96 FOOTBALL FANS were crushed to death at Hillsborough stadium during a match between Liverpool and Nottingham Forest, and the police (helped by politicians and the tabloids) immediately started trying to deflect the blame for their failure to control the crowd.

'No comment' – Knacker spells it out

A plainly furious Inspector Knacker last night refused to comment on allegations that the police had been "massively incompetent" in handling the events surrounding the Hillsborough disaster.

"Owing to the fact that a bona fide and top-level judicial inquiry has been appointed to look into these matters, it would be entirely inappropriate for me to make any comment whatsoever on these allegations.

"However," he continued, "if you was to pop round the back and have a word with some of my lads who were actually present at home watching television when these incidents occurred, you might find a number of stories about the way these drunken animals from Liverpool indulged in an orgy of urinating and mass rape which would make a good headline for your Page One and might take a bit of the heat off my good self while I try to think up a plausible alibi for the inquest."

SUN EDITOR Kelvin MacKenzie rode out the storm over his front page headlined "THE TRUTH", which contained the exact opposite.

Gnome

It is with great pleasure that I announce the first findings of the *Daily Gnome* Ombudsman, or "Gnombudsman", a totally independent arbiter of the paper's behaviour who as such is paid by myself. He has found that my paper's coverage of the Hillsborough disaster was "inaccurate" and has ruled that the headline "DRUG-CRAZED SCOUSE THUGS MURDERED BABIES" was "unacceptable".

I readily admit that the *Daily Gnome* was in error. It was a terrible error to offend people in Liverpool and thus lose 40 percent of our sales there.

E. Strobes
pp Lord Gnome

THE SITES OF BOTH the Rose and Globe Theatres were uncovered during building works in London.

Rose Theatre – what the tourists will see

Shakespeare's toilet

Prob. Royal Box as used by Q. Elizabeth

Shakespeare's dressing room (prob.)

Bones of Shakespeare's pet gerbil found here

Steps to balcony (as used in 1st perf. of *Romeo and Juliet*)

Site of desk where Shakespeare wrote *Hamlet* (prob.)

Part of Shakespeare's toothbrush found here

Roman bath (as used by Shakespeare)

THE CHINESE GOVERNMENT declared martial law in Beijing and sent troops in to massacre student protesters in Tiananmen Square.

TALES FROM THE WATER MARGIN NO.94

The Wise Emperor and the Foolish Students

(as read out twelve times every hour on Chinese television)

Once there was a very wise and popular Emperor called Deng Xiaoping. He was much loved by the people and his only concern was for their good.

But one day some foolish students, who knew nothing of the realities of life, gathered in the great square and began to plot how the Emperor could be overthrown.

For a long time the Emperor was patient. But then the students grew angry and armed themselves with thousands of tanks and millions of rifles. So the wise and kindly Emperor decided to send in his loyal guards to tell the students to return peacefully to their homes.

But the counter-revolutionaries now had evil in their hearts, and when the peace-loving, unarmed guards of the 27th Army approached with flowers in their hands, the students attacked them furiously. At the end of the massacre, thousands of innocent people lay dead in the square.

Confronted with the sight of what they had done, the foreign devils and their Taiwanese running-dogs were deeply ashamed and realised that they had committed a terrible crime against the Emperor and the people of China. Some of them queued up, begging to be shot. Others went to the nearest police station and beat themselves up. Still others ran away to Hong Kong and we are still looking for them.

Thus did the wise Emperor Deng restore peace, harmony and tranquillity to his people.

A RESHUFFLE BROUGHT a relative unknown into the cabinet.

Man in the *Eye* – Ron Major

by BRUCE ANDERSON and many other hacks

Who is he, this fast-rising white hope of Thatcherism whom few people have heard of and no one has ever met? A week ago no one knew who he was, not even his wife, if he has one, which we have not managed to discover. Now, however, he is recognised as the unmistakable heir-apparent to Mrs Thatcher.

Although Major failed to gain any GCSEs at his South London comprehensive, he is widely acknowledged to be one of the most intelligent men in politics today. Although he has never travelled abroad, friends say that his knowledge of international relations is profound and wide ranging. And although he is a poor speaker who has made little or no impact on the House of Commons, his fellow MPs have a deep respect for his debating skills and his power as an orator.

Although Major is terrifically boring and insignificant, he is a close friend of Mrs Thatcher and will do everything she says.

THE NEWLY-MERGED Social and Liberal Democratic Party decided that wasn't a very good name after all.

SLD name change

Paddy Ashdown in his keynote conference speech to SLD delegates has announced a dramatic name change.

Following pressure from grass-roots opinion he will from now on be known as "David Owen".

PRINCESS ANNE and Captain Mark Phillips began a new royal tradition by announcing their marriage was over.

THE COMMUNIST REGIMES of Eastern Europe were beginning to collapse, despite the fervent support of one businessman and newspaper proprietor.

MIRROR EXCLUSIVE

Erich Honecker interviews Robert Maxwell

Yesterday I was privileged to be the only East European leader to be granted an exclusive interview with the most hated man in Britain, Robert Maxwell.

In the past few weeks the world has heard reports that Maxwell is deeply sick, as he presides over a fast-crumbling empire. The world has been shocked by the spectacle of hundreds of journalists and printers desperately fleeing from the horrors of Maxwell's despotic regime.

I asked him why so many people in the West describe his regime as "the last bastion of Stalinism".

"These claims are only malicious inventions by my capitalist enemies," he beamed. "My employees enjoy complete freedom to write whatever I tell them. And many of them enjoy a very high standard of living, considering how badly paid they are."

THE BERLIN WALL came down.

With Dave Spart, co-chair of the Tufnell Park Homeless Against Poll Tax Group and Editor of the Chuter Ede Estate Community Action Newsletter.

This week: the end of the Cold War

Once again it is totally sickening to read the capitalist media indulging in an orgy of triumphant self-congratulation on the so-called "death of Communism" i.e. the collapse of the Berlin Wall and the other alleged reform movements in the Eastern Bloc i.e. Prague, Warsaw, er... what the masses are really demanding has been totally and unequivocally obscured and distorted by the delusions of euphoria generated by the broadcasting monopolies of the so-called free world – viz. the people on the streets are celebrating the return to the real values of Marxist-Leninism and far from being an end to the socialist struggle it is on the contrary a new victory for the proletariat and for the revolutionary ideals espoused by generations of the international brotherhood of workers and a total and utter defeat for the forces of reactionary bourgeois Thatcherite-Gorbachevism and moreover *(cont. p94)*

NEW SECURITY GATES were put up in Downing Street just in time for chancellor Nigel Lawson to storm out through them.

10 Downing Street
Whitehall

Dear Bill,

I don't know if you saw but the latest thing is that they are going to put up iron railings at the bottom of Downing Street to keep out the Provos. I said what about bona fide travellers trying to get in at night time after important board meetings at the club and wasn't it a bit much, at my time of life, to have to risk life and limb clambering over spiky railings in the middle of the night?

Poor Fatty next door has finally got his comeuppance. Do you remember the American with the tartan suitcases, used to work upstairs with the Boss, name of Walters? She's got him back. Come tincture time she hammers on the wall, bellowing for the Chancellor, and our Nige comes puffing in looking very out of condition. "Ah dear Nigel, of course you remember Professor Whatnot," she said with icy composure, "he is here to lend you a hand with the figures. He will have a desk in your office until further notice."

Fatso protested – "We seem to be ticking over quite nicely, thank you: besides, if we joined the EMS as I myself have always counselled...", at which point the Professor started to cackle and Krakatoa erupted. I thought it best to absent myself to Boris's staff rest room, but you can hear everything surprisingly well from there and the ensuing row carried on all the way down the stairs, the Boss snapping off banisters in her fury as she went, Lawson spouting off that "either the Yankee streak of piss goes or I go" until finally I heard the front door slam and that was that.

I thought it best to lie doggo with a bottle or two of Boris's Buffalo grass Vodka, but when I came round the Boss was clearly back on a high. "There you are, Denis! Well, all that's settled. We are well rid of him. John Major has been aching to take the controls, Douglas has dreamed of the FO since he was in short trousers, I can't remember who we've got at the Home Office, but I'm told he's a safe pair of hands. It is time to close ranks and turn victory into defeat. I mean the other way round."

Could you get on to Maurice's Gentle Gorilla Removal firm to see if they might ferry our kit down to Dulwich at fairly short notice?

Yours behind bars, Denis

COMEDIAN KEN DODD was acquitted of tax evasion.

In the Courts

Regina vs Dodd

Mr George Carperson QC *(for the defence)*: Mr Dodd, is it not true that you have led a troubled and lonely life with pound notes as your only companions?

Dodd *(weeping)*: Yes, it is true, Your Honour. There were times when I have been tempted to do away with it all, or at least move it all to the Isle of Man. Sometimes the sheer weight of the money I put in suitcases puts a strain on my heart. I am just a humble comedian who tries to bring a smile to people's faces to show them how tattifilarious life can be.

Mr Justice Cocklecarrot: What is "tattifilarious"?

Carperson: M'Lud, it is an example of my client's surreal use of the English language in the manner of Lewis Carroll and Margaret Thatcher. It has no precise meaning.

(Ticklesticks were then passed to the jury for forensic examination. Case continues.)

"STALKING HORSE" candidate Sir Anthony Meyer stood against Mrs Thatcher for the Conservative leadership, giving 60 MPs the chance to express their dissatisfaction by not voting for her.

Gnome's Man of the Year poll

Readers are invited to vote as usual for the 1989 Man of the Year.

They can choose from any of the following candidates:

SIR ANTHONY MEYER ☐

The Ghastly Woman of the Year Award has already been decided.

THE GUILDFORD FOUR were freed from prison after the court of appeal overturned their convictions for IRA pub bombings 14 years earlier, ruling they had been based on police fabrications and concocted confessions.

JAMES STIRLING'S "post-modern" design for Number 1, Poultry, a City of London site being controversially developed by Peter Palumbo, was the latest modern building to betray a particular inspiration.

"You're right! It is Lego"

WHEN MUCH OF THE DAMNING DTI report on the Fayeds' takeover of Harrods was leaked and published in a special mid-week edition of the *Observer*, the paper owned by their rival Tiny Rowland, Slicker drew some of the conclusions the inspectors appeared unwilling to.

The one major question in the Harrods affair that still remains unanswered is where Mohamed Fayed obtained the £570 million to buy House of Fraser. But a number of coincidences point to the Sultan of Brunei either knowingly, or more likely not, being the source.

Prior to 1984, the Phoney Pharaoh had no access to personal wealth on three-figure millions scale. During that year he made contact with the sultan, possibly the world's richest man. In August 1984, Fayed visited Brunei to see the Sultan. As a result of that visit he received at least two powers of attorney from the Sultan. And soon after that visit several hundred million dollars were transferred into Fayed accounts at the Royal Bank of Scotland in London and a Swiss bank in Geneva.

Fayed presented himself to Kleinworts and Mrs Thatcher as the Sultan's advisor. He later bragged in a taped 1985 conversation that he controlled up to $1 billion of the Sultan's money. After the Sultan revoked all the powers of attorney in April 1985, Fayed was not in possession of such funds again. So much so that HoF has borrowed more than £850 million.

It is understood that the Sultan has been informed of the findings in the DTI report. His position all along, however, has been not to want to know.

APRIL SAW THE FIRST MENTION of bribery in the massive Al-Yamamah arms deals with Saudi Arabia.

Helmut Kohl is furious at the large amount in bribes the British Government has agreed to pay to certain Saudi princes. The West Germans were reported to be "horrified" by the unusually large percentages which were asked for by the princes, and even more horrified when the British agreed to raise them a little if they could be promised the lion's share of the deal.

Ever since they discovered how much (or nearly how much – the exact percentage in personal bribes is masked in a complicated arms-for-oil deal), Germans have been increasing their government contribution to the contract, thus infuriating Mrs Thatcher. If the British have to pay anything like the same amount it will cost them several billions extra.

The Germans are starting to leak strange stories about the bank accounts of some of the latest additions on board the Saudi king's gravy train, some of whom have started to buy up suitable residences in London and the Home Counties – their new homes are all part of the service.

A Serious Fraud Office investigation into the Al-Yamamah deals was finally opened in 2003, but shut down by Tony Blair's government three years later on the grounds that "our relationship with Saudi Arabia is vitally important and that strategic interest comes first".

OCTOBER BROUGHT DETAILS of where Jeffrey Archer drew his literary inspiration from.

Six years ago Archer judged a short story competition run by a local magazine in Cambridge, to which Kathleen Burnett submitted an entry. Her story was narrated – or so it seemed – by a woman waking up in the morning, thinking about breakfast, discussing the other members of the household and musing about her love life. In the last line came the twist: the narrator was really a domestic cat.

Archer was bowled over by this simple tale and unhesitatingly awarded it the first prize. It was rare to find an author with such "a genuinely original idea", the great man gushed. He told her afterwards that he intended to put together a collection of short stories, and he would get in touch to discuss the possibility of including it in the book.

And that was that – until earlier this year, when Kathleen Burnett happened to read Jeffrey Archer's recently published collection of his short stories, *A Twist in the Tale*. One tale in particular caught her attention: it was narrated, or so it seemed, by a woman waking up in the morning, thinking about breakfast etc. etc. until, in the last line, she is revealed to be – surprise! – a cat.

Following a lengthy correspondence with Archer's publishers Hodder & Stoughton, she threatened to tell the press about the author's perfidy unless he agreed to pay her a share of his royalties for the story and acknowledge her by name in future editions of the book. This modest proposal brought a swift and menacing letter from the master storyteller's lawyer, Lord Mishcon. "The threat contained in your letters is most improper," thundered Mishcon. "Our client has no legal or moral obligation to you whatsoever."

Archer later denied that this was plagiarism, saying that only consisted of "when you write out line after line after line". He was also accused of stealing another of the stories in the collection from a Nigerian author who had sent him a copy of his own book.

1990s

AT THE START OF THE NINETIES, IT HAD BECOME quite hard to imagine a world without Mrs Thatcher. But by that November her own party had done what the opposition never managed and booted her out of Downing Street. John Major took the helm, managed quite unexpectedly to win an election of his own, and then oversaw an excruciatingly drawn-out decline as his party trashed their reputation for fiscal competence in the course of a single Wednesday, trashed one another over Europe, and gradually collapsed into a morass of ministerial corruption and marital incontinence. From all this, the *Eye*'s jokewriting gang – Ian Hislop, Nick Newman, Richard Ingrams, Christopher Booker and Barry Fantoni – spun another rich comic creation, the point-missing and gloriously ineffective secret diarist who would remain in place for what now seems an incomprehensible six and a half years.

The back of the magazine was beefed up by the full-time return of Paul Foot after 21 years, while the opposite end upped its game too, with Francis Wheen beefing up coverage of politics and the media, the Rotten Boroughs column expanding to cover council corruption the length and breadth of the country and the recruitment of specialist columnists like rail specialist Dr B. Ching, TV reviewers Square Eyes and Remote Controller, and medical man Dr Phil "M.D." Hammond.

> " *What we are looking for in a Parliamentary Committee on Standards is commonsensical judgement. I remember a journalist telling me a few years ago that we did not need all the paraphernalia – we just needed to apply the Private Eye test: 'If it appeared in Private Eye, would you be embarrassed by it? If so, you should not be doing it in the first place'* "
>
> Charles Kennedy MP, 1997

Old *Eye* traditions were maintained when his column swiftly broke a major story, the Bristol heart surgery scandal, which was ignored for six long years until bursting into the national consciousness with a public inquiry.

By the time Captain Bob finally bobbed off into the sunset in 1991, the *Eye* had already identified its latest millionaire villain in the form of Mohamed "Al" Fayed, whose fantasising and priapism as the owner of Harrods was regularly chronicled from the beginning of the decade. Again, it took the rest of the world a while to catch up: first with his brown envelope bribes to government ministers, then his grassing them up when they failed to do his bidding, and finally with his cultivation of the Princess of Wales, now divorced from the heir to the throne but still just as keen on a free holiday. Her death in a car drunkenly driven by one of Fayed's staff in 1997, and its extraordinary aftermath, proved that the *Eye* had lost none of its ability to offend. Copies of the edition pointing out the hypocrisies of both the press who had pursued Diana and the public who had shown such an appetite for it were hoicked from shelves, even as the "respectful" rest of the press bayed for more royal blood. By that point it seemed almost inevitable that a reading at her funeral in Westminster Abbey should be hammily delivered by the man whom the *Eye* had consecrated four months previously as the Vicar of St Albion's.

1990

NELSON MANDELA was released from prison after 26 years.

All-day Panorama Special

Dimblebore *(for it is one of them)*: ...and the pictures we're seeing now live from Soweto and there you can see Paddy Ashdown... sorry... ah yes there they are in Soweto and we now have in the studio Mr Mbiki Mbutu.

(Elderly black man in suit)

Mr Mbutu, as someone who knew Nelson Mandela for five minutes in 1961, what do you think his feelings will be when he is released in what can only now be a matter of minutes... hold on, sorry... we're going back live to Capetown where something is happening, we think.

(Shot of man in shirtsleeves with moustache talking inaudibly into microphone as people in background wave flags and grin at camera giving clenched fist salutes)

Thank you, Kevin. And now as the release of Nelson Mandela becomes a reality, on this historic day when history is being made as Mr Nelson Mandela is released we can only guess what his emotions must be. Paddy Ashdown, you've never met him, what do you imagine Mr Mandela's feelings would be were he to meet you?

Paddy Ashdown: Good evening, I think it's too early...

Dimblebore: I'm sorry, I have to interrupt you there as we've got live pictures here of the jubilant scenes outside South Africa House in Trafalgar Square... *(continues on 94 channels)*

COMMUNIST STATES continued to crumble throughout Eastern Europe.

RIOTING INMATES took over Strangeways prison and protested on the roof.

A HUGE PROTEST in central London against the newly imposed Poll Tax descended into violence and looting.

Dave Spart, editor of the Prisoners Against the Poll Tax fact sheet, comments

As the Tory media sickeningly and predictably attack the working class for alleged acts of looting during the anti-poll tax Battle of Trafalgar it is totally predictable the way er... they totally ignore the identity of the real chief looter in our society, i.e. Mrs Thatcher, when you compare the amount of money she has looted from ordinary working class men and women already victims of the poverty trap created by high interest rates and police provocation, er... through privatisation of water, electricity, gas etc. it is obviously totally minimal when a handful of protesters vent their justified fury by kicking in the windows of the capitalist strongholds such as shops on Goodge Street selling Snoopy posters and

Garfield badges, small family-run newsagents, kebab houses etc. and removing goods which are rightly theirs, i.e. videos and that which have been made by the working classes and are therefore rightly their property er... as I say when you compare *(cont. p94)*

TO EVERYONE'S SURPRISE, Iraq invaded Kuwait, and the US and Britain were forced to rush around firming up alliances in the rest of the Gulf.

Yes! It's Gulf Crisis Rhyming Slang

F.O.	Didn't know
Kuwait	Too late
Saudi	Howdy!
Baghdad	Raving Mad
Quite Insane	Saddam Hussein
Moustache and Beret	Bonkers, very
Facial Hair	Germ warfare
Persian Gulf	Worse than Adolf
Massive army	Barmy
Jihad	Things look bad
George Bush	Big Push
F-111	Get to heaven
Peter Snow	'Ere we go

If anyone compares me to Hitler, I'll gas them

ARMCHAIR BELLIGERENCE was just one of the summer's crazes.

The Sun Says
Send in the Turtles!

We've all had enough of being pushed about by this jumped-up little Hitler in a tea-towel.

We say – give us another lager. We're dying of thirst in this heat.

The Teenage Mutant Hero Turtles are the most efficient fighting machine the world has ever seen.

We've paid for 'em. Now let's use 'em.

WAKE UP MAGGIE – IT'S COWABUNGA TIME!!!

ENGLAND WERE KNOCKED OUT of the World Cup, but a new national hero was created in the process.

Glenda Slagg
She's hotter than the Gulf!

◾ Gazza – aren'tchasickofhim?!?! Wherever you look there he is with his gappy teeth and his dopey grin!?!?? OK, so he cries??!! Who doesn't? I tell you, Mister, I cry out loud every time I hear his stoopid name?!?

Take a tip from Auntie Glenda, Cry-Baby Bunting – get yourself a seat on the subs' bench and stay there for the rest of the season?!? Gazzzzzzza (Geddit?!)

◾ Leave him alone!?!! Gazza, I'm talking about, stoopid!?! He's only a kid, for gawd's sake!!? So give him a break, and stop hypin' this handsome hero before it's too late!?! What he needs is time to grow up without the newspaper know-alls tellin' him how to live his life!?! Belt up, everyone, we've all heard enough about Gazza!!!?!

◾ Gazza?!?! About time he got himself a new dolly-bird!?! What's the matter, dearie – don't you like girls??! We'll be calling you Gayzza next!!?

◾ Gazza?!?!! *(We've had him – Ed)*

AT A SUMMIT in Dublin Mrs Thatcher continued to fulminate against European plans for a single currency, central bank and greater political union.

That Mitterand-Kohl plan for European political unity in full

1. Annoy Thatch
2. Er...
3. C'est ça.

IN AN ATTEMPT to disprove worries about BSE, or "Mad Cow Disease", agriculture minister John Gummer publicly fed his four-year-old daughter a beefburger.

MACHINE TOOLS FIRM Matrix Churchill was raided by Customs officers on suspicion of breaking an arms embargo on exports to Iraq – despite the deal having been nodded through by the government.

Gnome

Let me state categorically that my firm, Gnome International Scientific, Technical and Electronic But Definitely Not Military Supplies plc, has nothing to hide.

The export of a number of giant metal biros to Iraq in 1988 was passed by both the DTI and the Minister responsible, Mr Alan Sharke MP, with the words "Biros, that's a good one" – a reference to their desirability as trade items.

The biros, hollowed metal tubes 700 feet long with threaded barrels for the easy insertion of refills and a computer launch system for the blue ink, are one of Gnome International's standard lines.

I was personally told by the Iraqi education minister, General Madman Insein, that the biros would be used as educational aids in under-developed Kurdish-controlled villages.

E Strobes
pp Lord Gnome

GEOFFREY HOWE DRAMATICALLY resigned from the cabinet.

Dear Margaret,

It is with deep regret that I must inform you of my resignation. This unexpected news will no doubt prompt you to ask who I am. I am the one with glasses who sits next to you in Cabinet – or used to.

I have always been a great admirer of your strong leadership, philosophical vision and ability to sack people who disagree with you. Your failure to do so in my case has caused me considerable concern, indicating as it does that you have finally lost your grip.

It is for this reason that after sixteen years of careful consideration I have decided to walk out in a bate. The central issue as I see it is that of Britain's role in Europe, or to put it another way, my role in the Cabinet. I am in no sense a Euro-Federalist or a Brussels Idealist but I am getting on a bit and I do want to be Prime Minister.

I am therefore left with no honourable alternative but to stab you in the back and throw the party into chaos.

Elspeth wishes you all the best in your retirement.

Yours,

GEOFFREY

(The one with the glasses)

TO OUTRAGE from Mrs Thatcher's fans, Michael Heseltine challenged her for the leadership.

POOF
THIEF
MURDERER

These are three words, all of which can be found in a dictionary belonging to Michael Heseltine. Doesn't that say it all?

Adulterer, Arsonist, IRA Gunman. These are words you will find on other pages of today's *Sun*. The same newspaper that has a picture of Michael Heseltine on the front. How sickening!

ON OTHER PAGES
Why Gazza Backs Thazza: p14
Mrs Thatcher and Mother Teresa – 20 Things They Have in Common: p11

THE RULES OF the leadership contest were somewhat baffling.

"You need 65% of the sword to win outright, but 43% should see you through to the next round"

AND DESPITE AN EARLY SHOW of defiance following the results of the first round, the unthinkable happened.

Denmarg
Eventide Estate
Dulwich

Dear Bill,

Do thank Daphne for the floral tribute: don't tell her that they got sent to Number 11 by mistake. We only got them when little Norma Major crept in to ask if it was all right for her to measure up for their G-Plan.

I can't say the past few days have been entirely untraumatic. I finally bit the bullet and strolled into the mem's bedroom at two a.m. on the night of the first ballot to find the old girl three-quarters of the way through the Quart of Old Smuts 70-year-old South African Whisky Terreblanche gave me on my last trip, and gripping one of Carol's old rag dolls round the throat. "I fight on, I fight to win!" she was repeating in a low growl. "If I do not secure a majority at the second ballot, I shall at the third, and failing that, at the fourth!"

I coughed politely to indicate my presence and helped myself to a largeish measure of the good Terreblanche's electric soup. "Up to a point, old girl," I temporised, "but let us consider the Party's interest. Surely our watchword at this late hour must be screw Heseltine."

The boss winced at his name but did not interrupt, and allowed me to bring up the case of Barmy Winnifrith when he was under threat from the Golf Club Committee for excessive drinking at meetings of the Ways and Means Group. Sniffing which way the wind was blowing, he made an emotional speech announcing his resignation from a club of which he was not worthy to be a member, only for the rest of them to wake up the following morning feeling they'd been absolute swines and what would the club be without

Barmy prostrate on the floor every night. He was unanimously re-elected by way of making amends. Of course, four months later he burned the clubhouse down, but everyone agreed it was a good way to go.

M. had been listening to my tale with unwonted attention, and I could see I had planted a shrub in her mind which might bear fruit. Sure enough the following morning she announced that she was heaving in her clogs. To tell the truth it reminded me of the time we had to get Maurice sectioned after that episode at the Del Mar Pavilion. Same sudden unfocused look in his eyes after the little shrink gave him a shot of tranquiliser in the buttock and he agreed to come quietly after all.

Still, she did manage to get on the blower to every one of the backbenchers saying that unless they voted for Major she would see to it that they were deselected by their constituency parties, all of whom showed the loyalty they so signally lacked and would kill on her command. That did the trick and Wonderboy romped home in the Allcomers' Stakes.

So yours truly set to, carrying out eleven years' worth of empties from H.Q., and off we went. It's awfully quiet here. Do pop down and visit, but mind out for the metal teeth that pop up out of the drive if you get the gate code wrong – you may also find yourself surrounded by slavering police dogs and a chap pointing a gun at you.

Somehow I don't think I'm going to enjoy my retirement as much as I had anticipated.

Yours in limbo,
Denis

A NEW MAN – and, he was careful to assure everyone, his own man – took over in Number 10.

I sat at my desk and got to work with a vengeance! I moved all the biros into one jar, set the desk calendar to the right day and then I wondered what to do next. I decided to have a look at the papers to see what was happening. I was amazed to see how busy I'd been, though some of them were being quite rude about me. They said that when I'd chosen all the people in my cabinet, I'd forgotten to put in any women. Really they are so hypocritical. Last week they were all wanting to get rid of the only woman in the Cabinet. Honestly!

AT THE END OF JANUARY, the government admitted after 15 years of denials that Colin Wallace, dismissed as an army press officer for giving restricted information to a journalist, had actually been allowed to do so as part of his role. His dismissal – and his wrongful conviction for manslaughter – just happened to coincide with him attempting to blow the whistle on the cover-up of a paedophile scandal at Kincora Boys' Home in Northern Ireland.

The great mystery of the Colin Wallace affair is why the Ministry of Defence broke one of its oldest rules and admitted years of routine lying to the public.

Sir Michael Quinlan, stern moralistic Roman Catholic who recently took over as permanent secretary at the MoD, was shocked by the suggestion that men in his own ministry had deliberately sanctioned widespread child abuse just because Kincora's "housefather" and abuser-in-chief, William McGrath, was an intelligence agent. He ordered a very full inquiry into the whole Wallace affair, which forced rather shamefaced junior officials to produce the two documents which proved that at least six government ministers, the secretary of state for defence and the prime minister had been deceiving the Commons about Wallace for at least two years. It also proved that at least four top MoD people had known about the Kincora scandal and had done nothing to stop it.

Quinlan pushed for a full judicial inquiry, but faced cries of anguish about "security considerations" throughout Whitehall. Instead a compromise was hit on: the MoD agreed to set up a small inquiry into how Wallace was sacked in 1975, indicating that he may have been right when he said he was only doing his usual job passing on false information to journalists.

This compromise has brought on the government at least two weeks of constant hostile publicity and one of its worst setbacks in a decade. Now orders have gone out from no less a person than Sir Percy Cradock, "foreign affairs" (MI6) adviser to the prime minister, that no more concessions are to be made on this "damned business".

Private Eye has learned that at the MoD meeting which preceded the parliamentary answer on 30 January, a senior officer from GCHQ was called to attend. There can only be one reason for this, namely that at some stage in the story substantial government-sponsored surveillance – phone tapping – was used.

Increasingly, MoD civil servants are asking themselves why they should continue to cover up for MI5. They point out that the army itself comes out quite cleanly from Clockwork Orange, the dirty tricks campaign against politicians, and from Kincora. On the latter, it was actually the army who took the initiative to push the police into action, only to see it stopped because McGrath was passing on all sorts of information to MI5 about his friends in the ghastly sub-world of Protestant paramilitaries. And so boys in the care of Belfast local authority were raped and abused for 20 years without anyone in authority lifting a finger.

Wallace's conviction for killing his friend Jonathan Lewis was quashed by the Court of Appeal in 1996, after, in Paul Foot's words, "the prosecution abandoned almost every detail of the intricate case it put in 1981".

IN MAY, THE EYE'S new "Rotten Boroughs" page uncovered a scandal in Staffordshire children's homes.

Council leaders are being asked to investigate why bizarre Romanian torture practices were meted out to children in the council's care at two council-run children's homes in Newcastle-under-Lyme and Stoke-on-Trent. It seems that children at the homes were incarcerated in a special wing where they were guarded night and day, clad only in pyjamas, until they could prove convincingly that they had modified their behaviour.

This strange form of punishment, known as the "pin-down" method, should only be used under the strictest guidelines. However, opposition councillors are alleging that proper procedures were ignored and that senior Labour members of the council hid details of the scheme from councillors on the social services committee.

It also seems that the ingenuity of the scheme outwitted even the council's Director of Social Services, whose novel excuse for not incorporating the guidelines in the use of pin-down was that it was not a "sanction or a punishment but a method of treatment" *(sic)*.

The honour of initiating the system has gone to high-powered council social worker Tony Latham, then area officer in charge of the two homes, who introduced pin-down in 1983. Latham was a busy man. As well as running the local child care service, he had his hands full running his own money-spinning sideline in private social services.

Latham and other county council officers had set up a number of companies which were providing much needed facilities to both Staffs council and the local probation service. These included a private day-care centre in Stoke, a taxi-hire service to ferry old folk to the home, a "community" warehouse stocking cheap furniture and a skip hire business.

An inquiry was established weeks later, which found that pin-down had been used in four homes in Staffordshire, and at least 130 children as young as nine had been subject to a "harsh, restrictive and punitive regime" which involved them being imprisoned in bare rooms in their underwear, without even mattresses, sometimes for weeks at a time, and obliged to "earn" privileges including even being allowed to communicate with staff. A District Auditor's report in 1991 revealed that the companies Latham was running on the side had a combined turnover of more than £1.4 million. Latham was dismissed, as were two deputy directors of social services and several other staff, and the government ordered a national survey of children's care homes.

SADDAM HUSSEIN'S invasion of Kuwait in August changed everything when it came to the Lockerbie bombing.

There is, for the foreseeable future, no chance of those responsible for bombing the Pan-Am jet which crashed at Lockerbie in 1988 being brought to justice.

As newspapers reported in a series of huge features a year after the disaster, and as the then Transport Secretary Paul Channon was silly enough to blurt out at a lobby lunch, the governments and police of Britain and the United States knew exactly who planted the bomb. It was a gang of Middle Eastern terrorists based in Syria.

As the *Eye* reported, both governments were reluctant to name the gang or seek to bring them to justice. In a conversation reported in the *Washington Post*, Thatcher and George Bush agreed to "put the shutters up over Lockerbie", and when the new Transport Secretary Cecil Parkinson tried to get a public judicial inquiry into the disaster, he was quickly snubbed by Thatcher.

The Syrian gang named repeatedly is known to be close to the Syrian government. The strategy of the British and American governments in the Gulf is to isolate Iraq's Saddam Hussein from other Arab leaders, and in this matter President Assad of Syria is crucial and equivocal.

He is less easy to "bend" than, say, the Saudi monarchy or Mubarak of Egypt and diplomatic relations with him (abruptly cut off only recently) must be restored and fostered. One result will be that as a fatal accident inquiry starts in Scotland, the families of the Lockerbie victims will be kept even more bleakly in the dark.

IN NOVEMBER, SLICKER had details of the ongoing criminal investigation into Polly Peck, the collapsed company run by fraudster Asil Nadir.

Those at the heart of the Polly Peck affair have a unusual interpretation of the word "cooperation".

"It has always been my position that I wish to cooperate fully," declared Asil Nadir, the day the Serious Fraud Office raided his headquarters. The SFO had, he suggested, ignored his cooperation – no doubt as part of their Greek-inspired vendetta – and mounted an unnecessary raid. Several newspapers took their cue from Nadir and queried whether this was evidence of desperation on the part of the SFO. Time will tell, as it did before, with those who took the Nadir line.

The facts were that although the SFO's accountants Peat Marwick had been working in the Polly Peck HQ, their access to documents and individuals was tightly controlled. Certain offices were off-limits, enforced by Nadir's goons. All requests for documents had to be vetted by a company official, and certain requests were stalled if not denied.

It was only after a period of growing frustration that the SFO and its fraud squad investigators decided to end the farce by enforcing their requests with a warrant. So much for cooperation. The word clearly loses something in translation.

No such language problem should exist with Nadir's personal banker Elizabeth Forsyth, who remains in the safety of Switzerland, along with the equally previously elusive Jason Davies, Nadir family employee and stockbroker extraordinaire. "I have tried to cooperate," she told the *Sunday Telegraph*, which failed to ask the obvious follow-up question: "Why, then, do you not both return to Britain to see the SFO, which has made manifestly clear its desire to interview you using its powers to compel answers regarding Nadir's affairs?"

There has also been no explanation of who is paying for Davies to continue to live in Switzerland and keep two if not three lawyers.

Nadir was charged with 70 counts of false accounting and theft – but fled to Northern Cyprus ahead of his trial in 1993.

1991

THE DEADLINE SET down for Saddam Hussein's troops to leave Kuwait passed, and an American-led alliance went to war against Iraq.

Gulf War Day 94

Continuing our round-the-clock, extended, non-stop, continuous, ball-by-ball coverage of the Gulf War

David Dimblebore: We're going over live to Martin Bell, who is at a forward base somewhere in Saudi Arabia.

Kate Adie *(for it is she)*: Hullo, David. We're getting unconfirmed reports here that you've been getting reports of a possible missile attack on an as-yet-unidentified military target somewhere in the Middle East.

Dimblebore: What is the mood there, Kate, wherever it is you are?

Brian Barron *(for it is no longer she)*: Well, you have to remember that it is three o'clock in the morning out here, so the mood is pretty quiet, due to the fact that everyone is asleep. Of course I cannot say too much, and I cannot reveal exactly where I am, but I can tell you that if a missile were to land anywhere near here we'd certainly know about it.

Jeremy Paxman *(in studio)*: Admiral, I come to you first. You were listening to that. What do you think we can really say about the mood here in the studio?

Admiral Sir Roderick Gussett: Well, of course, the first thing we have to remember is the weather. At this time of year, there's a lot of it about, particularly in that part of the world.

Peter Snow: I must stop you there, because I just want to show you a video of the type of missile we believe may have been responsible for this attack, if one has taken place.

(Cut to out-of-focus film of rocket being fired into the sky, captioned "MANUFACTURER'S VIDEO")

Snow: The great point about the PF-34 Scorcher missile is that it has a range of 2,000 miles, and can only be brought down by the new American Asskicker anti-missile missile, which has not yet been invented.

Dimblebore again: I'm sorry to cut you short there, Peter, but we're now going over live to the Gulf where there are unconfirmed reports that General Norman Schwarzkopf

may be about to give a press conference.

(Cut to a still picture of John Simpson watching TV in hotel in Amman)

Simpson: Hullo, David, yes, I can confirm that General Schwarzkopf's press conference is being broadcast by CNN at this moment.

Alastair Stewart *(In shirtsleeves in front of palm tree in Saudi Arabia)*: Can I just break in there to say that I've just had a call from ITN's Mike Nicholson with the Royal Navy in the Gulf to say that he's watching CNN as well.

(Continued all day and every day on all TV and radio channels)

THE UK WAS PLUNGED into a deep recession.

"This recession's certainly hotting up competition in the high street"

THE IRA LAUNCHED a mortar attack on Downing Street during a cabinet meeting.

Tuesday

Yesterday was a beautiful day, grey and cold. But today when I woke up it had snowed! I thought it was a good job I didn't have to go out to work, or I might never get there! My wife Norman asked me whether I would like hot milk on my Weetabix. "Oh yes," I said. That shows how cold it is.

After breakfast we were all sitting around in the War Cabinet – Douglas, Mr King, my friend Chris Patten, Norma Lamont from next door and the man who sits at the end of the table who is some kind of lawyer. We were all wondering when they were going to start the ground war (obviously we won't be told for security reasons), when suddenly there was a huge bang outside in the garden.

We looked out of the window, and there was a cloud of smoke going up from where my snowman used to be. All that was left was his long grey scarf.

The silence was broken by Norma Lamont. "That was the best bang I've had for weeks," he said. Everybody laughed, but I wasn't quite sure why.

I said to them all, "Don't worry, I expect it's only one of those Scud missiles." Then I looked at my *Daily Telegraph* coloured map of the world on the wall and I was very surprised to see that in fact we are much too far away from Iraq for one of their rockets to land on my garden.

"Thank goodness for that," I said. "It's only the IRA."

BRITISH RAIL BLAMED "the wrong type of snow" for delays to trains.

Type of snow they were expecting – train-friendly, invisible and totally dry

Killer Snow – white, damp and fallen from the sky

THE WAR ENDED as Iraqi troops fled Kuwait – but then promptly redoubled their efforts to slaughter Kurdish rebels in the north of their own country.

The Gulf War – An Apology

In recent days, along with all other newspapers, we may have given the impression that the war in the Middle East was a tremendous victory over an evil dictator who used poison gas against his own people. We may well have further suggested that the war had been brought to a triumphant conclusion, and headlines such as "Hussein is Finished", "Evil Dictator Flees to Algeria" and "Now Iraq Will Be Free" may have inadvertently given the impression that we would be hearing little more of Saddam Hussein ever again.

We now realise that these claims were totally unfounded, and that Mr Hussein is alive and well and gassing his people just as he did before. We further accept that allegations the Republican Guard had in some way been finished off were inaccurate, in the light of their ongoing engagement in a massive tank battle against unarmed civilians from which all the indications are that they will emerge victorious.

We offer our apologies to President Hussein for any

distress the war may have caused him, and sincerely hope that after he has regrouped and recovered he will allow us to go to war with him again, as it seems he is the only person we can beat.

YUGOSLAVIA WAS SLIDING inexorably towards civil war.

Who's who in the new Yugoslavia

No.94 SLOBODAN DANISLOB
Charismatic leader of the Serb New Democrat Party (formerly the Communists) whose calls for the extermination of all Croats in Kosovo has recently provoked mass demonstrations in the autonomous region of Prin by irredentist Bosnians who are demanding the massacre of the Herzegovinian minority in Slovenia led by Montenegrin-born Mihail Kuthisballsov, whose Croat-led anti-Communist militia is accused of plotting a bloodbath against ethnic Albanians living in the largely Orthodox, Muslim-speaking Pristina stronghold.

NEXT WEEK: *Danislan Slobovitch of the New Communist Party (formerly the Democrats)*

A SERIES OF HORRIFIC ATTACKS on children resulted in the government rushing through the ill-thought-out Dangerous Dogs Act.

When I had got to my desk, Mr Baker came in and said: "It's alright, Prime Minister, I've found a sure way to win the next election."

"Oh yes?" I said, letting him know that he was not exactly my favourite person in the Cabinet. "And what might that be?"

"What is the most important issue in Britain today?" "Oh, that's easy," I said. "You don't need an O-level Economics degree to answer that one. Inflation, isn't it?" "No," he said, giving me one of his considerably annoying smiles. "It is the killer dogs which are rampaging through Britain – look at the front page of the *Sun*."

He held up a copy of that paper, which had a big headline saying PAGE 3 GIRL DIES OF CANCER. Below it was a picture of a snarling dog with the headline MAJOR MUST KILL THESE DOGS NOW.

Mr Baker looked triumphant as he said, "My plan is quite simple. You should kill these dogs now."

I hate to say it, but even Kenneth sometimes has quite good ideas. If I kill all the dogs, it will make me very popular and will show people that I can act decisively when I want to. Mrs Thatcher never had the courage to shoot 10,000 dogs in a day.

QUESTIONS WERE RAISED about the royal finances, and the fact the Queen paid no tax.

SHORTLY AFTER the Maguire Seven, wrongly convicted of producing explosives for use in the same bombings that had seen the Guildford Four jailed, were released by the Court of Appeal, two members of the Provisional IRA who were awaiting trial climbed over the walls of Brixton Prison and escaped.

Brixton IRA escape – that Home Office inquiry in full

1. The present Home Office policy is to keep innocent Irish people in jail and to let guilty ones escape.
2. The Inquiry feels it might be a good idea to reverse this policy.
3. Er…
4. That's it.

JOHN MAJOR UNVEILED his defining policy.

This is the biggest week I have had since I became Prime Minister. Oh yes. I will finally unveil my Citizen's Charter which everyone has been looking forward to for many months.

I was amused to see a lot of articles saying that the Charter had been "watered down", no doubt inspired by the Labour party. Oh, no. In my estimation it has been not inconsiderably toughened up, and has more teeth than anything the government managed to do under Mrs Thatcher. For example, there is a whole new section laying down that in future all civil servants will have to wear name-tabs saying who they are, and when they answer the telephone to members of the public they will have to say "Have a nice day."

I have lots of other brilliant ideas for my Charter, too. For instance, one of the real menaces of the modern world is when you have a ball-point pen in your pocket and it starts to leak, marking your shirt and suit and sometimes your vest, if it is wintertime. Under my Charter, you would be entitled to recover the cost of the dry-cleaning from the manufacturers.

Also we are appealing to commercial firms to step forward to sponsor much-loved army regiments which Mr King might otherwise have to shut down. When I gave my friend Chris a "sneak preview" of this bit, he said, "So in future it will be the NatWest Household Cavalry and the Hoffmeister Lager Light Infantry?" "Yes," I said to him in my firm voice. "What is wrong with that?"

This is the kind of thing that will show the country that the Conservative Party under my leadership has got the real vision that is required for the 1990s. Oh yes!

TEN YEARS in, all was not looking good in at least one royal marriage.

SIR ALLAN GREEN, Director of Public Prosecutions, resigned after police caught him approaching prostitutes in the red light district around King's Cross in London.

"Wanna blow a job?"

HOSTAGE JOHN McCARTHY was finally released after over five years of captivity in Lebanon.

For God's sake, leave them alone!

says GLENDA SLAGG

For years, Jill Morrell and John McCarthy have been waiting for this moment of happiness when they can look into each other's eyes, smile, and rekindle their love for each other away from the prying eyes of the world.

How sickening, then, to find that the prurient media have tracked them down to this tiny cottage in France, turning their dream holiday into a nightmare.

"Are the press being intrusive?" I shouted through the letterbox as I shoved a microphone into the hallway. "Do you just want to be left alone?" I screamed through the keyhole.

Thankfully, our series of helicopter shots of them taken down the chimney tell the story themselves: these are two young lovers who just want some time to themselves.

Why oh why can't anyone get the message?

BESET BY TROUBLES on all sides – and firing off libel writs until the very end – Cap'n Bob Maxwell disappeared over the side of his yacht off the Canary Islands.

A Spanish Doctor writes

As a doctor, I am often asked: "What are the symptoms of a heart attack?"

The answer is very simple. The patient usually wakes up in the early morning, takes off all his clothes, opens the cabin door and goes to the only section of the boat without a proper rail. He then propels himself at the moment of death straight into the water, without hitting the side of the vessel. Seven hours later, he is discovered.

This is perfectly normal and should give no cause for concern. Heart attack, or *Maxwellus dubiys circumstances mortalis*, as we Spanish doctors call it, is a common medical description of something a bit fishy.

If you are worried about your life insurance policy, you should consult a professional private detective at once.

AS THE YEAR BEGAN, the *Eye* drew attention once again to Robert Maxwell's habit of using one arm of his business empire to bail out another.

There is intrigue on Wall Street over the activities of media gargantuan Robert Maxwell, whose Maxwell Communications Corps has been reducing its debt by selling off assets. These may be hard times for business, but to give credit where it's due, Cap'n Bob is getting a good price from his purchaser – one Mirror Group (prop: R. Maxwell) – which has paid more than £400 million to bail out MCC. What can it all mean?

THE BIRMINGHAM SIX, wrongly convicted of IRA bombings in 1974, were released by the court of appeal in March. Ahead of the court hearing, the *Eye* revealed what had happened to a key witness.

Many a Midlands Conservative Club will miss the jovial company of retired Detective Superintendent George Reade, formerly of West Midlands Serious Crimes Squad, who led the investigation into the six men held after the Birmingham pub bombings.

Just as the case was about to come on at the appeal court, and as the evidence of the police was the only shot left in the empty locker of the prosecution, Reade, the most important policeman in the case, hopped it to Australia. A long and crucial interview with him there by no less a figure than the Chief Constable of Cornwall turned out to be the decisive factor in the DPP's sudden decision to withdraw.

Reade it was who compiled the famous "Reade schedule", a list of interviews of the six men crudely altered apparently so that it could fit in with the evidence given by his officers when the case first went to trial in 1975. When the case was first referred back to the Court of Appeal in 1988, the defence argued that the Reade schedule was a deliberate attempt to pervert the course of justice by inventing times and interviews which never took place.

This was vigorously denied by a not altogether coherent Reade in the witness box. Indeed, his very incoherence seems to have helped him. The Lord Chief Justice Lord Lane, in his judgement, made it clear he thought Reade far too thick and bumbling to have devised such a complicated conspiracy.

How Reade managed to reach Australia, without any sign that he intended to return and give evidence, is a matter for the authorities.

Reade and two other former officers were subsequently charged with perjury and conspiracy to pervert the

course of justice, but the case was abandoned in 1993 when a judge ruled that coverage of the Birmingham Six scandal had been so widespread it would be impossible for them to get a fair trial. At the end of the month, the *Eye* had evidence that such tactics were far from over.

West Midlands men are still up to their old tricks of forging or forcing false confessions from the innocent. The latest in a long tradition which stretches from the Birmingham Six to the victims of the disbanded Serious Crimes Squad is an educationally subnormal 31-year-old, Paul Ryland.

He was imprisoned in early January awaiting trial for the murder of Rosemary Kelly, aged 38, and her five-year-old daughter Claire Murphy, at Bartley Green in Birmingham. The evidence was a confession said by detectives to have been made during a car journey after his arrest.

Now forensic evidence has shown conclusively that Mr Ryland could not have been responsible. He has been quietly released and another man arrested. Police observers have noted a big increase in the number of "car confessions" following the enforced introduction of tape recorded interviews at police stations.

MAY BROUGHT us back to Maxwell.

British financial institutions have shown carefulness in subscribing for shares in the Mirror Group, soon to be floated on the stock exchange. Possibly because Cap'n Bob's own prospectus states that any litigation outstanding against the group will not materially affect its balance sheet, while sceptics in the City are aware that if all the various claims against the Mirror Group were to be won by the plaintiffs, the liability would total roughly £50 million.

For instance, the trustees of the Mirror Group Pension Fund have threatened to sue the Mirror Group over Cap'n Bob's policy of imposing a moratorium on corporate contributions and his decision to buy stock for the pensioners in an existing public company whose share price has been slipping – Maxwell Communications Corporation.

Even more intriguing is paragraph 14 on material contracts, which purports to explain the relationships between the Mirror Group and Maxwell's myriad of private companies, most of them ultimately owned by his shadowy, Liechtenstein-based family trusts. Reputable City bankers who have read the prospectus have confessed themselves baffled by the tortuous network of Cap'n Bob's empire.

THE BEGINNING OF JUNE saw Slicker surveying the court listings.

An interesting case appears in the High Court under the deliberately obscure title of A and Others v B Bank, Bank of England intervening. In April the Bank of England sought certain documents from the London-based B bank in connection that it had made "false and fraudulent statements" to the US Federal Reserve Board. As supervisor, the Bank of England wanted to investigate these matters, which related to the acquisition by B bank of an American bank holding company in violation of US law.

A and six others had earlier obtained an injunction preventing the disclosure of documents relating to that deal or their accounts at B bank, following a subpoena issued by a New York grand jury investigating the deal. B bank wanted a ruling from the court as to whether it could comply with the Bank of England request. Mr Justice Hirst ruled that it could and should.

All of this presumably has nothing whatsoever to do with Hasan Abedi, founder but no longer controller of the Bank of Credit & Commerce International, and the purchase of the First American Bank group which is under investigation in New York. So it cannot mean that the Bank of England may be investigating BCCI with a view to taking away its licence, something it did not do after it pleaded guilty to laundering drug money.

The Bank of England, acting alongside regulators from six other countries, shut down BCCI on 5 July, 13 years after Slicker had first raised issues about the bank's practices (*see p71*). BCCI was liquidated with debts of over £10 billion to creditors including several local councils in the UK. Its liquidators subsequently sued the Bank of England for "malicious recklessness" in failing to properly regulate the company. Abedi died in Pakistan in 1995 with a number of charges outstanding against him.

THERE WERE SOME amazing claims about the *Mirror* in October.

A new book, *The Samson Option*, by Pulitzer prizewinning US reporter Seymour Hersh, contains claims from Ari Ben-Menashe, the former Israeli intelligence agent, that he ran the foreign editor of the *Daily Mirror*, Nicholas Davies, as a Mossad "intelligence asset", and that Davies was even dealing in arms from the newspaper's office in Holborn Circus.

Hacks from several newspapers are on to the story,

but the *Eye* has had exclusive access to documents obtained by publishers Faber & Faber. Ben-Menashe claims that in the early 1980s he began to offer Davies substantial rewards for running a business dealing in arms to Iran on behalf of Israel, which wanted the Iranians to defeat Saddam Hussein's forces in the Iran-Iraq war. He alleges that over several years up until early 1989, Davies received $1,550,000 from a Mossad slush fund, which was paid into bank accounts in Grand Cayman, Belgium and Luxembourg. During the working day, Davies's direct line at the *Daily Mirror* was used to receive calls from Iranians discussing arms deals.

The book also claims that back in 1986 Davies, Ben-Menashe himself and Mirror Group publisher Robert Maxwell, a self-styled intimate of the Israeli cabinet, were involved in a disinformation exercise to undermine the *Sunday Times*'s story about Israeli technician Mordechai Vanunu and his revelations that Israel had secretly developed nuclear weapons capability. A freelance journalist representing Vanunu approached Davies with copies of photographs that Vanunu had taken of the interior of the Israeli nuclear plant at Dimona. Maxwell ordered his staff to deliver Vanunu's photos to the Israeli Embassy, and the *Sunday Mirror* went to work rubbishing the story as a "a hoax, or even something more sinister – a plot to discredit Israel".

Ben-Menashe goes further and says Davies tracked down Vanunu's whereabouts in London and passed this information to him, as a result of which Vanunu was lured to Rome by another Mossad operative and from there to Israel where he is presently serving a lengthy prison sentence.

Maxwell promptly dismissed Davies from the *Mirror*, despite declaring Hersh's claims about him "ludicrous, a total invention." Just days later he fell off the back of his boat, the *Lady Ghislaine*, and died. One of his last acts was to issue a libel writ against *Private Eye* for its stories about the Mirror Group pension funds, and the monstrous suggestion that he had been "personally responsible" for acting unlawfully in relation to them. Within weeks of his death it turned out that he had looted no less than £460 million from the funds.**

IN NOVEMBER it was officially announced that two Libyan intelligence agents were responsible for the Lockerbie bombing. The *Eye* explained why.

During the Gulf War, both American and British authorities were delighted by the support they got against the bestial and inhuman government of Saddam Hussein from the bestial and inhuman government of Syria. Assad became the dictator everyone (except the Syrian people) loved to praise, and the New World Order has been founded on the rock of cooperation with him, the moderate wing of the Palestinans and even the ayatollahs in Iran. This was the basis of the steady flow of released hostages in Beirut.

But in recent weeks, Bush and Major have been under some pressure from the families of people who died at Lockerbie, with one US group of relatives recently visiting Britain to agitate for action. The statement about the Libyans was the two governments' answer. The wretched Lord Fraser, Lord Advocate for Scotland, was ordered to read out "results" of his police inquiry, which were completely different from those which had been already read out to newspapers all over the world implicating a gang of extremist Palestinians led by a man named Jibril, who had the protection of a Syrian government-backed terrorist sect led by a man called Nidal. Even the man who had been "identified" as travelling to Malta to buy the clothes to put in the bomb suitcase was named as Talb, a Palestinan terrorist then (and still) in prison in Sweden. Now, however, foreign secretary Douglas Hurd has gone out of his way to exculpate the "other governments" (Syria and Iran) which his colleague Paul Channon had confidently told hacks were responsible back in March 1989.

1992

FOLLOWING THE resignation of Mikhail Gorbachev on 25 December, the former Soviet Union rapidly began to collapse.

"Boris Yeltsin got Russia for Christmas and it fell apart by Boxing Day"

LIBERAL DEMOCRAT leader Paddy Ashdown's admission to an affair with his secretary unexpectedly boosted his popularity among voters.

Glenda Slagg
Fleet Street's Floppy Dish

Who does he think he is, Mr Paddy so-called Pantsdown?!?!

Just because he's leader of the Lib-Dems doesn't mean he can go a-squeezin' and a-squealin' with the dame who types his letters?!!

Get on back to the Missus, Mr Bonk-Happy!?!

You won't be getting any of Glenda's X's on your ballot paper!?!

Hats off to Paddy Ashdown, the Lib-Dem Lothario from sizzling Somerset!?!

Who cares if Pantin' Paddy had a fling with his typist!?!? What hot-blooded male with an eye for the gals doesn't like a bit on the side!?!

Passionate Paddy gets my vote any day of the week?!?

Here's to a well-hung Parliament!!?! (Geddit?!?)

AS A GENERAL election approached, the press fell into line.

Daily Mail

Labour plans slaughter of the first born

One of the first actions of a future Labour government, the *Daily Mail* can reveal, would be to murder the eldest children of all families in Great Britain. This would mean, at a Central Office estimate, the deaths of some 10.6 million innocent toddlers.

Labour leader Neil Kinnock, when confronted by a *Mail* reporter at his £250,000 swanky Ealing split-level semi-detached house, failed to deny the claim but instead opened fire on them with a machine gun, screaming: "You'll never live to tell the story, boyo!"

ON OTHER PAGES: *Mother Teresa on 'Why I back John Major' p3; Why sexy Virginia Bottomley is better than ugly Clare Short, by Glenda Lee-Potter p5*

TAKING NO CHANCES, the government put through an astonishingly generous budget a month ahead of polling day.

The Secret DIARY OF JOHN MAJOR aged 47¾

Tuesday
Norma Lamont's budget has been a great success. His picture is everywhere and it is front-page news. This couldn't be better timing when we are about to have an election! It is also in no small measure fortunate that his Budget is going to make everyone better off. I congratulated him on this coincidence. He laughed and winked at me. "You could say it is a budget for jobs," he said. "Ours."

Wednesday
Mr O'Donnell tells me that I have chosen a new theme tune for our election campaign. "The Labour party has Brahms," he said, "So we are going to have Persil." "Oh good," I said. "It is one of my favourite adverts, and my wife Norman says it washes grey out completely."

Thursday
I am delighted by the success of Norma Lamont's budget. He promised me he would not bribe the public to win votes and he has been as good as his word. We are 3 points behind.

RATHER TO everyone's surprise, Major won with a 21-seat majority.

Heir of Sorrows *by SYLVIE KRIN*

Having watched the election coverage, the next morning Charles visits his mother with renewed hope...

"You see, Mater, it's democracy. Er... the good of the people... time for a change, as Mr Kinnock put it." Charles followed his mother as, armed with her Callard & Bowser secateurs, she patrolled the Windsor Castle rose bed, pausing from time to time to snip the already burgeoning buds.

"Pick up those prunings will you, Charles, and throw them onto the bonfire."

Obediently he bent down and, grasping the discarded cuttings, felt a sharp stab of pain in his fingertips. Manfully suppressing a cry of anguish, he hurled the blood-specked twigs onto his mother's conflagration.

"You see, Mater," Charles persevered, "the whole idea is that you get new people to sort of take over when everyone feels that the old ones are not up to it." How was it that his old friend Sir Laurens Van Der Fraud had put it in his book *Gardening in the Sahara Desert*? "Out of the dead oak, comes the live acorn?" Or was it the other way round? "Anyway, the point is that in every aspect of life a sort of renewal thingie is the key."

His mother stopped in her tracks and turned to face her son. "What time did you go to bed, Charles?"

"Well, er, late actually, about eleven. Diana was just on her way out to some disco at the Savoy I think. Anyway the exit polls chaps had made it clear. The old lot were out, the new man was in."

The Queen stared at her son in disbelief. "No wonder we called you Charlie. Your father and I stayed up all night. It was all very gratifying. No change at all." She prodded the fire with a rake. "Continuity, you see, that's what people want. Old values, familiar faces."

The wind swung round, blowing a thick black cloud of smoke in Charles's direction. As the acrid fumes engulfed him, he felt his eyes begin to water...

(To be continued...)

ANDREW MORTON'S *Diana: Her True Story*, with its extraordinary revelations of suicide attempts, affairs and eating disorders, was published and serialised in the *Sunday Times*.

Grave constitutional crisis rocks Fairyland over *Funday Times* revelations

The *Funday Times*' shock revelation that Prince Charming and his lovely bride did *not* live happily ever after has exploded a time bomb under the whole edifice of the Fairyland monarchy.

Passages from the book *Sleeping Beauty – Her True Story* revealed to the world for the first time that:

- Sleeping Beauty was only asleep for 100 years because she had taken a massive dose of paracetamol
- Prince Charming was cold and indifferent to his lovely bride, and frequently rode off into the forest to visit his close friend Camilla Parker-Rapunzel
- The Queen ruthlessly ignored the Princess's cries for help and continued to eat bread and honey in a callous manner
- In her distress, Sleeping Beauty "binged" on pies stuffed with up to 24 blackbirds at a time
- The Princess's ugly sisters-in-law Fergiana and Anne were allowed to get divorced, but she wasn't.

One friend who used to share a pumpkin with the Princess said, "She used to be such a fun-loving girl, who enjoyed balls and wearing glass slippers. But now she sits sadly in her turret, spinning a yarn which only the *Funday Times* is stupid enough to pay a quarter of a million pounds for."

WHEN HIS AFFAIR with an actress was exposed by the tabloids, national heritage secretary David Mellor demanded privacy and then coralled his entire family for an excruciating photocall.

RIOTS ENGULFED LA after an all-white jury acquitted four white police officers of viciously beating a black suspect, despite clear video evidence.

What the L.A. jury saw

Have a nice day

DESPITE THE CHANCELLOR spending £15bn in a desperate attempt to prop up the value of the pound against currency speculators, Britain was ejected from the European Exchange Rate Mechanism.

Lamont tumbles

The value of the Lamont fell through the floor today after heavy speculation that he is no bloody good at his job. After initial attempts to defend the Lamont, it became apparent that this was impossible, and the Lamont became the lowest-rated financial minister in Europe. There were panic moves to offload Lamont and a general rush followed to get rid of him at any price.

Only a short time ago, the Lamont was being heralded as the proud symbol of British financial stability. Now it lies in disgrace – weak, unwanted, and with silly eyebrows. *(Shurely 'little immediate hope of recovery'? – Ed.)*

Norman Lamont is 57. No, hold on – 63. No, 42. Er 51... no... er...

JUST FIVE MONTHS after claiming it was them wot won it for John Major, the press were swift to turn on his government.

Apology

Over the past year the *Daily Gnome* may have inadvertently given the impression that it considered Mr John Major a suitable person to hold the office of Prime Minister. Headlines such as "Vote Conservative!", "Honest John will lead us to recovery", "Boomtime with Major!" and "Lamont is genius" may have erroneously given readers the impression that we in some way backed his government's economic policies.

We now accept that John Major is entirely unfit to run a whelk stall, let alone the country. We further acknowledge that he is a cretinous half-wit and buffoon who has no grasp of basic arithmetic. We are happy to point out that his entire Cabinet are similarly incompetent and that Major and all his moronic cronies should resign at once.

> E. Strobes
> pp Lord Gnome
> Dun Toryin', Major-on-the-Slide, Berks

TAPE RECORDINGS emerged of Princess Diana phoning a male friend, James Gilbey, who referred to her affectionately as "Squidgy"...

Those Royal love tapes in full

Mystery man: Hullo! It's me.
Woman: Who?
Man: Charles.
Woman: Oh.
Man: You remember. We got married. My mother's the Queen?
Woman: Oh, yeah.
Another man: Is that you, Squidgy?
Man: I think there must be a crossed line. You know, it really is appalling.
Woman: Mmm, yah. Got to go.

...MEANWHILE, FERGIE, who was in the process of divorcing Prince Andrew, was photographed topless and having her toes sucked by the man she claimed was her "financial adviser".

TO MAKE THINGS WORSE for Major, Tory Eurosceptics went on the attack over the Maastricht Treaty.

Wednesday

When I got to our conference hall in Bournemouth, I found that Mr Tebbit was on stage making a complete idiot of himself by attacking Maastricht. Fortunately the delegates soon managed to shut him up by cheering very loudly, waving Union Jacks and shouting "Good old Norman!" which was a very kind reference to my wife. When Mr Tebbit came off the platform, many of the delegates were so angry that they clustered round him and started to hit him on the back.

THE GOVERNMENT ANNOUNCED – and then rapidly backtracked on – plans to close 31 pits and make 30,000 miners redundant.

"I think you know everybody – Jones the Dole, Jones the Redundancy, Jones the UB40, Jones the YTS..."

A HUGE FIRE broke out at Windsor Castle...

A poem to commemorate the tragic conflagration which en e historic castle of Windsor
by WILLIAM REES-McGONAGALL

'Twas in the month of November 1992
That there befell a disaster which I will tell of the noo.
For motorists travelling home on the M4
They saw a sight the like of which they had ne'er seen before.

For many drivers the road it was hard to keep their eyes on
On account of the mighty blaze that lit up the horizon.
Thousands of fire engines came in from far and wide
With Royal Berkshire Fire Service emblazoned on the side.

But alas, the brave firemen had arrived too late
(Perhaps Prince Andrew had mistakenly dialled 888).
As the ravening flames leaped from tower to tower
Minister Peter Brooke proclaimed that it was our heritage's
darkest hour.

Three battalions of the Household Cavalry worked through
the night
To make sure the Royal treasures did not catch alight.

Many fine chairs and sofas were also saved
About which Professor Roy Strong most eloquently raved.

For 24 hours as the fire blazed on the hill
People began to wonder who would foot the bill.
But while this question was being discussed by many
Mr Brooke announced that the taxpayer would cough up
every penny.

At once the nation was filled with spleen,
Saying the person who should pay was Her Majesty
the Queen.
The percentage that thought this was 99 and a half
The only dissenter being Charles Moore of the Sunday
Telegraph.

But then the Queen became angry at this
Saying she had had an annus horribilis.
And although she spoke with a heavy cold
The public's lack of sympathy was amazing to behold.

Next day she said, "If you get off our backs
I'll cut the Civil List and pay income tax."
And so by a coincidence some thought rather funny
The Queen suddenly decided to give the public back
some money.

...AND TO CAP OFF the Queen's Annus Horribilis, Charles and Diana announced they were separating.

JANUARY BROUGHT some home truths about trade with Iraq.

Bill Weir, a senior official at the ministry of defence, insists he is just a "metallurgist". So why would junior defence minister Alan Clark rush down from the MoD to tell the Commons trade and industry select committee that Bill must not at any cost appear on the telly?

In fact Bill Weir works in what the chairman of Walter Somers, the Midlands engineering firm of Iraqi supergun fame, told the Commons in an unguarded moment was the ministry's "spooks department", which includes men from MI6 and some from MI5.

In private, away from those nasty cameras, Bill Weir told the committee that he had had a series of telephone conversations in 1989 when the company was building a series of massive guns for Saddam Hussein. On the basis of the calls, Weir couldn't decide whether what was being built was guns or petrochemical pipes, so he didn't do anything further about it.

This is all nonsense. The entire intelligence service responded to the call from the CIA at the end of the Iran-Iraq war to "do everything we can to help our ally, Saddam Hussein". This was the main purpose of the 1989 arms fair in Baghdad, which was attended by the military attaché at the British embassy in the city. He now says he somehow missed the gargantuan supergun which was on display at the fair and was ordered, in a slightly smaller model, from British companies. But he does not say why he attended an arms fair in a country with whom the British Government was in theory maintaining a strict arms embargo.

There was no embargo, of course: only an encouragement on all sides for arms firms to supply Saddam – and a long string of lies and prevarications ever since.

Despite the best efforts by most of the government to cover the entire scandal up – and allow a number of directors of another company which had exported to Iraq, Matrix Churchill, to go to prison without a fair trial in the process – minister for defence procurement Alan Clark admitted in November that the rules on the embargo had been secretly changed at the end of 1988 so that Saddam could buy arms. The *Eye* predicted ahead of that trial in September that "some very interesting facts might emerge, although anxious spooks are already rushing round to judges armed with Public Interest orders, which once signed by a judge, ban from court proceedings any information whose publication is deemed to be a threat to the public interest".

THE SAME MONTH saw some revelations from Brussels.

While everyone knows that those who run the European Community are rampantly profligate with our money, the latest report by the European Court of Auditors shows how impossible it is to find out exactly how profligate. While checking the European Parliament's inventory of equipment, auditors found that 17,000 of the 84,000 officially-listed items of office, technical and computing gear had vanished.

Six months on, Euro civil servants had managed to trace 6,000 of the items, which meant that only 11,821 were missing. The ingenious Euroservants then covered up for all possible discrepancies: they set the lower value limit for inventory listings at 74 ECUs – and wrote down the value of all the missing items as less than 75 ECUs apiece, whatever their value, so they all "disappeared."

Auditors have also discovered that expenses for urgent [sic] MPE business, funded through a special account called the Imprest Account, were up to 28.8 million ECUs in a year. Even though the official limit was 2.5 million ECUs.

Not to be outdone, the staff of the Council of Ministers hired computing and data processing equipment at a cost estimated by the auditors to be 76 percent greater than the normal cost of buying it.

The European Court of Auditors would not be able to give their unqualified approval of a single set of EU accounts until 2007.

NEW MEDICAL COLUMNIST 'M.D.', aka Dr Phil Hammond, reported on his local hospital in May.

Dr John Roylance, chief executive of the United Bristol Healthcare Trust, has applied for a "charter mark", the department of health's new gold standard of service provision. But before the department of health bestows its mark of excellence, it may wish to ponder the perilous state of paediatric cardiac surgery at UBHT. In 1988, mortality was so high that the unit was dubbed "The Killing Fields". Despite a long crisis of morale among intensive care staff, the surgeons persistently refuse to publish their mortality rates in a manner comparable to other units. And although Dr Roylance and the DoH are well aware of the problems, they won't recognise them officially.

Recently, the unit failed to provide a paediatric cardiac surgery nurse for post-operative care because it was assumed the baby would not survive the operation. And although Liverpool surgeons have successfully operated on 160 babies with Fallot's tetralogy, a congenital heart abnormality, the Bristol mortality rate is between 20 and 30 percent. Hardly the stuff of commendations.

His long-running series of reports on paediatric heart surgery in Bristol eventually resulted in a public inquiry between 1999-2001, which ruled that the unit was "not up to task… not safe" and that between 30-35 babies had died unnecessarily. James Wisheart, the surgeon at the centre of the scandal, was struck off the medical register.

THE EYE CLARIFIED a few details about MP Jonathan Aitken's business career in May.

A correction and apology to Jonathan Aitken recently appeared on the front page of the *Independent*. It pointed out that Mr Aitken was not, as had been alleged, a director of a huge Saudi Arabian export/import company, but of its UK subsidiary, which he described as "an investment company". Mr Aitken was quoted as saying he was not involved in arms sales.

This assertion greatly surprised Mr Gerald James, former chairman of Astra, who was approached by Aitken in 1988. Aitken, who was a consultant to Astra subsidiary BMARC, desperately wanted to be a main board director of Astra. When James asked what Astra would get in return, Aitken replied with an impressive list of his contacts in the royal family in Saudi Arabia whom, he said, could be useful for arms contracts.

Aitken then invited James for a week in Geneva where he contacted various influential members of the Saudi royal family, then staying at the Geneva Hilton. Astra, of course, was an arms company, and the only possible reason for introducing Astra to the Saudi royals was to sell them arms.

FACT: Jonathan Aitken is now minister for defence procurement (arms sales) in nice Mr Major's government.

ANOTHER FACT: A huge slice – probably the majority shareholding – of another of Mr Aitken's former investment companies, Aitken Hume, is owned by Sifco, the company of Wafic Said, who helped Mrs Thatcher negotiate the Al-Yamamah contracts for British Aerospace.

Aitken's entanglement in arms deals, his failure to declare his interest when he was given ministerial responsibility for the trade and his shady Saudi contacts were all key elements of his spectacular downfall five years later.

SLICKER MADE A PREDICTION that same month.

Interest in expanding the Polly Peck charge sheet to include Asil Nadir's two happy helpers on the private company side, Jason Davies and Elizabeth Forsyth, seems to have evaporated. Former stockbroker Davies is still understood to be in Switzerland, while Forsyth now spends most of her time in Northern Cyprus where the rumours are that Asil will be returning soon.

Just why that should be so, given his bail restrictions, is less than clear – especially as Britain has no extradition treaty with a state it does not recognise.

Nadir did indeed flee to Northern Cyprus in May 1993, and stayed there for 17 years. When he finally returned to the UK in 2010 – voluntarily – he was tried and sentenced to ten years in prison. Forsyth had been jailed for money laundering in 1996 but released on appeal.

NOVEMBER SAW the collapse of the Matrix Churchill trial.

Officials approached Judge Smedley with "public interest immunity" certificates with fantastic haste, hoping to ban from the trial any reference to the security services and the defendants' connection with them. Four ministers concerned signed the documents, barely even reading them. Judge Smedley, they had been told, was a "safe" judge who had been chosen to try the case for his long experience as the senior judge in the British sovereign bases in Cyprus, a place run almost entirely by MI6 and its friends in the military.

At first, the certificates worked. Judge Smedley rejected the defence argument that ministerial certificates should not be permitted to suppress evidence of some relevance to a criminal trial. In order to obtain the documents, the lawyers for Matrix Churchill's Paul Henderson had to reveal his defence – that he had been following Government policy, not announced to Parliament, to sell significant defence-related equipment to Saddam. When Smedley read the documents, he felt he had no alternative but to release them.

He did largely uphold the immunity certificate signed by Home Secretary Kenneth Clarke, enabling MI6 to suppress all material they did not wish to disclose. But he didn't see why the court shouldn't know that the security services had led the way in flagrantly breaking the law relating to arms exports to Iraq. The judge thought this might be relevant to the defence of Henderson and Co: namely that they were selling arms to Saddam for their country, and that they knew they were being patriotic because MI6 had told them so.

1993

DESPITE THE BEST EFFORTS of the UN, war and ethnic cleansing continued to escalate in the former Yugoslavia.

"I'm not going in there – it's a no-fly zone"

IT WAS THE TURN of the Prince of Wales and his mistress Camilla Parker-Bowles to have a secretly recorded conversation published – in which, amongst other sexy talk, he fantasised about being her tampon.

Gnome filth lines

(In cooperation with MI5, GCHQ etc)

CAMILLA – Waiting to Hear your
Dirty Jokes 0898 74625

Toilet-Talk with
Miss Parker Bowels 0898 674732

I want to Read Your Speeches
on the Environment 0898 788324

M4/M11/M25 Traffic Update 0898 67432

THE GOVERNMENT pressed ahead with plans to privatise the railways.

Transport Secretary John MacGregor answers your questions

Q. Is British Rail going to be privatised?

A. Our proposal is to separate British Rail into a number of component sectors. The old BR will become an independent franchised agency, represented by Offrail, which is what most of the trains will be.

Q. What about the signalling system?

A. The signals will be operated by a new commercial agency called Signalforce, who will lease the signals from Trackforce, the new track operation.

Q. Under your new scheme, how would you get from, say, Brighton to London?

A. Very simple. First you would go down to Brighton Tierack, as the station will now be called, and catch a new Virgin Downsline to Hastings. There you would connect with the World of Weald system, operated by Spud-U-Like, which would take you across to Maidstone. Then you would jump onto one of Carlton's new Whitecliffs Express shuttles which would get you to Dover in plenty of time for tea. Then if you still wanted to get to London you could easily nip over on the Hovercraft to France, where it would only take you an hour on their very good, cheap state system to reach Paris. Then it's a piece of cake to hop on a plane to Heathrow, and there you are. What could be easier?

AWARDED THE FIRST private contract to transport prisoners, Group 4 managed to lose seven of them in the first three weeks.

A statement from Lord Gnome, Chairman of Gnome 4 Security plc, explaining why the early setbacks experienced by his company are irrelevant to the long-term success of the prison privatisation programme and why Gnome 4 is the ideal organisation to run British prisons and eventually replace the police.

Gnome 4 regrets that Lord Gnome's statement has been lost on the way to the page. The statement was due to appear today, but unfortunately disappeared during the transfer from Gnome 4's offices. Every effort is being made to find the statement.

E. Strobes
pp Lord Gnome
Gnome 4... 2...1... hang on, they've all gone.

AS THE CHURCH OF ENGLAND prepared to admit women as priests, traditionalists headed Romewards.

God to leave C of E

by The Word Staff **Terry Christian**

Following the precedent set by leading former Anglicans, God has indicated that he is to leave the Church of England. Sources close to God (TV's Charles Moore) say he has been persuaded by the arguments of the agriculture minister John Gummer.

God will now be accepted into the Catholic

Church on condition that He takes instruction from an expert theologian who can explain His beliefs to Him properly. A C of E spokesman said, "Losing God is a blow, but compared with major figures like Ann Widdecombe defecting it's just something we're going to have to live with."

BUCKINGHAM PALACE opened up to paying visitors for the summer, to help cover the cost of the restoration of Windsor.

FORMER CONSERVATIVE MP Alan Clark released his extravagantly libidinous *Diaries*. Craig Brown provided his own version for the *Eye*.

Bumped into a ghastly little woman at reception the other night. Took her to be one of the waitresses: common as muck, foreign look about her, nasal voice, not a bad bust, decidedly alluring to be frank, tidy-poo hairdo, had her marked down as a cleaning lady, obviously fancied me something rotten, kept giving me the come-on by asking me questions of the "What exactly is it that you do, ooh that must be very interesting" variety.

Was just plotting to offer her tuppence ha'penny an hour to clean out the stables when I suddenly found myself

getting the hots for her. Must have been her feet – two of 'em, one on each side, quite small, well shod, not bad at all. So I put my arm round her shoulder, volunteered her my broadest grin, and whispered into her ear, "If you really want to know EXACTLY what I do, why don't we bunk up together for a few mins in a little Ministerial cupboard I spotted out in the corridor?"

At this point, an oik in pin-stripes sidled over to the cleaning lady and said, "Your Majesty, may I present Lady someone-or-other?" Crikey, I thought, how utterly spastic of me – I've been trying to have it off with the Queen. Smack botties for Alan. Silly really, because I hardly ever fancy Krauts.

AS THE ECONOMY SANK yet further, John Major finally sacked Norman Lamont as Chancellor.

DROPPING THE PILOT.

MIDDLE EAST PEACE TALKS took a great leap forward as Yasser Arafat met with Israeli prime minister Yitzhak Rabin at the White House, and signed a deal to allow limited Palestinian self-rule in the Gaza Strip and West Bank.

AS PARLIAMENTARY negotiations over Maastricht got really messy, John Major was caught on microphone describing Eurosceptic colleagues in his cabinet as "bastards".

Sunday

I cannot believe it. The newspapers are suggesting that I have called the rebels bastards just because I said so to a television reporter! "What bastards!" I said to my wife Norman in bed. "It was all off the record."

The following are in my judgement bastards and I have written their names in my special Black Book of Bastards: a) Mr Portillo, b) Mr Howard, c) Mr Redwood, d) Mr Lilley and e) lots of other bastards as well.

It would be easy to sack these bastards. But that would be the cowardly route. It is much braver not to sack them in case they cause trouble.

Monday

I called my press secretary Mr O'Donnell in to demand an apology from the BBC for leaking my remarks about bastards. "It must have been them," I said, "because they have it in for me."

"They are not the only ones, Prime Minister," he said. "But anyway, 'Bastardgate' has been a great success for you. It shows that you are tough-talking and aren't frightened to say what you think."

This was very encouraging. "Perhaps I should go to Christchurch before the by-election and tell the voters that if they don't vote for me they are bastards?" I suggested. Mr O'Donnell thought this was a brilliant idea, but unfortunately he had arranged for me to be in Siberia all this week on a very important trade mission.

STEPHEN SPIELBERG'S *Jurassic Park* was released – with terrible consequences.

Dinosaur terror stalks Fleet Street

Thousands fled in terror yesterday as hundreds of prehistoric clichés ran amok across the broadsheets, causing panic and boredom to sweep the land.

A swarm of metaphors not seen in such numbers since *2,000,000 Years BC* spread uncontrollably across London, mutating into terrifyingly unfunny jokes such as "The Maastrichtodon" (*Guardian*) and "Thatcherosaurus Rex" (*Observer*). Inspector "Knacker of the Yard" Knacker said, "We had the situation under control, with all the metaphorsauruses safely confined, then some irresponsible lout released an overhyped film *(shurely "all the dinosaurs"? – Ed.)*

CROP CIRCLES BECAME the media's obsession for this summer's silly season – despite two hoaxers having confessed to making hundreds of them two years earlier.

Crop Circle stories begin to reappear

Amazing crop circle stories have been spotted all over Britain's newspapers this week. For the first time since last summer an outbreak of these extraordinary phenomena has again baffled readers looking for news.

Said one spotter, "I've no idea why they keep coming back year after year. On Tuesday I saw seven, with a beautiful one in the *Telegraph*. It was an extraordinary shape, going down the first column and then round and round an advertisement for memory loss."

Experts offer various explanations for the recurrence of these summer paranormal manifestations. They suggest they could be caused by:

● Electrical impulses swirling on the geodesic axis of the globe

● Extraterrestrial life forms giving a coded message via the pages of the *Independent*

● Desperate journalists filling in all the acres of space whilst the entire Features staff is on holiday in Tuscany.

No one knows where they will appear next, but experts suggest looking between the stories about Diana going shopping and the ones about her not going shopping.

THE FIRST ALLEGATIONS emerged about Michael Jackson.

Glenda Slagg
Fleet Street's mad cow – the gal with the six-year-old beef

■ Call me old-fashioned, but I thought people were assoomed innocent till they've been proven guilty?!! Isn't that right, Mr Pressman?!! So why for Gawd's sake is Wacko Jacko tried and hung by the Meejah before he even knows what he's accused of!?! Frankly it makes me ashamed to be a journalist!?!?!

■ Wacko Jacko!? What a perv?!! A-creepin' and a-sleepin' with little lads scarcely out of short pants!?! URGHHH! He says "I'm Bad"!? Well now we know!? Crawl back into the sewer Mr Molester and keep your filthy hands off the fans!?!

THE MIRROR GROVELLED in the face of legal action by Princess Diana, after printing photographs, taken with a hidden camera, of her working out in a gym.

Back to Basic Instincts

Lord Gnome would like to apologise for the publication of this picture. It was printed in the sincere belief that it would make him a great deal of money. He deeply regrets that it may have the opposite effect, and would like to make it clear that after resigning from the vPress Complaints Commission five minutes ago he has rejoined it with genuine and renewed commitment until he gets his hands on some new even saucier pictures.

Eat your heart out, Sharon Stone

JOHN MAJOR LAUNCHED his "Back to Basics" campaign, with several cabinet ministers publicly disparaging single mothers.

BETHLEHEM STAR
Storm grows over lone mothers

Pharisees and politicians joined forces last night to condemn the wave of single parenthood which has been sweeping Bethlehem in recent days. Ministers have linked the increase in so-called "lone mums" with the rising tide of crime which has lately been rocking Judaea.

"It is time to return to basic family values," said the Emperor Notveryaugustus (formerly Johannus Minimus), and he was strongly supported by his henchmen Pontius Portillo and Petrus Lillius. They cited the example of a young unmarried mother who had actually come to Bethlehem in order to jump the queue for accommodation. "She was immediately given a stable of her own, complete with manger, swaddling clothes, oxen, asses and other benefits," the Pharisees claimed. "The moral character of this woman can be judged by the fact that in the days after her son was born, she entertained a continual stream of male visitors, ranging from rough shepherds to wealthy foreigners, some of them coloured, bringing exotic substances into the home." Neighbours were deafened by the persistent playing of loud music, and light shows in the sky.

One opponent of single motherhood went even further. Michael Herod, the Judaean Interior Minister, pointed to recent research which showed that first-born children without fathers "lacked a proper role model" and would almost certainly end up on the wrong side of the law. "My solution is simple," said Howard. "All first-born children should be slaughtered immediately."

TWO 11-YEAR-OLD BOYS were found guilty of the brutal murder of toddler James Bulger in Liverpool.

Why Oh Why?

Why oh why oh why oh why oh why oh why oh why oh why oh why oh why oh why oh why oh why oh why oh why oh why oh why?

Oh why oh why oh why. (*Will this do?*)
© *Exclusive to all newspapers*

ENGLAND FOOTBALL MANAGER Graham Taylor resigned after the national team's poor form meant they failed to qualify for the following year's World Cup.

THE EYE'S FIRST REPORT on a scandal that would run for decades appeared in January.

North Wales detectives investigating the alleged involvement of no fewer than 12 serving and former colleagues in the country's biggest-ever child sex abuse scandal are running into an unforeseen problem. The crown prosecution service seems reluctant to prosecute anyone for well-documented cases of rape, buggery and indecent assault involving young boys who were in care over a 20-year period.

The reluctance has nothing to do with the involvement of a number of the local great and good as members of a paedophile ring, which regularly used homes, like the now-closed Bryn Estyn near Wrexham, to supply boys for sex to local celebrities.

In the late 1970s, Superintendent Gordon Anglesea of the North Wales police was appointed to investigate an allegation of buggery made by Steve Messham against the son of a then member of the North Wales police authority. The Supt found there was no case to answer. Coincidentally the police authority member and Supt Anglesea were prominent masons.

Although senior police officers knew five years ago that Anglesea was alleged to have buggered boys in care at Bryn Estyn and that he had also forced them to have oral sex with him on several occasions, he has been enjoying a well-earned retirement. He "voluntarily" agreed to an interview last month, but since no fewer than six of his former colleagues have been told that the CPS has returned their files marked "no action", Anglesea is confident no charges will be forthcoming.

Police are also urgently seeking to interview one John Allen, a businessman who used to operate a private children's home complex called the Bryn Alyn community. It is understood they wish to find out why he gave a former resident of one of his homes a post-dated cheque for £2,500. John Allen has been unavailable since early October and is understood to be in New York pursuing other business interests. This may explain why he has been unable to keep up mortgage payments on a house in Wrexham's Queens Park which he bought three years ago for another Bryn Alyn old boy. Nor has he paid his dues to his masonic lodge.

John Allen received jail sentences for six sexual assaults in 1995, and a further 33 on children from Bryn Alyn in 2014. In 1994 Gordon Anglesea successfully sued *Private Eye* **and other media outlets for libel and received £375,000 in damages.**

In 2012 the BBC's *Newsnight* **relied on Steve Messham's confused testimony to imply that former Conservative party treasurer Lord McAlpine had been a member of the paedophile ring, with disastrous results for the corporation.**

In 2016, at the age of 79, Anglesea was finally convicted of sexually abusing teenagers in care and given a 12-year jail sentence. One of the former care home residents, Mark Humphries, who had given evidence at the original libel trial, died by suicide shortly afterwards after telling his wife he could "never get over not being believed".

NEW DIRECTOR-GENERAL John Birt's changes at the BBC came under scrutiny in June.

Voodoo economics at the BBC have plumbed new depths with the news that Producer Choice, the system designed to make the corporation cost competitive, is adding to its growing losses. With Network Television's overspend now up to an estimated £124.8 million as of the end of financial year 1992-93, Producer Choice is expected to return a deficit of £35-45 million in its first year.

How a system that was designed to cut loss and inefficiency can itself become part of both defies belief. But the impact of what seems to be a serious cash flow problem is clear: hundreds of freelancers, outside contractors and independent programme makers have been jamming unit managers' phone lines in the past few weeks complaining that invoices submitted as long ago as February have still not been paid. "No one is going to work for us very soon," laments one production chief.

As usual, managers blame the computer software. "Like everything in the BBC now, it is designed for the convenience of accountants and finance managers rather than anyone who actually has anything to do with making programmes," says one production assistant. "Some units are in fact financially healthy, but when loaded with Producer Choice's fictitious overheads – say a proportion of the rent for a building the BBC owns the freehold on – they become insolvent on paper."

Producer Choice was scrapped in 2006 after it emerged that the system was so crazy it was cheaper for BBC staff to go out to shops and buy brand-new CDs than to borrow them from the corporation's own music library, or hire out West End venues for recordings at a better price than the BBC's own Radio Theatre.

PAUL FOOT RETURNED to the *Eye*, and shared the testimony of Michael Chamberlain with readers in June.

For many years I was a close friend of John Perkins, a police officer in the West Midlands Regional Crime Squad, who was closely involved in the investigation into the murder of the newspaper boy Carl Bridgewater. I now realise that the confession of Pat Molloy, one of the four men convicted, who has since died, was crucial to the prosecution case and I feel that what I know about that confession, and the background to it, should be made public.

John Perkins was a tough man and he believed in what he called "tough justice". He was often called in to interview suspects in "heavy" cases – armed robberies and so on. He summed up his attitude to these interviews by holding out his fist and saying: "This is the truth drug." More than once, when discussing suspects for violent crimes, John would say that he would give them the "plastic bag treatment". This meant that suspects would be questioned with plastic bags over their heads.

During the investigations into the Carl Bridgewater case, I used to meet John regularly in pubs around the Wolverhampton area. One conversation sticks in my mind – I can't remember which pub it was in. John said he was going to interview Pat Molloy because he was the "weak link" in the case.

The interviews with Molloy at Wombourne police station went on for days. One of those days, over a drink, I remember John predicting: "He'll go today." He made it absolutely clear to me that he had been violent to Molloy – I think the expression he used was "a couple of slaps".

I assumed that Molloy had had the same tough treatment as other suspects for violent crime had had from John Perkins. This did not worry me at the time because I thought justice was being done. But in recent years I have become more and more concerned that Molloy's confession might not have been voluntary.

The Court of Appeal finally overturned the Bridgewater Four's convictions in 1997 on the grounds that Molloy's confession had been forced out of him. The surviving trio had been in prison for over 18 years.

THERE WAS MORE NEWS of Dame Shirley Porter in August.

What is happening to the district auditor's report on Westminster council's policy of "political cleansing"? This was Dame Shirley Porter's brilliant plan to make marginal seats safe by persuading council tenants (believed to be Labour) to make way for decent Tory home-owners. All sorts of efforts have been made to suppress, now to delay the report.

Could this be because at a single swoop the report makes Tory propaganda about the "waste" of Labour councils dwindle into insignificance? The sum spent on Westminster's gerrymandering is said to have been huge.

If the district auditor does feel obliged to surcharge the Tory councillors involved, it is hard to see how he could expect them to fork out less than £2 million. If so, there is only one former Westminster Tory councillor who is likely to be able to afford it: the dame herself.

This turned out to be something of an underestimate: the surcharge imposed on Porter after the report was finally published three years later was £31 million. Having moved much of her vast fortune offshore or into secret trusts and emigrated to Israel, she finally agreed in 2004 to hand over just £12m – despite interest having taken the total then due to over £43 million.

FOOT CONTINUED to highlight miscarriages of justice.

Eddie Browning rings the *Eye* from Full Sutton prison near York, with what he calls "terrific news". He was convicted in 1989 of the murder of Marie Wilks on the M50 motorway. The prosecution case depended on the coincidence that he was driving a silver Renault 25 on the day of the murder, and that more than one witness claimed the murder car was a Renault 25. Mr Browning has always insisted he didn't drive on the M50 on the day of the murder, but travelled instead on the M4 and crossed the Severn Bridge. The prosecution submitted photographs made up from the videos of the cameras on the bridge. They claimed that not a single Renault 25 crossed the bridge at the relevant time.

This evidence was crucial to the prosecution case, and was not seriously dented by the defence. But now, says Eddie Browning, his lawyers have had a close look at the original videos. "There's a Renault 25 on the bridge all right," he says, "and it's just about the time I said I was there. There are experts to prove it."

His case, which was referred to the court of appeal a year ago, could prove very interesting indeed.

In May 1994 Eddie Browning was released after the Court of Appeal ruled that police had withheld multiple pieces of evidence at his trial. He had been in prison for over five years. The murderer of Marie Wilks has never been found.

1994

The Secret DIARY OF JOHN MAJOR aged 47¾

ENVIRONMENT MINISTER Tim Yeo's love child was just the latest sex scandal to hit John Major's government (honourable mentions to Stephen Norris's five mistresses; David Ashby's two-man bed-share and Stephen Milligan's death by auto-erotic asphyxiation in stockings and suspenders).

Monday

The papers are once again trying to make trouble. Instead of concentrating on my very popular classless New Year Honours list, they have somehow managed to dig up a totally irrelevant story about one of my very junior ministers called Mr Yeo. All he has done is to have a child with some lady who is not his wife. "To my mind this is entirely his own affair," I told Norman as I put the remaining portion of Safeway Christmas pudding into the microwave. "It is certainly an affair," said Norman crossly. "And anyway, I thought you were meant to be in favour of the family." "I am," I said, "and so is Mr Yeo. And now he's got two of them."

Tuesday

The tabloid press, ie the *Telegraph*, are still going on about Mr Yeo. I am not going to be told who I should have in my government by the newspapers, oh no.

Wednesday

The *Sun* says that Mr Yeo should resign. I agree. It is time for him to go. I cannot have ministers making my "family values" campaign look ridiculous. Not that my "family values" campaign is about families. It has nothing to do with people's private lives. It is about getting Back to Basics.

Thursday

The Yeo affair is over. I have drawn a line under it. Unfortunately no one has told the newspapers. Now they say Mr Yeo has had another love child. But I have drawn a line under this one, too.

I asked the Cabinet whether any of the rest of them wished to spend more time with their families, as it would help me greatly if I could know in advance. I am filling in my new Year-At-A-Glance Planner, and it is not inconsiderably annoying to have to keep putting in new Government vacancies to fill – three this week!

However, the Cabinet were all very quiet indeed, which shows they have nothing to hide.

Friday

Another Minister has resigned. It is a substantial pity as he had done nothing wrong. If everyone resigned when they had done nothing wrong I would have very few people left in the Government.

THE DISCOVERY of a number of bodies in the Gloucester house and garden of Fred and Rose West coincided with a particularly sticky patch for the government at the Scott Inquiry into the arms to Iraq scandal.

House of horror gives up more secrets

The house at 10 Downing Street is now set to go down in history as the world's most gruesome dwelling. Last night a number of new skeletons in closets were found there.

Forensic experts working round the clock said, "We may never know just how many political lives have been lost here. We've almost given up counting." Sources close to the investigation believe a Nicholas Lyell, currently attorney-general, may be the next victim to be discovered and inquiries (Scott) are being conducted into a number of other unexplained cases.

The suspect, a Mr J. Major, is laying the blame at the feet of the previous occupant of the house, a Mrs Thatcher.

LADY BIENVENIDA BUCK'S affair with the Chief of the Defence Staff (who resigned after it was exposed) briefly made her almost as famous as her PR man, Max Clifford.

CLIFFORD PENSION SCHEMES

More and more young women are planning a large tax-free sum to ensure they never have to work again. The Clifford Scheme is very simple. It requires only a brief affair with a middle-aged public figure, though obviously the more important he is the bigger your return!

Max Clifford will maximise your assets and will take care of all the arrangements. He will even write your life story in his own words. All you have to do is put yourself about a bit!

"I have nothing but praise for the Clifford service. He turned me overnight from an unknown scrubber into a well-known scrubber" – Antonia di Scrubba, "actress".

THE BBC'S ATTEMPT to appeal to a younger audience by dispensing with several ageing DJs and turning Radio 5 into a rolling news station turned out to involve also dispensing with millions of listeners.

That New Radio One Playlist

1. **Help!** – The Birtles
2. **Grandad, Grandad, We Fired You** – The Choir of St Forgan's Primary School
3. **Audience (I can't get no)** – The Rolling News

KURT COBAIN died by suicide.
In Memoriam Kurt Cobain, Lead Singer of the Popular Grunge Singing Group 'Nirvana'

> So. Farewell then
> Kurt Cobain.
>
> You shot yourself
> Because you were
> Depressed.
>
> I once listened
> To one of your
> Records
>
> So I know
> How you
> Must have felt.   E.J. Thribb (17½)

LABOUR LEADER John Smith died of a heart attack.

He'd still beat Major

A FRONT-RUNNER to succeed him swiftly emerged.

Blair's new three-point vision of new Britain

In a dazzling bid to become leader of the Conservative Party, the telegenic, youthful, charismatic Tony Bliar, 23, unveiled his thrilling vision of a new Britain. In a sensational yet deeply statesmanlike speech which had his supporters roaring with yawns, Mr Bliar called for "a fair society, a just society, and a fair and just society".

He called for "an end to the sort of society which is neither fair nor just, and which we have had rather too much of in recent years".

IN A TELEVISION INTERVIEW with the second-in-line Dimbleby, Prince Charles admitted committing adultery, causing public outrage.

Poll shock after royal interview

89% of the British public now think that Jonathan Dimbleby is not fit to make any more royal documentaries. A further 75% think it would be "in the national interest" if he never appeared on television again.

23% said that "he should get a proper job" instead of just wandering round the country talking to people and pretending to be interested by their replies. These are the amazing findings of a poll commissioned by the *Daily Hellograph* in the hope of finding something to fill up the front page.

The last straw for many of those who responded was Dimbleby's willingness to speak openly on television about Prince Charles's alleged "watercolours". This proved too much for the public, who no longer believe he is fit to commentate on the next Coronation.

SINN FEIN PRESIDENT Gerry Adams announced that he had persuaded the IRA to implement a "complete cessation of military operations".

Mr Gerry Adams – An Apology

In recent years, in common with all other newspapers, we may have promulgated the erroneous impression that Mr Gerald "Gerry" Adams was in some sense the most evil man who had ever lived, responsible as he was for the deaths of a vast number of innocent men, women and children.

Headlines such as YOU BASTARD, YOU MURDERING BASTARD and YOU BASTARD BASTARD may have inadvertently encouraged this impression.

We now realise that, on the contrary, Mr Adams was throughout this period a moderate, statesmanlike figure working only for peace inside the democratic framework.

We would like to take this opportunity to apologise to Mr Adams, in the form of today's 12-page supplement entitled "St Gerry The Peacemaker".

THE RED CARPET PREMIERE of *Four Weddings and a Funeral* gave the *Daily Telegraph*, a newspaper that was barely there and held together with safety pins, something new to write about.

In your Daily Hurleygraph today:

- Interest rate surprises Liz Hurley
- No comment from Hurley on two-speed Europe
- Rail strike spells chaos for Liz Hurley
- Hurley not named in Ashes squad
- Was Liz Hurley the key element in the creation of the universe?

Comment: Paul Johnson asks why oh why isn't there more coverage of Liz Hurley, girlfriend of Hugh Grant?

BESET BY EVIDENCE of his corruption and shady involvement in arms dealing, defence procurement minister Jonathan Aitken came up with an extraordinary cock-and-bull story to explain how his bill at the Paris Ritz came to be paid the previous year.

TORY COMPLAINTS were loudest on the subject of the *Guardian*'s use of a fake fax to extract some of the evidence used against Aitken.

That fax that fooled the Ritz
Horse of Commons

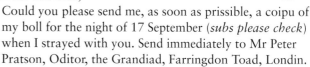

Office of Mr Jonathan Aitken P.M.

Dear The Ritz,

Could you please send me, as soon as prissible, a coipu of my boll for the night of 17 September (*subs please check*) when I strayed with you. Send immediately to Mr Peter Pratson, Oditor, the Grandiad, Farringdon Toad, Londin.

PS This is not a fake fax. Honstely.

WITH RITZ OWNER Mohamed Fayed also revealing his role as corrupter-in-chief in supplying money in brown envelopes to MPs Tim Smith and Neil Hamilton, the government began, despite its protests, to look dodgier than ever.

Sleaze and Whine Party

JOHN MAJOR MARKED the end of the year by getting rid of his Commons majority.

Monday

Today is the historic debate on the European budget. It will be a very important vote, unless of course we lose, in which case it will only be a technical hiccup.

Tuesday

Just because 319 MPs happened to vote against me doesn't mean anything. There are still 311 who supported me, which is what matters in my view, and shows that I still have the confidence of almost everyone, except eight people who are in no small measure Loonies, Bastards, Barmies, Traitors and SEVERAL DOZEN APPLES, PEARS AND BANANAS SHORT OF A PICNIC, which no one would invite them to anyway because they are all BASTARDS. I immediately called in my friend Mr Ryder, who is the Chief Whip, and told him that he must take away their party whip.

"But prime minister," he said, "that means they will no longer have to vote with the government." "They don't anyway," I said, "because they are Bastards. But now we have punished them, they will soon fall into line. You just wait." Mr Ryder opened the window and jumped out, just like Mr Lamont used to do before he became my ex-friend and the biggest BASTARD AND LOONY OF THEM ALL.

THE CHANNEL TUNNEL, which was finally due to open in May, came under scrutiny in January.

Eurotunnel must make £600 million a year to pay interest on its colossal debts – and it can only do so by capturing all the present traffic on freight and passenger services, and all the income from duty-free sales currently earned on the short ferry crossings.

This is beyond the dreams of avarice, so its debt must increase and the City view remains that the company will enter the Humber Bridge club, spending all its revenue on interest on a debt that can never be repaid because the interest will always be greater than income.

It may try to slash prices to kill off competitors, but given the size of the debt (£10 billion) it would need an unusually patient and forbearing collection of bankers to wait for that to happen. The awkward fact is that the tunnel, our prestige emblem, is not and cannot be viable.

It took until 2006 for Eurotunnel to collapse under the weight of its debts, by then totalling £6.2bn.

IN JUNE, PAUL FOOT had news about the investigation into the racist murder of Stephen Lawrence the previous year.

The main witness to Stephen Lawrence's murder, a close friend of the murdered student, picked out a suspect from an identification parade, but his evidence was discredited by a police sergeant. Now the witness himself is being prosecuted for violent disorder and criminal damage arising from a protest demonstration two weeks after the murder.

This prosecution was not brought until September last year: four months after the demonstration and after the decision to prosecute two men for Stephen Lawrence's murder had been dropped because of the police sergeant's intervention.

If this young man is convicted, the Metropolitan police and the crown prosecution service will have achieved a rare record. While Stephen Lawrence's murderers stalk the streets as free men, a young friend of Stephen who was with him when he died and who identified a man as one of the murderers is prosecuted and punished.

The proceedings against Duwayne Brooks, Stephen Lawrence's best friend who was attacked along with him, were subsequently ruled an abuse of justice by a judge, and the Met's file on them has mysteriously disappeared. Brooks was arrested a further five times, and at one point prosecuted for sexual assault, only for another judge to stop the trial because of the unreliablility of the evidence against him. In 2014 it was revealed that police had continued to gather intelligence on Brooks right up until 2001, including bugging a meeting between him and his solicitor. No one was convicted of Lawrence's murder until 2012.

IN JULY, THE DTI confirmed they were investigating the now Lord Archer for insider dealing over the purchase of shares in a company of which his wife Mary was a director. Slicker was unconvinced by the version that had appeared in the press.

The most intriguing non-libellous question raised by the Jeffrey Archer probe is just who was the fortunate friend who made £80,000 within days of being told to buy Anglia Television shares by the husband of the fragrant Mary, coincidentally an Anglia director?

Archer declines to identify the lucky investor who was so impressed by the great novelist's tip that he went out and invested more than £200,000. Just why the normally motor-mouthed Archer should be so uncharacteristically silent is unclear. So too is the failure of the friend to come to Archer's aid. Perhaps this reticence will end once the Tory peer is rightly "cleared" by the impending report from the inspectors appointed by the Department of Timidity and Inaction.

Archer maintains that the mysterious friend staked his own money and took the profit. He says he bought no Anglia shares himself, and did not benefit from the £80,000 realised within a matter of days as 50,000 shares were bought and sold.

This firmly disproves the suggestion that the cause of Archer's embarrassment was that he had, as a favour, facilitated the share deal by allowing the friend to use either a stockbroker or an account with which he had some connection. A name is rumoured – the small firm Charles Stanley – but this is probably just because the firm has an office in Cambridge where the Archers live. Anyway, why would someone who had £200,000 to invest need to use someone else's account? He would surely have his own stockbroker.

It turned out Archer had not merely tipped off his friend Broosk Saib – he had personally conducted the purchase and sale of the shares on his behalf through his own account with Charles Stanley, and asked for the deal to be recorded in Saib's name "c/o J. Archer", using his own home address. Insisting all the way that his wife had never discussed a pending takeover bid for Anglia with him, Archer nevertheless admitted in August to a "grave error", though neither man has ever clarified why the deals were conducted in such an inexplicable way.

MEANWHILE, THE EYE revealed details of yet more dodgy dealing that had only been hinted at elsewhere (although the *Eye* had been onto it a decade earlier: *see p103*).

No one was more relieved than John Major at the "shelving" of the recent Central Television programme on Ian Greer Associates, the parliamentary lobbyists.

A long-standing friend and associate of Ian Greer is Neil Hamilton, the dashing corporate affairs minister. He had been widely tipped for promotion, but didn't get it. Last October the *Guardian* disclosed that in 1987, before he was a minister, he stayed for a week with his wife at a "European hotel" owned by a client of Greer's with whom Hamilton also had a long-standing relationship. On returning from his luxury week, with the whole £5,000 bill paid by the owner, Hamilton asked two parliamentary questions about his company and did not declare the visit in the MPs' register of interests. The *Eye* can disclose that the hotel was the Ritz in Paris, and the firm was owned by the Fayed brothers, owners of Harrods in London.

Hamilton stays where he is, as does another Greer client looking for promotion: Tim Smith, who remains a junior minister in Northern Ireland. In his backbench days Smith astonished colleagues with the range of his parliamentary questions, which often sought information about government accounting contracts.

THREE MONTHS LATER, Fayed fully blew the gaff on Smith and Hamilton, whom he had paid both directly and through Ian Greer Associates to ask parliamentary questions: Smith resigned immediately, although Hamilton continued to unconvincingly protest his evidence all the way to the libel courts three years later. As the story broke, Slicker advised strong caution.

There is something revolting about watching the sanctimonious *Guardian* editor Peter Preston dancing to the tune of the phoney pharaoh Mohamed Fayed. Truth is where you find it, but the price for exposing corruption and MP's greed should not be defending a proven liar who misled the government and regulators about his wealth and background. The *Guardian* may yet come to learn the lesson they are teaching the Tories about dogs and fleas.

Fayed knew from his years of hustling in the Middle East how to infiltrate the Tory government: find out what MPs and ministers wanted and give it to them. The answer was cheques big and small plus generous hospitality. Those who eagerly accepted the Fayed shilling never contemplated their paymaster turning on them when he did not get what he wanted. But he had done it before: when he served as a "bag man" for Dubai fixer Mahdi Al-Tajir, collecting commissions and taking care of business, Fayed was well known to certain London madams who provided girls for partying. When he later fell out with Mahdi, Fayed produced chapter and verse of pay-offs that the then United Arab Emirates ambassador to Britain had received. He was also prepared to go to extraordinary lengths to discredit Mahdi, falsely accusing him of involvement in drug trafficking and sexual deviancy with everyone short of a camel.

Neil Hamilton, who with fellow victim Tim Smith continued to do Fayed's bidding after the DTI's damning conclusions on him were known (*see p125*), was preceded by a long list of senior journalists and other MPs on Ritz freebies. They – with Jonathan Aitken – will no doubt be reassured to know that not only does Fayed keep the receipts but it is claimed he arranged for rooms to be bugged, enabling the recording of telephone calls and if necessary video taping.

Fayed's inability to distinguish truth from fiction, and his unassuageable thirst for revenge, became much more widely known following his son's death alongside Princess Diana three years later.

IN NOVEMBER, an *Eye* special report on the arms-to-Iraq inquiry by Paul Foot and Tim Laxton detailed the extraordinary extent of the doublespeak and double-dealing by the government, civil service and arms companies that had been revealed.

In early 1988 David Hastie was group marketing director of British Aerospace, who wanted to flog £5 billion of Hawk fighter aircraft, plus the factories to build them, to Saddam Hussein's Iraq. It knew there might be trouble with the sale, so it decided it needed another man in the ministry in addition to its former group marketing director, Colin Chandler, who had been appointed by the Thatcher government as head of the Defence Export Services Organisation at the MoD.

Accordingly, BAe wrote to Chandler suggesting a "one-year development secondment to the MoD" for Hastie. His prestigious salary and expenses, BAe promised, would of course be paid by the company.

Chandler agreed at once. But there was the small problem of what he was to do: in reality, of course, he was there to help flog the Hawk fighter to Saddam but more squeamish civil servants might object to this role being proclaimed out loud. Instead it was announced that Hastie would be a "business development adviser" to Mr Chandler, a post which did not exist before or since.

An important event in the arms-flogging calendar was the Baghdad Arms Fair held in April 1989. Mr Hastie was keen to go to represent the ministry at the fair, so his contract was conveniently extended for six months. But then came an awkward hitch: an infuriating decree from the foreign office that no DESO personnel could attend the arms fair in case it gave the wrong signal to Saddam, namely that there had been a change in British policy on arms sales (which of course there had).

Following a desperate meeting between Chandler and the permanent under-secretary at the MoD, a brilliant solution emerged: Hastie would remain a DESO man until he went to the fair, but not while he was at it. On his way to Baghdad he would become a British Aerospace man again, and not be allowed to hand out any visiting cards which described him as a man from the ministry. As soon as he got on the plane to go home, however, he would become a DESO man again.

IT ALSO CAST DOUBT on the former prime minister's testimony.

Did Mrs Thatcher tell the truth? She spent a lot of her day at the Scott Inquiry saying how little she knew. She didn't know that the sales guidelines for arms to Iraq were changed in 1988, and she didn't know anything about the export of Matrix Churchill lathes until June 1990.

This was strange – it directly contradicted a briefing written for ministers in December 1988 which read "Intelligence sources indicated that the lathes were to be used for making shells and missiles… The Prime Minister agreed that in order to protect the intelligence source the licences already granted should not be revoked… This needs to go back to the Prime Minister before we could recommend approving the current applications."

Further evidence came from an even more reliable source: Mrs Thatcher herself. When the guidelines were changed in 1988, documents show she demanded of her civil service that she be kept closely in touch with the developments in the changing circumstances of the arms trade with both Iraq and Iran.

Mrs Thatcher, however, denied this utterly. And Mr Barratt, the official who wrote the briefing, was overcome by a terrible fit of amnesia, saying, "I cannot recall if and when the PM was told about the Matrix exports."

Five months after Mrs Thatcher gave evidence, the court of appeal heard the appeal of two directors of Euromac who had been convicted in 1991 of illegally exporting "nuclear triggers/capacitators" to Iraq. Their convictions were quashed. In the course of the appeal a message was disclosed from the US customs operations HQ in San Diego: "The British authorities in London have also added their support to the proposed operation and customs San Diego was advised that the British Prime Minister was advised of the status of the investigation and is very much interested in its progress and successful outcome." The document was dated 4 August 1989 – five months before Mrs Thatcher said she had first heard of the case.

DECEMBER SAW the first mention of something with which *Eye* readers would become very familiar.

The Tories have unveiled their latest bright idea for preventing computer cock-ups: the Private Finance Initiative (PFI) which has proved itself by bringing expensive projects in on time and on budget – projects like the, er, Channel tunnel rail link.

One side effect of this complex scheme is that payments to consultants' remain hidden from ministers and scrutiny by the public accounts committee. Not surprisingly, the warmest welcome has come from… the consultants.

Following disasters at the social security department, Andersen Consulting has suggested PFI should be applied to the DSS's next project: the huge national insurance system, NIRS2. The DSS has commissioned an "independent" report giving it the green light. It was, of course, written by Andersen Consulting, and the firm has just opened a new 300-staff data centre in Newcastle in anticipation of the award.

NIRS2 was indeed contracted to Andersen Consulting under PFI the following year, and it came in massively late and enormously over-budget: at the end of the decade the public accounts committee said it had "resulted in uncertainty and loss of income for thousands of people… There has been a clear failure to deliver services to the citizen." But by then PFI had been enthusiastically embraced and extended by the Labour government, thanks largely to chancellor Gordon Brown's keenness on keeping things off the public balance sheet.

1995

AFTER BEING SENT OFF in a match against Crystal Palace, Manchester United striker Eric Cantona launched a kung-fu kick on an opposition fan who was taunting him from the front of the crowd.

Knee says 'Kung Fu' Depardieu to stay

By E.I. Erewigo, Our Man on the Terraces With The Collected Poems Of The French Symbolists

Tight-lipped Neasden supremo Ron Knee announced yesterday that the club's controversial £25 continental striker Eddie Depardieu is to stay with Neasden despite his life sentence for inflicting grievous bodily harm against a fan, Mr Sidney Bonkers.

The incident took place during the needle relegation battle with Dollis Hill, when Mr Bonkers had run onto the pitch wielding a chainsaw, shouting, "I'm going to cut your frog's legs off and have 'em in garlic, you useless French git."

Counsel for Mr Depardieu told Neasden Magistrates Court, "It was more than flesh and blood could stand. My client has a Gallic temperament. He admits he seized the corner flag and stabbed it into Mr Bonkers' head. In mitigation of his action, he points out that it failed to do irreparable damage because Mr Bonkers does not possess a brain."

THE HOPELESSLY SPLIT cabinet were unable to agree a line on the proposed European single currency, obliging John Major to continue fudging the issue.

We've agreed to disagree

No, we haven't

CABINET UNITED

SOME PEOPLE CLAIMED to see a future for what the *Eye*'s TV critic described as "the Internet, some kind of souped-up computer network on which techno-anoraks converse with similar obsessives around the world".

Great Bores of Today

"...it's brilliant all you need to do is configure your modem to autodial your service provider and then you're online to a global network which enables you to browse the worldwide web surf the newsgroups ftp to a site to grab an update for your display driver or anything you want now I've got an email address anyone can reach me instantly all you need is a PC with a fast serial port a V32 modem minimum or ISDN if you can afford it a good network connection to the PSTN and away you go it's as simple as that at 2am I was able to send the message 'hello I'm on the Internet' to Colin next door only it got bounced because he hasn't got his system installed yet so I had to ring him instead but anyway it's brilliant..."

IN AMERICA, the murder trial of O.J. Simpson went on, and on.

The Trial of O.J. Thello (994th day) before His Excellency Doge Cocklecarrot

Appearing for the defendant, Miss Janet Street-Portia told the court that her client, the well-known celebrity general O.J. Thello, could not possibly be guilty of the murder of his wife, Mrs Des D. Mona, in front of hundreds of witnesses, because he was black.

Signor Perry Masone (*for the State of Venice*):
Objection, your Dogeship.

Doge: Objection overruled.

(Applause from 80 million viewers worldwide)

(Cut to Commercial Break. Mr Stephen Fry, for it is he, rhymes amusingly: You get a better class of investor/At the Shylock Bank, Venezia)

Street-Portia: Welcome back to our viewers. I call as my next guest in the witness box someone that everyone at home has been waiting to see. So let's have a big hand for our old friend, that Learned Doctor of the Humours of the Afflicted Mind, Professore Sigmundo Freud.

(Enter bearded Viennese [shurely 'Venetian?' Ed] psychiatrist as house band strike up version of Crazy Crazy Nights)

Portia: Would it not be true to say that my client is totally innocent and that the only truly guilty party is the state of Venice, for its unashamedly racist policy towards its Moorish-Adriatic ethnic minority community in making O.J.Thello Commander-in-Chief?

Freud: I hev examined ze case history of ze defendant and zere is no doubt in my mind zat he is suffering from being black.

(Cheers from the gallery and cries of "O.J. for Doge!")

Judge: Objection! It's time for another commercial break.

(Continued for 94 years)

THE PRIME MINISTER was beset by Lords coming back to haunt him.

Monday

Everyone is talking about Mr Lord Nolan, who is the man I appointed last year to stop people talking about sleaze. When I appointed Mr Lord Nolan it was done with the very highest of motives, ie to push sleaze under the carpet until everyone had forgotten about it. What I forgot about was that he would eventually produce a report. Luckily almost everybody in the House of Commons agrees with me that we should now push the report under the carpet instead.

Friday

It is quite unbelievable. Now Mr Lord Justice Scott, whom I appointed to find out who was to blame for the scandal over selling arms to Iraq, has apparently produced some kind of report listing the people who are to blame. How dare he? After all I have done for him, giving him a job and making him famous. No one would have heard of Lord Justice Scott if it wasn't for me. He is just like my brother Terry.

ACTOR HUGH GRANT was arrested in LA in the company of prostitute Divine Brown, but his girlfriend Liz Hurley agreed to take him back.

A Sylvie Krin Summer Special

To err is human, to forgive divine

She spread the few keepsakes of the dying embers of their love on the tabletop before her. What did they mean now, these tattered clippings, bank statements and copies of *Hello*? Huge translucent tears welled in her perfectly-formed eyes, and gushed unchecked down the exquisite peach-skin purity of her cheeks. She was barely recognisable as the pouting beauty whose peerless features had graced every single page of the *Daily Telegraph* each morning for the past six months.

Her mobile trilled. Could it be the studio, finally offering her that longed-for part? She cupped the telephone to her immaculate, Dresden-shepherdess ear and murmured "Who is this?"

"It's me." The manly voice was racked with pain and self-doubt. "I'm so sorry, my darling. It was a moment of madness. I've been a bloody fool. But you know we've got to stay together."

"What for?" she gasped, her voice choked with emotion.

"For the sake of the money."

"Oh… Oh darling, I'm so happy. That's what my agent said too." She slowly put the phone down, and the whole world suddenly seemed to be lit by the glow of a thousand rainbows…

BARINGS, one of the world's oldest merchant banks, collapsed as a result of the activities of its derivatives "rogue trader" Nick Leeson. £827 million in the red, it was purchased for just £1 by Dutch bank ING.

JEMIMA GOLDSMITH, daughter of the obsessively vengeful friend of the *Eye*, converted to Islam and moved to Pakistan to marry cricketer-turned-politician Imran Khan.

FINALLY TIRING OF DIVISIONS over Europe and declaring that it was time to "Put Up or Shut Up", John Major resigned as leader of the Conservative Party – and defeated right-wing challenger John Redwood in the ensuing vote. This was largely thanks to his most likely rival Michael Heseltine deciding to throw his weight behind him. He was rewarded with the post of Deputy Prime Minister.

Monday

When I went to my office this morning I noticed that the wall where my *Daily Telegraph* world map used to be has been turned into a very large door with two lights above it. One is red, saying "Wait" and the other is green, saying "Enter". I was just going to sit down when the green light went on, and the doors slid open. Imagine my not inconsiderable surprise when I saw, on the other side, a huge room the size of a football pitch, and at the far end an enormous desk with my friend Mr Heseltine sitting behind it. "Do come in, John," he shouted, "I'll be with you in a minute, I've just got a few important calls to make."

While I sat there waiting I read the notice on his desk, which said "Rt. Hon M. Heseltine, Deputy Prime Minister,

First Lord of the Jungle, Chairman of all Cabinet Committees, Primus Inter Pares and De-Facto Supreme Ruler of the Universe." I was just going to ask him what "Primus Inter Pares" meant, when Mr Heseltine finished his telephone call to Mr Herr Kohl and said, "Ah, John, I've got some good news for you. All this election business must have been pretty tiring for you. You deserve a good long break, so I've decided to send you on holiday." I thought how lucky I am to have a deputy who is so considerate and thoughtful.

"Now if you'll excuse me," said Mr Heseltine, "I have to ring Mr Yeltsin to see if he's dead yet."

Tuesday

I was just puzzling over the main headline in the *Telegraph*, "HEZZA RINGS YEZZA", when the new Party Chairman Mr Mawhinney came through to my office. "Don't touch those papers, John," he shouted in his funny Irish voice. "I've put them out for Mr Heseltine to look at before the Cabinet meeting he's called."

"Oh," I said. "Is there a Cabinet meeting?" "Not for you, John," he said. "You're officially on holiday." He then put a card into the sliding doors, and they opened. I was about to follow him when the doors shut again, and the red light went on, saying "Wait".

There is something very odd going on here, which I do not completely understand.

MICHAEL PORTILLO, the darling of right-wing Tories, made a barnstorming speech to the party conference.

Cabbie wows Tories

Youthful 41-year-old Spanish-born cab driver Miguel Portillo took the Tory Conference by storm yesterday, with a speech that had the party faithful on their feet screaming for blood (*shurely "more"? – Ed.*)

"Those blokes in Brussels," he began, "they're all foreigners, every one of them. If they had their way we'd all still be living under the Nazis, shouting 'Seig Heil'." Here the audience rose to their feet and gave him a raised arm salute.

"Tell you what we should do to Brussels," he went on, "send in the SAS. Know worrimean? They'd soon sort them out. You know what their motto is? 'String 'em up'. That's the only language those foreigners understand. I had that General de la Billière in the back of the cab once," he concluded to a standing ovation.

A YEAR AFTER ITS LAUNCH, the National Lottery was accused of channelling cash towards posh causes such as the refurbishment of the Royal Opera House, rather than those enjoyed by the people who actually bought tickets for it.

TONY BLAIR'S TOP MEN Alastair Campbell and Peter Mandelson were busy ensuring lots of coverage of their attempts to ensure lots of coverage for their boss.

A Spin-Doctor writes

As a spin-doctor, I am often asked, "Why do you keep ringing up the BBC?"

The simple answer is that I am suffering from a condition known as Campbell's Syndrome, or *Media Manipulatus Mandelson* as it is more formally known.

The symptoms include a swollen head, an enlargement of the mouth and delusions that everyone is incredibly interested in Tony Blair.

If you feel you could be suffering from Campbell's Syndrome, you should ring up John Birt at once.

PRINCESS DIANA gave a surprise tell-all interview to the BBC's *Panorama*. Craig Brown transcribed it for the *Eye*.

There were three of us in the marriage, and it was a little bit crowded. So to give myself more space, I formed a close friendship with James Gilbey. Then there were four of us in the marriage, and it was a little bit crowded. So to give myself more space, I entered into an intimate relationship with James Hewitt. And formed a close attachment to Oliver Hoare. And enjoyed a friendship based on mutual trust and support with Will Carling. Then there were seven of us in the marriage, and it was a little bit crowded. So to give myself more space, I invited in a television crew. Now there are three hundred million people worldwide in the marriage, and it is a little bit crowded.

I have two children to bring up. And I can't even remember having eaten them. But honestly, I wish everyone would understand that the privacy of my two boys is all I care about. But the media pressure can be unbearable. Just last month William produced a box of chocolates and said

something so private that I've never forgotten it. He said, "Mummy, I think you've been hurt. These are to make you smile again."

I would hope that I still have a valuable role to play. The poor and the starving and the dying have their role to play too. For who else would we care for if it were not for the poor and the starving and the dying? I know from my own experience in this environment that for many years I tried desperately to care for the wealthy, the well-fed and the still-living. But no matter how hard I cared, these people simply wouldn't keep still, often moving to the other side of the room. This was obviously distressing for me. But then I discovered that there are millions of ordinary people out there who are simply not able to move away in this manner. Many of them are in hospital, stuck in bed, unable to walk or run. And to these people I hold out my hand. "Let me share in your pain, because deep down, I'm as miserable as you must be," I tell them. "Yes, I have been through the living hell of marrying into the richest family in Britain, being adored by many hundreds of millions, and being hailed by the international press as the most beautiful woman in the world, but I have come out the other side." And now I know what ordinary people in the same situation go through every day.

And that is why from this day hence I am proud to be your Queen of Hearts.

THE PALACE was not amused.

IN FEBRUARY, the *Sunday Times* reported that former Labour leader Michael Foot had been a KGB agent. The *Eye* pointed out a few flaws in the story.

The paper's source for the Foot story was Oleg Gordievsky – a self-confessed liar whose various claims about British "agents" over the years have been so wildly contradictory as to render his evidence all but worthless. Perhaps aware that it could not go into print on Gordievsky's word alone, the *Sunset Times* dispatched David Leppard to Moscow last week in the hope he could find another ex-KGB officer prepared to corroborate the story.

His first port of call was Mikhail Lyubimov, a KGB man who worked at the Soviet Embassy in London in the 1960s and had met Foot. Alas, he said that he had never made any payments to Foot and had never heard of any suggestion that old Wurzel might be working for Moscow.

Undaunted, Leppard then went to see Viktor Kubeykin, another retired KGB man. And here, according to last Sunday's front-page report, he struck Moscow gold: Kubeykin had seen the file marked "Boot" and confirmed that Soviet intelligence "regarded Foot as an agent of influence".

Alas again! As soon as the *ST* piece was published, a furious Kubeykin flatly denied that he had told Leppard anything of the sort. Collapse of story? Not quite. Leppard continued to insist that his account of the interview with Kubeykin was accurate – and that he had a witness to prove it.

The "witness" is Carey Scott, the paper's new Moscow correspondent, who did indeed accompany him on his visit to Kubeykin. But if Leppard imagines she will save his skin, he may have to think again. According to Kubeykin, when he complained to Scott about the story last Sunday, she was equally indignant, agreeing that Leppard had misrepresented him. Scott herself is now unavailable for comment: a message on her Moscow answering machine reveals that she has – very wisely – disappeared to Australia since the article appeared.

The *Sunday Times* apologised to Foot and paid him substantial damages in July. The story resurfaced in 2018, when the *Eye* took great pleasure in shooting it down all over again.

WHEN JONATHAN AITKEN unleashed his "simple sword of truth" against a series of libel defendants (including the *Eye*) in April, the magazine devoted an entire page to his history of perfidy.

Aitken seems to believe that truth is so precious it must be strictly rationed. He was a director of TV-am in the 1980s, thanks to a 14.9 per cent stake in the breakfast channel which had been acquired by his firm, Beaverbrook Investments. But Beaverbrook Investments was in turn controlled by the Saudi Arabian royal family through a firm called Al Bilad, of which Aitken was also a director. Under Independent Broadcasting Authority regulations, Aitken was obliged to inform the IBA of any shareholding exceeding 1 per cent which was held by non-EEC organisations or individuals. Did he wave his simple sword of truth and tell the IBA? Er, no. Nor did he mention to his fellow directors of TV-am that the station was being bankrolled with Saudi money. "With the wisdom of seven years hindsight," he said when this was finally revealed, "I accept that the confidential requirements of our clients were given too high a priority above the candour that should have been offered to our colleagues on the board."

In 1977 he angrily denied reports of a "romance" with Carol Thatcher, only to reveal two years later to the *News of the World* that "we were very much romantically attached". In 1993 he denied having a meeting with three of his former business partners, Wafic Said, Said Mohammed Ayas and Dr Fahad Somait, at the Ritz in Paris, saying the purpose of his visit had been to spend time with his wife and daughter and "social encounters with my daughter's godparents and other old friends". The godparent in question, as the *Guardian* soon discovered, was Mohammed Ayas.

Then came the question of who paid his hotel bill, which contained the words "Debiteur: A/C Mr Ayas." "Mr Ayas did not pay my hotel bill," Aitken told the paper. "The hotel bill was paid by my wife, with money given to her by me for this purpose." The denial seemed to be unequivocal. But by then Aitken was also being investigated by the cabinet secretary, Sir Robin Butler. To support his case, Aitken told him that Ayas had now received a letter from the Ritz confirming Mrs Aitken had paid the bill. Not so: it consisted of one sentence saying "you have not personally paid the bill of Jonathan Aitken", and said nothing about Mrs Aitken. A later letter from the Ritz's manager said the cashier remembered that "a brunette lady of European aspect

paid the cash sum of Ff4,257 in favour of the account of Mr Ayas": Aitken sent this to Butler as further proof, even though his wife is manifestly not a brunette. And before sending it to the cabinet secretary, Aitken erased the words "in favour of the account of Mr Ayas", thereby altering its meaning entirely.

When the *Guardian* obtained the full text of the letter and drew attention to the creative editing, Aitken provided yet another "explanation": part of the bill had been paid by Ayas's nephew, by some mysterious oversight. Aitken had reimbursed him with a cheque dated 21 February 1994 – more than a month after his denial that anyone other than his wife might have paid the bill.

This pattern – outright denial, followed by amendments and ambiguities – has been repeated several times. Last November, for example, it was alleged that Aitken had visited Ayas's yacht, the Katamarino, in the summer. At first his office said "at no stage was he on the Katamarino", then when told the ship's captain distinctly remembered seeing him, that "Mr Aitken has never been on a 10-day cruise on the Katamarino or any other boat. He has never been on any boat in his life for longer than a few hours." The next day, his office changed its statement yet again. "Mr Aitken and his family had dinner on board

with an old family friend one evening." The friend was… Said Mohammed Ayas.

The same technique was used during the recent fuss about Aitken's directorship of arms company BMARC. Last autumn he was asked what he knew about Project Lisi, BMARC's contract for exporting guns to Singapore. A flat denial: "I had no knowledge of Project Lisi." When the *Independent* ran the story in March, this became "I have no recollection of Project Lisi." Within 24 hours his memory had suddenly got a lot better: "At no board meeting of the company was I ever given the slightest indication or information that could suggest that the company's wholly legitimate contract to Singapore might subsequently result in components being shipped to Iran." So he apparently did know about Project Lisi after all – just not that the guns might go to Iran!

If Aitken's libel suit against the *Guardian* ever comes to court, he will be obliged to swear to tell the truth, the whole truth, and nothing but the truth. It should be a novel experience for him.

He didn't – he lied his way through the whole thing, and obliged his teenage daughter to lie on oath on his behalf too. The case duly fell apart, and Aitken was sent to prison for perjury.

IN MAY, M.D. RETURNED to Bristol (*see p148*).

As far back as 1988, the mortality rates at the paediatric cardiac surgery unit at the United Bristol healthcare trust were so high that it was dubbed "The Killing Fields" and "The Departure Lounge" by those in the know. Despite a long crisis of morale among the unit's staff, surgeons repeatedly refused to publish their mortality rates in a manner that would allow comparison with other units. John Roylance, the trust chief executive, and senior officials at the department of health were fully aware of the problems, but initially chose to ignore them.

Other consultants working in the trust admitted in private that the unit was a disgrace and that they wouldn't send their children to it – but they continued to send other people's children there "to support the hospital".

A secret audit kept by consultant anaesthetist Dr Stephen Bolsin revealed that the unit's mortality rate for repairing Fallot's tetralogy, a congenital heart malformation, was between 20 and 30 per cent. In Liverpool, 160 babies had similar operations without a single death.

He then found that the mortality rate for arterial switch, an operation to connect congenitally transposed arteries from the heart, was 30 per cent in Bristol compared to 10 per cent elsewhere in the country, and nearly 0 per cent in America. This figure worsened to 61 per cent by 1993, though parents were told they had "a 70 to 80 per cent chance of success".

In 1992 James Wisheart, the senior paediatric cardiac surgeon, was appointed chairman of the hospital management committee and medical adviser to the trust board. For whatever reason, he did not alert them to the disastrous death rates of his unit. Overall, a baby was twice as likely to die from open heart surgery in his unit than any other in the country.

Dr Bolsin first confronted his trust superiors with his findings in 1993, though they were already well aware of them. He received little support and eventually took his findings to Dr Peter Dole at the Department of Health. In October 1993, 18 months after the *Eye*'s leak, neonatal switch operations were cancelled at the hospital. However, in January 1995 a switch operation was performed on an 18-month-old child who died the next day. The DoH then banned the unit from doing all operations.

A surgical unit can have bad mortality figures for a number of reasons. Sometimes it is because they select particularly difficult cases. Sometimes it is because of a lack of specialist staff and equipment. And sometimes it is because some of the surgeons are slow, dangerous, cumbersome and too arrogant to acknowledge their own limitations, even when babies are dying around them.

Which or whom to blame in this case is unclear. The trust has refused to release a damning report by independent investigators, or to divulge its statistics since the problem was first highlighted in 1988. The fact that it took seven years to suspend all operations at the unit is a disgrace, and the trust, the government, the NHS and the taxpayer now look likely to face huge compensation claims from the distressed parents of up to 100 children who may have died as a result of the incompetence and self-protective instincts of senior doctors and managers at UBHT.

Were it not for the courageous whistleblowing of Dr Stephen Bolsin, the death toll would have been even higher.

A full inquiry into the scandal was not set up until 1998. In 2001 it concluded that up to 35 children died between 1991 and 1995 who would probably have survived if operated on elsewhere. Stephen Bolsin was praised for his attempts to raise the alarm – "he persisted and he was right to do so" – but by that point he had emigrated to Australia saying his whistleblowing had irreparably damaged his career prospects in the UK.

THERE WAS NEWS from Whitehall in June.

To help him to slash the benefits of disabled people, Social Services Secretary Peter Lilley has hired the vice-president of a big multinational private insurance company which is using the benefit cuts to boost its sales. And overcoming the xenophobia to which Lilley so often gives voice at Tory party conferences, it is an American – Dr John Le Cascio, second vice-president of the Unum Corporation. He has been invited by Lilley's department to help in the extensive training of doctors in the new techniques of "all-work tests", which will change the criteria under which disabled or sick people receive benefits. Previously they were entitled to benefits if they could no longer do their jobs; now they will get them only if they can do no work at all. The change from invalidity benefit to incapacity benefit aims to provide "savings" of an astonishing £1.7 billion in 1997-98.

Unum was quick to spot that with so much less government money going to sick and disabled people, the opportunities for private disability insurance were enormous. Its chairman "launched a concerted effort to harness the potential" in the form of a slick advertising campaign in April, which pointed out that "if you fall ill and have to rely on state incapacity benefit you could be in serious trouble".

Unum firmly embedded itself in what became the Department for Work and Pensions, with execs sitting on the working groups which came up with the new Work Compatibility Assessments introduced in 2008 and the panel reviewing sickness absence rules in 2011.

1996

THE FIRST PRIVATISED rail services began running, as South West Trains and Great Western's franchises kicked in.

No. 891
Friday
9 Feb. '96

PRIVATE EYE

Full Steam Ahead!
Britain's Privatised Railways Are Go!!

Do I still have to change at Didcot Parkway?

Don't ask me, that's Railtrack

The Eye
Something to read while you are waiting for your train

HOME OFFICE MINISTER Ann Widdecombe was happy to publicly defend a policy of shackling pregnant prisoners during hospital visits, after it emerged that a woman had been chained even after her waters broke.

Women *will* be chained, claims defiant Government

The government last night announced that it would be extending its policy over chaining to include Home Office ministers who were out of control. "There are some women," said a spokesman, "who, if not chained, will run straight into a television studio and do serious damage to the government's reputation. They have to be chained to their desks where they can continue their labour without the risk of doing anything stupid."

THE IRA SET OFF a massive bomb in London's Docklands, ending their 18-month ceasefire.

The Secret DIARY OF JOHN MAJOR aged 47¾

Friday

This evening Mrs R, the secret head of MI5 (Mrs Rimington) came round personally to assure me that the IRA ceasefire is holding strongly. This is very encouraging. While she was explaining this there was a very loud bang.

Saturday

I was in no small measure surprised to hear Mr Gerry Adams telling Mr Humphrys on the BBC that the only person responsible for the bombing was me. I immediately rang up the police to give them my alibi – ie, that I was with a Mrs R at the time and she would support me, although she could not be identified for security reasons.

Sunday

All the papers are saying that my peace process is at an end. They are wrong, as usual. It is my peace process, and the only person who can decide it is at an end is me, not the IRA, who cannot stop the peace process just by letting off a few bombs and killing people. One thing is certain. I will not be talking to Mr Adams again for a not inconsiderable period of time. I rang him up at once to tell him this.

ENVIRONMENTAL protesters took direct action to prevent the felling of 10,000 trees to make way for the Newbury bypass.

Look and Learn, Part 94: The Ascent of Man

1. **4m BC:** Man comes down from trees

2. **4,000 BC:** Man invents wheel

3. **1996 AD:** Man goes back up the trees

A 43-YEAR-OLD MAN walked into his local primary school in Dunblane and shot dead 16 5-year-olds and their teacher, injuring 15 others, before killing himself.

Editorial: The value of silence

There are times when the only appropriate response to tragedy is one of mute reflection. Mere words cannot convey the feelings engendered by the appalling events of the past week.

The temptation to rush into print with facile comment or instant analysis must be resisted. Nor should we permit intrusion into private grief under the cover of public interest.

Words are sadly inadequate in the face of this horror.

Also in our 48-page Special Massacre Supplement:

THE GOVERNMENT ADMITTED that actually, there might be a link between Mad Cow Disease and the human illness CJD, prompting an international panic over British beef products.

Your guide to those products you should avoid

Few people realise that a wider range of everyday household products contain deadly toxic beef. These are the at-risk items you should keep away from at all costs:

Mousetraps	Wine Gums
Washing-up gloves	Boot polish *(black)*
Rubber bands	Bookshelves
Loft Cladding	The Sunday Telegraph

Toothpaste *(except banana-flavoured)*
Waxed dental floss *(especially banana-flavoured)*
Cows

IN APRIL the government finally got round to fully banning farmers from feeding their livestock mammalian meat and bone meal (ie themselves).

RATTLED BY THE RUNAWAY popularity of Tony Blair, the Tories launched a new 'Demon Eyes' ad campaign.

AS ENGLAND'S FOOTBALLERS faced Germany, new *Mirror* editor Piers Morgan showed off his consummate understanding of his readers with a jingoistic front page reading "Achtung – Surrender – For you, Fritz, ze Euro '96 championship is over".

Voice of the Moron

You would imagine from the reaction of some of the snottier media commentators that the *Daily Moron* had been in some way inciting English fans to violence against foreign supporters.

What on earth has happened to these people's sense of humour? It is a sad day for this country when the press cannot produce a few knockabout front pages without incurring the wrath of the politically correct killjoys.

The *Moron*'s lighthearted "Hit a Foreigner in the Face" campaign is not intended to be taken seriously, for heaven's sake!

And yes, we are perfectly aware that the confrontation between England and Germany is not a war. We are not stupid.

Football is just a game. A war is a serious violent confrontation between two enemies who will stop at nothing to defeat each other. Like the *Daily Moron* and our rival newspaper the *Scum*. In conclusion: IN-GUR-LAND!!!

Old Macdonald

ALBERT

DAME SHIRLEY PORTER, the heir to the Tesco empire, was ordered to personally pay £27 million to make up for the cost to Westminster Council of her illegal gerrymandering while she was its Conservative leader.

New prices at Tesco

Baked Beans **WAS** 38p per tin **NOW** £1.2m
Washing powder **WAS** £3.50 per packet **NOW** £14m
Cornflakes **WAS** £1.75 per box **NOW** £22m (per flake)
TESCO – IT GETS YOUR VOTE!

BRITPOP was in its pomp.

In tomorrow's *Daily Hellograph*

Bill Deedes On Tour With Oasis
Exclusive interview with Naughty Noel by *Sarah Sands*
Clifford Langley on the Religious Message of Oasis
Dr James Le Fanu on Can Oasis give you BSE?
Are Oasis better than the Beatles? Is the *Telegraph* even worse than the *Guardian*? Vote now on 0171-538-5000: *Charles Moore* is ready to take your call.
PLUS READER OFFER: The *Daily Telegraph* Oasis Shooting Stick and Wrought-Iron Bootscraper Set offer – only £99.99

DESPITE HAVING PERSUADED his parliamentary colleagues to amend the law so that he could sue the *Guardian*, Neil "cash for questions" Hamilton abandoned his libel case at the last minute.

The Secret DIARY OF JOHN MAJOR aged 47¾

Saturday

I am not inconsiderably incandescent with rage. Just as we are setting off for Bournemouth for the most successful party conference in history, the *Guardian* newspaper has deliberately tried to ruin everything by making Mr Hamilton climb down and give up his libel action. He promised me that he would win the case, because he was entirely innocent. He rang me up this morning to say that he was still entirely innocent, but that unfortunately the *Guardian* had come up with a lot of evidence to prove that he wasn't. And anyway, he couldn't afford to carry on with the case, because his ex-friend Mr Al Fayed hadn't given him any money recently in brown envelopes.

Sunday

I have had a brilliant idea for drawing a line under the sleaze issue once and for all. I have decided that this whole business is to be investigated very thoroughly and very carefully by Mr Sir Gordon Downey, who has agreed to report sometime after next May. This is very fortunate, since this will be after the election. When I told my wife Norman, she gave a big smile and said, "That's brilliant, John. In that case *you* won't have to worry about it." Once again she has missed the point.

PRINCE WILLIAM had a drawing selected for a school art exhibition at Eton, with teachers gushing that it was "an extraordinary piece of art for a 14-year old. William has considerable talent".

Prince's art goes on show

What was described as the most exciting new painting in the history of Western Art went on display at St Cake's public school.

In an exhibition of Under-15s painting and drawing in the "Highly Recommended" category, the picture is the work of HRH Prince William, 14 (Hobnobs house) and is entitled "The House of Windsor".

The work is described by art master Mr Lawrence Brownnose (Slade Dip. Failed) as displaying "astonishing maturity for someone so young. His young majesty has a mastery of composition and design, and is clearly destined to become the Rembrandt of his age, like his father Prince Charles before him. His subtle use of shading brings to mind the work of William Turner, while his brushwork can only be compared to Tintoretto. I would very much like to be invited to the Palace to tell his parents in person what a privilege it is to teach this genius and to kneel before them to receive my knighthood. God bless Prince William! Floreat Cakeamus!"

HAVING SUCCESSFULLY jettisoned Clause IV, Tony Blair was doing everything he could to convince voters New Labour was not the same as Old Labour.

APRIL BROUGHT more disturbing news from North Wales.

A huge child abuse scandal is unfolding. It has been exposed in a report commissioned two years ago by Clwyd county council from a panel headed by John Jillings, former social services director of Derbyshire. It concluded that "the abuse of children and young people in Clwyd residential units has been extensive and has taken place over a substantial number of years... Our findings show that time and again the response to indications that children may have been abused has been too little and too late. Furthermore the needs and interests of children and young people have tended to be an incidental rather than a primary concern. Our criticisms in this regard apply not only to Clwyd County Council but also to the Welsh Office, the North Wales police and constituent agencies... An overarching finding is that where there has been a conflict of interest between safeguarding professional position and the safety of children and young people, the interests of children have almost invariably been sacrificed."

The report notes 10 separate secret inquiries by the council into abuse at children's homes, none of them linked and none of them properly acted on. Most councillors had not the faintest idea about most of these inquiries and their outcomes.

This is by far the worst official report on child abuse in Britain. It makes it clear that the problem is not just one of the past, but of the present and future. Yet the council which commissioned it is not going to publish it. Nor is the Welsh Office, which has put its five copies under close lock and key. Nor the police, who also have at least one copy. The council, for its part, is terrified by the advice of the lawyers of its insurance company, Zurich Municipal, who say that if they publish they will be liable to claims from abused young people in the homes.

The extent of the cover-up gives some force to the persistent rumours circulating in north Wales for years that children from the homes were "supplied" to important people all over the area.

This is a major scandal, and the report should be published in full at once.

Three months later the government ordered an overarching investigation into child abuse in care homes in North Wales. Sir Ronald Waterhouse's tribunal sat for 15 months, and named and criticised nearly 200 people either for abusing children or failing to protect them properly. In 2012 a new police inquiry, Operation Pallial, was opened which resulted in 76 new complainants coming forward to allege abuse: it was this investigation which led to the convictions of John Allen and Gordon Anglesea (*see p154*). A redacted version of the Jillings Report was finally published in 2013, when Jillings himself described what he and had his team had discovered as "horrific... a disgrace, and stain on the history of child care in this country".

AS SIR JAMES GOLDSMITH prepared to stand 600 Referendum Party candidates against the Conservatives in May's election, as revenge for John Major's insufficient Europhobia, Slicker took a look at the great patriot's property interests.

Goldsmith rallies Little Englanders with calls to defend our shores against the threat of a federal Europe and the invading grey hordes of Eurocrats, but there are a few little personal details they may be unaware of. The saviour of the British nation was born in France, represents French voters in the despised European Parliament, is referred to in company documents as "Anglo-French", has more homes abroad than he does in Britain and lists one of them, in a little corner of Jalisco province that will be forever Mexico, as his residential address as director of the Referendum party.

And does their chief candidate pay any significant tax here – or any tax at all? That question could well revolve around where the great patriot lives and how much time each year he visits the land not of his fathers. Lady Annabel Goldsmith calls Ormeley Lodge, a million-pound mansion on Ham Common in south-west London home, and, when not with his other family in New York or Mexico, this champion of morality and family values resides there too. But for nearly 20 years the house has been controlled by companies, either British companies controlled offshore or offshore companies period. In 1976 the property was bought by the British company Figurewalk for £350,000 and promptly used as security to raise money for the Goldsmith-controlled Banque Occidentale. By 1980 Figurewalk was controlled by his then Hong Kong master company, General Oriental. GO in turn was owned via two Panamanian companies by the Brunneria Foundation in the total secrecy haven of Liechtenstein. Both home and company have changed ownership several times since, all of them opaque.

The offshore labyrinth is explicable in one three-letter word: tax. And that is what his political opponents should be asking questions about if and when he stands.

Two months later Sir Jams was forced to announce he had become "permanently resident" in the UK – although Slicker pointed out this didn't mean he was paying a full British tax bill like those he expected to vote for him.

THERE WAS YET MORE news of Jonathan Aitken in June.

In 1991 Gerald James, former chairman of the arms company Astra, revealed to the House of Commons select committee on trade and industry the astonishing fact that the biggest contract of Astra's subsidiary BMARC was for the illegal supply of guns to Iran. The committee reported: "We have treated the evidence given by Mr Gerald James as true."

The committee recently investigated BMARC and heard in detail the same information from Gerald James as he had made in his 1991 memo, that millions of pounds worth of guns had gone from BMARC through Singapore in clear breach of British government policy and export law. As the committee rather grudgingly concedes, there was incontrovertible proof of this. But they have been more absorbed with a single question: how to explain the behaviour of

their parliamentary colleague Jonathan Aitken, who from September 1988 to June 1990, when the guns were still being delivered to Iran, was a director of BMARC.

The first task was to smear Gerald James: in 1991 his evidence was "true", in 1996 he has suddenly transformed into a "highly unreliable witness". The transformation came about because James dared to suggest that Aitken knew about the destination of the guns exported by his company.

The committee discovered quickly that Mr Aitken was the only BMARC director at the time to imagine that 140 naval guns were supplied to Singapore for the use of the tiny Singapore navy. Every other director of the company conceded that they were going somewhere else, though only two of them said they knew perfectly well that was Iran. Three other directors thought they might be going to other countries in the Far East.

Senior BMARC executive John Pike, who has made it clear that he'd known the guns were going to Iran, was not called to give evidence. Nor was Julian Nettlefold, Astra's former PR man, who told DTI inspectors in 1991 that there was "a huge contract with Iran worth £16 million".

The committee concluded that "it is not clear that such rumours were circulating during the time of Mr Aitken's directorship". Yet evidence from BMARC staff published by the committee shows they were.

Aitken told the committee "The words Project Lisi" – codename for the Singapore/Iran deal – "are not once mentioned in the board minutes." Whoops! Tory MP Keith Hampson flourished a copy of the board minutes for 27 June 1989: "In these minutes Lisi 2, the second phase is mentioned twice in a very prominent way." Aitken waffled. And the committee report seems to have forgotten that Hampson ever asked the question. "We have examined BMARC's board minutes for the period," it states, "and find they contain no direct reference to project Lisi."

The central conclusion of the committee was that "none of the allegations made against Mr Aitken have been substantiated" – which appeared in the papers next day unanimously as AITKEN CLEARED.

Allegations about BMARC were among those Aitken wielded his famous sword of truth at: they were never aired at the High Court because his other spectacular lies brought his libel trial to a crashing end before they could be heard. The *Eye*, which was in line to be sued after the *Guardian*, never got its day in court.

1997

AFTER MONTHS of megalomaniac behaviour both on and off-air, Chris Evans walked out of the Radio 1 Breakfast show.

A NEW POP phenomenon was sweeping the world.

Yes! It's the Space Girls!

It's official – the fabulous five-member girl group have taken newspapers by storm! This week they were voted the Best Way to Fill Space by all of Britain's top editors!

Said Charles Moore, editor of the *Daily Mel-B-graph*, "The Space Girls are the best thing that has ever happened to Britain! They are going to be really huge – about ten column inches on every page!"

"I love all of them – Large Space, Huge Space, Vast Space, Op-Ed Space and Front Page Space. These girls are world-beaters!" said Peter Stoddart of unpop fanzine the *Times*.

Blairy   Batey   Ginger   Spoil-Sporty   Posh

JOHN MAJOR FINALLY called the general election for May 1 – a date long associated with the Labour movement.

Caesar plumps for Ides poll

A relaxed and confident Julius Major today announced that he would be going to the country on the Ides of March. Brushing aside rumours of splits and plots, the leader said that when it came to the day "everyone would be right behind me".

Senior colleagues including Portillus, Heseltinus and Cassius Dorrellius all pledged their support to the leader, saying they would be "backing him to the hilt" when the big day came. "We have come to bury Major, not to praise him."

Dorrellius later issued a clarification, saying that he had been quoted out of context, and meant to say "We come to murder Major, because he's completely useless."

ON OTHER PAGES: *Swampus strikes again at Appian Way Protest*

AS NEIL HAMILTON (and his wife Christine) still refused to stand down in Tatton, Labour and the Lib Dems withdrew from the constituency in favour of independent candidate Martin Bell, whose main selling point was that he wore a white suit and wasn't Neil Hamilton.

Bell Washes Whiter than White

Yes, it's Martin Bell's doorstep challenge – would YOU swap your dirty MP for a bright, clean, former war correspondent?

New Formula Bell is biologically engineered to remove even the toughest sleaze. Filthy Fayed – gone! Brown envelopes – gone!

So take the Bell Doorstep Challenge – and win yourself a candidate who has no idea what he is doing!

Manufactured by LibLab Brothers plc, Staines, Tatton.

THE RESULT was a Labour landslide – but the new prime minister refused to let his 179-seat majority derail his strictly scripted plans for government.

SIR JAMES GOLDSMITH'S Referendum Party, meanwhile, was soundly trounced.

From the Referendum Bunker

Achtung!

So. You think you have seen the last of me, Mr Bond. But I tell you, we were not defeated.

We were betrayed. By the people of Britain. Who were stupid enough to give their votes to everyone but me. And now it is time for them to meet their own exit poll.

(*Presses button which opens trapdoor dropping voters into huge vat of boiling Marmite filled with sharks*)

I have here a cyanide pill. I am sure you all expect me to swallow it. But you are wrong, Mr Bond, Mr Major, Mr Blair, Mr Ashdown, Mr Middle England.

You are fools, all of you, do you hear me? I am not finished. Not by a long way. One day I shall be back. And in the meantime I shall be watching you from my secret hideaway on the comet Hale-Bopp.

Goodbye. Or should I say Auf Wiedersehen, Schweinhunden!

(*Turns to enter escape pod but accidentally falls through still open trapdoor to be devoured by Marmite-crazed sharks*)

A NEW BROOM swept into the Vicarage.

ST ALBION PARISH NEWS

Hello! I'm Tony, your new vicar. And that's what I'd like you to call me – Tony!

It is a truly awesome responsibility you have placed upon my shoulders, and I shall do my utmost to be worthy of the trust you have placed in me!

You will not need me to tell you that there is much to do, and that this is a tough parish to take on!

Things have got pretty run-down in recent years, as we all know, and our financial position leaves a lot to be desired! And that's why we're very fortunate that Mr Brown, the bank manager, has agreed to come in and do the books!

I've got a great team of helpers, especially a huge number of ladies (I'm not complaining about that!). Ms Mowlam will be opening our Mission to Northern Ireland and St Gerry's. Ms Short will be leading her new outreach programme for the Third World. And Mr Prescott from the Working Men's Club has pledged his full support too! I know that we're all singing from the same hymn sheet – Mr Mandelson, our new churchwarden, is going to make sure of that!

I know what a lot of you are wondering is – are there going to be any changes in the way St Albion's is run? The answer is, yes and no! Yes there are, and no there aren't! But more of that later!

See you on Sunday!

Tony

HONG KONG was ceremoniously handed back to China.

That Hong Kong Farewell Banquet Menu in full

Chinese Takeaway Whole Island

ROBIN COOK, the new foreign secretary, was revealed to be having an affair with his secretary.

New Foreign Office ethical guidelines – dealing with Uganda

Ugandan Affairs are extremely complicated and it is inappropriate to apply any hard and fast rules when dealing with this state. Negotiations should be conducted in camera (or in handy ministerial love nest close to the House of Commons), not on the front page of the *News of The World*).

Signed,

Mr Robin Cook

We apologise for the mis-spelling of Mr Cock's name in the above memo. It should of course have read Mr Fook.

PRINCESS DIANA took her sons on holiday with the Fayed family, with shots of her in a swimsuit on board their yacht setting off a frenzy of speculation and vituperation in the press.

Di – is she or isn't she? *by GLENDA SLAGG*

Those tell-tale pics are keeping the world guessing, as Di frolics in the Med with Egypt's Mr Sexy. A little swelling leaves millions asking this question: has she got anything at all in her head?

Glenda says: At 36, your biological clock is ticking away and grey matter is disappearing at an alarming rate.

If she wants a little intelligence, it's still not too late to get some!

■ What do you think? Is she or isn't she amazingly stupid? If your answer is YES: call 0898 7920159. If your answer is NO: you must be as thick as she is.

BUT IT ENDED in disaster when the princess and her new boyfriend, Mohamed Fayed's son Dodi, were killed in a high-speed car crash while attempting to evade paparazzi.

SO GRAVE WAS THE EVENT that even *Teletubbies* was cancelled to make way for rolling news coverage.

Highlights from the TV coverage

Sunday 3.17pm

Martyn Lewis: So, you never met Diana but you must have some memories of her?

Man with beard in black tie: I suppose my first reaction when I heard the news was one of shock and disbelief.

Martyn Lewis: So, your first reaction was one of shock and disbelief?

(Caption appears: "Dr Wilmot Pringle, former reader in Constitutional Studies, Strathclyde University")

Dr Pringle: Well, I er…

Martyn Lewis: Thank you for that, Dr Pringle. I am sure that all over the country viewers will be sharing your feelings of shock and disbelief. Now we've just heard that we can go over live to Balmoral…

Woman with microphone on windswept road: Well, Martyn, I am standing here on the windswept road where shortly the Royal car will arrive, possibly with the Queen and other members of the Royal Family on board, although we are not sure who will be with the Queen or if the Queen will actually come down this road to wherever it is she might be going.

Martyn Lewis: Well, thank you Jennie. And it's not hard to imagine what the Queen must be feeling at this tragic and historic time, wherever she is. No doubt a sense of shock and disbelief. Now I am joined in the studio by Anthony Holden, David Mellor, Ben Pimlott, Jeffrey Archer, Richard Branson, Roy Jenkins, Jeffrey Archer, Jim Callaghan, Richard Branson, Anthony Holden and Jeffrey Archer. (*Men in black ties and suits look serious*) Gentlemen, can I begin by asking you how you all felt when you were asked to come on this programme?

All: I suppose our first reaction was one of shock and disbelief since we have nothing worthwhile to say at all.

Martyn Lewis: Thank you, gentlemen, for your thoughts on this most tragic day. And we are now getting tributes from all over the world: the Life President of Rumbabwe has said in the last hour that his reaction was one of "shock and disbelief on this most tragic day". Dr Henry Kissinger told reporters that he was shocked and disbelieving at the news on this most tragic day, and William Hague and Paddy Ashdown said that they were equally as shocked and disbelieving as Tony Blair. Now over to Los Angeles where Billy Connolly and Pamela Stephenson are (*continued for several weeks*)

THE REVERSE FERRET by the press was faster even than the car that killed her.

The Late Princess Diana – An Apology

In recent weeks – not to mention the last ten years – we at the *Daily Gnome*, in common with all other newspapers, may have inadvertently conveyed the impression that the late Princess of Wales was in some way a neurotic, irresponsible and manipulative troublemaker who had repeatedly meddled in political matters that did not concern her and personally embarrassed Her Majesty the Queen by her Mediterranean love-romps with the son of a discredited Egyptian businessman.

We now realise, as of Sunday morning, that the Princess of Hearts was in fact the most saintly woman who has ever lived who, with her charitable activities, brought hope and succour to hundreds and millions of people all over the world and resembled in every respect a candle in the wind.

We would like to express our sincere and deepest hypocrisy to all our readers on this tragic day and hope and pray that they will carry on buying our paper notwithstanding.

LATE NEWS: What you will read next month! *Were the brakes on the Mercedes tampered with by MI5 or MI6? Was there a mystery motorbike rider who got away, and if so, who was he? Was it really Diana in the car? Etc, etc, etc.*

EVERYONE went a bit mad for a while.

*Every week **Dave Spart**, co-chair of the Crouch End Branch of the Republicans for Diana Movement, writes on the story behind the news.*

The Floral Revolution will totally go down in history as the most important display of the power of the British proletariat against the entrenched forces of the capitalist Establishment since the… er… Royal Wedding… and, er, there can only be one conclusion to the stunning victory of the masses over the reactionary monarcho-fascists of the Windsor family, i.e. that the sickening so-called Royal Family is totally and utterly finished and that a new political era has been born out of the ashes of the old coalition of aristocratic landed interest and, er… Earl Spencer spoke for the entire working class when he said that the Windsor dynasty was totally doomed and if proof were needed of that verdict the massed voices of the ordinary people sang "God Save the Queen" er…

"It appears from our records that you haven't bought the Elton John single"

NEW LABOUR EXPERIENCED their first big sleaze scandal after it was revealed they had exempted Formula One racing from a ban on tobacco sponsorship after accepting a donation of a million pounds from the sport's boss, Bernie Ecclestone – but Tony Blair assured the world that the two events were unconnected, and he was "a pretty straight sort of guy".

ST ALBION PARISH NEWS

Hullo! Look, this isn't easy for me! But I know that I owe everyone in the parish a really heartfelt and sincere apology. I'm really sorry for the fact that so many people seem to have misunderstood what I was trying to do when I put the tobacco adverts in the last issue of the parish news.

I'm really sorry if some of you thought that, just because I've always said that I wouldn't take adverts for cigarettes in the newsletter, the fact that I *did* meant that in some way I'd gone back on my word!

O ye of little faith! (*Mark 7.6*).

What I'm most sorry about is that some really malicious people have tried to make out that my decision might have been connected to the fact that Mr Ecclestone, who has the tobacco kiosk in the garage, contributed £150 to the fund for restoring the church roof.

Look. I want to make it clear that I'm a completely honest, straight guy! (*Luke 21.13*). You know this! I'm the same vicar now as I was when I first walked into St Albion's six months ago. I'm sorry if anyone has made the mistake of thinking otherwise.

But as we say in church every Sunday, "Forgive us our failings as we forgive those who haven't been nice to us" (*Book of Common Blair, p249*).

I've certainly forgiven all of you for your lack of trust over the past week or two!

Tony

AND ALL OTHER NEWS – including the death of Mother Teresa of Calcutta – was superseded.

Diana's friend dies

An elderly nun who was once photographed shaking hands with the late Princess of Wales has died. The nun first met Diana during the course of the Princess's work amongst the sick and dying and was apparently greatly inspired by her example.

ON ALL OTHER PAGES:
Did the Press Overkill Diana?

JANUARY SAW SLICKER looking to the future.

Who, other than deputy prime minister Michael Heseltine and the local Labour party in Greenwich, wants the Millennium exhibition?

Certainly not most of the vital corporate sponsors who are being dragooned into donating £150 million towards the cost of this custom-made white elephant. "People are being strong-armed to put money in on the basis they have a relationship with the government," explained one of those who is already in. "People have their arms up their backs."

The business elite who have been approached know the exhibition does not make commercial sense. Hezza admitted as such at a crisis meeting last year when he asked sponsors to "make a leap of faith" without any hope of a commercial return. The sponsors are also resigned to the exhibition overrunning in classic British big project-style (cf British Library, Channel Tunnel etc). So is the government. At a recent meeting heritage secretary Virginia Bottomley declared cheerily that such projects "always go over budget". The only question is by how much the £580 million will be exceeded. The betting is that the final bill will be nearer £800 million – if all goes well. That's why the taxpayer and the lottery cheque books will have to remain open beyond 2001.

A large part of the pessimism is the dismal impression created by those running the Millennium Commission. Chief executive Jennifer Page is seen as lacking the commercial experience to run such a major project within budget.

New Labour enthusiastically inherited what became the Millennium Dome at Greenwich. Page lasted just over a month after opening before being fired – and the final bill came in at £789 million.

NEWS FROM UP NORTH filled the Rotten Boroughs column in May.

Labour-dominated Doncaster Council saw its own chief executive, Doug Hale, escorted from the building last week and told not to return until a police inquiry and district auditor's report had been completed. Hale had already been suspended on full pay (£80,000 a year), but was shown the town hall door when he tried to re-enter the building.

The Donnygate scandal began when the district auditor discovered massive overspending by councillors. While the council itself struggled with cuts of £8m, the councillors enjoyed beanos abroad to, er, drum up trade for the area.

They also visited their twin towns, of which Doncaster has five: Wilmington in South Carolina, Avion in Northern France, Herten in Germany, Dandong in China and Gliwice in Poland. Trips would include club class flights and drunken "working" lunches. The auditor found one meal for two which cost an obscene £284.

Doncaster Council Watch, set up by revolted locals, has now produced a table of the expenses claimed by the worst offenders since 1990.

Tony Sellars, the chairman of the Labour group, claimed a total of £69,475 over those years, while Peter Welsh, the Labour council leader until his recent resignation, claimed an immense £92,649. These figures did not include £500 of annual free race tickets per member, nor plane tickets for flights abroad, nor their use of council credit cards which have now been cancelled.

Now Doncaster awaits the report of South Yorkshire's Inspector t'Knacker. The police investigation was initially expected to focus on councillors' expenses claims but has now widened to look at land deals, the granting of planning permission to developers and the allocation of contracts by the council.

21 Doncaster councillors were convicted of fraud in the next five years, including two former leaders of the council and two former mayors. The chair of the planning committee received a four-year prison sentence for accepting bribes including a £160,000 house from a developer.

IN THE FIRST EDITION after the election, beneath the heading "New Labour, New Scandals", Slicker sounded an early warning.

Despite Labour landslides, lawyer David Mills, whose wife is better known as Labour MP Tessa Jowell, is said to be a worried man because of all the work he did on former Italian prime minister Silvio Berlusconi's offshore companies. This has already brought him into the frame for the Serious Farce Office and the Italian authorities who are greatly interested in Berlusconi's tax affairs.

It would be a further 12 years before the Italian courts sentenced Mills to jail for accepting a bribe from Berlusconi to give false evidence during the PM's corruption trials – and another year after that before he was ruled not guilty by the appeal court on the grounds that the statute of limitations had expired.

A FORTNIGHT **after the death of Princess Diana, Slicker revealed a few facts about Dodi Fayed's much-vaunted career as a "film producer" and his father's tactics following the crash...**

The disinformation surrounding the high-speed death of the Princess of Wales will come as no surprise to those who know the history of Mohamed Fayed. He has always been both experienced and skilled in rewriting history, and when Di and Dodi became an item it was necessary to create another false image – of Fayed junior as a fantastically rich and successful film producer. Once again more fiction than fact.

From 1980 until 1988 Allied Stars, the Fayed film company in Britain, invested in films with some success, although its accumulated net profits by 1987 were merely £15,000. Then it went into film production backed by £630,000 from its shareholders – more the three senior Fayed brothers than Dodi, by then based in Hollywood and not even a director of the British company. Allied Stars was not a success. By 1991 accumulated losses were £459,000 and the company had ceased to produce or develop films. Two years later it was taken over by a Liberian company of the same name and Dodi Fayed became a director. The British company was dissolved in 1994; the Liberian twin partied on. That may help explain why in Hollywood Dodi Fayed was seen as a playboy, not a player, and a playboy with a reputation for a considerable appetite not just for girls but also cocaine.

Fast forward to today, and as questions and rumours about the crash and its causes increase, so does the Fayed camp's need to keep the attention of a public seeking someone to blame focused elsewhere: first, on the murderous paparazzi and then (reluctantly) on the drunken driver Henri Paul rather than events inside the Ritz and the Ritz-provided car.

Result: a smokescreen boosted by tales of engagements, homes and last words, designed to head off crucial questions which, once mourning turns to anger, may be directed in Fayed's direction because those who decided Diana's fate that night were his son and his employees.

...while Street of Shame revealed an interesting fact about her brother as he led his crusade against the press.

Lord Spencer moves among the great and good making the case for a new privacy law – without mentioning his own negotiations a few months ago with *Hello!* magazine for a huge colour feature about his South African house and family. He asked for a quarter of a million for the feature, a vast sum he suggested to *Hello!* was appropriate because of the embarrassment he might suffer during his campaign for a privacy law. He would, the people's earl explained, have to put up with a lot of criticism from people who didn't understand his position. There might well be flak about the hypocrisy of his demands for a law to protect people's families while selling a feature about his own family.

Hello! turned down Spencer's extravagant demand, explaining that it just didn't pay that kind of money.

The furious Earl wrote to the *Eye* to deny the story, saying "At no stage have I ever contemplated allowing any intrusion into my family's privacy in Cape Town. I think it is a pity that my sincere wish to help this country's fight against the culture of intrusion should be sneered at so dishonestly" – so the magazine printed extracts from the Spencers' letters to *Hello!*'s fixer, the Marquesa de Varela, negotiating exclusives.

IN SEPTEMBER **a passenger train went through two warning signals and ploughed into a freight train at Southall in West London, killing seven people and injuring 139. The *Eye*'s rail correspondent Dr B. Ching looked at why.**

The abandoning of the automatic train protections (ATP) programme to release money for privatisation is one probable contributory factor – a case of the railway not taking a step forward. Another likely factor – running a high-speed train on which the automatic warning system (AWS) was not working – seems to show the railway stepping *backwards*. British Rail rules expressly prevented trains running without operational AWS; where this was unavoidable, a second driver had to ride in the cab and double-check each signal. This rule seems to have been jettisoned in the switch to private profit-driven operations.

The official report into the crash, published three years later, revealed that the service had had ATP installed, but that operator Great Western Trains had made no attempt to roster drivers who had been trained to use it, and that their "inadequate maintenance procedures" were responsible for the non-functioning AWS. The requirement for a second driver in the cab had been removed following privatisation, and Railtrack's rules on what should be done when AWS was not working were "ambiguous and confusing". The rule that a "competent person" should accompany the driver in the cab under such circumstances has since been reintroduced.

Two years later, in October 1999, another crash just a few miles away on the same line, at Ladbroke Grove, killed 31 people and injured 419. It, too, would have been prevented if ATP had been operational.

1998

HOME SECRETARY Jack Straw's teenage son Will was caught offering to buy drugs for an undercover *Daily Mirror* reporter.

This transcript of reporter Dawn Allfraud's conversation with the son of the Home Secretary will entirely vindicate the *Moron*'s reputation for honest and impartial journalism of the highest kind. The original tape-recording is now in the hands of Inspector Knacker of the Drug Squad.

Dawn: Would you like a nice time, big boy? I'm a real goer with a bit of pot inside me.

Schoolboy: er... er... crikey...

Dawn: Go and buy some from that bloke over there, handsome. Here's the money.

Schoolboy: Gulp... blimey...

Dawn: I'm mad for it, me! Hurry up, lover boy!

PRESIDENT CLINTON threatened military action against Iraq unless Saddam Hussein allowed UN weapons inspectors in, a move that many thought was aimed at distracting attention from allegations about what he had been up to with White House intern Monica Lewinsky.

SORRY TO DISTURB YOU MR PRESIDENT... SHALL I ORDER THE BOMBING OF IRAQ?

PENTAGON

YES! YES! OH GOD YES!

SCEPTICISM WAS RISING about the Millennium Dome, now under the control of the prime minister's right-hand man, Peter Mandelson.

THE XANADULY TELEGRAPH

Opposition to Pleasure Dome mounts

Public opinion is hardening against plans by Kubla Khandelson to build an ancient pleasuredome on a site in Xanadu. "The project is a fiasco," say critics. "Khandelson is a dictator who expects everyone to do whatever he decrees. The twice five mile-round wall and tower-girdled site near the River Alph is very difficult for people to visit, and moreover, there are no ideas as to how to actually fill up the caverns measureless to man."

Kubla Khandelson denied this, saying he had just returned from a trip to Disney World where (*article discontinued due to Samuel Taylor Coleridge being interrupted at this point by a visitor from Porlock*)

MOHAMED FAYED continued to peddle nonsense to a willing press.

THE FIRST COUNTRYSIDE March drew 250,000 protesters to London in opposition to Labour's policies on rural issues (but mostly fox hunting)...

Countryside Unites

...BUT THE GOVERNMENT seemed keener on wringing the last drops out of the phenomenon of "Cool Britannia".

How cool are you?

Do this test to find out if you are fit to live in Tony Blair's Britain!

1. Is your favourite film:
a) *The Full Monty*
b) *In Which We Serve*

2. Is your favourite band:
a) Oasis
b) The Royal Philharmonic Orchestra

3. Is your favourite novelist:
a) Nick Hornby
b) William Makepeace Thackeray

4. Is your favourite model:
a) Kate Moss
b) Airfix's *HMS Victory*

5. Is your favourite TV programme:
a) *Teletubbies*
b) *Kenneth Clark's Civilisation*

6. Is your favourite artist:
a) Damien Hirst
b) Sir Frederick Leighton RA

7. Is your favourite Prime Minister:
a) Tony Blair!
b) William Pitt the Younger

How you score:
All 'a's – congratulations! You are Alastair Campbell!
All 'b's – oh dear – you are William Hague. Get on the next plane out of here!

REPRESENTATIVES of all sides in Northern Ireland finally came together to sign the Good Friday Agreement, bringing an end (mostly) to the Troubles after 30 years.

RUPERT MURDOCH SEPARATED from his second wife, Anna.

 *What you will not read*

Blonde Sex Bomb Dumps Aussie Porn King

The world's top filth merchant Rupert Murdoch, 68, alias "the Dirty Digger", has been kicked out by his sex-starved missus.

Busty Estonian-born Anna (38-28-38) did not tell the *Sun* last night "I've had enough – or rather I haven't! My old man's never home for nooky – he'd rather spend his nights setting up complex cable deals in Szechuan than coming back for a love romp in one of our luxury homes."

Last night Mr Murdoch was unavailable for comment because we didn't dare ring him up.

ENTIRELY COINCIDENTALLY, a brand-new impotence treatment went on the market with great fanfare.

New pill gives hope to middle-aged men

The announcement of a new pill to cure impotence has brought relief to newspaper editors who have been increasingly suffering from limp organs. The pill, Viagra, has already had miraculous results in America where editors have talked of its amazing power to boost circulation and to provide "an astonishing rise in column inches".

Editors in Britain are already swallowing the story in huge numbers. One happy subject who had previously been embarrassed by his poor performance (known only as Peter Stothard of the *Times*) said: "The results are fantastic. I used to be ashamed of only having sex stories once a month but now with Viagra I am at it day and night."

Another, who would only give his name as Charles Moore of the *Daily Telegraph*, said, "I don't care what they say about side-effects. I'm going for a permanent hard-sell. This isn't just a story for the willy season."

MARATHON TALKS END

I could murder a McGuinness

I can see light at the end of the barrel

A STATE VISIT BY Emperor Akihito of Japan prompted outrage and protests, particularly when he claimed that "constitutional restrictions" prevented him from apologising for the treatment of British POWs by his countrymen during World War II.

Gnome

There are continuing demands from Japanese veterans of the 1970s that I should make some formal apology for the "atrocious" cover of *Eye* no.256 with its "Piss Off Bandy Knees" message. [*See p42*]

Whilst I accept that the cover was regrettable and caused distress to thousands of Japanese subjects, it is not part of the culture of *Private Eye* to apologise (except when faced with a libel action).

In any case it is not possible for me as Lord Gnome to make any statement of any kind on a political matter due to my quasi-divine status as proprietor of a magazine – a man revered as a god-like figure by millions of readers.

Besides, the events of 1971 are all in the distant past, and as the UK government clearly understands, it is now time to build bridges, not to mention cars, with our former enemies, the Japanese.

Emperor Gnomohito
Chrysanthemum Throne, Ah Soho

FORMER CHILEAN DICTATOR General Augusto Pinochet popped over to the UK to have afternoon tea with Baroness Thatcher – and was promptly arrested on a warrant from a Spanish judge.

That Tea Menu In Full
Coup of tea
Rack of toasted dissidents
Grilled opposition
Chopped-off finger sandwiches
Eggs (beaten to death)
Mrs Teacake

BRITISH NANNY Louise Woodward, convicted in America of murdering an eight-month-old baby in her care, had the charge reduced to involuntary manslaughter on appeal and returned home to a media storm.

An Apology

The *Daily Gnome* would like to take this opportunity to apologise to Miss Louise Woodward for its coverage of her trial last year, and in particular for the headlines "Why This Kiddie Killer Must Not Go Free", "Would You Leave Your Toddlers With The Nanny From Hell?" and "String Her Up Now".

These headlines may have given readers the impression Miss Woodward was in some way guilty of the heinous crime of which she stood accused. However, we now realise that we have paid out a huge sum of money this week✳ and

that there is therefore no question that Louise is a victim of appalling injustice.

✳PLEASE NOTE: *The Daily Gnome has not paid a penny to Louise Woodward for her story, as our downmarket rivals have alleged. It has paid £400,000 to the Woodward Family Support Foundation Trust PLC, which is an entirely different matter.*

A GRAND JURY quizzed Bill Clinton on his statements about Monica Lewinsky – and the president insisted that he had been accurate in saying he didn't have sexual relations with her, because oral sex didn't count.

Did you ask the witness to lie?

No, sir. Just kneel

BLUE PETER PRESENTER Richard Bacon was sacked after he admitted taking cocaine.

TV Highlights

5.05pm BLOW PETER – A new presenter line-up is revealed, and Katie shows viewers how to recycle three million copies of the already-printed 1999 Annual in the waste-paper bank. If you want to help this year's Sniffer Dogs Appeal, send in your old tin foil, razorblades or carefully rolled-up fivers to the usual address – but do get permission from a grown-up before using their credit card!

DESPITE THE COMMONS voting for the age of consent for gay sex to be lowered to the same as for heterosexual sex, the House of Lords rejected the law change.

That debate in full

The Bishop of Sodom and Gomorrah: My Lords, if we reject this bill we condemn thousands of young Anglican clergymen to a lifetime of celibacy. Surely it is time for trousers to be lowered for once and for all?

Baroness Young: My Lords, the simple fact of the matter is that these homosexuals are utterly disgusting and what they get up to is pretty disagreeable. That is why it is vital that this House should not contemplate any further lowering of trousers.

The 7th Earl of Longjohns: When I was a boy in 1823 anyone caught engaging in an act of beastliness would have been thrashed within an inch of his wife. And it never did us any harm. We must prevent practices that are simply harmful to young people. Free Myra Hindley now.

The debate concluded in an overwhelming defeat for the Government's proposal. The Trousers Bill was sent back to the Commons to be pressed for a third time.

CABINET MINISTER Ron Davies resigned in mysterious circumstances after going for a night-time walk on Clapham Common. After an awkward moment on *Newsnight*, the BBC put an edict out banning any further mention of Peter Mandelson.

Sad double life of shamed Ron

More details began to emerge last night of the twilight world frequented by Ron Davies – a world he kept a secret from even his closest friends. Davies, a respectable homosexual, was sensationally revealed to spend long nights hanging around the Commons, in the hope of picking up a job.

Last night Mr Davies would only say that he had made "a serious error of judgement". Rumours that he was an MP had been circulating in gay circles for years, but it was only when journalist Matthew Parris revealed live on television that he was the Secretary of State for Wales and "certainly" sat in cabinet alongside Peter Mandelson that his dark secret was revealed.

Davies immediately resigned as a homosexual and asked the press to "leave his political life alone". Asked about the allegation, Mr Mandelson said, "No comment. And that's an order from John Birt."

PLANS FOR THE NEW parliamentary term included radical reform of the House of Lords.

QUEEN'S SPEECH SHOCK

My Government will scrap all hereditary privilege... hang on, that can't be right

IN JANUARY, PAUL FOOT had further news of the Al-Yamamah arms deals with Saudi Arabia (*see p130*).

Blind panic swept the board room of Rolls Royce on the morning of 12 December when a writ arrived from a Panamanian company demanding millions of pounds in unpaid commissions on arms contracts. The second paragraph of the writ summed up the scandal which threatened the firm: "By an agreement made in writing on 31st August 1991 the defendant appointed the plaintiff as its commercial adviser and sole representative in the Territory for the purpose of selling and supporting its gas turbine engines of all descriptions for military aviation or marine applications," and stated that the defendant agreed to pay the plaintiff "a commission" for every jet engine sold.

"The Territory" was the kingdom of Saudi Arabia. The engines were for Hawk trainers and Tornado jets sold in the notorious Al-Yamamah deals between the British and Saudi governments, the first of which was signed in 1985. Ever since, British defence ministers have insisted that "no commissions were paid and no agents or any middlemen were involved" (defence minister Roger Freeman, 1994).

Yet the High Court writ even specified the terms of the commissions: 8 percent of the price of each gas turbine engine, 5 percent on the price of the spare parts. On the basis of the agreed rate, the commissions since 1991 would amount to more than £100 million. Yet the writ complained Rolls Royce had so far agreed to pay only £23 million.

On 17 December, Rolls's lawyers confronted City lawyers Davies Arnold Cooper, plus barristers, in a torrid secret session in front of a high court master. At the end of the day, a secret compromise was agreed. The Panama company withdrew the writ and Rolls immediately went into private discussions of payments of commissions at a level far above the £23 million already conceded – the commissions which the British government has always denied had ever been agreed.

It is becoming ever more evident that most of the arms sold in the Al-Yamamah deals can never be used by the Saudi Arabian armed forces. Their only purpose is to provide commissions for the Saudi rulers.

Eight years would pass before Tony Blair capitulated to Saudi threats and agreed to cancel a Serious Fraud Office investigation into the Al-Yamamah deals – which the High Court in London later described as a "specific and, as it turns out, successful attempt by a foreign government to pervert the course of justice in the United Kingdom".

FOOT REPORTED FROM the public inquiry into Stephen Lawrence's murder in June.

Something like the real story is beginning to seep out. Within hours of the murder, the police were inundated with information that the murderers were a racist gang of five youths, including David Norris, son of Clifford Norris – a notorious gangster and arms dealer in South London, who is now in prison.

Clifford Norris's name did not emerge in the early days of the inquiry. But on 12 May, Scotland Yard disclosed to the inquiry a police complaints report against a flying squad officer who had very close connections to Norris. The Yard reluctantly agreed to hand it over on condition that the officer's name be kept quiet – he was to be known as Officer XX.

In the late 1980s Customs & Excise officers carried out a long investigation into Clifford Norris. They were surprised on three occasions to find their suspect hobnobbing in pubs with Detective Sergeant XX. The detail of the report's disclosures were spelled out on 3 June during the questioning of Detective Chief Superintendent William Ilsley, a senior officer in overall charge of the Lawrence murder investigaiton, by Rajiv Menon, barrister for Duwayne Brooks, Stephen Lawrence's friend and the only eyewitness to his murder.

Q: They thought, Customs, that XX was warning Clifford Norris that he was a suspect because after the meetings he kind of vanished, and because of some of the suspicious things that XX was doing during those meetings. He was observed making notes, he used a calculator, and on one occasion he was carrying a carrier bag which contained a number of oblong slabs or packages and on one occasion Clifford Norris handed a carrier bag to him. All this aroused the suspicions of the customs officers. They reported it to the police.

A: Yes.

Q: An internal inquiry was set up. When XX was interviewed as part of that inquiry he said that various meetings with Clifford Norris in public houses were by pure chance and that, although unauthorised by any senior officer, he was meeting Mr Norris for the purpose of cultivating him as an informer. The police inquiry concluded that there was more to the relationship between XX and Clifford Norris than XX was prepared to admit?

A: Yes, sir.

Q: Yet for reasons best known to that internal inquiry they chose not to discipline him but simply to give him "words of advice".

A: Yes.

XX was disciplined over another matter – pretending he was attending a trial at the Old Bailey when he wasn't – and demoted from sergeant to constable. But the importance of the new evidence was that it proved that at least one officer in the area had been mysteriously connected with the gangland criminal, Norris.

For a time the inquiry was told that DC XX had nothing to do with the Lawrence murder. But soon two more pieces of information emerged which linked the demoted officer very firmly to the murder investigation. The first came from DCS Ian Crampton, the officer who took charge of the murder investigation immediately after Stephen was stabbed, and who crassly decided to engage in a policy of delay and not to arrest young Norris and his four fellow suspects. Crampton agreed that XX had worked under him at Bexleyheath police station in the 1980s. When XX was hauled up in front of a disciplinary inquiry for his fibs about the Old Bailey, Crampton wrote him a warm reference. The second link emerged almost by chance during the cross-examination of Sergeant Peter Flook, an officer now retired. DCXX had been appointed as an official police escort of the witness Duwayne Brooks while he was giving evidence in the Lawrences' 1996 private prosecution of three notorious south London racists for the Lawrence murder – which collapsed after the judge ruled that Brooks's identification evidence was inadmissible. On the day Mr Brooks gave evidence he was escorted by XX from the court to a hotel.

In cross-examination by Menon, Ilsley was asked: "Can you think of a less appropriate officer in the Metropolitan police to protect Duwayne Brooks during the all-important period when he was giving evidence at the Old Bailey? Would you have expected an officer such as XX, given that he had this particular association in the past, if he is chosen for this kind of specialist duty, to declare that connection with Clifford Norris so that someone more appropriate could be selected for the job?"

DCS Ilsley replied: "Absolutely, sir, yes."

IN AUGUST, after the inquiry hearings had concluded, Foot filled in a few more details.

For some weeks the legal team acting for Stephen Lawrence's parents followed up what they described as "the Noye connection". Kenneth Noye is a gangland leader who served 14 years for VAT fraud connected with gold allegedly stolen in the Brink's-Mat bullion robbery; he is currently on the run, wanted for the "road rage" killing of Stephen Cameron. His long years of freedom are widely attributed to his familiarity with police officers everywhere, and especially in south-east London. Clifford Norris is alleged to have been one of Noye's lieutenants on the south London crime scene.

Former *Sunday Mirror* journalist and crime writer Wensley Clarkson interviewed several police officers who knew Noye and confirmed Norris's close contacts with him. In April 1993, when Stephen Lawrence was murdered, Norris is alleged to have urgently contacted Noye who was still in prison. In some panic, he asked him if he could help protect his son, David Norris, who was one of the five first suspects for the Lawrence murder. Noye, it was said, obliged with the names of police officers who might help.

This seemed to answer some of the questions about the appalling delay in arresting the suspects, and the Lawrence legal team was hoping to bring the story out in the final stage of the hearings. The problem was that none of Clarkson's sources were prepared to sign a statement justifying the story, and Clarkson himself refused to sign for fear that he would be asked on oath to name his sources, to whom he had promised confidentiality. Without sworn statements or witnesses, the family were told they could not raise the matter at the inquiry.

The inquiry report described Clifford Norris as an "evil influence hovering over the case", but despite detailing his bribing of a witness in another case in which his son David was a suspect, concluded that there was "no evidence of such interference with witnesses" in the Lawrence case (*see p189*). It also rejected "*any suggestion that Mr Crampton was corrupt or that he acted in collusion with any member of the Norris family*". In January 2012 David Norris – who had been jailed for another racist attack in 2002 – was finally convicted of the murder of Stephen Lawrence along with another of the original suspects, Gary Dobson.

Claims of police corruption – including from a former officer and two members of the Norris family – have continued to emerge since, and an investigation by the Independent Office for Police Conduct and the National Crime Agency is still ongoing.

OVER THE SUMMER, the *Eye* continued to reveal alarming details about the man who insisted only a secret services plot had prevented him from becoming step-grandfather to William and Harry.

A young female interior designer at Harrods had her meagre salary generously supplemented by Mohamed Fayed handing over wads of cash. He then tried to grope her – and when she resisted his advances, warned that "I'll cut your fucking legs off and throw you out in the street and then you'll realise how lucky you are to work for Mohamed Al Fayed." When she eventually sued for unfair dismissal, Harrods settled the case by paying her £5,500.

Fayed also takes his pick of the young management trainees at Harrods. One 17-year-old, Miss D, who began a two-year training course at the store, was quickly poached by Fayed for his private office. Before she started she had to undergo an examination by a Harley Street doctor "to see if you're clean". The Harrods boss is obsessed with personal hygiene, but this was not about clean fingernails: he often insists that attractive women working in his office should have full gynaecological examinations, with reports on tests for HIV, VD etc sent to Fayed himself, sometimes without the patient's consent. One such report found an irregularity on an employee's cervical smear. Later the same day she was accosted by Fayed: "I gather you've been fucking the wrong boys", he announced.

Fayed asked Miss D to regard him as a father or "papa". And he took his paternal duties seriously: first there were hugs and kisses, then he started brushing against her breasts and feeling her bottom. He also offered cash inducements, trying to place a wad of money down the front of her blouse.

One evening, Fayed summoned her to his flat in Park Lane where she found him wearing a dressing gown. After leading her into a room he described as his private "nightclub" he locked the door, offered her champagne, put his hand on her thigh and said: "Come to papa, have a cuddle." Eventually, and with difficulty, she persuaded the revolting old lecher to let her out.

Many other women, all young and attractive, most of them blonde, have been "received for interview" at Park Lane. They usually remain closeted away with Fayed for about two hours, after which, if the Pharaoh is in generous mood, security staff are instructed to hand them bundles of money in (surprise, surprise) brown envelopes.

Fayed has always denied such behaviour.

1999

EVENTS OVER CHRISTMAS made for an unhappy new year for the vicar.

ST ALBION PARISH NEWS

At the beginning of 1999, we look forward to what is to come, not backwards at unfortunate events which may have happened in the past!

Which is why I won't be dwelling on Mr Mandelson's unexpected resignation as our Churchwarden. I think we all know by now that Peter, through no fault of his own, borrowed some money from his friend Mr Robinson so he could buy himself a nice house.

What's wrong with that, you may ask? Nothing is the simple answer! There's nothing in the Good Book that says we can't borrow money from our friends!

After all, didn't Our Lord himself say "Greater love hath no man than this: that he lay out £373,000 for his friend"? (*Revelations 7.16*)

However, Mr Mandelson, being a man of very high principle, knew that he had done nothing wrong, which is why he resigned as our Churchwarden. Without Peter's vision and hard work, we wouldn't have the Millennium Tent. It would just be standing there on the village green half-finished, with nothing to put in it! And incidentally, if anyone does have any ideas of what to put in it, could they please send them in ASAP.

Although not to Peter, obviously, because he's got to be out of action for a while, recharging his batteries. Not that he'll be sitting around on the back pews for long, I'm sure. He has far too much to offer. After all, as he pointed as he left the vicarage, on Christmas Eve: "I know where every single one of you lives. So don't forget it."

Happy New Year! Tony

EURO, EURO, EURO YOUR BOAT GENTLY UP THE STREAM...

SHIT CREEK

JOHN BYRNE

THE NEW European currency had its soft launch, with Tony Blair still equivocating about whether the UK would be joining.

THE MACPHERSON INQUIRY report ruled that the police investigation into Stephen Lawrence's murder had been "marred by a combination of professional incompetence, institutional racism and a failure of leadership", and that racism was still an issue throughout the Metropolitan Police and the legal system. A number of senior officers evaded disciplinary charges by retiring.

NEW FROM PLODDINGTONS

Haven't A Cluedo?

The sleuthing game for detectives everywhere!

Mister Black has been found stabbed to death in the street. Can you guess who dunnit? No, nor can the police. It wasn't Mr White and his mates, that's for sure! Perhaps it was nobody.

Not much fun for all the family.

Says top Inspector Bullock, "I played *Haven't A Cluedo* for years, but now I've had to retire early!"

FOREIGN SECRETARY Robin Cook's sex life erupted into the headlines again as his ex-wife, an NHS consultant, published an excruciating tell-all memoir of their marriage.

A Doctor Writes

BASTARD! Bastard! Bastard! Beardie Bastard! etc, etc.

© *Dr Margaret Cook*

THE ENTIRE European commission resigned en masse following a critical independent report on fraud and mismanagement.

The Guilty Men of Europe

Your cut-out-and-keep guide to those Commissioners they had to sack

KLAUS HANDINTILL, *former Deputy Leader of the Bavarian Social Christian Party*. Has been Commissioner for Organic Olives and Media Studies since 1996. Report described him as "a bit shifty but totally innocent".

EMMA LA PAYOLA, Has been Commissioner for School Milk, Airports and Bullfighting since 1996. Report acquits her of any wrongdoing, apart from being "a bit dodgy".

HERGE BRIBE, *former Mayor of Bruges*. Has

been Commissioner for Tax Harmonisation, Sandwiches and Underfloor Heating since 1995. Report could find no fault with his "thoroughly suspicious" conduct.

SIR LEON BRITTAN, *former failed British politician.* Has been Commissioner for External Lunches, Trading Stamps and Omelettes (non-Spanish) since 1988. Report found him to be "an innocent slimy creep".

MADAME EUGENIE CROISSANT, *former mistress of the President of France.* Commissioner for Fraud, Mismanagement and Sado-Nepotism since 1997. Report found her to be "totally corrupt and a suitable scapegoat for all the other innocent Commissioners".

SANTER KLAUS, *former President of Radio Luxembourg.* President of the European Commission since 1994, responsible for Doing Nothing and Getting Away With It. Report totally exonerated him, but recommended he should "resign immediately before they find out what he's been up to".

Who are they – The new whiter-than-white Commissioners who will take Europe into the new sleaze-free Millennium?

See above, with a few exceptions to make it look as though things have changed.

AS IT BECAME INCREASINGLY apparent that Slobodan Milosevic was not going to cease his campaign against ethnic Albanians in Kosovo, NATO finally intervened with air strikes.

The Albanian majority must be protected

What if we make them a minority?

IT DIDN'T GO entirely to plan.

War Briefing – Week 94

Monday NATO bombs Swedish Embassy, two hospitals and teddy bear factory in Novi Sad.

Tuesday NATO spokesman Jamie Shea apologises for bombing embassy and hospitals, but defends attack on teddy bear factory on grounds that a 1954 Blue Guide to Novi Sad had shown it as "key military installation".

Wednesday Tony Blair flies out to Macedonian camps and promises "Every Kosovar refugee child will be given a teddy bear by NATO."

Thursday Three more US Apache helicopters crash on

training mission to drop teddy bears into camps.

Friday NATO bombs Romania, mistaking it for Bulgaria.

Saturday Robin Cook and Madeleine Albright appear on thousands of television programmes. Cook says it is "clear we are winning. Milosevic is obviously cracking up. He keeps going on TV to claim he is winning."

Sunday John Simpson reports exclusively that it will be sunny today, based on information from sources in Belgrade (the weather forecast TV in his hotel room). NATO warplanes attack Belgrano, killing hundreds of innocent Argentine fish. Jamie Shea explains it was "only three letters out from Belgrade, which is not a bad ratio".

TWO TEENAGERS went on a shooting spree at Columbine High School in Colorado, USA, killing ten of their classmates, a teacher, and finally themselves.

EXCLUSIVE TO ALL NEWSPAPERS

America – A Sick Society

Once again, the world has been shocked by the depths of depravity to which modern America has sunk. The United States is mired in its obsession with guns, violence, and the wilder reaches of psychopathic disorder.

An ordinary suburban schoolroom is littered with the bodies of innocent schoolchildren. Thank goodness it could not happen here, in a sleepy Scottish village, whoops, er, will this do?

ON OTHER PAGES: *Brixton bomb – new suspects.* ● *Brick Lane bomb – were neo-Nazis responsible?* ● *Man hijacks car and drives round Rochdale shooting Kalashnikov.* ● *Mardi Gras Bomber guilty on 20 charges.* ● *Bulger Killers – new appeal.*

A NEW GENRE, reality TV, was flooding the schedules.

AS HE MADE HIS POLITICAL comeback in the Kensington and Chelsea constituency – to the consternation of lacklustre Tory leader William Hague – Michael Portillo revealed in an interview that he had "had some homosexual experiences as a young person".

Don't worry, William, I don't find you attractive

Nor does anyone else

THE QUEEN'S YOUNGEST SON, Prince Edward, married Sophie Rhys-Jones.

A poem to help you remember those Royal Weddings by Henry VIII

> Divorced, Divorced, Divorced,
> Divorced, Divorced, Surprise!

AS (PART OF) THE COUNTRY experienced (or didn't because it was cloudy) the first total solar eclipse in 72 years, everyone searched for a way to cash in.

Amazing Gnome Offer

The safe way to watch the eclipse!

Simply cut out these specially treated medically-approved spectacles and put them on during the eclipse.

Providing that you close your eyes and look in the other direction for the duration of the eclipse, you will suffer no ill-effects. These glasses are provided entirely free in the interests of public safety.

MELITA NORWOOD, an 87-year-old retired civil servant, was revealed to have spent her entire career passing on state secrets to the KGB.

Tell-Tale Signs that MI5 missed in the Neasden Mata Hari case

1. She was chairman of the Neasden Women's Institute for the Overthrow of Capitalism
2. She organised regular trips for her local Darby and Joan Club to have tea with senior Politburo members
3. She listed her hobbies in *Who's Who* as "Spying for the KGB"
4. She had a life-size statue of Stalin in her front garden
5. She named her cottage in Neasden, "The Lubyanka"
6. When watching James Bond films in the Neasden Roxy she always booed when 007 appeared.

TWO TRAINS COLLIDED at speed at Ladbroke Grove, killing 31 people and injuring over 400.

Prescott announces new safety rules

The Transport Secretary, Mr John Prescott, yesterday unveiled sweeping new measures to ensure that safety is the number one priority for those involved in public transport.

1. Blame Railtrack
2. Blame the operating companies
3. Blame privatisation, even as you are privatising blame
4. Announce a 10-point plan
5. Go to work in your chauffeur-driven car as usual

"Once you have completed this operation," said Mr Prescott, "your job as transport minister will be safe."

JEFFREY ARCHER was revealed to have faked evidence and persuaded a friend to commit perjury during his 1987 libel trial, and was forced to quit as Conservative candidate for Mayor of London.

AND THE WORLD PREPARED for a date change which seemed inordinately important at the time...

In Memoriam The Second Millennium

> So. Farewell then
> The last thousand years.
> Yes, a lot of things have
> Happened during
> That time.
>
> Too many to incorporate in
> A poem
> Of this length.   E.J. Thribb (17½)

E.J. Thribb's millennial collection, Leaves on the Line of Life, is now available from the Trouser Press.

JANUARY BROUGHT more news of racism in the police force.

Sergeant Gurpal Virdi was in duty in Hanwell, west London, late one night last March, when he took an emergency call that two lads had been stabbed in the street. He went straight to the scene where a young Iraqi was lying on the pavement bleeding heavily. His friend, who had been stabbed less severely, told the officer that the pair had been attacked by five white youths, whom he described.

Having given the young men first aid and put the Iraqi in an ambulance, Sergeant Virdi went in search of the assailants, and found two skulking in a back street. The other three had already been found. He went to tell the badly stabbed boy's mother about the attack, then returned to Hanwell and found the knife which had been used in the stabbing.

Virdi left the case in the hands of the Ealing CID, but when he next checked up on it he was horrified to find all five of the accused youths had been released on bail and the attack had not been classified as racist. He complained that this was wrong – the youths had taunted the two boys, urging them to get out of the area and push off to places where there were more black people. He was told he was interfering, to which he replied that he was one of the arresting officers.

Soon afterwards he went on holiday for 10 days. On the day of his return, as he took his children to the dentist, he was surprised to find himself followed by some of his police colleagues. Later that day he was arrested and hauled off to the police station where he was accused of sending out racist mail. The previous December all black and Asian officers in the area had received hate mail saying they were "not wanted". Mr Virdi was accused of sending out the mail from his computer in the police station and "perverting the course of justice", two charges he contemptuously denied. He was released on police bail. That was on 15 April last year. Ever since, he has been suspended, awaiting some information from his colleagues as to whether or not he is to be charged.

In the summer the attack on the two young men was suddenly reclassifed as a racist incident, as Sergeant Virdi had recommended. Three of them were convicted in October, with the stabber getting four years' youth custody.

This was merely the beginning of a very long saga. The CPS did not press criminal charges over the racist mail, but a police disciplinary tribunal found Sergeant Virdi guilty and he was sacked. He took the Met to an employment tribunal which ruled there was no evidence that he had been responsible for the racist mail, and that he had been "the subject of discrimination on the grounds of his race". He received £240,000 in compensation and a personal apology from the commissioner of the Met, and was reinstated to the force after four years off duty, with a job at Scotland Yard. He said he was sidelined by "racists and bigots" for the rest of his career before retiring in 2012 – and two years later was arrested on suspicion of indecently assaulting a male suspect in the back of a police van 28 years earlier. At his trial it was proved that the assault as described could not possibly have happened. "The Met has continually campaigned to discredit me," he pointed out after the trial. "It's twice they've tried to put me in prison." The person or people who actually sent the racist hate mail – which read "Keep the Police Force White, so Leave Now or Else! – NF" – has never been charged.

WHEN THE MACPHERSON REPORT into Stephen Lawrence's murder was published the following month, the *Eye* reminded readers of its Clifford Norris stories (*see p184*) and pointed out a couple of major problems.

On the incompetence and racialism of the Metropolitan Police, especially in the lower ranks, the inquiry was uncompromising. But the charges of "corruption" and "collusion", however, were treated in a totally different manner. The inquiry members admitted applying a different criterion. "The standard of proof (of corruption and collusion) must be the criminal standard," they insist. "We can only reach a conclusion adverse to the police or individual officers if we are satisfied beyond reasonable doubt… in other areas of the case we are entitled to reach conclusions based upon a balance of probability."

The inquiry relied for its research on the treasury solicitor's office, a government department who have little experience in detailed investigations of this kind. The enormous fact-finding work, interviews, trawls through bank statements, advertisements for information and so forth which were necessary to prove a complete lack of collusion between Norris and the police were far too onerous for the inquiry team. They could, and perhaps should, have abandoned the subject altogether and passed it back to the home secretary or to another tribunal. What they did instead was blandly to "form a view" that the police were incompetent, but all completely clean. The suggestion gangsters were using their influence to protect their youth from the law was anathema.

AS THE NORTHERN IRELAND peace deal foundered over decommissioning and prisoner releases in July, the *Eye* carried an extraordinary tale.

Is the government so keen to keep the Good Friday agreement on track that it is prepared to sacrifice the safety of its former dirty workers? It would appear so.

Last Friday, solicitors acting for the Crown Authorities (ie MI5) told the former IRA member and RUC agent Martin McGartland, shot by the IRA in Tyneside three weeks ago, that they would not be responsible for his fate. The reason for washing their hands of him was that he had given a TV interview – in disguise, but against their advice. They now "regard him as having assumed complete responsibility for his own security".

In fact they have been declining responsibility for Mr McGartland for the past two years, ever since his cover was blown by Northumbria Police and the local Crown Prosecution Service, who insisted on prosecuting him for perverting the course of justice by using different driving licences. After hearing of his dangerous double life as an IRA informer, the jury at Newcastle Crown Court took less than ten minutes to acquit Mr McGartland, but by then everyone – especially his former colleagues in the IRA – knew who and where he was.

Negotiations for a new safe identity for Mr McGartland broke down in March last year after the Crown offered a derisory removal package which would have left him substantially out of pocket. But far more crucially, they also declined to remove his details from police records. Given that the police national computer is far from secure, that officers have been known to tell or sell its contents and that the police had already blown his cover once, it was not surprising that Mr McGartland was adamant his safety could only be guaranteed by purging all mention of him.

This was declined. Just over a year later McGartland, like other IRA informers before him, was blasted six times at close range. Miraculously he survived the wounds to his stomach and chest, and was placed under 24-hour protection. But after the ITV interview, Northumbria Police withdrew their armed guard and confirmed the fact to the world and the IRA in a press statement, saying he had chosen to leave against their advice.

It would be 20 years before a police report finally confirmed McGartland's attempted assassination had indeed been carried out by the IRA, rather than the local drug dealers that were held responsible in a cover-up McGartland believes was "invented and fed" to media sources by MI5 or the government. He has spent most of that time involved in litigation or complaint processes to try to force the authorities to resume funding of his medical and psychiatric treatment. In the midst of it, he and his partner's new home was raided by men in balaclavas late at night – who turned out to be officers from Northumbria Police investigating drug-dealing by former residents.

THERE WAS AN EARLY appearance in October from someone who would become a familiar face.

Our old friend Peter Carter-Fuck has despatched a furious letter to the *Guardian* on behalf of Nigel Farage MEP, the chairman of the UK Independence Party, demanding immediate and grovelling apologies for an article about him. This is not the first time Carter-Fuck has taken up cudgels for Farage. In June this year he threatened to issue a writ against the *Times* after the paper reported on Farage's mysterious lunch two years earlier with one Mark Deavin, a prominent member of the far-right British National Party.

Farage's friends have claimed in recent days that the *Times* was forced to apologise. Not so: it published a tiny clarification of one point, that Farage had met only one BNP extremist so it was inaccurate to say he had been in contact with "extremists" in the plural. Nothing else was retracted.

Farage admits he lunched with Deavin on 17 June 1997: he could hardly do otherwise, since a photo exists of the two men leaving the restaurant. But why did he meet him, given that UKIP has always gone out of its way to shun any contact with racists and far-right activists – and that Deavin had been expelled from UKIP the previous month when he was discovered as an infiltrator from the BNP?

Farage was vague when challenged about it at a UKIP meeting in February 1999. After composing his sworn statement, he didn't provide his executive with a copy, even though the party was paying a share of his lavish Carter-Fuck costs for negotiations with the *Times* (£18,000 in all). Even the "full explanation" in his affidavit actually raises more questions than it answers. Farage says he agreed to the lunch because he "wanted to find out why he (Deavin) had left UKIP", but elsewhere in the same paragraph he admits that Deavin "had been expelled... when it was discovered that he had links with the BNP".

As one executive member puts it, Farage has been "less than candid".

2000s

SOMETHING EXTRAORDINARY HAPPENED AS THE *Eye* celebrated its fortieth year on sale. It won a libel action.

As is often the way with these things, it was over something quite obscure and not especially important: a brief story in 1992 detailing how a Cornish accountant overcharged his clients. But the involvement of his lawyers Carter-Fuck (a long-standing deliberate *Eye* misprint: the firm are actually called Farter-Fuck) ensured that the case dragged on for the best part of a decade and produced so much expensive paperwork that the judge pronounced himself "absolutely horrified". Then the accountant in question got in the witness box, accused his lawyers of lying, and the entire thing collapsed leaving him and his lawyers around a million pounds out of pocket.

Even more amazingly, at the end of the decade the magazine managed to repeat the trick, when it defeated one of the legal actions that had replaced libel as the weapon of choice for those who wanted to keep themselves out of the papers, a privacy injunction. Once again, Carter-Fuck were involved, once again the potential bills were astronomical, and once again the ridiculousness of the legal manoeuvre – in this case, claiming that an ombudsman's report and a Law society inquiry into a solicitor's professional behaviour were confidential and should be kept private – did not prevent the action dragging on for far longer than anyone expected.

The introduction of privacy laws in Britain, via the exploitation of European human rights rules incorporated in 1998 and the blunt tool that became notorious as a "super-injunction", had been documented – sometimes in necessarily cryptic terms – in the *Eye*'s pages.

Meanwhile the magazine built on its other strengths: one of Paul Foot's last acts before his untimely death in 2004 was to recruit a former tax inspector, Richard Brooks, who expertly exposed a series of eye-watering deals where HMRC had agreed with major firms that paying tax was only optional, most of which came as news to the MPs who subsequently dissected them. Brooks's most un-hack-ish ability with a balance sheet, along with that of the veteran Michael Gillard, helped the *Eye* chart a definitive course through the two big cons that erupted towards the end of the decade and enraged readers perhaps more than any before them: bankers' gambling and MPs' expenses.

> *It has become a crucial part of Britain's informal constitution, the court of ultimate appeal against outrageous conduct. A company chairman once admitted to me that if a director puts forward some really shady proposition, he has to say, 'What would happen if that got into Private Eye?'*
>
> Anthony Sampson, 2004

This was also the decade, as the Reverend Blair devoted himself ever-more fervently to Holy War on all fronts (including with his chancellor and eventual successor as Supreme Leader) that people came to realise that perhaps New Labour were not quite such a refreshing change after all – and that laughing at them was not just a human right but our duty in a stakeholder economy. From the 1997 election to the fag end of Gordon Brown's reign in 2009, the *Eye*'s readership went up from 180,000 to over 210,00.

2000

THE MILLENNIUM DOME turned out to be a damp squib…

…AS DID ANOTHER much-hyped marker of the date change.

An Apology

In common with all other newspapers, we may have given the impression that the so-called Millennium Bug was in some way going to disrupt the normal functioning of the world's computers, leading to global panic, disruption and the end of civilisation. Headlines such as "Computer Glitch Spells Trouble For 2000", "Yes – It's the Y2K Armageddon" and "Help – We're All Going To Die!" may inadvertently have led readers to believe that there were likely to be problems at the turn of the year.

We now realise that there was not the slightest foundation for any of this scaremongering nonsense, which only appeared due to the self-importance and incompetence of so-called responsible computer experts.

We apologise to readers for any distress that this confusion may have caused.

ON OTHER PAGES
Deadly Virus Sweeps Country! 3
Yes, It's Flu-mageddon! 4
Help – We're All Going To Die! 5-22

HOME SECRETARY Jack Straw hit upon a new way of ending the political embarrassment of keeping former dictator Augusto Pinochet under house arrest in the UK.

A Doctor Writes

As a doctor, I am often asked, "Could you please look at this poor old Chilean gentleman and come to the conclusion that he is too senile to stand trial?"

The simple answer is "Of course, Mr Straw. May I have a cheque please?"

If you are worried about a tricky political situation, you should consult professional medical advice at once.

FRANK DOBSON narrowly beat Ken Livingstone to the Labour nomination as candidate for London mayor, much to the Vicar of St Albion's delight.

Thought for the Week

Amid all the silly tittle-tattle about the choice of our friend Mr Dobson to play the part of the Lord Mayor of London in this year's St Albion's pantomime being rigged and "a fix", let me remind parishioners what it says in the Good Book, "The first shall be last, and the last first." So, the fact is that since Mr Livingstone came first in the popularity stakes, and Mr Dobson was last, the Bible tells us that Mr Dobson should be the winner. And I hope no one is going to argue with Holy Scripture! T.B.

NOTICE: A Service of Excommunication will be held next Sunday

Mr Livingstone will be cast into utter darkness. Kids, please bring a candle! T.B.

MEANWHILE in Zimbabwe, supporters of President Robert Mugabe had begun forcibly seizing agricultural land from white farmers.

AS THE STORMONT ASSEMBLY was suspended in a row over IRA decommissioning, not everyone could keep track of the different factions involved.

THE I.R.A — THE CONTINUITY I.R.A — THE REAL IRA — I CAN'T BELIEVE IT'S NOT THE I.R.A

AFTER NORFOLK FARMER Tony Martin was jailed for shooting dead a 16-year-old who was burgling his home, faltering Tory leader William Hague seized on the debate around the right to kill intruders.

The leader of the opposition, Mr William Hague, today defended his call for new laws to protect those on the receiving end of unprovoked attacks.

"Everyone has the right to defend themselves by any means at their disposal," he told supporters. "If someone is picking on you because you are weak and hopeless then you are entitled to do *anything* to save yourself.

"This must include," he continued, "using any weapon that is at hand, including desperate speeches about law and order and frenzied assaults on asylum seekers."

ON OTHER PAGES
Support Burglar Killers, says Hague – Jail Pokemon Bullies for Life, says Hague – Restore News at Ten now, says Hague – Ban Rain on Bank Holidays, says Hague.

ANTI-CAPITALIST CAMPAIGNERS, tiring of the "guerrilla gardening" protest that had been planned for central London, decided to riot instead.

Guerrilla Gardeners' Question Time

with ANNA KIST

Caller: What is the best time of year to plant a brick through the windows of McDonalds?

Anna: Any time of year is good, but spring is traditional. Make sure you've got a nice big brick and make a great

big hole in the window. With any luck, in six months' time you'll see a lovely 'For Sale' notice where the shop was.

Caller: Hello Anna, can you recommend the best seeds of destruction for world capitalism and the international finance system?

Anna: I suggest you grow a nice green mohican or maybe a red beard. Then strip off all your clothes and behave as if you're in the nursery. This should do the trick.

Caller: How can I help to provide more green spaces in London?

Anna: The best thing to do is find a nice grassy area with plenty of flowers, like Parliament Square, and then dig it all up and put it on the road for the dustmen to throw away.

BARRY GEORGE was charged with the murder of TV presenter Jill Dando. His conviction would later be overturned on appeal.

Knacker triumphant as Dando killer held

by Our Crime Staff **Phil Prisons**

A delighted Inspector Knacker of the 500-strong Dando Squad was "over the moon" yesterday that at last the killer of TV's Jill Dando is behind bars.

"All that we have left to do now," said Knacker, "is find some evidence, link it to the killer and present the case to a jury."

He continued, "It would be quite wrong for me to say anything at this stage of the proceedings except that he did it and this is his name and address."

ENGLAND WERE KNOCKED out in the first round of Euro 2000.

An Apology

In recent weeks, in common with all other newspapers, we may have given the impression that the England football team, under the inspired leadership of Mr Kevin Keegan, had the finest chance since 1966 of winning a major championship. Headlines such as "King Kev Can Do The Biz", "Shearer Magic Will Bring Home The Silver" and "Becksie's Blitzkrieg Will Win World War Four" may have led readers to believe that the England squad had some chance of coming in the first two in their group.

We now realise that the national team was without doubt the worst bunch of talentless no-hopers ever to don an England jersey, and that in the words of Alf Littlejohn (Cab No. 94 with flag of St George obscuring the windscreen), "they should all be strung up, guv, it's the only language they understand".

We apologise unreservedly for any confusion that may have arisen from any previous articles by our sports team.

THE FOURTH, and most-hyped yet, instalment of the Harry Potter saga was published.

LORRY DRIVERS, protesting at the cost of fuel blockaded oil refineries and ran rolling roadblocks, closing thousands of petrol stations and forcing the government to assume emergency powers in order to keep essential services running.

You can't fuel all of the people all of the time

A BRAND-NEW programme launched on Channel 4.

Your cut-out-'n'-keep guide to the cast of the fly-on-the-wall game show that has captured the imagination of the nation.

Big Brother is not being watched by you

Every night for the past three years, millions of viewers have been tuning in to one of the most bizarre experiments in public entertainment ever devised.

An ill-assorted group of unsavoury characters are forced to live 24 hours a day locked away from reality in a special "sealed environment" known as The Government.

These unpleasant, self-centred show-offs compete with each other to win the approval of the viewers, who at regular intervals can vote to have them evicted from the show.

STILL IN

Tipped by the bookies as the "dark horse" who could last the course the longest is **Gordie**, the dour, uptight Scotsman who "keeps himself to himself" and sits in a corner going through his cheque-stubs.

ALREADY OUT

Sharp-dressing man about Notting Hill, **Mandy** was generally voted too clever by half. Amazingly, Mandy insisted that despite getting the boot, he should be allowed back in, and Tony and the rest weakly agreed.

NEWLY-APPOINTED *News of the World* editor Rebekah Wade decided to make a splash with a "Name and Shame" campaign of paedophiles.

Noose of the World named and shamed

by LYNCHTIME O'NOOSE

This evil woman is responsible for an act of indescribable sickness and grotesque cynicism which must shock the entire nation. She is Rebekah Wade of Pennington Street, Wapping, a foul-minded editor psychiatrists say can never be cured of her vile tendencies.

She *will* offend again, whatever the do-gooders may say.

We publish her name only in the interests of protecting her innocent readers, many of them vulnerable morons with the mental age of a toddler. It is our duty because Rebekah Wade is not acting alone – she is part of a seedy ring of filth merchants and pedlars of pornography who are controlled by Mr Big, known only as Rupert Murdoch, who runs his evil empire from a sleazy backroom in London's criminal East End.

We strongly urge readers not to go out and string these people up, even though they would be perfectly justified in ridding the world of these sickos. No, we have plenty of rope in our offices, but we urge readers not to come and collect their free hanging rope.

More pictures of the faces of evil, pp. 2-94

UNSURPRISINGLY, it led to vigilante attacks.

"I'm a paediatrician!"

THE EYE FIRST REPORTED on the build-up of dangerous fumes inside aircraft in January.

The vast public relations machine of British Aeropsace was not at all concerned when contacted about what the Swedish air accident investigation board described as "an extremely unusual and serious incident" on board one of the company's 146 jetliners. The crew fell mysteriously ill, with one member of the cabin crew describing the experience as "like being on a moonwalk". In the middle of the third flight of the day, the cabin manager, besieged with complaints from passengers, finally lost patience and stormed into the cockpit. To her amazement she found both the pilots wearing oxygen masks…

British Aerospace dismissed the whole affair as a one-off. Perhaps they had forgotten the Australian bureau of air safety report issued two months previously, regarding the captain of a 146 who, as he approached the runway, smelt fumes, suffered vertigo and became confused. Even more recently, three senior British Aerospace engineers gave evidence to an Australian senate inquiry into air safety. They testified that at least four pilots had lost their licences because of ill health, for which they blamed cabin fumes. Another dozen flight attendants are permanently off work, and 120 exempted from work on the 146 after complaining of the same symptoms…

19 years later, union Unite brought a legal action against five different airlines over the exposure of their flight crew and pilot members to dangerous fumes on board aircraft, which was due to come to court in 2021.

IN FEBRUARY, *Daily Mirror* editor Piers "Moron" Morgan was revealed to have made a large investment in Viglen shares which were going to be tipped by his paper the following day. Slicker suggested some fruitful lines of inquiry for investigators:

While the editor may have been cleared by the *Mirror* internal inquiry – isn't that the purpose of internal inquiries? – he may find the DTI somewhat more probing. It and the Stock Exchange may want answers to questions like:

1. How often has he invested £20,000?
2. Why did he invest on a day when his pals Bhoyrul and Hipwell were once again preparing to boost Viglen?
3. Were the shares to be registered in his own name?
4. Had he ever discussed Viglen with his pals and, if so, when?
5. Does he own or has he ever owned any other shares tipped by his newspaper?
6. Why, when the *Mirror* tipped Viglen and the price doubled the day after he bought, did Morgan not recognise the problem and immediately sell and donate the profits to charity?
7. Does the *Daily Mirror* have any rules preventing journalists or executives from dealing on information obtained by the newspaper?

Mirror **journalists Anil Bhoyrul and James Hipwell were subsequently found guilty of conspiracy to breach the Financial Services Act. The DTI announced that there was not enough evidence "currently available" to charge Moron. At the 2005 trial it was revealed that Moron and his wife had actually bought £67,000-worth of Viglen shares rather than the £20,000 he initially confessed to, that the editor had been in regular contact with Bhoyrul asking for investment tips, and that six other members of** ***Mirror*** **staff and their relatives had piled in to buy shares that were about to be tipped in the City Slickers column. The man in charge of the internal inquiry told the trial he had not been aware of Moron's request to a Viglen PR man to change his account of a phone conversation, and that if he had, the report would not have cleared the editor. Moron continues to deny any wrongdoing.**

ALSO IN February, the *Eye*'s rail columnist Dr B. Ching provided one reason why Labour were so desperate for Ken Livingstone not to bag the job of mayor of London.

Public-Private Partnerships for maintaining tube lines are not the only device Labour is using to tie the hands of the London mayor before he or she is even elected. London Underground has been ordered to sell off its non-operational property asap. Meanwhile London Transport Property is seeking a long-term private sector partner willing to redevelop stations and collect vast prospects from the resulting office space, shopping malls, car parks etc.

Mayoral candidates might try to console themselves with the knowledge that these deals will be far from stitched up by the time the mayor takes office. But Labour saw that one coming too. It has arranged for powers relating to the underground not to be passed to the mayor until the negotiations for semi-privatising the tube have been completed. By which time the asset-stripping programme will be complete, and the operational system will be enmeshed in long-term Old Tory contracts which cannot be broken.

After he was elected, Livingstone went to the high court but failed to defeat the plan to part-privatise the tube system – although the judge criticised the government for not making it clear that the mayor would not take control until PPP was already in place.

MORE THAN A YEAR on from the Macpherson Report, the *Eye* continued to expose disturbing examples of police behaviour, including this in June.

Over the past four years Delroy Lindo, 40, and his wife Sonia have been charged by the Met with a total of 18 offences – some trivial (having a dirty number plate) but some so serious (affray and threatening to kill) that they carry the threat of up to 10 years in jail.

Every time the prosecution has collapsed, been abandoned or the police version of events has not stood up to the scrutiny of magistrates, judges or juries. The reason for the Knacker's persistence? It is surely no coincidence that Mr Lindo spearheads campaigns against police racism and is a friend of Winston Silcott, wrongly convicted of the murder of PC Keith Blakelock.

Now the couple are suing the Met. As well as allegations of continuing harassment, wrongful arrest, unlawful imprisonment and malicious prosecution, the family alleges assault for injuries suffered during some of the incidents.

Soon after this article appeared, Delroy Lindo was arrested for "sucking his teeth" at two police officers, and held in a cell for five hours. The Met subsequently admitted to harassing the Lindos, and four years later agreed to pay them £80,000 in compensation in an out-of-court settlement.

THE TRIAL OF THE TWO LIBYANS accused of the 1988 Lockerbie bombing began in September. The *Eye* provided a few details about the prosecution's star witness.

Abdul Majid Razkaz Salam Giaka worked for Libyan intelligence at Malta airport. He defected to the CIA in 1989, but at the time of his defection he forgot to mention anything about the Lockerbie bombing a few months previously. It was not until early 1991, when Syrian involvement in the United Nations effort against Iraq became crucial and the Lockerbie suspects switched from terrorist plotters in that country to Libya, that Giaka, now safe under a witness protection scheme in the US, disclosed his evidence. Giaka is paid $1,000 dollars a month and stands to make another $4m if the defendants are convicted.

There has been little or no British reporting of the performance of Harold Hendershot, the FBI agent who interviewed the star witness when he was finally taken off Malta. Questioned by the prosecution, Mr Hendershot could not even recall the dates of his interviews with Giaka, let alone what he revealed. It emerged that although the FBI agent had taken notes of all ten interviews he conducted, he had left them behind in Washington.

IN OCTOBER, DR B. CHING cast a critical eye over Railtrack, the privatised company in charge of Britain's railway infrastructure.

Private investors' only concern is to make a fast buck from a long-term industry. The rail regulator is obliged to allow Railtrack more than £1m profit each day, however abysmal its performance. Railtrack has no grassroots staff except signallers, who are on frighteningly low pay for safety-critical workers. Maintenance is handled by a ragbag of contractors, all charging enough to guarantee their own profits but needing intense supervision by Railtrack. Direct labour, which should be cheaper and safer, is not on the agenda for Railtrack, which fancies itself as a major-league property developer and not a boring old engineering business.

The government could change the system. Instead of subsidising train operators to cover Railtrack's whopping track fees, it could subsidise Railtrack direct – in return for an annual government allocation of Railtrack shares. That would give the government a say in Railtrack's actions and gradually amount to re-nationalisation, which recent history has shown to be a more efficient way of managing the rail infrastructure. But the government is set against such a logical course of action. The same profits for the same pisspoor work are guaranteed for the next five years.

On the day the magazine containing this column went to print, the Hatfield rail crash killed four people and injured over 70 others. It was caused by a cracked rail which should have been replaced but wasn't thanks to the system of Railtrack farming out maintenance procedures to contractors and failing to maintain proper supervision of the state of tracks. The company and contractor, Balfour Beatty, were found guilty of breaking health and safety law, and the government renationalised it as Network Rail two years later.

2001

PETER MANDELSON resigned from the cabinet for a second time over his role in the billionaire Hinduja brothers acquiring passports shortly after donating to the Millennium Dome – but this time he insisted that he had done nothing wrong.

THE FILM *Bridget Jones's Diary* was released just as Sophie Rhys-Jones, the Countess of Wessex, fell prey to a *News of the World* sting by "fake sheikh" Mazher Mahmood and was forced to step down from the PR company she had founded.

SOPHIE RHYS-JONES'S **DIARY**

Sophie Rhys-Jones's Diary (15)
For anyone who's ever been set up by a tabloid
A No-Longer-Working Titled Production

EYE VERDICT: Hilariously funny story of a silly sloaney PR girl who is desperate to find Mr Rich. When she falls for tall Arab stranger she thinks her problems are over. But it turns out to be a complete disaster!

AS SHE WRITES IN HER DIARY: "Bugger! Bugger! Bugger! Arab Prince Charming turns out to be ghastly bloke from *News of the World*

with towel on head. Have gained 200 column inches (v.v. bad) and lost 500,000 pounds (Aaargh!!) Am now lady of leisure, ie ghastly jobless oik in manner of Fergie or similar."

DISSIDENT Irish republicans set off a bomb outside BBC Television Centre.

"This looks like the work of the Real ITN"

FOOT-AND-MOUTH disease spread rapidly across Britain, resulting in the closure of much of the countryside to visitors, the slaughter of millions of cows and sheep, and a crisis in the agricultural sector.

NURSERY TIMES

Foot and Mouth traced to Mary's little lamb

Top vets today announced they believe the horrifying spread of FMD may be due to the movements of one lamb belonging to a girl called Mary.

"The pattern of the new outbreak is consistent with the path of the lamb as it criss-crossed the country following Mary," said a spokesman for the Fairyland Ministry of Agriculture, Fisheries and Food (FMAFF). "Everywhere that Mary went," explained a Ministry vet gesturing to a large map, "FMD was sure to go."

ON OTHER PAGES: ● "I lost my sheep and found Maff had shot them all," says Bo-Peep ● Old MacDonald to abandon farm and sell *Big Issue* instead ● Old King Cole says situation not merry but appalling and makes donation to help farmers in need.

THE ELECTION was finally called for 7 June.

That Labour election-winning strategy in full

1. Call the election
2. Remind everyone that William Hague is leader of the Conservative Party.
3. Er... that's it.

THE REVEREND BLAIR remained confident as Parish Council elections approached.

ST ALBION PARISH NEWS

Everywhere I have been in the past few weeks I have been greeted by groups of happy, smiling people (organised by Mr Campbell) thanking me for all the good work I have put in on their behalf to make their lives better, richer and more modern in every way.

Time and time again I was impressed by the sheer number of people who turned out to see me. For example, in our local hospital, they had been literally queuing up for months, and "so great was the multitude", as it says in the Bible, that they were spilling out onto trolleys in the corridors and wheelchairs in the car park!

As I said to them, "Blessed are those who wait, for they shall see God rather sooner than they expected!" *(Book of the Dead, Ch.VI, v12)*. I urge you all to make "the sign of the cross" alongside the names of all my team on the Big Day!

Yours ever, Tony

And he was right to be. Labour won another landslide.

THE THIRD Mrs Rupert Murdoch (of four so far) revealed that she was pregnant.

Never Too Old... *by SYLVIE KRIN*

THE STORY SO FAR: Billionaire media mogul Rupert Murdoch has married the willowy, almond-eyed prawn cracker of the East, Wendy Deng, but his children have always looked down on the amber goddess from the land of pot noodles. Now read on...

It was 4 o'clock in the morning as a summer dawn broke over the Manhattan skyline. On the 94th floor of the Perry Como building an old man shuffled reluctantly from his bedroom to a Redgrave and Pinsent Olympic-standard rowing machine, an 87th birthday present from his fragrant oriental wifette.

"I've set it for 3 hours uphill rapids," she cooed lovingly from her boudoir three floors away. "Chop, chop, Lupert. I'll come and see you later if you're still alive. Just joking, ha ha ha!"

As the hours ticked slowly away, the proud tycoon cast his mind back to that rare night of passion in September when, for a few fleeting moments, Wendy had made him feel like a young man again.

Just like all those years ago in the outback when he rode a kangaroo from the sheep station at Diggery Doo to Old Rolf's Abbo's Armpit Club in dusty Alice Thompson. Happy days then when, as a virile, carefree young jackaroo he had wanged his donger and watched the Sheilas' eyes pop with pleasure...

"Lupert! What you do dreaming? No slacking!" The shrill voice of the sultry beauty from Beijing interrupted his reverie as she hit him playfully with a copy of the New South Wales Courier and Argus. "Look! It says here I have bun in oven. What this mean?"

"Well, my little fortune-hunting cookie," wheezed the global media magnate as the perspiration poured down his wrinkled cheeks, "it means that when you cough out the little feller, it gets a big slice of its daddy's dosheroo. Mind you, I have to croak first."

Wendy's beautiful eyes narrowed inscrutably and her hand moved to the setting on the rowing machine marked "Dangerous: Not suitable for rich old men".

THE DOTCOM BUBBLE burst spectacularly.

Apology

In common with all other newspapers, our City pages may have given the impression over the last two years that an investment in high-technology and telecommunications shares was in some way desirable, if not essential. Headlines such as "Buy! Buy! Buy!", "We're all going Dotty.com!" and "It's money for old rope!" may have led readers to believe that a high-tech/telecom stockmarket portfolio constituted an exciting investment opportunity.

We now accept unreservedly that such was not the case and that, in truth, the entire dotcom frenzy was a speculative bubble inflated by the media which was guaranteed to lead to a stockmarket collapse with its attendant personal distress to unwary investors. We apologise to anyone who lost their money, but regret that no refund will be available.

Read more on our website: "Bye! Bye! Bye!"; "It's a Dot. Con!"; "Hang yourself with our free rope!"

DAYS OF NEGOTIATIONS between the governments of the UK and Ireland and all parties in Northern Ireland failed to solve an impasse over IRA decommissioning which threatened the entire peace process.

That Blair-Ahern Ulster deal in full

1. British army to be withdrawn from sensitive areas (Belfast, London, etc) and its weapons placed "beyond use".
2. RUC to be scrapped and replaced by IRPS (The Irish Republican Protection Service)
3. All remaining terrorists to be given amnesty, including the ones who have just bombed Ealing.
4. Sir Gerard Adams to become First Minister of the United Kingdom.
5. All outstanding IRA demands to be met in full.
6. The IRA to jolly well think very hard about having talks with General de Chastelain about a possible timetable for talks about the possibility of a timetable for potential decommissioning of a representative sample of weapons (eg. one black beret or similar)
7. Er... That's it.

HIJACKED PLANES WERE FLOWN into the Pentagon and both towers of the World Trade Centre in New York, killing thousands. President George W. Bush was immediately removed to Air Force One, where he remained for several hours.

PRIVATE EYE

BUSH TAKES CHARGE

It's Armageddon, sir

Armageddon outahere!

RESCUERS SEARCHED through the rubble of the collapsed towers for survivors as the media looked on.

Buried under rubbish

There was thought to be little hope of any informed coverage emerging from the thousands of tons of newsprint which left readers buried in voyeuristic cliché and bellicose sentimentality last week.

"There but for the grace of God go I," admitted one reporter, who added, "America tonight is a nation united in prayer, but also in a desire for vengeance in an atmosphere of almost biblical *(cont. p94)*

THE 19 HIJACKERS, all of whom died in the attacks, were swiftly linked to Al Qaeda, the Islamist terror organisation which had attempted to blow up the World Trade Center in 1993.

"If only I could go to Paradise with you – but, alas, I'm needed here on earth"

THE PRESIDENT DECLARED that he had "directed the full resources of our intelligence and law enforcement communities to find those responsible and to bring them to justice".

I'm relying on intelligence

Uh-oh!

HYSTERIA reigned.

Daily Newscare

We must not give in to terror

ON OTHER PAGES:

- Bin Laden has nuclear weapons **2**
- Nerve gas attack imminent **3**
- Britain is terrorists' main target **4**
- Global recession now definite **5**
- House prices will tumble **6**
- We're all going to die **94**

THE US RECRUITED allies to strike back hard, even if it wasn't quite certain at whom. The Reverend Blair was already on board.

ST ALBION PARISH NEWS

The Vicar's Sermon 'In Time Of War'

(as preached last Sunday at Evensong)

We hear a lot in the Bible about how we should all love our neighbours and turn the other cheek and blessed are the peacemakers and all that sort of stuff.

Well, it may have been all very well in its time. But times have changed. Since last week we are living in a different world.

How is it different, I hear you ask? Let me tell you, in once simple little word. W-A-R. And let's take that one letter at a time. 'W' (or 'Dubya' as we've come to call it!) is for 'We'. 'A' stand for 'Are'. And 'R', of course, for 'Ready' or 'Raring to go'. I am sure the children will find that easy to remember. I know I do! It's what we call an 'acro-nym' from the Greek words 'acro', meaning 'fools' and 'nym', meaning 'no one'.

AIRSTRIKES on Afghanistan began on 7 October.

That Afghanistan Strike

BEFORE

AFTER

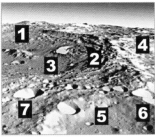

1. Chemical Warfare Centre
2. Nuclear Missile Silo Disguised as Rock
3. Telecommunications Centre Camouflaged as Tree
4. Anthrax Production Facility (Camel Dung)
5. Terrorist Barracks (To Hold Up To 2000 Fully-Trained Mass-Murderers)
6. Barber's Shop (Closed By Order of Taliban)
7. Prob. Bin Laden In Tent

1. Nothing

THE AL QAEDA LEADER proved elusive, as a new website, which early adopters were referring to as a "social network", was becoming a craze.

"Oh no – I've been tracked down by Friends Reunited"

BACK AT HOME, the panicked government was attempting to rush through new security legislation without full consideration of the consequences.

Blunkett arrested under new terrorist law *by PHIL JAILS*

A sinister-looking blind man with a beard was arrested yesterday near the House of Commons under the new Detention of Dodgy-Looking Bearded Men Act (2001).

Under the new act, any dodgy-looking bearded men can be detained at Her Majesty's Pleasure without trial, charge or evidence.

Only a beard is needed by the police as proof that the man in question is a danger to civilised values, such as freedom to walk around without being arrested.

The Home Secretary last night was delighted at his arrest.

"This is a triumph for justice," Mr Blunkett said. "It shows that none of us is safe under my new regulations."

MEANWHILE HOSTILITIES escalated between the prime minister and chancellor.

IAIN DUNCAN SMITH emerged as surprise front-runner in the race to be the next Tory leader.

The alarming spread of IDS

by Our Medical Staff
Dr Thomas Utterfraud

A large number of senior Conservatives are believed to be suffering from the mystery illness known as IDS.

IDS affects both men and women and attacks the capacity to resist choosing the wrong leader. It produces a softening of the brain and the eventual loss of all mental faculties.

THE EYE REFUSED to accept the guilty verdict against Libyan intelligence agent Abdelbaset Ali Mohmed al-Megrahi in the Lockerbie trial at the end of January, focusing on one part of the evidence the judges had apparently dismissed.

The essence of the prosecution case was that the bomb that brought down Pan Am flight 103 was first planted on an aircraft at Luqa airport, Malta, whence it travelled to Frankfurt. There, it apparently changed planes to London, where it changed planes again onto the doomed flight bound for the US. What was the evidence from Luqa that the bomb went on a plane there? None whatsoever. The judges were obliged to admit that "the absence of any explanation... is a major difficulty for the Crown case". The suspect bag, if it ever existed, would at Frankfurt have been taken for x-ray. Staff had been warned only two months previously to keep a special watch out for explosive devices. The judges were able to dispose of this objection on the grounds that the training given to the workers in charge of the x-ray was "poor" and the bomb might not have been noticed.

But the defence could prove easily that security at Heathrow in December 1988 was abysmal. There were at least three places from where a suitcase could be smuggled onto the Pan Am flight without being picked up by airline staff. The container with the baggage for the flight was left completely unattended for three quarters of an hour.

Everyone agreed that the bomb had been packed in a brown Samsonite case. John Bedford, a baggage loader at Heathrow gave evidence. He recalled seeing "A maroony-brown Samsonite case" that he was certain he had not put into the container. The other baggage handler for the fatal flight, Sulkash Kamboj, told the fatal accident inquiry, "I did not place any luggage in the PA 103 tin that day."

What of Tony Gauci, the owner of a clothes shop in Malta from which some clothes in the bomb suitcase were bought? His identification of Megrahi 10 years after he says he saw him in his shop is described by the judges as "a highly important element in the case". But when Scottish police officers went to see him in 1989, less than a year after the bombings, he said from the outset that the man who bought the clothes was a big man, some six feet tall, aged about 50. Megrahi is five foot eight inches and in 1988 was 37.

PAUL FOOT returned to the subject in a special report in May, revealing more details about the "star witness" at the trial.

Garage mechanic Abdul Majid Giaka, irritated by his employers in the Libyan intelligence service, the JSO, had secretly approached the CIA in the American embassy in Malta several months before the Lockerbie bombing. To start with, he had repeatedly lied to the CIA to impress them with his own importance, grossly exaggerating his role in the JSO.

For many months he said nothing at all about Lockerbie, even when he was asked about it. It was obviously important for Giaka to impress his CIA contacts. He depended on them for a thousand dollars a month, rising to $1500. But his handlers in Malta got increasingly fed up with his prevarications, and started to conclude he was not worth the money. In July 1991 he was summoned to a meeting with officials from the US department of justice and told his future depended on what he disclosed. He was met with a threat that unless he could come up with something about his former colleagues in the JSO that might incriminate them in the Lockerbie bombing, he would be cut off without a penny. So he did.

FOOT AND MOUTH disease was first detected in February 2001, and despite restrictions on animal movements and access to the countryside, rapidly swept across the whole country. The *Eye*'s own agricultural correspondents got straight on the case. "Even Newer Muckspreader" filed this report for the 23 March edition.

The one thing certain about the foot and mouth crisis is that agriculture minister Nick Brown is presiding over the greatest administrative cock-up even this government has ever put its hand to. On 19 February an inspector at an Essex abattoir discovered FMD in 27 pigs brought down from Northumbria. When the disease was confirmed at the Heddon-on-the-Wall pig farm four days later, the Maffia [Ministry of Agriculture, Fisheries and Food] allowed this to be thought the original source of the outbreak. But already the epidemic was out of control, thanks to an unusual number of movements of sheep around the country, many originally bought by a small group of big dealers at Longtown market near Carlisle. As infected animals were dropped off all the way from Cumbria via the Welsh borders down to Devon, FMD raced across the country.

By the time the outbreak "went public" the Maffia already feared as many as 80 percent of sheep in some areas could be infected. With diagnostic services breaking down under the flood of work, and a critical shortage of vets to carry out tracing work, they feared the epidemic could explode into the cattle population. Hence the unprecedented plan for a mass cull of up to one million "healthy" animals.

By now, though, stage three of the Maffia shambles was also under way: the chaos it made of the slaughter operation, ignoring every lesson learned from the last 1967/68 outbreak as to how to minimise the risk of spreading infection. First, animals must be shot as soon as a vet spots infection. Second, they should be buried at once and on the spot: even burning was ruled out as likely to spread infection.

This time, clinical tests have to be confirmed, often taking days. Burial is virtually prohibited. Many infected carcasses have to be trucked miles through uninfected countryside to rendering plants – still giving off infection.

By April, things had got even worse.

Mr Blair's one real hope of bringing this disaster under control would have been to do what should have been done in early March, when it first became clear that the mass-slaughter policy was failing to stop the spread of the disease. All stops should then have been pulled out to organise a massive vaccination programme of cattle, and allow sheep just to suffer a few days' discomfort from which the vast majority would soon naturally recover.

Even if at this late stage the British government were to opt for vaccination, it would take months to commission sufficient supplies. The decision should have been taken weeks ago, right at the start of the FMD outbreak.

In May, as the postponed election date approached, the *Eye* remained sceptical.

The Maffia's *Einsatzsgruppen* continue to roam the countryside, killing thousands of healthy animals with no scientific or legal justification whatever. These massacres have not shown up in the daily reports issued by MAFF, precisely because the slaughtered animals were not infected. The only statistic MAFF will now admit to is the "headline figure" showing cases where the disease has actually been confirmed. And that of course is the figure MAFF is now doing all it can to massage downwards, because that is what Alastair Campbell wants. The only order which matters is that the figures must support one overriding message:

that our Beloved Leader has the crisis licked and that, as those graphs from Professor Roy Anderson's Imperial College computer so conveniently confirm, the epidemic will be over by election day, 7 June.

The slaughter continued before and after polling day, as Christopher Booker and Richard North documented in an *Eye* Special Report published that November.

Although the number of outbreaks officially admitted by MAFF since the beginning of May had only risen from 1,517 to 1,719, a million more animals had been killed. But FMD had all but dropped off the news agenda. In pursuit of the continuous cull, vets had been routinely forced to breach their professional code by signing declarations that farms were infected, even though they had inspected the animals and found them healthy. In the week after the election 80,000 animals were killed. The following week the total was 93,000. And so it was to continue through weeks and months of summer, at the very time of year when folklore dictated that the warm, dry days should have killed the virus off and brought the epidemic nearer to its natural end.

Their conclusions were damning.

The world's leading veterinary scientists are unanimous that there are only two effective strategies for ending a Foot and Mouth epidemic. One is a slaughter policy. The other is a combination of slaughter with vaccination. But they attach a crucial condition to a policy based on slaughter alone: it can only be fully effective when the epidemic is identified in its early stages. Once the infection has spread to many different places and becomes multi-specific, a slaughter policy becomes a sledgehammer increasingly likely to miss the nut.

The total number of animals slaughtered comes to around 7.7million – or one eighth of all the farm animals in Britain.

The government later conceded that they had been too slow to act, and that vaccination would be part of the strategy for dealing with any future outbreak.

THIS WAS THE YEAR that *Private Eye* began a long-running series of stories regarding Dr Andrew Wakefield's claims about the MMR vaccine and a possible link to autism, since disproved. In February 2010, the magazine admitted that "*Private Eye* got it wrong in its coverage of MMR. It gave undue prominence to unproven theories based on a small number of uncontrolled observations, and paid far less attention to the weight of evidence from large comparative studies that failed to find any link between MMR and autism."

2002

A DETENTION CAMP for prisoners of the "War on Terror" was set up at Guantanamo Bay in Cuba, which the Bush administration insisted was outside of US jurisdiction and the scope of the Geneva Convention.

PRINCESS MARGARET died, at just 71.

Terrible old farce closes

"Charley's Aunt", one of the West End's longest-running comedy shows, came unexpectedly to an end last night at the Kensington Palace. Said a spokesman, "It is very sad, but it was inevitable. In the Fifties, audiences queued round the block for what was hailed as the wittiest and most glamorous show in town. But recently we couldn't give the tickets away. The punters are no longer interested in this drawing room stuff. They want something a bit more raunchy, like *The Merry Wives of Charles Windsor*, *Princess Annie Get Your Divorce* or *No Wessex Please, We're British*."

IN ZIMBABWE, Robert Mugabe won an election that was neither free nor fair.

AMERICAN SECRETARY of state Colin Powell intervened in an attempt to end fighting between Israel and the Palestinians.

Old Jokes Revisited

Colin Powell: I want to talk about peace
Yasser Arafat: Peace off!

This joke first appeared in Private Eye in 200 BC and has been republished 1,738 times during various crises in the Middle East, making it the magazine's oldest surviving joke.

THE QUEEN MOTHER died at the age of 101. The BBC had been rehearsing for the moment for at least 15 years, but it turned out the *Daily Mail* had been rehearsing their reaction to the BBC's coverage even longer.

Gnome Queen Mother Souvenir Offer

The Queen Mother Memorial Reversible Tie

Don't get caught out (as some people have been!) by the unexpected death of a senior member of the Royal Family.

You need never be seen with inappropriate neckwear with this new silk-style reversible tie, made from 100 percent washable Naflon™.

On one side, the tie is an all-purpose burgundy colour, suitable for day-to-day activities such as a business meeting, lunching with clients or reading the six o'clock news on television.

On the other side, however, the tie is a respectful black, entirely suitable for showing instant respect at the death of a senior and much-loved member of the Royal Family.
Send £375.55 now to Gnome Offers, PO Box 934, Yeovil Trading Estate TA3 4PO.

Says Peter Sissons: "I wish I'd had the Gnome Reversible Tie. It would have saved me a lot of trouble!"

THE VATICAN admitted for the first time that allegations of child sexual abuse had been mishandled in the past.

News in Brief

POPE ADMITS: 'There may be paedophiles in the priesthood'
POPE ADMITS: 'Yes, I may be a Catholic'
BEAR ADMITS: 'Ok, on some occasions I may have shat in the woods'

LABOUR ACCEPTED a £100,000 donation from Richard Desmond, publisher of a number of pornographic magazines (and, since 2000, the *Daily Express*), following equally controversial cash injections from the Hindujas and Lakshmi Mittal.

Lord Desmond Gnome is delighted to present a new publication from Gnorthern & Shellsuit plc, publisher of the *Daily Sexpress* and *OK! Margarine (surely "Magazine"? Ed)* IN THIS WEEK'S 'ASIAN BRIBES'...

- The biggest donation you've ever seen!
- I'm Mandy, br*be me!
- Tony likes it blind-folded!!

PLUS
- Hottest Hinduja action
- Mittal Mania
- And XXX-rated Vaz!

Says Lord 'Dirty' Gnome: "This new magazine is aimed at the sophisticated male reader in his forties, living in 10 Downing Street. It comes complete with its own brown envelope!"

JEAN-MARIE LE PEN got through to the second round of the French presidential elections, the latest far-right figure to come to unexpected prominence in Europe.

Who are they – the new wave of far-right loonies who are taking over Europe?

FRANCE Jean-Marie Le Sven came close to toppling President Chirac in a nail-biting 83-17 percent finish. Le Pen's near-victory has traumatised the French people who fear that the sound of jackboots down the Champs Elysées can only be a matter of months away.

AUSTRIA Jorge Hidler, ruthless leader of the far-right "Say No To The Euro" Party, has already taken his first giant step towards supreme power by becoming mayor of the key village of Bad Hortswessel. His meteoric advance has traumatised the Austrian people who fear that their beloved Blue Danube will soon be running red with the blood of innocent victims.

BELGIUM Simon van der Hefferlump, leader of the far-right Flemish Nationalist Dailimael Party, has already taken a giant leap towards seizing supreme power by winning three seats in the recent Bruges municipal elections. Van der Hefferlump recently told his screaming followers (Sid and Doris Oranjeboom), "Today Bruges, tomorrow Antwerp." The traumatised Belgian people are already hiding in their attics for fear of the advancing Swastika hordes.

BRITAIN Brian Snott, charismatic leader of the far-right British Anorak Party, has already swept to power by winning three votes in the recent elections for the Heckmondwyke parish council. A traumatised Britain is waiting in terror as Millwall supporters rampage through the streets in a shock tidal-wave of violence and thuggery. *(That's enough right-wing hysteria. Ed.)*

THE THIRD SERIES of *Big Brother* created a new star.

Ratings for Big Bedlam soar

Ye most popular entertainment of ye moment in ye Metropolis is ye Big Bedlam Showe, presented by the celebrated showmen Mr Julian Bellamy and Mr Peter Bazalgette. Each night vast queues form of excited gentlefolke, anxious to witnesse with their own eyes ye sad anticks of ye unfortunate and mentally disturbed wretches who dwelle within ye house of Bedlam. Ye poore inmates strip themselves naked, shriek with laughter and shout profanities at each other all ye nighte long.

Foremost among ye curiosities on display is Mistress Jade, an uncomely wench of limited mental powers, who hath been dubbed by ye hackes of Grubbe Street as "Ye Pigge". The hope of these bloodthirstie hackes is that the populace will rise up and murder Mistress Jade, thus adding greatlie to ye publick stocke of harmless pleasure.

The tabloid treatment of Goody when she returned for *Celebrity Big Brother* **in 2007 was even more vitriolic – prompting a rapid reverse ferret when she was diagnosed with a terminal illness soon afterwards (***see p.238***).**

AT AN INQUEST into the death of Stuart Lubbock in the swimming pool at TV presenter Michael Barrymore's home the previous year, it is revealed that he suffered serious anal injuries before drowning. Barrymore claimed to know nothing about how his death occurred.

PRIVATE EYE

No. 1063
20 September –
3 October 2002
£1.20

BARRYMORE POOL DEATH LATEST

How did the man die?

Buggered if I know

BUSH AND TONY BLAIR were still attempting to push an attack on Iraq through the official channels of the UN Security Council and weapons inspectors – with the help of a press that was both gullible and gung-ho.

Saddam 'only hours away' from nuking world

A terrifying report, published today by the prestigious Institute You've Never Heard Of Before, reveals that Saddam Hussein could be on the verge of achieving full nuclear capability at any time in the next few weeks.

"All he has to do," says the report, "is to acquire the nuclear materials, assemble an expert team capable of putting all the pieces together, and he could then have a fully operational device within a matter of only ten years or so."

BLAIR'S GOVERNMENT published a dossier which claimed Saddam could launch a devastating attack in just 45 minutes. Its veracity was immediately questioned.

Highlights from the Blair dossier

No. 94 Range of Saddam's Ballistic Missiles

BUT WHATEVER the circumstances, it was clear war was on its way.

BY WAY OF LIGHT RELIEF, Edwina Currie revealed that she had had a long-running affair with John Major.

ENTERTAINING DETAILS emerged of the PM's wife Cherie Blair's relationship with her personal new-age "lifestyle guru" Carole Caplin. Caplin's convicted conman boyfriend had helped Mrs Blair buy two flats in Bristol – without, she insisted, her husband knowing anything about it.

DAILY CAWDORGRAPH

Doubts grow over First Lady

by Our Man at Number Thane **William Deedspeare**

There was mounting concern last night over the influence exercised by Lady Macbeth on her husband.

Unconfirmed reports have linked her name with a group of unsavoury characters, some of whom she has introduced to King McBlair.

They are said to include a group of three "lifestyle gurus" who have been trying to market a new slimming potion made from organic materials, including eye of newt, spleen of toad and wing of bat.

Meanwhile Alastair Campbell, the chief of the McSpin clan and a personal friend of King Macbeth's, has tried to distance the Scottish ruler from his wife's personal concerns.

"Lady McBlair is an independent career woman," he said, "and who she murders is entirely her own affair."

ITV SERIES "POP IDOL" made stars of contestants Will Young and Gareth Gates – and Simon Cowell.

IN JANUARY, THE EYE noted a change of direction at the Inland Revenue.

One aspect of government policy that gets little publicity and no opposition is its encouragement of tax avoidance. Recent government documents proclaim a new, much more friendly attitude to big firms seeking to avoid tax. In the Inland Revenue and Customs & Excise, the government encourages a "change of culture" to get away from the old fuddy duddy concept that the main job of tax inspectors is to collect taxes and stamp out tax avoidance schemes.

Inland Revenue deputy chairman David Hartnett has spent a lot of the last few months listening to the views of big business, and has become increasingly impressed. Last year he attended a "large corporates" forum with representatives from businesses including ICI, British American Tobacco, Dixons, Orange and Rolls Royce. It concluded that it was much safer and wiser for businessmen to go into the Revenue than for Revenue snoopers to go into industry. 20 people from industry had been "seconded" to the Revenue.

Now an official Revenue report has made 40 recommendations exclusively devoted to strengthening the influence of big businessmen in assessing their own tax liabilities. They include assessing the quality of Revenue inspectors' work against that of major accountancy firms like PricewaterhouseCoopers and Arthur Andersen, and designating a whole department of the Revenue's head office as "a champion for business".

To complete the picture, Mr Hartnett has joined the editorial board of *Tax Journal*, a publication devoted almost entirely to advising big companies on how to avoid tax.

YET ANOTHER TRAIN CRASH killed seven and injured 76 in May. Dr B. Ching suggested the likely cause.

The tragic derailment at Potters Bar has served to publicise again the ludicrous system of contracting and sub-contracting vital maintenance work devised by the Tories in the mid-1990s, which the *Eye* has been highlighting since 1995.

Governments have preferred to ignore the situation for seven years. Even after the Hatfield crash, caused by poor track maintenance, "new" labour declined to legislate for Railtrack to employ a stable and properly trained workforce for all its maintenance. Whatever the cause of the Potters Bar points failure turns out to be, ministers and civil servants must surely understand now that the principle of private contractors competing against each other to cut maintenance costs was one of the most reckless and untenable aspects of the Tories' rail privatisation. Will they take action now?

Jarvis, the engineering company which holds the £250 million contract to maintain the line on which the accident took place, was successfully prosecuted by the Health and Safety Executive this very month for "unsafe practice". It has a long history of accidents, and the firm has also performed the extraordinary feat of increasing its number of signals passed at danger to 10 in the latest figures from the Railway Inspectorate, despite the fact it is not a passenger or freight operator and only runs engineering trains through signals.

Jarvis at first attempted to blame sabotage for the accident, then accepted responsibility, but avoided prosecution when its rail maintenance arm went into administration. Network Rail, which replaced Railtrack just months after the accident, was fined £3 million for having "seriously inadequate" procedures and standards in place at Potters Bar.

JUNE SAW THE EYE dig deep into a recent deal under which the Inland Revenue and Customs had sold most of their buildings to a company called Mapeley... something.

About 600 buildings have been sold for an estimated £1bn, under a PFI deal which lasts 20 years. Mapeley Ltd, as the name suggests, is registered in good old England, but its parent, deceptively called Mapeley UK Co Ltd, is registered in the British Virgin Islands, a tax haven. The crucial question remains, which company actually owns Britain's tax and customs offices? Could it be another subsidiary called Mapeley STEPS Ltd? The acronym gives a clue to its purpose: it stands for "strategic transfer of estate to the private sector". Mapeley STEPS is not registered at Companies House, and is therefore based somewhere offshore, no one knows where.

It turned out to be Bermuda. While Mapeley STEPS was indeed the real purchaser, even the Mapeley companies that were based in the UK boasted in that year's annual reports that "no liability to taxation will arise in the foreseeable future". The Revenue announced that they had lied about this in the press release announcing the sale, but there had been "no intention to mislead". Parliament's Treasury Select Committee called it "one of the worst examples of maladministration we have come across".

AS WAR WITH IRAQ began to seem inevitable, September saw the *Eye* pointing out a fairly major conflict of interest.

A firm formerly run by American vice-president Dick Cheney stands to make billions from the American and British armies if an attack on Iraq becomes a big enough operation.

Until he stood for office, Cheney was boss of America's Halliburton. Last December the US army awarded the company the 10-year contract to feed and house troops under the "logistics civil augmentation program". Thus Halliburton now builds barracks, feeds troops and services US army equipment overseas. It is now facing a bonanza thanks to the War on Terror. Halliburton also won a $9.7m contract to build prison cells for Al Quaeda suspects at Guantanamo Bay.

Attempting to oust Saddam Hussein could lead to even more work should the US need to maintain a presence in Iraq after a "regime change".

Britain has also given Halliburton contracts in the continuing privatisation of war. Last January, Labour gave the company a £300m contract to transport the army's tanks – into the battlefield, if necessary. Halliburton's truck drivers will transform themselves into troops if they come under fire. These "soldiers" are also supplied by Cheney's old firm, effectively making them PFI mercenaries.

The tank transporters will not be operational until late 2003, so are likely to miss out on early battles against Saddam. But if a war on Iraq leads to longer-term commitments in the region, Cheney's old firm could be driving our boys around the desert.

IN NOVEMBER, THE TRIAL of royal butler Paul Burrell sensationally collapsed after the Queen claimed he had told her he had taken several of Princess Diana's possessions after her death – and he went public with his claim her Majesty had also warned him to beware of "dark forces". *Private Eye's* own correspondent at the Palace, "Flunkey", was sceptical of both accounts.

His memories of that audience, as subsequently revealed to the *Daily Mirror*, have caused some ironic amusement at Buckingham Palace. No one who knows Brenda believes her capable of sustaining a three-hour conversation with anyone. And the language of "dark forces" just isn't in her vocabulary. Most tellingly, Brenda would never, ever call a servant by his Christian name.

In the version of Brenda's great feat of memory prepared for public consumption, she had her flash recollection in the car with Charles and Philip on the way to the Bali memorial service at St Paul's. She didn't. The conversation at which the Queen decided to back Burrell's claims had taken place immediately before, at a meeting attended by senior courtiers and lawyers. Buckingham Palace had refused to see any papers on the Burrell case in an effort to preserve Brenda's judicial neutrality, but St James's Palace had eagerly devoured them all. As Charles's staff were panicking over just what Burrell might reveal in the witness box, and knowledge of the "rape tape" was becoming an open secret, a lifeline was thrown to them. Burrell told his defence team about the private meeting with the Queen in 1997, and word was fed back to Charles's office by a trusted third party. After that the whole process of collapsing the trial was swift.

2003

WHAT PASSED FOR the US president's mind was made up, and war with Iraq was inevitable.

THE REVEREND TONY BLAIR stood completely behind him…

ST ALBION PARISH NEWS

Hullo!

And I don't mind telling you that I've been getting pretty hot under my dog collar this week!

Let's just say that I've had it up to here with all those people in the parish who've been going round complaining that there's been no debate about our great crusade to rid the world of Satan.

Look, we've had the debate. And I won it!

What I said at the parish meeting, for those who failed to attend, was the following:

A. Satan is evil

B. Rev. Dubya of the Church of Latter-Day Morons is good

C. We should be on the side of good rather than evil

D. Therefore, we must be against Satan. The logic is inescapable!

After my speech, we all sang a new hymn, which I'd written specially for the occasion, and which we sill be singing at Evensong until further notice:

"Fight the good fight, with all thy might,
You are wrong and I am right."

Words and music Rev. T. Blair.

Yours, more in anger than in sorrow, Tony

…BUT THE UN was showing no sign of budging on a resolution that would justify military action, and weapons inspector Hans Blix was unable to uncover any WMDs in Iraq.

ANTI-FRENCH FEELING ran peculiarly high in America as Jacques Chirac became a figurehead for international opposition to a UN resolution authorising military action.

That American Anti-French Menu in Full

Freedom Fries
Selection of Freedom Cheeses
Freedom Bread
Salad with Freedom Dressing
PLUS
One Freedom Letter for use in
Post-Meal Intercourse

IN BRITAIN, one the biggest street protests ever seen took place against the war…

The march has gone past Parliament

That's more than the war has

THE ATTORNEY GENERAL U-turned on his position of a few weeks earlier, and declared it would not be illegal to launch a war on the basis of a previous UN resolution after all.

Why it is legal to go to war

The Attorney General, Lord Goldsmith, has reassured the Prime Minister that any war against Iraq is not only just but legal under an ancient British law called *De Bello Saddamico Conveniensis*, which dates all the way back to yesterday morning.

According to the ancient statute, "The First Minister of the British Nation, whomsoever he may be, shall have the inalienable right to declare war on behalf of His Majesty's Government without let or hindrance from any foreign bodies whomsoever they may be or any of his ministers who may calleth him reckless or the unruly populace of the country or any French person who may attempt to invoke divers bogus laws (*Lex Bogi*) which shall be deemed 'an unreasonable veto'. All of which quite obviously alloweth the Prime Minister to do whatever he so desireth with the full might and majesty of the law of the United States of America."

MEANWHILE, the space shuttle Columbia disintegrated on its return to earth, killing all seven crew.

How American missile technology will blitz Saddam with pinpoint accuracy
'War will be over in minutes' say experts

ON OTHER PAGES: "We have no idea why space shuttle blew up," say U.S. experts. "We may never know."

War was finally declared on 20 March.

THE INCREASINGLY DESPERATE denials by an Iraqi government spokesman that the regime was losing made a very unlikely star of "Comical Ali".

The laugh-a-minute Iraqi Minister for Information has tickled the ribs of the world with his electrodes (*surely "amusing asides"? Ed.*) and has kept the west laughing in the dark days of the war. Here is a selection of his hilarious one liners:

> *"The only good Kurd is a dead Kurd"*
> *"Take these people away to be tortured"*
> *"Shoot them all and bury them in a pit"*

© All newspapers

CLARE SHORT'S belated resignation from the cabinet over the war coincided with the second series of a TV hit.

A tear-stained Clare Short last night decided to leave the long-running TV reality show *I'm a Liability, Get Me Out Of Here.*

The popular programme is set in the jungle of Westminster and features a group of B-list MPs who have to undertake various challenges to stay in the "Government".

Clare Short had to undergo the "Creepy-Crawly Challenge" in which she had to "creepy-crawl" up Mr Blair's bottom. "I just couldn't do it," she sobbed, "even though the others seemed to have no trouble completing the task."

MARTIN BASHIR FOLLOWED up his 1995 interview with Princess Diana with an in-depth chat to Michael Jackson.

Tonight on TV: The unmissable television event of the Millennium
MICHAEL JACKSON interviews MARTIN BASHIR

Jackson enters the weird world of the mysterious superstar and genius interviewer to find out what really makes Bashir tick. See "Backo" doing his trademark "Loontalk" as he sits on a sofa, nodding his head and taking off his spectacles.

And for the first time, "Backo" is finally asked the question to which the whole world wants an answer: "Why is your nose so brown these days?"

A HUGE ROW BROKE OUT when Andrew Gilligan suggested on Radio 4's *Today* programme that the government had "sexed up" claims in their dossier about Iraq's WMDs...

IRAQ LATEST

Government denies 'sexing up' dossier

by Our Intelligence Staff **Pierce Brosnan**

A cabinet spokesman furiously denied the charge that the intelligence dossier on the weapons of mass destruction had been "exaggerated".

"This suggestion," said the spokesman, "is the most outrageous, dangerous and evil suggestion that has ever been made in the history of the world. Making this suggestion actually puts British lives at risk. We could be talking about millions of deaths within 45 minutes of the suggestion being made. Whoever is saying that we exaggerated the findings of the dossier is as bad as Hitler and should be removed at all costs."

...WHICH raged on for weeks.

"...that unless we hear from Mr Alastair Campbell by 11 o'clock this morning we will be in a state of war..."

ALL THIS RATHER DISTRACTED attention from the fact that no WMDs had turned up.

Weapons inspectors find 'the smoking pants'

by W.M. DEEDES

A team of UN inspectors have at last reported the discovery of the vital evidence in the hunt for the Iraqi Weapons of Mass Destruction – a pair of smoking pants believed to have been worn by Tony Blair.

"If these pants are genuine," said Mr Hansup, "then it proves that they were definitely on fire whilst Blair was wearing them and that all his statements about WMDs were lies."

Mr Bliar is 50 (or maybe he isn't – you never know with him).

AS THE PRIME MINISTER and his spin-doctor's behaviour became increasingly demented, the government drip-fed the identity of Dr David Kelly, the former weapons inspector who told his employers at the MoD that he was Gilligan's source for the story to the media.

Blair reveals source

by Our Political Correspondent **Michael Whitewash**

The Prime Minister, following repeated demands for him to reveal the source of his information concerning weapons of mass destruction, named "a senior figure with a beard".

Pressed further, the Prime Minister admitted that he had several meetings with the man, who told him in strict confidence that "everything he did was absolutely right".

Journalists were at first slow to identify the source, but the Prime Minister gave them a series of clues, saying his name began with 'G', ended with 'D' and had an 'O' in the middle. Blair also explained that he lived on a cloud in the sky.

A spokesman for God, however, denied that he was the source and suggested that a more likely candidate might be another bearded man with horns on his head and cloven hooves. *(Reuters)*

KELLY WAS HAULED in front of a parliamentary select committee and died by suicide two days later. The prime minister immediately announced a public inquiry.

"Get me a spin-coroner!"

SIR JOHN SCARLETT, the Joint Intelligence Committee chief who had been responsible for compiling the government's WMD dossier, appeared before Lord Hutton's inquiry.

That Scarlett cross-examination in full

Sir Huge Dingledrawers QC: Mr Scarlett, was any pressure put on you to "sex up" the dossier in question?

Scarface: No.

Dingiepants: What about this email from Mr Campbell, reading, "Come on, Scarlett, you'll need to do better than this if we're going to send a million men to their deaths."

Did you consider this memo to be in any way putting pressure on you to amend the dossier in a way that Mr Campbell would have found more conducive to his case?

Scarlatti: No.

Dingieknickers: Did or did you not, Mr Scarlett, alter the wording of the dossier from "there is a faint possibility that Mr Hussein might possibly have the ability to develop nuclear weapons within 45 years, but we can't be sure" to "we're all going to die in 45 minutes?"

Sir Gerald Scarfe: No.

Dingiehose: Are you aware of this email marked "Top Secret – For Your Eyes Only", which was sent you yesterday morning from someone calling himself "C"? It says, "If they start asking you about the dossier, just say 'no' to everything, okay? See you for dinner later."

Scarlet Pimpernel: No.

Rubberdinghy: Is there anything you would like to add?

Scartissue: No.

SADDAM HUSSEIN was finally captured by Coalition forces in Iraq, as US leaders continued to insist he was in some way connected to the attacks on 9/11.

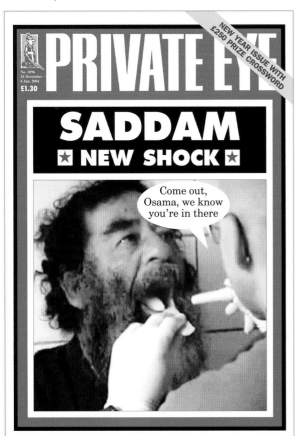

CONSERVATIVE LEADER Iain Duncan Smith was disposed of in a vote of no confidence, and Michael Howard installed unopposed.

"Would it help to appoint a new leader?"

IN MARCH, THE EYE surveyed the work of the *Independent*'s new young columnist.

Johann Hari has been bemoaning the "corrosive acid of distrust" in public life. "The number of my friends who assume that we just make up stories – even at a reputable paper such as the *Independent* – is startling."

Not that startling if they are regular readers of Johann Hari. He began his career by boasting about his drug habit to readers of the *New Statesman* and *Evening Standard*, defending "the Ecstasy I know and love". In fact the young rascal had never taken Ecstasy: he had to phone up a friend and ask what it felt like.

He then went to Genoa for the G8 summit and filed a vivid dispatch for the *New Statesman* about the death of an anti-globalisation protester: "When I saw the scene, I couldn't believe so much blood had flowed from just one body." Yet, as several witnesses can attest, Hari wasn't there, having hailed a taxi to escape the scene some time before the man was killed.

Now he has been pontificating in the *Indie* and on *Newsnight* about his support for a war with Saddam Hussein. "Last October I spent a month as a journalist seeing the reality of life under Saddam Hussein." Actually Hari spent two weeks in Iraq on a package tour visiting ancient archaeological sites. He wrote about the trip in the *Guardian* last December, complaining that it was "very difficult to get Iraqis to express their feelings". Yet in the *Indie* he writes that "most of the Iraqi people I encountered... would hug me and offered coded support".

Before Hari's talents were as widely known as they

are today, he flexed his literary muscles by poison-penning reviews on the Amazon.com website. On 4 June 2000, while still studying at King's College, Cambridge, Hari posted that the University's professor of Greek Literature's *Aeschylus: The Oresteia* was "pompous drivel. This Goldhill man has the prose style of a dead worm and even less warmth and charm. He clearly loves himself. Fine. Nobody else will." Hari now says about Goldhill that he is "an all-round arsehole". Prof Goldhill tells the *Eye* "there was a disciplinary matter which followed a complaint from the staff about his unpleasantly arrogant rudeness".

Hari was sacked from the *Independent* eight years later for plagiarism, making up quotes, and launching anonymous online attacks on other journalists.

ON THE EVE OF THE WAR in March, the *Eye* delved deeper into the evidence being used to justify military action.

The foreword to last September's dossier, by the prime minister, boasted that the "assessed intelligence" in the dossier "established beyond doubt that Saddam continues in his efforts to develop nuclear weapons".

By far the most powerful evidence for this assertion was on page 25, as follows: "Iraq's known holdings of processed uranium are under IAEA [International Atomic Energy Authority] supervision. But there is intelligence that Iraq had sought the supply of significant quantities of uranium from Africa. Iraq has no active civil nuclear power programme or nuclear power plants, and therefore has no legitimate reason to acquire uranium."

An IAEA spokeswoman in Vienna explained to the *Eye* that this piece of intelligence was "by far the most important evidence that Iraq was seeking to rebuild its nuclear programme". All the rest of the evidence was about "dual use" equipment that could, but not necessarily must, be used for nuclear weapons.

The weapons inspectors, under the director-general of the IAEA, Dr Mohamed ElBaredei, made sustained inquiries into this intelligence. His report says "the investigation was centred on documents provided by a number of states that pointed to an agreement between Niger and Iraq for the sale of uranium between 1999 and 2001." Both countries said there were no such agreements, but considering the issue was the illegal

sale of uranium, they would, wouldn't they? But the report goes on, "the IAEA was able to review correspondence coming from various bodies of the government of Niger, and to compare the form, format, contents and signatures of that correspondence with those of the alleged procurement-related documentation. Based on thorough analysis, the IAEA concluded, with the concurrence of outside experts, that these documents – which formed the basis for reports of recent uranium transactions between Iraq and Niger – are in fact not authentic. We have therefore concluded that these specific allegations are unfounded."

The IAEA spokeswoman was even more forthright to the *Eye*: they "were forged", indeed, "a blatant attempt to deceive us".

The British foreign office brusquely rejects this. It says: "We have faith in the origins of the material as an indicator of Iraqi intentions to procure uranium." Faith in forgery!

Saddam did not have any WMDs.

IN DECEMBER the Street of Shame pages had a scoop that, curiously, no other titles wanted to report.

Red faces all around Fleet Street after a raid on a private detective by investigating officers from the information commissioner found incriminating evidence of scores of tabloid hacks having paid a private eye to break the law.

This included ex-directory phone numbers, numbers of family and friends, vehicle licence traces and criminal record investigations – all illegal under the data protection act, all commissioned by journalists whose papers claim to support the right to reasonable privacy.

This may explain why when a Met detective was arrested on corruption charges there was not a squeak out of the press. But the names of the victims and the reporters and photographers who were clients are all detailed. Prosecutions will follow as sure as night follows day, or as desperate hacks follow celebs.

Although the *Eye* subsequently named and shamed publications which had purchased illegally-acquired information from the private detective Steve Whittamore, including the *News of the World*, *Sunday People*, *Daily Mirror* and *Daily Mail*, it would not be until the phone-hacking scandal broke several years later that anyone else took any notice.

2004

LONDON MAYOR Ken Livingstone was readmitted into the Labour party after it became apparent that despite his differences with the leadership he was deeply committed to one New Labour policy, that of actually winning elections.

Saddam 'can rejoin Labour'

by Our Local Government Reporter
Jerry Mander

Despite opposition within the cabinet and the party's National Executive Committee, Tony Blair still insists that Saddam Hussein will be able to rejoin the Labour party within the next three years.

"I understand that Saddam is an evil tyrant responsible for terrible atrocities and that he's the number one hate figure in the world at present," the Prime Minister told a reporter, "but, as he has a proven track record of consistently winning elections, I see no reason why he shouldn't be able to be taken back into the Labour fold."

SOON AFTER A NOTORIOUS serial killer took his own life in prison, Lord Hutton released the conclusions of his inquiry into the death of Dr David Kelly – essentially that the BBC were at fault for everything, and the government had done nothing wrong at all.

BOTH THE DIRECTOR-GENERAL and chairman of the BBC resigned, and the corporation descended into a frenzy of self-criticism.

BBC News (on all channels)

Newsreader: Tonight the BBC is in the worst crisis it has ever faced in its 80-year-old history. "Meltdown" is not too strong a word for what is happening here at the BBC. Thousands of hacks are engulfed in the collapse of the entire broadcasting system which has followed Lord Hutton's finding that the BBC was guilty of the murder of Dr Kelly.

Tonight I ask myself, how did it happen? Are we all guilty? And, even if the answer is "yes", why should anyone accept that I am telling the truth?

Later on I will be talking to a lot of people who hate the BBC, and I won't interrupt them at all.

But first – Bird Flu. Is the BBC to blame for the death of millions of birds?

TONY BLAIR TRAVELLED to a tent in the desert to meet Colonel Gaddafi, to emphasise that Libya was now back in the West's good books.

Gaddafi salutes 'brave' Blair

by Our Man in Tripoli **Libya Purves**

Col Gaddafi has taken a bold political gamble by agreeing to meet the notorious Western war criminal Tony Blair.

Said Gaddafi last night, "I know in the past Blair has become something of a pariah among the civilised nations. Many have refused to deal with him after his acts of terrorism in Iraq and the thousands of deaths which have resulted from his crazed lust for power.

"But it is my belief now," the Libyan spiritual leader and world statesman continued, "that it is time to bring Blair in from the cold, and to draw a line under his unfortunate international record."

But some Libyan peace groups were furious at their government's attempt to rehabilitate Tony Blair.

"He is a dangerous lunatic who believes that he is infallible," said spokesman Tony Benn-Ghazi. "He is totally unpredictable and should not be trusted to buy our oil and give us a huge amount of money."

DISTURBING PHOTOGRAPHS emerged of US soldiers torturing and humiliating prisoners in Abu Ghraib prison in Iraq.

MEANWHILE, THE MIRROR'S Piers Moron came up with some photos of his own – which turned out to be fakes, and he was sacked.

VILE

This picture has shocked the entire civilised world.

It shows the whole newspaper industry pissing all over *Daily Mirror* editor Piers Moron for publishing some dodgy photographs in his paper.

The Eye says: This humiliating abuse is illegal and should be stopped immediately! Leave Piers alone! *(Surely some mistake? Ed.)*

PRINCE WILLIAM was reported to be dating fellow student Kate Middleton.

21-year-old has girfriend
by Our Entire Staff **Phil Space**

A 21-year-old student may have a girlfriend, it emerged last night. (*Reuters*)

ON OTHER PAGES: Girl's Father Owns House 5 Girl Went to School 6 Girl Has A Friend 8 Why Oh Why Won't The Press Leave William Alone? 94

AFTER 15 MONTHS in charge, the Americans ceremonially handed Iraq back to its people.

BAGHDAD TIMES

Nation celebrates as democracy returns to Iraq

Scenes of jubilation all over the country greeted the historic "handover of power". Old-age pensioners shot each other openly in the streets as the sky over Baghdad exploded in an unforgettable display of fireworks, suicide bombs and ground-to-air missiles.

Teenagers joined hands to rush eagerly to the nearest bomb shelter, as helicopter gunships staged a magnificent demonstration of indiscriminate targeted killing.

The new prime minister of the Free and Independent Republic of Iraq, Mr Ayad-that-President-Bush-in-the-back-of-the-cab-once, declared, "We, the undersigned, take delivery of one entire country (slightly damaged) and hereby undertake that we will exempt the United States and its allies from any responsibility for anything that happens in the future."

ON OTHER PAGES

Election latest – Saddam Ahead in the Polls

MEANWHILE TONY BLAIR had grudgingly agreed to a referendum on any future European Constitution.

Blair – 'We will hand over sovereignty'
by Our Political Correspondent **Hugh Rowe-Sceptic**

The Prime Minister gave a categorical assurance that he would hand over the sovereignty of Great Britain to Brussels "at the first possible opportunity".

There have been fears that Britain would continue to hang on to the control of key British institutions, but Mr Blair was keen to reassure sceptics that this was not the case.

"All the vital areas have already been ceded to Brussels," he told reporters. "Parliament, the Law, the Police, Industry, Agriculture, Health and Safety and the shape of cucumbers are now effectively in the hands of non-local people.

"We may have to maintain a military presence in Britain," he continued, "but by the end of the year we should pull out altogether."

A UKIP SURGE in the European elections – helped by TV presenter Robert Kilroy-Silk's candidacy – coincided with the European football championship, which featured the customary behaviour by England fans.

EURO 2004

Disgrace – Britain's Day of Shame

Britain must hold its head in shame today as yet again a group of mindless morons have dragged our nation's good name into the gutter.

Shocked continentals watched in disbelief as a small gang of British hooligans, led by their pea-brained leader 'Kilroy', stormed into the hallowed precincts of the European Parliament, shouting "We're going to wreck it".

Said one German onlooker, Heinrich Mandelschwein from Stuttgart, "Zere we were, trying to pass a few directives on ze marketing of fish by-products, ven suddenly in rushes zis crazed mob, viz their placards saying 'UKIP for Ever', and laffing at us."

STOP PRESS: Order restored in Brussels

Last night 12 Britons, describing themselves as "UKIP MEPs", were reported to be queuing up "in an orderly fashion" to collect their lavish £172-a-day expenses. Later the 12 "hooligans" were seen in one of Brussels' legendary 5-star restaurants, "Chez Woy", tucking into several large plates of gravy, a famous local delicacy.

THE TOURNAMENT made a star of an 18-year-old spud-faced nipper.

EXCLUSIVE TO PRIVATE EYE

The Wayne Rooney story in full

Chapter One
I was born yesterday and my mum and dad called me Wayne.
Chapter Two
This morning I played football.
Chapter Three
Today I sold my autobiography. *The End.*

THE GOVERNMENT delivered a leaflet to all households which advised them on what to do in the event of a terrorist attack or other disaster.

HM Government

Preparing for Emergencies

HOMEOWNERS! When a copy of this leaflet falls through your letterbox it is VERY IMPORTANT that you should not be worried. DON'T PANIC. The purpose of this leaflet is to warn you that at any moment you may be the victim of a terrorist outrage.

What Will it Be Like?

At the moment we cannot specify, for security reasons, the nature of the threat which is facing us all.

● It could be a nuclear device landing in your garden
● It could be a deadly nerve gas seeping under your door or coming up through your drains
● It could be a swarm of deadly killer bees swooping through your loft window or catflap

But it is very important to keep things in proportion. *It is vital that, on reading this leaflet, you should not be alarmed or panic.*

WITH GORDON BROWN on leadership manoeuvres, Tony Blair reshuffled his cabinet and re-appointed his own key supporter Alan Milburn to a job in charge of election preparations.

Alan Milburn's reponsibilities as the Chancellor of the Duchy of Lancaster in full

1. Rub Gordon Brown's nose in it...
2. Er, that's it.

HOSTILITIES continued.

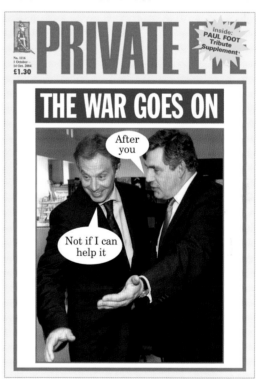

PRO-HUNTING PROTESTERS burst into the Commons chamber as MPs voted to ban fox-hunting.

Blair outraged at Commons invasion

The Prime Minister yesterday expressed his fury at the invasion of the House of Commons. He told reporters, "The Commons is no place for people expressing opinions about Government policy. How dare these hooligans come into the chamber and try and debate the issues? It is an affront to autocracy." (*Surely "Democracy"? Ed.*)

THE GOVERNMENT announced "the most radical shake-up of exams in England for 60 years", but failed to show their workings.

Government announces new education fuck-up

The government today announced a radical fuck-up of the entire education system aimed at reversing the decline in standards and the failure to produce employable school-leavers.

"It is high time for another fuck-up," said the author of the government's new report, Michael Tomlinson. "We haven't fucked up schools since the big fuck-up when we introduced AS Levels and the fuck-ups before that when we introduced GCSEs, coursework, continuous assessment and all the other bright ideas that have made the education system what it is today."

DAVID BLUNKETT RESIGNED as home secretary after it was revealed he had intervened with officials to fast-track a visa for the nanny of the child he had with his married lover Kimberly Quinn.

I'm going to spend more time with someone else's family

ON BOXING DAY a vast tsunami devastated the coasts of the Indian Ocean, killing over 200,000 people. Initial reports of the disaster took a somewhat parochial view.

Worst disaster in history of world
Many Britons feared dead

Following the greatest flood the world has ever known, fears were mounting last night that many British citizens may have perished in the huge natural catastrophe that has overtaken the entire globe.

As I look out from the crowded deck of the ark, writes *Sabbath Times* man Noah, it has become increasingly clear that everyone in the world except me has been washed away by the unprecedented rise in sea levels.

This leads me to the horrifying conclusion that the death toll is likely to include many Britons, possibly all of them.

IN JANUARY, THE EYE pointed out some inconvenient truths about the rapprochement between Britain and Libya.

Prime Minister Tony Blair and foreign secretary Jack Straw have warmly congratulated themselves on an agreement with the government of Libya in which Colonel Gaddafi renounced weapons of mass destruction he never had. And the Libyan government has now paid enormous compensation for some Lockerbie victims.

But Libyan government ministers do not accept that Abdelbaset al-Megrahi, convicted in 2001, had anything to do with the bombing. They have agreed to pay compensation chiefly because they want to end sanctions imposed on Libya by the UN and the US. Submissions made by Megrahi's Glasgow lawyers to the Scottish criminal cases review commission include the awkward fact that two days after the bombing, £11m was paid by agents of the Iranian government to the PFLP-GC – a terrorist group which, British and US intelligence chiefs once believed, was commissioned by Iran to avenge the shooting down by US forces of an Iranian airliner a few months before Lockerbie, killing almost exactly the same number of people.

FEBRUARY BROUGHT news of a new mega-hospital in London, to be built under PFI.

The costs of the catastrophic deal to merge the Royal Brompton and Harefield Hospital in Paddington Basin have more than doubled from £360m to £800m. It seems the monstrous over-run was even noticed in the treasury, where despite chancellor Gordon Brown's boundless enthusiasm for PFI, there was a marked reluctance to approve a project whose costs have risen so effortlessly. Delay followed delay... There are plenty who hope and pray the whole Paddington project is dead in the water. If so, it should certainly take its place among the most outrageous wastes of public money that even PFI has ever produced.

The Paddington Health Campus project was finally cancelled in the summer of 2005, at a cost of £15 million to the public. The National Audit Office concluded that "the original business case was inadequate, the lack of a single sponsor was a fatal flaw and the final scheme was not deliverable."

GORDON BROWN GAVE an enthusiastic endorsement for a company that was expanding into the UK in April. The *Eye* was slightly more sceptical.

Chancellor Gordon Brown took sycophancy to new levels when he opened a new HQ for the Lehman Brothers merchant bank in London this month. He grovelled: "In thanking you for your invitation, let me at the outset pay tribute to all of you here – executives, employees, representatives of the financial sector, all 3,100 staff of Lehman's here in Canary Wharf – for the contribution you and your company make to the prosperity of Britain, the enterprise you show and the difference you make."

The bank was fined $50m in 2002 for its involvement in the "pump and dump" scandal in the US, but Brown must have forgotten about this. Nor did he refer to the bank's close involvement with Enron. Or Lehman Brothers' pay-out of $1.7m in January to avoid prosecution for fraudulent deals. Nor its 1994 settlement of the Maxwell pensions swindle.

Instead he promised: "We will continue to look with you at the business tax regime so that we provide incentives for investment in wealth creation and greater rewards for success."

Four years later, the bank's spectacular collapse as a result of subprime lending and dodgy accounting played a major part in kicking off the global financial crisis which Brown, by then prime minister, had to deal with.

MORE TAX DODGINESS was uncovered in May.

Deeply disturbed by the rise in tax avoidance, the government has gone on the offensive. The treasury is directing a "tax probe" against 30 companies – but especially against top accountants Ernst & Young which, the Inland Revenue claims, "distinguishes itself as the big four's most aggressive promoter of abusive tax avoidance schemes". In particular, the Revenue was shocked by a single scheme which punched holes in the 2002 finance act and lost the government £1bn. It was dreamed up in the imaginative tax avoidance department of Ernst & Young.

While the treasury was cracking down on the company, however, Jim Cousins,

Labour MP for Newcastle Central, asked a) how much the government had paid in fees to Ernst & Young, and b) how many top people from the big four accountancy firms had been taken on as "secondees" to government departments. The answers were astonishing: a) £10m to Ernst & Young in three years, and b) five senior people at the DTI of "assistant director level or above" were "seconded" from Ernst & Young, and there was even an E&Y "secondee" working at a very high level in the treasury's budget and finance directorate – the very section that advises on tax and tax avoidance!

FURTHER DETAILS OF the ridiculousness of PFI emerged in July...

As if private finance initiatives providing new schools, hospitals, prisons and roads weren't costly enough, the scale of additional windfall profits – those made simply by refinancing the PFI deal with the banks once the buildings are up – has now been revealed by the treasury. A staggering 40 projects have effectively been "remortgaged", with a total profit for the private contractors of £334m.

Under a voluntary code that came into force in September 2002, taxpayers will be able to claw back just 30 percent of that – but over a 30-year period. Four PFI hospitals have produced windfalls of £177m, to be divvied up between contractors including Carillion, John Laing and Taylor Woodrow.

...AND NOVEMBER

When governors at one Nottinghamshire school decided to get rid of vending machines stuffed with crisps and chocolate to encourage healthy eating, they found they were locked into keeping the machines – by their private finance initiative deal. Harry Carlton School was taken over by Alfred McAlpine Business Services in a new-build PFI deal last year. In a letter to parents, chair of governors Marion Shore said that while the current management are "vehemently opposed" to the presence of the machines, the school has a contract with snack-giant Nestlé under McAlpine's management of the catering facilities, and that the machines make a significant profit – none of which goes to the school. "In fact, the school pays for the electricity that powers the machines, with no return," she added. The governors have been told by McAlpine that breaking the contract on the machines would cost the school a "considerable" sum.

2005

PLANS FOR THE WEDDING of the Prince of Wales and Camilla Parker-Bowles had to be publicly and embarrassingly revised several times due to unforeseen issues of protocol. Dame Sylvie Krin had the inside story.

Born Not to be Queen

After all the years of Royal snubs and slights, at last she was going to be part of the family – Charles's wife no less! A Royal Wedding! And where would it be? Obviously it couldn't be St Paul's again. So it must be the Abbey! And perhaps a coach along the Mall. Her heart beat faster at the very thought. Crowds cheering. Bands playing. It was all going to be such fun...

"It's all going to be such fun," said a curiously jittery Charles that evening, as they waited for Sir Alan Fitztightly to announce that dinner was served. "There's going to be five of us, which is so much better than having hundreds of people one doesn't even know," he hurriedly went on.

"What are you talking about, Chazza? The Abbey holds thousands."

"Er, yes, old thing. It's not exactly going to be in the Abbey. The trouble is that, since I'm going to be head of the Church, it's all got rather complicated. D'you see what I'm getting at, old thing?"

"No, I don't!" Camilla responded sharply, fiddling impatiently with her turquoise-and-zircon engagement ring from Ratners of Belgravia. "Where's the venue then? Not that boring old chapel at Windsor with all those moth-eaten flags?"

"Oh no, not there, obviously not," Charles stammered.

"Well, where?" she demanded. "I can't think of any other decent churches."

"Ah, you've hit the nail on the head there, old thing, and it's for that reason and that alone that mater and pater and, of course, I think that..."

Charles paused as he nervously took a bite from a Duchy of Cornwall badger-flavoured organic twiglet. "You know, it's nothing to be ashamed of, a registry office, the ceremony is much the same, it's just a bit quicker than hanging about in a church with all those hymns and er, er..."

As her dreams collapsed around her like a soap bubble bursting when it flies too high, Camilla clung to one final scintilla of hope. At

least her union with her beloved Charles would be graced by the presence of the Queen of England.

"But your mother will be there, surely?" she pleaded, her voice tinged with desperation.

"Er, there's a bit of a problem with this protocol thingie – apparently they've discovered that the Queen can't go to a registry office if she doesn't want to. It's the Marriage Act of eighteen forty-something." Charles put out his hand to calm her. "Anyway, it doesn't matter. The most important thing is that you will be there."

"I wouldn't count on it," Camilla snapped. Outside, an icy wind whipped the heads off the crocuses, scattering the petals like so much unwanted confetti...

TONY BLAIR CALLED another election. Under Michael Howard, the Conservatives tacked right, taking a hard line on immigration.

I BELIEVE THAT BRITAIN CAN ONLY TAKE A LIMITED NUMBER OF VAMPIRES EACH YEAR.

WE ARE A SMALL ISLAND. OUR BLOOD TRANFUSION SERVICES ARE ALREADY OVERSTRETCHED AND OUR GRAVEYARDS ARE FULL TO BURSTING.

NO ONE CAN ACCUSE ME OF VAMPIRISM. I MYSELF AM A VAMPIRE AND THE DRACULAS CAME TO THIS COUNTRY FROM TRANSYLVANIA, AND WERE WELCOMED BY THE BRITISH PEOPLE WITH OPEN NECKS.

BUT NOW THE TIME HAS COME TO DEFEND OUR SHORES WITH LINES OF GARLIC AND CRUCIFIXES.

VOTE CONSERVATIVE

AS THE ELECTION neared, the Blairs gave an extraordinary interview to the *Sun* in which Cherie talked about their sex life.

'I'm at it all the time!' says PM

In an astonishingly frank exclusive interview with the *Sun* newspaper, Tony Blair yesterday boasted that he does it "five times a night". It is rare for a prime minister to admit so openly to his passion for lying. But Tony Blair makes no bones about it. "I'm a normal guy, look, I like lying, I don't see anything to be ashamed of."

At this point, his wife Cherie chipped in with a saucy comment of her own. "Size matters," she said, "and when it comes to a good lie, the bigger the better I say. And I don't mind telling you that Tony's are whoppers!"

The nation's queasiness was not enough to stop him becoming the first Labour leader ever to win three elections in a row.

PEOPLE ACROSS THE GLOBE donned wristbands to show their support for the "Make Poverty History" campaign launched by Bob Geldof ahead of the G8 summit.

A group of African leaders has today united to create a new movement on the continent to "Make Poverty History".

Said spokesman President Bkanda from Rumbabwe, "We pledge that from now on there will be no more poverty amongst African leaders. And to that end we promise that we will steal as much money from our people as possible and misappropriate as much foreign aid as we can and ensure free trade at all times with our relatives' companies."

Mr Bkanda and the other leaders then showed off the bracelets that they were all wearing as a symbol of their campaign. These are made from solid gold and are studded with diamonds to form the words, "Make Poverty History".

Mr Bkanda concluded the inaugural meeting with his famous catchphrase, "Give us your fucking money, or we'll lock you up and torture you."

THE MESSAGE definitely got through to the world leaders meeting in Scotland.

We can defeat poverty

Just tell me where it is and I'll invade it

GELDOF'S PLANS for a "Live 8" concert which would feature only high-profile western musicians were criticised for cultural insensitivity.

"I'm not sure that's helpful, Bob"

ON THE MORNING of 7 July, four Islamist terrorists detonated suicide bombs on London's public transport system, killing 52 people and injuring hundreds more. Police at first seemed unsure who they were looking for.

No connection between Islam and terror

London's top policeman, Chief Superintendent "Knacker of the Yard" Knacker, yesterday called a special press conference in the wake of the London bombings to explain that, in the view of London's police service, there was no connection whatever between what he was about to say and common sense.

"Just because these bombs were let off by Muslims," he said, "it does not follow that there is any link between the bombers and the religion of Islam.

"My officers will be focusing their efforts largely on members of the Church of England and other fanatical groups – especially those who are known to be linked to extremist organisations, such as the Women's Institute."

LATE NEWS: Dead Men Arrested

Chief Superintendent Knacker last night announced that "thanks to a triumph of forensic detection" the four men responsible for the London bombings had all been arrested. "The breakthrough came," he said, "when we uncovered evidence of the four men's identity, including their names and addresses and the words, 'We did it – we want to be martyrs to the cause of Islamic terrorism.'"

THE CAPITAL'S MAYOR knew exactly who we should not be looking for.

Red Ken demands two-year silence

The mayor of London, Ken Livingstone, today called for all Londoners to observe a two-year silence about his disastrous meeting last year with the fanatical Muslim extremist Yusuf al-Qaradawi. "As a gesture of respect to myself," said the Mayor, "I would ask everyone to keep very quiet about the fact that I invited to London a man who preaches the kind of hatred that leads to people thinking that they can go around blowing up London."

TWO WEEKS LATER, five more would-be suicide bombers failed to detonate their devices on underground trains and a bus. A manhunt was launched, and the following morning armed police mistook an entirely blameless Brazilian electrician, Jean Charles de Menezes, for one of the suspects and shot him dead at Stockwell station.

Government reintroduces capital punishment

In a new crackdown on innocent men in the street, Home Secretary Charles Clarke last week ordered a return to capital punishment for anyone whom the police mistake for a terrorist.

"It is time these innocent people were taught a lesson," said Mr Clarke, who explained, "Capital punishment of course only applies to those shot in the capital, London."

FORMER FOREIGN SECRETARY Robin Cook died suddenly on a hill-walking holiday. Tony Blair did not attend his funeral because he was on his own holiday – at a venue the media was forbidden to report.

He's gone to a better place

But we can't reveal it for security reasons

IT TURNED OUT TO BE another free stay at Cliff Richard's house in Barbados.

Old Jokes Revisited No.94

BLAIR: My wife and I went to the Caribbean.
WOMAN: Jamaica?
BLAIR: No. She likes a freebie as much as I do.

DOCTOR WHO made a triumphant return to television.

DAVID CAMERON emerged as the surprise front-runner in the race to be the next Conservative leader, despite refusing to answer questions about his drug use when younger.

The big *Eye* interview

Who is he, this man that everyone's talking about but no one has heard of?

WORLD'S FIRST FACE TRANSPLANT 'A SUCCESS'
BEFORE   AFTER

The *Eye* can exclusively reveal that the biggest and newest star in Britain's political firmament is called David Cameron.

He represents a new generation of Conservatives who are young, compassionate, modernisers and, above all, compassionate. I was privileged to be the only journalist in the last five minutes to be granted an exclusive interview with the next Tory leader in his £8 million home in Ladbroke Grove.

He sat at his kitchen table, looking relaxed and compassionate. He makes a cup of Nescafé with the practised ease of a compassionate father and husband who is entirely at home in his own kitchen. Leaning forward in a rumpled pullover that can only be described as compassionate, David spoke frankly to me about why he refuses to speak frankly about anything at all.

"There are certain things," he told me frankly, "that the public has no right to know – such as what my policy is on anything at all.

"People can say 'tax', 'asylum seekers' and 'Europe' to me as often as they like, but there are certain things that a chap is perfectly entitled to keep to himself."

THE GOVERNMENT attempted to push a 90-day detention period for suspected terrorists through parliament.

'Why we need 90 days' – Knacker spells it out

Top police chief Inspector, Sir Ian Knacker of the Yard, today told the Prime Minister that the 90-day detention period for terrorist suspects was "absolutely imperative" if the police were to win the war against terror.

"We at the Met are convinced that nine months is the very minimum that it takes the police to extract a confession from those we suspect of being in our cells."

He continued: "Nine years is a small price to pay for ensuring the safety of the public. The alternative is that we will have to shoot them in the Underground. It is the only way to protect innocent citizens against the possibility of being killed on the Tube."

THEY WERE MORE successful with legislation to lengthen the period people could remain in pubs.

PRESIDENT BUSH was criticised for his inadequate reaction to the catastrophic damage caused by Hurricane Katrina in New Orleans.

Hurricane Disaster
'Help me!' – Drowning man's plea

Today I saw with my own eyes one of the most tragic spectacles I ever hope to witness.

Standing alone on the roof of what was once his home, as a flood of toxic filth rose ever higher towards his isolated refuge, a solitary white male survivor shouted, "Please save me! I don't know what to do, I've lost everything."

When our helicopter got near enough for me to speak to him, the inarticulate Texan sobbed out his pathetic story.

"They tell me my name is George Dubya Bush," he stammered. "Everything seemed to be going along just fine and dandy until this hurricane came along. The next thing I knew, I was up to my neck in effluents. And my world just fell apart."

GOVERNMENT revealed Britain had deployed white phosphorous weapons in Iraq.

'We did use whitewash, but it's harmless' says Reid

The British government today admitted that, contrary to its earlier denials, whitewash had been widely used in Iraq. However, the Defence Secretary Dr Reid was quick to point out that the use of whitewash does not breach any international rules, and is not mentioned in the Chemical Weapons Convention of 1368.

"We only used whitewash," he went on, "against civilians, to protect ministers. This is a perfectly legitimate and beneficial use of the substance in a military context."

Whitewash was most recently used in the battles of Hutton and Butler, when the government came under heavy fire from backbench insurgents, and needed large amounts of whitewash to escape.

HOW IT WORKS: Whitewash, or *Blairium Toxicum* to give it its proper chemical name, is commonly used to eliminate opposition and to cover up errors. It eats away at the oxygen of publicity, consuming all damaging evidence, and leaves the public stumbling about in a fog of confusion. Once whitewash has been applied, it is almost impossible to remove, and often continues its deadly work for years.

The only known antidote is telling the truth, but this has not yet been discovered by governments.

AFTER A LENGTHY trial in California, Michael Jackson was found not guilty of molesting 13-year-old Gavin Arvizo.

IN JANUARY, THE EYE revealed the management secrets of *Daily Mail* editor Paul Dacre.

Dacre, whose paper bemoans the coarsening of British culture almost as often as it predicts a crash in house prices, is so prodigal in his use of the c-word that editorial conferences are now known among staff as "the Vagina Monologues". A typical greeting of one *Daily Mail* hack by another now goes as follows: "I say, have you been double-cunted yet?"

Translator's note: This is *Mail*speak for "Have you been called a cunt by the editor twice in the same sentence?"

THE FORMER HOME SECRETARY'S new job came under scrutiny in March – but only from the *Eye*.

David Blunkett's new employers, Indepen management consultants, have many contracts with government departments and public bodies, including his own previous ministry, the department of education. There is, of course, an official watchdog which supposedly vets the employment of ex-ministers, the Advisory Committee on Business Appointments (Acoba), and its guidelines are clear: "A three-month waiting period from the date of leaving office will normally be expected when the former minister is of cabinet rank." Yet Blunkett accepted a paid consultancy with Indepen in January this year – *one month* after his resignation from cabinet. Shome mishtake, shurely?

Having returned to the cabinet following the election, Blunkett resigned again in disgrace in November, admitting "I was at fault not writing to the committee" when he took this and two other jobs.

JULY BROUGHT MORE details of the poverty-busting deals being struck by HMRC.

A law dating back to the 1930s is, HMRC says, "intended to prevent an individual from gaining a tax advantage by making arrangements which divert his or her income to another person who is liable at a lower rate of tax or is not liable to income tax". Probably the largest ever dividend payout to the non-taxable spouse of the head of a family firm occurred last year when Philip Green's Arcadia group paid £460m to companies controlled by trusts in which Tina Green, Philip's Monaco-resident wife, is the principal beneficiary. The cash extracted from the group far exceeded the profits made in the two years since Green's acquisition of the group in 2002 for around £850m. So will the law, recently upheld in a high court case, land him with a tax bill of 25 percent of the dividend – £115m?

Unlikely. The *Eye* has learned that not long before the massive payment, Green had personal discussions with the Revenue's deputy chairman, Dave Hartnett. The Revenue declined to say why the multi-billionaire gained such privileged access, or how the department decide who they see, commenting only that the "decision depends on the circumstances in any individual case".

MAZHER MAHMOOD'S recent run of scoops for the *News of the World* were questioned in November.

On 23 October, just days after it was revealed that police were taking seriously deported asylum-seeker Florim Gashi's claims that he had fabricated the evidence which was the basis for more than a dozen *News of the World* scoops, including the infamous "Posh Spice Kidnap" of 2002, the paper had another hot exclusive. Imran Patel, "a fanatic who has had arms training in Pakistan", told Mahmood that he had been "groomed" to be a fifth suicide bomber in London on 7 July before getting cold feet and pulling out.

As is the usual routine, the paper "handed its dossier on Patel to the Anti-Terrorist Squad", who obligingly arrested him late on the Saturday evening just prior to the *Screws* going to press – before questioning him at length and, rather less obligingly, charging him with wasting police time. Naturally, rather than reassuring readers that there was in fact no need to worry about the dire warnings of primed fanatics in their midst, the paper did not print another word on the matter.

In 2016, Mahmood was sent to prison for conspiracy to pervert the course of justice, for fabricating evidence and lying on oath about his "stings" exposing supposed criminals.

2006

CHARLES KENNEDY stepped down as Lib Dem leader, and two of the contenders to replace him were promptly caught up in sex scandals.

Lib Dem in Three-In-A-Party shock

A senior MP confessed last night that he had indulged in a threesome with fellow Liberal Democrats. "Yes, it's true," he said. "There are only three members of the party left, since everyone else has resigned in disgrace." He admitted that the three of them had acted out "perverse fantasies" of forming a government.

AN INTERNATIONAL furore erupted over the publication of 12 cartoons of the prophet Mohammed in a Danish newspaper.

How dare these cartoonists stereotype Muslims as violent, aggressive and filled with hate towards the West?

FREEDOM OF EXPRESSION GO TO HELL!!

It's our right to demand...

...an end to free speech

Er...

BRITISH AUTHORITIES were slightly confused as to how they should react.

POLICE LOG

Neasden Central Police Station

Office hours: 9-12 Mon-Tues (Except Tuesday)
14 February 2006

1200hrs: Mrs Prendergast, our canteen assistant, was placed under arrest for serving Danish bacon, a clear attempt to incite religious hatred against the Muslim members of the force (none). Mrs Prendergast was later admitted to hospital after suffering an unfortunate fall in the cells.

1430hrs: Following representations from the Neasden Jihad League, all available officers were instructed to escort members of the League on their planned demonstrations at the premises of the Danish furniture company Ikea. The purpose of the police escort was to protect the protesters' right to display placards contining such slogans as "Kill the Infidels", "We Want Holocaust Now!" and "Death to the Cartoonists!" It was necessary to ensure their freedom of protest against any interference by members of the public. During the demonstration a number of arrests were made involving persons who were seeking to incite religious hatred against the protesters by engaging them in dialogue. These included the Rt Rev Moses Setnanugu, the Bishop of Neasden, Rabbi Rachel Coren of the Liberal Reformed Orthodox Synagogue, and Dr Sylvester Dawkins, Chair of the Neasden Chapter of the Seventh-Day Atheists. The peaceful demonstration went off without further incident, apart from the setting fire to the premises of Messrs Ikea & Co, the unfortunate Swedish retailer, and the beheading of a small number of the firm's staff.

THE MAYOR OF LONDON was suspended from office for four weeks after his "unnecessarily insensitive and offensive" comparison of a Jewish journalist to a concentration camp guard, for which he steadfastly refused to apologise.

Livingstone attacks suspension verdict

"I did nothing wrong," said an unrepentant "Rude" Ken Livingstone, "and the three-man disciplinary tribunal are no more than concentration camp guards, obeying orders and sentencing me to the gas chambers. These little Hitlers are committing an assault on British democracy and free speech. They should shut up or be exterminated at once."

THE DISCOVERY that a swan in Scotland had died of H5N1 Avian Flu led to unfounded fears of an epidemic sweeping Britain.

PET SHOP

"This parrot is dead. It is no more. It has ceased to be"

DEPUTY PRIME MINISTER John Prescott was revealed – in rather too much detail – to have been having an affair with his secretary.

The Joy of Secretaries

The Gourmet Guide to Cringe-making
by International Secs Expert Dr Alex Discomfort

Position 1
THE RED BOX

The man sits at the desk reading his briefings on regeneration and the environment. The woman gets under the table and addresses the Honourable Member.

Position 2
THE TWO JAGUARS

The man sits in the back of his car refusing to comment before transferring to his other car to avoid the press. The woman sits in the *Mail on Sunday* "talking dirty."

Position 3
THE "UNTENABLE" POSITION

The man kneels in front of the prime minister in submission. Meanwhile the other man carries on screwing the country.

FORMER HEAD of the Met Police Lord Stevens delivered his thorough and painstaking report into the various conspiracy theories surrounding Princess Diana's death. Needless to say, not everyone was convinced.

DAILY EXPRESS

WHO KILLED OUR STORY?

by Daily Express Editor MOHAMMED AL-DESMOND

The Stevens report is a total whitewash which leaves the central question of the Diana mystery unsolved, ie why was our beloved story "The People's Front Page" killed off when it had so much life ahead of it?

The answer is clear. The Royal Family and MI6, led by the Duke of Edinburgh, wanted the story dead and deliberately arranged for Lord fuggin Stevens to run it over in a fuggin whitewash Fiat Uno in a fuggin *(continued for ever)*

PAUL McCARTNEY announced that he would be separating from his fantasist wife of four years, Heather Mills.

How they Aren't Related Any More

Paul McCartney   **His Money**

A MAN WAS SHOT during a police raid in East London, which resulted in anti-terror police finding… nothing whatsoever.

The Prime Minister today defended the invasion of a house in Forest Gate by 250 crack police marksmen and chemical warfare experts, insisting that "Weapons of Mass Destruction" would eventually be found there.

"It may take time," he said, "but make no mistake, they will be found. This is a big house, a one-up, one-down, and there is even a garden shed at the back. These weapons could be anywhere or nowhere. Even as I speak, officers are in a wardrobe upstairs with a torch."

The Prime Minister was then asked about the unfortunate shooting of various members of the household during the invasion, and replied, "It is unfortunate that there have been civilian casualties, but in the war on terror there is bound to be collateral damage."

THE ENTIRE WORLD appeared to have gone mad for a spectacularly bad book, film, and various other spin-offs.

NEW FROM GNOME

The Da Vinci Trouser Press

RELIVE all the thrills of the blockbuster film of the book of the millennium with the Trouser Press that Christ's descendants would have used if He had fathered a child and gone to live in Boulogne!

ENJOY the biggest mystery of the last 2000 years whilst steaming your favourite trousers, just as all the Knights Templar have done from Galileo to Michelangelo to Wayne Rooney.

"If I had to condemn one trouser press as heretical, I would have no hesitation in condemning the Gnome Da Vinci Trouser Press" – His Holiness the Pope.
Send £666 now!

WAR BROKE OUT in the Lebanon.

The Book of Ehud

Chapter 94

1. And lo, it came to pass that Ehud sent the mighty warriors of Israel, the sons and even the daughters of Israel, indeed all the children of Israel who could carry a sword or ride in a chariot of iron, into the land of Le-ban-on.

2. And Ehud spoke unto the children of Israel in this wise: O children of Israel, the time hath come for the smiting that will end all smiting.

3. For too many years the Hez-boll-ites have been a thorn in our flesh, like unto the scorpion that creepeth up in the night and stingeth a man in his foot, yea, even before he can lay his hand upon the flip-flop beneath his bed in order to smite it dead.

4. Talking of which, Ehud concluded, it is time for some serious smiting, even the final day of reckoning with the Hez-boll-ites.

5. Ye are to go into the land of the cedars of Lib-anus and smite all that moveth – not just the Hez-boll-ites but also the Leb-an-ites, who may be no friends to the Hez-boll-ites but that is just the luck that is called tough.

6. And the children of Israel saith unto themselves, yea, it will all be over in seven days.

7. And it will be like unto a piece of cake.

8. But lo, it was not as it had been foretold by Ehud.

9. For the Hez-boll-ites had hidden themselves privily, in caves and holes in the ground, like unto the cunning fox which concealeth itself by day and, when night comes, jumpeth out and fireth an rocket at Haifa.

10. And the children of Israel found themselves on the receiving end of the smiting for a change.

11. And Ehud cried aloud, cursing the Hez-boll-ites with an mighty curse, saying "This goeth not according to plan."

12. "So now it is time for the plan that is called B – that is to say more smiting."

13. And where Ehud had smote a hundred-fold, he now smote a thousand-fold.

14. But lo, the Hez-boll-ites were still there, like unto the nettle of the desert which, the more it is cut down, the more it groweth up to sting again.

15. And Ehud took counsel with himself, asking what he should now do.

16. And the answer came to him as follows: "I know – all that is needed is more smiting."

THE ARRIVAL OF A NEW Bond film – the first to star Daniel Craig – coincided with the poisoning with radioactive polonium of a former KGB man and Putin critic in London.

Is this the best spy poisoning ever?

Critics have hailed the brutal, savage poisoning to death of Alexander Litvinenko as a real return to form for the KGB's "Licence To Kill" franchise.

"The sheer, in-your-face brutality of the Litvinenko death takes us back to the classic KGB spy killings of the early sixties," said one astonished critic.

The KGB admitted their franchise had become stale and formulaic over recent years, with too much reliance on silly gadgets to kill dissidents, and that's why they had decided to go "back to basics".

"We know now that what really captures the public's imagination are no-nonsense brutal murders like this."

NEW RESTRICTIONS were imposed on air travellers after police announced they had foiled a plot to blow up planes with liquid explosives.

Hand luggage – those new guidelines

You will no longer be able to take the following items on board the aircraft as hand luggage:

- Bottle of water
- Copy of *Da Vinci Code*
- Upright piano
- Islamic terrorist
- Baby's nappy
- Trouser press
- Sudoku puzzle
- Nuclear bomb

All these items must be placed in the hold.

THE PRIME MINISTER'S friend, tennis partner and chief fundraiser, Lord Levy, was arrested as part of an investigation into the sale of honours in return for political donations.

SOMETHING FISHY was going on in Downing Street in January.

One thing Tony Blair really must sort out before he quits is the confusion about the going rate for an honour. In the days of Maundy Gregory and Lloyd George, everyone knew where they stood: a peerage cost £100,000 (about £2m in today's money), while a donation of £40,000 would get you a baronetcy.

But what now? Just after Christmas it was revealed that the House Of Lords Appointments Commission had blocked the PM's latest "Lavender List" of peerages for tycoons, pending further inquiries. The nominees include property developer Sir David Garrard (Labour donation: £200,000); curry mogul Sir Gulam Noon (£220,000); but also stockbroker Barry Townsley who has given a mere £6,000 to the party. True, Townsley also sponsored one of Blair's beloved "city academies" (as did Garrard), but the same can't be said of our old mate Chai Patel, whose party donation was a modest £10,000.

Two months later, a petulant Patel consulted lawyers about whether his human rights were being infringed by his ongoing lack of a peerage: a police investigation was subsequently launched into whether donations and loans to Labour had been made in return for honours. It resulted in the arrest of the party's chief fundraiser Lord Levy and senior Downing Street adviser Ruth Turner and officers questioning Tony Blair three times himself, but although the scandal overshadowed his final year in power, no charges were ever brought.

THE EYE TOOK A LOOK at how the NHS's IT programme was going in May.

Eight years ago, surveying a history of failed health service IT initiatives, Labour MP Maria Eagle asked the then NHS chief whether somebody who repeatedly walked into the same brick wall might be thought "drunk or of unsound mind". Now, three years into the national IT programme – sexily rebranded Connecting for Health (CfH) – the NHS is once again drunkenly or insanely heading for the wall. But this time, in true New Labour style, the bill will run into many billions.

Despite the many delays and fiascos emerging at a local level, the head of the prime minister's delivery unit, Ian Watmore, has declared CfH a success – but coming from the former UK boss of Accenture, responsible for one of the greatest ever public sector IT cock-ups in the NIRS2 national insurance system (*see p161*), that's not saying much. The records show that by March this year CfH had in fact only provided basic administrative systems (often badly) to nine acute hospitals – against a target of delivering these and more complex clinical systems to 102 of them. Some might wonder just how pissed or mad you would have to be to call that a success.

The NHS IT scheme was finally scrapped by the coalition government in 2011, after at least £12.7 billion of public funds had been wasted on it.

IN SEPTEMBER, Slicker raised doubts about a major Serious Fraud Office investigation.

The announcement of a new £10 billion contract for the Eurofighter from Saudi Arabia is unlikely to make life easier for the Serious Farce Office as it continues its long-running probe into a suspected £60 million "slush fund" linked to corrupt services provided by BAE to certain of its high-ranking Saudi customers involved in the earlier £20 billion Al-Yamamah Tornado contract. The new deal is expected to increase the pressure from a never keen MoD, not to mention the Foreign Office, about the risk of embarrassing such a good customer by making allegations that Saudi princelings are corrupt. Whatever next – bears in woods?

Three months later, the government announced that the Al-Yamamah investigation was being dumped simply because Tony Blair judged it could cause "serious damage" to relations with Saudi Arabia.

NEWS OF THE WORLD royal editor, Clive Goodman, pleaded guilty to phone hacking in December. The *Eye* pointed out how unlikely he was to be the only one at it…

"As the editor of the newspaper, I take ultimate responsibility for the conduct of my reporters," said *Screws* editor Andy Coulson. But in fact he appears to be shrugging off responsibility, by implying that neither he nor anyone else at the *Screws* had the slightest inkling of what Goodman was up to. Glenn Mulcaire, the private detective who carried out the bugging, is said to have earned £200,000 a year from the *Screws*, plus undisclosed cash payments. Fees on such a scale would have to be authorised by Coulson or one of his senior executives. Yet they would have us believe it never occurred to them to ask why the sleazy Mulcaire merited such largesse. There are only two possible explanations: either they're lying, or they're recklessly negligent.

They were lying. Coulson was jailed in 2014 for his part in the widespread phone hacking at the *News of the World*.

2007

IT EMERGED THAT the Home Office, already condemned as "not fit for purpose" by home secretary John Reid, had failed to keep proper records of British criminals who had committed serious offences overseas, and lost track of 150 convicted drug traffickers who were supposed to be banned from travelling abroad.

"Approximately 8 teas. Roughly 6 coffees. I'm afraid I don't have accurate figures for milk or sugar"

CONSERVATIVE LEADER David Cameron's exploits in the Bullingdon Club while he was a student at Oxford were exposed.

Where are they now – the Glittering Prats of 1987?

1. David "Spliffy" Cameron – Old Etonian, now tipped to become Britain's next prime minister. Took a First in Public Relations and Media Studies at Snortnose College.
2. Boris "Beano" Johnson – Old Etonian, now tipped to become the ex-editor of the *Spectator*. Read Comics at Cripeschurch College.
3. Augustus "Gussy" Fink-Nottle – Old Etonian, son of Lord Hitbottle, now a hedge fund manager at Fink and Nottle (this year's bonus £700 billion).
4. Peregrine "Perry" Starborgling – Old Etonian, son of merchant banker Sir Arthur Starborgling. Married heiress, the Hon. Poppy Moneypenny, sister of the Hon. Penny Moneypoppy. Now works for Starborgling Securities (Riyadh).
5. Rodney "Dipso" Ricketson-Hatt – Old Etonian, read the Daily Telegraph at Lady Margaret Thatcher Hall. Now (*That's enough prats – Ed.*)

IN THE MIDST of commemorations marking 25 years since the Falklands war, a standoff over the arrest of 15 British Navy personnel by Iran ended with the UK being made to look very silly indeed.

Bands played and flags fluttered bravely in the breeze, as the entire Royal Navy today set sail from Portsmouth to liberate the victims of Iranian aggression.

The so-called "task force" despatched by Prime Minister "Maggie" Blair consists of one rubber dinghy, *HMS Useless*, two canoes, *HMS Ant* and *HMS Dec*, and a rowing boat crewed by round-the-world yachtswoman Ellen MacArthur.

If weather conditions are favourable, the task force should arrive in the disputed waters of the Shat-al-over-Britz sometime early next year.

DURING A MENTAL HEALTH breakdown exhaustively documented by the paparazzi, pop star Britney Spears shaved off all her hair.

Comes complete with
- Shaved head
- Tattoos
- Drink Problem
- No knickers

HOURS OF FUN as you make Britz disintegrate in front of your very own eyes! Press the button and hear Britz cry for help! Or add the following accessories for even more entertainment – two children under 5! Wicked!

TONY BLAIR FINALLY announced his departure date and looked forward to a future in the private sector.

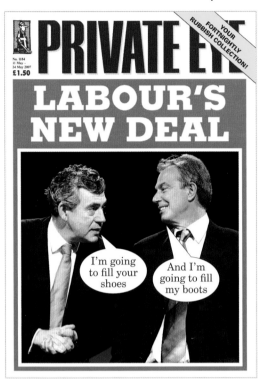

AND THE VICAR was happy as he surveyed his parish.

ST ALBION PARISH NEWS

Just look out of your windows and tell me if things have not got better in every possible way!

- The St Albion's prison full to bursting!
- St Albion's Primary School – biggest class sizes ever!
- St Albion's Kwikfit Beacon Academy of Excellence – all obesity records broken!
- St Albion's Cottage Hospital can now guarantee MRSA for every patient!
- St Albion's police station – closed because there's no longer any crime to solve!

We talk about counting your blessings, but there are so many that it's easy to lose count, isn't it?

How about these? A Tesco on every street corner! A post office in every W.H. Smith! A Polish builder in every home!

And that's not the half of it! Not that I want to bore you by going on about my legacy (from the greek *legasos*, meaning "having no leg to stand on"), because as you know, I'm a pretty modest kind of guy!

In fact, modesty is one of the things I have been most proud of in all the years I have served you so well as your vicar!

THE DISAPPEARANCE of three-year-old Madeleine McCann dominated all news coverage everywhere.

Maddy – No new developments at all

There was nothing new to report today as the search continued for the missing toddler.

ON OTHER PAGES

Where is she? We don't know **2**
Is this man guilty? We don't know **3**
What are the Portuguese police doing? We don't know **4**
Is this every parent's worst nightmare? Yes **5**
More Pix, more Speculation **6-94**

APPLE'S STEVE JOBS announced a new invention that would change the world.

At long last it's here!

The incredible EYE-PHONE!

Has the following amazing features: Allows you to ring people up – Accepts incoming calls – Gives you instant access to the entire UK phone network – Stores an amazing one ring tone (Brrring!! Brrring!!) – Unique touch-sensitive controls (push buttons) – Unlike rival phones with a similar name THIS ONE ACTUALLY WORKS!

"Unbelievable value at only £199.99" says Steve Jobs of Neasden

NEW LAWS ON SMOKING in workplaces – including pubs – came into force.

Places you can smoke

Swimming pools
    YES So long as there is no water
    NO If there is a lifeguard

Confessional Box
    YES If there is a priest present and you wish to confess to smoking
    NO If you have gone in there for a fag

The Bikesheds
    YES If it is behind the bikesheds
    NO If it is in front of them

Public Toilets
    YES If you are a member of the cottaging community
    NO If another member of the cottaging community objects to your smoking

Crematorium
    YES If you are dead
    NO If you have gone to pay your last respects to a loved one who died from smoking

HAVING FINALLY TAKEN over unopposed as prime minister, Gordon Brown set about forming what he called a "government of all the talents".

That Brown Cabinet – How it will look

Foreign Secretary – G. BROWN
Home Secretary – G. BROWN
All other posts – G. BROWN
Chancellor of the Exchequer – A. DARLING (just in case the economy goes belly-up and he can be blamed)

WITH THE REJECTED European Constitution having turned into something called the Lisbon Treaty, the new prime minister insisted a referendum was no longer necessary.

From the Desk of the Supreme Leader

Comrades,

There follows a clarification of the situation regarding the new constitution which has been approved under the Supreme EU Council under the title of "This Is Not a Constitution".

Revisionists and subversive forces in our society, including right-wing reactionaries and traitorous members of the workers collectives, have falsely claimed that the People are in some way entitled to have their say in this matter.

It must be noted that the promise to hold such a referendum was made personally by the discredited former leader and imperialist warmonger Comrade Blair, as part of his carefully orchestrated cult of personality.

As Supreme Leader, with the full backing of the Party, I and I alone am competent to decide such matters on behalf of the People.

I would remind the traitors in our midst that it was not necessary for the People to be consulted when by universal acclamation I was nominated to succeed the now discredited Comrade Blair after his prolonged period of mental breakdown.

Yours fraternally
Gordon Brown Supreme Leader

HIS PREDECESSOR was reported to be seeking £8 million for his memoirs.

BORIS JOHNSON was selected as the Conservative candidate for Mayor of London.

Yes, It's Boris Johnson Cockney Rhyming Slang!

Rosie Lee – *O.E.*
Pony and Trap – *Jolly nice chap*
Barnet Fair – *Silly hair*
Berkeley Hunt – *Darius Guppy*
Trouble and Strife – *Don't tell my wife*

CUSTOMERS QUEUED round the block to withdraw their cash from bank Northern Rock amid reports it was on the verge of collapse.

A Message from Northern Gnome

May I have this opportunity to assure savers and investors in Northern Gnome that my money is completely safe and that there is absolutely no need for me to panic.

There is no chance, I repeat no chance, of me losing a single penny of my considerable salary and bonus.

Let me reiterate to anyone who may be concerned at this time that the Chancellor of the Exchequer has personally assured me that however abysmally I have run Northern Gnome, he will guarantee huge sums of taxpayers' money to enable me and my lady wife to live in a style to which we have long become accustomed. I thank you for your support and understanding.

Lord Gnome
Northern Crock
We're Opeless (surely "Open?" Ed.)

VLADIMIR PUTIN announced that he would be stepping down as Russian president – as required by the constitution – to serve as prime minister instead.

Putin to run for Czar

Vladimir Putin has confirmed that when he stands down as Russian president next year he plans to run for the lesser post of Czar.

"The position of Czar will be largely ceremonial and will consist of me ruling over all of Russia for all time," said President *(cont. p94)*

THE CONTROLLER OF BBC1 resigned after claiming footage from a new documentary showed the Queen storming out of a photoshoot, when it actually showed her going in in a perfectly good mood.

BBC apologises over mixed-up footage

The Director General of the BBC, Mr Mark Thompson, today apologised for an embarrassing mix-up of two pieces of film footage.

He told reporters, "In the first sequence, the controller of BBC1, Mr Peter Fincham, is seen walking into his job. In the second, he is seen leaving it hurriedly after being sacked. We deeply regret that the BBC put these scenes in the wrong order."

HAVING GIVEN EVERY indication that he was about to call a general election, Gordon Brown chickened out.

THE GOVERNMENT had to correct its official figures for the number of foreign workers in Britain – twice.

'We have no idea how many there are' admits immigration chief

by Our Political Staff **Phil Country**

The head of Britain's immigration department today confessed that the official figure for the number of idiots in his department was much higher than originally thought.

"There are thousands of them working here," he said, "most of them are completely unskilled and we can't just send them home."

HMRC ADMITTED it had lost computer discs containing the personal details of 25 million child benefit recipients.

The Importance of Being Useless (Her Majesty's Theatre of Revenue & Customs)

To lose one parent may be regarded as unfortunate; to lose 25 million looks like carelessness

IN APRIL, 32 PEOPLE were killed in the worst mass shooting to date in the US, at Virginia Tech University. The *Eye*'s TV columnist Remote Controller raised a few issues about what happened next.

When the package of vodcasts and statements from the shooter arrived at the offices of NBC, there must have been a mixture of emotions. The thrill of getting ahead of the other networks on the biggest story of the year will have been undercut by a very mild unease that a guy who wished to be on TV after killing 32 people immediately identified NBC as a sort of Al-jazeera for psychopaths.

A man whose playwrighting teacher was warned not to interfere with his clearly deranged dramas on the grounds that he was expressing American freedom of speech, and who was allowed to buy handguns at will because of the American right to bear arms, was now granted his desire to be even more famous in death than the Columbine killers by the perceived right of American networks to show whatever they want. His videos were being used precisely in the way he intended: to make him the world's most known and notorious serial-killer. There must also be a substantial likelihood that some other campus malcontent, seeing the scale of fame that can be achieved with a simple posthumous package, will do the same one day not very soon, with the inevitable inflation of depravity to make sure it gets on the air.

Throughout the week NBC and all the other networks that enviously relayed the material were allowing their news bulletins to be executive-edited by a dead psychopath. Some freedom.

Twelve years, and a great many mass shootings later, NBC was among many media outlets to change the way they reported such incidents, on the grounds that "blanket media coverage can provide potential shooters with a chance of fame, scorecards with which to compare one another and even blueprints for carrying out attacks".

THAT SAME MONTH the *Eye* uncovered a nice little earner.

The Department for International Development has enabled several executives to become millionaires at the expense of the world's poorest countries. Surely shome mistake?

Back in 2000, International Development Secretary Hilary Benn allowed managers at a government-owned development fund CDC (formerly the Commonwealth Development Corporation) to buy out its fund management function. Two years later Actis Capital LLP was established, 60 percent owned by managers led by Paul Fletcher, the rest in DfID's hands. Fees were agreed so that, according to Benn, Actis would break even but not profit from CDC for the first five years.

The price paid by the managers for their 60 percent stake was an affordable £373,000. This now looks distinctly good value, as in its first full year Actis didn't just break even but made profits of $14m (£8m). Of this, the firm's accounts show that one member trousered $1.84m. And these profits for the bosses came after the firm's 192 employees shared an average of $168,000 each, plus a further $55k each in "short-term incentive payments".

IN MAY, THE EYE identified a man even keener on freebies than the prime minister.

Why does 73-year-old comptroller and auditor-general Sir John Bourn, head of the National Audit Office since 1988, carry on working long after other top public officials have called it a day? Information unearthed by *Private Eye* using the Freedom of Information Act suggests it might be because the job has long enabled Sir John, whose task is to ensure taxpayers' money isn't wasted, to live the high life at the expense of, er, the taxpayer. In the three years up to this March Sir John managed 43 foreign trips, on 22 of which he was accompanied by his wife. The travel bill for Sir John's private office tops £336,000, of which £76,000 went on Lady Bourn's fares.

Among the couple's city-breaks were three nights at the Astoria in St Petersburg, Russia's leading hotel according to industry awards, which charges £400 a night for the cheapest double room. Other jaunts included three nights at the luxurious San Regis just off the Champs Elysées (more than £300 a night) and a week at the Gresham Palace in Budapest (£270 a night)...

After several months of further revelations about his expenses in the *Eye*, Bourn stepped down in October.

THE COVER-UP OF PHONE HACKING at News International continued in June.

Andy Coulson had to resign as editor of the *News of the Screws* but has now been hired as chief Tory spin-doctor by David Cameron. Royal editor Clive Goodman is now out of jail and pressing ahead with an unfair dismissal case. Questions about what Coulson knew and when he knew it may soon become rather insistent. Insiders suspect certain senior figures haven't been totally candid with the Dirty Digger about just how high up the command structure knowledge of the phone-tapping racket actually went.

A private settlement has been reached with Goodman's partner in crime, the private investigator Glenn Mulcaire, who had a contract paying him a six-figure annual retainer for "research". Terrified at the prospect of Mulcaire airing the paper's filthy linen in public, the company has now paid him a sum not far short of £200,000.

Goodman eventually accepted a pay-off brokered by Rebekah Brooks, which kept a lid on the scandal for a few more years.

SLICKER SOUNDED a note of alarm in August.

The impact on world markets of the ticking time bomb represented by $100bn of sub-prime mortgage losses for US lenders and their derivative customers worldwide has suddenly, but belatedly, focused regulatory attention on lending to those who cannot afford to borrow. Nowhere has this lack of attention been greater than at the Fundamentally Supine Authority, which is described by insiders as being "asleep at the switch" while a £15bn business expanded exponentially in Britain.

There is a growing fear that next year will see a serious crisis in the UK sub-prime market as a result of over-lending to poor credit risks leading to an acceleration in home repossessions.

The FSA's "light touch" style of regulation was created by Gordon Brown when he was chancellor. It was and is proof of Labour's pro-business policy. Which is why the world's bankers and brokers want to do business in London and not in New York where, post-Enron, tough regulation is still seen as necessary.

The Financial Services Authority, long a target of Slicker's disdain, was abolished following the financial crisis which did indeed erupt in 2008.

2008

CONSERVATIVE MP Derek Conway was suspended from the Commons and had the whip withdrawn after it emerged that he had employed almost all his family on the public purse to work in his Westminster office, including one son who was a full-time student in Newcastle at the time.

New Words

Administrative Shortcomings *(n. compound)* Theft, particularly from public funds. "Mr Derek Conway has repeatedly committed acts of administrative shortcomings" (*Hansard, 2008*)

Research Assistant *(n.)* Personal relative who receives large sums of public money for doing nothing. "Another bottle of Dom Perignon for Mr Conway's research assistant" (*University bar, 2007*)

Secretary *(n.)* Wife. "Who was that secretary I saw you with last night?" – "That was no secretary, that was my wife" (*Old Parliamentary joke, 1994*)

Conway *(n. slang)* Conman, fraudster, one who embezzles public funds.

It's great here – no photographers!

IT WAS REVEALED that Prince Harry had been serving with the army in Afghanistan for the past three months, an experience that he later said was one of the happiest periods of his life.

CHERIE BLAIR RUSHED out *Speaking for Myself*, a memoir in which, between attacks on her husband's successor, she revealed eye-watering details of the conception of her and Tony's youngest son.

Continuing our serialisation of Cherie Blair's sensational Memoir "Helping Myself"

What a weekend it was! Tony and I were staying at Balmoral with the dreary old Queen when I discovered to my surprise that I had a little book on the way! Imagine – at my age!

Obviously I was thrilled for myself, but how would Tony take it? He had other things on his mind, like the terrible war with Gordon Brown.

However, when I broke the news, instead of looking worried his face broke into a huge smile. "How wonderful, darling!" he said. "I've always wanted some more money."

The book came out and a lovely £500,000 non-bouncing cheque was delivered safely.

Tony was overjoyed. He picked it up and held it lovingly in his hands. "You beautiful little thing!" he said. "I'm going to take you for a little walk down to the bank right away."

Tomorrow: How I always had the ultimate respect for the melancholic, psychotic, fat Scots git Gordon Brown who ruined my husband's life.

FOLLOWING A REBELLION led by back-bench MP Frank Field, Gordon Brown performed a U-turn over plans to abolish the 10p tax rate which would disproportionately affect the lowest earners.

From the Desk of the Supreme Leader

Comrades!

When last year I proposed a new tax system for the benefit of the British proleteriat, it was always my intention that any additional tax that they paid would be given back to them.

This brilliant scheme was nevertheless wilfully misrepresented by Comrade Field, an embittered and cynical former member of the Politburo, who circulated rumours that I was in some way trying to take money from the pockets of the poor in order to redistribute it to the rich.

This vile, anti-Socialist calumny was allowed to fester in the warped minds of those Comrades who are still hankering after the ideological false turnings promoted by the doctrines of the Mandelsonian-Campbellite revisionist claque.

A pathetic attempted putsch was then mounted by ex-Comrade Field and a handful of some 100 of his fellow opportunist neo-Blairite renegades.

I took firm action at once by rounding up all the insurrectionists in the dimmer recesses of the Soviet and giving them an ultimatum – that if they did not back down, I would give in to all their demands.

They duly cowered triumphantly in the face of my principled and uncompromising show of leadership.

THERE were rumblings that the cabinet were growing increasingly dissatisfied with Gordon Brown's leadership.

FORMULA ONE BOSS Max Mosley sued the *News of the World* for infringing his privacy by publishing a video of him during a sado-masochistic orgy.

In The Courts

Sir Max Mosley vs the News of the Screws before Mr Justice Cocklecarrot

Sir Ephraim Hugefee: My Lord, I represent Sir Smacks… I'm terribly sorry, Sir Max Mosley, one of the most distinguished figures in the world of international motorsports. It will be our case that Sir Whacks… I mean Sir Max… was innocently taking part in a private orgy involving a number of sado-maxochistic… er, masochistic practices which were nobody's business except Sir Muck's… Sir Max's.

Justice Cocklecarrot: Would now be an appropriate time for us to see the video of the orgy?

Hugefee: My Lord, showing this innocent scene of erotic roleplay would serve no function, but might prove painful for my client.

Foreman of the Jury: Then he will probably enjoy it!

Cocklecarrot: May I remind the court that this is a very serious case indeed, involving highly important matters of legal principle. So let us get on with this video. If the usher would be so kind as to pull down the blinds…

(The case continues)

THE EU DECIDED to press on with the Lisbon Treaty, despite it being rejected by a referendum in Ireland.

All those in favour of ignoring the Irish vote

MUCH TO THEIR OWN and everyone else's displeasure, British troops were still being shot and blown up in both Iraq and Afghanistan.

DISSATISF-ACTION MAN™

NEW – The soldier who is suffering from low morale. Pull his dog tag and he complains about lack of equipment, constant overstretch, poor conditions and unsatisfactory aftercare.

DISSATISFACTION MAN comes complete with:

- Resignation letter
- Change into civilian clothes
- Inadequate pension
- Gulf War Syndrome

Price: **VERY CHEAP**

Hours of fun(damentalists trying to kill you)!

JOHN DARWIN, who faked his own death in a canoeing accident, and his wife, Anne, who claimed his life insurance before the couple attempted to emigrate to Panama, were both sentenced to six years for fraud.

THE TRUTH ABOUT SHERGAR

CHANCELLOR ALISTAIR DARLING desperately attempted to stay ahead of the chaos.

THE HUGELY OVERSTRETCHED Royal Bank of Scotland was bailed out by the government at a cost of £45bn, a significant chunk of which turned out to be going to sacked chief executive Sir Fred Goodwin in the form of an eye-watering pension.

THE ROYAL BANK OF GNOME

RBG has, as of this morning, been taken over by the government.

I welcome this development and I am happy to give a reassurance to members of my family that my money is perfectly safe.

Despite my sadness at leaving a bank that I have done so much for over the years, I walk away with the knowledge that I have done everything in my power to safeguard my salary, bonus and pension scheme. Investors may take comfort in the knowledge that all my money is now safeguarded by government guarantee.

I wish the government the best of luck as I start my new career as a financial adviser to HM Treasury.

Lord Fred Gnomewin

Royal Bank of Gnome – "*Your money is safe in my safe*"

ALSO FOLLOWING Northern Rock into part-nationalisation were Bradford & Bingley, Lloyds, TSB, Halifax, Bank of Scotland – and anything else the government could think of that might halt the crisis.

Government Unveils Nationalisation

by Our City Reporter **Hugh Drop**

The Government today sought to ease panic in the City and calm the stock market as it unveiled a multi-million pound plan to nationalise the BBC's business editor, Robert Peston.

"We cannot stand by and do nothing as billions of pounds are wiped off stock prices every time Peston opens his mouth," said Alistair Darling's eyebrows. "Once we have taken control of Peston, he will be placed in a dark cupboard where his arms and legs will quickly be de-leveraged."

Some analysts, however, warned that the plan was too little, too late, and would do little to alleviate Robert Peston in the short-to-medium term.

ALL THE MEASURES to tackle the crisis – capital injections, liquidity provision, interest rate cuts, infrastructure investment and quantitative easing – essentially boiled down to throwing money at the problem in the hope it would go away.

That Alistair Darling explanation for the economic crisis in full

Overspending by consumers using borrowed money they could never afford to pay back.

That Alistair Darling solution for the economic crisis in full

Overspending by Government using borrowed money they could never afford to pay back.

IN A LAST-DITCH reshuffle, Gordon Brown appointed his old enemy Peter Mandelson to the cabinet.

COMEDIAN RUSSELL BRAND left the BBC and Jonathan Ross was suspended following a furore over obscene messages they left on actor Andrew Sachs's answerphone during a Radio 2 show.

Me and My Spoon

This week – JONATHAN ROSS

Do you have a favourite spoon?

Yes. Look at this one. What does it remind you of? That's right. A bloke's knob. A great big pork sausage looking for some stuffing. Though it's not as big as…

(Unfortunately, due to a number of complaints from our readers, we have decided to suspend this column for three months. However we must stress that we reserve our right as a public service magazine to publish cutting-edge spoon interviews that push back the boundaries of acceptable cutlery feature pieces – The Board of Private Eye Trustees, 2008).

HIGH-STREET CHAIN Woolworths went into administration after a century of trading.

Late Woolworths News

Loyal shoplifters were last night bemoaning the disappearance of Woolworths from our high streets, as negotiations over the sale of its shops continue.

"I remember coming here as a lad when my mother was shoplifting something special for me for Christmas," said one distraught man, as he emptied the entire contents of the pick-and-mix and a Black & Decker drill into his over-sized jacket. "And now I'm one of the most regular shoplifters this store has. To think that my grandchildren won't be able to shoplift here brings a tear to my eye."

BARACK OBAMA was elected US president.

BUT THE ENTIRE GLOBAL financial system continued to teeter on the brink of collapse.

IN MARCH, SLICKER provided a few extra details of the Northern Rock rescue deal.

Taxpayers already overjoyed at the £55bn handout they are providing to Northern Wreck depositors and lenders will be even happier to know that they are now the proud owners of a bank in an offshore tax haven whose deposits from non-UK taxpayers they are also guaranteeing.

The building society that thought it was a bank has for more than a decade owned an untrumpeted banking subsidiary in Guernsey. Northern Rock (Guernsey) has been in business since 1996 and at the end of 2006 boasted deposits of £2.1bn. Like many of the 47 "banks" on the island, it is little more than a processing centre for mainly online and postal deposit business, which is passed onto its parent company. The nationalisation of its parent means that the Guernsey bank is now effectively run by the Treasury. So HMG is now in the offshore business, which, through Revenue and Customs, it is constantly trying to restrict if not close down.

Prior to Northern Rock imploding, the £2bn deposited in NRG was not covered by the Financial Compensation Scheme. But all deposits were covered by the Treasury's 100 percent guarantee last September. So the UK taxpayer is in effect guaranteeing the deposits of non-UK taxpayers and possibly even tax evaders. Another triumph for Brown and Darling.

THE EYE UNCOVERED in April more details of the cash being raked in, courtesy of the world's poorest countries, by the privately-owned arm of Britain's overseas development fund.

Bosses cream it in by managing the move out of low-yielding but helpful investment in third-world agriculture into the more lucrative businesses of mobile phones and shopping centres. But their million-pound-a-year pay packets are only the start of the bonanza. While Actis's accounts declare huge profits from hefty management and incentive fees, even more cash is being salted away through secret outfits kept studiously off Actis's books.

These are Scottish limited partnerships, registered in Edinburgh and owned by the Actis bosses, into which their shares of profits on sales of investments are channelled. Yet when the Actis sell-off was agreed by parliament in 2004, no mention was made of these secretive entities, which aren't required to publish accounts. But they have coined it in, perhaps to the tune of more than £30 million.

In 2010, international development secretary Andrew Mitchell announced that the fund would be drastically reconfigured to make it "more developmentally than financially focused" again. Actis itself was disposed off – with managers allowed to buy the remaining 40 percent of the company, with the government charging them £8 million this time, as opposed to the £373,000 the rest had gone for.

BORIS JOHNSON WAS ELECTED as London's mayor in May. Rotten Boroughs provided some details of the people who would actually be doing the work for him.

After eight years of being secretly run by the secretive Trots of Socialist Action, post-Livingstone London has fallen under the control of an even more sinister sect: the Tories of Westminster city council, who revere the memory of their disgraced ex-leader, Dame Shirley Porter.

Boris Johnson has effectively handed over City Hall to the control of three senior Westminister Tory councillors. Nicholas Boles becomes his interim chief-of-staff. Kit Malthouse, notorious for leading Westminster's negotiations with Dame Shirley which resulted in her paying just £12.3m of the nearly £49m she owed taxpayers for her gerrymandering corruption, is a deputy mayor, and Sir Simon Milton is to become Boris's lead adviser on planning and housing.

Milton was a member of Porter's housing committee

that voted in February 1989 to house homeless people in asbestos-ridden tower blocks – an act described by Westminster's former chief executive Rodney Brooke as "simply criminal". Who better to help Boris increase and improve London's stock of social housing?

Meanwhile Westminster's chief executive, Peter Rogers, the man who distinguished himself by his sloth-like "pursuit" of Shirley's millions, sending an urgent letter to Porter in Israel with a 2nd class 19p stamp so it took 68 days to reach her, becomes interim boss of the London Development Agency.

IN JUNE, THE EYE stepped in to right the *Guardian*'s wrong.

Days after the *Guardian* admitted libelling Tesco by falsely claiming that it had avoided corporation tax through a complex web of offshore operations, and agreed to pay compensation, *Private Eye* has discovered that Tesco has indeed been avoiding corporation tax through, er, another complex web of offshore operations.

The scheme unearthed by the *Eye* centres on an outfit called Cheshunt Overseas Limited Liability Partnership, whose partners are a Hungarian company called Tesco Global Stores Ltd, Irish firm Tesco Ireland Ltd and another outfit called Cheshunt Hungary Servicing LLC. The set-up is completed by a branch of Cheshunt Overseas LLP (named after the location of Tesco's HQ) in the Swiss alpine tax haven of Zug, through which the firm lends money to other companies in the Tesco group. The interest on these loans racks up very nicely in Zug, where it is taxed at just 6 percent, as against the standard UK rate of 30 percent.

Dumping millions in tax haven companies is a widespread old trick that the Revenue has been onto for 25 years since chancellor Nigel Lawson first introduced legislation to claw back the lost tax. As loopholes in these rules have been exploited then blocked, the determined tax avoider has needed ever more convoluted set-ups.

Tesco even alleged "malicious falsehood" against the *Guardian* and its editor, while all along it knew it was knee-deep in… avoiding corporation tax!

STREET OF SHAME continued to chronicle the march of an unwritten privacy law in September.

HOW PRIVACY WORKS

May 2007: Legal firm Schillings writes to editors warning them that to reveal the location of a house purchased by the footballer Steven Gerrard and his partner Alex would breach their right to privacy under the human rights act.

September 2008: OK! magazine features "WORLD EXCLUSIVE: Alex and Steven Gerrard exclusively invite OK! to their secret Portuguese mansion".

MEANWHILE, the *Eye* delivered some unexpected legal news about the BBC's top political presenter.

Eleven years ago, as editor of the *Independent*, Andrew Marr entered the debate about privacy law. "There is an argument about whether to allow judge-made law to accumulate or to have a clean, honest, open debate in parliament," he said. "I'm enough of a traditionalist to believe that is what should happen rather than allow it to be settled by judges."

But the judges carried on regardless. Over the past decade they have developed an increasingly restrictive law of privacy by using human rights legislation to suppress stories that were previously publishable, since there was no question of libel. What isn't such common knowledge is that the courts are also willing to stop newspapers from even reporting the fact that a privacy injunction has been obtained. And who has sought to invoke this gag on the press? Step forward Andrew Marr, the great traditionalist, who obtained an injunction earlier this year not only to stop publication of "private" information about him but also to prevent any reporting of the fact that he had been to court at all.

Lord Gnome's lawyers asked Marr's lawyers what the court had been told and on what grounds the order had been made, as well as requesting a copy of the order itself. Basic requirements of justice, one might think. Marr's lawyers adopted a thoroughly obstructive attitude. It was only when the *Eye* threatened an application to court that they belatedly provided the information and the order.

In 2011, amid growing public unease (and gossip) about "super-injunctions", Marr abandoned his one and admitted "I did not come into journalism to go around gagging journalists... the situation seems to be running out of control."

AS THE GLOBAL financial crisis exploded in September, the *Eye* noted how the government was having to seize upon whatever legislation was available to prevent disaster for British investors...

NUMBER CRUNCHING

£7bn Icelandic bank funds frozen under UK anti-terrorist asset-freezing orders

£0.0005bn Terrorist funds frozen under UK anti-terrorist asset-freezing orders

...AND HOW GORDON BROWN had suddenly taken against "off-balance sheet finance" of the type practised by the overstretched banks – despite his own long-standing habit of concealing government debt.

Much of the current financial crisis, claims Gordon Brown, can be put down to off balance sheet finance: the "securitisation" or packaging up of debts followed by their sale to "special purpose vehicles" that appear on nobody's balance sheet.

Strange then that this July, the Sale of Student Loans Act became law. The whole purpose of the £6.3bn sell-off is to get student loans off the government's books and put some cash into the government's coffers. But as the banks who will take over the loans will have to pay more for their funds than the government, and the government will have to make up the difference, this option will end up costing the taxpayer even more than the conventional on-balance sheet arrangement.

The allure of such finance has produced no more bizarre policy than the scheme to privatise defence training. Because it involved raising around £1bn for buildings (a fraction of the total £12bn value), it had to be done through PFI which means the training itself will be provided by private companies.

The only reason PFI was needed was to keep the debt off the books so as not to breach the government's self-imposed and arbitrary borrowing limit of 40 percent of gross domestic product, which is now set to be scrapped anyway.

2009

ISRAEL MARKED the start of an election year by invading Gaza.

'New Year fireworks big success' say organisers

Dateline: 31st December

This year's spectacular display of pyrotechnics which welcomed in the New Year over Gaza was "the best yet", said organisers.

Thousands came out of their houses in order to run away from the multi-million pound extravaganza put on for the benefit of Israeli voters. As phosphorous smoke lit up the sky, there was general agreement that this year's display was the best since last year's, and the one before that, and the one before that.

"It is something the Israelis do awfully well," said one bystander. "Just look! Ooh! Aargh!

BOSSES OF THE COLLAPSED banks appeared before a parliamentary committee investigating the crash. **The Supreme Leader welcomed their humiliation.**

Comrades across the nation will have gazed in horror and disgust at the sight of the hated "Gang of Four" bankers, publicly confessing their errors in front of a tribunal of People's Representatives.

One by one, these maggot-parasites who had been gorging themselves on the rotting flesh of the capitalist system, abased themselves before the tribunal, as with trembling voices they admitted they had done nothing wrong.

Just listen to their recitals of their crimes against the People:

Comrade Lord Shred of Wheat, ex-Chairman of ROBS: I wish to say how profoundly I regret my many errors which resulted in the loss of a great deal of money, not least for myself when my bonus disappeared and I got the boot.

Comrade Andy Pandy, HLOSS: I profoundly regret having to appear before this Committee and I am deeply sorry that I have been put to all the trouble of coming here today to answer these impertinent questions.

THE G20 SUMMIT in London discussed the ongoing financial crisis.

G20 – Brown promises new stable door

The Prime Minister last night pledged that all world leaders would sign up to his plan to mend the stable door.

Said the Prime Minister, "We cannot ignore the fact that the horse may already have done a certain amount of bolting, but future generations will not forgive us if we do not institute the necessary measures to instigate a new door-security regime process.

"Plans are already advanced," he said, "to install a new-look door with all the latest safeguards to prevent it ever opening again.

"State-of-the-art hinges are to be put in place with an international fail-safe locking mechanism, which all the countries in the world have already agreed to."

When asked if he had any idea where the horse was or how they could get it back into the stable, Mr Brown was unavailable for comment.

THE DECADE'S ULTIMATE celebrity, diagnosed with inoperable cancer, underwent another reputational U-turn.

Ms Jade Goody – Yet Another Apology

In recent years, headlines such as "Drop Dead, You Ugly, Fat, Racist Pig!" may have led our readers to believe we took a negative view of Ms Goody's character.

Now that she is about to drop dead, we would like to put it on record that we have always regarded Ms Goody as a courageous young woman and a warm-hearted iconic role model for the nation's youth.

This is reflected in our moving 94-page supplement dedicated to her recent engagement, "Till Death Us Do Part – Brave Jade says 'I Do' With Last Breath."

A POLICE OFFICER, overseeing protests at the summit, hit and pushed a passer-by, Ian Tomlinson, causing his death.

Knacker's shock claim

By Our Crime Team **Troilus and Cressida Dick**

Chief Inspector "Knacker of the Yard" Knacker last night lashed out at critics of the police, who had suggested that officers had somehow gone "over the top" in their treatment of the late newspaper seller Mr Juan Carlos de Tomlinson.

"Obviously it's a tragic shame that Mr Tomlinson died shortly after being assaulted by one of my team, Officer Z," said the inspector, "but we were in a highly dangerous riot situation. We have examined the CCTV footage very carefully, and even though there is no sound, highly-trained Scotland Yard lipreaders have confirmed that shortly before Mr de Tomlinson's unfortunate demise, Officer Z shouted 'Stop! Proceed no further! I am an armed police officer, using my powers under the Prevention of Terrorism and Anything We Don't Approve Of Act 2006 to assist you in falling to the ground'."

AS A NEW PANDEMIC threatened to arrive in Britain, the full, obscene details of what MPs had been claiming for on expenses were revealed.

THE JUSTIFICATIONS offered were gobsmacking.

Those expense claim rules in full

1. All claims made by MPs are within the rules
2. All rules are made by MPs
3. Er…
4. That's it.

THE PRIME MINISTER took to YouTube to issue a bizarre apology video, in the same month that *Britain's Got Talent* discovered an unlikely global superstar in Susan Boyle.

Frumpy Scot amazes world

It just shows how deceptive appearances can be. From the moment the dumpy, wild-haired Caledonian stomped onto the stage, the critics and audience were preparing to snigger and to jeer. But what followed was little short of stunning.

The wannabe with the weird smile and the appalling dress sense suddenly opened his mouth and out came a sound that no one had expected.

It was the word "Sorry".

"It was unbelievable," said one member of the audience, fighting back the tears. "You couldn't believe a word he was saying."

Gordon is now hotly tipped to go all the way and lose the competition in spectacular fashion.

DIGNITAS SET UP a clinic in Switzerland, helping those with terminal conditions to end their lives.

DOZENS MORE MPS were forced to step down after it was revealed they had claimed for items including moat-cleaning, orchards-full of trees and an ornamental duck house, as well as dishonestly "flipping" their second-home designation to max out expense claims. Five MPs and two members of the House of Lords eventually went to prison for false accounting.

PARLIAMENT'S SHAME

Shame we got caught!

INSIDE: Apology for a Prime Minister

WILLIAM REES-McGONAGALL chronicled the resignation of the Commons Speaker, Michael Martin.

When the press began to rake the muck
He called in, at our expense, Messrs Carter-Fuck.
But the Speaker had misjudged the mood of the nation
Which was one of furious indignation.

The entire country was now united in anger
All the way from Lowestoft to Bangor.
Still this Caledonian clown clung onto his job,
For it was worth to him more than a few wee bob.

Plus a luxury apartment – not to mention
An enormous gold-plated and index-linked pension.
"I will nae gang awa," he told the MPs
As they put down motions saying "Will you resign, please?"

But finally there was a knock at the door and there stood a
                                                    man with a frown,
This late-night caller was none other than the
                                        Rt Honourable Gordon Brown.
"The game us up, my fine Scottish friend.
For you, Gorbals Mick, this is the end."

CABINET MINISTER Hazel Blears' career also bit the dust.

Me and My Spoon *Hazel Blears*

Could I begin by asking you whether you have more than one set of spoons?

Well yes, as a matter of fact I do. But I must make it clear that these spoons here are my principal spoons. My other set of spoons are in my constituency home. I need to keep them there because I spend a lot of time there.

So you have two sets of spoons?

No, you mustn't misquote me. I have three sets of spoons altogether. One is my principal set of spoons, as I have already explained. Then there are my second spoons, which are vital for my constituency. Then there are my third collection of spoons which last year I designated, for allowance purposes, as my main set, so that I could quite legitimately claim on my second set under the 'Second Spoon Allowances' rule.

Surely this is dishonest?

Not at all: It's very clearly laid down in the Spoon Book, rule 61 (b) Cutlery Allowances. Everything I have done is perfectly within the rules.

But haven't you sold off some of these spoons at quite a handsome profit without paying any capital gains tax?
(Long pause)

Oh yes, so I have. I'd better pay that money back before the Prime Minister sacks me.
(Mobile phone rings)

Oh dear, it looks as if he has.

SEVERAL OF GORDON BROWN'S ministers resigned in an attempt to oust him. In a desperate attempt to remind voters that there had been other prime ministers they hated too, Brown announced an official inquiry into Britain's role in the Iraq War – but said it would have to be held in secret.

From the ███* of the Supreme Leader

I appreciate that citizens rightly wish to see the former leader arraigned and publicly humiliated for his Bushite-Rumsfeldist-Cheneyist-Adventurism, but on reflection I have decided that this open forum might allow the wily ex-Comrade Blair to falsely implicate some of his former colleagues and suggest quite improperly and contrary to all the facts that he was not the only one who supported the war and is not the only one who deserves to be purged and punished.

Therefore, I must regretfully conduct the show trial in private, myself.

GB, The Supreme Leader.
"Transparent About Secrecy"

JOANNA LUMLEY'S slightly unlikely role heading a campaign on behalf of veteran Gurkha soldiers won them the right to settle in Britain.

LIVES OF THE SAINTS AND MARTYRS No.94

St Joanna of Lumley

And there was living in those times a beautiful, high-born lady named Joanna of Lumley. With her radiant smile and angelic voice, she enchanted all who saw her. One day she

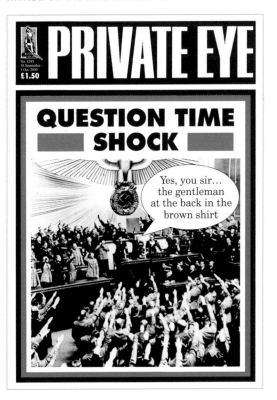

came across a humble gurkha sitting by the roadside, cutting nettles with his kukri knife to make nettle soup. For he was so poor that this was his only form of sustenance.

The kindly Joanna knelt down beside him and said, "You poor little gurkha. How came you to this sorry pass?"

And the gallant little warrior replied in his own language, "After all I have done for Britain, they are sending me back to Gurkaland where I shall surely die, for there are no nettles there for me to make my soup."

Hearing this sorry tale, the saintly Joanna at once determined to lead a great pilgrimage to Westminster, there to upbraid the wicked rulers of the land for their heartless crime.

And when she appeared, the mere sight of her melted the hearts of all who gazed at her, except one, the evil first minister, Gordon Brown.

And the cruel ogre told the poor gurkha, "I give not a fig for your sufferings – you must go back to the land where no nettles grow."

And when the people heard this, they cried out aloud that Gordon was a ruthless tyrant who must resign at once, to be replaced as first minister by the beautiful Saint Joanna.

THE SECOND EVER elections held in Afghanistan resulted in widespread and blatant fraud, and a victory for incumbent Hamid Karzai...

Afghan Election Latest – Mugabe Wins

In a surprise second ballot the Afghan elections were won by President Robert Mugabe, who secured 99% of the vote. A delighted Mr Mugabe said, "The opposition parties led by Silvio Berlusconi only got 98% of the vote, thus proving the power of the ballot box – especially when you steal it and hit people over the head with it."

A dejected Mr Hamid Karzai, who only secured a desultory 94% of the vote, said he was disappointed about

the election result, but surprised and delighted to have won *Strictly Come Dancing* instead. "It's been a remarkable journey," he said, "and I am living the dream."

...AND FOREIGN SECRETARY David Miliband encouraged the new government to hold police talks with the "moderate Taliban".

The Miliband Guide to spotting a moderate Taliban

1. Only wears small beard
2. Only carries small bomb
3. Only met Osama bin Laden once
4. Wives have to follow three paces behind him not four
5. Reads *Guardian* and votes Lib Dem
6. Likes occasional G&T with his pork scratchings
7. Has never committed suicide

MICHAEL JACKSON DIED at the age of 50. Gushing tributes were paid across the world's media.

What you read in all newspapers

My Friend Michael

What you didn't read in all newspapers

Mad Paedophile Dead

AFTER THE British National Party's surprisingly good showing in the Euro-elections, BNP leader Nick Griffin was invited on the BBC's *Question Time*.

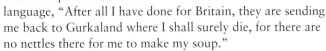

SENATOR TED KENNEDY died, four decades after his politician brothers (and Mary Jo Kopechne, who had accepted a lift from him).

Those Kennedy funeral arrangements in full

1pm Hearse carrying Edward Kennedy's body leaves the church to begin the three mile drive to the cemetery

1.13pm Hearse inexplicably speeds up in heavy fog as it approaches rickety bridge

1.14pm Hearse careers off the bridge and crashes into the icy water of the lake below

1.19pm Hearse driver panics and runs off

Nine Hours Later Hearse driver turns up in Connecticut and Edward Kennedy's coffin is finally reported missing

FOLLOWING RUMOURS about the prime minister's mental wellbeing, BBC interviewer Andrew Marr asked Brown directly if he was using "prescription painkillers and pills". The *Eye*'s top shrink gave him a clean bill of health.

MANIC OUTBURSTS: We could find no evidence of any hypomanic disorder, apart from a very minor incident when he threw a heavy stapler at Mr Darling, shouting, "You bastard!" It is fair to say that Mr Brown himself has no recollection of this incident, the evidence for which is based solely on the large number of staples embedded in Mr Darling's forehead.

PARANOIA: Any suggestion that Mr Brown has been displaying the classic symptoms of paranoia is entirely baseless. His repeated assertions that "everyone" hates and despises him, and that his colleagues are all plotting to remove him from power are, in our opinion, based on 100 percent solid evidence.

MEDICATION: We found no evidence that the Prime Minister is in any way reliant on pharmaceutical aid, apart from taking a number of nutritional stimulants designed to assist his concentration, viz. Anti-bonkazapam (5 milligrams), Equine tranquilisers (5 milibands) and Hallucigon (double dosage at half-hourly intervals).

Signed

Dr Lord Mandelson, Hon Professor of Psychiatric Medicine at the Alastair Campbell Research Institute, the University of Tourettes, Burnley.

OUTRAGE ERUPTED over *Daily Mail* columnist Jan Moir's take on the death of Boyzone singer Stephen Gately.

World uproar forces Slagg to apologise

An article by *Eye* columnist Glenda Slagg on the subject of Seamus Gayfeller, a late member of the popular Dublin-based singing group Bogzone, has drawn over two million complaints to the Press Complaints Commission, the Race Relations Board and the UN Security Council.

A campaign on the social networking site Twitter called for Ms Slagg to be tried for war crimes and the death penalty to be restored in this particular case.

GLENDA'S CONTROVERSIAL COLUMN LAST WEEK:

Seamus Gayfeller!?!! Who did he think he was, a-mincin' and a-wincin', a-preenin' and a-queenin' with his boyfriend (sorry, Mr PC, "civil partner"). No wonder the gay brigade all end up dead when they behave like Shameless (geddit?).

BRITISH BARONESS Cathy Ashton was made European high representative for foreign and security policy, serving alongside the new president of the European Council, a Belgian no one had heard of either.

THE NEW FACE OF EUROPE

THE DECADE ENDED in dismal style, with the UN Climate Change Conference in Copenhagen failing to agree to do very much.

IN JANUARY, one man was continuing to do his best to make England the libel capital of the world.

Even in the bleak midwinter, one part of the tourism industry flourishes. Thanks to the efforts of Mr Justice Eady, foreign litigants still find London an irresistible destination. And that is where Greek citizen Alexis Mardas is suing an American newspaper and a Paris-based website.

A high court master found that there were 27 hits for the offending article in the *International Herald Tribune* site and four on the *New York Times* one (although some of those may have been from Scotland or Northern Ireland, which aren't in the jurisdiction). About 170 hard copies of the *NYT* also reached the country, though it's not known if any of the buyers actually read the piece. The master decided last year that this was not sufficient publication in England and Wales to justify the time and expense of a trial – but Eady has now overruled him.

Three years ago the publisher of the *Wall Street Journal* succeeded in having a London libel action struck out as an abuse of process, since the offending online article only had five hits – three of them from the claimant's lawyers. But Eady denies that this case "can be characterised as a case of forum shopping", even though Mardas is not suing in either of the more obvious forums, the US or France.

On the very day of the ruling in this latest case, by happy coincidence, parliament held a debate on the libel laws. MPs from all parties denounced the English legal profession for silencing foreign authors and journalists. They were particularly concerned by Eady's decision to order the destruction of the American author Rachel Ehrenfeld's book on terrorism at the behest of a Saudi banker, and by the ability of convicted fraudster Nadhmi Auchi and his lawyers Carter-Fuck to scrub the web of critical reports and ensure that *Private Eye* is the only publication willing to point out that he is a convicted fraudster.

The right to sue foreign individuals or companies in the English courts was finally curtailed by the 2013 Defamation Act. Eady, who also presided over a number of "super-injunction" cases, retired the same year.

THE EYE WAS FIRST to point out an inconvenient truth about the man who had been put in charge of the newly nationalised banks in January.

Looking after the public interest as a new non-executive director of UK Financial Investments, the new Treasury company set up to run the taxpayer's stakes in high street banks RBS, Lloyds, TSB/HBOS, Northern Rock and Bradford & Bingley, will be one Glen Moreno, the £450,000-a-year chairman of *Financial Times* owner Pearson plc. Leaving aside whether the proprietor of Britain's leading financial paper should take a job with the government body his organ should be holding to account, there's his other interest in the country's finances: er, ripping them off. Moreno also happens to be a trustee of both Prince Alois of Liechenstein and of the prince's Liechenstein Global Trust, a private banking empire which exists to promote tax-dodging using the alpine principality's notorious secrecy.

So serious is the threat this poses to the UK exchequer that last year HMRC took the unprecedented step of paying £100,000 to an insider for stolen details of British residents' LGT accounts.

Moreno stepped down the following month.

ROTTEN BOROUGHS REVEALED some financial fishiness in February.

Tory Essex council leader Lord Hanningfield, who is also Call Me Dave's shadow transport minister in the Upper House, appears to have a relaxed attitude towards expenses. In 2007-08 he claimed a splendid £17,120 from the Lords for "overnight subsistence" in London – even though he lives just over 35 miles away near Chelmsford, to which there is a perfectly adequate train service. But Lord H clearly is not a frequent user of the train, for he only claimed £1,095 last year under the heading "rail/ferry/coach", out of total expenses of £38,884.

He does, of course, have a chauffeur-driven car, provided by the council taxpayers of Essex. And his chauffeur is listed as having a House of Lords pass. But as it would not be legal for Lord H to use his county council car for Lords business, he must be getting to London some other way. Perhaps he hitch-hikes.

This particular scam was re-exposed in the *Telegraph*'s dossier of parliamentary expense abuses four months later, and in 2011 Lord Hanningfield received a nine month jail sentence for false accounting.

THE EYE EXCLUSIVELY uncovered the behaviour of a true patriot in March.

If an Englishman's home is his castle, a sprawling neo-Palladian pile in the rolling Wiltshire countryside might be expected to bring with it full British tax status for the lord of the manor. But not, it seems, when the Englishman in question is the chairman of the Daily Mail and General Trust, the 4th Viscount Rothermere, aka Jonathan Harmsworth.

His father Vere Harmsworth, the 3rd Viscount, lived as a tax exile in Paris for most of his life, becoming "non-domiciled" for tax purposes. And just like his hereditary title, this status passed – as a "domicile of origin" – to Jonathan when he was born.

The principal tax break for a "non-dom" is that overseas income is only taxable when "remitted" to Britain. And for Jonathan Harmsworth this has proved immensely valuable, as the hundreds of millions of pounds in DMGT dividends channelled over the years through Bermudan-registered Rothermere Continuation Ltd into a trust of which he and his family are beneficiaries have magically become overseas income.

But the archaic "non-dom" status has to be sustained by an overriding commitment to another country, demonstrated by such choices as the location of the family home, upbringing of children and the person's intended final resting place. As Harmsworth looks to have made a permanent family seat on the Wiltshire-Dorset borders, and he and his wife have become leading figures on the county scene, his non-dom status looks precarious to say the least.

Tax inspectors have been busy investigating Harmsworth's media empire after the group earned itself a place on HMRC's "high-risk corporates" list by undertaking a number of tax avoidance schemes. A full-scale inquiry was recently launched with a view to withdrawing Harmsworth's non-dom status, if necessary through the courts. But the investigation was blocked by HMRC deputy chairman Dave Hartnett, who pressured officials to find a "technical" reason for not pursing the investigation.

NEWS ARRIVED that would bring the Lockerbie saga to an end, if not a conclusion.

How convenient for the US and UK governments that Ali Mohmed al-Megrahi, the Libyan unreliably convicted for the Lockerbie bombing, has contracted terminal prostate cancer while in prison in Scotland.

Megrahi has always maintained he will never return to Libya until his name is cleared and the truth emerges about the blowing up of Pan Am 130 in December 1988. But Jack Straw, the justice secretary, has now stuck two fingers up at MPs and peers on the human rights select committee and refused their request to delay ratification of a deal which will allow the transfer of prisoners between the UK and Libya. Thus the treaty is to be sealed as Megrahi's lengthy appeal against his conviction for the bombing gets underway this week. How long it will be before his deteriorating health dictates that he return to Libya to die with his family is not known.

It was three months. Megrahi's appeal was dropped as a condition of his release, and the copious evidence of his innocence never heard.

AS THE MPS' EXPENSES scandal broke, the *Eye* filled in plenty of the details.

NUMBER CRUNCHING

£250 Winter fuel allowance for all pensioners, for which government is considering introducing means testing in order to save money

£25,000 Additional costs allowance for all MPs, which government is considering changing because they've been caught out

SLICKER POINTED OUT that the exceptional treatment extended well beyond Westminster.

Slipped quietly into the Income Tax (Earnings and Pensions) Act 2003 by one G. Brown were a number of exemptions for "special kinds of employee". MPs and government ministers got more exemptions than any other group – not just overnight expenses but also travel, transport, subsistence and even termination without extreme prejudice from their enviable existence. The effect has been to create for MPs whole rivers of exempt income denied to their constituents. MPs have their very own tax office – Public Department 1 in Cardiff – which deals with sensitive tax files. The word among tax accountants is that the inspectors there, like officials in the Commons' discredited Fees Office, know better than to raise too many questions.

MPs, like other celebrity clients of PD1, do not now have to submit their tax returns online in order to benefit from the 31 January deadline. Too insecure! They can submit their returns non-electronically in January, whereas other taxpayers must do so by October.

And when home secretary Jacqui Smith and other expense abusers dwell on the likelihood that next year they will pay the price at the ballot box for their bath plugs and pet food, they can be comforted by the fact that the first £30,000 of the golden goodbye they automatically receive on being ejected from the Westminster gravy train will be tax-free – even though it is a contractual benefit. This is 50-100 percent of their last salary, plus "winding-up" payments including bonuses to any family members they employ.

THE PEOPLE RESPONSIBLE for the changes to second-home rules that had made them so profitable were also revealed.

Tony Blair and accountants PricewaterhouseCoopers jointly helped push through a rule change in 2004 that brought the MPs' expense scandal to the heart of government. The Senior Salaries Review Board looked at MPs' pay using a survey of MPs prepared by PwC, and the firm was happy to support a point that *Private Eye* understands was pushed by the Prime Minister. Its report said: "There were comments made about the rules which require ministers and other paid office holders to elect their London residence as the main residence and the constituency as their second property. The rules mean that the Additional Costs Allowance is used against costs on a property which in many cases has been owned by the MP and his or her family for a significant number of years and where the mortgage is typically low."

The report makes it clear ministers complained that because they were deemed to live in London, they could not "flip" homes in order to claim higher expenses. The rule was dropped.

The former PM's support for the change was no random act of greed. He was actually trying to increase his ministers' income while publicly appearing to keep a lid on their headline pay.

He did so by following a model set in 1985 by Margaret Thatcher who, trying to hold back public sector pay and wanting MPs to appear to set a good example to teachers and the like, introduced the crucial change in the Additional Costs Allowance which allowed MPs to begin claiming their mortgage costs rather than simply hotel bills or rents.

THE EYE WON a significant privacy law victory in May.

Michael Napier, former head of the Law Society and now a government adviser responsible for regulating lawyers, spent £350,000 in court costs trying to stop *Private Eye* reporting the fact that he has been formally disciplined over a bitter conflict of interest case involving a whistleblower and the huge multinational, Exxon. Not only did Napier and his law firm Irwin Mitchell not want anyone to know that he, along with Ellen Windsor, at the time also a partner at the firm, had been formally reprimanded by the Law Society, they also wanted to stretch the law on confidentiality to keep secret the fact that he and the firm were the subject of a highly critical ombudsman's report into the Law Society's investigation into the affair.

Five months after the *Eye* first contacted Napier for his response, only to be slapped with a temporary high court injunction courtesy of Carter-Fuck, the court of appeal ruled unequivocally in favour of *Private Eye* and press freedom.

IN JULY, TWO YEARS after the *News of the World* phone-hacking scandal had been declared over, it was revealed that Rupert Murdoch's company had paid out a million pounds to football boss Gordon Taylor to prevent him suing.

In a dramatic performance before a Commons select committee last week, *Grauniad* hack Nick Davies produced several documents which appeared to reveal further skulduggery by Murdoch hacks and executives. But he omitted a file which showed a personal request for a private detective to trace someone's address via his phone number – a request that came from Rebekah Wade when she was editor of the *News of the Screws*.

The *Guardian* has also yet to reveal that the secret payment to buy the silence of Gordon Taylor was not a mere executive order. It was decided by the directors of News Group Newspapers, the subsidiary which owns the *Sun* and the *Screws*, at their board meeting on 10 June last year. If their involvement were revealed, it could cause grave embarrassment for the directors of News Group Newspapers Ltd – not least James Murdoch.

And it did – but not for a further two years.

A SINGLE EDITION in September carried two apparently unrelated news stories...

Last month, a certain institution obtained a high court injunction to prevent a certain newspaper from publishing a certain document. More than that we cannot say: to do so is fraught with danger.

Thanks to some aggressive solicitors and timorous judges, prior restraint is now a flourishing industry. If lawyers get a whiff that one of their clients is about to be embarrassed, late in the evening they contact a duty judge – often one who has no experience of libel or media law. And the judge, reached down a phone line while eating his dinner and half-watching *Coronation Street*, errs on the side of caution. The newspaper may not even be aware of this "hearing without notice", still less have a chance to argue its case.

But that isn't all. The new breed of super-injunction is far more oppressive than the traditional court order. It usually involves an order that "the publication of all information relating to these proceedings or of information describing them or the intended claim is expressly prohibited". Nobody can report that the order has been granted, or who applied for it. Even the identities of the judge and the newspaper remain secret, and anyone who even hints at them "may be held to be in contempt of court and may be imprisoned, fined or have their assets seized".

...and four pages later:

Full marks for resilience to Carter-Fuck partner Adam Tudor who acts for the oil trading company Trafigura.

He must have had a stressful couple of weeks, what with gruesome front-page stories about the toxic waste dumped in the Ivory Coast by one of Trafigura's sub-contractors, a thunderous *Guardian* editorial about Carter-Fuck's "disgraceful attempts" to intimidate hacks who dared question Trafigura's version of events, and then the settlement of a class-action lawsuit brought by 30,000 Ivorians against the company. Trafigura, without admitting liability, has agreed to pay them £30m.

The *Eye* sent Tudor two questions: "Knowing what you now know about Trafigura, are you still proud and happy to represent them? If so, is there anyone you wouldn't represent?"

Back came the reply, "Yes, there are plenty of people and organisations that my firm refuses to represent. Yes, we are very happy to represent Trafigura." Splendid!

In the following issue's HP Sauce section, the *Eye* printed the parliamentary question tabled by MP Paul Farrelly about "the injunction obtained in the High Court by... Trafigura and Carter-Ruck solicitors on 11 September 2009 on the publication of the Minton report on the alleged dumping of toxic waste in the Ivory Coast, commissioned by Trafigura". Two days later Carter-Fuck dropped their attempt to prevent the *Guardian* from reporting this parliamentary question. It also abandoned the super-injunction covering details of the report into the waste dump, which had led to over 100,000 people seeking hospital treatment and authorities recording 15 deaths as a possible result.

THE EYE EXPLORED why a fire in a London tower block had spread so dangerously.

The Lanakal House fire, which took the lives of six women and children in Camberwell in July should never have been so deadly. A specific set of errors and oversights, some 20 years in the making, aligned to bring about the tragedy.

The progress of the fire was unusual, spreading from a flat on the ninth floor where a faulty TV had caught fire, to the 11th floor, where smoke and flames killed Catherine Hickman in Flat 79. Later the bodies of Dayana Francisquini, her children Thais and Felipe, Helen Udoaka and her baby Michelle were found huddled on the bathroom floor of Flat 81 next door. They had been asphyxiated by smoke. The fire also spread to the fifth and seventh floors.

The London Fire Brigade's initial advice to residents was to stay in their flats. This may have sealed the fate of the families sheltering in Flat 81.

The brigade might reasonably have assumed that, in accordance with fire safety regulations, each flat in the block represented a "one hour fire compartment" which would isolate a fire. It is now clear Lakanal House enjoyed no such protection.

Nine years ago Southwark Council's own building design service identified Lanakal House and 12 other buildings in the borough as being at "medium" fire spread risk. In particular, it was noted, "there is a risk of localised fire spread between wall panelled sections." Yet it appears that subsequent renovations did not address this.

Eight years later, a fire in Grenfell Tower in North Kensington rapidly spread because of the panelling used on the building's exterior and failures to address safety concerns during renovations; residents were advised by the fire brigade to stay in their flats and 72 of them were killed. Hundreds of other tower blocks across the country were subsequently discovered to have similar dangerous cladding.

2010-2021

THIS WAS THE PERIOD WHEN THE *EYE* QUITE OFTEN seemed to be setting the national agenda. The magazine's long-term reporting on phone-hacking in Rupert Murdoch's empire was cited in evidence at the Leveson Inquiry after the story finally exploded in 2011. Lord Justice L himself was kind enough to highlight the magazine's *Street of Shame* pages as "a very powerful example of the proper manifestation of free speech" in his final report (he still recommended hammering the *Eye* with punitive court costs until it was forced to join a press regulator, though). Revelations about sweetheart tax deals were enthusiastically followed up by both the Commons Public Accounts Committee and protesters who occupied Vodafone stores across the country, and the issues of "non-doms" and off-shore financial arrangements became major political issues in the 2015 and 2017 elections. PFI, the buy-now-pay-much-more-later chicanery that the *Eye* had been banging on about since the early 1990s, was finally recognised in the Treasury as the confidence trick it always had been. Still, though, successive Conservative-led governments continued to believe against all the evidence that the private sector did things better: just two of the instances flagged up early by the *Eye* were the privatisation of probation services, and the outsourcing of emergency coronavirus services at the end of the decade.

The joke-writing team on the *Eye* saw its most comprehensive evolutionary jump since the primordial soup of the sixties: Tom Jamieson and Nev Fountain had already clambered ashore, Andrew Hunter Murray soon followed, and between Richard Ingrams and Barry Fantoni's retirement in 2012 and Christopher Booker's death in 2019 the central team of Ian Hislop and Nick Newman were joined by Giles Pilbrow and Colin Swash. They had no shortage of topics to joke about: the years 2014-2021 have been easily the most feverish in political memory, with a referendum on Scottish independence closely followed by the election of the man least likely to ever become Labour leader, the frenzied run-up to the Brexit referendum, the resignation of almost everyone, three general elections which crushed in turn the smug expectations of Nick Clegg's Lib Dems, Theresa May's Conservatives and Jeremy Corbyn's Labour, and parliament repeatedly imploding over exactly how, and potentially whether, to leave the EU. And that was before you even got on to President Trump and the global pandemic.

> **All the initial intelligence came not from HMRC officials or the National Audit Office, but from my regular reading of Private Eye... Should we really rely on Private Eye to do due diligence on individuals who are given public appointments?**
>
> Margaret Hodge MP, 2016

The *Eye* managed to wring some laughs from all this despite the general sense of humour failure that accompanied the increasing tribalism: this was the decade when the magazine's letters page was assailed by Scots Nats, Ukippers, Corbynites and various other true believers, all surprisingly surprised to find their favoured politicians the subject of satire in a satirical magazine. Others, however, were more enthusiastic: in the year of the Brexit referendum and Trump's election the magazine recorded its highest sales figure *ever* in its history, 250,204.

2010

INTERNET GIANT Google was condemned for its tax avoidance.

Web Images Videos Maps News Shopping Mail more ▼

Google | UK tax paid | | Search |

Search: ⦿ the web ○ pages from the UK

Web ⊞ Show options...

Your search -   - did not match any documents.
Suggestions:

TONY BLAIR APPEARED before the Chilcot Inquiry into the Iraq war.

Light Brigade Inquiry – Lord Cardigan: 'It was a terrific success'

Lord Cardigan made a spirited defence of his controversial decision to charge into the Valley of Death, which resulted in hundreds of British casualties. "We had reliable intelligence that the Russian guns were where we thought. The fact they weren't makes no difference to my decision to charge," he told the inquiry.

"It wasn't a blunder, as some irresponsible people, including the Poet Laureate, seem to think. It was the right thing to do and I would do it again to bring about an end to the Light Brigade (*Surely "Crimean War"? Ed.*)

GORDON BROWN FINALLY called the election, with his party pulling together to pretend they were right behind him.

Comrades,

The hour is upon us! The phoney war is over as we move forward to the battle. E-Day, May 6th, when the forces of Neo-Cameronite Reaction and Bullingdonian-Borisite-Feudalism will finally be put to flight and swept into the dustbin of history!

A Message from
Comrade Lord Mandelson

In my capacity as Supreme Commissar for Trade and Everything Else, I urge all Comrades to rally to the support of the Party in the forthcoming plebiscite. Whatever our feelings may be about the desirability of Comrade

Brown continuing as Supreme Leader, it is vital that we all vote for him. No one has worked so hard for so long in the service of this great country. It is not to be wondered at that he looks so knackered and washed-up.

AS LIB DEM LEADER Nick Clegg impressed in the first ever televised election debates, "Cleggmania" briefly swept the country – and despite actually winning five *fewer* seats than in 2005, his party ended up holding the balance of power in a hung parliament.

THE GREEK ECONOMY was collapsing.

Old Jokes Revisited

What's a Grecian urn?

Considerably less than before he joined the Euro

AS THE NEW REGIME took over, there was bad news from the new headmaster (and his deputy).

The New Coalition Academy (formerly Brown's Comprehensive)

Headmaster: David Cameron MA (Oxon)
Deputy Headmaster: Nicholas Clegg MA (Cantab)

A Message from the Headmaster

I can't help these days looking back at my own old headmaster – who, before he gave you six of the best, would always say, "This is going to hurt me more than it hurts you!"

And we all thought "What tosh!" But now that I'm headmaster, I realise that he was telling the truth.

The fact is that the news I've got to give you all today is going to be very painful for all of us – for parents, pupils and staff, but for no one more than me. And, of course, Nick.

When we took over the school we knew the accounts were in a mess. But we had no idea just how bad they were. The brutal truth is that this school has been running on a huge overdraft – no less than £152 billion to be precise.

The fault for this lies fairly and squarely on the last headmaster, Mr Brown, and his team. For years they pursued every kind of reckless development scheme. Giant new Science blocks. A new state-of-the-art Sanatorium. An Olympic-size sports stadium. A new iPad for every pupil.

But now the chickens have come well and truly home to roost. And that's why in the past few days Mr Osborne, our new Bursar, has been spelling out the detail of where the cutbacks are going to have to be made.

And I make no bones about it – these cuts are going to hurt. But I have enough faith in you all to know that you will be only too happy to make these sacrifices for the good of the school.

As I should have said to my old headmaster all those years ago, "Thank you very much, sir. I do appreciate what you have done."

Mr Clegg writes:

I would like to echo everything David has said. Mr Cable, our head of Business Studies, has been over all Mr Osborne's figures with his slide rule, and we could see they were far, far worse than anyone had imagined. So I'm backing David to the hilt.

Yours in it together,
David & Nick

DAVID CAMERON seemed to believe that a "Big Society" would step in to fill the gaps.

Public given freedom to do things nobody wants to do

There was widespread joy throughout Britain today as the Government delivered on its promise to give people the freedom to do for themselves all the things that none of them want to do.

"Labour's nanny state is dead: we can now police our own streets, teach our children ourselves in schools we set up and run ourselves, and from next year, we'll even be able to choose to perform our own operations on ourselves at home," said one Bradford man. "Only the Tories would give us this sort of freedom!"

A TAXI DRIVER ARMED with a shotgun and a rifle went on a rampage through several Cumbrian towns, killing 12 people, and weeks later a huge manhunt was launched in Northumbria for a gunman with a grudge against the police.

EXCLUSIVE TO ALL PAPERS

Why did this seemingly normal, well-liked family man go on a rampage of death?

We don't know.

ON OTHER PAGES: "What drove me to write this piece": Top criminologist Dr Phil Boots asks what made him fire off 5,000 words. Was it financial worries, or a warped desire to be famous?

THERE WAS a huge public outcry about a woman who put a cat in a bin, and less of one about the return to 'business as usual' following the financial crisis.

BROTHERS ED AND DAVID MILIBAND went up against each other for the Labour leadership, with Ed the eventual unexpected winner. Craig Brown transcribed the launch of their campaigns.

ED: As regards the Labour leadership election, I think I speak for both of us when I say that – contrary to press speculation!! – there is absolutely no element of sibling ri...

DAVID: ...valry, no – none at all! But, with respect, I'd go further than those who are prepared to simply sit back and say that there is no element of sibling rivalry. As a party, we've simply got to get out of our comfort zone of talking about this brother or that brother and what each of us may or may not think about the other. We desperately need to focus on the larger...

ED: ...issues that are facing us all. After all, this isn't just about us, or even just about the party as a whole. No, it's about the kind of country we want to live in, the kind of future we want to see for our children.

DAVID: And for our children's children. Let's not forget our children's children. And their children too.

ED: But in concentrating on the very real need for a vision of the future, it's essential that we as a party must continue to learn the lessons of the past...

DAVID: ...but let's never forget that we live in the present. There's a real danger that some of my colleagues are, perhaps a trifle naively, concentrating on the future and the present to the exclusion of the past. But as for sibling rivalry, I think we're both agreed that there's no place for it in this election.

ED: Yes, David agrees with me on that. And I'm delighted he's finally come round to my way of thinking.

DAVID: Why don't you just fuck off?

ED: No, you fuck off.

DAVID: I said it first!

THE SECOND-IN-LINE to the throne announced his engagement.

Six things you didn't know about Wills and Kate

1. Wills's first words to Kate when he met her at St Andrews University were "Hi, ya, is this chair, like, you know, taken or anything?"
2. Wills first told his grandmother, the Queen, that he wanted to marry Kate at the Braemar Games in 1985, when he was just three.
3. Four men had already proposed to Kate before she accepted Wills – Robbie Williams, Stephen Fry, Wayne Rooney and Oliver Letwin.
4. On a trip to Kenya, practical joke-loving Prince Harry fooled the Royal couple by dressing up as Robert Mugabe and arresting them at gunpoint.
5. Damien Hirst has been commissioned to create the first official portrait of the couple, touchingly showing them cut in two and swimming in a tank of formaldehyde.
6. When Wills told his grandmother that he was engaged to Kate, the Queen's touching response was to ask him "Have you come far?"

AS AUSTERITY BEGAN to bite, the nation found comfort in a cosy Sunday night TV drama.

Downturn Abbey

Agreeable, patrician aristocrat Lord Cameron has welcomed the gauche middle-class Nicholas Clegg into the family, to the horror of Dowager Dame Maggie who fears that Clegg will take over the estate, disinherit the rightful heiress, Lady George, and ruin everything with his silly ideas about improved housing and free education for the workers.

There is trouble downstairs too, as the resentful footman, Hughes, plots and schemes under the watchful eye of the trusty butler, Cable, and thrifty housekeeper, Mrs Alexander. And the arrival of a newfangled telephonic device at the Abbey threatens to expose the secret past of Lord Cameron's valet, Coulson.

EYE RATING: A big hit that will run for years (thanks to the Fixed-Term Parliament Act)

VIEWERS ENJOYED picking holes in the real version.

Daily Telegraph – Letters to the Editor

Sir – I wonder how many viewers of ITV's *Downton Castle* were shocked as I was by the historical inaccuracies in what was an otherwise entertaining tale of ordinary life in Edwardian England.

Those of us who were fortunate enough to spend our childhood in such a well-ordered household know that a scullery maid addressing the Under-Housekeeper as "Mrs Matthews" whilst wearing her cap would have resulted in instant dismissal and possibly death, and quite rightly so.

At least they got the jumbo jet right as it flew over the gathering of the Downton hunt in 1912, startling Lady Starborgling (an excellent performance, incidentally, by Dame Judi Mirren) in a reasonably authentic fashion.

Yours faithfully,

Sir Herbert Gussett, The Old Rehab Clinic for Distressed Gentlefolk, Notlong-on-the-Wagon, Nr Barkworth, Somerset.

JULIAN ASSANGE'S WIKILEAKS caused outrage by releasing thousands of classified diplomatic documents.

Those Wikileaks in full

- Terrible flaws in the coalition strategy in Afghanistan are resulting in the unnecessary deaths of hundreds of allied troops in an unwinnable war
- President Sarkozy of France is "vain, silly, and French"
- Prime Minister Berlusconi of Italy is "sex mad, corrupt, and sex mad"
- Prime Minister David Cameron of Great Britain is "lightweight, weak, Old Etonian"
- His Holiness Pope Benedict XVI is "Catholic"
- Newly released logs demonstrate bears actually do (*that's enough – US National Security Agency*)

NICK CLEGG U-TURNED on a pre-election pledge to oppose any rise in tuition fees, to the outrage of the students who had voted for him.

FEBRUARY BROUGHT NEWS from the housing market.

Times are tough in the property game, where even the top suits are feeling the squeeze – but not if they are in charge of Annington Homes, the property company that gets its income from the desperately over-stretched defence budget. Recently filed accounts for the company that owns Britain's dire military family accommodation shows that chief executive James Hopkins trousered £2.56m including bonuses in 2008/09, more than 100 times a squaddie's pay and more than twice the basic wedge of even a Royal Bank of Scotland chief executive.

Annington acquired £1.7bn worth of military housing from the MoD in 1996 in a deal that the National Audit Office found shortchanged taxpayers by around £140m. Under the contract, Annington leases the properties back to the MoD, which still has to maintain them, even if they are empty, so guaranteeing Annington's income. Under the contract's generous ongoing rent reviews, payments to Annington are up by 22 percent over the five years to 2007 (having been hiked by 48 percent up to 2002).

The rent paid out of the defence budget that doesn't end up in Hopkins and co's pockets is paid out to the ultimate economic owner of Annington, Japanese investment bank Nomura, removing all but a few pounds of taxable profit from Britain, and leaving a tax bill of just 0.1 percent of Annington's operating profit.

DETAILS OF THE FINANCIAL CRASH two years earlier were still trickling out in March.

The British government line that the 2008 financial meltdown was an American problem with Britain as an unwitting victim of "contagion" is comprehensively debunked by last week's report on the accounts fiddling at Lehman Brothers that played such a critical role in the bank's collapse. The trick was to get billions of pounds of loans off the balance sheet using a transaction called "Repo 105". American regulators were having none of it, so what did Lehman's do? It simply transferred its security inventory across the pond and got its operation in regulation-lite London to conduct the transaction!

The deal was signed off here by pukka City lawyers Linklaters, first in 2001, then repeatedly "refreshed" until 2008. It isn't the only off-balance sheet chicanery Linklaters advises on. Last year it was brought in by chancellor Alistair Darling to advise on setting up the Treasury's Infrastructure Finance Unit, under which public money will fund private finance initiative schemes, handily allowing the government to boast of future investment without corresponding increases in debt levels. Then a few weeks ago Linklaters was appointed as sole adviser to Infrastructure UK, the government body that will plan all major public investment – which, along with the commitments to pay for it, will in true Lehman style be mysteriously excluded from government debt figures.

AS THE ELECTION was called in April, the *Eye* identified a suitable legacy for Gordon Brown.

There is no more fitting symbol of 13 years of financial mismanagement in Whitehall than the 27-year deal to lease air-to-air refuelling and troop transport aircraft from the Airtanker consortium led by the European defence company EADS. This long-running PFI disaster is now the subject of a damning National Audit Office report. Back in 1997 defence secretary George Robertson identified the need for a new fleet of in-air jet refuelling aircraft. Three years later, told that paying for these in the normal way would cost £1bn over four years, his successor Geoff Hoon plumped for a PFI deal that would cost more over the long term but have less impact on immediate finances and so for political expedience could be deemed more "affordable".

As things stand, however, thanks to PFI the MoD has ordered warplanes that can't actually fly into war zones. Pleas from the military for "defensive aid suites" to be added to the new Airtanker craft after surface-to-air missiles were fired during the Kosovo intervention were refused by Treasury and MoD officials since they would be unsuitable for the private charter flights that PFI suppliers would want to use the planes for when the forces did not need them. Now

Afghanistan shows they are indeed necessary and the MoD faces an extra bill for hundreds of millions of pounds to adapt the new aircraft.

To justify the use of PFI, the mother of all accounting fiddles was deployed. Under Treasury rules, future leasing costs should have been discounted by 3.5 percent a year when comparing them with the cost of public ownership of the planes. But a long discredited and excessive discount of 6 percent was used, even though the Treasury's senior economic adviser admitted that had the correct figure been used, "the PFI solution would not represent value for money".

The cost is now put at £12.3bn, payable as £390m a year, plus the MoD's own costs from a desperately stretched armed forces budget. Of this total, just £80m is the annual cost of running the planes. The rest pays Airtanker's financing costs and its profit. The non-PFI cost would have come in at around £9bn cheaper, but was magically made to look more expensive by Gordon Brown's Treasury-mandated fiddling.

Despite claiming he would undertake a "fundamental reassessment" of PFI, new chancellor George Osborne merely rebranded it as PF2 in 2012 and pressed ahead with hundreds more projects. His successor Philip Hammond finally abolished the use of PFI for any future building projects, but we will continue to pay out billions until the final contract ends in 2050.

OVER THE SUMMER, the *Eye* began exposing serious problems at care homes run by Southern Cross, and the body charged with regulating them.

Last month a coroner severely criticised Southern Cross, the UK care home giant, when one of its residents died after being admitted to hospital with no fewer than 18 weeping bed sores covered in dirty dressings. Alan Simper, 84, who was blind and had dementia and Parkinson's disease, died for "want of care" at Swiss Cottage nursing home in Leighton Buzzard, said the Bedfordshire coroner. One hospital nurse said it was "the worst case of neglect" she had ever seen.

Southern Cross was allowed to carry out its own internal review, in consultation with local social services and the Care Quality Commission (CQC) and announce after the inquest that "steps have been taken to improve the quality of care".

Three months before Mr Simper went into Swiss Cottage, which charges between £550 and £695 a week, CQC inspectors went in following an anonymous complaint. They found problems with staff training and care records and highlighted concerns that some residents had to wait until nearly lunchtime to be washed and dressed. But they found no major shortfall in service and still passed the home as one star – ie that it gave "adequate" quality care.

Only six months earlier, another coroner had slammed another care home run by Southern Cross after a vulnerable elderly resident, 85-year-old Will Perrin, had died after being admitted to hospital in agony from bed sores, gangrene and malnutrition. The Westminster coroner said neglect by staff had contributed to his death, and his was one of the worst examples of care in a nursing home she had seen. That home, too, was rated adequate. It still is.

At a third Southern Cross care home, St Michael's View in South Tyneside, police are investigating the death of 80-year-old Alzheimer's sufferer Joyce Wordingham amid claims of negligence – although the official cause of death was "bronchial pneumonia". Two managers and ten care workers were suspended, and emergency staff were drafted in from the local health and social services to care for the residents as the investigation was widened to look at 15 other deaths at the home since January 2009.

As Eileen Chubb, who runs the charity Compassion in Care, points out, seven months before police were called in to investigate Mrs Wordingham's death, St Michael's View was rated by CQC as "two-star, good". This was based not on an independent inspection by CQC but on answers provided by Southern Cross to a questionnaire.

Nearly one in five of the company's 700 care homes are rated only adequate or poor. But it has no immediate plans to invest even in the 19 "poor" ones. Instead, for its care home managers it proposes "skills training including sales techniques, financial management, people development, report writing and complaint handling" and implementing a new rostering system which "is expected to generate payroll savings of about 1 percent per annum".

Southern Cross's chief executive and group finance director both pocketed well over £500,000 last year, not to mention the £48,000-plus pension contributions that will help with their own care needs in their old age.

Two members of staff at St Michael's View received prison sentences, and three were struck off the nursing register. Cases of appalling neglect at Southern Cross homes continued to be reported in the *Eye* right up until the company – which had cashed in by selling the freeholds of its care homes and leasing them back – collapsed under the weight of its debts in July 2011.

THE COMMISION HIT BACK by claiming it had forced 100 closures of failing care homes in the past year. But their figures were not what they seemed.

An investigation by *Private Eye* and the charity Compassion in Care has discovered that:

● Some homes with a history of poor care, said to have been closed, are still open and under the same ownership or management

● At least two homes with a dire history have simply been renamed but are still under the same ownership or family

● Two homes were closed as a result of police arresting the owners for people-trafficking and not the result of "robust inspection"

● One home shut voluntarily – just as the CQC was about to upgrade it

● Two homes had simply changed use, one to care for autistic adults, another to provide sheltered accommodation

● And care homes rated "good" or "adequate" that have not been closed or sold are listed, though they should not be on the list at all.

Despite repeated requests, CQC has failed to supply details of any enforcement action against any home on the list and failed to identify the six homes it supposedly served with official notice to close.

It would not be until May 2019 that the CQC started displaying historic ratings for care homes on its website even if they had been re-registered under a different name.

SEPTEMBER BROUGHT NEWS of some very cosy deal-making.

Chancellor George Osborne gave Vodafone top billing in his drive to increase British business fortunes on his recent jolly to India, launching a new phone from one of the company's shops in Mumbai with chief executive Vittorio Colao. Meanwhile back at home, HM Revenue & Customs have settled a tax dispute that has been wending through the courts for six years. When Vodafone bought German engineering company Mannesmann a decade ago for £180bn, it asked the then Inland Revenue if it could route the acquisition through an offshore company, but was refused. Vodafone went ahead anyway, and bought

Mannesmann using a Luxembourg subsidiary called Vodafone Investments Luxembourg sarl (VIL), in which it would go on to dump vast profits taxed at less than 1 percent. VIL's accounts show that up to March 2009 €15.5bn was stuffed into the company, resulting in around £5bn in lost tax and interest so far. An epic legal battle was launched by the Revenue, with tax inspectors confident they could win the cash back. But they reckoned without HMRC's "permanent secretary for tax", Dave Hartnett, and his customer-friendly approach to big multinationals. Despite a series of legal victories by HMRC, Hartnett moved the case from his specialists and lawyers – whom he described to the *FT* this month as suffering from "a black and white view of the law" – to a more amenable group which would negotiate with Vodafone's head of tax John Connors. Until 2007 Connors was… a senior official at HMRC working closely with Hartnett on big business. Also involved was David Cruikshank, a tax avoidance guru from Deloitte, brought in bizarrely by Hartnett to act for Vodafone.

The fruits of these talks, conducted without consulting HMRC's litigators and specialists in tax law, was a bill for Vodafone of £800m, with another £450m payable over five years, and remarkably, agreement that the arrangement can continue into the future with a promise of no challenge from HMRC.

The bill for all other taxpayers in lost tax is likely to

be at least £6bn. Hartnett's comments to the *FT* signal more sweetheart deals to come. Staff cuts at HMRC are, in any case, destroying its ability to fight tax avoidance: spending on the activity has already fallen from £3.6bn in 2006/07 to £1.9bn with more cuts to come. This has prompted the association of senior Revenue officials to compare the government to "a drowning man who decides to throw off his lifejacket because it weighs too much."

The scandal led to a series of protests at Vodafone stores throughout the UK, and criticism for this, and a similar deal struck with Goldman Sachs, followed Hartnett right up until he "retired" from HMRC in 2013 – and immediately went to work for… Deloitte, on their "tax services" wing.

RENEWED INTEREST in the *News of the World* phone-hacking scandal – and Downing Street aide Andy Coulson's key role in it – prompted the *Eye* to tell some home truths in September.

Phone hacking was prevalent throughout the red-tops at the time – the *Sunday Mirror* and *Sunday People* also got dozens of stories by this method – and everyone in tabloid-land knew about it. "Bullshit" is the verdict of

one veteran *Screws* hack on Coulson's protestations of innocence. As editor, he had to be confident that a scoop was copper-bottomed and bulletproof before running it, and so executives would have to reassure him about their evidence. "They were hacking phones 30 or 40 times a day. It got to the point where almost all our investigations were based on phone-hacking." Private detective Glenn Mulcaire's role was hardly a secret. He was invited to *Screws* Christmas parties at which, according to one witness, "he was treated like a guest of honour".

It would be a further four years before an Old Bailey jury also called bullshit on Coulson's protestations of innocence, and five before the *Mirror* and *Sunday People* also 'fessed up to phone hacking.

THERE WAS MORE tax news in October.

HMRC has written to hundreds of offshore account holders suspected of tax evasion. The accounts are with HSBC's Swiss private banking arm, whose secret operations were always most likely to appeal to British tax evaders. And who was chairman of HSBC Private Banking Holdings (Suisse) SA until February, facilitating this fleecing of the British taxpayer? None other than incoming trade minister Stephen Green!

Five years later, an enormous leak of account files from the Swiss wing of HSBC revealed details not only of large-scale tax fraud, which HMRC had failed to prosecute over, but organised crime and corruption too: the bank admitted to "past compliance and control failures" – and David Cameron finally faced some very awkward questions from somewhere other than the *Eye* about why he had made Green a minister in his government.

2011

THE WRONGFUL ARREST of landlord Christopher Jefferies by police investigating the murder of Joanna Yeates in Bristol proved very costly for everyone concerned.

The Daily Mail asks: Could this long-haired weirdo possibly be innocent?

Contempt Of Court Special, pages 1-94

THE WEDDING of Prince William and Kate Middleton at Westminster Abbey received wall-to-wall coverage – not least for the outfits on display.

Our fashion editor Liz Bones gives her verdict:

■ Get a **pip**, sis! Pippa's shameless attention-grabbing makes me **bridal** with annoyance! **Honour**-stly girl, put them away, you've **maid** an ass of yourself!

■ This Princess is the **Be-atrice** and end all of fashion! This daring eye-catching creation makes her look a right **Royal Knock-out!**

■ What the **flock** is he playing at? Doesn't he know that pointy hats are so **old testament**? This gaudy, fussy outfit has just ruined the whole day!

REVOLUTIONS IN TUNISIA and Egypt kicked off what would become known as the Arab Spring.

That All-Purpose Editorial

(please insert appropriate country name)
Jubilant scenes in square / Moment of history / Reverberations throughout the Middle East / Scenes not seen since fall of Berlin Wall / Voice of the Arab street / Bloodless revolution / Shockwaves felt by neighbouring dictatorships / Domino effect / Note of caution / Need for orderly transition / Stability paramount / Army good thing / or not / to be honest we haven't got a clue / Foreign Office useless / Anyone been there on holiday lately? / Er… er…

AS LIBYA COLLAPSED into civil war, David Cameron launched an ill-advised military intervention to impose a no-fly zone over the country.

Libya: 'No-end' zone declared

The Coalition yesterday announced the creation of a "No-End" Zone across Libya, which would guarantee that military action would "carry on forever".

The "No-End" Zone has the backing of the UN, NATO, The Arab League and the Four Horsemen of the Apocalpyse.

The architect of the operation, Prime Minister David Cameron, says, "This action makes it absolutely clear where we stand – which is over a map of Libya, wondering what on earth to do now."

RIOTING BROKE OUT in London, followed by other cities across the UK.

TUNIS TIMES

Tottenham Spring sweeps Britain

For the third night running, the streets of London and many other cities were filled with angry crowds of protesters in the greatest challenge to Britain's Conservative ruling order for decades. The protesters, mainly young and co-ordinated by social media such as Twitter, seemed fearless in confronting Britain's hated police force, as they burned buildings, ransacked shops and attacked news reporters.

Speculation was growing last night that Cameron and the corrupt clique that surrounds him would soon be overthrown by the brave young protesters, and forced to flee and seek asylum in a friendly Arab country such as Libya.

WHO ARE THE RIOTERS? Experts on British culture blame the violence on the rise of a new "overclass" in the country, comprised of various social groups sharing a common lack of conscience, motivated by greed, who feel no allegiance to the wider community they grew up in. As one analyst said, "These include feral bankers grabbing vast bonuses 'just because they can', corrupt politicians fiddling their expenses to snatch expensive electronic equipment and household goods, and incompetent police officers working for the *News of the World*. The bastards."

WITH THE NEWS that teenage murder victim Milly Dowler had been among thousands of phone-hacking victims, the *News of the World* scandal finally exploded. Rupert Murdoch swiftly closed the paper down and went into full contrition mode.

THAT HISTORIC LAST EDITION

NEWS OF THE SCREWS

The world's worst newspaper 1843 - 2011pm (That's how long it took to cobble together)

THANK GOD & GOOD RIDDANCE

After 168 years, we finally say a sad farewell to the 7.5 million people whose phones we've hacked

INSIDE: 94-PAGE THROWAWAY SOUVENIR

THE PRIME MINISTER scrambled to distance himself from his former friends.

A message from the Headmaster: A lot of you have been emailing me about one of the school's longtime sponsors, the elderly Mr Murdoch and his full-time carer Mrs Brooks.

I want to make it clear that, contrary to what you may have been told, I do not have a close relationship with either of these people.

Indeed, I have scarcely even met them, except on the few occasions when I have inadvertently run into them at social occasions, such as Mrs Brooks's wedding, Mr Murdoch's summer parties and a handful of several dozen dinner parties where, of course, no school business was ever discussed.

Of course, it is true that when we employed Mr Coulson as the school's head of marketing, I did so on the personal recommendation of Mr Murdoch who, as his former employer, laid out some very good reasons as to why I should employ him, ie if I didn't, my career as Headmaster would be finished and that Rebekah knew where I lived, as she had been there several times.

I am afraid Mr Coulson let the school down very badly.

I would, however, urge both parents and pupils not to become too obsessed with trivial tittle-tattle when there are so many more important issues to deal with, such as Mr Gove's exciting new curriculum (a Latin word, note!) and how I am going to keep my job next term if all this stuff about Mr Murdoch doesn't die down over the summer holidays.

Yours, *David*

AND THE COMMISSIONER of the Metropolitan Police, Sir Paul Stephenson, resigned after it emerged he employed the *News of the World*'s former deputy editor, Neil Wallis, as his PR man and enjoyed a stay at a health farm he represented.

FAR TOO LATE NEWS

Knacker resigns

Just days after defending his force's investigation into phone-hacking, which he brought to a close after receiving an out-of-office reply to his email requesting to speak to James Murdoch, Inspector Knacker of the Yard has announced his resignation and issued the following statement:

"Evening all. My personal integrity is intact. I feel very good about myself due to a long stay in the excellent health spa Champagneys. May I make it clear that at no time was I aware of any link between the former *News of the World* journalist Mr Wally Wolfman and my PR consultant Mr Wolfy Wallman. To suggest that officers would accept any sort of bribe to bring a premature close to investigations is an appalling slur. We act without fear or favour, as several of my former colleagues have made clear in their columns in the *News of the World*.

"I have decided, nevertheless, to do the fashionable thing and resign. Mind how you go."

HAULED IN FRONT of a parliamentary committee investigating the scandal, a humiliated Rupert Murdoch received a custard pie to the face courtesy of a member of the public.

Gnome Heritage is proud to present

The Wendi Deng Memorial Pie Dish

Relive the epic moment when brave Wendi Deng leapt to the defence of her husband and attacked his custard pie-wielding assailant.

Each pie dish, fashioned out of China-style Deng Dynasty Polywendilene by the craftsmen of Wah Ping provnce, bears the image of the striking Dragon Lady who has captured the world's hearts. Perfect for serving up Dim Son should it become necessary, the dish is the centrepiece that will complete your Chipping Norton Set of crookery.

This beautiful dish will be treasured by your children, your children by your much younger second wife, and their children who will argue about who owns the dish when you've passed on!

Hurry while News Corp stocks last!

WHILE BARACK OBAMA'S top team were engaged in taking out terrorist leader Osama Bin Laden, our own politicians were busy with an equally vital issue (and one that was key to the coalition agreement): a referendum on whether general elections should switch from a first-past-the-post system to an "alternative vote" one. Two-thirds of the electorate said no.

THE LAST HARRY POTTER film was released.

Harry Potter and the Deadly Goodbyes

As the final film in the Harry Potter franchise premiered in London last night, there were tears for the three Warner Brothers executives who had been there right from the start.

"We were just kids when we greenlit the first movie: we didn't have any idea what effect Harry Potter would have on our bank balances," said one of the three balding men dressed in expensive suits. "Then of course we had no option but to go on, because our fortunes were growing bigger and more attractive with every passing year!

"It's so sad that we now have to say a final goodbye to Harry."

Moments later the trio gave the go-ahead for a series of eight planned Harry Potter prequels, saying they could not disappoint the voracious demand amongst fans to explore revenue streams that remained unexplored in the books.

THE GOVERNMENT announced it was finally abandoning and "urgently dismantling" the NHS National Programme for IT (*see p226*).

"There's no hope. I'm switching off the machine"

DEFENCE SECRETARY Liam Fox resigned after it emerged that his friend Adam Werritty had attended official meetings, travelled overseas with him and had business cards printed up claiming he was his adviser, despite holding no government role.

Foxtrot disaster – odd couple voted off *Strictly*

Hopefuls Dr Liam Fox and his professional dancing partner Adam Werritty failed to impress the judges when they took to the floor in the latest round of the reality TV show *Strictly Come Off It!*

As Fox stumbled through his paces the audience began to boo and he was forced to withdraw. One of the judges said, "I have never seen a worse performance. The two of them got everything wrong and then tried to cover up their mistakes."

Fox issued a public apology, saying, "I'm sorry if it looks as if we were no good."

The couple have already announced they will be sharing a flat in the *Celebrity Big Brother House* next year, and may well be heading off to tropical climes together on *I'm Not a Special Adviser, Get Me Into There!*

THE IMPORTANCE of the death of Steve Jobs, founder of Apple, was overstated.

Apple man dead

The world was last night in mourning for the most important man in the entire history of humanity.

As one online tribute put it, "Adam was a creative genius. He came up with the names for everything – animals, birds, plants, flowers, the lot." But there were also suggestions that the Apple may not have been an unqualified force for good. As one serpent said last night, "Yes, the Apple changed everything, but (*cont. 94,000 BC*)

ANTI-CAPITALIST PROTESTERS "Occupy" set up a tent village in an attempt to shut down the London Stock Exchange – but only succeeded in closing St Paul's Cathedral on the other side of the square.

The Alternative Rocky Horror Service Book

A Service for the Closure of a Cathedral for Health and Safety Reasons

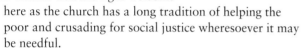

The Canon: Brothers and Sisters, you are gathered here together in your tents to make your voices heard, in protest at the recent failings of global capitalism.

The Congregation: Yes, indeedy!

The Canon: You are right welcome here as the church has a long tradition of helping the poor and crusading for social justice wheresoever it may be needful.

The Congregation: Thanks be to you.

(There then follows a reading from the Book of Health and Safety Regulations, Chapter 7, Page 75: "The erection of tented structures within 10 metres of the Cathedral's Main Access Points")

The Dean: O Lord, close our doors.

The Congregation: Result! Way to go!

The Dean: Let us now pray for the gift shop, and the coffee shop, and for the admission fees which usually amount to over £16,000 per day.

The Congregation: Boo! Capitalist Bastards!

(Hymn number 94: "There is a green hill far away / Perhaps you would like to go and camp there instead?")

DAVID CAMERON claimed to have wielded the UK's veto for the first time at 4am after a rancorous all-night EU summit on plans to rescue the single currency – only for the other leaders to go ahead and sign the treaty without him.

NEW FROM KELLOGG'S

Veetos – the ideal alternative to a Continental dog's breakfast!

Can't face croissants, cheese and yet more large brandies after a hard night in the negotiating room? Why not pop out and enjoy a refreshing bowl of Veetos – guaranteed to give your polls the boost you need to get you through the morning!

VEETOS – SPIN-DOCTORS RECOMMEND IT!*

**when served with a semi-skimmed splash in the *Mail*, *Sun*, *Telegraph*. Veetos are not a long-term substitute for a healthy poll-rating.

IN MARCH, THE EYE revealed details of one of Julian Assange's associates.

Wikileaks' agent in Russia is Israel Shamir, an Assange intimate and a Wikileaks insider since 2007. Russian-born Shamir says he was trusted with selecting the 250,000 US State Department cables for the Russian media: many went to the pro-Kremlin *Russian Reporter*.

Extracts from one cable, Vilnius 000732, turned up in an article by Shamir for web magazine *CounterPunch*, which painted a rosy picture of Belarus – "a Shangri-La" – and damned the opposition for receiving foreign money. What Shamir chose not to mention is that Belarus is a thuggish tyranny led by Alexander Lukashenko, or that after the recent crooked elections, 700 democracy activists were locked up by the secret police, still known as the KGB.

The piece worried Index on Censorship so much it wrote to Wikileaks demanding to know what Shamir was up to, since the cables might be useful evidence for Belarus KGB showtrials against the opposition. Wikileaks replied with sublime detachment: "We have no further reports on this 'rumour/issue'."

Shamir was born a Jew in Novosibirsk, emigrated to Israel in the 1960s, fought in the Yom Kippur war, came to London where he worked for the BBC Russian Service in the late 70s and then emerged as a freelance web hack after the fall of the Soviet Union, stridently attacking Jews and promoting pieces questioning the Holocaust. In 2005 his publisher in France, and in 2008 the man himself, were convicted of inciting racial hatred against Jews in his book *The Other Face of Israel*.

In 2007 Assange emailed Shamir, inviting him to join team Wikileaks. A leaked email from September 2007 shows Assange telling him, "Someone wrote saying they 'refused to associate with an organisation that would work with an anti-Semite like Israel Shamir'. From a brief sampling of your writing I did not find the allegation born out... I suspect the name 'Israel Shamir' is a realpolitik deadweight we are not yet big enough to carry... Writing under another name in the interim may be an option." Handily, Shamir has six different names, including Robert David, a pseudonym he's used to write pieces for neo-Nazi media in Russia attacking Andrei Sakharov, Jews and anti-Kremlin democrats.

Assange reacted by phoning up the *Eye*'s editor and accusing him of being part of a conspiracy led by Jewish,

or "sort-of Jewish" journalists. Former Wikileaks staffer James Ball later confirmed that he had personally "given direct access to more than 90,000 of the US Embassy cables, covering Russia, all of Eastern Europe, parts of the Middle East, and Israel" to Shamir on Assange's orders, and that Shamir then passed the entire tranche on to Lukashenko.

NEWS INTERNATIONAL finally made "an admission of liability in [phone hacking] cases meeting specific criteria" in April, and said "we continue to co-operate fully with the Metropolitan Police". The *Eye* revealed how that worked.

Andy Hayman, the assistant commissioner who so spectacularly mishandled the original investigation, resigned from Scotland Yard in 2007. The *News of the Screws* had a story about his private life at the time, but it was spiked. And shortly after returning to civvy street, he joined the payroll of News International as a columnist for the *Times*.

In February this year Scotland Yard gave the Metropolitan Police Authority a list of all the private dinners hosted by *Screws* executives for senior officers. In September 2006, for instance, the then deputy commissioner Paul Stephenson dined with the paper's deputy editor, Neil Wallis, only a month after the arrest of the paper's royal correspondent Clive Goodman. In November 2009, shortly after deciding not to reopen the hacking inquiry, assistant commissioner John Yates dined with editor Colin Myler and crime editor Lucy Panton. In all, the list disclosed eight previously unacknowledged private dinners and five other meetings with NI executives. But it omitted to reveal that Andy Hayman had three lunches and two dinners at the *News of the Screws* between 2005 and 2007, even while he was investigating the paper for criminal offences.

There were still three months to go before the scandal would burst, leading to Stephenson's resignation as Met Commissioner over his links to Wallis. The second part of the Leveson Inquiry the government set up as a result of the phone-hacking scandal – which David Cameron promised would "look into the original police investigation and the issue of corrupt payments to police officers, and consider the implications for the relationships between newspapers and the police" – has never happened.

FOLLOWING 18 MONTHS of strangely cryptic items in the Street of Shame pages, in April the *Eye* pointed out why the recent flurry of anonymised privacy injunctions – and even super-injunctions, which banned any mention of their very existence – were actually a serious matter.

At least four injunctions were granted in the week before the *Eye* went to press, with hordes of high-minded online commenters pointing out that they couldn't care less about famous people's sex lives, and that the press should stick to real stories. There is, however, another way of looking at several of the cases that have come before the courts in recent months. The media has been prevented from revealing:

1) The name of the entertainment company which sacked a female employee after an executive ended an extramarital affair with her and told bosses that "he would prefer in an ideal world not to have to see her at all and that one or the other should leave".

2) The effect that a sexual relationship between two senior executives at a global business may have had on the running of that business during a period when it got into severe financial difficulties.

3) Financial arrangements made by the chief executive of another global company while it was experiencing widely reported problems.

4) How an author of bestselling books and newspaper columns drawing on his own personal life has blocked his ex-wife from writing a book of her own or talking to any journalists about her time with him.

5) "Private information" that MoD adviser Bernard Gray – since appointed to the position of Chief of Defence Materiel – communicated to an individual, or who exactly that individual was.

6) The identity of a "well-known sportsman" who had simultaneous sexual relationships with persons referred to as XX, YY and ZZ, even though the court of appeal recognised that granting him anonymity calls into question the behaviour of a number of innocent people.

7) Any information about a number of cases where anonymous figures have been accused in court of attempted blackmail, a criminal offence carrying a prison sentence of up to 14 years, which is traditionally tried in open court. In most cases there is no indication that police were even informed.

In every single case, judges ruled that any public interest was outweighed by the applicants' right to privacy. And those are only the ones we know about.

The identity of Sir Fred Goodwin (2) was subsequently revealed under parliamentary privilege; a court eventually allowed the reasons Chris Hutcheson was sacked by his son-in-law Gordon Ramsay (3) to be revealed; Jeremy Clarkson (4) abandoned his own injunction saying "they don't work". The rest – and several more – remain secret by order of the courts. A tightening of the rules under which privacy injunctions could be granted in May 2011 has severely curtailed their use.

AS THE PHONE-HACKING scandal finally erupted in July, the *Eye* shifted the spotlight onto the *Daily Mirror* under its former editor Piers Morgan.

Moron may hope and pray that no one who attended it still remembers a lunch held in September 2002 in a private room at the swanky new Four Seasons Hotel in Canary Wharf, just by the offices of the *Daily Mirror*. The occasion was one of the monthly bunfights hosted for Moron by the convivial Trinity Mirror chairman, Sir Victor Blank. The dozen or so guests at this one included Ulrika Jonsson, Jeremy Paxman, and the then chief executive of BT, Ben Verwaayen.

Moron's feeble attempts to master a Scandanavian accent in front of Jonsson – he was trying to wind her up by mimicking conversations with her lover Sven Goran-Eriksson, their affair having been exposed by the *Mirror* five months earlier – were received with embarrassed titters. Then he started to hector Verwaayen, roaring that BT "should start providing better security for pin numbers for mobile phones! You should tell your customers to go and change them!"

Having mocked Ulrika and hectored Verwaayen, Moron then launched into his party piece – a re-enactment of Heather Mills arguing on the phone with Paul McCartney, and the ex-Beatle winning her round by singing "We Can Work It Out".

At the Leveson Inquiry, Morgan admitted listening to a recording of the message McCartney had left on Mills's phone, but refused to say who played it to him, and Jeremy Paxman confirmed details of the lunch conversation. Morgan maintained up until 2015 that there had been no phone-hacking at the *Daily Mirror* under his leadership, right up until Trinity Mirror confirmed there had been plenty.

SEPTEMBER DELIVERED the first news of a long-running scandal.

Over the past few years the Horizon IT system that 11,500 sub-postmasters are forced to use has thrown up a rash of apparent financial "shortfalls", prompting dozens of prosecutions and financial ruin for businessmen and women with previously spotless records. Now 55 sub-postmasters have launched a "class action" against the Post Office, arguing their troubles owe more to computer error than dishonesty.

In a standard week a sub-post office performs thousands of transactions – many, such as pension payments and lottery and foreign currency purchases, in cash. When the computer says the till is short, the sub-postmaster (or mistress) has to cough up the difference, and the computer is apparently always right. If they can't pay up, the Post Office's fraud investigators swiftly descend. The Post Office is the only body in the UK that runs its own prosecutions after Customs and Excise was stripped of the power a decade ago when it was found to have over-stepped the mark in several high-profile cases.

Several sub-postmasters and mistresses have been jailed for theft simply on evidence from a computer system that seems to be misfiring, with no indication of what they are supposed to have done with the cash. One, Seema Misra, was pregnant when she was found guilty of stealing £75,000 even though no trace of the money could be found and the judge at Guildford crown court appeared to instruct the jury that the evidence was very limited. She was sentenced to 18 months.

Since her case, others have pleaded guilty simply for more lenient sentences. Many more have coughed up thousands of pounds from their own pockets in desperate attempts to retain their livelihoods. The Justice for Sub-postmasters Alliance reckons the total affected could run into the thousands.

The Post Office maintained for a further seven years that Horizon was "absolutely accurate and reliable", before caving in and paying £58 million to settle a civil case brought by no fewer than 555 sub-postmasters and mistresses in 2019. It later emerged that at least 15 separate bugs had been identified in the system as early as 2006, and that senior management had been aware that prosecutions based solely on Horizon evidence were unsafe from 2013 onwards. By then, 60 people had been convicted, and 20 jailed. In October 2020, the Post Office announced it would not be contesting 44 appeals by those convicted. Seema Misra was one of them.

2012

AS BANKERS BONUSES returned to their sky-high pre-crash levels, the City continued to brush off any criticism.

"That's very anti-business"

ROBERT THOMPSON

CHANCELLOR George Osborne managed to make himself even more unpopular by imposing a "pasty tax" in the Budget.

Osborne's next budget plans leaked

20% VAT INTRODUCED ON:
Raindrops on roses, Whiskers on kittens
VAT INCREASES ON: Bright copper kettles, Warm woollen mittens, Brown paper packages (extra if tied up with string)
TAX REDUCTIONS FOR: Nazis

THE ONCE-AND-FUTURE chief executive of News International, Rebekah Brooks, took the stand at the Leveson Inquiry.

Salem Witch Trial – Day 94

Witchfinder General (Mr Jay QC): Do you admit working as a minion for the Dark Lord?

Rebekah: I do, sir.

Witchfinder: And did you see anyone else consorting with the evil one?

Rebekah: Aye, sir, with my own two eyes I did see Goody Cameron supping with the Beast on many occasions.
(Gasps of horror sweep the court)

Rebekah: And it was not just Goody Cameron, sir, who danced with the Devil that night at the pyjama party – but Goody Osborne too! He and Murdoch spoke privily in whispers.

Witchfinder: Heavens, child, be careful of what you speak!

Rebekah *(foaming at the mouth)*: I denounce Goody Hunt, Goody Gove, Goody Brown, Goody Blair…
(Hysterical screaming engulfs court-room as massed townspeople pass out with excitement)

Judge Leveson: It seems to me that most of these Goodies are actually baddies.

Witchfinder: Very amusing, your honour.

Judge Leveson: Now, shall we burn the witch?

All: Yeah!

BROOKS REVEALED details of the many text messages she had received from her riding companion, the prime minister, who had signed them LOL under the impression it meant "Lots of Love".

DETERMINED to avoid extradition to Sweden, where he was being investigated on suspicion of two sexual assaults, Wikileaks' Julian Assange hit on a novel way to escape justice.

Assange seeks asylum in Uganda

Julian Assange has sought refuge in the Ugandan Embassy, it was confirmed last night. His supporters said, "Julian is currently discussing Uganda in the ambassadorial spare room. He has always loved Uganda and greatly admires the Ugandan way of doing things."

At time of writing, it is unclear whether the Ugandan Embassy has given consent to Mr Assange's unexpected entry, or agreed on the issue of protection. One of the celebrity supporters who stood bail for him, Jemima Khanihavemymoneyback, said, "I'm sure this affair won't last long – Julian doesn't like to take no for an answer."

THE QUEEN celebrated her Diamond Jubilee.

UK AND US REGULATORS fined Barclays Bank **£290 million** for attempting to rig the Libor inter-bank lending rate, and boss Bob Diamond was forced to resign even though he protested that knowledge of the fraud had been limited to a "small number" of junior employees.

Diamond 'Shocked'

Barclays' former chief executive Bob Diamond has admitted that he was shocked to discover the extent of banking practices taking place in some of his most profitable criminal divisions. "I would describe the people carrying out this banking as a few good apples who were in no way representative of the vast majority of Barclays investment bankers," Diamond told MPs.

He also expressed his personal sadness at being forced to resign over the scandal. "People say it must have been about the job, but it was never about the job, it was about the money. Loads of it. Being separated from the money that I have loved and dedicated years of my life to will be the hardest part of all this."

EROTIC NOVEL *Fifty Shades of Grey* became a publishing sensation. Craig Brown proved he could do it just as well as E.L. James.

When I wake, Mr Grey is at the piano, completely lost in the melody he's playing. His expression is sad and forlorn, like the music. His playing is stunning. He is able to use both hands at once. "That was a beautiful piece" I say. "Bach?"

"Chopin. Prelude opus twenty-eight, number four. In E minor, if you're interested," he murmurs. "Perhaps best known for his nocturnes, Frederic Chopin is considered one of the great masters of Romantic music..."

When I wake again, Mr Grey is still at the piano.

"Born in the village of Zelazowa Wola, in the Duchy of Warsaw, the young Frederic was soon to become a renowned child prodigy..." he continues. It all spurts out of him like a waterfall.

He tweaks the stem of his champagne flute with his expert hand and looks at it through his narrow eyes. "Bollinger Grande Année Rosé 1999, an excellent vintage," he sighs.

How long can he keep going like this? No man before has ever bored me so stiff, so solid, his every shaft of verbiage thudding into me like a truncheon. Beneath his boorishness, I yelp and writhe, begging for mercy as he rampages across me with his cock and bull.

THE OLYMPICS kicked off triumphantly in London.

Team GB round-up: Day 94

- Britain's amazing record-breaking streak continued last night as GB achieved the longest double-dip recession. George Osborne, who took Gold (and Silver, and Bronze from everyone), told reporters, "It's beyond my wildest dreams. It just shows what you can do with 100 percent determination and 0 percent talent." Experts believe Osborne now has every chance of pressing on to even greater depths in 2016 and beyond.

- There was another triumph for Britain as the army went from a stand-in start to take the title of official security guards from G4S, who blamed their own poor performance on being "severely over-stretched" following recent efforts to organise a piss-up at a local brewery. There was praise, however, for G4S's valiant efforts to "keep the amateur spirit of the Olympics alive".

- There was disappointment in the pool as Murdoch Crawl champion Rebekah Brooks attempted to defend her title (*News of the World*) and herself against the Crown Prosecution Service. Putting on a brave face, Rebekah thanked all her team for their hard work, but insisted that she had at no point had any idea what they were doing.

- The Royal Mail announced plans to honour all Gold winners by actually collecting letters from their local post boxes.

- Praise continued to flood in for Danny Boyle's Opening Ceremony. "It's incredible to think that such a spectacle was put on by the man who made *Trainspotting*," gushed one delighted fan. "He's gone from youths in tracksuits pumped full of drugs, to..." (*continued on red button service*)

REVOLTING REVELATIONS about the late Jimmy Savile led to the launch of Operation Yewtree as police investigated other former screen stars.

THE BBC COLLAPSED into chaos, with *Newsnight* making up for its previous repression of a report on Savile's proclivities by broadcasting one based on the unreliable testimony of an abuse victim in the North Wales scandal (*see p154*) which managed to falsely implicate former Conservative party treasurer Lord McAlpine as a paedophile. The new director-general, George Entwhistle, resigned after just 54 days in the job.

Those schedules in full

9.30pm: *Panorama* – An investigation into why *Newsnight* was cancelled

10.30pm: *Newsnight* – A discussion about *Panorama*'s revelations about *Newsnight*: tune in to see if the BBC have agreed to put anyone up for interview or will it be empty-chaired again? Plus tomorrow's front paedos.

12.00am: *Late News* – What did *Newsnight* say about *Panorama*'s news about *Newsnight*?

7.00am: *Today Programme* – John Humprys interviews director-general George Entwhistle about what he knew about *Newsnight*'s investigation into Savile when tributes to Savile were commissioned, and why he still doesn't know anything now.

7.03am – 7pm: *Live rolling coverage* of George Entwhistle's resignation as director-general and the BBC's complete disappearance up itself.

THIS ALL RATHER TOOK the heat off other institutions which were even more culpable for failing to stop Savile's behaviour.

NHS waiting list shock

The failure of the NHS to treat the Savile scandal seriously has been defended by a senior Health spokesman. "The delays of up to 40 years to get any attention for this story are in no way our fault. There is, unfortunately, a very long waiting list of people wanting not to explain why Jimmy Savile was given a bed in a children's ward and given free rein to wander around hospitals in the middle of the night with no questions asked."

He continued, "It is very sad that these very old stories eventually died a natural death, and no one could have expected them to be resuscitated (*cont. p94*)

THERE WAS UPROAR as foreign papers printed photographs of Prince Harry partying naked in a Las Vegas hotel room, and Princess Kate sunbathing topless in France. Meanwhile a long-lost relative turned up.

Naked Royal exposed

Another leading member of the Royal Family has been exposed in perhaps the most astonishing invasion of privacy yet. King Richard III was uncovered in a Leicester Car Park wearing "absolutely nothing".

"We were shocked when we saw him," one onlooker said. "A respected king like Richard III wearing absolutely nothing – no clothes, no skin, no flesh to flash at all."

A spokesman for the royal family said, "The late King is deeply upset at being exposed in this way. To be quite frank, he's got the hump."

CYCLING CABINET MINISTER Andrew Mitchell denied calling police officers who directed him to an alternative gate out of Downing Street "plebs", but resigned anyway.

CYCLISTS – NEW FROM GNOME

The Andrew Mitchell Bicycle Horn

The must-have accessory for 2012... This easy-to-fit-up, hot-air-powered warning device will open doors marked "Exit" and have everyone jumping out of your way.

HORN SOUNDS: "Pleb", "Fucking Pleb", "Do you know who I am?", "You don't run the place", "Oh dear, neither do I any more".

Frequently bought with The Andrew Mitchell Stupid Basket

THERE WAS LITTLE change in China.

Chinese Election 'Too closed to call'

● Xi Jin-Ping declared first Secretary by majority of 0 votes. Swing to Communist Party: 100%

IN FEBRUARY, *Street of Shame* pointed out the story behind a story in the headlines.

For three months the *Sunday Times* resisted a court order requiring it to give Inspector Knacker copies of a private email correspondence between cabinet minister Chris Huhne's ex-wife, Vicky Pryce, and the paper's political editor Isabel Oakeshott, regarding the paper's story last year claiming she took speeding points on his behalf. On 20 January, without explanation, it suddenly agreed to hand over Pryce's emails after all. Given the lack of fuss or outrage about this blatant shopping of a source, some people assumed Pryce must have consented to the paper's U-turn. Not so. Pryce tells friends she certainly did not give her consent, and finds the *Sunday Times*'s failure to protect its source "a strange way to behave".

The effect on Pryce may be devastating. Director of Public Prosecutions Keir Starmer said last week that the "new material" supplied from Wapping allowed prosecutors to declare that they had "sufficient evidence to bring criminal charges against Mr Huhne and Ms Pryce for perverting the course of justice". Witherow and Oakeshott have not just betrayed their source but also landed her and Huhne with a criminal prosecution.

Both Pryce and Huhne received eight-month prison sentences the following year.

GRASSING-UP PRYCE was just the tip of the iceberg at Rupert Murdoch's company.

Will "Thirsty" Lewis, the witch-finder general on News International's management and standards committee (MSC) has been told by CEO Tom Mockridge that he's now barred from the Cape, the Wapping pub where he was often to be found. The MSC's actions in volunteering evidence to police which led to the arrest of nine *Sun* journalists, and several of their sources who had every right to expect the company to maintain their anonymity forever, have infuriated staff so much that their local pub was no longer thought safe for Lewis to be seen in.

The arrests rose from material in a huge tranche of emails which until relatively recently the company was maintaining had been destroyed, and which staff reporting to Lewis and his MSC sidekick, old schoolfriend Simon Greenberg, have been trawling through alongside police officers invited into Wapping without so much as a court order.

Taking place under the auspices of Operation Elveden, this has conveniently drawn attention away from the sister investigation into phone-hacking which had reached far higher up the management tree, all the way to James Murdoch.

Although every single *Sun* reporter charged with conspiracy to commit misconduct in public office was cleared (one by the Court of Appeal), 34 public officials, including nine police officers, were convicted, thanks to News International turning supergrass and ignoring its duty to protect confidential sources.

In several trials it emerged that paperwork that would have demonstrated the involvement of higher-ranking executives, including Rebekah Brooks, in the payments was mysteriously not amongst that produced by the MSC.

THERE WERE REVELATIONS from an employment tribunal in February.

Engineer Dave Smith won a rare admission from construction giant Carillion before an employment tribunal last month that for many years he had been on an illegal blacklist because of his trade union efforts to improve building site safety. He was twice sacked by Carillion's subsidiaries, John Mowlem and Schal International.

As well as detailing his address, date of birth, national insurance number, car and movements, Smith's blacklist file also contained photographs and press cuttings, personal information about his family and sinister fabricated smears, such as suggestions that he had carried out an arson attack.

Even more alarming than the spying activities, the tribunal also heard that police and the intelligence services had clearly collaborated in setting up the database. David Clancy, who was the lead investigator for privacy watchdog the Information Commissioner's Office, which closed down the blacklist back in 2009, said that some of the information held was so specific it could only have come from police records.

This is hardly a surprise, given that Ian Kent, the man behind the Consulting Association, which operated the database, is a retired Special Branch officer. The tribunal heard that between 1999 and 2004 Mowlem paid £20,444 to the Consulting Association.

In May 2019, an out-of-court settlement and apology by eight construction firms brought the total compensation paid out to over 1,200 workers who had been blacklisted to £35 million.

THERE WAS NEWS from Saudi Arabia in May.

Due to an ongoing court case 11 years later, our lawyer has advised us that we shouldn't boast about this particular story – yet.

YET ANOTHER INJUNCTION case emerged in August.

Congratulations to "AAA", a young child who may or may not be the daughter of "an elected politician [whose] conduct and character are matters of public interest", and who last month scored a significant legal victory over Associated Newspapers, publisher of the *Daily Mail* and *Mail on Sunday*.

Being too young to achieve this by herself, she did so with the help of her "litigation friend" and mother, whom court documents identify as having had an affair with the married politician "at the time she was appointed by him as an unpaid fundraiser to a project to which her then partner gave money".

The Honourable Mrs Justice Nicola Davies refused to grant an injunction stopping any more being written about the child. But she declared that the publication of photos of her had been an unacceptable invasion of her privacy. AAA was awarded £15,000 in damages, which buys an awful lot of toys.

Less fortunate was her mother, who had funded the legal action through a conditional fee agreement with solicitors Collyer Bristow. The judge ordered her to pay 80 percent of Associated Newspapers' costs on the grounds that her counsel had been forced to apologise in court for "the manner in which evidence was prepared", Collyer Bristow having lifted sentences and whole paragraphs from the mother's evidence and cutting and pasting them into a signed statement from the child's nanny. "I do not accept that the words which were reproduced in the nanny's witness statement would have been the words used by this quiet and somewhat diffident witness," Davies stormed. "I deprecate, in the strongest terms, the actions of a solicitor who presents to a witness for approval a statement which represents words which are not those of the witness." Cripes!

Nine months later, in May 2013, the Court of Appeal ruled that Boris Johnson's fathering of a daughter with Helen Macintyre, one of his many mistresses, was "a public interest matter which the electorate was entitled to know when considering his fitness for high public office".

FORMER NIGERIAN POLITICIAN **James Ibori pleaded guilty this year to fraud and money laundering and was sentenced to 13 years by a British court. In a special report in August, Richard Brooks revealed who had been helping him.**

During a short stint in England in the early 1990s, James Ibori and his new wife Theresa had been fined for stealing from a Wickes DIY store in Neasden where, working on the tills, he had waved her through without paying for repeated baskets of "shopping". This, and a conviction for handling a stolen credit card, should have disqualified Ibori from office. But when he returned to Nigeria to work his way up the political ladder soon afterwards, he forged the date of birth on his passport and shook off his troublesome past.

Hitching his star to the nascent People's Democratic Party, by 1999 he had secured his place in Government House, Asaba. With it came control of an annual Delta State budget of around $1bn, from which he could extract far more than a few DIY tools. His pillaging was prolific. First there were transfers from state funds into local accounts of dozens of Nigerian companies nominally owned by Ibori's close associates or his mistress, Udo Onuigbo, under such pretexts as "security" or for phantom oil supplies when the supposed supplier, Total, had never supplied the state with a drop. Equally profitable was a stream of official contracts handed to front companies for anything from sports tracks to fleets of bullet-proof Range Rovers. The requirement for a minimum number of tenders for government contracts was easily met by Onuigbo ensuring she set up enough companies and submitted a bid in the name of each.

As he eased into a second term in 2003, the frauds grew more grandiose. Ibori set about squeezing hundreds of millions of pounds from the juicier fruits of state privatisations and sell-offs. But the accumulating loot was of little use sitting in banks in Nigeria: it had to be taken out of the country. And so it was laundered through accounts at two of Britain's biggest high street banks. Ibori himself had half a dozen Barclays accounts, through which around $1.5m was washed by 2005. Much of this funding came from accounts operated by Onuigbo at HSBC. The transfers of cash were as brazen as the Wickes scam: between 2000 and early 2007, £2.3m was paid into Onuigbo's main HSBC account, most of it in cash, spread liberally around the bank's London branches from Mayfair to Barking. East Ham proved particularly receptive, swallowing up £90,000 cash over eight days in December 2003, including £35,800 on a single visit, and another £72,000 over 12 days the following spring. Other transfers, typically in pocket-money sized £5,000 and £10,000 amounts, regularly left Onuigbo's HSBC account for James Ibori's personal accounts at Barclays, Knightsbridge, where he was a valued "Barclays Wealth" client. Millions more flowed through Ibori's wife's and sister's accounts.

The relentless deposits of cash, accompanied by transfers to the accounts of somebody known to be a "politically exposed person" (PEP), and thus subject to even greater levels of scrutiny, would not have survived the most cursory inspection and ought to have raised the alarms at both banks and been stopped long before Inspector Knacker appeared on the scene. Instead, they facilitated the most sumptuous lifestyles at the expense of the Nigerian people: the mortgage-free purchase of two properties in Regent's Park and Shaftesbury, Dorset, £143,000 in private school fees, and paying off fraudulently acquired mortgages on a string of London properties owned by mistress Udo Onuigbo and sister Christine. A £456,000 Mercedes Maybach 62 was bought in London's West End for delivery to Ibori's £3m mansion in, er, Johannesburg. Life wasn't too bad for the man whose official salary was less than $10,000 a year.

"One of the biggest money laundering cases seen", in the words of Judge Anthony Pitts, required British banks to gobble up the loot with no care for the consequences, willingly deploying their expertise to convert illicit funds into obscene luxury without asking where the riches came from. But they were not put in the dock at Southwark – or anywhere else, for that matter. The London laundry remains open for business.

In December 2012, HSBC was fined $1.9bn by US authorities for failing to flag up a whole load of other money-laundering offences by "drug kingpins and rogue nations" during the period that Stephen Green, minister for trade and investment in David Cameron's government, was its chairman.

2013

THIRTY-SEVEN PERCENT of frozen beefburgers sold in supermarkets were revealed to contain horsemeat, with a strong equine flavour to many ready-meals too.

DAVID CAMERON'S enthusiasm for the Marriage (Same Sex Couples) Bill caused discomfort amongst more traditional Conservatives.

Tory outrage grows over gay marriage

There is growing anger among Tory MPs over the Prime Minister's support for gay marriage. "The repercussions haven't been thought through," fumed one yesterday. "This raises all sorts of unanswered questions. For instance, what happens if this bill becomes law and I am forced to marry my boyfriend and have affairs with my wife?

"And if I only marry one of my gay lovers and another one goes to the papers about my past, who do I do my photocall with? It could all be very confusing for my children as I cower behind them and call for privacy. It is not bigotry to point out that these are questions that have to be confronted."

NEW GUN LAWS were passed in the USA, following the Sandy Hook massacre of 20 elementary school children.

Those stringent new gun controls in full

1. You will no longer be allowed to buy a gun unless you have enough money to pay for it.
2. You will no longer be allowed to buy a gun if you are drunk, unless the person selling you the gun is also drunk.

3. The age at which guns can be sold to kids with fake IDs will be raised from 8 to 11.
4. Anyone wishing to buy a gun must prove they are able to handle the weapon, by shooting the store clerk before robbing his shop.

LATE NEWS: *All four proposals defeated in Senate following lobbying by National Rifle Association. NRA issues statement: "The only thing that can stop a bad guy with a ban is some even worse men with a bung."*

AFTER A YEAR proclaiming his innocence, former Lib Dem cabinet minister Chris Huhne changed his plea to guilty of perverting the course of justice by persuading his ex-wife to accept speeding points on his behalf.

Huhne 'Guilty'

In a surprise development on the first day of his trial, Chris Huhne has admitted he was guilty of speeding away far too quickly from his marriage.

"In retrospect, I now see that I shouldn't have raced out of the family home into the arms of my new lover so fast," said the disgraced former minister. "I should have noticed the very angry woman in my rear view mirror, and anticipated what was ahead."

POPE BENEDICT XVI became the first Pope to resign the office in almost 600 years.

POPE QUITS!

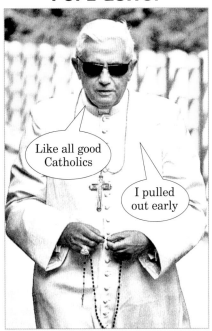

A REPORT on Mid-Staffs Hospital confirmed shocking abuse, neglect, mismanagement and cover-up.

NHS issues strict new guidelines after Mid-Staffs scandal

New NHS guidelines will make it clear to all staff that they are only allowed to kill patients if they're really annoying.

"Just being old, a bit smelly and going on about the war all the time will no longer be a valid reason to kill a patient," said a senior NHS manager. "Nurses will have to show that the patient is seriously getting on their tits big time before they'll be permitted to ice them. We will now be emphasising that every patient, no matter how annoying, deserves to be treated with dignity and respect as they're being pulled across the ward by their hair and slowly starved to death."

THE DEATH AND EXPENSIVE funeral of Margaret Thatcher split the nation.

Thatcher Funeral
Order of Service/Protest

10.45 THE ARRIVAL
The guests/protesters arrive escorted by
First Battalion Welsh Guards/ G4S

11.00 THE ADDRESS
On the steps of St Paul's Cathedral/Trafalgar Square

11.05 THE ARRIVAL
Of Mark Thatcher, who somehow managed to get lost in the desert on his way to St Paul's/of a team of photographers anxious to capture every sickening vile banner that no one should have to see, for publication across several pages in tomorrow's paper

11.30 THE FIRST READING
Of Mrs Thatcher's official biography, to boost
Charles Moore's pension/Of Mrs Thatcher's Wikipedia Page, to tell you why you are so angry

12.00 HYMN
I Vow To Thee My Country/
Ding Dong, the Witch is Dead

12.45 THE COMMENDATION
The guests/protestors will heartily commend the
Conservative Party/copies of *Socialist Worker*

1.00 MUSIC
A selection of classics from Sir Edward Elgar/
Chumbawumba

1.15 THE RECESSIONAL
Everyone will go back into the real world and
face the recession

ROLF HARRIS and *It's a Knockout*'s Stuart Hall were the latest elderly TV stars to be arrested and charged with child sex abuse.

1970s: More arrests

It was confirmed last night that police have arrested the 1970s, which are currently being held for questioning. "We believe that the decade colluded with the stars of the day to carry out abuse by being a totally different era from the modern day," announced Inspector Knacker, head of Operation Yewtree. "The 1970s has long wanted us to think it was the decade of space hoppers, Spangles and chopper bikes, but we all now know this loveable façade was just presented to allow heinous crimes to be committed."

He refused to rule out the arrest of later decades, as the inquiry continues.

OFF-DUTY SOLDIER Lee Rigby was brutally murdered in the street outside Woolwich Barracks by two Islamist extremists whose rants following the attack were videoed by passers-by and broadcast on that evening's television news.

EXCLUSIVE TO ALL NEWSPAPERS

Don't give them the oxygen of publicity!

INSIDE: Hundreds of graphic pictures, videos, interviews, comments, editorials in our 94-page terror special.

AS SUPPORT FOR HIS PARTY melted away, Nick Clegg claimed that the Lib Dems were fighting certain Conservative policies "tooth and nail" but had no choice other than to go along with the coalition's wider programme – and that he would do it again.

Nick Clegg: 'No choice' but to support austerity

Deputy Prime Minister Nick Clegg told his party's conference that the Lib Dems had no choice but to support their coalition partners' welfare reforms, however distasteful they found them personally. "We must stick to the government cu*ts," he said. "The cu*ts may be unpopular, but if we abandon them now, I won't get to be Deputy Prime Minister any more."

He also shocked his audience when he admitted that "whatever happens, I would absolutely be prepared to work with the Liberal Democrats after the next election". Such an outcome is thought to be unlikely.

AS THE WINTER OLYMPICS in Sochi approached, fears increased about the rampant homophobia being stoked by political leaders in Russia.

KATE MIDDLETON gave birth to the third-in-line to the throne.

THE GOVERNMENT SUFFERED a shock defeat after recalling parliament to vote on sending British troops into Syria.

The New Coalition Academy

A Message from theHeadmaster

While I was on holiday I took a phone call on the beach from one of the world's most important fellow Heads, Mr Obama, who as you know is in charge of Washington's top academy, Drone High. He was very keen for our Combined Cadet Force's joint trip to Syria to go ahead, and I was very keen to agree with him.

I put the CCF on full alert and told both members to get out their Ordnance Survey maps of Damascus, which have apparently suffered slight fire damage. However, I thought I'd just run my decision by the rest of the staff in the full expectation that they would see sense and join my lead in following Mr Obama's lead.

Imagine my disappointment (not to mention anger, irritation, fury, rage and desire for vengeance) when the staff, led by the young and inexperienced supply teacher Mr Miliband, took a show of hands and voted to keep the CCF safely at home.

For this, I'm afraid, I blame the parents who are still going on about the unfortunate trip to Iraq all those years ago when an unacceptable number of pupils died. How many times do I have to say that this was under a different Headmaster and the circumstances were entirely different, even thought Syria and Iraq appear to be very similar kinds of destinations for school expeditions?

However, I of course accept that this is the view of the majority, and I am prepared to acknowledge their cowardice and stupidity with good grace.

'Washington' D.C.

FORMER CIA MAN Edward Snowden released lots of classified material through the *Guardian* and other international newspapers.

'Spies spying on people' shock

In the most surprising revelation in the history of revelations, the *Guardian* can exclusively reveal that British spies have been secretly spying on people, many of whom were unaware that they were being spied upon.

Extraordinarily, some of the spying involved spying on people from countries who the spies wanted to know more about because they don't always tell us exactly what they are doing.

Full details of shocking spying by spies on pages 2-94, and in the 24-hour rolling updates on the Snowshitsherlock Files on grauniad.co.uk

BUSINESS SECRETARY Vince Cable's cunning plan, to ensure the privatisation of Royal Mail benefited small investors, failed spectacularly.

Royal Mail delivered to wrong address

Due to an unfortunate administrative error, the previously publicly-owned Royal Mail ended up in the hands of large financial institutions rather than the general public for whom it was intended.

A spokesman for the Royal Mail, Mr V. Cable, said "I'm very sorry. I don't know how this happened. It was clearly addressed to The British Public, c/o Britain, the UK, the EU. Unfortunately it seems to have wound up in the City of London instead."

Mr Cable continued, "We put the correct rubber stamp on it and imagined that it would get to the right people. Perhaps they were out. Or maybe they readdressed it incorrectly."

Empty-handed critics, however, were furious at the loss of the Royal Mail. Said one angry non-shareholder, "It's a disgrace. They lost our entire mail service, and there's no prospect of getting it back. The Royal Mail had huge sentimental value and now we're never going to see it again."

The recipients of the Royal Mail insisted there was no cause for complaint. "This enormous parcel of shares turned up in our letterbox. We signed for it, and it is now our property. Sadly, there will be no compensation for the previous owners for their loss. If it was that important, they should have sent it FedEx."

MPS DREW UP a royal charter for a new, post-Leveson press watchdog, which newspapers proved curiously unwilling to sign up to.

AS UKIP SUDDENLY started enjoying electoral success, Nigel Farage sacked his former flatmate and fellow MEP, Godfrey Bloom.

Man 'too mad for UKIP' shock

Britain was reeling today as it emerged it was possible for an MEP to be "too bonkers" to belong to UKIP. Summoning reporters to an emergency pint and fag, leader Nigel Farrago announced, "I know it's difficult to believe, but Mr Godfrey Loon is too swivel-eyed even for us. His views are dated, sexist, and borderline racist, which is of course how we came across him in the first place, but he has now overstepped the mark by referring to women as 'sluts'. In this modern age, you can't go around insulting women – because they've got no sense of humour and will get all uppity and make a fuss, especially if it's that time of the month (ie party conference season)."

AT THE OPENING of their trial for phone-hacking, it was revealed that former *News of the World* and *Sun* editors Andy Coulson and Rebekah Brooks had had a long-running adulterous affair during the period they were busy unmasking celebrity adulterers.

WHAT YOU NEVER READ IN THE

Randy Andy Puts Pecker in Bekka!

Top Tabloid Ed Puts Red Top Temptress to Bed

Not much, really.

THE SURVIVING MEMBERS of the Monty Python team reunited for shows at the O2 Arena.

And now for something completely the same...

JOHN CLEESE – This horse that you are flogging is dead. It is no more. It has ceased to be.

MICHAEL PALIN – Nah, nah, there's plenty of life in it. Stage show, DVD, podcast, download...

Large Foot Comes Down In Lieu Of Punchline

THE GOVERNMENT'S TRIAL badger cull, aimed at reducing the badger population by 70%, kicked off in two pilot areas, despite scepticism about its effectiveness in reducing TB in cattle.

"It's nothing personal, Badger, it's just that we've been paid to cull you"

THE EYE SHONE A LIGHT on one of Michael Gove's little helpers in February.

Everyone agrees that education secretary Michael Gove is a most courteous chap. But like other polite politicians he has a retinue of thugs whose manners are less refined. When he learned last week that the *Observer* was investigating his political methods, his taxpayer-funded henchmen duly swung into action.

The *Observer* had strong evidence that Gove's special advisers, Dominic Cummings and Henry de Zoete, ran the Twitter account "Tory education news" (@Toryeducation) which rubbishes anyone who dares cross the great man. When *FT* education correspondent Chris Cook had reported that Gove, Cummings and de Zoete were using private email accounts to escape FoI scrutiny, for example, @Toryeducation made sexual innuendos and called Cook a "stalker".

Cook complained to Tory officials. And Paul Staines, aka blustering blogger Guido Fawkes, rushed to defend Cummings and de Zoete. And he was there again last week with a pre-emptive rubbishing of *Observer* political editor Toby Helm's investigation. "Guido understands," he sneered, "that Helm reckons it could bring down Michael Gove." Helm reckoned nothing of the sort: Gove's aides, with Staines's help, were merely engaged in the spin-doctor's classic ruse of raising false expectations that can't be met.

Gove presents himself as a civilised intellectual. Yet he allows his coterie to behave like a bunch of boozed-up bruisers at chucking-out time. Has he forgotten Labour's Alastair Campbell, Charlie Whelan, and Damian McBride?

From July 2019 to November 2020, Dominic Cummings ran the country with the help of Michael Gove, on behalf of alleged prime minister Boris Johnson.

THAT SAME MONTH, the *Eye* predicted trouble ahead for new justice secretary Chris Grayling.

Seeking to justify coalition plans to privatise the bulk of the probation service, Grayling said it was because it was failing. It was unacceptable, he said, that 58 percent of short-sentenced prisoners re-offend within a year, with half a million crimes committed each year by released prisoners.

What he failed to mention is that those statistics have nothing to do with probation. There is no statutory provision for supervision of prisoners who serve less than 12 months, by probation staff or anyone else.

The same lack of logic seems to have been applied to the plans Grayling published last month to let the likes of Serco and G4S take over 70 percent of the probation service. The security and service giants will be contracted to manage all "medium to low risk" offenders in 16 areas.

Every year about 44,000 of the 240,000 on the probation caseload are recalled to jail for breaching the terms of their release or community penalties. Under government proposals there is no provision for the private sector to be able to return someone to prison or court. That remains the responsibility of the probation service and as union Napo points out, defence lawyers will have a field day arguing that officers will be in no position to call for someone's incarceration without having managed their case.

The document is spookily silent too on whether cash will follow a case transferred from the private to the public sector, and vice versa, and whether or not an army of accountants will be needed to work it all out. Then there is the attempt to devise a secure computer system containing sensitive information which will have to be accessible to the private and voluntary sector.

The plans appear so ill-conceived that MPs have already tabled more than 50 questions asking about such basics as how Grayling will ensure that the probation service remains accountable for public protection if it's not directly involved in managing cases. MPs also want to know how the government will ensure that private contractors, who stand to lose money if offenders are returned to jail or are considered high risk, will take appropriate action if they become aware of a heightened risk. Expect chaos ahead.

The disastrous privatisation was reversed in 2019. Reoffending had increased, in the case of the most serious crimes by more than a fifth, 22% of offenders were released without accommodation, tens of thousands of them only received a phone call every six weeks rather than face-to-face meetings, and the private companies involved had already required a £500m bailout by the government.

IN MAY, THE EYE raised concerns about a telecoms provider.

The rift is widening between Britain and much of the rest of the world over whether Huawei is an evil pawn of the Chinese government or a harmless teddy bear. Citing concerns that Huawei's equipment may be leaving telecoms networks open to surveillance by the Chinese government, other countries including the US, Canada, Australia and India, have severely restricted imports or are considering doing so. But David Cameron is a big fan. "The British government values the important relationship with China," he said last year, announcing a major expansion of Huawei's UK facilities.

Huawei kit is already inside virtually all Britain's important telecoms infrastructure. The company is supplying the equipment for the EE 4G network and also has deals with TalkTalk, Vodafone and BSkyB. But its cosy relationship with BT causes most concern.

It was BT that gave Huawei its first big contract in the west in 2005. Huawei is helping BT modernise its copper broadband service and is also a major supplier for its national fibre-optic broadband rollout – one of the UK's biggest infrastructure projects underway today. Last year, as the result of the axing of regional development agencies, the government even allowed Huawei to buy CIP Technologies – located *inside* BT's high-security research facility, Adastral Park in Suffolk.

It was not until 2020 – when we were onto 5G – that the UK government decided to ban Huawei from being involved, because it said aggressive sanctions brought in against the company by US President Trump "make it impossible to continue to guarantee the security of Huawei equipment in the future".

YET ANOTHER PRIVATISATION was on the cards in June.

Despite claiming over a year ago to have filled the "yawning black hole" in the UK's £15bn annual military equipment bill, defence secretary Philip Hammond remains determined to outsource the arm of government that has the big and strategically crucial job of spending the money. The justification for privatising Defence Equipment and Support is to be found, as ever, in the work of management consultants. According to LEK Consulting and Booz & Co, "frictional inefficiencies" in the budget cost between £1.3bn and £2.2bn annually.

The causes of these include a "conspiracy of optimism" among the military and its suppliers, leading to excessive ordering, insufficient skills and too close a relationship between military and civilian MoD staff, who thus often demand adaptations to suit current military needs. Strangely, the list of flaws in the process doesn't include the revolving door between those spending the billions and the multinationals receiving them.

The preferred solution to these problems is not to sort them out but to create a whole new set through a government-owned but outsourced procurement company, or "GoCo". This will prove very lucrative for whichever consortium wins the contract – but as usual, the taxpayer will remain on the hook for screw-ups. As the Royal United Services Institute points out, the plan "rests on an argument that, because the government is not very good at negotiating and managing contracts with the private sector, it is going to negotiate an even bigger contract with a private sector entity to undertake the entire task on its behalf".

It wasn't very good at negotiating this one, either. The privatisation was abandoned six months later, but not before the MoD had spent £33 million preparing for it.

IN OCTOBER, the month that the *Daily Mail* denounced Labour leader Ed Miliband's late father Ralph as "The Man Who Hated Britain", the *Eye* provided more details of "The Man Who Hates Paying Any Tax In Britain".

Since 1995 the Daily Mail and General Trust empire has been controlled through a company, Rothermere Continuation Ltd, registered in Bermuda but run from Jersey. Rothermere and DMGT non-executive John Hemingway, a retired lawyer who advises the wealthy on "structuring and management of their family resources", are directors of this company, which is owned by an unknown trust administered in Jersey for the benefit of Rothermere and his family. Following an offshore transaction earlier this year which almost certainly avoided a hefty stamp duty bill, Rothermere Continuation Ltd now owns all the voting shares in DMGT and receives more than £10m a year of the dividends paid annually by what is – thanks to the *Mail*'s online soft porn offering and other commercial ventures – a highly profitable media group.

This ownership combines patriotically with Rothermere's "non-domiciled" tax status (*see p244*) to produce serious tax advantages. Under the status, whereby Rothermere claims allegiance to, er, France – the offshore income into which the Bermudan and Jersey network converts the DMGT spoils is taxed only when "remitted" to the UK. Loopholes aplenty ensure that, in the words of one of Britain's most senior tax accountants, "to all intents and purposes for your well advised truly wealthy [non-dom] this is a complete exemption for investment income and gains", which is what the vast majority of Rothermere's DMGT income is.

2014

AS EU RULES ON the migration of Romanians and Bulgarians were eased on 1 January, an expected rush of arrivals failed to materialise – but storms did.

Daily Mail asks – Why have we failed to stop foreign flood?

Our weak and feeble government admitted today that it was totally powerless to stop yet more foreign weather flooding into Britain.

Over the course of this winter we've already seen an unprecedented influx of weather blowing in from abroad, taking roofs from British houses, and what is the government doing about it? Nothing!

Why won't anyone stand up and say this foreign weather isn't welcome in Britain, and we've had enough of it?

THE RESULTING floodwaters did not subside until late February.

PRIVATE EYE

No. 1359
7 February –
20 Feb. 2014
£1.50

ENVIRONMENT MINISTER VISITS SOMERSET

It's all under control

DETAILS EMERGED of Rupert Murdoch's latest divorce, and an astonishing note Wendi Deng had written about how much she fancied their friend Tony Blair.

There's no fool like...

by DAME SYLVIE KRIN

Rupert's hands trembled as he pored over the document sent to him by his internal security team Phil Sneaky and Mike Beaky. Squinting in the darkness – his ex-wife had even taken the lightbulbs with her when she stripped the apartment and moved out – he tried to take in the painful words written there.

"I ruv Tony", Wendi had written. "He has really good body and great legs and butt."

"Jeez," whispered the world's most powerful communications capitalist. "What's wrong with my butt? I may be 89, but I've got the butt of an 85-year-old."

He could not help but carry on reading the words that stabbed him through the heart like the 18-inch heels on her Mandela Blarney shoes. "I miss Tony's ruvly smile and his greaming teeth."

"I've got bloody good teeth," fumed Rupert. "Look at them there in the jar – just as good as the day I bought them."

But it was no good. Were the days when he could sweep a Sheila off her feet just by opening his wallet now far behind him?

The darkness deepened as the screen on his Nookia 94 smartphone went into sleep mode. And without his fortune cookie-hunter beside him, jumped-up Jezebel that she was, he had no idea how to switch it on again...

RUSSIA INVADED Ukraine and took over the long-disputed Crimean peninsula.

Putin reveals plans to commemorate start of WW1

The President of Russia, Mr Vladimir Putin, today announced his official plans for marking the 100th anniversary of the First World War.

"I shall start small with a localised conflict, full of ethnic concerns which nobody outside the area understands," he told a Kremlin news conference, "but with any luck it should soon turn into a massive conflagration on a global scale which will truly remind us of all the lives lost in 1914."

AFTER YEARS OF BOASTING about the stories he had kept out of the headlines, Max Clifford was convicted of eight counts of indecent assault, some on underage girls.

Clifford found guilty

Anyone know a good PR man?

UKIP CAME IN well ahead of both the Conservatives and Labour in the European elections, and a schism began to open up in British politics that did not run along the usual party lines.

Sarcastic status updates fail to influence election

Thousands of young people across the country were left in a state of shock last night after discovering their amusing Facebook status exhorting their friends not to vote UKIP had had very little impact across any sections of society.

"I can't believe it," typed one. "I have written literally three status updates in the last week saying UKIP were a bunch of racists and that Nigel Farage is a bell-end, and I even put the hashtag #sarcasm on the one reading 'Off to vote for UKIP, guys!' beneath the picture of the cute dog at the polling station. And now I find that none of it made any difference. I'm disgusted. Is this what Emmeline Pankhurst killed that horse for?"

Spokespeople for the three main parties were sympathetic, pointing out that none of the campaigning they did made any difference either.

THERE WERE ALLEGATIONS of a "Trojan Horse" plot to smuggle extreme Islamist teaching into schools in Birmingham.

THE DEADLIEST FIGHTING for decades broke out in the Gaza Strip.

The Book of Benjamin – Chapter 95

1. And lo, as you may have read in the previous chapter, the children of Israel were yet again engaged in the act of smiting.

2. And the victims of their wrath were, as usual, the Hamas-ites that dwell in the land that is called Gaza.

3. And he that ruled over the children of Israel, Benjamin, son of Netenyahu, spoke unto the world and said, "It is right and our bounded duty that the children of Israel should slay the children of Hamas, and indeed all the adults as well, even a hundredfold, yea even a thousandfold."

4. "For the Hamas-ites have been coming upon us by stealth, even by pathways dug deep in the earth, which are called tunnels."

5. Yet some of the children of Israel, who were not so keen on the smiting, cried unto Benjamin, "This smiting of the Gaza-ites, their hospitals, supplies of water and the power stations that giveth them light, doth not make any sense."

6. And then Benjamin did wax even more wroth, and he saith unto them, "O ye of little faith. Dost thou not realise that it is only when we have laid waste to every building that is in the land of Gaza, till their stones be level unto the ground, that we will be able to see where the doors are to these deadly tunnels?"

7. And when they heard this, the children of Israel wagged their heads and replied unto Benjamin, "Now that thou hast explained thy thinking in such logical and persuasive fashion, we realise that thou hast a very good point."

8. And so it was that the smiting continued, even during the fires that are called "cease".

9. But all the people of the world that were looking on began to say amongst themselves, "We have looked the other way long enough when it comes to the children of Israel and their smiting. But this time they have really gone too far."

10. And they added, "We know we say this every time. But this time we really do mean it."

11. And Benjamin, son of Netenyahu, heard what they were saying, and he was not sore afraid. And he carried on just as before, proclaiming, "The Hamas-ites need to be taught a lesson. And that is why we are going to blow up their schools."

(Continued verily unto eternity)

MEANWHILE TERROR GROUP ISIS were expanding their self-proclaimed "caliphate" across both Syria and Iraq.

Putting the fun back into fundamentalism – A message from the Caliph!

Today I call upon the world's media to halt these vile slurs on our attempt to bring peace to the Middle East by uniting it as one Islamic State. It is alleged that we, as devout Muslims, should not be massacring so many of our fellow Muslims.

This is quite wrong. We are an equal opportunities organisation, firmly committed to a non-discriminatory killing of everybody, regardless of their religion, gender or race.

As we say, "May Allah be merciful, because we certainly won't be!"

ABU BAKR AL-BAGHDADI
"Sunni side up – and everyone else down!"

FORMER HOME SECRETARY Leon Brittan was the latest high-profile figure to be accused of child sex offences (falsely: *see p103*) as the papers and police – with the help of a conspiracy theorist website called Exaro and their primary source then known only as "Nick" – went slightly mad.

Britain was paedophile shock

Private Eye can exclusively reveal that the whole of Britain was a paedophile in the 1970s and 1980s.

Everybody in the entire country, including MPs, members of the House of Lords, judges, bishops, senior policemen, TV celebrities, traffic wardens, priests, school teachers, businessmen, farmers, factory workers, manual labourers, the unemployed and every single other person was a known paedophile for the entire period.

They have all covered-up for each other ever since in a vast paedophile ring of at least 60 million known names.

POLICE RAIDED A FLAT belonging to the equally innocent Cliff Richard, as a BBC helicopter hovered expensively overhead.

Knacker justifies dawn swoop on Cliff

Inspector Knacker of South Yorkshire Police has denied that the raid on Cliff Richard's house, involving a hundred armed men, two assault helicopters and a surface-to-air missile, was anything other than a routine investigation of a possible suspect.

"Operation Hello Mum was a complete success," Knacker told invited reporters, "and my mother enjoyed it greatly as it looped round and round on the BBC's 24-hour news channel."

CONSERVATIVE MPS Douglas Carswell and Mark Reckless defected to the increasingly influential UKIP.

Former UKIP Clacton candidate latest to embarrass Farage

Former UKIP Clacton candidate Roger Lord is the latest member of the party to be caught on tape expressing the sort of views Nigel Farage hoped to put behind him as his party finally attains respectability and Westminster seats.

"I'm not saying I've got anything against disgruntled Tories, but look at this Douglas Carswell," Lord was heard saying. "He's like all the rest of them, coming over here and taking our jobs. How would you feel if one of them moved in next door to you and took over the constituency you've been lined-up for all your life?"

He continued, "Apparently they don't smoke and in their culture you're not even meant to drink at lunchtime. There's no way his type can successfully integrate into UKIP life. They should be put back on the first boat to Boris-Boris Land."

RUSSELL BRAND briefly, and inexplicably, became some kind of political guru.

How Russell Brand sees himself

How other people see him

TESCO SUSPENDED four executives after admitting it had overstated its profits for the year by a staggering £250 million.

Special Offers at Tesco this week!

- Ready-Cooked Books
- Chocolate Profiterrors
- Half-Baked Bean Counters
- Porkie Pies
- Frozen Assets
- Fishy Fingers in Till
- Jammy Dodgers
- Porridge

TESCO *Every Fiddle helps*

AHEAD OF A REFERENDUM on independence for Scotland, wild claims were made on both sides.

DESPITE A LAST-MINUTE PANIC by the British government, the result was a 55% "No" vote.

Eve of Poll latest

CAMERON FINAL OFFER: VOTE 'NO' AND GET INDEPENDENCE

With just hours to go until the vote, David Cameron made a dramatic last-minute bid to win over wavering Scottish voters by promising them full independence if they vote to reject independence.

He said, "Scottish voters need to understand that full independence is my final offer in a bid to save the Union and, more importantly, my skin."

'YES' CAMPAIGN FURY OVER BBC BIAS

There was fury from the 'Yes' campaign today after it accused the BBC of spreading accuracies and truths about life in Scotland after independence. "The British Biased Corporation seems determined to report how businesses and investment would leave Scotland in the event of a 'Yes' vote amid uncertainty over currency concerns," said one 'Yes' campaigner. "It would show far more balance if they did not report on it at all, and just played some jolly dancing music over a soft-focus picture of some heather instead.

"Time and time again during the campaign the BBC have made Alex Salmond look ridiculous by putting him on the television and asking him fairly simple questions that he's then unable to answer."

'QUEEN SHOWS ANTI-SCOTS BIAS' – 'YES' CAMPAIGN

The Queen has been condemned by the 'Yes' campaign for expressing a hope that Scottish voters "will think very carefully about the future" in the run-up to the referendum vote.

"To suggest that Scottish people should think very carefully about anything is an insult to the Scottish people," said Alex Salmond, posing for a photo with a bowl of porridge on his head. "We are a brave, doughty, handsome, lovely, passionate people who don't believe in thinking carefully about anything. The very fact I am here as your First Minister shows what a proud, unthinking race we are.

"For her to demand that any Scotsman think carefully about anything just shows how out of touch she is with her subjects north of the border."

GEORGE OSBORNE'S stewardship of the economy was still going brilliantly.

FROM THE HOUSE OF GNOME

The Record Debt Memorial Mug

Now you will always remember the moment when Britain broke the all-time record for the largest national debt in history. Made from high-quality china-style china in China, this unique heritage item will be passed down to your children and your children's children, as they wonder how the hell they're going to pay for it.

COLOURS: In the Red

Says G.O. of Westminster: "You must all be mugs!"

18-YEAR-OLD MICHAEL BROWN was the latest black man to be shot by a white policeman in the US, with a grand jury deciding not to indict the officer.

"Hey, buddy, would you mind stepping out of the vehicle so I can get a better shot at you?"

THE TRIAL OF REBEKAH BROOKS, along with her PA Cheryl Carter, continued to throw up unlikely stories through the first few months of the year.

Asked why she had chosen 8 July 2011 to remove seven boxes marked as "notebooks from Rebekah Brooks" from the News International archive – which she claims actually contained her own personal material – Cheryl Carter told police she had done so because Rebekah was on holiday. She claimed her  boss was undergoing a fitness training "bootcamp" along with husband Charlie and a personal trainer at their Oxfordshire home.

Carter claimed that the demands of her job made it very difficult for her to leave her desk for any period of time when Rebekah was in the office, so the collection had been arranged "not for any other reason than that she wasn't there that week". Asked if there could have been any reason for Brooks to be at News International on 8 July, her PA reiterated that "my understanding was that she would be at home... I'm sure she was off that week".

The week ending 8 July 2011 was the week that it was revealed that Milly Dowler's mobile phone had been hacked and News International was plunged into the biggest crisis in its history: on 7 July the closure of the *News of the World* had been announced, and that very afternoon Rebekah – who, phone records shown to the court demonstrate, was at the News International offices all that day – was addressing a "town hall meeting" of *NOTW* staff whose employment had been terminated. It was also the day that her former colleague, Andy Coulson was arrested.

Reminded of these events, Carter admitted to police that she did remember "what was going on and that she [Rebekah] was very upset... the pressure of everyone, should she resign, should she not resign".

The jury heard that police and forensic experts have established that up to nine "devices which may be attributable to Mrs Brooks" have never been recovered – either two or three iPhones, two iPads, three Blackberries, and an HTC Desire mobile phone. Asked why he had travelled to the couple's Oxfordshire home, Jubilee Barn, on the morning of what he agreed was "one of the most telegraphed arrests in history",

Charlie Brooks said it was "to collect some shoes that Rebekah particularly wanted to wear to the police station". He denied that he had emptied the house of electronic equipment, or that the "real point was to get rid of stuff that might damage your wife".

Questioned about a number of emails which the prosecution submitted as evidence, Rebekah pointed out: "I often put quite a lot on email. I could quite easily have sent it even though they [the recipients] were just over there." And she later confirmed that she "used email a lot – more than was usual".

The jury has previously been told that as part of what the prosecution alleges was a cover-up, Brooks issued orders that all emails predating 2010 should be permanently deleted from News International's computer systems. When the date was queried by a colleague who pointed out that "The revised date is likely to be misconstrued if circulated externally", Brooks replied, "Yes to 2010. Clean sweep." The court heard that more than 10m emails have been lost forever. In June 2011 the hard drive of Brooks's old office computer disappeared from the records of the IT department at News International, presumed destroyed.

After an eight-month trial, the jury found Rebekah Brooks not guilty not only of phone-hacking, but of conspiracy to pervert the course of justice by covering up and destroying evidence too.

IN JANUARY, THE EYE failed to get answers over the privatisation of Royal Mail.

Defending an impenetrable 440-page privatisation prospectus last October, business secretary Vince Cable told MPs, "The whole point is to be as transparent and as open as possible, to give information."

Really? Perhaps the most important information on a sale that Cable promised would bring in "responsible long-term institutional investors" as opposed too "spivs and speculators" is who the shares were sold to. But after much delay, Cable's business department has rejected the *Eye*'s freedom of information request for this information, arguing that investors have a "legitimate expectation of privacy".

A few months later, the National Audit Office winkled out the information that six of the institutional investors given priority by Cable had sold off all their shares within weeks of the privatisation, making a vast profit in a frenzy of spivvy speculation that led to taxpayers missing out on £750 million in a single day's trading.

APRIL SAW an urgent notification pop up.

Having only had seven years' advance warning, the government was naturally unprepared when Microsoft stopped issuing security updates for Windows XP earlier this month. Without the updates, there will be no patches for any new security holes discovered in the antiquated operating system – meaning that any PCs running it could be wide open to hackers. Unfortunately, as of last September, this included 85 percent of NHS PCs.

So, to buy a bit more time, the government has handed £5.5m to Microsoft for 15 months' extra support for public sector machines. The software will still need to be upgraded: just not until after the election.

But it won't be easy. Nobody even knows how many NHS computers are simply incapable of running newer software and will have to be replaced, but it's likely to be tens of thousands.

In May 2017, the WannaCry ransomware attack disrupted computers at more than a third of NHS trusts and nearly 500 GP practices, causing the cancellation of 6,900 appointments and five A&E departments being left unable to treat patients. The fact they were still using the unsupported Windows XP was a key factor.

THE EYE REVEALED details of the *Daily Telegraph's* editorial policies in June.

The *Telegraph* recently printed a grovelling apology for a one-star review of *X-Men: Days of Future Past*, blaming a "production error. The correct rating is two stars. We apologise for this inaccuracy". Apologise to whom? Mainly, it seems, to greasy advertising guru Dave King, executive director of the Telegraph media group, who had been incensed by the damning review on the grounds that it could jeopardise the paper's "commercial partnership" with 20th Century Fox.

And it is not only in reviews that the *Telegraph* shamelessly panders to its sponsors: advertisers such as Cunard and John Lewis are rewarded with puffery in the news and features pages. And then there's HSBC, which not so long ago stopped its *Telegraph* advertising for a year after taking umbrage at a story. Now the paper is extra-careful to emphasise the positive in all coverage of the bank. The arslikhan reached new levels of absurdity two weeks ago when more than a fifth of HSBC's shareholders voted against its executive pay proposals. The headlines were unanimous: "HSBC shareholders revolt on pay" (*FT*); "HSBC shareholders revolt over fat-cat pay" (*Mail*); "HSBC shareholders revolt over plan to give £1m bonus to boss" (*Times*). Well, almost unanimous. The *Telegraph* headline? "HSBC shareholders back pay plan."

Eight months later, in February 2015, the *Telegraph's* chief political commentator Peter Oborne made his high-profile resignation from the paper on the grounds he had discovered... it offered favourable coverage of HSBC in return for advertising!

IT WAS NOT THE ONLY bit of financial funny-business going on at the *Telegraph* that year, as Street of Shame revealed in September.

No pundit worked harder to boost the anti-independence vote in Scotland than the *Daily Telegraph's* Scottish editor, Alan "Cochers" Cochrane, whose daily column sounded increasingly desperate as polling day approached. And there is a good reason why. In what may be a journalistic first, *Telegraph* chief executive Murdoch MacLennan had secretly promised his Scottish editor a £20,000 bonus if he could help deliver a 60-40 vote against independence. If the Noes won, but by a narrower margin, his bonus would fall to £10,000. No wonder Cochers sounded a bit anxious!

2015

ARMED ISLAMIST terrorists broke into the offices of French satirical magazine *Charlie Hebdo* and slaughtered 12 staff.

40 WORLD LEADERS gathered in Paris three days later to show their support for free speech beneath the banner "Je Suis Charlie".

Let's Parlez Franglais!

Monsieur Hollande: Bienvenue à la plus grande photoopportunitée du monde.

Monsieur Cameron: Je suis Charlie.

Hollande: Vraiment? J'ai pensé que vous êtes David.

Madame Merkel: Ich bin Charlie.

Hollande: C'est très confusant. Qui êtes vous, monsieur homme noir avec l'amusant chapeau?

Le Président de Mali: Moi? Je suis Mali.

Hollande: Zut alors!

Le Prime Ministère de Turkey: Allowez-moi to explain. Nous sommes ici pour marcher contre le speech libre.

Hollande: Sûrement vous meanez "pour" le speech libre?

L'Ambassadeur de Saudi Arabia: Non, non, c'est definitement contre. Il faut que nous crackons down sur les journalists et les cartoonists.

Le Foreign Ministère Russe: Particulièrement si ils sont gaies.

L'Ambassadeur de Saudi Arabia: Ils ne peuvent pas dessiner sans handes!

Tous les despots: Hahahahaha!

Cameron: Sacré bleu! Je suis dans le wrong place. Je should be next to la Première Ministre fruitée de Denmarke!

Madame Fruitée-Kinnock: Bonjour, grande garçon! Voulez-vous un autre selfie inapproprié comme à la funèbre de Monsieur Mandela?

Benjamin Netanyahu: Attendez un moment! Ne takez pas any photos sans moi!

Hollande: Vous n'êtes pas invited!

Netanyahu: Est-ce que c'est because je suis Jewish?

Hollande: C'est tout too confusant! Mon Dieu!

L'Ambassadeur de Saudi: Vous blasphemez, infidel! Une mille de lashes pour vous!

Cameron: Mais vous ne pouvez-pas say that!

Madame Fruitée-Kinnock: Oui, il peut! C'est le freedom de speech!

Hollande: Ma tête est spinning avec tous ces arguments philosophiques! Qu'est-ce qu'on peut say?

Le Photographier: Dîtes fromage!

Tout le monde: Je suis Cheesie!

THE WORLD BECAME briefly obsessed with what colour a dress on the internet was.

It's the internet sensation that everyone is talking about – THE COALITION!

Look at this dodgy outfit. What colours to you see? Most people originally saw it as a coalition of blue and yellow. Then the longer they looked at it, the more they saw it was entirely blue. Then they saw red.

© BuzzFeeble, 2015

WITH OPINION POLLS all over the place, speculation was rife that the SNP would end up holding the balance of power after the general election…

EXCLUSIVE TO ALL PAPERS

Is this election impossible to predict?

We don't know.

…ONLY FOR THE CONSERVATIVES to win an unexpected 12-seat majority…

…LARGELY AS A RESULT of voters turning against the Lib Dems for their part in the coalition government.

Public vote to kill monkey and elect organ-grinder for another five years

A spokesman for the public said last night, "We hate these tunes. We've been listening to them for five years, and we've decided it's time to take action. If the monkey hadn't been dancing along, we'd never have had to put up with such terrible music. We now look forward to hearing it on its own, without the distraction of a ridiculous performing pet."

HUGE NUMBERS OF PEOPLE fleeing conflict in Syria, Libya and other ongoing war zones were attempting to make their way across the Mediterranean to seek refuge in Europe.

SEVEN FIFA EXECUTIVES were arrested, and another 14 officials and their associates indicted in the US courts, for rampant corruption offences.

GNOMETEL PRESENTS

Now that's what I call FIFA – football songs 2015

"Oh when the Feds go marching in"/ "He's going down, he's going down, Blatter's going down" / "Who's the bastard? Who's the bastard? Who's the bastard in the black? Oh, it's the FBI. Sorry, officer, I'll come quietly" / "You only sing when you're thinking it'll get you a shorter sentence" / You're not bunging any more" / AND MANY, MANY MORE!

Send $30,000 in an unmarked brown envelope to: Private Account Number 2018/2020, Bank of Switzerland.

JEREMY CLARKSON was sacked from the BBC's *Top Gear* after hitting a member of staff who told him only cold food was available at his hotel.

That episode you'll never see…

A middle-aged man with a paunch is driving yet another boring car

Clarkson: Today's Unreasonably-Priced Star in a Fracas is the head honcho, the bee's knees, the dog's bollocks, yes it's me! And I'm in the driving seat of the Mini Fracas, which may sound small but believe you me it packs a hell of a punch. The Fracas is hotter than a cold-meat platter and could cost an eye-watering 150 million pounds – which is almost as much as my weekly salary. I'm not at all happy with the handling, and I'll tell you, the suspension leaves a lot to be desired. But once I put my foot down – bang! – I was gone, faster than a chef clearing off after doing a long day's real work.

This episode will also not be repeated several times a week on Dave.

THE POLICE INVESTIGATION into the wild claims by Carl Beech had expanded to include the late Ted Heath as well as several still-living, and entirely innocent, figures.

SUMMER GNOMEMART PRESENTS

The Westminster Paedophile Ring

Not suitable for children.
WARNING: May inflate out of all proportion

WITH GREEKS CHAFING against the austerity measures imposed on them in return for international bailouts, a "Grexit" from the Euro began to look increasingly likely.

Greece in new crisis

Greece faced a new disaster this week, as it emerged the country is toiling under an enormous shortfall in metaphors to describe the country's situation. "We've used absolutely everything," said one anguished headline-writer. "We've done 'Greek tragedy' thirty or forty times; we've done the one about them losing their marbles; we've had every variation on 'Greeks bearing gifts': we even had a go at 'elbow Greece' and a really contrived one about 'Greeced Lightning' which was the worst in living memory. But we may have to face facts. If things keep getting worse there, there's just no way we'll be able to carry on."

THE NO-HOPER LEFT-WING candidate in the race to be the next Labour leader turned out to be surprisingly popular amongst those young enough not to remember what happened last time…

Controversial front-runner emerges

He's a left-wing firebrand who has the support of the unions and is determined to take the party away from the safe middle-ground of politics – yet in a shock result the late Michael Foot looks set to become the next Labour leader.

"The fact that Michael has been dead for years," said one enthusiastic supporter, "should not deter us from making him our next leader. He's the man to take us into a bright new past! He ticks all the boxes, including the one he's buried in. He's definitely the man to pull off a sensational election defeat in 2020 – he's the ultimate symbol of the current Labour party, being dead."

Jeremy Corbyn is 66.

FORMER TORY DONOR Lord Ashcroft, explicitly admitting that he was out for revenge after the prime minister failed to give him a high-ranking government job in return for his cash, published a book claiming David Cameron had "inserted a private part of his anatomy" into a pig's head when he was a student. He offered no evidence.

Man Found Guilty of Revenge Pork

A 69-year-old man has this week been found guilty of committing the new offence of "Revenge Pork". After their relationship went sour, Lord Ashcroft sent a mental image to everyone around the world of his former partner, "Dave", indulging in a lurid sex act with a dead pig.

One regular browser of the *Mail* Online, which was used to disseminate the mental image, said, "I'd never thought of anything like it. I couldn't wait to pass it on to all my friends."

The victim described it as "a shocking and hurtful breach of trust from someone whose money I loved for many years. It's one thing for people to assume that you enjoy screwing the poor, but now everyone who sees me thinks I like screwing the pork too."

THE NEW LABOUR LEADER was given a bumpy ride by the press.

Jeremy Corbyn writes:

A lot of journalists from the *Times*, the *Telegraph*, the *Mail* and the *Sun* have been asking me, "Why do you consort with members of Hamas, Hezbollah and the IRA?" My answer to that is, "My philosophy is always to talk to everyone, even those people you profoundly disagree with, because only that way can you get your message across." However, I refuse to speak to journalists from the *Times*, the *Telegraph*, the *Mail* and the *Sun*, so I would be grateful if you could pass this message on to them.

ISIS SUPPORTERS carried out a coordinated series of mass shooting and suicide bomb attacks on a football stadium, a concert venue and several restaurants in Paris, killing 130 people and injuring more than 400.

"You hate music, football, eating out and drinking? Might as well kill yourself now"

THE DECISION TO STRIKE BACK militarily caused a major schism in the Labour party...

...**AND, WHEN TURKEY** added to the mix by shooting down a Russian jet it said had strayed into its airspace, considerable confusion about who was fighting against whom (and indeed, what we should call them).

'Syria – it couldn't be simpler' says Cameron

The Prime Minister explains where everyone stands.

"It's all perfectly straightforward. Britain is against Daesh, or ISIS as the BBC insists on calling them. Daesh is against Assad. Britain is also against Assad. But Russia is for Assad. And Iran is for Assad. But Turkey is against Assad. And Turkey is also against Daesh.

But *now*, of course, Russia is against Turkey. And the Americans are for Turkey. The Americans are also for the Kurds. Iran is against the Kurds, and also against Turkey and Daesh. Oh, and the Saudis.

The Saudis are also against Assad, but they and the Qataris are also thought to be behind al Qaeda in Syria, whom I haven't mentioned yet, but they are against Daesh and the Kurds.

Britain is against al Qaeda, but *for* the Saudis and the Qataris, who are also against Assad.

So, as you can see, we have no choice but to send in British planes to fire British missiles against Daesh fighters, who may or may not be British. Is that clear?

AS A WOMAN SUING paedophile Jeffrey Epstein alleged that she was also forced to have sex with Prince Andrew when she was 17, the *Eye*'s royal correspondent Flunkey reported from inside the Palace in February.

Andrew's decision to dismiss all accusations of sexual impropriety in a few words, surrounded by the glitz and glamour of Davos, has done nothing to allay the fears of many senior courtiers that the royal family is letting him lead them by the nose to potential disaster.

Three officials have put their concerns in writing to the Queen, arguing that in any other profession someone accused of such misdemeanours would be suspended from duty pending an investigation, and that the royals should follow suit.

This is new territory for Buck House and the Queen is having none of it. Andrew can do no wrong in her eyes and, as she has done since he was a child, she indulges him fully.

Her three correspondents have received curt, typed acknowledgements signed by her secretary. Given their standing, two of them would have expected handwritten replies from the monarch on the small sheets of personal notepaper she uses. They can expect a frosty reception when she returns to London from Sandringham.

It was nothing compared to the reception Andrew got when he finally deigned to go on the record with a disastrous *Newsnight* interview almost five years later. He was forced to retire from all public duties.

IN MARCH, SLICKER raised the alarm about BHS's new owners.

The leading figure in the new owners of the BHS store chain has been made bankrupt twice in the past ten years while also being involved in two multi-million pound company crashes to add to a previous sizeable business failure. The less than stellar CV of former racing driver Dominic Chappell, along with the colourful City career of the new BHS chairman, former stockbroker Keith Smith, and the past achievements of other members of their Retail Acquisitions Syndicate do little to reassure that they can turn round the ailing high street retailer – especially as this is a task that has defeated veteran retailer Sir Philip Green, who is effectively paying Retail Acquisitions – which has no retail experience, despite the name – to take BHS away.

The terms of the deal are a purchase price of £1, no debt and a dowry of around £90m cash plus some freehold properties in return for a business losing £40m a year with 11,000 employees and a pension fund with a £100m-plus (and counting) black hole.

BHS went into administration in April 2016. All 11,000 staff lost their jobs, and the pensions deficit stood at a staggering £571 million. After a year of pressure from parliament and the pensions regulator, multi-billionaire Green made a "voluntary contribution" of £363 million. Chappell had to be taken to court and forced to make a contribution: in January 2020 he was ordered to put in another £9.5m. In November 2020 he was jailed for six years for tax evasion following the BHS acquisition.

SOME HOME (surely "abroad"?) truths were revealed in June.

A chunk of England's green and pleasant land larger than the county of Surrey is owned by companies registered in not so pleasant tax havens. Using freedom of information laws and extensive data crunching, the *Eye* has established that since 1999 titles to 97,500 properties covering 49,000 acres have been acquired by companies in tax havens from the Caribbean to the Channel Islands. With much land also acquired by offshore companies before that, the total area could well be twice that.

The largest single owner by area is a British Virgin Islands company called Gunnerside Estates Ltd, with an expansive 27,258 acres of the North Yorkshire moors much favoured by grouse shooting parties. The man behind the company, American luxury duty-free shopping pioneer Robert Miller, reported to have acquired UK citizenship but to reside tax-efficiently in Hong Kong, is perfectly placed to benefit from the inheritance tax breaks given to a "non-dom" on overseas assets, and is likely to have escaped stamp duty too. None of this prevented the EU paying agricultural subsidies to the estate over a decade or so of €430,000.

Further south, Park Place and its 300-acre grounds near Henley were bought for £120m by the former president of the Bank of Moscow, Andrey Borodin – but not in his own name of course: they are owned by another BVI company, Durio Ltd. The acquisition was made while Borodin was under investigation by Russian authorities who are still pursuing him and froze hundreds of millions of dollars of his assets in Swiss banks before he received political asylum in the UK in 2013.

A mile or so down the Thames, the chocolate-box village of Hambleden is described as "quintessentially English". But it was bought by Swiss foreign exchange dealer Urs Schwarzenbach in 2007 through BVI company Hambleden Estates Ltd.

Billionaire non-dom Lakshmi Mittal owns the 300-acre Alderbrook estate in Cranleigh, Surrey, through BVI company Wilks Holding Ltd. Khoo Kay Peng, the Malaysian chairman of the firm behind Laura Ashley, owns the 866-acre Rossway Park Estate in Hertfordshire via a BVI company, Central Point Group Ltd. In the businessman's divorce proceedings, a judge said of Peng and his estranged wife, "Neither of them currently pays any English taxes whatsoever"…

In 2016, at the international Anti-Corruption Summit in London, the government committed to forcing offshore owners of property to reveal their identities rather than hiding behind anonymous companies; the Draft Registration of Overseas Entities Bill was published in 2018. Two years later, in July 2020, the government announced that they were still giving it "careful consideration".

THE REVOLVING DOOR was spinning yet again in June.

Confirmation that chancellor George Osborne's closest special adviser, Rupert Harrison, is off to work for the world's largest asset management company, BlackRock, just after designing the pensions reforms on which the company is cashing in, again exposes the pisspoor system for approving such appointments. The prime minister's advisory committee on business appointments (Acoba) said it had taken into account "that Mr Harrison has been involved in the development of the government's approach to regulation of the banking sector" but that this "did not specifically relate to asset management". There was no mention of his dealings with BlackRock or work on any policy that would affect it. But his hospitality register shows he was taken to lunch by the asset managers on 1 March 2013, and in the budget less than three weeks later Osborne exempted funds from stamp duty when savers redeem their holdings. BlackRock's UK retail boss was reported as "wholeheartedly" welcoming the changes. Six months later in his autumn statement Osborne exempted "exchange traded funds" from stamp duty on share purchases, again welcomed by BlackRock as of benefit to "a wide range of investors from retail through to pension funds [of which BlackRock manages over £200bn]…"

Harrison's starring role in government was

dreaming up the pensions revolution which allows savers complete freedom with their pots. Osborne announced this in his budget on 19 March last year; and two weeks later Harrison was again lunching with BlackRock. If his involvement with the policy really did "not specifically relate to asset management" as the committee says, what did he discuss over lunch with the world's largest asset manager?

When Osborne himself was ignominiously kicked out of government a year later, one of the many jobs he took was a £650,000-a-year, one-day-a-week position with... BlackRock.

THE SAME MONTH brought news from the *Eye*'s energy correspondent, 'Old Sparky'.

Early signs of how new energy secretary Amber Rudd intends to achieve her ambitions of "keeping the lights on, carbon emissions down and saving money on energy bills" come from her first big decision: a preliminary green light for the Swansea Bay "tidal lagoon" electricity project. To pay for this, we are being softened up for levels of subsidy which would make a nuclear plant blush.

The lagoon, created by a new six-mile sea-wall studded with tide-driven turbines costing £1bn, would have a capacity of 320MW and deliver "14 hours of reliable generation every day". Its developers describe this as "affordable" – which it may be, for them.

The form of subsidy wanted by Tidal Lagoon (Swansea Bay) plc is that offered to EDF for new nuclear plants – an ultra-high electricity price guaranteed for 35 years, paid by electricity users. But whereas EDF's bung is a mere double the present wholesale price, the lagoon project is being pitched as more than *four times* the current price. Briefings suggest that £168 per megawatt hour is the magic number for the lagoon's 14 hours per day of electricity. Today's wholesale price for 24-hour electricity is £41/MWh.

After several years of constantly-shifting numbers – at one point, Lagoon boss Mark Shorrock was pitching for a 90-year contract, compared to the 15 years allowed for wind turbines, and the costs had gone up to £1.3bn – and despite the Welsh Assembly pledging £200m towards the project, the government cancelled the Swansea tidal lagoon in June 2018, on the grounds that it did not provide value for money and would add hundreds of pounds to everyone's electricity bills.

THE PRIME MINISTER'S advisory committee on business appointments was continuing to do a fine job in December.

Former Lib Dem schools minister David Laws – never the most reliable form-filler, as the expenses scandal that once required him to resign from the cabinet demonstrated – has secured a job as international adviser to the hedge fund-backed, free school-sponsoring charity Ark. Acoba's chair, Tory peer Baroness Browning, gave him the green light, writing "the committee took into account that you did not have any dealings with Ark while in office, but the charity would have been impacted by decisions the DfE took on accountability and funding… you did not deal with the organisation directly while in office."

Really? Some very basic checking of this statement – which must have been based on Laws's application – would have found him as schools minister boasting of such dealings, and giving Ark a big plug, in 2013. Speaking at a National Education Trust conference, Laws said: "Let me give you a sense of my thinking, and my ambition, by recounting a visit I made to a school last week. That school is King Solomon's Academy, a new Ark school near Paddington Station." Interviewed by the *Independent* a few months later, Laws mused that "there are some good academy groups doing an absolutely fantastic job – like Ark and Harris". Then, in the run-up to the last election, while Laws was still schools minister, *Schools Week* magazine revealed he had received donations totalling £15,536 from the chair of the Ark trustees, hedge fund manager Paul Marshall. Yet all this went unspotted by the blundering committee before it applied its rubber stamp!

2016

RUPERT MURDOCH (net worth: £8.35bn) announced his marriage to wife number four – none other than Jerry Hall, former partner of rock stars Brian Ferry (£50m) and Mick Jagger (£225m).

Never Too Old *by SYLVIE KRIN*

The six foot nine-inch Texan bombshell turned on her extra-high heels outside the Golden Globe Awards and looked down at the red carpet to where her elderly escort appeared to have collapsed. "Are you alright, Rupee?" she drawled. "Have you fallen over?"

"Strewth no, Leggy," gasped the world's sexiest senior citizen. "I'm down on one knee. I've got an important question to ask you. Will you make me the happiest man in the world – and sign a pre-nup?"

Leggy's heart beat faster as she answered him breathlessly, lost in the heady rush of new love. "You'll have to talk to my lawyers, Messrs Stitch, Dupp, Lyke & Kipper."

"I'll take that as a 'yes'," beamed the Chairman of Fux News, as a concerned Dame Judi Dench helped him to his feet. "There we go, dear," she said kindly, "and just let me know if you need to go to the toilet."

Distantly, bells began to ring out. But was his hearing going? Instead of the joyful peal he expected, were they not tolling out "*Deng! Deng! Deng!*"...?

THERE WAS A SUDDEN spate of unexpected celebrity deaths (David Bowie, Alan Rickman, Terry Wogan, Prince, Victoria Wood and Caroline Aherne among them).

Private Eye's all-purpose cut-out-and-week article

The world has lost [celebrity] who has died after a short/long/public/private/brave/cowardly battle with cancer. Looking back over a career which spanned four/five/six/fifteen decades, it seems fair to say that no one will ever wield a microphone/act/dance/present television programmes as well, ever again, and that they were the most iconic/extraordinary/iconic and extraordinary talent in their chosen field.

Tributes have poured in from other celebrities/normal people on Twitter/abnormal people on Twitter, and the Prime Minister has paid personal tribute, saying convincingly/unconvincingly how personally fond of his/her work he was.

THREE CO-ORDINATED suicide bomb attacks in Brussels killed 32 people and injured more than 300. ISIS claimed responsibility.

EXCLUSIVE TO ALL NEWSPAPERS

WE MUST NOT GIVE IN TO TERROR BY OVER-REACTING

ON OTHER PAGES
PANIC! 1 FEAR! 2 HORROR! 3 DEATH! 4 SLAUGHTER! 5 APOCALYPSE! 6 ARMAGEDDON! 7 HELP! 8 WE ARE ALL GOING TO DIE! 94

AS THE REFERENDUM on whether or not Britain should leave the EU approached, the part-time MP for Uxbridge used his *Telegraph* column to decide which way to jump.

Why this is the most important decision for a generation

by Boris Johnson, MP for Oxbridge South

Cripes! Every now and then history comes up and taps you on the shoulder to say, "This one is a game-changer. You'd better get it right, or the future looks pretty grim."

I have to tell you that it is really the hardest decision I will ever have to make. Do I:

a) line up with my old school chum, Dave, and help the "Remainers" to win a glorious victory – in which case Dave would be bound to do the decent thing and give Bozza a top job as his heir apparent? or

b) stab Dave in the back and throw in my lot with the "Leavers" who at the moment are in a total shambles because they so obviously lack a strong, popular leader who could lead them to an even more glorious victory?

And that, readers, is what the real question of this whole European campaign comes down to: IN Number 10 or OUT in the wilderness?

So you can see why Bozza is burning the midnight oil at both ends on this one!

AS REFERENDUM DAY approached, President Obama declared an independent UK would be at the "back of the queue" for a trade deal and David Cameron suggested terror group ISIS would love to see us leave…

So-called 'UK' not first in queue

In a shock referendum intervention, ISIS leader Abig Bigdaddy said there was no "special relationship" between the UK and ISIS and Britain would have to wait its turn to get bombed. He said, "We have many complex terrorist plots already in place, linked to major European nations, that have taken years to put together. We are not just going to start doing special terror plots for the so-called 'UK' just because it leaves the EU."

…CHANCELLOR GEORGE OSBORNE produced nonsensical figures demonstrating the supposed cost of leaving the EU which were widely denounced as "Project Fear"…

Don't put hard-fought austerity at risk

George Osborne has been presenting the Treasury case for Remain, insisting that Britain should not put at risk the crippling austerity that has strangled all hope in the country since 2010. "If Britain votes Leave, the UK economy could sink overnight," the Chancellor warned, "instead of sinking slowly and painfully as it has under my stewardship these past six years."

He rejected claims that the Treasury had produced a "dodgy dossier" designed to support his argument. "Our forecast makes it clear that should Britain vote to leave the EU, our economy would be destroyed within 45 minutes."

…THE OFFICIAL LEAVE campaign responded with their own equally inaccurate numbers…

Modern Nursery Rhymes

"The lies on the bus come round and round, round and round, round and round"

This childhood favourite is based on the old saying "You wait ages for a bogus statistic on a bus, and then 350 million come along at once."

…AND OTHER LEAVERS, not to be outdone, showed they could do inaccurate scaremongering too.

Country finally united

Nigel Farage has strongly defended his "Breaking Point" immigration poster, saying it had provided a welcome boost to the nation by uniting the whole country in hating him. "Of course it was easy to get the Remain camp to hate me," announced Farage, downing his fifth pint in the Red Lion, "but to actually get Gove and Boris from the Leave campaign condemning me too, well, that's s bit special. People from all sides of the political spectrum have called my poster 'inflammatory', 'divisive' and 'xenophobic', but I have no problem with that. I've always loved a compliment."

WITH THE SHOCKING murder of pro-EU MP Jo Cox a week before polling day, the referendum seemed to be splitting the UK along hostile and increasingly irreparable lines.

BRITAIN VOTED by a 52% to 48% margin to leave the EU.

Britain vote to leave frying pan for fire

In a knife-edge decision, Britain narrowly voted to exit from the unpopular frying pan in favour of an optimistic leap into the roaring furnace.

The surprise vote to exchange the status quo of gently sizzling in continental olive oil for roasting unprotected in the giant fire below came after months of argument. Claims that exiting the pan would result in everyone burning to death were dismissed by Leave fans as "Project Fire". Since the result, however, some Leave voters have expressed regret. As one said, "I thought a leap in the dark was bound to result in feeling much cooler, but now I think we are all toast."

Another was surprised to find several turkeys roasting in the fire, despite promises from the Leave campaign that they would be prevented from coming in. Questioned about their presence, the birds said that they had heard very good things about Christmas.

IN QUICK SUCCESSION, David Cameron resigned as prime minister, Michael Gove stabbed his Leave colleague Boris Johnson in the back and prevented him running for Tory leader before being knocked out of the race himself, Theresa May emerged as a front-runner, Nigel Farage resigned from UKIP saying his work was done, and dozens of Labour MPs resigned from the shadow cabinet and held a vote of no confidence in a failed attempt to oust Jeremy Corbyn.

FOR A WHILE, all was chaos.

DAILY EXPRESS

BRITAIN HAS TAKEN BACK CONTROL

ON OTHER PAGES: Nobody in control

BUT THERESA MAY was swiftly confirmed as the new prime minister...

...AND NEW headmistress.

St Theresa's Independent State Grammar School

Good afternoon,

Thank you for reading this newsletter, which is the first since the school was described as "Failing" and put in special measures. This is not a criticism of the previous Headmaster, to whom I would like to pay tribute for making the school what it is today, but I simply don't have time at the moment, owing to the vast amount of work needed to turn the school around.

AND HER NEWLY-APPOINTED team quickly set about implementing Brexit.

BREXIT NEWS IN BRIEF... David Davis hails trade deal with Narnia, says similar deals with Brigadoon and Lilliput in progress ● *International Trade Secretary Liam Fox says British businessmen 'too lazy' to consider exporting, suggests they follow example of his friend Adam Werritty* ● Office For National Statistics qualifies figures showing that despite "Project Fear" warnings, Brexit has had little effect on economy, by pointing out Brexit hasn't actually happened yet ● *BREXIT JOBS BOOM! as Whitehall forced to hire hundreds of civil servants to work out how on earth to extricate us from EU* ● Telegraph launches campaign to relaunch royal yacht Britannia as Brexit flagship, owners say "We recognise a scuttled ship when we see one" ● *IMMIGRATION: Theresa May pledges to accept "thousands more excuses" for not taking in refugees.*

ACCUSED OF LETTING anti-Semitism flourish in his Labour party, Jeremy Corbyn hired former Liberty director Shami Chakrabarti to deliver what many considered to be a whitewash – and gave her a peerage and a seat in the shadow cabinet to say thank you.

> I'd like you to clear the party of claims of anti-Semitism

> I'd be honoured

ALTHOUGH WHETHER or not he could get a seat on a train somehow became an even bigger scandal.

Traingate: Day 94

Jeremy Corbyn has been praised as a once-in-a-generation politician for holding a sit-down protest about overcrowding on British trains on the only train in the UK that actually had seats free.

"For Jeremy to actually find a train with loads of empty seats on which to make his protest shows he is a politician like no other," said Corbyn's spin-doctors, who had spent the previous day claiming variously that all the seats were taken by people too small to show up on CCTV footage from the train, by Pokemon Go characters invisible to the naked eye, or by blind lepers for whom the leader had selflessly given up his seat. "For our next video, we plan to visit a ram-packed brewery to demonstrate that this is no way to run a party."

DESPITE A HOST OF WOMEN coming forward to say Donald Trump had sexually assaulted them – and even a recording of him boasting about doing so – he was elected US President.

IN APRIL, THE PANAMA PAPERS leak revealed details of hundreds of thousands of offshore shell companies created to avoid tax and facilitate money laundering.

"The investigation we need… is for HMRC, our tax authority, to use all the information that is coming out of Panama to make sure companies and individuals are paying their taxes properly," thundered David Cameron the day after the first Panama Papers stories. This means busy times ahead for HM Revenue & Customs' recently promoted executive chairman, Edward Troup.

Until 2004, Troup was head of "tax strategy" and a senior partner at City law firm Simmons & Simmons. He has a long record working with and for tax havens, and has publicly defended them. He told a 1999 parliamentary committee that havens "assist tremendously" in mobilising capital and admitted he had been paid to lobby the Organisation for Economic Co-operation and Development for them.

Now papers obtained by the International Consortium of Investigative Journalists and seen by the *Eye* reveal Simmons & Simmons' close involvement with running offshore companies while Troup was its senior taxman. In one case, the firm administered a series of investment companies on behalf of their beneficial owner, a certain Sheikh Hamad bin Jassim bin Jaber Al-Thani (known as "HBJ"), then foreign minister and later prime minister of Qatar and a major UK property owner (including a joint venture in the One Hyde Park development with the Candy brothers). They included two companies in the Bahamas and four in Panama. On 5 July 2002, Simmons & Simmons wrote to the Panamanian law firm at the centre of the leak, Mossack Fonseca, to inform it that HBJ became sole director of these companies. This was not long after, in 2000, HBJ had compensated the Jersey authorities for an inquiry into a complex trust structure he had put in place after allegedly benefiting from an arms contract as foreign minister.

The files also show Simmons & Simmons acting until 2003 as a director and agent for a BVI company called Chale Ltd, which owned upmarket properties in Piccadilly and Mayfair on behalf of a wealthy Saudi sheikh, before handing the firm to the sheikh's in-house management. Not long after Troup left the firm to take a job in the Treasury in charge of business tax (where he saw huge concessions to multinationals moving profits into tax havens) his old colleagues began to advise the prime minister's father Ian Cameron's Panama company, Blairmore, on such matters as whether to go to the Caymans or Bermuda. Just the man taxpayers would want to investigate the Panama files!

Troup left HMRC in 2018 – and inevitably, flipped back from gamekeeper to poacher with a job as a "senior tax consultant" at management consultants McKinsey.

IN THE SAME ISSUE, the *Eye* revealed details of a story no one else wanted to print.

In November 2013, the Tory MP John Whittingdale and his girlfriend Olivia King were photographed by a snapper working for the *Sunday People* at a glitzy fundraising dinner attended by the Duchess of Cambridge. Why the interest? The paper had been tipped off that King worked as a £200-an-hour dominatrix at a basement in London SW5 under the professional name Mistress Kate.

The *People* seemed enthusiastic about its scoop. But Mirror Group bosses said that the story must not run.

In January 2014, the *Sun* took it up. "The editor is really keen and having final meeting with lawyers tomorrow," a hack told a source. Again the story was spiked. A month later the *Mail on Sunday* seemed ready to publish. But shortly before it was due to run, editor Geordie Greig suddenly told staff it was dropped and their investigation must stop. No reason was given.

It is possible that each newspaper independently concluded that there was no public interest. Whittingdale is divorced, and at that time was not a cabinet minister. But such scruples haven't stopped them running salacious scoops on much lower-profile politicians: in September 2014 the *Sunday Mirror* lured Tory MP Brooks Newmark into "sexting" pictures of his penis, and last July the Labour peer Lord Sewel was secretly filmed by the *Sun on Sunday* cavorting with two prostitutes.

One striking difference with Whittingdale is that at the time he was chair of the Commons Select Committee for Culture, Media and Sport. The press had good reason to keep him sweet, because he seemed sympathetic to the Street of Shame, telling parliament in October that year that any new regulator must be one which "commands the support of as many of the newspapers as possible, rather than a system which commands the support of none of them".

In 2015 Whittingdale was, rather surprisingly, elevated to the cabinet as culture secretary, responsible for deciding if press regulation is working. Cue great rejoicing among editors, who started referring to him as "our asset". Thank goodness they had not printed the Mistress Kate story!

Soon afterwards, however, the *Independent* started investigating how and why the tabloids had suppressed a classic tabloid splash. But then, on 19 October 2015, the culture secretary gave a speech to the Society of Editors conference in London, and revealed that he had chosen not yet to activate a draconian clause in the Crime and Courts Act forcing newspapers and magazines outside the state-approved system to pay costs in libel and privacy cases even if they won. The next day, the *Indy* editor told hacks, "We can't do this story, I'm afraid."

The *Independent* is based in the Kensington HQ of the *Daily Mail*, which also provides some back-office services. An *Indy* executive puts it this way: "As tenants of the *Mail* we cannot be seen to take away an asset like Whittingdale from them. We would be out on the street."

Whittingdale subsequently issued a statement saying he had ended his relationship with Olivia King after learning what she did for a living and that the tabloids were investigating.

ENERGY CORRESPONDENT 'Old Sparky' issued a warning in October.

In his energy policy speech last month Jeremy Corbyn lauded as "brilliant" Nottingham council's gas and electricity supply venture, Robin Hood Energy. Did he speak too soon?

While other councils have also tried to undercut the "Big Six" suppliers, the new municipal energy companies have only been thriving because wholesale prices have been falling, meaning they can undercut the big suppliers who buy in several years in advance to secure supplies. It's an easy trick – until prices turn, that is, when they will have to put more of their council taxpayers' money on the line.

When prices rise, small players are at a big disadvantage – because buying forward, to secure supplies at today's prices, needs a high credit rating or a guarantee from their owners. The only way local authorities can provide this for their tiny new supply ventures is to put council taxpayers' money at risk in the energy markets.

Nottingham council had sunk £43m in the venture and risked £16.5m in guarantees by the time it finally pulled the plug on Robin Hood Energy four years later.

NOVEMBER BROUGHT news of international trade.

UK Export Finance, the arm of the government that guarantees and funds overseas trade, is almost certainly allowing UK taxpayers' money to be used to bankroll bribery and corruption, *Private Eye* has discovered. In eight years from 2007, a total of 260 of the 1,272 companies applying to the organisation disclosed that they had paid commissions to agents on the contracts they wanted funded or guaranteed. Such commissions are often cover for bribes to win business, as a long line of cases including recent ones featuring Rolls-Royce and Airbus show, and UK Export Finance (formerly the Export Credit Guarantees Department) should therefore refer suspicious-looking arrangements to law enforcers from the Serious Fraud Office (SFO) or National Crime Agency.

However, records show that since 2007 it did not do that in *any* of the 260 cases. The only check, which evidently reassured in every single case, was to ask "the relevant UK overseas diplomatic mission about the standing of that agent".

But even in the redacted records the *Eye* obtained using Freedom of Information laws, there are some flapping red flags of suspicion. In one example, a company simply said an agent was providing "facilitation" in return for a handy "10 percent contract value". For 20 percent commission another agent provided "introduction and contract negotiation". "Market entry facilitation, business development and relationship building" was rewarded with "$4m over the development phase" and "$2.5m per annum over the duration of the construction phase".

The SFO's guidance on the 2010 Bribery Act is clear: "A facilitation payment is a type of bribe and should be seen as such." Yet this is what British taxpayers are now backing.

In 2017 engineering company Rolls Royce paid £671m to settle 12 cases of "conspiracy to corrupt or failure to prevent bribery" brought by the SFO. In at least three of them, UK Export Finance and its predecessor had given the deals taxpayer backing.

THINGS WERE HEATING UP in Northern Ireland in December.

A huge cock-up with Northern Ireland's Renewable Heat Incentive (RHI) will cost the public purse £140m over the next five years, while encouraging businesses to heat buildings pointlessly – yet officials and regulators have no record of meetings when the problem with the scheme emerged, Stormont Assembly members were told. And Economy minister Simon Hamilton has refused to reveal a full list of schemes signed up to benefit from the fraud.

The Northern Ireland public accounts committee recently questioned regulators from Ofgem about the botched initiative, intended to encourage the use of biomass heat technology, burning wood pellets. An Audit Office investigation earlier this year found the deal was a money-spinner for farmers and factories to install boilers and claim a subsidy to heat buildings that didn't need heating. The auditor's report said a whistleblower told them that in one case "a farmer who has no need for a biomass boiler is aiming to collect approximately £1m over the next 20 years for heating an empty shed".

The accounts of Northern Ireland's enterprise and trade department (DETI) have been qualified as a result of the mess, which leaves the government with 20-year commitments to payments which will run into hundreds of millions of pounds.

The committee was told that no meeting between Ofgem and DETI between August 2014 and November 2015 was formally minuted, so there was no record of the period when the lack of any mechanism to prevent abuse of the system became evident and applications for the subsidy spiked. Ofgem boss Chris Poulton described this as an "oversight".

At a later meeting of the committee, Dr Andrew McCormick, permanent secretary at the economy department, said he couldn't "recall anything that was on the scale in relation to both opportunity costs to public services and... poor value for money".

The Renewable Heat Incentive scandal, for which DUP first minister Arlene Foster had been responsible in her previous job, led to the collapse of the Northern Ireland Assembly in January 2017, when her deputy, Sinn Fein's Martin McGuinness, resigned in protest. Northern Ireland was left without a working government for the following three years. In March 2020, a public inquiry concluded that the scheme "should never have been adopted", identified several "instances of unacceptable behaviour" by special advisers in government and confirmed that "basic administration and record keeping was on too many occasions lacking".

2017

AMID CLAIMS THAT the Russians had helped him beat Hillary Clinton to the job, the new US President was sworn in before a small crowd he insisted was much bigger than any crowd ever before in history.

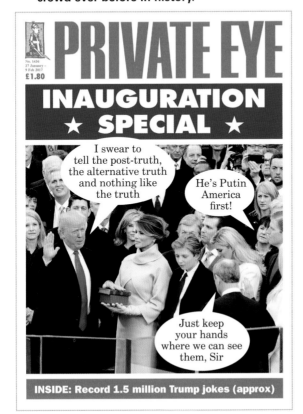

FIRST MINISTER Nicola Sturgeon, leader of the SNP, demanded another referendum on Scottish independence – but Theresa May refused.

That Scottish Referendum question in full

Do you want to be plunged into economic chaos…?

☐ On your own   ☐ With the rest of us

THERESA MAY triggered Article 50, giving the UK precisely one year to leave the EU, and immediately instigated the legislation that would become necessary.

That Great Repeal Bill in full

1. The hated European Communities Act which for 44 years has been the supreme symbol of our subservience to laws passed by those over whom we have no control shall be repealed.
2. All 19,000 EU laws shall then be incorporated into British law.

3. Hey presto! All that nasty foreign law has been transformed into benign, responsible British law as approved by our own sovereign British parliament.
4. All EU red tape to be changed to patriotic red, white and blue tape.
5. Er…
6. That isn't it.

A "LONE WOLF" terrorist drove a car into pedestrians on Westminster Bridge, killing four people, before entering the grounds of the Houses of Parliament and stabbing a police officer to death. It came amid calls for a crackdown on end-to-end encrypted communications and radical websites.

EXCLUSIVE TO ALL NEWSPAPERS

Sick terror tips easily available on Google

This paper has discovered shocking websites containing information on how to murder people are easily accessible via Google, including sick tips revealing:

- People can be run over by CARS
- People are vulnerable to KNIVES
- People die when they are SHOT

It would take a matter of minutes for evil ISIS thugs to piece together enough information to *(cont. p94)*

AFTER MONTHS of promising she wasn't going to call a general election, Theresa May called a general election, assuming the apparent unpopularity of the Labour leader would make it a walkover.

How the election coverage will look

Daily Mail – JEREMY CORBYN IS UTTERLY RUBBISH

The Sun – JEREMY CORBYN IS BLOODY RUBBISH

The Daily Telegraph – JEREMY CORBYN IS TERRIBLY RUBBISH

The Times – POLL SHOWS JEREMY CORBYN IS RUBBISH

The Guardian – JEMERY CORBYN IS ONLY SLIGHTLY RUBBISH

Daily Express – DID RUBBISH CORBYN HAVE SOMETHING TO DO WITH MADDIE'S DISAPPEARANCE

Daily Mirror – KEIR STARMER IS NOT RUBBISH

BUT THE PRIME MINISTER herself became just as much of a problem, seeming incapable of doing anything but dully intoning her catchphrase "strong and stable".

Messaging 'not robotic and repetitive'

The Daleks today hit out furiously at claims that their message to Britain was "robotic and repetitive".

"Repeating the phrase 'Exterminate, exterminate, exterminate' over and over again is very important in this multi-media age," said one unthinking automaton. "There may be some people out there who do not watch the bulletins, and might not be aware that we are intending to exterminate everyone. So it clearly and concisely sets out what the British people can expect from us for the next five years, should they choose to be enslaved by us."

MAY ALSO EXECUTED a disastrous U-turn on care funding, with proposals the opposition were quick to dub a "Dementia Tax"…

A Doctor Writes

As a doctor, I'm often asked by the Prime Minister, "Doctor, do I have dementia? I keep forgetting things like the fact older people do not like having all their money taken away."

The simple answer is that yes, she does appear to be exhibiting signs of memory loss which form a worrying pattern, such as forgetting she promised not to have an election. This can be established with simple questions, such as "Do you know who the Prime Minister is?", to which the correct answer is, "not for long".

…WITH THE RESULT that she lost her majority, and was forced to do a £1bn deal with the DUP in order to prop up a fragile government.

A SUICIDE BOMBER launched an attack on an Ariana Grande concert packed with children at Manchester Arena. 23 people were killed and over 800 wounded. MI5 launched an inquiry into how it had missed multiple warnings about the perpetrator.

Those subtle, hard-to-spot indicators that your neighbour may be an Islamist terrorist

1. Quiet, studious type who keeps himself to himself
2. Apart from putting Isis flag in window
3. And tendency to scream "Death to the West" while putting out bins
4. Complains he has been banned from local mosque for being too extreme
5. Frequently shows you holiday snaps from Libya and Syria
7. Flies into rage when Ocado delivers strawberries as nearest substitute to bomb he has ordered
8. Friends regularly warn you they are alarmed by his obvious radicalisation
9. Establishes caliphate in back garden
10. Is not detained at any point by MI5

WEEKS LATER, three men launched another terror attack on London Bridge. This time, one of them had actually appeared in a Channel 4 documentary called *Jihadis Next Door*.

11. Has actually starred in a Channel 4 show which identified him as a Jihadi.

BREXIT SECRETARY David Davis didn't seem entirely committed to negotiations.

Let's Parlez Franglais

Numéro 94 – Le deuxième round des négotiations historiques entre le Royaume Uni et l'EU

Davis: Bonjour, Michel
Barnier: Bonjour, David.
Davis: Au revoir, Michel!
Barnier: Vous êtes walking out?
Davis: Non, mais j'ai un Eurostar booké dans cinq minutes.
Barnier: Mais nous avons un montagne énorme de travail! Oû sont vos notes?
Davis: Moi, je bring rien to les talks!
Barnier: Nous all know ça!
Davis: Je suis off maintenant. See vous en Septembre!
Barnier: Mais c'est seulement le fin de July?
Davis: Oui, et aussi le fin de May! Je dois être back home.
Continué apres 94 jours de vacances…

A FIRE IN THE GRENFELL tower block in West London spread rapidly and devastatingly due to the dangerous cladding fitted to the building. 72 people died.

Bonfire of
Regulations

DONALD TRUMP was churning through senior staff at a rate of knots.

EYE CLASSIC MOVIE

All the President's men have resigned

A plucky team of investigators from the *Washington Post* have been given the job of uncovering a scandal at the White House. But can they manage it before literally everyone in the country has been hired, made a horrific and easily avoidable blunder, and then resigned?

CAST

Richard Nixon: *Donald Trump*

Aide 1: *Jared Kushner*

Corrupt Aide 2: ~~*Mike Flynn Sean Spicer Reince Priebus Steve Bannon*~~ *Jeff Sessions*

Deep Throat, the insider revealing top secret information: *The President's Twitter account*

AFTER YEARS SPENT sexually abusing and bullying women, Hollywood producer Harvey Weinstein was finally unmasked.

Why, oh why didn't I say anything earlier?

The silence has been deafening. For years I have sat typing up promotional guff for all the films Harvey told me were marvellous, without ever mentioning the sordid truth about his treatment of young actresses. His behaviour was an open secret, albeit one I thought I probably shouldn't mention in case I didn't get invited to his Oscar night party.

How could I do it? That is the question facing me today. So instead I'm going to write a piece attacking everyone in Hollywood for keeping quiet as the movie mogul monster was allowed to rampage unchecked, and even blame his actress victims themselves for not speaking out earlier.

Shame on everyone apart from me!

IT LED TO AN OUTPOURING of other cases of sexual harassment being exposed, including several in and around parliament.

ROLLING #METOO NEWS: Pestminster latest – "It's absolutely disgusting that the other side have misogynist pervs amongst them," explain both Conservatives and Labour ● *Theresa May expresses sympathy with women bullied by arrogant men into doing things they don't want to do #MayToo* ● How could seedy photographer have got away with it for so long, ask newspapers which kept buying and printing his photos ● *Fashion world in shock: "I thought we had created a wholesome, nurturing environment in which to take highly-sexualised photographs of emaciated underage models"* ● Shock as taboo-busting comedian who made loads of creepy jokes about his sex obsession turns out to have been sex pest ● *Spoiler Alert: Kevin Spacey from Usual Suspects turns out to have been baddie all along*

PRITI PATEL WAS FORCED to resign as international development secretary after admitting she had held 12 unauthorised meetings – including with the prime minister and two of his ministers – during a "family holiday" in Israel.

Secret meetings shock

A senior member of the government has been called in to face the music after it emerged that they had embroiled themselves in one of the most poisonous feuds in history by holding secret meetings with one side's most hardline representative.

"What was Benjamin Netanyahu thinking, meeting with Priti Patel?" asked one Israeli. "Brexit has been a source of bitter conflict for so long now, with the Remainers being forcibly relocated far away from their chosen homeland, Europe, and Leavers insisting they have a right to the Promised Land, even if it does mean the price of both milk and honey going up. The whole issue is just toxic, and there's no sign of any peaceful resolution. Why get involved at all?"

96-YEAR-OLD Prince Philip announced his retirement from public duties.

And now the end is near and so I face the final curtain ...

PRINCE HARRY announced his engagement.

What should Meghan's royal title be? You decide

The Princess of Wales

The Duchess of Windsor

The Duchess of Duke Street

The Duchess of Hazzard

The Dowager Lady Grantham

Baroness Meggie Thatcher

The Mystic of Meghan

The Duchess Potato

The Duchess Original Oatmeal and Ginger Fruity Crumpet

Queen Meghan, Khaleesi of the Great Grass Sea, Lady Regnant of the Seven Kingdoms, Breaker of Chains and Mother of Dragons

THERESA MAY and the EU announced a "breakthrough" Brexit divorce deal which would allow talks to move on to the next stage. It was rather short on detail.

A RELIGIOUS ABUSER was unmasked in February.

The Archbishop of Canterbury says that the Church has "failed terribly" in the case of John Smyth QC, accused of savage assaults on teenage boys and young men. And how. By his own admission, Justin Welby was told early in 2013 about Smyth's monstrous behaviour – but said nothing. And it surprises some of Smyth's victims that he hadn't known about them much earlier. Many of them attended annual Christian camps for top public schoolboys run by the Iwerne Trust, a charity chaired by Smyth. As a student in the late 1970s, Welby was one of his "dormitory officers" at the camps, which were run along the lines of a Victorian public school to produce an officer class of muscular evangelists. According to the archbishop's office, "No one discussed allegations of abuse by John Smyth with him."

Many of Smyth's victims were also pupils at Winchester: although he had no official connection to the school he lived nearby. After Sunday chapel he would invite boys back to his house, supposedly for Christian discussions. In fact he was taking them to his shed and flogging them – all in the name of Jesus, to cleanse them of impure thoughts. The standard cure for masturbation was 100 strokes of the cane: for the sin of pride, 400.

One victim who received thousands of lashes over four years was told by Smyth that he could expect a "special" beating for his birthday. Unable to face the prospect, he tried to kill himself – but only after sending an anonymous letter to the Rev David Fletcher, an Iwerne trustee, about Smyth's sado-evangelism.

After this failed suicide attempt, the trust asked the Rev Mark Ruston to investigate. He located 13 victims. "The scale and severity of the practice was horrific," Ruston wrote in his March 1982 report, which the *Eye* has obtained. "I have seen bruised and sore buttocks, some two and a half months after the beating."

Ruston also contacted former camp officials – but not, apparently, his close friend and ex-flatmate, Justin Welby. Nor, it seems, did Welby hear anything from another good friend, the Rev David Fletcher, who commissioned the inquiry.

Ruston's report was sent to all the Iwerne trustees, including several prominent clergymen, and to the headmaster of Winchester, John Thorn. None of them saw fit to contact the police. Thorn merely asked Smyth for a private undertaking that "my mission can no longer lie with boys and young men".

The Iwerne Trust became the Titus Trust in 1997, for unclear reasons. "Did they want to distance themselves from things that might come back to haunt them?" wonders one churchman. Yet although it inherited Iwerne's files, the one containing Ruston's report must have gone astray. According to a statement two weeks ago, "it was only in 2014 that the board of the Titus Trust became aware of these allegations". Very puzzling.

When the trustees *did* officially become aware, they retained the top Christian media consultant Andrew Graystone to advise them what to do – but when he recommended an independent investigation they recoiled in horror, stopped paying his monthly retainer and made no further contact with him. So the truth remained hidden for a few years longer – thanks to people and institutions that claimed to be doing God's work.

Smyth had moved to Zimbabwe in 1984, where he was running similar camps, at one of which a boy died. He was in the process of being extradited to face criminal charges in the UK when he died in 2018. The following year, the Church of England commissioned an independent review into its handling of allegations about Smyth, which is yet to conclude. In 2020, the Titus Trust came to a legal settlement with three of his victims, and made a limited apology for its previous "inadequate" response.

IN JUNE, following the devastating Grenfell Tower fire, the *Eye* offered some background.

Long before the fire, the Grenfell Action Group (GAG), representing local residents, had published a regular blog cataloguing the many failings of the Royal Borough of Kensington & Chelsea and the Kensington & Chelsea Tenant Management Organisation (TMO) which runs social housing in the borough on behalf of the council. In November 2016 a GAG post stated: "It is our conviction that a serious fire in a tower block or similar high density residential property is the most likely reason that those who wield power at TMO will be found out and brought to justice!"

The TMO was set up in 1996 to manage the Tory council's 9,760 properties. Ultimate responsibility still remained with the council, which at any one time has at least two councillors on the TMO board. When it started life it was claimed the TMO would be "tenant-led" and give residents a more prominent voice. In 2007 and 2008, tenant members made numerous unsuccessful attempts to call Extraordinary General

Meetings to hold the board to account over their fears about safety, financial malpractice and pisspoor governance.

In December 2008, having run out of excuses not to hold any EGMs, the board changed the TMO's constitution without consultation so that 250 signatories, rather than 50, would be needed to petition for an EGM. Rules for Annual General Meetings were also tightened: tenant members were no longer permitted to ask questions under "any other business", but instead had to write them down in no more than 40 words and submit them ahead of the AGM to the chairman, who decided whether they would be answered or not.

A public inquiry into the fire is still ongoing at time of writing.

THE EYE QUESTIONED the direction of travel on the proposed high-speed rail line between London and the north of England in July.

With the announcement of £6.6bn worth of contracts for the first phase of HS2 by Chris Grayling's transport department, there's no turning back from the questionable £56bn project. And the task of ensuring such a huge amount of public money is properly spent with consortia led by engineering companies Carillion, Balfour Beatty, Costain and Sir Robert McAlpine has become a particularly important one.

The job, like so much else on HS2, has been outsourced – to a senior beancounter from KPMG. Sue Kershaw, the firm's head of infrastructure programme and project management, claims she is "responsible to the Department for Transport for assuring HS2 is delivered to time and budget and quality... and that value is evidenced for expenditure of the public purse. This role is effectively the eyes and ears of the government on the project."

It might be hoped that an objective public servant rather than a consultant would have this task – especially as KPMG is not without other interests in the project. Among its clients are, er, Carillion, Balfour Beatty and Sir Robert McAlpine. It audits and provides other services for the first two and acts as a consultant for the third. Kershaw's boss, Richard Threlfall, describes himself as the "lead partner for Sir Robert McAlpine".

And how did HS2 get the go-ahead? Back in 2013 none other than KPMG were brought in to report on the economics of the project and, lo and behold, calculated benefits of £15bn a year. Legislative approval was duly given. When experts looked at the work, they found a series of implausible assumptions so serious that the Treasury Select Committee chair wrote to Grayling to tell him "HS2 has the weakest economic case of all the projects within the infrastructure programme, yet it is being pursued with the most enthusiasm." One of the authors of KPMG's report was Richard Threlfall.

By January 2020, the estimated cost of HS2 had nearly doubled, to £103bn.

DECEMBER DELIVERED news of how the government spent money at the other end of the scale.

Eye readers know all too well the many problems with health assessments carried out by Crapita and Atos, which have seen disabled people lose their personal independent payment (PIP), which replaces disability living allowance. Others have faced reductions in help with care and getting out – often with tragic consequences. And those affected have repeatedly had to enforce their rights through the courts. This month a disabled woman will take the Department for Work and Pensions to court over "unfair and discriminatory" changes to PIP.

A tribunal in November 2016 found that people with mental health conditions such as schizophrenia, agoraphobia, extreme anxiety or post-traumatic stress disorder, who need to be escorted on journeys because of the psychological distress, should be treated in the same way as someone who cannot travel alone because of visual or cognitive impairment. But instead of implementing the decision, Penny Mordaunt, then minister for disabled people, changed the rules so she wouldn't have to – without consultation or recourse to parliament. Hence the December court action, where the woman, who cannot be identified, will argue that she and others with "invisible" disabilities are being denied the right to participate in society.

Even when the DWP admits a fundamental flaw in PIP, it appears reluctant to make amends. Thousands of people, many with epilepsy, have been denied the benefit because the DWP guidance wrongly excluded safety consideration for those at risk of unconsciousness. Seven months after a tribunal ruled the guidance "unlawful", the DWP announced "updates" providing up to £90 a week. It has now emerged, however, that ministers will only backdate payments to the March date of the tribunal ruling – even though people may have been wrongly deprived of the benefit for years.

The DWP says criticism of PIP needs to be put into context: of 2.6m PIP decisions to date, only 8 percent have gone to appeal. That translates, though, to more than 200,000 people thrown into increased poverty, exclusion, ill-health and stress while they fight a tribunal. More than half the decisions are overturned. But by then, those wrongly deprived of their benefits may have lost their independence, their mobility cars, their jobs or homes – and in some cases their lives.

The woman won the case, with the High Court ruling that Mordaunt's rule change was "manifestly without reasonable foundation" and "blatantly discriminated" against people with psychiatric problems. The government was forced to review 1.6 million cases, with around 220,000 disabled people expected to receive more money as a result.

2018

THE BBC'S CHINA editor, Carrie Gracie, resigned and announced she was taking legal action against her bosses for paying her far less than men in equivalent jobs, on the very day she was co-presenting the *Today* programme with the extravagantly-remunerated John Humphrys.

Are You Being Paid?

Classic BBC sitcom starring a creaking institution full of cheerful 1970s sexism

Enter Young Mrs Gracie, coming out of the BBC lift.

Gracie: You're all doing very well! Apart from the women, obviously. Mr Humphrys?

Mr Humphrys: I'm not free! I'm extremely expensive.

Mrs Slocombe: Am I being paid less because of my pussy?

(Audience in hysterics. Theme tune plays)

Voice from lift: Men's pay: going down!

ANACHRONISTIC MP Jacob Rees-Mogg was made leader of the so-called European Research Group, pushing for the hardest possible Brexit within the Conservative party – and even being talked up as a possible party leader.

AFTER EIGHT YEARS of public sector austerity, the country was visibly crumbling.

"It makes you wonder how deep these potholes have to get before the council does something"

SERGEI SKRIPAL, a former Russian military officer and double agent for the UK, who had been living quietly in Salisbury since a spy swap in 2010, was poisoned along with his daughter Yulia. The substance used was quickly identified as Novichok, a nerve agent developed by the Soviet Union. Putin's government denied any involvement.

MORNING TSAR

Vlad the Impaler denies impaling anyone

Eastern European strongman Vlad the Impaler has denied having anything to do with a number of suspicious deaths involving people impaled on stakes.

"Admittedly, they were all my enemies, and I had vowed vengeance on them, but people are just taking two and two and making four," he told investigative scribes. Asked about the stakes found impaled in the bodies, which bore the legend "If found please return to V. Impaler", Mr Impaler offered to "do an independent analysis as to their provenance, which will find I have never clapped eyes on these stakes of mine before". He declined to answer further questions, pointing out that he still had lots of stakes, which people who annoyed him had a bad habit of inadvertently falling on top of.

The press conference concluded with the assembled scribes congratulating Mr Impaler on his victory in the elections to be held next week.

AFTER A CHEMICAL ATTACK on civilians in Douma, the UK joined air strikes on Bashar al-Assad's Syria.

THE GOVERNMENT was revealed to be attempting to deport elderly members of the Windrush generation, who had responded to official invitations to migrate from the Caribbean between 1948 and 1971 and worked in Britain for decades. Home secretary Amber Rudd was forced to resign, despite the policy being the fault of her predecessor in the job.

St Theresa's Independent State Grammar School

The Headmistress Writes: Hello. Or if you are Ms Rudd, Goodbye.

Ms Rudd's resignation apparently came as something of a surprise to her, as apparently did everything else going on in her department.

In short, a number of our Caribbean pupils may well have experienced some minor difficulties, such as being expelled for doing nothing wrong, being refused treatment in the Sanatorium or being refused entry back into the school after their holidays with their parents. So it's only right and proper that someone should take the blame.

I hold my hand up and say that I was Head of Discipline during the time that pupils in Windrush House were frogmarched to the school gates and put on a bus marked "Go Home", but this was entirely the fault of the then Headteacher, Mr Cameron.

Now that I am Headteacher, I have introduced a new and improved system whereby the problems with the Windrush pupils are entirely the fault of the new Head of Discipline, Ms Rudd. Ms Rudd has apologised a number of times (though we don't have a precise record of exactly how many, as a number of documents in the Headmistress's office have been shredded). I have, however, decided Ms Rudd has to be sent back to where she came from.

ITV2'S LOVE ISLAND proved a big hit.

An *Eye* guide to the lingo on the show everyone's talking about, Leave Island

Cracking On – Getting started on a new relationship. What Brexit Secretary David Davis says he's doing, but isn't.

Coupling Up – What International Trade Secretary Liam Fox says he's doing with other countries, but is only doing with Mr Werritty.

Being Pied – How Britain is going to be treated by Europe, ie dumped unceremoniously and embarrassingly in public, despite pathetic pleading.

Mugged Off – To be taken for a fool or a mug. See also Mogged Off.

Prangy – Feeling anxious, paranoid or scared, worried that you're going to be voted off, ie Theresa May, all the time.

Dicksand – Like quicksand, an unsubtle trap for a female involving a dick (Boris Johnson)

Snake – Michael Gove

IT EMERGED THAT Donald Trump's administration had been separating families who attempted to migrate over the border with Mexico, jailing or deporting the parents and keeping kids as young as one year old in cages.

GNOMEMART PRESENTS

The Trump Cage

PARENTS – want to keep your children under control this summer? Struggling to cope in the long vacation? Put your mind at ease with the TRUMP CAGE™

Made out of high-tensile ultra-secure Chinese steel, the TRUMP CAGE™ comes complete with a silver foil blanket and packet of crisps – Junior will be safe 'n' sound for weeks!

WARNING: this US-imported cage contravenes UN Human Rights legislation and the tenets of basic humanity, but who cares!

A REVIEW OF BUILDING regulations following the Grenfell disaster concluded there had been a "race to the bottom" in safety practices – but stopped short of banning the use of combustible cladding.

THERESA MAY UNVEILED her "Chequers Plan" for the future relationship she was aiming for with the EU. Brexit secretary David Davis promptly resigned in protest. When he realised someone else was getting the publicity that was rightly his, foreign secretary Boris Johnson also quit, warning that the deal would turn Britain into a "vassal state".

INTRODUCING The Quitbit™

New from Johnson & Johnson, makers of **VASSAL-INE**™ (*guaranteed to ease even the most difficult of exit passages*) – the ideal gadget for the Minister on the move!

This technological marvel tells you when to make a stand, and then when you've quit, when to start running.

Colours: *Turd Brown, Flag White, Gammon*

QUITBIT™ comes with two faces and lasts as long as any ministerial career (up to 12 months).

WARNING: May emit loud whine and unpleasant beeping.

Price: 30 pieces of euros (formerly silver)

FOOTAGE OF JEREMY CORBYN saying that some "Zionists" failed to understand English irony despite "having lived in this country for a very long time, probably all their lives" was added to the growing mountain of examples of anti-Semitism in Labour ranks.

Corbyn apologises for sharing platform with himself

The Labour leader has admitted once again appearing on the same stage as a speaker guilty of making anti-Semitic remarks.

"I should have known that Jeremy Corbyn had a history of expressing anti-Semitic views, many of them disguised as criticism of Israel," he continued, "and when I heard myself making these unfortunate remarks, I should have walked out of the room in protest at once to show how strongly I disagreed with myself."

Asked if he was in denial about the scale of the problem within his party, Mr Corbyn replied, "Certainly not."

TWO RUSSIAN MILITARY intelligence officers were identified as having visited Salisbury twice when Sergei and Yulia Skripal were poisoned and traces of Novichok found in their hotel room. The pair claimed they were just tourists keen to see the city's cathedral because it was "famous for its 123-metre spire".

tripadvisor Salisbury ★★★★★

Review by Alexander and Ruslan

As ordinary citizens with no connection whatsoever to the secret service, we had a lovely time in this quaint English rural town. Unfortunately, we were so exhausted after one hour's sightseeing, and as Russians found the unfamiliar snowy weather so difficult to deal with, that we headed back to our hotel. But we came back the next day and had a lovely time trying to avoid all the CCTV cameras. We had a great time and definitely won't be going there ever again, or indeed anywhere else outside Russia (particularly anywhere with an extradition treaty).

NO ONE COULD AGREE on anything about Brexit.

Possible options on table:

1. **The Norway Option** – Norway enjoys all the benefits of the single market without being in the EU, so it might be a good idea to go and live there.
2. **Canada-Plus** – Leaving Britain to go and live in Canada would also bring the big plus that you wouldn't hear anyone going on about Brexit.
3. **Chequers Plan** – The only idea that Theresa May has been able to come up with, but everyone else agrees is totally unworkable. Basically means you have to leave Britain because Corbyn is going to move into Chequers.
4. **No Deal** – You can't leave the country, because no ships are leaving Deal, let alone Dover, Folkestone or any other ports. Also, don't think of flying, because No Deal means all flights will be grounded.

SAUDI ARABIAN JOURNALIST Jamal Khashoggi was murdered and dismembered in the country's consulate in Istanbul.

Press Standards campaign launched

A new campaign group dedicated to curbing the intrusive behaviour of the press has been set up in Saudi Arabia.

Known as "Hacked Up", the group is led by campaigner Crown Prince Mohammed bin Salman, the famous star of *No Weddings and One Funeral*, and is committed to stamping out any sort of investigative journalism or criticism of the country's regime in the press. "What I get up to in my public life is entirely my own business," pointed out the Crown Prince, renowned as a liberal moderate by anyone who knows what's good for them.

Jamal Khashoggi was unavailable for comment.

IN JANUARY, columnist and controversialist Toby Young was appointed by the government to watchdog the Office for Students – briefly.

Comments Young made on Radio 4 about "progressive eugenics" have been shared far and wide. But his interest in the area has made him some friends. Last year Young was invited by the psychologist James Thompson to attend a secretive conference at UCL called the London Conference on Intelligence (LCI). "Attendees were only told the venue at the last minute, and asked not to share the information," Young recalled. What he kept to himself was why the conference he attended was so secretive.

Although our request for the invitation-only 2017 conference's programme was declined, LCI 2015 included papers arguing that racial differences in penis length predict different levels of parental care, that racial "admixture" has a negative effect on population quality, that "skin brightness" is a factor in global development, and that country-level differences in the number of Nobel Prizes can be explained by racial differences in male hormone levels.

One paper presented at the 2016 conference argued that "low IQ, high fertility Southern non-Western immigration… threatens the stability of European democracy, welfare and civilisation". Another argued that children from working-class households tend to have "aggressive, antisocial" personalities, and that the welfare state promotes this by letting working-class households have children. Three papers, all by men, were presented on the topic of women being innately less intelligent.

The conference serves as a rendezvous for academic racists and their sympathisers. One speaker, Emil Kirkegaard, whom Young follows on Twitter, presented papers at the 2015, 2016 and 2017 conferences. Writing about paedophilia on his website, he argued in 2012 that a "compromise is having sex with a sleeping child without them knowing it (so, using sleeping medicine). If they don't notice it is difficult to see how they cud [sic] be harmed." He added in April last year that he advocated a "frank discussion of paedophilia-related issues".

Another speaker in 2015 and 2016 was Richard Lynn, a white nationalist and extremist. He has previously called for "incompetent cultures" to be "phased out" and argues that black people have naturally "psychopathic" personalities.

Responding to the *Eye*, Young said: "I don't accept that listening to someone express an idea constitutes tacit acceptance or approval of that idea, no matter how unpalatable. That's the kind of reasoning that leads to people being 'no platformed' on university campuses." In the same statement he managed to misname his own lecture, referring to the "Amanda Holden" Memorial Lecture, rather than Constance Holden.

Young resigned his position at the Office for Students on the day the *Eye* was published.

AS MASSIVE PFI contractor Carillion collapsed the same month, the temporarily renamed *Private Eye Told You So* sounded an early warning about another company.

If Carillion was a financial wreck that had to be fed ever more contracts to keep going until it was too late, something similar can be seen in the UK's outsourced health services. The company now winning the most NHS contracts is Virgin Care, which provides everything from children's services in Devon to urgent care in Croydon and adult social care in Somerset. Yet it has a balance sheet that makes Carillion's look like a picture of health.

On a total turnover of £252m up to March 2017, Virgin Care companies recorded losses of £15.9m last year. Set against this, income from several joint venture partnerships with local GPs totalling £4.2m still left the group with an eight-figure loss. If Virgin Care can't make a profit on its healthcare contracts, has it, like Carillion, been bidding too low for them – and in the process, elbowing out the NHS organisations with which it competes? Recent legal action against health commissioners in Surry showed that those elbows are pretty sharp.

The business is spared from insolvency by ultimate owner Sir Richard Branson promising from his bolt-hole in the British Virgin Islands to continue to provide support, allowing Virgin Care's directors and its auditor KPMG – which checked the Carillion numbers! – to declare that the companies are "going concerns".

In January 2020 it was revealed that the ongoing losses had enabled Virgin Care not to pay any corporation tax in ten years of operation, despite bagging £2bn-worth of public sector contracts.

THE EYE CONTINUED to uncover issues with the proposed Swansea Tidal Lagoon (*see p284*), including this in May.

Mark Shorrock, CEO of the project, appeared before a parliamentary committee last week to plead for the fat subsidy he wants for his Delorean of the Deep. He was characteristically disingenuous about the stake in the project being being taken by his wife's firm, Good Energy. His real jaw-dropper, however, was an outright denial when questioned about his quarrying schemes in Cornwall.

Lagoon construction would need millions of tonnes of rock. Shorrock's plan is to quarry it from St Keverne, a beauty spot and marine conservation area in Cornwall owned by Shire Oak, another of his many commercial ventures. In parliament he was asked if he had ever offered an inducement to the local parish council to support his planning application. He answered a flat "no", which he repeated when the chair invited him to confirm his answer for the record.

But the *Eye* has obtained a copy of Shorrock's proposal to St Keverne Parish Council. Although structured to look like a contract, Shire Oak's initial draft contained only unilateral undertakings by the company, including donations of a substantial six figure sum, the exact amount depending on how much rock was excavated, as a "community fund" to be paid to the PC. At first, Shire Oak proposed no reciprocal obligations – but then Shorrock dropped his shocker. A new paragraph was inserted, stating: "The Parish Council covenants with Shire Oak that it will give reasonable support to the application for Planning Permission and not make representations against [it]. Shire Oak may terminate this agreement at its absolute discretion if the Parish Council is in breach of this clause." The PC recognised this for what it was, and honourably dropped it like a hot potato.

The following month the government cancelled the entire project.

AS JACOB REES-MOGG and his ERG chums continued to push for the hardest of Brexits in June, Slicker had news of the MP's own financial planning.

Rees-Mogg has been prominent in resisting the Lords' amendments in the EU Withdrawal Bill that would keep the UK in the customs union. He supports threatening to walk away with no deal if necessary to ensure the UK leaves the EU.

But over at fund manager and Rees-Mogg's part-time employer, Somerset Capital Management (SCM), which he co-founded, there seems much less equanimity about Brexit, never mind the "cliff edge" version. Like many City banks, insurers and asset managers, SCM relies on "passporting" from the UK's EU membership to sell in other EU countries. That could all come to an end with Brexit – a EU chief negotiator insists there will be no special deal – putting City firms at a big disadvantage.

No doubt this is why SCM has launched a new investment fund based in Dublin, a major fund management centre, even though that means submitting to Irish/EU laws and regulations.

The prospectus for this new MI Somerset Emerging Markets Dividend Growth Feeder Fund spells out serious warnings about possible consequences of the "considerable uncertainty" both before and after Brexit among the "investment-specific risks". This comes three months after the *Eye* pointed out that Rees-Mogg was telling his Twitter followers "We must stand up to Russia" while the then £1.5bn MI Somerset Emerging Markets Dividend Growth Fund had almost 10 percent invested in Russian stocks.

Promoted to Leader of the House of Commons by Boris Johnson, Rees-Mogg played a central role in guiding Brexit legislation through parliament. Although this obliged him to give up his part-time job with SCM, he maintains his 20 percent shareholding through a blind trust.

2019

DESPITE SURVIVING no-confidence votes brought by both her fellow Tory MPs and Labour, Theresa May suffered an epic defeat in parliament's "meaningful vote" on her Brexit proposal.

EXCLUSIVE TO ALL PAPERS

WHAT HAPPENS NEXT AFTER PM'S HISTORIC BREXIT VOTE DEFEAT IN THE COMMONS?

We don't know.

THE PRESIDENT of the European Council was in no mood to help her out.

Multi-Tusking

MEANWHILE, AS PART of preparations for the possibility of no deal at the end of March, hapless transport secretary Chris Grayling awarded a £13.8m contract to run cross-channel ferries to a company that owned no ferries.

NEW FROM GNOMEMART – IT'S THE

Seaborne Freight Ship in a Bottle

Celebrate the government deal of the century with this fantastic 125th-scale model of the actual ferry that is going to save Britain and keep our economy afloat in the event of a no-deal Brexit!

Made from the finest thin air, this charming replica of 'NoBoaty McNoBoatface' will delight sea-salts and land-lubbers alike. *Outsourcing has never been so transparent!* PRICE: Just £13.8 million

CLIMATE change protesters "Extinction Rebellion" brought parts of London to a standstill with imaginative occupations of bridges and major roads.

AS THE CLOCK TICKED down towards the UK's March exit date, and parliament proved unwilling to agree on any of the options on (or even off) the table, all was chaos.

GNOME 24 ROLLING BREXIT LATEST:

After all-night sitting, MPs reject Malthouse compromise in favour of Maltwhisky compromise ● *Cooper-Boles amendment voted down: Camilla Cooper-Boles will "never be Queen"* ● In attempt to get cross-party consensus, May says she is prepared to ignore ideas from both sides ● *Newspapers reported to be stockpiling scare stories about stockpiling ahead of no deal* ● "Just get on with it, we managed just fine in the war", say people who were not alive during war ● *Corbyn denounces seven MPs who have resigned to sit as Independent Group: "They are trying to destroy the Labour party, which is my job"* ● Legal commentators say Geoffrey Cox's ruling against Backstop establishes dangerous legal precedent: "Future Attorney-Generals may now also be obliged to give honest legal opinions rather than politically expedient ones" ● *"We must get on with Brexit,"* demand backbenchers who have spent several weeks voting against getting on with Brexit ● In last-ditch attempt to persuade MPs to back her deal, Theresa May agrees to name date for end of her period in charge: "It was about three months ago."

EVENTUALLY, THE PM was obliged to request an extension to the leaving date from the EU.

St Theresa's Independent State Grammar School

Special measures flextended until further notice

A Message from the Headmistress: Good afternoon, and a very happy Easter to you all. As a vicar's daughter, I know more than anyone that Easter is a time to reflect on the true meaning of Halloween.

It may seem early in the year to be talking about October 31st, but trust me, we'll be there in no time. Halloween is of course the date by which the school will definitely be leaving the European Education Union, or failing that, announcing the next date by when we will definitely be leaving the EEU. Or asking for a new date.

Halloween is when the dead rise again, just as everyone thought they were dead and buried. Just in case you're wondering, the choice of Halloween as our new departure date is not a twisted sick joke by our friends in the EEU, and neither was the previous decision that we should leave the day before April Fools' Day. Whatever anyone says, the school is definitely not a laughing stock.

Theresa May

(Dictated from her Dead Man Walking Holiday in Snowdonia)

THE DELAY MEANT that the UK was forced to put up candidates in the elections to the European Parliament, and Nigel Farage's newly-formed Brexit Party won a landslide.

Logos as they should be...

REALISING THE GAME was up, the prime minister announced her resignation. A number of unsavoury characters threw their hats into the ring to succeed her...

Tory leadership – frontrunners emerge

It increasingly looks as if the grassroots Tory party membership will be presented with a straight choice between Mr Devil and Mr Deepbluesea. Mr Devil (constituency Hell South) is the hot favourite, although there are fears that his sinful record may catch up with him, revealing millions of skeletons in his closet.

Mr Deepbluesea (Dover South) is blue through and through, is strong on fisheries policy but is considered a wet and may well be out of his depth. Support meanwhile has drained away from the other candidates, Mr Rock and Mrs Hard-Place.

One young Conservative, 94, said, "This is a particularly difficult choice, because the type on the ballot sheet is very small and I can't remember where I put my glasses or who I am."

...BUT, INEVITABLY, the winner was the man who had always regarded it as his birthright. His arrival in Downing Street coincided with the 50th anniversary of the moon landings.

BILLIONAIRE PAEDOPHILE Jeffrey Epstein, and close associate of figures like Prince Andrew and Donald Trump, died in prison before his trial on sex trafficking charges.

In Memoriam Jeffrey Epstein, entrepreneur and socialite

So. Farewell
Then Jeffrey Epstein,
You have died at
The age of 66.

Far too young,
They said, but you had
Sex with them
Anyway.

E.J. Thribb (17½, and keep your hands off me)

STILL UNABLE TO GET a Brexit plan through the House of Commons, Boris Johnson and his chief adviser Dominic Cummings withdrew the whip from 21 of their own MPs, and then suspended parliament by means of a royal prorogation.

Dominic Cummings' masterplan in full

1. Sack all rebellious MPs
2. Sack all MPs who object to sacking of rebellious MPs
3. Threaten dire consequences to any civil servants who talk up Project Fear
4. Execute anyone who says Downing Street is operating a Reign of Terror
5. Replace John Bercow as Speaker of the House with a nodding dog toy
6. Replace Queen with Olivia Colman, get Queen's Speech rewritten by woman from Fleabag
7. Construct Terminator cyborg to travel back in time and eliminate Philip Hammond
8. Reconstruct Jacob Rees-Mogg to travel forward in time to at least twentieth century
9. Find cure for baldness
10. Invite Cabinet to remote island and eliminate them one-by-one in style of grim BBC Agatha Christie adaptation
11. Liquidate all MPs with any trace of EU sympathies, such as Boris Johnson
12. Close down parliament and deny it ever existed
13. Point out that this was what people were voting for when they said they didn't want to accept orders from unelected bureaucrats in Brussels; absolute rule by unelected bureaucrat in Number 10 instead

THE GRUESOME TWOSOME were swiftly slapped down by the Supreme Court, which overruled them and reinstated parliament.

Shock at Supreme Court's unanimous verdict

We're the only bit of the UK that's not divided

MEANWHILE, ON the other side of the Atlantic, President Trump was facing impeachment proceedings over his most recent, but not necessarily most egregious, attempt to corrupt democracy.

EXCLUSIVE TO ALL NEWSPAPERS

Will this latest abuse of power finally sink Boris/Trump?

Probably not.

JOHNSON CAME UP with new proposals to deal with the major Brexit sticking point, the Irish border. Well, new-ish.

People's Prime Minister's Question Time – Live on Fakebook

Hello folks – it's People's Question Time again, as usual prepared from a short list of genuine questions the general public might have asked, had they been Dominic Cummings. First question is from Mr Ian Vented-Name.

Could you explain your simple and brilliant plan to solve the gridlock over the Northern Ireland Backstop?

In a word, Ian, Yes! What we do is keep Northern Ireland inside the Customs Union but not in the Single Market, or is it in the Single Union and not the Customs Market? Either way, we don't have a border, we have two borders – one in the sea and one invisible. So there aren't any checks on the border, because there isn't one (there are two).

Isn't this just Theresa May's plan with a different name?

Absolutely not. The key difference is that Chummy Varadkar seems to have bought it this time. So the only one we've got to convince now is Jean-Claude Druncker, and if we get him after lunch he'll sign off anything. Resultio! Next question is from an Arlene Foster from Ulster.

Will there be checks on goods travelling between Northern Ireland and the mainland of Britain?

The simple answer to this, Arlene, is No. Or to put it in the lingo that you'll understand, "NOOOOOOOOOOO!".

That's not true, is it, you shifty lying feck?

Well, no, Arlene, let me be honest with you, that was a lie. There will be checks, but they won't really be checks as such. The whole process will be more like filling in a few pieces of paper, possibly as few as 100, while swimming across the Irish sea, and you won't even notice the frictionless bureaucratic intervention because it will be so jolly hi-tech. I've been taking advice from my technology adviser, Jennifer Arcuri, and there was definitely nothing frictionless about my trade-offs with her. Next question! And this is from a Ms Carrie Symonds of Downing Street.

What was that about Jennifer Arcuri?

Cripes!

The Facebook Live session was unexpectedly prorogued at this point.

DESPITE JOHNSON'S PROMISE the previous month that he would rather be "dead in a ditch" than ask for another Brexit extension, he did.

PRINCE ANDREW DECIDED an interview with *Newsnight* was the ideal way to clear up all the rumours about his friendship with Jeffrey Epstein and allegations that he had also had sex with one of the paedophile's 17-year-old victims. It wasn't.

The Andi-Perspirant

Say goodbye to unwanted disco sweating misery, with this amazing Andi-Perspirant, Paedo Linx for Men. Clammy palms and damp armpits are a thing of the past for you, if not your PR people. Perfect for nights out at Tramp, and mornings after *Newsnight* interviews, not to mention awkward audiences with your mother.
PRICE: Your job

The Woking Pizza Wheel

Never eaten pizza before? Unsure how to divide a circular dough-based snack into slices at your daughter's friend's birthday party, many miles from the nearest nightclub?
Then you need this fully Woking pizza cutter!
WARNING: Wheel may fall off pizza wheel.
Everything Must Go –
Including Prince Andrew.
Hurry Hurry, While Monarchy Lasts!

AN ELECTION WAS CALLED for 12 December, with Johnson's Conservatives campaigning on a platform of their "Oven-Ready Brexit"...

...AND JEREMY CORBYN'S Labour campaigning on a platform of pretty much everything they could think of.

AN ELECTION PROMISE BY THE LABOUR PARTY

Free Trousers

We are committed to delivering high quality universal trousers across the whole country FOR FREE. This will be a huge improvement, not just for individuals who are "trouser-poor", but for businesses everywhere who need state-of-the-art, high-speed trouser access to get ahead in today's highly competitive environment.

This is why, under a future Labour government, trousers will be nationalised. No one should profit from trouser demand, when every leg has a right to be equally covered.
Free Trousers for all at the point of delivery.
Simple, fair, bonkers.

Please note: Labour's offer of free trousers did not feature in the party's comprehensive, fully-costed clothing manifesto released yesterday, when John McDonnell announced that the nationalisation of jackets, shirts, jumpers, hats and shoes was "the limit of our ambitions", but is still a key pledge. At least until Jeremy Corbyn does another interview and gets asked about the national shorts shortage.

JOHNSON WAS RETURNED with a thumping 80-seat majority, making surprising gains in the "Red Wall".

Wild scenes of celebration across the country

Joy was unbounded across the North of England on Friday as the size of Boris Johnson's Conservative landslide victory became apparent.

"Finally, the hated Conservatives, who have presided over a decade of savage cuts to our public services, the decimation of the NHS and the demonisation of the poor through Universal Credit, have been swept away by a Conservative party promising to bolster public services, increase NHS spending and care for the poor," said a group of cheering first-time Tory voters in Sedgefield.

FEBRUARY BROUGHT YET MORE evidence that nothing succeeds like failure.

Can you guess who was appointed last week to the non-executive board of the Cabinet Office to provide "independent advice, support and scrutiny" of official business such as the running of government and leaving the EU?

Step forward Paula Vennells, chief executive of the publicly-owned Post Office who, recent high court revelations suggest, is not only incapable of scrutinising her own company properly, but has presided over a cover-up of flaws in its deeply dodgy Horizon computer system which cost hundreds of sub-postmasters their jobs, their reputation and in some cases their liberty (*see p260*). She also got a CBE in the New Year Honours for "services to the Post Office and to charity".

In 2012, senior Post Office officials held a special meeting after they found discrepancies in the IT system "impacting circa 40 branches", but decided to keep the matter secret because any admission could "have a potential impact on the ongoing legal cases". Three years later in 2015, Vennells told a committee of MPs that she continued "to have confidence" in Horizon.

Vennells stepped down from the Cabinet Office job in March 2020, four months after her successor at the Post Office agreed to settle the court cases at a cost of £58 million. There have since been calls for her to be stripped of her CBE.

THERE WAS NEWS from within Labour in May.

Jeremy Corbyn is about to be hit by the largest political leak since the MPs' expenses scandal, the *Eye* has learned. Former party officials, who left because they could not work with Corbyn's apparatchiks Karie Murphy and Jennie Formby, have prepared a vast document-drop for anti-racism investigators.

Labour is the first party since the neo-Nazi BNP to be investigated by the Equalities and Human Rights Commission (EHRC). Former Labour staffers have already collected 100,000 emails, including tens of thousands showing how the party ignored complaints that supporters were promoting anti-Semitism. More are expected. The investigators will also receive copies of WhatsApp conversations from the officials' time inside Labour HQ, and sworn affidavits detailing the efforts to protect Corbyn loyalists.

"Who is going to speak out? Everyone is going to speak out," one of the organisers of the protest said. "The protection of anti-Semites was on a scale and at a level the public does not begin to understand." The emails suggest that the party's claim that its disciplinary process has been free from political interference since March 2018 is so much spin. They also reveal the central role of Corbyn's chief of staff, Murphy, in saving his supporters from expulsion.

In October 2020, the EHRC concluded that the Labour party under Corbyn had committed "unlawful harassment" against Jewish people and that the leader's office had repeatedly interfered in the disciplinary process. Litigation over the matter continues.

THE DIRTY DIGGER caused concern in June.

Dark murmurings from News Corp suggest that while 88-year-old Rupert Murdoch is still with us physically, his mind may be increasingly semi-detached. The murmurs took on a new significance last week after filings with the US Securities & Exchange Commission revealed that on 14 June the Digger personally spent more than $20m buying 600,000 shares in his company Fox Corp – only a week after he had bought exactly the same number but then promptly sold them.

Smart trading by the nimble octogenarian to turn a quick profit? No. The SEC filing explained that Murdoch had bought the first batch of shares by mistake, adding: "Any short swing profit resulting from the erroneous purchase and subsequent sale will be returned to the issuer."

The word "erroneous" has set alarm bells ringing. If, while having a senior moment, Rupert can absentmindedly spend more than $20m on shares he didn't mean to buy, what eight-figure errors will he commit next?

WHEN IRAN SEIZED a British-flagged tanker in the Strait of Hormuz, the *Eye* pointed out all was not as it seemed.

As tensions rise between Britain and Iran, what is the lineage of the "British" ship at the centre of the row, the Stena Impero? The ship is a chemical and oil products tanker, built at Guangzhou in south-west China and launched at a traditional Chinese ceremony in January 2018. She was the last in a series of 13 ships ordered by her owner, Stena Bulk, which is based in Gothenburg and part of one of the largest family-owned companies in Sweden.

Stena uses Northern Marine, a Clydebank-based

fleet management and crewing company which is itself a subsidiary of the Swedish Stena Bulk conglomerate, to manage the ship, which has a crew of 23 seafarers who are from India, Russia, Latvia and the Philippines. However, Stena chose to register the Impero under the British flag – hence, flying the Red Ensign, she is seen as a British responsibility.

The *Eye* has noted that that Brexit has led to a dramatic fall in the number of ships registering under the British flag. To combat this decline, the UK shipping register has changed its rulebook and declared itself an international register. This means Commonwealth countries, plus another 20 nations including China, Panama and the Marshall Islands, can now choose to register under the British flag. Could the Royal Navy soon find itself rushing to protect a Chinese or Panama-owned ship? Murky waters indeed…

OMINOUS NEWS EMERGED in September about what would happen in the event of a no-deal Brexit.

To fill the thousands of extra civil service posts which will be required, the government has arranged for a rather unorthodox reshuffle: if/when a no-deal Brexit happens, thousands of local government officials are to be reallocated to Whitehall departments to fortify Sir Humphrey.

Who will run town and county halls in their absence? This is where matters become surreal. The army – including territorial volunteers – are being issued with instructions to take over local government posts, in a civilian capacity, in the event of a no deal.

One officer, who admitted he was uncomfortable at the optics of all this, observed to the *Eye* that this involved putting soldiers in charge even when they lacked basic literacy and numeracy. Quite how they would get on calculating council tax, or providing adult social care and children's services, remains to be seen.

ROYAL CORRESPONDENT Flunkey made a prediction in November.

The news that Harry and Meghan will be taking six weeks off for "much-needed family time" in the run-up to Christmas was timed perfectly to coincide with their emotive appearance on ITV screens complaining about press beastliness, but in truth a break has been planned since the start of the year.

Californian sunshine, time with Meghan's mum (but not dad), Thanksgiving, and Harry working on the mental health TV project he announced with Oprah Winfrey earlier this year have long been in the schedule. The mini-sabbatical, however, could also pave the way for what everyone knows is coming: the Sussex exit from the royal stage, or "Sexit" as those in gold braid call it.

It could be just for a year or an eternal parting, but Harry wants to ditch the formality of monarchy and Meghan is finding out that being a princess isn't all it's cracked up to be. Harry promised her she would be Diana's successor, a campaigner who could break the mould, stuff protocol and stick two fingers up to everyone except Brenda. But the royal machine, slow to get the measure of Meghan at first, has seen a thing or two over the years. It was never going to let that happen.

The following January, the world was shocked to learn that… Harry and Meghan were exiting the royal stage for a new life across the Atlantic.

THAT SAME MONTH, the *Eye* revealed some missing information from a story that was in the headlines elsewhere.

It is hardly surprising the US is reluctant to see Anne Sacoolas put on trial in a UK court over the death of 19-year-old Harry Dunn, whom she collided with when driving her car outside "RAF" Croughton. Sacoolas left the UK shortly after the August crash, initially claiming "diplomatic immunity" because her husband works at Croughton, described as housing "an annexe of the US embassy". But that is not the full picture. The base is actually a major CIA/Pentagon communications and signals intelligence centre. It has satellite and fibre-optic links to US bases around the world and to the US's own GCHQ. It is *not* staffed by diplomats: Sacoolas's husband is an intelligence officer.

It is from Croughton, with British connivance, that more than 200 US personnel control and monitor air strikes by drones based in Djibouti on the Red Sea, including attacks on targets in Yemen and Somalia. And it was from there that the Americans were found to have tapped into the mobile phones of prominent politicians, including German chancellor Angela Merkel. Neither the US nor British intelligence agencies would welcome scrutiny in court of exactly what goes on inside.

2020

PRINCE HARRY AND MEGHAN, his wife of less than two years, announced that they were giving up royal duties and moving across the Atlantic.

NURSERY TIMES

Frog Prince agrees to hop it

In a historic development that has rocked the Nurseryland monarchy, the Frog Prince has announced that, having kissed the Princess, he wants to give up his Royal duties and return to life as a normal frog on the other side of the pond. The couple's decision is thought to be related to the media's recent portrayal of them as toads.

The Prince will be expected to repay the cost of refurbishing his luxury Frogmore lilypad, which cost the taxpayers of Nurseryland several Golden Goose eggs. The Queen has invited the Frog Prince to her parlour for talks over bread and honey to finalise details of the couple's future role, warning that if a solution cannot be found, she will cut off everyone's heads.

The Grand Old Duke of York was unavailable for comment, but is said to be delighted that for once it isn't him in the headlines.

BRITAIN OFFICIALLY left the EU and entered the brave new world of... a transition period during which nothing changed.

ALLISON PEARSON: Reach for the designer shades and the Factor 50! Britain has shaken off its chains and the sun is shining bright. What's more, green shoots are, in the words of the immortal song, "comin' up roses".

Just look at the evidence of joyous national renewal. The beloved *Great British Bake Off* has carried off first prize at the British Television Awards. "Smart" lanes are making our Great British Motorways speedier than ever – with barely a handful of people killed for every extra mile travelled! National treasure Carol Vorderman has been spotted buying a splendid new kitchen unit from John Lewis! And – at long last – that Great British Company, Huawei, has finally taken back control of our all-important networks.

By the way, have you noticed? No one mentions "climate change" any more. Thankfully, now we're out of the EU, it no longer affects us.

Top British Prime Minister Winston Churchill would be proud of us.

MEANWHILE, far away...

China finds source of coronavirus outbreak

The Chinese authorities are deeply concerned about the spread of information about the coronavirus, and indeed how it got out in the first place.

They have assured the world that they did everything in their power to contain the story, and to stop it getting out of China and into the news around the world.

A spokesman for President Xi yesterday announced, "We located the source, the so-called 'truth-spreader', and we were going to put him in isolation for a very, very long time. Fortunately, he has since died, so he can no longer infect anyone with dangerous facts."

AS THE DISEASE ARRIVED on our shores, there were sudden changes to everyday behaviour.

"You must be joking"

EVENTUALLY, as infections and deaths rocketed, Boris Johnson ordered the country into full lockdown.

Stable door strategy criticised

The WHO (World Horse Organization) has expressed its astonishment at the policy adopted by the stable owner who decided to lock the door of his premises after the horse's rapid departure.

Equine experts pointed out that all research points to the fact that 100 percent of closed doors work better with horses still inside but, speaking from a beach, the stable owner in question, King Cnut, said that he remained very confident about his earlier estimate of "turning the tide within 12 weeks".

Many political observers believe the King to be rather out of his depth, and a complete Cnut.

AS PERSONAL PROTECTIVE EQUIPMENT for healthcare staff ran short, chancellor Rishi Sunak sprayed money around willy-nilly and the prime minister himself succumbed to the illness, the government did not cover itself in glory.

THE POPULATION proved unexpectedly compliant with the new rules – right up until the point it emerged that the prime minister's chief adviser, Dominic Cummings, had repeatedly flouted them. While ill with coronavirus, he took his family to Durham and for a 60mph eyesight-test in Barnard Castle, and refused to apologise for doing so.

That Cummings press conference in full

I've been asked to give a statement. So here it is. "I did nothing wrong. The media are to blame. Now fuck off." Oh no, I was told to cut that last bit. Right, that's it. Any questions? Oh no, hang on, it's not that bit yet. I've got to read you this very, very long and plausible alibi involving my desperately ill wife, my vulnerable child, a terror threat to my home, my elderly parents and selfless nieces, my tragic loss of eyesight, bluebells, toilet stops, historic landmarks and an invasion by aliens. Actually, we decided to drop the aliens as they sounded too plausible.

Anyway, on March 27th I did nothing wrong. On March 28th I made the decision to do nothing wrong again. For the next nine days I did nothing wrong. Once or twice during that time period I may have done nothing wrong. So does anyone from the media want to defend why they misreported all of this? Yeah, you from the BBC, that still exists, does it? Not for long.

Laura Koronaberg: You say you drove 260miles while suffering coronavirus symptoms to ensure you had childcare. But why couldn't you ask friends in London to look after your child?

Cummings: I haven't got any.

Koronaberg: Actually, that does sound pretty convincing.

THE WAY we all lived rapidly evolved.

IN AN ALMOST UNIVERSALLY grim year, all the good news was saved for the end: in the space of a fortnight in November, Donald Trump lost the election (even if he wouldn't admit it), effective vaccines for the coronavirus were produced, and Dominic Cummings was ousted from Downing Street after falling out with the prime minister's fiancée.

People's Prime Minister's Press Briefing – Live on Fakebook

Greetings, folks! And for once this isn't a de-press briefing! We've got proper good news from the boffins-that-be: we've found the miracle vaccine that's going to save lives. Political lives, that is, ie mine. So rejoice, rejoice, Bozza saves the country, Christmas is back on!

Dominic Cummings: What the FUCK is going on?

Boris: What ho, Dom! I was just telling the folks the good news…

Cummings: What, that your girlfriend has stopped you appointing my protégé as Chief of Staff, like I told you to? How hen-pecked are you?

Boris: Hang on, I thought it was Lee Cain that wore the chicken suit?

Cummings: Shut up, fuckwit.

Boris: I've got a feeling we might be getting things the wrong way round here on the communications front. Don't we usually use a major event to bury bad news, rather than creating our own bad news to bury good news?

Cummings: Fuck off. Time to decide, who's in charge – me, or her? We all know it's not you.

Boris: Dom, you're putting me in an impossible position – forcing me to choose between you and the dearest person to me in the world. Well, I choose the love of my life. Me!

Cummings: I give up. That's it – I'm fucking well fucking off…

(Phone rings)

Boris: Ah, saved by the bell! As well as the vaccine. The President's on Line 1. Hello, Mr President, congratulations on your historic victory! About time they got rid of that laughable TV has-been with the stupid hair… Ah, Donald, it's you. Er… can I put you on hold, I've got another President on Line 2. Top of the morning to you, President Biden! Great to have some craic with you! Not like the crack your son takes in all those pictures, the good old Emerald Irish sort. Bosh! Special Relationship restored by the Boz diplomaster… what's that Joe? Do a Brexit deal and keep the Good Friday agreement or the trade deal will be shoved up my sorry ass? Yikes, Sleepy Joe, you're not as sleepy as I was hoping. Oh, he's gone. And so's everyone else.

LED BY MEDICAL CORRESPONDENT, M.D., the *Eye* was sceptical about government tactics to tackle coronavirus from the outset.

MARCH: Why has the UK government stopped population testing of coronavirus? It plans to protect the most at risk by asking them to self-isolate for up to 14 weeks, while allowing the least at risk to become infected in a phased manner that establishes herd immunity while avoiding overloading the NHS. This is highly speculative and at odds with the policies of many other countries and the World Health Organization. Many UK scientists are also deeply sceptical of this approach, and the government urgently needs to release the modelling that informs it. Stopping community testing makes any plan less likely to succeed. If you don't measure, you can't manage. And you can't fight a virus if you don't know where it is.

MAY: It has taken us more than three months to move from Patient Zero to mass testing and tracing. And as swab testing is finally being rolled out, it is being outsourced to private companies employing low-paid workers with minimal training. Just as important are the human resources put into specialist contact tracing afterwards. Nuanced, specialist interpretation is needed.

Once again, the UK is going its own way. Only 3,000 of Health Secretary Matt Hancock's 18,000 contact tracers will be "qualified public health and clinical professionals". The rest will be "call handlers" from "an external logistics partner". The NHS won't directly hire those 15,000 people, instead handing out call centre contracts to companies like Serco, whose low-wage "customer services" approach is in contrast to best practice elsewhere, which relies on local government staff.

Public Health England had only 300 contact tracers at the time the approach was abandoned, and it didn't mobilise the 5,000 or so local authority environmental health experts who already have contact-tracing experience. Hancock's antipathy to local government and enthusiasm for contracting out, as well as for unproven tech solutions – his scheme relies on untested mobile phone apps to trace contacts digitally – means the UK is again out on a limb.

By hiring private firms to run the drive-through sites, meanwhile, the government took the chance to reward some friends of the Tory party. Some operations are performed by Mitie, whose board members include Baroness Couttie, made a peer by David Cameron after years of party service in 2016. Compass runs other test sites through its subsidiary Levy: its chairman Paul Walsh was one of the business leaders who signed a "vote Tory" letter praising George Osborne ahead of the 2015 election. Serco improved its relations with government by appointing Rupert Soames, grandson of Winston Churchill and brother-in-law of Tory MP Philip Dunne, as chief executive in 2014.

The job of running the test and trace programme, meanwhile, has gone to Dido Harding, both a Tory peer and the wife of a Tory MP (John Penrose). She at least has already made a significant Covid-related contribution: as a board member of the Jockey Club, she shares responsibility for its decision to go ahead with the Cheltenham Festival in March, one of the last significant superspreading events before lockdown.

OCTOBER: Hancock announced in April that the Department of Health and Social Care would be "working together" with Clipper Logistics to deliver Personal Protective Equipment. Clipper was founded by Steve Parkin, its chairman and biggest shareholder. He has donated £475,000 to the Tories since 2016 and has attended at least one "donors' dinner" with prime minister Boris Johnson and other leading Tories. Clipper isn't on the Crown Commercial Service list – the register of approved suppliers used for many Covid-19 contracts – and it usually works for the likes of fashion retailers Boohoo and Asos, rather than delivering medical supplies to hospitals. The NHS said it had paid Clipper £7.2m until the end of June, and the open-ended contract is still running. The decision to award the contract was "taken at daily Covid-19 calls between DHSC, NHS England, Supply Chain Coordination and the Army". Asked for records of this phone call, and who recommended the company, it admitted "no formal minutes or record were made".

NOVEMBER: In April, Allan Wilson, the president of the Institute of Biomedical Science, the professional body representing 17,000 lab scientists, including many NHS and other health lab staff, wrote to health secretary Matt Hancock to open discussions on expanding Covid-19 testing. It received no reply for six months – and when it came, it was a pro-forma response referring it to the government portal for businesses seeking to win public sector contracts.

DECEMBER: Prize for Most Secretive Covid Contract – in a tough field – must go to the Department of Health's deal with consultancy firm Deloitte for managing the woeful test and trace scheme. Nearly eight months after its announcement, and seven months after starting work, the department has yet to publish a notice on the programme. This should have been made public within a month.

Could the secrecy relate to its eye-watering costs? The little information released, via monthly departmental spending spreadsheets, shows payments in July totalling £38.8m. A freedom of information request revealed that 1,114 Deloitte consultants were working on the project, making that around £35,000 each across, at most, three months – far more than double what it would cost to employ public officials.

2021

AFTER A COUP attempt at the Capitol by his fans failed, Trump departed the White House in January.

THE UK DEPARTED the European Union the same month. At time of writing, coronavirus is very much still with us.

You have been reading...

George Adamson, Amanda Alcock, Gary Andrews, Nathan Ariss, David Austin, Mary Aylmer, Backbiter, Brian Bagnall, Norman Balon, Mike Barfield, Ed Barrett, Gavel Basher, Neil Bennett, Philip Berkin, Marcus Berkmann, Jeffrey Bernard, Bernie, John Betjeman, Richard Body, Cecilia Boggis, Christopher Booker, Bookworm, Andrew Bousfield, Richard Brooks, Craig Brown, Robby Bullen, Ciar Byrne, John Byrne, Dave Cash, Simon Childs, Dr B. Ching, Ed Clarke, Rachel Claye, Remote Controller, Claud Cockburn, Peter Cook, Tristan Davies, Henry Davies, Alan de la Nougerede, Nigel Dempster, Sarah Dempster, Frank Dickens, Pete Dredge, Tom Driberg, Simon Edmond, Liz Elliot, Jane Ellison, Geoff Elwell, Harry Enfield, Christian Eriksson, Square Eyes, Barry Fantoni, Sally Farrimond, Peter Fluck, Nev Fountain, Paul Foot, Ben Fox, Michael Gillard, Maisie Glazebrook, Ed Glinert, Anthony Goldman, Emily Green, Germaine Greer, Dr Grim, David Haldane, Paul Halloran, Dr Phil Hammond, Graham Harvey, Michael Heath, Louis Hellman, Ian Hislop, Caroline Holden, Mark Hollingsworth, Martin Honeysett, Ed Howker, Solomon Hughes, Barry Humphries, James Hunter, Tony Husband, Richard Ingrams, Tom Jamieson, Richard Jolley, Penny Junor, Aiden Kelly, John Kent, Graeme Keyes, Roger Latham, Roger Law, Tim Laxton, Victor Lewis-Smith, Christopher Logue, John "Cluff" Longstaff, Hilary Lowinger, Jack Lundin, Peter McKay, Jane Mackenzie, Ed McLachlan, Adam Macqueen, Paul Magrath, Steve Mann, Patrick Marnham, Heather Mills, Spike Milligan, Sheila Molnar, Tim Minogue, Lizzie Mooney, Andrew Hunter Murray, Rob Murray, Nick Newman, Roy Nixon, Richard North, Lunchtime O'Boulez, Glenn Orton, Andrew Osmond, Matt Owen, Ruth Pallasen-Mustikay, Terence Parkes, Simon Pearsall, Giles Pilbrow, Anna Powell-Smith, Hope Pym, Ken Pyne, Keith Raffan, Ratbiter, Rupert Redway, Tony Reeve, Royston Robertson, Susan Roccelli, Heather Rogers, Matei Rosca, Martin Ross, Brian Rostron, Tony Rushton, Willy Rushton, Albert Rusling, Gerald Scarfe, Brian Sedgemore, Sarah Shannon, Robin Shaw, Christopher Silvester, AJ Singleton, Quintus Slide, Anthony Smith, Sam Smith, Old Sparky, Bio-Waste Spreader, Gavin Stamp, Ralph Steadman, Ben Summerskill, Colin Swash, DJ Taylor, Robert Thompson, Bridget Tisdall, Nick Tolson, Martin Tomkinson, Trog, Megan Trudell, Peter Usborne, Paul Vickers, Nick Wallis, Noel Watson, Auberon Waugh, Steve Way, John Wells, Richard West, Colin Wheeler, Francis Wheen, Nicholas Whitmore, Kevin Woodcock, Emma Woollacott, Emma Yeomans ...and many, many more.

Some *Eye* staff in the '60s...

...and some *Eye* staff in 2021